Mastering Windows Security and Hardening

Secure and protect your Windows environment from intruders, malware attacks, and other cyber threats

Mark Dunkerley

Matt Tumbarello

BIRMINGHAM—MUMBAI

Mastering Windows Security and Hardening

Copyright © 2020 Packt Publishing

All rights reserved. No part of this book may be reproduced, stored in a retrieval system, or transmitted in any form or by any means, without the prior written permission of the publisher, except in the case of brief quotations embedded in critical articles or reviews.

Every effort has been made in the preparation of this book to ensure the accuracy of the information presented. However, the information contained in this book is sold without warranty, either express or implied. Neither the author(s), nor Packt Publishing or its dealers and distributors, will be held liable for any damages caused or alleged to have been caused directly or indirectly by this book.

Packt Publishing has endeavored to provide trademark information about all of the companies and products mentioned in this book by the appropriate use of capitals. However, Packt Publishing cannot guarantee the accuracy of this information.

Commissioning Editor: Vijin Boricha
Acquisition Editor: Meeta Rajani
Senior Editor: Richard Brookes-Bland
Content Development Editor: Ronn Kurien
Technical Editor: Sarvesh Jaywant
Copy Editor: Safis Editing
Project Coordinator: Neil Dmello
Proofreader: Safis Editing
Indexer: Tejal Daruwale Soni
Production Designer: Jyoti Chauhan

First published: July 2020

Production reference: 1070720

Published by Packt Publishing Ltd.
Livery Place
35 Livery Street
Birmingham
B3 2PB, UK.

ISBN 978-1-83921-641-1

www.packt.com

Packt.com

Subscribe to our online digital library for full access to over 7,000 books and videos, as well as industry leading tools to help you plan your personal development and advance your career. For more information, please visit our website.

Why subscribe?

- Spend less time learning and more time coding with practical eBooks and Videos from over 4,000 industry professionals
- Improve your learning with Skill Plans built especially for you
- Get a free eBook or video every month
- Fully searchable for easy access to vital information
- Copy and paste, print, and bookmark content

Did you know that Packt offers eBook versions of every book published, with PDF and ePub files available? You can upgrade to the eBook version at packt.com and as a print book customer, you are entitled to a discount on the eBook copy. Get in touch with us at customercare@packtpub.com for more details.

At www.packt.com, you can also read a collection of free technical articles, sign up for a range of free newsletters, and receive exclusive discounts and offers on Packt books and eBooks.

Contributors

About the authors

Mark Dunkerley is a highly motivated and passionate technology leader. Mark was born in Newcastle Upon Tyne, UK, and resides in Orlando, Florida. He holds a bachelor's degree in business administration and a master's degree in business administration. He has worked in the technology field for 20 years and has experience in several technical areas. He has earned certifications from (ISC)², AirWatch, Microsoft, CompTIA, VMware, AXELOS, Cisco, and EMC. Mark has been invited to speak at multiple conferences, including Microsoft and VMware events, is the author of *Learning AirWatch* published by *Packt Publishing*, and has published a number of case studies.

Matt Tumbarello is a resident of Atlanta, Georgia, and a passionate solutions architect. He has been in the technology field for 15 years and has experience in working with products from Microsoft, VMware, Dell, and Citrix. He also has a background of working directly with Fortune 500 executives in a technical enablement role. Matthew was recently invited to Redmond and participates in Microsoft's Customer Connection program. He has published reviews for Azure security products, privileged access management tools, and mobile threat defense solutions. He also holds several Microsoft certifications.

About the reviewer

Steve Hardee is an information security professional with over 15 years of experience in IT, currently leading a security team at one of the largest healthcare systems in the nation. Steve has broad knowledge of securing enterprises through incident response, penetration testing, threat hunting, table-top exercises, enterprise architecture, and IT operations. He holds a degree in cyber security and has received extensive training and certifications through SANS, Microsoft, EC-Council, and ISC2. He is a technology board member at Full Sail University, is a staff member of a local security conference, BSides, and has spoken at multiple events as an information security expert.

> *I would like to thank my partner for her continued support and encouragement with everything that I do. You have always pushed me toward new adventures, accomplishing my goals, and doing what is right. I genuinely appreciate what you have done for us and I love you.*
>
> *To my parents and brother, who raised me to be who I am today. You are always there for me, you are amazing, and your efforts have not gone unnoticed. I greatly appreciate and love you.*

Packt is searching for authors like you

If you're interested in becoming an author for Packt, please visit `authors.packtpub.com` and apply today. We have worked with thousands of developers and tech professionals, just like you, to help them share their insight with the global tech community. You can make a general application, apply for a specific hot topic that we are recruiting an author for, or submit your own idea.

Table of Contents

Preface

Section 1: Getting Started

1
Fundamentals of Windows Security

Understanding the security transformation	22	Recognizing breaches	34
		Current security challenges	36
Living in today's digital world	24	Implementing a Zero Trust approach	39
Today's threats	28		
Identifying vulnerabilities	30	Summary	40

2
Building a Baseline

Introduction to baselining	42	framework	49
Policies, standards, procedures, and guidelines	44	Building baseline controls	52
		CIS	52
Defining policies	44	Windows security baselines	53
Setting standards	45	Implementing a baseline	54
Creating procedures	46	CIS	54
Recommending guidelines	46	Microsoft SCT	57
Incorporating change management	48	Incorporating best practices	59
Implementing a security		Summary	60

3
Server Infrastructure Management

Technical requirements	62	management tools	76
Overview of the data center and the cloud	62	Introducing Server Manager	76
		Looking at Event Viewer	79
Types of data center	63	Using Windows Server Update Services	82
		Introducing Windows Admin Center	84
Implementing access management in Windows servers	68	Using Azure services to manage Windows servers	85
Physical and user access security	68	The Azure portal and Marketplace	86
Privileged Access Management, Just-in-Time Access, and Privileged Identity Management	69	Implementing role-based access control	87
		Azure Resource Manager	91
Using a tiered model for privileged access	70	Understanding Azure Backup	91
		Introducing Azure Update Management	94
Enhanced security administrative environment	74	Leveraging Azure Site Recovery	97
Access management best practices	75	Summary	99

Understanding Windows Server

4
End User Device Management

Technical requirements	102	Windows Autopilot	117
Device management evolution	103	Microsoft Endpoint Configuration Manager	119
Device Imaging and Windows Autopilot	104		
		Securely deploying clients for Configuration Manager	120
Windows Assessment and Deployment Kit (Windows ADK)	110	Client collections, settings, and communications	123
Windows Configuration Designer	111	Intune Mobile Device Management (MDM)	129
Microsoft Deployment Toolkit	113		
Windows Deployment Services	115		
MDT and Configuration Manager	116	Configuration Service Provider	129
		Mobile Device Management versus	

Mobile Application Management	132	Introducing Microsoft Endpoint Manager	134
Windows enrollment methods	133	Summary	138

Section 2: Applying Security and Hardening

5

Hardware and Virtualization

Technical requirements	142	UEFI Secure Boot	160
Physical servers and virtualization	143	Trusted Platform Module (TPM 2.0)	162
		Advanced protection with VBS	164
Microsoft virtualization	144	Credential Guard	166
Hardware security concerns	151	Device Guard	171
Virtualization security concerns	153	Windows Defender Application Guard	175
Cloud hardware and virtualization	154	Hypervisor-Protected Code Integrity	177
Introduction to hardware certification	154	Windows Defender System Guard	180
BIOS and UEFI, TPM 2.0, and Secure Boot	158	Hardware security recommendations and best practices	182
Unified Extensible Firmware Interface	159	Summary	182

6

Network Fundamentals for Hardening Windows

Technical requirements	186	Configuring a firewall rule with Group Policy	204
Network security fundamentals	187		
Understanding Windows Network Security	191	Windows Defender Exploit Guard Network Protection	207
Network baselining	192	Introducing Azure network security	211
Windows 10	193		
Windows Server	198	Network Security Groups (NSGs)	211
Networking and Hyper-V	201	Summary	218
Network troubleshooting	202		
Windows Defender Firewall and Advanced Security	202		

7
Identity and Access Management

Technical requirements	220	Implementing PAM security tools (PAM, PIM, and JIT)	240
Identity and access management overview	221	Using Azure RBAC	245
Identity	221	Understanding authentication, MFA, and going passwordless	246
Authentication	222		
Authorization	223	Securing your passwords	247
Accountability	223	Introducing SSPR	250
Implementing account and access management	225	Using Azure AD Seamless SSO	254
		Configuring Azure SSO	257
HR and identity management	226	Configuring MFA	258
Integrating directory services	227	Introducing Windows Hello	262
Using local administrative accounts	231	Understanding going passwordless	262
Managing Azure external user access (B2B)	233	Using Conditional Access and Identity Protection	264
Understanding the Azure cloud administrative roles	236	Summary	269

8
Administration and Remote Management

Technical requirements	272	Connecting securely to servers remotely	306
Understanding device administration	273	Remote management and support tools	306
Differences between domain join, hybrid, and Azure AD joined devices	273	Using Azure Security Center Just-in-Time access	307
Enforcing policies with MDM	275	Connecting with Azure Bastion	311
Creating compliance settings with Configuration Manager	275	Introducing PowerShell security	313
		Configuring PowerShell logging	314
Creating Policies with Intune	286	Using PowerShell Constrained Language Mode	315
Building security baselines	295	Enabling script execution	316
Using the Microsoft Security Compliance Toolkit	295	Summary	317
Creating a Configuration Baseline from a GPO	301		

9
Keeping Your Windows Client Secure

Technical requirements	320	Disabling the Web Proxy Autodiscovery Protocol (WPAD)	352
Securing your Windows clients	320	Configuring Office security baselines	354
Introducing Windows Update for Business	321	Hardening Google Chrome	360
Configuring Windows updates in Intune	323	Preventing user access to the registry	363
		Windows Defender Application Control	364
Advanced Windows hardening configurations	327	Windows 10 privacy	366
Enabling Windows Hello for Business	328	Controlling the privacy settings for each app	367
Managing BitLocker encryption	331	Additional privacy settings	368
Configuring Windows Defender AV	334	Privacy settings for Microsoft Edge	372
Enabling Microsoft Defender SmartScreen	336	Summary	374
Preventing name resolution poisoning	338		

10
Keeping Your Windows Server Secure

Technical requirements	376	Defender ATP	392
Windows Server versions	377	Onboarding with Group Policy	393
Installing Windows Server roles and features	378	Onboarding with Configuration Manager	397
Reducing the Windows Server footprint	379	Hardening Windows Server	400
Installing Nano Server 2019	379	Implementing a security baseline	400
Configuring Windows updates	381	Using Azure Disk Encryption	409
Implementing Windows Server Update Services (WSUS)	381	Deploying Windows Defender Application Control	415
Deploying Azure Update Management	387	Summary	422
Connecting to Microsoft			

Section 3: Protecting, Detecting, and Responding for Windows Environments

11
Security Monitoring and Reporting

Technical requirements	426	Installing gallery solutions	441
Monitoring with MDATP	426	**Monitoring with Azure Monitor and activity logs**	**448**
Investigating an alert	427	Secure access to Azure Monitor	449
Onboarding workstations to the MDATP service	433	Monitoring Azure activity logs	449
Enabling the Microsoft Intune connection	435	**Configuring ASC**	**451**
Creating a machine risk compliance policy	436	**Creating performance baselines**	**455**
Enabling advanced features	439	**Summary**	**458**
Deploying Log Analytics	**439**		

12
Security Operations

Technical requirements	460	**Investigating threats with Azure Security Center**	**486**
Introducing the SOC	461	**Introducing Azure Sentinel**	**488**
Using the M365 security portal	462	Creating the connection	489
Understanding Microsoft Secure Score	464	**Microsoft Defender Security Center**	**492**
Classifying your data	467	Assigning permissions and machine groups	492
Using MCAS	**469**	Reviewing the alerts queue	496
Reviewing the activity log	471	Automated Investigations	498
Looking at a user's activity	473		
Configuring Azure ATP	**476**	**Planning for business continuity and DR**	**504**
Planning for Azure ATP	477	**Summary**	**507**
Activating your instance	478		
Understanding the kill chain	478		
Looking at alerts	480		

13
Testing and Auditing

Technical requirements	510	Executing a penetration test	523
Validating controls	511	Reviewing the findings	525
Vulnerability scanning	517	Security awareness and training	526
Preparing for a vulnerability scan	517	Summary	529
Planning for penetration testing	520		

14
Top 10 Recommendations and the Future

The 10 most important to-dos	532	Always encrypt your devices	536
Implementing identity protection and privileged access	532	Enable endpoint protection	537
		Deploy security monitoring solutions	537
Enact a Zero Trust access model	534	Other important items	537
Define a security framework	534	The future of device security and management	540
Get current and stay current	535		
Make use of modern management tools	535	Security and the future	544
Certify your physical hardware devices	536	Summary	546
Administer network security	536		

Other Books You May Enjoy

Leave a review - let other readers know what you think   548

Index

Preface

Throughout this book, you will be provided with the knowledge needed to protect your Windows environment and the users that access it. It will cover a variety of topics that go beyond the hardening of just the operating system, including the management of devices, baselining, hardware, virtualization, networking, identity management, security operations, monitoring, auditing, and testing. The goal is to ensure that you understand the foundation of and multiple layers involved in providing improved protection for your Windows systems.

Since this is a book about security, it's important to understand what the core principles are that form an information security model and foundation. These principles are known as the CIA triad, which represents confidentiality, integrity, and availability. If you have pursued a security certification, such as the CISSP or Security +, certification for example, you will be very familiar with this model. If not, it is recommended that you familiarize yourself with it as a security professional. This book will not go into detail about the CIA triad but, as with any security, the concepts provided in this book will help you to ensure the confidentiality, integrity, and availability of information on the Windows systems you manage. At a high level, CIA represents the following:

- **Confidentiality** involves ensuring that no one other than those authorized access information.
- **Integrity** involves ensuring that the information being protected is original and has not been modified without the correct authorization.
- **Availability** involves ensuring that information is always available when access is needed.

The book is split into three sections to help guide you and provide the understanding and knowledge needed to implement a solid Windows security foundation within your organization. The first section provides an overview of the fundamentals, including an overview of the management tools for the Windows server and client environment, and a review of the management models used to manage Windows systems and the importance of each of them. This section will also cover the concept of baselining and the importance of following a standard with defined procedures and processes that have leadership support and sign-off.

In the second section, we will dive into the technical aspects of what is needed to apply security and hardening to your Windows environment. This section will not only provide the technical details of how to harden both the Windows server and client OS, but we will review all the different management scenarios and the importance of administration and remote management from a security standpoint. Most importantly, ensuring secure administration and the remote management of your Windows systems is vital. We will review the networking components as they relate to the hardening of Windows and then provide information about identity and access management and how critical the protection of identity has become in the digital world today.

The final section provides more of an operational focus on how to best protect and monitor your Windows environment. It is critical for your security program to not only implement the recommended security controls but validate that controls are in place. To do this effectively, we need to perform auditing and testing against the configurations implemented to harden Windows environments. In addition, it's just as important to monitor environments and provide reporting. We will look at an in-depth overview of the security operations program and discuss the tools that can be used for efficient incident management.

We will primarily focus on the most current versions of Windows available today, including Windows Server 2019, Windows 10, and the resources available within Microsoft Azure. We understand migrating to the latest Windows OS and shifting workloads from on-premises to the cloud is not an overnight task and may take years. In general, the concepts we provide throughout this book can be used within most configurations of Windows but could vary slightly depending on the build or version. Upgrading to the latest version of Windows is critical to the overall hardening of your systems and should be a driving factor to push your migrations forward. It is strongly recommended to upgrade as soon as possible as Microsoft will no longer release security patches or offer support for deprecated versions.

Who this book is for

This book is intended to educate the technical and security community, which includes the following roles:

- Microsoft security, cloud, and technical roles such as engineers, analysts, architects, and administrators
- Anyone involved with the management of a Windows environment
- All technical related security roles
- Technical/security managers and directors

What this book covers

Chapter 1, *Fundamentals of Windows Security*, provides an introduction to the security world within IT and enterprises. We will cover how security is transforming the way we manage technology and discuss threats and breaches that are relevant today. We will look at current challenges and discuss a concept known as zero trust.

Chapter 2, *Building a Baseline*, provides an overview of baselining and the importance of building a standard to be approved by leadership and adopted by everyone. We will cover what frameworks are and provide an overview of the more common frameworks for security and hardening an environment. We will then look at best practices within enterprises and cover the importance of change management to ensure that anything that falls outside the scope of policy receives the correct approvals.

Chapter 3, *Server Infrastructure Management*, provides an overview of the data center and cloud models that are used today. We will then go into detail on each of the current models as they pertain to the cloud and review secure access management to Windows Server. We will also provide an overview of Windows Server management tools, as well as Azure services for managing Windows servers.

Chapter 4, *End User Device Management*, provides an overview of the end user computing landscape. We will discuss the evolution of device management and review some major models that have emerged over the years. You will learn the importance of a centralized management solution as it pertains to security and how device management solutions are critical for a robust and compliant model. The management solutions covered include device imaging, Windows Autopilot, Microsoft Endpoint Configuration Manager (formerly SCCM), Intune **Mobile Device Management (MDM)**, and Microsoft Endpoint Manager Admin Center.

Chapter 5, *Hardware and Virtualization*, provides an overview of physical servers and virtualization. The chapter will cover hardware certification, enhancements in hardware security, and **Virtualization-Based Security (VBS)** concepts to secure and harden devices, including BIOS, UEFI, TPM 2.0, Secure Boot, and advanced protection with VBS.

Chapter 6, *Network Fundamentals for Hardening Windows*, provides an overview of networking components and how they play a big role in hardening and securing your Windows environment. You will learn about Windows Defender Firewall and Advanced Security, Windows Defender Exploit Guard Network Protection, and how to configure them on your Windows devices. Additionally, you will be provided with the knowledge needed to understand the latest technology from Microsoft as it relates to network security for your Windows VMs in Azure.

Chapter 7, *Identity and Access Management*, provides a comprehensive overview of identity management and the importance it plays in securing and hardening your Windows systems. Identity has become the foundation of securing users – this chapter will cover everything you need to do within the identity and access management area. We will provide more details on account and access management, authentication, MFA, passwordless authentication, conditional access, and identity protection.

Chapter 8, *Administration and Remote Management*, provides details on different methods for administration and remote management as they relate to the Windows infrastructure. You will be provided with the knowledge needed to ensure that best practices are applied and will learn how to apply those best practices. The topics covered include enforcing policies with Configuration Manager and Intune, building security baselines, connecting securely to servers remotely, and an overview of PowerShell security.

Chapter 9, *Keeping Your Windows Client Secure*, covers Windows clients and the different solutions used to keep them secure and updated. You will also learn hardening techniques to secure exploits commonly used by attackers. The chapter also covers onboarding machines to Microsoft Defender ATP and Windows Update for Business, and provides details on advanced Windows hardening configurations for Windows 10 privacy.

Chapter 10, *Keeping Your Windows Server Secure*, looks at the Windows Server OS and introduces server roles and the security-related features of Windows Server 2019. You will learn about techniques used to keep your Windows server secure by implementing **Windows Server Update Services (WSUS)** and Azure Update Management, onboarding machines to Microsoft Defender ATP, and enforcing a security baseline. You will also learn how to deploy a Windows Defender application control policy.

Chapter 11, *Security Monitoring and Reporting*, talks about the different tools available that provide telemetry as well as insights and recommendations to help secure your environment. This chapter will inform you about the ways to act on recommendations to help secure your environment. Technologies covered include Microsoft Defender ATP, Log Analytics, Azure Monitor, and Azure Security Center.

Chapter 12, *Security Operations*, talks about the **Security Operations Center (SOC)** in an organization and discusses various tools used to ingest and analyze data to detect, protect, and alert you to incidents.

Chapter 13, *Testing and Auditing*, goes through validating that controls are in place and enforced. You will also learn about the importance of continual vulnerability scanning and testing in addition to the importance of penetration testing to ensure that the environment is assessed in terms of its ability to protect against the latest threats.

Chapter 14, *Top 10 Recommendations and the Future*, provides recommendations and actions to take away after reading this book. It also provides some insight into the direction of where the future of device security and management is headed, as well as some insight into our thoughts on the importance of security in the future.

To get the most out of this book

In order to get the most out of this book, the following items will be needed to follow along with the examples provided. Thanks to cloud technology, you will be able to quickly enable an environment to build the infrastructure and foundation needed to support your journey throughout this book.

It is recommended that you set up an Office 365 subscription (add your own custom domain), which will in turn create an **Azure Active Directory** (**AAD**) tenant. Once the AAD tenant has been set up, this will allow you to add an Azure subscription to begin consuming Azure resources tied to your Office 365 subscription and your custom domains.

Office 365 E5 30-day free trial: `https://go.microsoft.com/fwlink/p/?LinkID=698279&culture=en-US&country=US`

Azure account with $200 credit for 30 days: `https://azure.microsoft.com/en-us/free/`

Cloud subscriptions required

- An Azure subscription
- Microsoft Enterprise E5
- An Intune subscription and license
- Microsoft Defender ATP licensing (Windows 10 E5 or M365 E5)
- Enterprise Mobility + Security E3 or E5 (includes AAD Premium P2)

Permissions

- Global administrator rights to your Office 365 subscription
- Owner role or appropriate RBAC to your Azure subscription to deploy resources
- Domain admin rights on your domain controller or equivalent rights to modify Group Policy

Azure resources

- Azure VMs (Windows 10 and Windows Server 2019 Core and Desktop versions from Marketplace)
- A virtual network, subnet, network security group, and resource group
- AAD
- Azure Security Center Standard
- Azure Sentinel
- Azure Bastion
- Microsoft Cloud App Security
- A Log Analytics workspace
- An Azure Automation account
- Azure Update Management
- Azure Privileged Identity Management

Applications, tools, and services

- PowerShell (version 5.1 recommended) with the AAD module and the Azure PowerShell Az module
- Text viewer to edit and open JSON files
- Windows Assessment and Deployment Kit
- Windows Deployment Services (Windows Server roles and features)
- Microsoft Deployment Toolkit
- System Center (Configuration Manager) hierarchy
- Windows 2016 Active Directory and domain functional level
- Microsoft Security Compliance Toolkit
- WSUS
- Windows 10 Pro/Enterprise, Windows Server 2016+ Core/Datacenter

All licensing and pricing is subject to change by Microsoft. Additionally, many of the products that are mentioned are covered under a license bundle, or available à la carte if you only want to enable a small subset of features.

For information about licensing Microsoft 365, visit this link:

`http://download.microsoft.com/download/8/7/7/877B1713-671E-43AA-BB79-AF8478C64AFF/Licensing-Microsoft-365.pdf`

To compare the different products available in the Microsoft 365 plans, visit this link:

`https://www.microsoft.com/en-us/microsoft-365/compare-microsoft-365-enterprise-plans`

For AAD pricing and features, visit this link:

`https://azure.microsoft.com/en-us/pricing/details/active-directory/`

If you are using the digital version of this book, we advise you to type the code yourself. Doing so will help you avoid any potential errors related to the copying and pasting of code.

Code in Action

Code in Action videos for this book can be viewed at (`https://bit.ly/2VEPO3t`).

Download the color images

We also provide a PDF file that has color images of the screenshots/diagrams used in this book. You can download it here: `http://www.packtpub.com/sites/default/files/downloads/9781839216411_ColorImages.pdf`.

Conventions used

There are a number of text conventions used throughout this book.

`Code in text`: Indicates code words in text, database table names, folder names, filenames, file extensions, pathnames, dummy URLs, user input, and Twitter handles. Here is an example: "Mount the downloaded `WebStorm-10*.dmg` disk image file as another disk in your system."

A block of code is set as follows:

```
html, body, #map {
  height: 100%;
  margin: 0;
  padding: 0
}
```

When we wish to draw your attention to a particular part of a code block, the relevant lines or items are set in bold:

```
[default]
exten => s,1,Dial(Zap/1|30)
exten => s,2,Voicemail(u100)
exten => s,102,Voicemail(b100)
exten => i,1,Voicemail(s0)
```

Any command-line input or output is written as follows:

```
$ mkdir css
$ cd css
```

Bold: Indicates a new term, an important word, or words that you see onscreen. For example, words in menus or dialog boxes appear in the text like this. Here is an example: "Select **System info** from the **Administration** panel."

> **Tips or important notes**
> Appear like this.

Get in touch

Feedback from our readers is always welcome.

General feedback: If you have questions about any aspect of this book, mention the book title in the subject of your message and email us at customercare@packtpub.com.

Errata: Although we have taken every care to ensure the accuracy of our content, mistakes do happen. If you have found a mistake in this book, we would be grateful if you would report this to us. Please visit www.packtpub.com/support/errata, selecting your book, clicking on the Errata Submission Form link, and entering the details.

Piracy: If you come across any illegal copies of our works in any form on the Internet, we would be grateful if you would provide us with the location address or website name. Please contact us at copyright@packt.com with a link to the material.

If you are interested in becoming an author: If there is a topic that you have expertise in and you are interested in either writing or contributing to a book, please visit authors.packtpub.com.

Reviews

Please leave a review. Once you have read and used this book, why not leave a review on the site that you purchased it from? Potential readers can then see and use your unbiased opinion to make purchase decisions, we at Packt can understand what you think about our products, and our authors can see your feedback on their book. Thank you!

For more information about Packt, please visit packt.com.

Section 1: Getting Started

This section will provide you with an overview of security fundamentals and the importance of building a baseline. It will also provide information on infrastructure models, and talk about end user computing evolutions and the solutions we can use to manage them.

This section includes the following chapters:

- *Chapter 1, Fundamentals of Windows Security*
- *Chapter 2, Building a Baseline*
- *Chapter 3, Server Infrastructure Management*
- *Chapter 4, End User Device Management*

1
Fundamentals of Windows Security

Nowadays, the conversation of cybersecurity has become a hot topic throughout the world. And even more so with leadership teams and board members of many major organizations asking the question, are we secure? The short answer is no: no one is secure in today's digital world, and there has never been a more critical time to ensure that you are doing everything within your power to protect your organization and its users.

As we continue to receive daily news of breaches throughout the world, it is clear how severe the issue of cybercrime has become. To put it bluntly, we simply need to do a better job of protecting the data that we collect and manage within our organizations today. This isn't an easy task, especially with the advancement of organized cyber and state-sponsored groups with budgets, most likely, far exceeding that of most organizations. As security professionals, we need to do our due diligence and ensure we identify all risks within the organization. Once identified, they will need to be addressed or accepted as a risk by leadership.

As a consumer, it is most likely that your data has already been breached, and there's a chance your account information and passwords are sitting on the dark web somewhere. We need to work with the assumption that our personal data has already been breached and build better barriers around our data and account information. For example, in the U.S., purchasing identity protection as a service to monitor your identity can serve as an insurance policy if you incur any damages. In addition to this, the ability to place your credit reports on hold to prevent bad actors from opening accounts under your name is another example of a defensive approach that you can take to protect your personal identity.

As the cybersecurity workforce continues to evolve and strengthen with more and more talented individuals, we want to help contribute to the importance of securing our data, and we hope this book provides you with the necessary knowledge to do the right thing for your organization. As you read this book, you will not only learn the technical aspects of securing Windows, but you will also learn what else is necessary to ensure the protection of Windows and the users that use it. Protecting Windows has become a lot more than making a few simple configuration changes and installing an **antivirus (AV)** tool. There is an entire ecosystem of controls, tools, and technology to help protect your Windows systems and users.

As you read through this chapter, you will learn about the broader fundamentals of security and the principles behind the foundation that is needed to protect your Windows environment. Specifically, you will learn about the following:

- An overview of the security transformation within the industry
- A look at security trends as they relate to today's digital world
- A review of the current threat landscape and common vulnerabilities
- An overview of some recent publicly known breaches
- An overview of the current security challenges faced today
- What Zero Trust security is, and why we need to adopt this approach moving forward

Understanding the security transformation

Over the years, security has evolved from being just a shared role or a role that didn't even exist within a business. Today, well-defined teams and organizational structures do actually exist or are being created to focus solely on security. Not only are these teams maturing constantly, but the **Chief Information Security Officer (CISO)** has become a person of significant importance who may report directly to a **Chief Executive Officer (CEO)** within an organization and not the CIO.

Over the years, many roles that never existed before have begun to appear within the security world, and new skill sets are always in demand. As an overview, the following is a list of some of the more common security roles that you can expect to see within a security program:

- CISO/CSO (Chief Information Security Officer/Chief Security Officer)
- IT Security Director
- IT Security Manager
- Security Architect/Engineer
- Security Analyst
- Security/Compliance Officer
- Security Administrator
- Security Engineer
- Software/Application Security Developer
- Software/Application Security Engineer
- Cryptographer/Cryptologist
- Security Consultant/Specialist
- Network Security Engineer
- Cloud Security Architect

One thing to point out, in regard to these roles, is the major shortage of the cybersecurity workforce throughout the world. A cybersecurity workforce study by (ISC)² shows that a worldwide growth of 145% is needed to meet the demand for cyber experts. In the US, this number needs to grow by 62%. These numbers clearly show the demand for skilled cybersecurity experts along with opportunities for growth. The challenge with this growth is that new positions are continuously being created as new skills are needed, which makes it difficult to find well-seasoned talent (read more about the (ISC)² 2019 Cybersecurity Workforce Study here: `https://www.isc2.org/Research/Workforce-Study`).

One of the primary factors for the growing need of security experts correlates to the advancement of the PC (or personal computer) and its evolution throughout the years. The PC has changed the way we connect. And, with this evolution comes the supporting infrastructure, which has evolved into many data centers seen throughout the world.

As we are all aware, Windows has been the victim of numerous vulnerabilities over the years and continues to be a victim even today. The initial idea behind the Windows **Operating System (OS)** was a strong focus on usability and productivity. As a result of its success and adoption across the globe, it became a common target for exploits. This, in turn, created many gaps in the security of Windows that have traditionally been filled by many other companies. A good example is a need for third-party AV software. As the world has turned more toward digitization over the years, and the adoption of Windows usage has continued to grow, so has the need for improved security along with dedicated roles within this area. Protecting Windows has not been an easy task, and it continues to be an ongoing challenge.

Living in today's digital world

Today, we are more reliant on technology than ever and live in a world where businesses cannot survive without it. As our younger generations grow up, there is greater demand for the use of advanced technology. One scary thought is how fast the world has grown within the previous 100 years compared to the overall history of mankind. Technology continues to push the boundaries of innovation, and a significant portion of that change must include the securing of this technology. Especially since the world has become a more connected place with the advancement of the internet.

To give you a rough idea of technology usage today, let's take a look at the current desktop usage throughout the world. For these statistics, we will reference an online service, called Statcounter GlobalStats: https://gs.statcounter.com/. This dataset is not all-inclusive, but there is a very large sampling of data used to give us a good idea of worldwide usage. Statcounter GlobalStats collects its data through web analytics via tracking code on over 2 million websites globally. The aggregation of this data equates to more than 10 billion page views per month. The following screenshot shows the OS market share that is in use worldwide. More information from Statcounter can be viewed at https://gs.statcounter.com/os-market-share/desktop/worldwide:

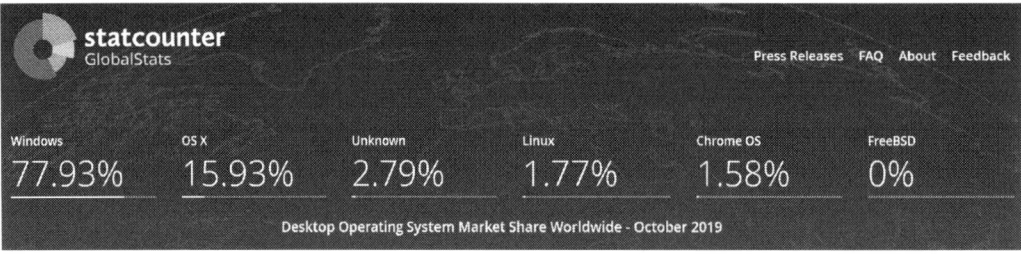

Figure 1.1 – Statcounter Desktop Operating System Market Share Worldwide

As you can see, the Windows desktop market is more widely adopted than any other OS available today. Seemingly, Windows has always had negative connotations because of its ongoing vulnerabilities in comparison to other OSes. Part of this is due to how widely used Windows actually is. A hacker isn't going to waste their time on an OS that isn't widely adopted. We can assume there would be a direct correlation between OS adoption rates and available security vulnerabilities. Additionally, the Windows OS is supported across many types of hardware, which opens up opportunities for exploits to be developed. One reason as to why we see significantly fewer macOS vulnerabilities is due to the hardware control with which Apple allows its software to run. As the platform has grown, though, we have seen an increase of vulnerabilities within its OS too. The point we're making is that we tend to focus our efforts on areas where it makes sense, and Windows has continued to be a leader in the desktop space, making it a very attractive source to be attacked. This, in turn, has created an ecosystem of vendors and products over the years, all aimed at helping to protect and secure Windows' systems.

Let's take a look at the current adoption of the different Windows OSes in use. The following screenshot from Statcounter shows the current Windows desktop version usage around the world today. To view these statistics, visit `https://gs.statcounter.com/os-version-market-share/windows/desktop/worldwide`:

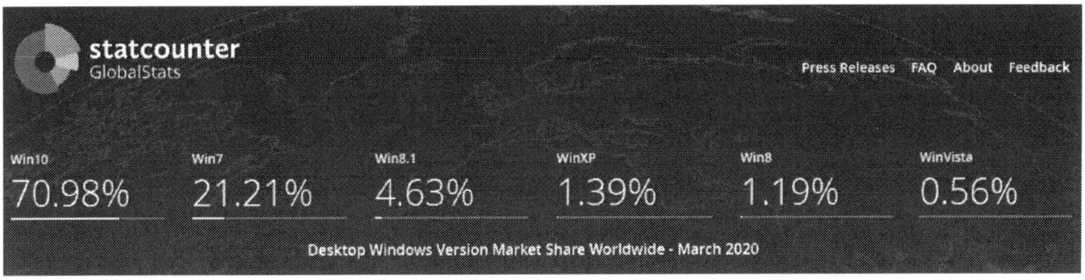

Win10	Win7	Win8.1	WinXP	Win8	WinVista
70.98%	21.21%	4.63%	1.39%	1.19%	0.56%

Desktop Windows Version Market Share Worldwide - March 2020

Figure 1.2 – Desktop Windows Version Market Share Worldwide

As you can see, Windows 10 has become the most adopted OS. Microsoft continues to push more users and organizations to Windows 10, and this is where they spend the majority of their development resources. There are also major changes to Windows 10 compared to older versions, which is why it is critical to migrate from older versions, especially for security-specific reasons. Microsoft ended its support (including security updates) for Windows XP in April 2014 and Windows 7 in January 2020.

NetMarketShare is another analytical site similar to Statcounter GlobalStats with its own set of statistics for reference: `https://netmarketshare.com/`.

A recent buzz term you have most likely heard in recent years is that of **digital transformation**. This refers to the shift from a legacy on-premises infrastructure to a modernized cloud-first strategy to support the evolving need of big data, machine learning, **Artificial Intelligence** (**AI**), and more. A significant part of this shift also falls within Windows systems and management. In *Chapter 3, Server Infrastructure Management,* we will look at the differences between a data center and a cloud model, including where the responsibilities fall for maintaining and securing underlying systems. Prior to digital transformation, we relied heavily on the four walls of the corporation and its network to protect a data center and its systems. This included a requirement for client devices to be physically on the corporate network in order to access data and services. With this model, our devices were a little easier to manage and lock down, as they never left the corporate office. Today, the dynamics have changed, and, referencing back to Statcounter in the following screenshot, you can see a significant shift from traditional desktop usage to a more mobile experience and requirement. To view the source of this diagram, visit https://gs.statcounter.com/platform-market-share/desktop-mobile-tablet/worldwide/#monthly-200901-202003:

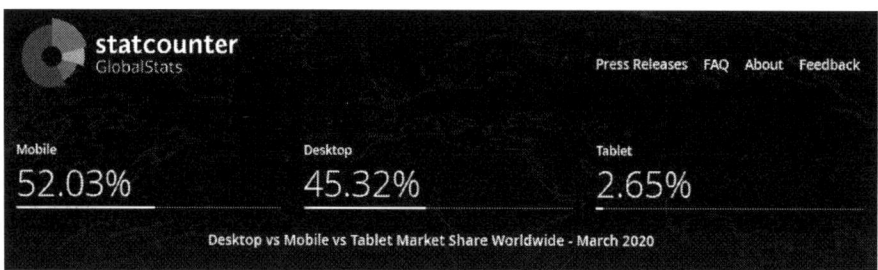

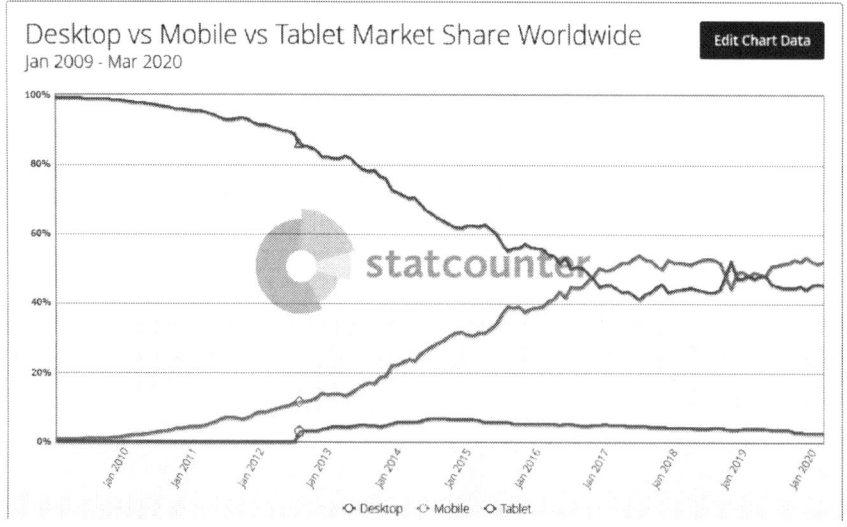

Figure 1.3 – Statcounter platform comparison Jan 2009 – Mar 2020

Focusing on Windows security, the traditional model of an organization would have typically included the following security tools as part of its baseline:

- AV (antivirus software)
- Windows Firewall
- Internet proxy service
- Windows updates

Depending on your organization or industry, there may have been additional tools. However, for the most part, I'd imagine the preceding list was the extent of most organizations' security tools on Windows client devices. The same would have most likely applied to the Windows servers in the traditional model. As this digital transformation has brought change, the traditional method of Windows management has become a legacy. There is an expectation that we can work and access data from anywhere at any time. We live in an internet-connected world, and, when we plug our device in, we expect to access our data with ease. With this shift, there is a major change in the security of the systems we manage and, specifically, the Windows server and client. As we shift our infrastructure to the cloud and enable our users to become less restricted, the focus of security revolves not only around the device itself but that of the user's identity and, more importantly, the data. Today, the items that we listed earlier will not suffice. The following tools are those that would be needed to better protect your Windows devices:

- **Advanced Threat Protection (ATP)**: AV and threat protection, advanced analytics and behavioral monitoring, network protection, exploit protection, and more
- Advanced data loss prevention
- Information protection
- Identity protection: biometric technology, multi-factor authentication, and more
- Application control
- Machine learning and advanced AI security services

Today's threats

The threat landscape within the cyber world is extremely diverse and is continually becoming more complex. The task of protecting users, data, and systems is becoming more difficult and requires the advancement of even more intelligent tools to keep the bad actors out. Today, criminals are more sophisticated, and large groups have formed with significant financial backing to support the wrongdoings of these groups. The following is a list of cyber threats:

- National governments
- Nationstates
- Terrorists
- Spies
- Organized crime groups
- Hacktivists
- Hackers
- Business competitors
- Insiders/internal employees

> **Tip**
> To learn more about these cyber threat sources, the Department of Homeland Security has a great reference here: `https://www.us-cert.gov/ics/content/cyber-threat-source-descriptions`.

To shed some light on real-world examples of data breach sources today, Verizon has created a *2020 Data Breach Investigations Report* (`https://enterprise.verizon.com/resources/reports/dbir/`). The report is built on a set of real-world data and contains some eye-opening data on attack sources:

- External actors: 70%
- Organized criminal groups: 55%
- Internal actors: 30%
- Partners: 1%
- Multiple parties involved: 1%

The full report can be found here:

`https://enterprise.verizon.com/resources/reports/2020-data-breach-investigations-report.pdf`

There are many types of cyberattacks in the world today, and this creates a diverse set of challenges for organizations. While not all threats are Windows-specific, there's a chance that Windows is the median or attack vector in which an attacker gains access by exploiting a vulnerability. An example of this could be an unpatched OS or an out-of-date application. The following list contains many common types of threats that could cause damage directly from a vulnerability within the Windows OS or by using the Windows OS as an attack vector.

Malware is software or code designed with malicious intent that exploits vulnerabilities found within the system. The following types of threats are considered malware:

- Adware
- Spyware
- Virus (polymorphic, multipartite, macro, or boot sector)
- Worm
- Trojan
- Rootkit
- Bots/botnets
- Ransomware
- Logic bomb

In addition to malware, the following are types of attack techniques that can be used to exploit vulnerabilities:

- Keylogger
- Phishing
- Spear phishing
- Whale phishing
- SQL injection attack
- **Cross-Site Scripting (XSS)**
- **Denial of Service (DoS)**

- Session hijacking
- **Man-in-the-Middle Attacks (MITM)**
- Password attacks (brute-force, dictionary, or birthday attacks)
- Credential reuse
- Identity theft
- Advanced persistent threats
- **Distributed Denial of Service (DDoS)**
- Intellectual property theft
- Shoulder surfing
- Golden Ticket: Kerberos attacks

> **Tip**
> To learn more about the threats listed earlier, the **National Institute of Standards and Technology** (**NIST**) contains a glossary that provides more information on most, if not all, of the preceding list: `https://csrc.nist.gov/glossary`.

Identifying vulnerabilities

Now that we know more about the threats, it's even more important for you to know where to access information about these vulnerabilities. You also need to be aware of any resources that are available so that you can educate yourself on what's required to remediate any vulnerabilities. As you are already aware, Windows is renowned for its ongoing vulnerabilities, and patching/updating these systems has morphed into a full-time and very specialized role over the years. The following website is the authoritative source with regard to Microsoft security updates: `https://portal.msrc.microsoft.com/en-us/security-guidance`.

> **Useful information**
> Here is the link to the **Microsoft Security Response Center** (**MSRC**): `https://www.microsoft.com/en-us/msrc?rtc=1`.

As shown in the following screenshot, you will be provided with a list of all identified vulnerabilities from Microsoft within a selected time range with additional filtering options. To give you an idea of the risk profile for Windows, the following filter is scoped to Windows 10 for x64-based systems over the last month, which returned 47 uniquely addressed vulnerabilities:

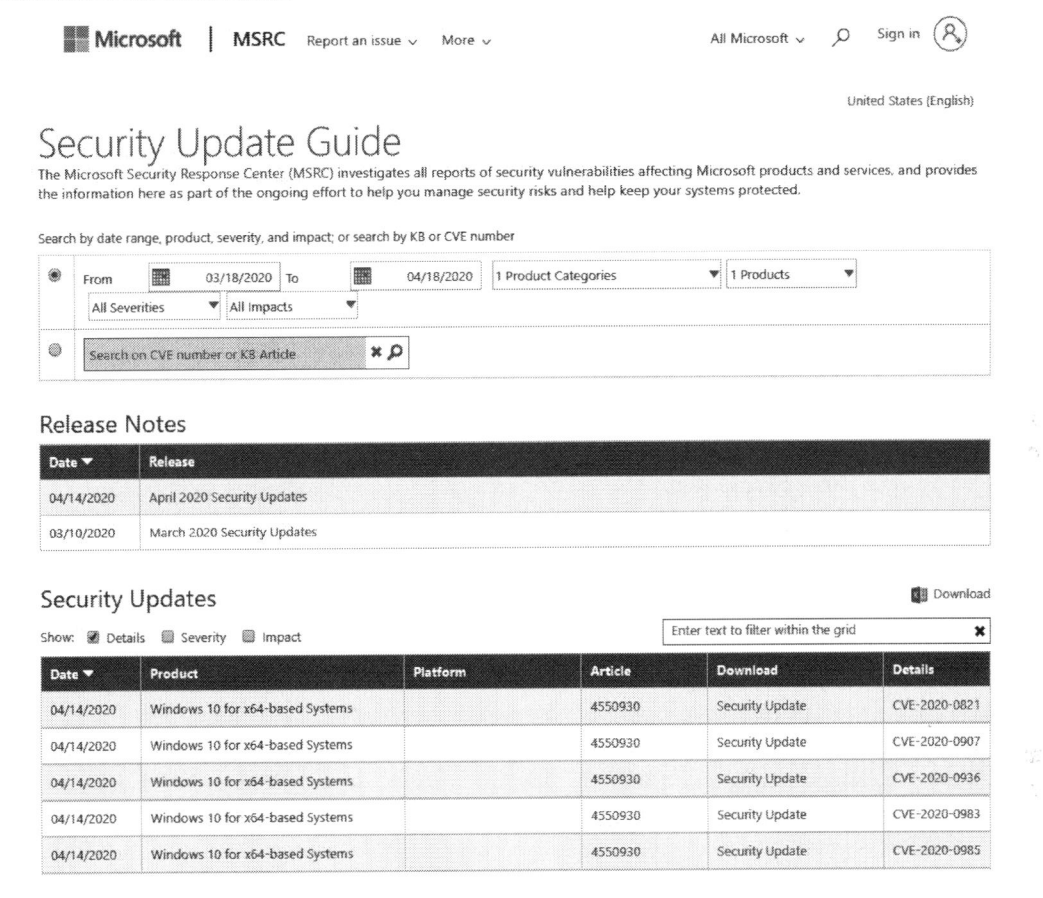

Figure 1.4 – Microsoft Security Update Guide

One term you may have heard as part of vulnerability management with Microsoft is the famous Patch Tuesday (also referred to as Update Tuesday). Patch Tuesday occurs on the second Tuesday of every month and is the day that Microsoft releases its monthly patches for Windows and other Microsoft products. There are many references on the internet for Patch Tuesday in addition to the MSRC. One example of a common resource used to track Patch Tuesday releases is the Patch Tuesday Dashboard: `https://patchtuesdaydashboard.com/`. Another example to better manage your notifications when vulnerabilities are released is `PatchManagement.org`: `http://patchmanagement.org/`.

As you review the updates needed for your Windows systems, you will notice that each of them has a unique identifier to reference the update beginning with CVE®. **CVE** stands for **Common Vulnerabilities and Exposures** and is the standard for vulnerability management, allowing one source to catalog and uniquely identify vulnerabilities. CVE is not a database of vulnerabilities but a dictionary providing definitions for vulnerabilities and exposures that have been publicly disclosed. The U.S. **Department of Homeland Security (DHS)** and the **Cybersecurity and Infrastructure Security Agency (CISA)** sponsor the CVE.

> **Tip**
>
> Visit this website to learn more about CVE: `https://cve.mitre.org/about/index.html`.

The following screenshot shows an overview of what the CVE provides and can be found at `https://cve.mitre.org/cgi-bin/cvekey.cgi?keyword=Windows`:

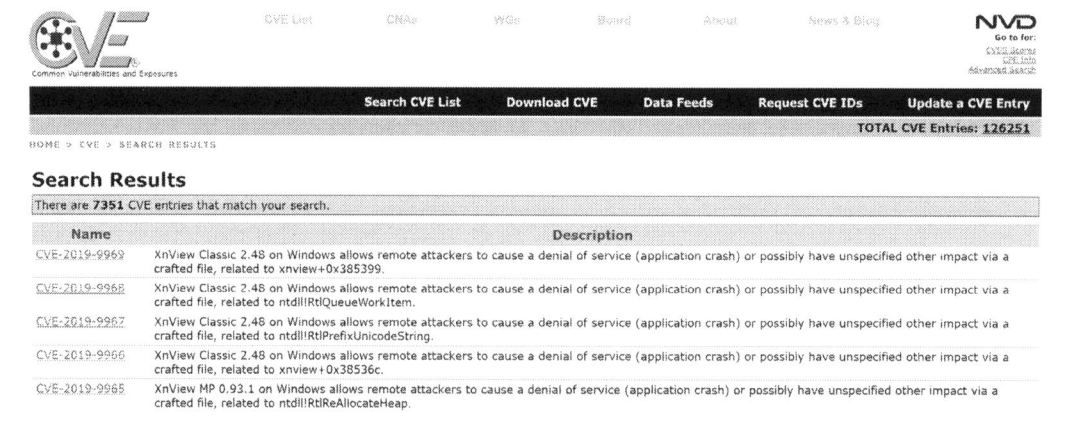

Figure 1.5 – CVE® Windows Search Results

In addition to the CVE there's the NVD. The **NVD** is the **National Vulnerability Database**, which is an additional resource for vulnerability management provided by NIST. The NVD is synced with the CVE to ensure the latest updates appear within its repository. The NVD provides additional analysis of the vulnerabilities listed in the CVE dictionary by using the following:

- **Common Vulnerability Scoring System (CVSS)** for impact analysis
- **Common Weakness Enumeration (CWE)** for vulnerability types
- **Common Platform Enumeration (CPE)** for a structured naming standard

Identifying vulnerabilities 33

The following screenshot shows an overview of what the NVD provides and can be found via `https://nvd.nist.gov/vuln/search/results?form_type=Basic&results_type=overview&query=Windows&search_type=all`:

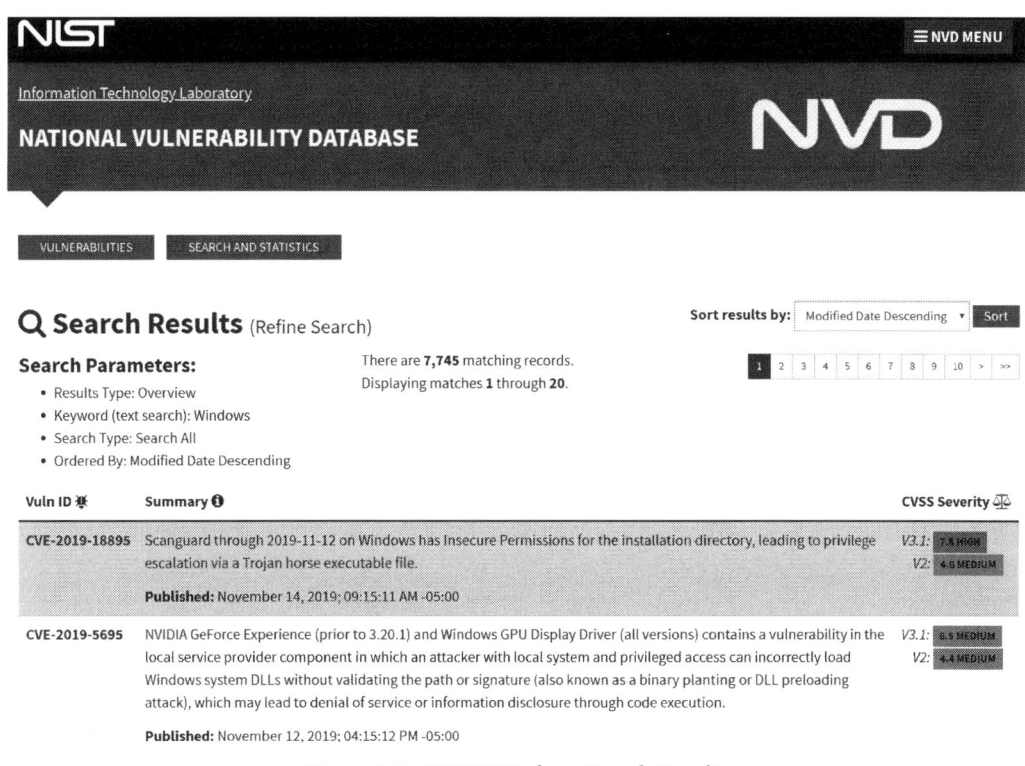

Figure 1.6 – NVD Windows Search Results

One additional resource that we should mention is the **Open Web Application Security Project** (**OWASP**). OWASP is a nonprofit organization to help improve the security of software for individuals and enterprises. They provide a tremendous amount of resources such as tools, documentation, and a community of professionals all looking to continually enhance software security. Although application and web-specific, there is a high possibility that the application or web app will be running on both your Windows server and Windows client. Because of this, it is critical, as a security professional, for you to be able to intelligently discuss these concerns and challenges with the business, developer(s), and application/web app owners.

> **Tip**
> You can find more information about OWASP at `https://www.owasp.org/index.php/Main_Page`.

One of the more common projects that OWASP provides is the OWASP Top 10, which provides the most critical web application security risks. The latest version available was published in 2017 and is presented here:

1. Injection
2. Broken authentication
3. Sensitive data exposure
4. **XML External Entities (XXE)**
5. Broken access control
6. Security misconfiguration
7. **Cross-Site Scripting (XSS)**
8. Insecure deserialization
9. Using components with known vulnerabilities
10. Insufficient logging and monitoring

> **Tip**
> View OWASP Top 10 2017 – The Ten Most Critical Web Application Security Risks here: `https://owasp.org/www-project-top-ten/OWASP_Top_Ten_2017/`.

Recognizing breaches

If you follow the news, you are probably aware that there is no shortage of breaches today. They are happening so frequently that it is not uncommon for several breaches to occur weekly or even daily. What is an even scarier thought is these are just the ones that we hear about. To give you an idea of how serious the issue has become, the following list has some of the more notable breaches that are documented on Wikipedia's *List of data breaches* page. There are many sources on the internet of top breaches, but Wikipedia has the most comprehensive I have found with references to each of the listings:

Company	Year	# breached records	Reason
Yahoo	2013	3,000,000,000	Hacked
First American Corporation	2019	885,000,000	Poor security
Facebook	2019	540,000,000	Poor security
Marriott International	2018	500,000,000	Hacked
Yahoo	2014	500,000,000	Hacked
Friend Finder Networks	2016	412,214,295	Poor security / Hacked
Zynga	2019	218,000,000	Hacked
Adobe Systems	2013	152,000,000	Hacked
Under Armour	2018	150,000,000	Hacked
eBay	2014	145,000,000	Hacked
Equifax	2017	143,000,000	Poor security
Canva	2019	140,000,000	Hacked
Heartland	2009	130,000,000	Hacked
Target Corporation	2013	110,000,000	Hacked
Capital One	2019	106,000,000	Hacked
Quora	2018	100,000,000	Hacked

Figure 1.7 – Wikipedia List of data breaches

You can find the source for the preceding screenshot here: `https://en.wikipedia.org/wiki/List_of_data_breaches`.

As you review the breaches and understand how they occurred, you will see a common trend where, for the most part, the breach occurred from hacking or poor security practices. You might also notice that other common methods of breaches include lost or stolen equipment. These statistics are alarming, and they indicate how critical it is to secure and harden our systems as best as possible.

To give you an idea of the importance of securing and hardening your environment, the article referenced next shows that the cost of a user record from a data breach is $242 per record. A quick calculation of this multiplied by 100,000 customers calculates a potential loss estimated at $24.2 million. When you look at the number of breached records shown in the table, you will understand how this could be extremely damaging to a business's value and reputation.

View the table at *What's the Real Cost of a Data Breach?* here: `https://www.pkware.com/blog/what-s-the-real-cost-of-a-data-breach`.

> **Tip**
> An interesting site for reference is *Have I Been Pwned*. This site will show you whether your email has ever been breached and, if so, where it was breached: `https://haveibeenpwned.com/`. You can also sign up for notifications for any breaches related to a specific domain.

There are many sources available where you can view security news and follow the latest trends and best practices. The following are some of the resources used to keep up to date with what is happening in the security world today:

- DarkReading: `https://www.darkreading.com/`
- Cyware: `https://cyware.com/cyber-security-news-articles` (recommended phone app)
- Business Insider: `https://www.businessinsider.com/sai`
- ZDNet: `https://www.zdnet.com/topic/security/`
- Newsfusion Cyber Security News: `https://www.newsfusion.com/cyber-security` (recommended phone app)
- BBC: `https://www.bbc.com/news/technology`
- The Hacker News: `https://thehackernews.com/`

Current security challenges

By the time you finish reading through the chapter, you will have hopefully been provided with a sense of how important security has become today and the challenges that come with it. We are continually becoming more reliant on technology than ever before with no signs of slowing down. We have an expectancy of everything being digitized, and, as IoT begins to take off, everything around us will be connected to the internet, thus creating even more challenges to ensure security is efficient.

As we briefly covered earlier, attacks are becoming more and more sophisticated every day. There is an ever-growing army of bad actors working around the clock trying to breach any data they can get their hands on because the cost of private data is very expensive. With the advancement of cloud technology, supercomputers, and the reality of quantum computing coming to light, hackers and organized groups are easily able to crack passwords and their hashes much more easily, making them obsolete as the only factor of authentication. No one should be using only passwords anymore; however, the reality is, most still are. The same applies to encryption. The advancement of computers is making algorithms insecure with the ongoing need for stronger encryption. These are just some of the ongoing challenges we are faced with when protecting our assets.

Keeping up with vulnerabilities today is a full-time role. It's critical that we keep on top of what they are, and which Windows systems need to be updated. We will discuss the management of Windows updates later in the book, but having a program in place to manage the overwhelming amount of Windows updates is critical. Additionally, third-party applications will need to be carefully monitored and updated accordingly. An example of a commonly used application is Adobe Acrobat Reader DC to view PDFs. The following screenshot is a vulnerability report from Microsoft Defender Security Center. It provides a software inventory of all machines with the application installed and lists the number of vulnerabilities detected across all machines in your organization:

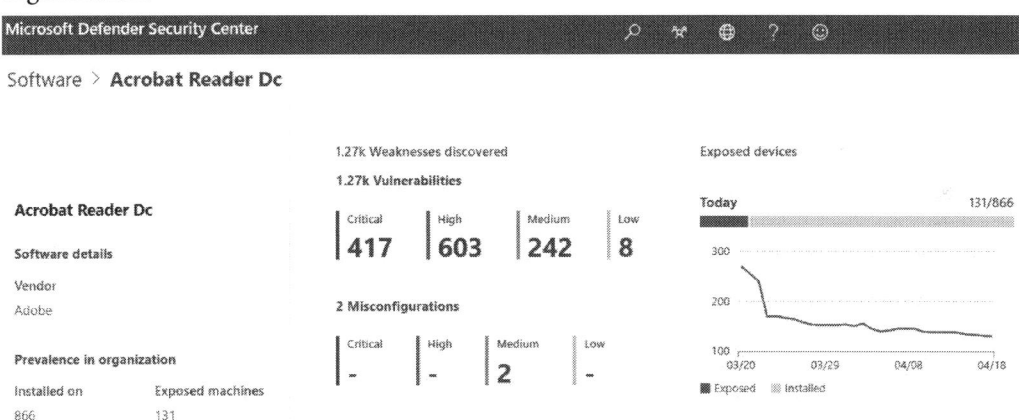

Figure 1.8 – Acrobat Reader DC identified vulnerabilities

As you can see, out-of-date applications have critical known vulnerabilities that are used by attackers.

Most organizations are reluctant to release the latest Windows updates to their servers straight away because of the risk that a patch could break a production system. The downside to this is that your system will have a known vulnerability, which opens an opportunity for it to be exploited between the time of the patch release and the system being patched. Another challenge we are faced with is zero-day vulnerabilities. A zero-day vulnerability is one that has been identified but, currently, has no remediation or mitigation available from the vendor. Because of these challenges, it is critical we build in a layered defense strategy with our Windows clients and servers. For example, never make your database server accessible via the internet, encrypt the traffic to your web servers, and only open the ports needed to communicate, such as only allowing port 443 for secure (HTTPS) traffic only.

As we focus on securing Windows devices within our environments, we can't turn a blind eye to the fundamentals, including the overarching ecosystem that also needs to be considered when protecting your Windows devices. This book will cover a lot of detail on the specifics of securing and hardening your Windows systems and devices, but we also want to ensure the bigger picture is covered; for example, simple concepts of identity and access management. A user whose account has been compromised to allow an intruder on your Windows system has just made all the securing and hardening of that system irrelevant. The concept of weak physical access controls and policies could allow someone to simply walk into a server room and gain physical access to your systems. Other examples are allowing a developer to install an insecure web app with vulnerabilities on it, or a business that develops a process without security best practices in mind. All the controls you put in place with Windows become irrelevant as an educated hacker could use the web app or exploit a process as an attack vector to gain access to your system. These examples show the criticality of not only being familiar with how to secure and harden the Windows OS, but all the other factors that fall within a mature security platform to ensure your environment is as secure as possible. This, of course, doesn't come easily, and it is critical you stay current and continue to learn and learn and learn!

Managing and securing your Windows systems is not a simple task, especially if you are working toward securing them correctly. There is a lot involved, and in order to efficiently and effectively secure your Windows systems, you need well-defined policies, procedures, and standards in place along with a rigorous change control process to ensure anything that falls outside of the standards receives the appropriate approval to minimize risk. Full-time roles exist today to manage and secure your Windows systems along with specialized roles that are necessary to manage your Windows environments. Examples include Windows desktop engineers, Windows server engineers, Windows update administrators, Windows security administrators, Windows Intune/MDM engineers, and others. As part of these roles, it is critical that the staff are continuously educated and trained to provide the best security for Windows. The landscape is changing daily, and if your staff isn't dynamic or doesn't stay educated, mistakes and gaps will occur with your security posture.

Other tasks to think about that must be addressed with your Windows devices are inventory management, that is, ensuring you know where all your devices are and who has access to them. Even more important is ensuring that devices are collected upon any terminations, especially those pertaining to disgruntled employees. Enforcing policies on your Windows devices is also another challenge; for instance, how do you ensure all your devices have the latest policies and how can you ensure accurate reporting on non-compliant devices? Remote management can also be a challenge, that is, to make sure that not just anyone can remotely access your devices, including the auditing of support staff for anything that they shouldn't be doing. Running legacy applications on your Windows devices creates an instant security concern and making sure they are patched to the latest supported version is critical. This list goes on, and we will be diving in much greater detail in the following chapters to help provide the information you need to protect your Windows environment.

Before we move on to the last topic, one additional challenge that needs mentioning is Shadow IT. In short, Shadow IT is the setup and use of servers and infrastructure without IT or the security team's approval or knowledge, for example, a business function. This instantly creates a significant security concern as Windows systems will most likely be used with no standards or hardening in place. This can be a challenge to manage, but it is something that needs to be understood and prevented within any business.

Implementing a Zero Trust approach

To close out the chapter, we wanted to touch on a concept known as **Zero Trust**. The Zero Trust architecture model was created by John Kindervag while he was at Forrester Research Inc. back in 2010. You may be wondering what exactly Zero Trust is. Essentially, it is a model where we trust no one until we can validate who they are, who they are meant to be, and whether they are authorized to have access to the system or information. Effectively implementing a Zero Trust model is going to require a multilayered approach to the security strategy along with the use of the most current and modern technology available. The method of allowing a user to access the environment with only a username and password is outdated and insecure. With Microsoft's version of a Zero Trust model, they are recommending the use of a strong identity, ensuring devices are enrolled within a management tool, enforcing the concept of least privilege, and verifying the health of both devices and services. To support this model, some of the technologies include Azure Active Directory, multi-factor authentication, biometrics, Conditional Access, Microsoft Intune, and Microsoft Defender ATP. As you read through this book, you will find the guidance and instructions that are provided will ultimately lead to a Zero Trust model.

> **Tip**
>
> You can read more about the Zero Trust Microsoft model here: `https://www.microsoft.com/en-us/itshowcase/implementing-a-zero-trust-security-model-at-microsoft`.

Summary

In this chapter, we covered, at a high level, what you can expect to read throughout this book. We provided an overview of the security in an enterprise and briefly covered the different roles that you can expect to see within security departments. Next, we looked at how security relates to the digital world and how relevant it's become as the world becomes more digital. We also looked at the usage of the Windows OS throughout the world to better understand the adoption by users.

We then reviewed the current threat landscape and the types of cyber threat sources. We moved on to provide an overview of the threats we typically see in an enterprise today. We then provided details on where you can go to learn and view all of the recent Microsoft vulnerabilities with correlating patches and instructions on how to keep your devices up to date. In addition to Microsoft's vulnerability resources, we provided additional insight into where the patches get their naming standards via CVE along with NVD, which is provided by NIST. Next, we looked at some of the biggest breaches that have occurred to date and provided some popular sources to keep you up to date with the latest cyber news. We finished the chapter with an insight into some of today's general security challenges and, more specifically, those with Windows systems, before closing with an overview of Zero Trust security and what it entails.

In the next chapter, we will review building a baseline. The chapter will review what a baseline is, and then go into detail as to why a baseline must be formed. As part of the baseline, you need to ensure your policies, standards, and procedures are in place, that they are well-defined, and that they are signed off by the leadership and all the stakeholders who are liable for protecting the data. Having these documented is important for security reasons as well as for compliance and auditing purposes. Following this, we will briefly cover change management and its importance as it relates to baselining. We will then review frameworks and what they entail before moving on to some common frameworks that should be referenced to build your baseline. We will finish the chapter with a review of baseline controls and how to implement them before providing the best practices around baselining.

2
Building a Baseline

In this chapter, we are going to cover the importance of building a baseline for your Windows systems. As you deploy tens to hundreds to thousands of Windows devices, you need to ensure that you are deploying your devices pre-hardened and secured. In addition to this, you need to ensure consistency with every system that is deployed. This is where building a foundation is critical and must be followed. In addition to the baseline requirements, very stringent policies, standards, and procedures must be followed. Anyone falling outside of these boundaries will create additional risk to the organization, so it is critical that a well-defined program is put in place early on with the backing of support and leadership.

As you read through this chapter, you will learn the following:

- An introduction and overview of baselining and its importance
- Policies, standards, procedures, and guidelines used within an enterprise and their relation to baselining
- Incorporating change management
- Implementing a security framework
- Building baseline controls
- Implementing a baseline
- Incorporating best practices

Introduction to baselining

Security baselining is the practice of implementing a minimum set of standards and configuration within your environment; more specifically, capturing a minimum configuration for your Windows devices. Building a baseline provides a minimum defined standard, which will help ensure a more secure environment as you deploy systems and devices within your enterprise. Depending on the size of your organization, baselines could vary from checklists or spreadsheets that someone follows to ensure the predefined security controls are in place to a captured snapshot or image that is already preconfigured with the predefined security controls. In addition to the starting baseline, there are additional management tools to layer and enforce baseline configurations. A couple of examples include **Group Policy Objects (GPOs)** and **Mobile Device Management (MDM)**.

Unless you are a small business with under 100 employees, it would be impractical to deploy any type of system or device and individually configure it every time a new version is built, especially if your user counts and servers start reaching the hundreds to thousands, with an extremely high volume of device deployments carried out on a day-to-day basis. This could also be very error-prone. Because of this, it is extremely important that a well-defined program is put in place to minimize the potential error-prone steps involved with deploying systems, and to ensure that devices receive their baseline and hardening configurations systematically.

Another important factor to consider with baselining is that your organization may be required to follow strict regulatory compliance regulations that will enforce the need to ensure specific security requirements are adhered to. Baselines help when you are audited or when the need to provide evidence arises. Some regulatory compliance examples include the following:

- **Payment Card Industry Data Security Standard (PCI DSS)**
- **Health Insurance Portability and Accountability Act (HIPAA)**
- **Federal Information Security Management Act (FISMA)**
- **The Sarbanes-Oxley Act**
- **General Data Protection Regulation (GDPR)**
- **California Consumer Privacy Act (CCPA)**

We can expect this to continue to grow as privacy continues to become a big discussion point and challenge. It is important to have a minimum understanding of what regulatory compliances are, especially when they directly relate to your organization's sector. They will play a big part in planning your overall security baselining.

As you begin to define and deploy your baselines, you will find that one baseline will not fit all situations. You will need to document and build them for different use cases. The following list gives some examples of where unique baselines may need to be defined:

- Network devices, such as switches, routers, firewalls, and so on
- Windows systems, such as servers and clients
- Linux/Unix systems
- Storage/file servers
- Database servers
- Web servers
- Application servers

As we look more specifically at the Windows environment, you may end up with baselines for different architectures.

For Windows Server, you have the following:

- The Windows **Domain Controller** (**DC**) server
- Windows Server **Internet Information Services** (**IIS**)
- The Windows SQL database server
- The Windows DNS server
- Windows Remote Desktop services

For the Windows client, you have the following:

- The standard Windows client (the user workstation)
- **Privileged Access Workstation** (**PAW**)
- The Windows Virtual client

Now that we've provided an overview of what baselines are, the next few sections will cover items that provide detail around the foundation and overall strategy that support the ability to build well-defined baselines and ensure consistency. Deploying baselines without well-defined policies, processes, and a framework will not be successful in the long term and can leave your organization vulnerable. In addition, having these foundations in place provides a platform to ensure leadership engagement and sign-off, which drives a consistent message to the organization about the importance that each associate has in its success.

Policies, standards, procedures, and guidelines

A follow-on to the previous section is policies, standards, procedures, and guidelines. This section works hand-in-hand with baselining and holds extreme importance within an organization. It is critical that as part of your security program well-defined policies, standards, and procedures are in place and are followed by everyone. In addition, it is important that policies are signed off on and enforced by leadership. Without this support, it becomes more difficult to enforce and collectively get behind security from an organizational level.

Start by defining and creating your company policies. As a result, your standards can then be built to form the foundation of your baselines. Once these baselines are created, procedures and guidelines can be built to implement the baselines and help accomplish the end goal. Keeping this strategy in mind will drive compliance with your company policies.

The following section provides a brief overview of policies, with recommendations of policies, standards, procedures, and guidelines.

Defining policies

A security policy is the first level of formalized documentation for your organization's security program and is mandatory. Policies are a critical component of your overall security program and require sign-off and support from the leadership team to ensure success. Policies should be very broad and general with no direct tie to the technology or solutions within the organization. In general, they should not change often but periodic review is critical. Some examples of policies may include an acceptable use policy, a change management policy, a disaster recovery policy, a privacy policy, an information security program policy, and so on.

If you don't have any policies in place that relate to your Windows security, it is highly recommended that you begin with some basics. The following, as a minimum, should be included to secure your devices and should be referenced in a policy:

- Security updates
- Encryption
- Firewall
- A password policy, **multi-factor authentication** (**MFA**), and biometrics
- A local administrative access strategy
- Security protection tools and antivirus

- Compliance and protection policies
- Data loss prevention and information protection

An example of a policy may include one that requires all systems to be kept up to date with the most recent security updates.

Next, let's look at setting standards to follow the defined policies.

Setting standards

Standards follow policies as they define the specifics of each policy and are mandatory. They provide the direction needed to support the policies. Standards help enforce consistency throughout an organization and provide specifics on the technology to be deployed.

The following are examples of standards for the recommended items listed in the previous section:

- All Windows 10 workstations will be configured using Windows Update for Business and Windows servers will use **Windows Server Update Services** (**WSUS**) or Azure Update Management. Update schedules will be defined and documented by the business use case.
- All Windows servers and end user workstations will be encrypted using BitLocker and/or Azure Disk Encryption.
- The Windows firewall will be enabled and configured on all Windows end user devices and servers. Connection rules will be documented.
- PINs and biometrics with Windows Hello will be set up and accounts will be required to use a password with a minimum of 12 characters. Passwords must contain lowercase, uppercase, numerical, and special characters and will be required to be changed annually.
- MFA will be required for all users accessing the corporate environment and resources.
- There will be no standard user accounts assigned with local admin access on any Windows device.
- All Windows end user devices and servers will have Windows Defender **Advanced Threat Protection** (**ATP**) applied to them.

- Compliance policies for conditions such as device risk and a minimum OS version will be assigned and enforced with Conditional Access on Windows devices
- Unified labeling with data loss prevention and information protection will be deployed to all Windows end user devices.

Next, let's look at building procedures to define a set of instructions used to accomplish tasks.

Creating procedures

Procedures are the step-by-step instructions used to accomplish a repeatable task or process. These instructions are intended to achieve a specific goal and assist with implementing the defined policies and standards, as well as any guidelines that may apply. Procedures can change frequently as software versions change, hardware is replaced, and so on. To help become better organized at following procedures, you may want to look at a third-party tool to help. One example is a tool known as Nintex Promapp, which helps document and share your organization processes. It can be found at `https://www.promapp.com/`.

An example of a procedure is as follows:

1. Deploy a new device with Windows 10.
2. Ensure the device is connected to the internet.
3. Validate the device configurations, that applications have been installed, and so on.
4. Check that the device is compliant.

Finally, let's look at creating guidelines to act as recommended best practices.

Recommending guidelines

Guidelines provide recommendations or best practices and are not mandatory requirements. They can be complementary controls, in addition to standards, or even provide guidance where a standard may not apply.

An example of a guideline may include ensuring that you save and close all documents and programs before rebooting after receiving the latest Windows updates.

Although they are not mandatory, guidelines provide a lot of value to users to help them be more productive with technology. When building guidelines, it's important to think about how to efficiently make the guidelines visible and accessible to users. An effective communication plan is critical in order to ensure users read and use the guidelines. The following is five ideas to help with communicating your guidelines:

- Build a theme around your guideline communications—for example, smart tech guidelines.
- Insert a section of the guidelines in the company newsletters and/or communications.
- Link your guidelines back to a central repository for users to come back to and access.
- Keep your guidelines short and to-the-point.
- Make your guidelines relevant to both professional and personal usage.

The following diagram illustrates a hierarchy of policies, standards, procedures, and guidelines, as well as highlights where baselines fall within the model:

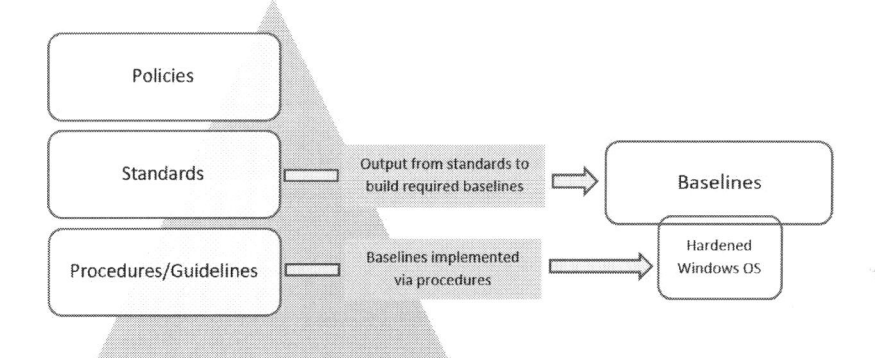

Figure 2.1 – Policies, standards, procedures, guidelines, and baselines

In the next section, we will provide an overview of the change management process. It's important to follow a change control process whenever implementing change in the environment.

Incorporating change management

We won't go into detail about change management, but it is critical that you understand the importance of change management and its place in the overall security program. Your organization most likely has some form of change control process in place today. If not, it is highly recommended and critical that one is enabled to provide a more structured and reliable environment.

The following diagram provides an example of a change flow process that you could implement if you don't already have one in your environment:

Submit Request → Review with Change Board → Receive Approval → Implement and Test Change → Validate Change → Close Request

Figure 2.2 – The change management flow process

Change management is typically part of a larger program, more specifically around service management. One of the more common frameworks to help with change management is **Information Technology Infrastructure Library (ITIL)**.

> **Tip**
> To learn more about ITIL, go to `https://www.axelos.com/best-practice-solutions/itil/what-is-itil`.

As part of your security program, you will want to ensure that all of your baselines are signed off by management and are well documented. More importantly, you will need to ensure that the baselines are implemented with every deployment. If any exceptions or deviations from the baselines are needed, it is extremely important that the requests are pushed through the change management process and are audited. They will need to be reviewed and approved by the appropriate teams, which will most likely include sign off from someone in the security team who is part of the change process. The same will apply to any changes needed to the baselines. As hardware, software, and operating systems change, there will be a need to modify the baseline to adjust to the changes. These changes should also go through a change control process to ensure everyone agrees to and approves the changes.

> **Important note**
> If a security incident occurs on a system where a baseline isn't correctly applied and approvals are not received for that exception, you could be putting your company and, more importantly, your own role at risk.

Next, let's take a look at security frameworks and widely adopted frameworks that can be incorporated into your own security program.

Implementing a security framework

There's a possibility that your organization may have an information security framework in place today. If not, it's highly recommended that you begin to implement one straight away to help lay the foundation of your security program and strategy. There are many different frameworks available for implementation and the direction you take may depend on multiple factors as it relates to your business type, industry requirements, and regulations.

An information security framework is designed to build a well-defined basis for your organization's security program. One of the primary reasons to implement an information security framework is to help reduce risk as much as possible. It will help cover the foundation of everything you need to be aware of within your security program and help to identify any gaps within the organization.

Implementing an information security framework isn't done easily and can be extremely complex and require a major investment of time. Implementing a framework won't just happen overnight; it will take a lot of planning and many months, and even years, to implement correctly. It is important to think of the framework as a journey as you continue to evolve and improve over time.

A significant benefit of implementing a framework within your organization is the ability to provide a well-constructed overview of your security program and strategy to executive management and leadership. A framework will help provide the executive team with a comprehensive overview of what security controls are in place and a road map of work to be completed. This will also allow them to provide feedback, prioritize needs, and provide valuable input. The ability to provide transparency about your security program and strategy with a framework to leadership is a significant advantage.

The following are some of the more common and widely adopted frameworks available today:

- **Control Objectives for Information and Related Technology (COBIT)**: `http://www.isaca.org/cobit/pages/default.aspx`
- **International Standards Organization (ISO)** 27000 Family: `https://www.iso.org/isoiec-27001-information-security.html`
- The **National Institute of Standards and Technology (NIST)** framework for improving critical infrastructure cybersecurity: `https://www.nist.gov/cyberframework`

- NIST SP 800-53, *Security and Privacy Controls for Federal Information Systems and Organizations*: `https://csrc.nist.gov/publications/detail/sp/800-53/rev-4/final`
- NIST SP 800-171, *Protecting Controlled Unclassified Information in Nonfederal Systems and Organizations*: `https://csrc.nist.gov/publications/detail/sp/800-171/rev-2/final`
- **Health Information Trust Alliance Common Security Framework (HITRUST)** CSF: `https://hitrustalliance.net/hitrust-csf/`

Your industry and location within the world may dictate which framework is to be used, but in general, they can all be used throughout any industry as a foundation. As an example, a healthcare organization will most likely adopt the HITRUST framework. ISO 27000 and COBIT will most likely have a more global presence over NIST, which is primarily leveraged by the US government.

To help with your implementation, let's take a closer look at the NIST framework for improving critical infrastructure cybersecurity. Although the framework was initially created for critical infrastructure, it can be used by any organization of any industry and size. This framework has gained a lot of popularity and has been adopted by many. The NIST cybersecurity framework is built around five core functions, as shown:

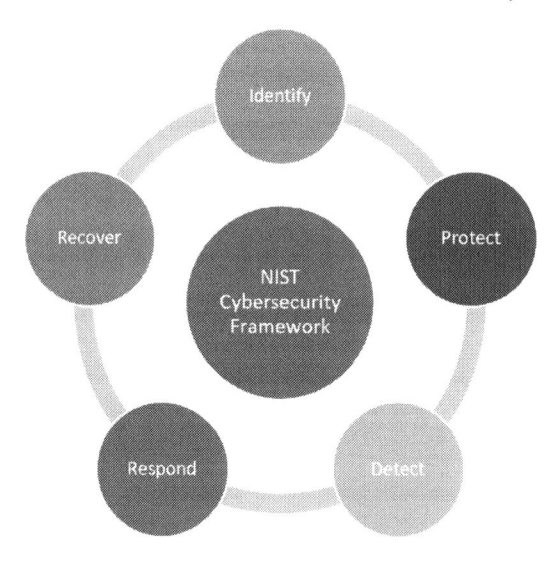

Figure 2.3 – The NIST cybersecurity framework core functions

More information about the five functions in the NIST framework can be found at `https://www.nist.gov/cyberframework/online-learning/five-functions`.

Within these functions are subcategories that provide a set of references on how to manage the risk within that given subcategory. To take this a step further, let's review the specific category that relates to the baseline configuration that you will follow as part of your overall implementation. The following table breaks down the **Protect** function of the NIST framework:

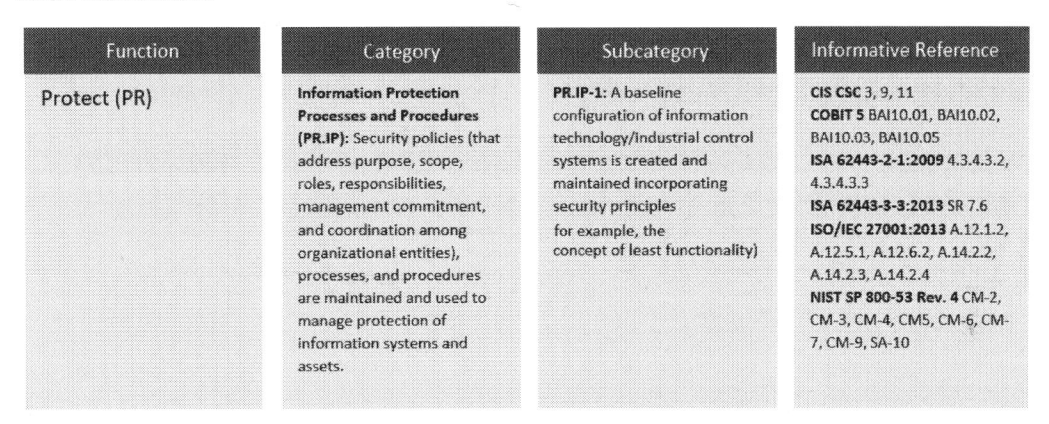

Function	Category	Subcategory	Informative Reference
Protect (PR)	**Information Protection Processes and Procedures (PR.IP):** Security policies (that address purpose, scope, roles, responsibilities, management commitment, and coordination among organizational entities), processes, and procedures are maintained and used to manage protection of information systems and assets.	**PR.IP-1:** A baseline configuration of information technology/industrial control systems is created and maintained incorporating security principles for example, the concept of least functionality)	**CIS CSC** 3, 9, 11 **COBIT 5** BAI10.01, BAI10.02, BAI10.03, BAI10.05 **ISA 62443-2-1:2009** 4.3.4.3.2, 4.3.4.3.3 **ISA 62443-3-3:2013** SR 7.6 **ISO/IEC 27001:2013** A.12.1.2, A.12.5.1, A.12.6.2, A.14.2.2, A.14.2.3, A.14.2.4 **NIST SP 800-53 Rev. 4** CM-2, CM-3, CM-4, CM5, CM-6, CM-7, CM-9, SA-10

Figure 2.4 – Example of the NIST cybersecurity framework

> **Important note**
> The NIST framework for improving critical infrastructure cybersecurity web page that contains the preceding example can be found at `https://nvlpubs.nist.gov/nistpubs/CSWP/NIST.CSWP.04162018.pdf`.

As you can see from the preceding table, the NIST cybersecurity framework provides guidance and resources that can be used to meet the controls. Ensuring a framework is adopted will build a solid foundation to ensure that the required baseline controls to strengthen your systems are put into place. Frameworks represent the overall controls at a higher level and help ensure that there are no gaps in your security program, including any gaps in your Windows infrastructure.

Next, let's look at baseline controls. Baseline controls are set to define a standard set of configurations for your devices.

Building baseline controls

Moving on, we will cover some more details about the baseline controls that can be used o your Windows devices. Here, we will cover the following:

- **Center for Internet Security (CIS®)**
- The Windows security baselines

CIS

First, we will look at CIS. You may already be familiar with CIS and you will often see CIS listed on a lot of lists of the most preferred frameworks, although it's not a full comprehensive framework like the others that we previously listed. Instead, CIS is more of a tactical compilation of controls and guidelines that allows organizations to meet the requirements of a chosen framework. The following screenshot is of the current CIS home page and can be reached by going to https://www.cisecurity.org/:

Figure 2.5 – The CIS home page

CIS is a non-profit organization comprising a global community to provide protection against the ongoing cybersecurity threat landscape. More specifically, the CIS mission is as follows:

- To identify, develop, validate, promote, and sustain best-practice solutions for cyber defense
- To build and lead communities to enable an environment of trust in cyberspace

> **Tip**
> To learn more about CIS, go to `https://www.cisecurity.org/about-us/`.

CIS has an overwhelming number of tools and resources available, many of them being free of charge. More specifically, CIS provides two sets of best practices that are widely adopted throughout the world: CIS controls™ and CIS benchmarks™. CIS controls are a broader set of 20 foundational and advanced controls that provide a more comprehensive approach to overall security protection for your organization, whereas CIS benchmarks are focused more on the specific strengthening of your systems, software, and networks.

> **Tip**
> The CIS cybersecurity best practices can be found at `https://www.cisecurity.org/cybersecurity-best-practices/`.

Next, let's look at the security baselines that are specifically for Windows and the tools we can use to enforce them.

Windows security baselines

Next, we will look at the Microsoft options for baseline controls. As part of their services, Microsoft offers Windows security baselines that provide recommended configurations to provide additional hardening of your Windows systems. The Windows security baselines apply to the following:

- Windows 10
- Windows Server
- Office 365 ProPlus

To give you an idea of the complexity of securing Windows, there are over 3,000 GPO settings for Windows 10 and over 1,800 for Internet Explorer 11. This clearly shows the need to leverage predefined baselines to help strengthen your Windows devices. The more common Microsoft tools used to implement these baselines consist of the following:

- Microsoft Intune
- GPOs
- Microsoft Endpoint or System Center Configuration Manager

> **Tip**
> Go to the following link to view additional information on Windows security baselines: `https://docs.microsoft.com/en-us/windows/security/threat-protection/windows-security-baselines`.

In the next section, we will discuss implementing a baseline using the CIS benchmarks and the Microsoft **Security Compliance Toolkit (SCT)**.

Implementing a baseline

Once a direction has been determined on which baseline controls to use within your organization, you need to review the controls and deploy them throughout your organization, as well as build them into your current process moving forward.

CIS

If you opt to move forward with CIS benchmarks, you will need to download the checklist and customize them for your specific needs. CIS also has the option of purchasing hardened images to provide an easier deployment.

To download the latest CIS benchmarks, follow these steps:

1. Open a browser and navigate to `https://www.cisecurity.org/`.
2. Click on **Cybersecurity Tools**.
3. Click on **Download** under **CIS Benchmarks**.

4. Enter the required information, agree to the terms, then click on **Get Free Benchmarks Now**:

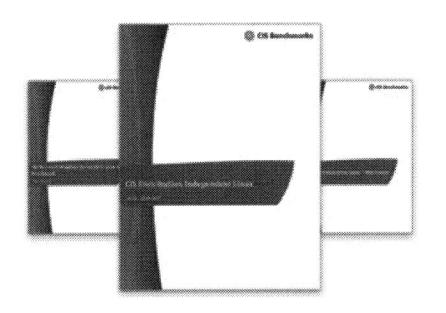

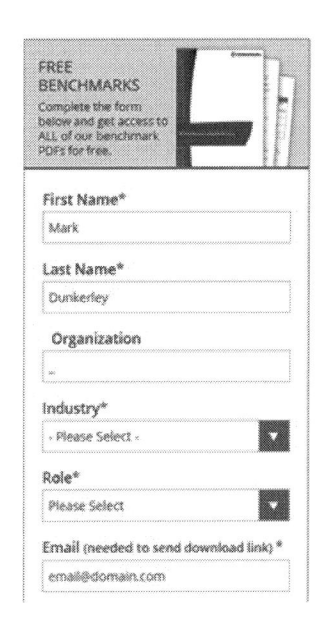

Figure 2.6 – The CIS Benchmarks download page.

5. Go to your mailbox and look for an email from CIS (check your **Junk** email folder too).
6. Open the email and click on **Access PDFs**. You will be provided with a list of all the available CIS benchmarks in PDF format.

7. Scroll down and you will see the Windows Server benchmarks:

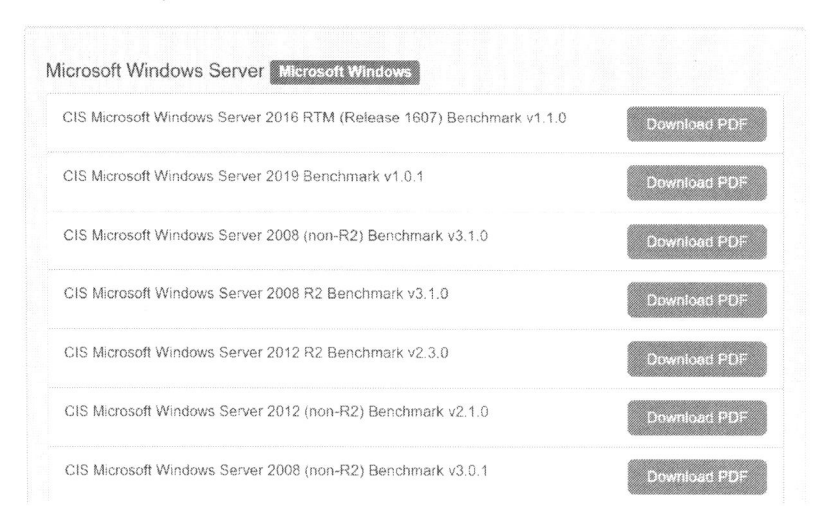

Figure 2.7 – The CIS benchmarks PDF

8. Keep scrolling down and you will also see the Azure benchmarks:

Figure 2.8 – The CIS benchmarks PDFs

9. In addition, there are many more Windows-specific benchmarks for specific roles, such as IIS, SQL, Exchange, and so on.

10. Once you have downloaded the PDFs, follow and implement the recommendations on them to strengthen your systems.

> **Tip**
> Visit the following link to access the CIS hardened images that map back to the CIS benchmarks: `https://www.cisecurity.org/cis-hardened-images/`.

Next, let's look at using the Microsoft SCT to download baselines for Windows.

Microsoft SCT

If you go down the Microsoft route with Windows security baselines, they provide a repository of resources that can be downloaded to allow the implementation of a baseline. To download these resources, follow these steps:

1. Browse to `https://docs.microsoft.com/en-us/windows/security/threat-protection/security-compliance-toolkit-10`.
2. Scroll down and click on **download the tools**.
3. Click **Download**:

Figure 2.9 – Microsoft SCT 1.0 download

4. Select the desired versions or click on the box next to the filename to select them all.
5. Click **Next**. You will receive all the toolkits in `.zip` format.

58　Building a Baseline

Downloading the preceding referenced toolkit will provide you with everything you need to deploy the recommended baselines from Microsoft. The following screenshot provides a quick overview of the baseline settings that can be deployed using the provided GPOs within the toolkit in Excel format. Notice that Microsoft provides separate settings not just for Windows 10 but also for a member server versus a **Domain Controller (DC)** server, providing additional settings specifically for your DCs. Also, if you look at the bottom of the spreadsheet, you will see the different categories that the strengthening is being applied to:

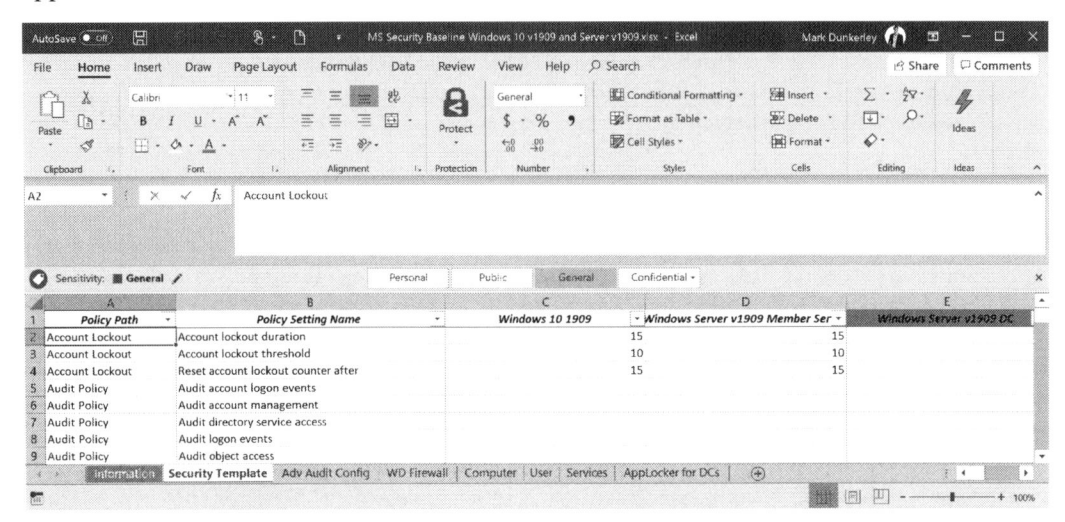

Figure 2.10 – The MS Security Baseline Windows 10 v1909 and Server v1909.xlsx spreadsheet

The referenced spreadsheet is `MS Security Baseline Windows 10 v1909 and Server v1909.xlsx` from the downloaded `.zip` files from the Windows 10 version 1909 and Windows Server version 1909 security baseline ZIP files referenced in the preceding steps. *Chapters 8, Administration and Remote Management, Chapter 9, Keeping Your Windows Client Secure,* and *Chapter 10, Keeping Your Windows Server Secure,* will provide more details on the implementation of security controls.

> **Tip**
> Microsoft SCT also provides additional details on the available tools to more efficiently manage your Windows baselines. You can find these details at `https://docs.microsoft.com/en-us/windows/security/threat-protection/security-compliance-toolkit-10`.

It is highly recommended that if you make any configuration changes from newly released baselines, you ease them into production and thoroughly test them first. In addition, ensure any changes go through your change control process for tracking and to offer transparency to your business.

Next, let's recap what we have covered in this chapter by providing a checklist of best practices that will help when building a security framework and implementing your baselines.

Incorporating best practices

To finish off this chapter, we wanted to provide a checklist of the most important items that will help enforce your security baselines. The following list is ranked in order of importance as you look to build and enforce your baselines:

- Select and deploy a framework to build a foundation.
- Select a baseline foundation. We covered CIS and Windows security baselines in this chapter.
- For your Windows devices, use the policy analyzer from the Microsoft SCT to review your baselines.
- Create or use a **Golden Image** template for each use case that you can reuse and always keep up to date with the latest updates.
- Build well-documented and easy-to-follow procedures that others can use and follow.
- Use the automation of controls and tools to re-enforce the baseline—for example, MDM with Intune or Active Directory Group Policy.
- Use compliance policies to validate whether controls are in place. This will also help with auditing devices that are non-compliant.
- Implement a quarantine or risk access policy with non-compliant devices.
- Implement efficient monitoring and reporting for device compliance. Power BI is a great way to visually provide reports.
- Always keep up to date with both the Windows versions and the technology used to manage the devices. The modern world is very dynamic and moves at an extremely fast pace.

It's important to note that while creating a security framework and enforcing controls with full compliance is desirable, exceptions will need to be accounted for. It is recommended that your organization also includes a risk register that clearly documents the systems and applications that do not comply with the defined policies and standards. The register should identify all the risks as well as rate the implication or severity of each risk and its potential impact on the organization. These implications should not only be viewed from a security lens but should also identify potential legal liabilities and costs implications if the risks were exploited. Leadership should be made aware of these risks and should sign off on their acceptance. Furthermore, a stakeholder should be named as the accountable party and the register should be reviewed frequently to identify any possible solutions to mitigate the risks.

Summary

Throughout this chapter, we have provided an overview of baselining to help you understand its importance and its role within the overall security program. You have learned about policies, standards, procedures, and guidelines, as well as their importance as part of your overall security strategy. We also looked at how these policies, standards, procedures, and guidelines interact with and build on each other to structure the baseline model. We then covered the change management process with regard to baseline management.

Finally, we reviewed frameworks and their role within the security function of your organization, discussing the more widely adopted frameworks that are implemented. Following this section was an overview of the baseline controls that are available for Windows. These options include CIS and the Windows security baselines, as well as directions on where to retrieve predefined templates, configurations, and images before outlining the best practices of baselining.

In the next chapter, we will cover server infrastructure management. This chapter will provide an overview of the data center and the cloud, along with the models that are available. You will learn about the different tools available for Windows server management, including the traditional on-premises and hybrid solutions available in Azure that extend your workloads to the cloud.

3
Server Infrastructure Management

The data center is constantly evolving and services traditionally used by hosting servers in physical data centers are now virtualized and using serverless computing models in the cloud. No matter how your infrastructure is deployed or what infrastructure is used, each presents a unique security challenge for an organization. In this chapter, we will provide an overview of the data center and cloud models as they exist today. We will discuss security access strategies for Windows servers as they are relevant to all infrastructure models to ensure not just anyone can access Windows without going through the proper access controls. You will learn about the available management tools used for on-premises, hybrid, and cloud deployments, as well as how to leverage Azure services to expand your data center reach to the cloud. Then, we will provide an overview of the Azure services that are used to manage Windows servers, including the Azure portal and Azure Resource Manager. It's important to understand the existence of these tools and services so that you have a high-level understanding of each when building out your security program. Depending on the size of your organization, services such as these may require several teams to control access, including physical security, a **security operations center** (SOC), and identity and access management teams. All of these play a vital role in ensuring your Windows systems are properly managed and protected.

In this chapter, we will cover the following topics:

- Overview of the data center and the cloud (IaaS, PaaS, SaaS)
- Implementing access management in Windows servers
- Understanding Windows Server management tools
- Using Azure services to manage Windows servers

Technical requirements

Throughout this chapter, we will be referencing different services available in Azure. If you would like to follow along, you can sign up for a free Azure account for 30 days and get $200 credit at `https://azure.microsoft.com/en-us/free/`.

To complete the RBAC example provided later in this chapter, you will need the following:

- PowerShell (version 5.1 recommended) with the Azure AD module installed – `https://docs.microsoft.com/en-us/powershell/module/azuread/?view=azureadps-2.0`
- Global Administrator rights to your Azure subscription
- A text viewer to open **JavaScript Object Notation** (**JSON**) files

Check out the following video to see the Code in Action: `https://bit.ly/38t2Qq3`

Overview of the data center and the cloud

Over the years, we have shifted our data centers strategies quite significantly as it relates to the hardware our services run on. The OS types, versions, and virtualization of those services have recently shifted to fully cloud-based technologies. A traditional enterprise data center typically consisted of mainframes to store and access information. Data centers during these times were located on location or at a separate facility under management of the organization. As technology evolved, there was a shift from mainframe to server-based data centers. This is where the Windows Server family became widely adopted and grew in popularity.

Moving beyond standard hardware-based server models comes virtualization. The ability to run many servers on only a few physical servers changed the dynamics of the data center significantly. Today, we are in a major shift to cloud computing. Organizations are slowly moving away from the traditional on-premise data center and moving all their workloads into cloud environments. With the cloud data center, organizations can continue to run traditional servers and services, but the overhead of owning and managing physical infrastructure is greatly reduced or eliminated.

Another major change with a shift to the cloud is the elimination of onsite facility management and physical operations. Building and maintaining a data center is an enormous undertaking that is challenging and comes with substantial cost implications when designing for highly available services and disaster recovery as part of a business continuity plan. Moving to the cloud changes these dynamics significantly. Your cost model changes to a subscription model with no ownership of any hardware or physical facilities, and a robust business continuity plan becomes more feasible to design.

This shift also changes the dynamics of security for the data center. Traditionally, physical security with access controls, locks, badge readers, and security cameras was all that was needed. This goes away with the cloud, but how do you ensure the cloud provider is protecting the access and controls? How do you ensure your data is safe? These are all valid concerns and change the way we manage security as opposed to the traditional data center perspective. We will cover these questions in more detail throughout this book.

Next, let's look at the three common types of scenarios for the data center.

Types of data center

This section will provide an overview of each of the current scenarios mostly being used today.

On-premise

As mentioned previously, an on-premise data center is considered the traditional model. Organizations build out and operate their infrastructure on your business's property or off-site at a separate facility. In this model, you are fully responsible for everything in the physical infrastructure (building, power, cooling, hardware, security, access, and so on) and everything that runs on the hardware. The following is an example of a traditional on-premise model:

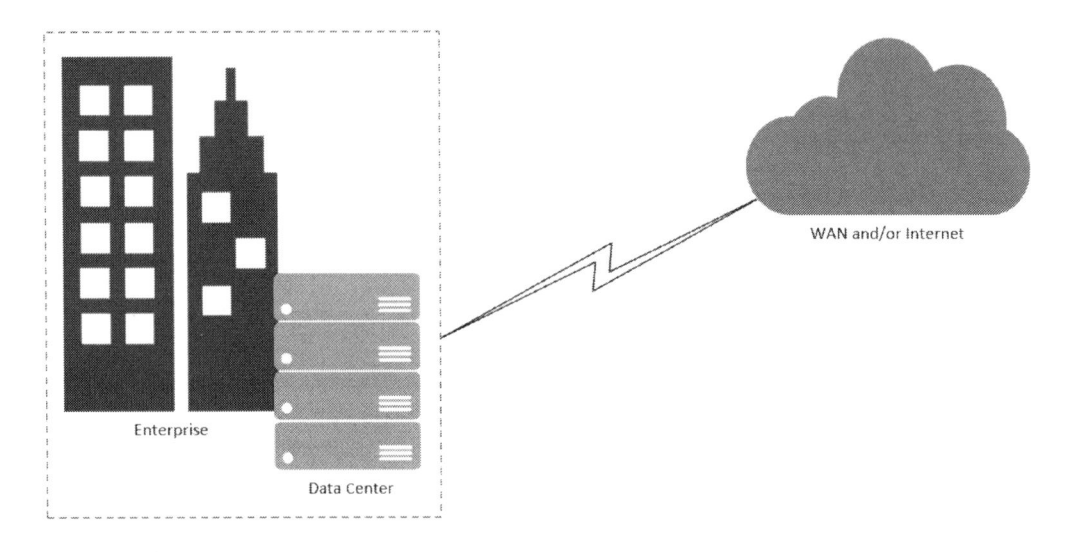

Figure 3.1 – On-premise data center

Cloud

As we look further into the cloud model, it is important to understand public and private cloud offerings. A public cloud is where the services are hosted by the provider and the underlying infrastructure is shared with other organizations. Your environment will be logically separated from other organizations, but the underlying hardware, network, and storage is shared with other subscribers on the same service. A private cloud offering is where the services are hosted in a dedicated environment and only your organization runs on the underlying services. Determining the appropriate model will most likely be dictated by your organization's industry and compliance requirements.

> **Tip**
> You can find more information on public versus private here: `https://azure.microsoft.com/en-us/overview/what-are-private-public-hybrid-clouds/`.

The following is an example of a cloud model:

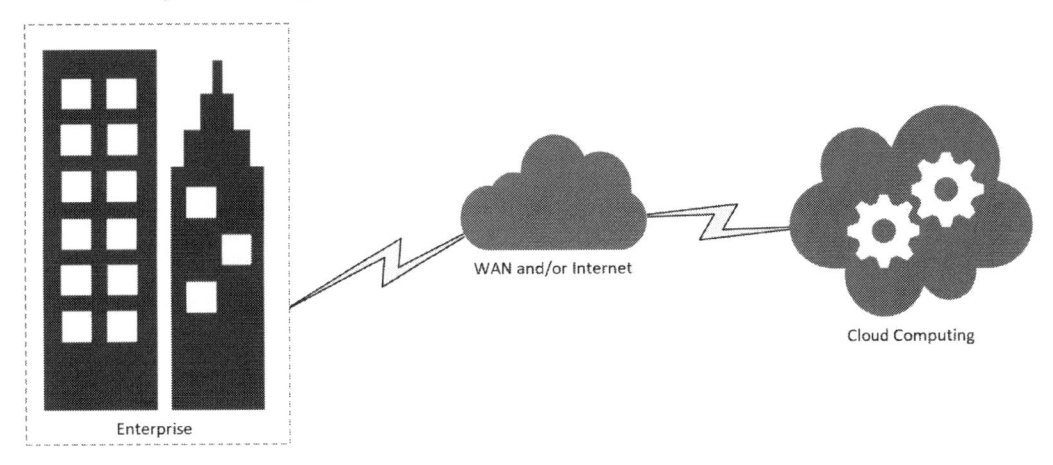

Figure 3.2 – Cloud model

Cloud solutions have three different types of primary services available for consumption:

- **Infrastructure as a Service (IaaS)**:

    IaaS requires the most involvement from your organization and is operated very similarly to a virtualized environment on-premises. The difference is that businesses have no responsibility for physical infrastructure and the servers, storage, and network are all managed by the hosting provider. You can simply turn on virtual machines and services as needed.

    > **Important note**
    > What is IaaS?: https://azure.microsoft.com/en-us/overview/what-is-iaas/.

- **Platform as a Service (PaaS)**:

    With PaaS, you are provided with the required platform from the cloud provider. In addition to the physical infrastructure, the operating system, middleware, and other tools to run services are also managed by the hosting provider. For example, in a traditional IaaS Windows environment, you would need to install **Internet Information Services (IIS)** to deploy a web server or install SQL to deploy a database server. With PaaS, you simply subscribe to an Azure Web App or Azure SQL database and you consume the service once it's available. There is no install or maintenance of any underlying software to run these apps.

> **Important note**
>
> What is PaaS?: https://azure.microsoft.com/en-us/overview/what-is-paas/.

- **Software as a Service (SaaS)**:

    The third available service is Software as a Service. This service requires the least involvement and essentially provides you with the entire software solution to be consumed. In addition to what is managed for both the IaaS and PaaS services, the hosting provider also maintains the application itself, including keeping it current and up-to-date. An example of a SaaS offering would be Exchange Online, in which your entire Exchange environment is hosted, kept up to date, and managed by Microsoft. You simply consume the email services for your organization.

    > **Important note**
    >
    > What is SaaS?: https://azure.microsoft.com/en-us/overview/what-is-saas/.

Now that we have covered what each of the cloud services are, let's look at some examples of what falls within the Microsoft ecosystem for each of these services. The following diagram provides some examples of what you can subscribe to within each of the services:

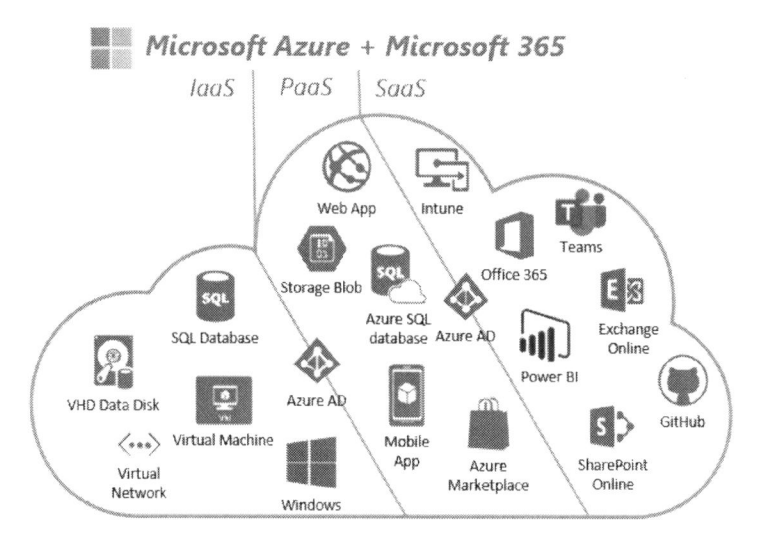

Figure 3.3 – Microsoft IaaS, PaaS, and SaaS examples

Hybrid

The last model we will review is the hybrid model. A hybrid model essentially combines the on-premise model with the cloud model, allowing an organization to use their on-premise data center at the same time as they're consuming cloud services. This model is most likely going to be preferred for most organizations simply because mature and expensive on-premise data centers can't easily be moved to a cloud model overnight. What the hybrid model does is allow a pathway from on-premise to the cloud while providing services from both environments.

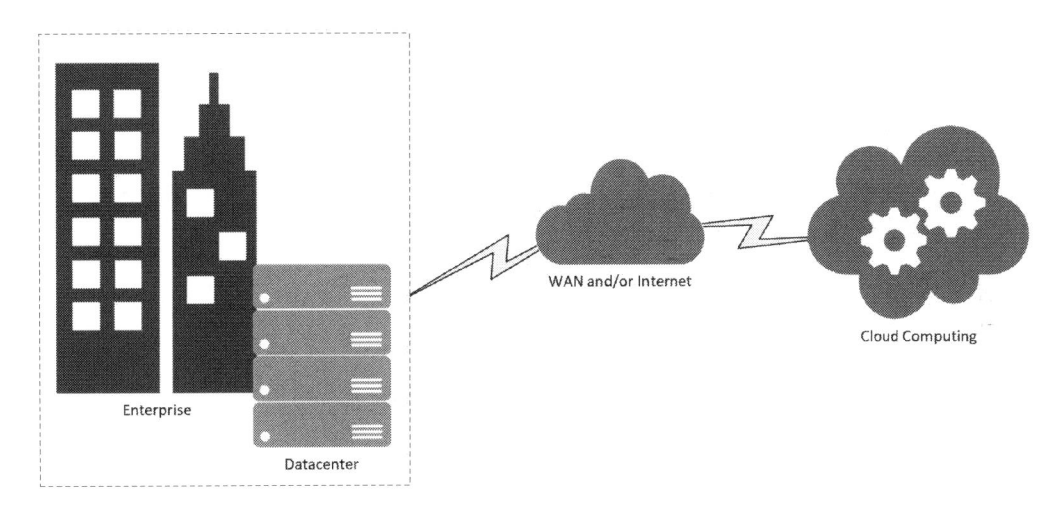

Figure 3.4 – Hybrid model

The focus of this book will be primarily around the on-premise, hybrid, and IaaS models as this is where your Windows servers will reside and operate. With the PaaS and SaaS models, the underlying OS is managed and secured by the service provider.

Now that we've covered the different models available for operating data centers, we will move on and discuss access management as it relates to Windows Server. In the next few sections, we will cover securing access to Windows Server and introduce common strategies and security access best practices used by organizations.

Implementing access management in Windows servers

The concept of building a solid access foundation is critical as it relates to server management as part of the overall infrastructure. You must consider everything, from physical access to the servers to protecting unified management consoles for managing multiple virtual servers at once. In the next few sections, we will discuss physical access and user access to the infrastructure and the importance of each. Next, we will discuss privileged isolation through a tiered model approach and provide an overview of **privileged access management** (**PAM**) and **privileged identity management** (**PIM**) solutions. Implementing these tools will help you provide a robust system of server access management. It is highly recommended that you become familiar with the topics mentioned in this section and understand how critical they are when implemented in your organization. First, let's look at physical access and security.

Physical and user access security

An important factor to consider with the on-premise model is to ensure all physical access to any server locations is protected and only accessible to those defined through their role. Your Windows servers and other physical infrastructure are typically located in a server room, a closet in your office building, or in a remote facility that is under your ownership. Because of this, it is equally important that well-enforced security access controls are in place, in addition to server hardening. The physical access needs to be locked down to avoid equipment being stolen and help prevent insider attacks that could open an opportunity for malware to be installed, such as a keylogger through a USB device. Encryption needs to be enabled on all Windows servers in the event theft does occur to help circumvent any information from being stolen.

> **Tip**
> Don't forget that your facility management and physical site access policies are just as important as your user access management to the servers.

As you make your move into the cloud world, your access management changes considerably. Physical access is now the responsibility of the cloud provider. The challenge is, how do you validate they are protecting your data with the utmost standards? This is where your contracts come into play, but more importantly, your due diligence, as it relates to audit requirements and SaaS questionnaires being provided by the cloud provider. We will cover audits in more detail in *Chapter 13, Testing and Auditing*.

The next consideration with the cloud model is management planes. On-premises deployments allows management solutions to be isolated from the internet and only accessible from your corporate network. With the cloud, the management pane and unified portals are internet-accessible and provide a single pane where you can access all your resources in one place, including your Windows servers. The downside? Anyone who compromises your access could have the keys to the kingdom. This is where a very stringent access policy is needed for your privileged identities. You need to ensure your regular user accounts are separate from your privileged accounts and that you enforce extremely strong access controls on your privileged accounts – no exceptions! The number of privileged accounts in your environment should be limited. **Role-based access control (RBAC)** needs to be defined if you wish to carve out a scope of who needs to access what resource.

> **Tip**
> Ensure that you separate privileged accounts from standard user accounts. No employee should ever use their regular identity to administer the environment.

Next, let's look at securing access using privileged access management, just-in-time access, and privileged identity management.

Privileged Access Management, Just-in-Time Access, and Privileged Identity Management

Continuing from the previous tip on identity, let's introduce three critical access models that need to be considered for implementation within your server environment. **Privileged Access Management (PAM)**, **Just-In-Time (JIT) access**, and **Privileged Identity Management (PIM)** are all privileged access models that provide an additional layer of protection to your admins while they access your infrastructure. These models help ensure that privileged user accounts are only available as needed, have an expiration date regarding their usage, and are fully audited and monitored when accessing Windows. Privileged accounts can be your weakest link if they're not protected properly and investing in these models should be a requirement.

We will cover each of these models in full detail in *Chapter 7, Identity and Access Management*.

Equally as important as implementing an access management solution is creating a segregation layer between your servers. To do this, organizations architect a tiering model to isolate different groups of servers based on its criticality to the infrastructure. In the next section, you will learn about using a tiered model and what it means for privileged access security.

Using a tiered model for privileged access

The concept of the tiered model is to isolate and build layers of containment between the Windows systems in your environment. This is accomplished through **Active Directory (AD) Organizational Units (OU)** by designing a structure that is divided into three or more parent containers. They are labeled tier 0, tier 1, and tier 2. Tier 0 contains the systems, accounts, and security groups of the highest security concern such as domain controllers, Azure AD connect servers, and identity management systems. The goal of this isolation or "tiered" approach is to prevent escalation by provisioning account access to only the tier they need access to in order to perform an operation. If an account from a lower tier gets compromised, its elevation will be restricted to its assigned tier or lower in the model. For example, a user account in tier 1 will only access systems in tier 1 or tier 2. They wouldn't be allowed access to tier 0. Let's review each of the tiers in a three-tier model in more detail.

Tier 0

Tier 0 (top level) typically contains a small number of assets and those deemed critical to your infrastructure. Admins in tier 0 usually have administrative rights to each level tier below. Here, an actor can exhibit domain dominance if breached and have direct control over your environment. We would want to limit the use of and accessibility to tier 0 servers as much as possible and limit the number of accounts with provisioned access. Further logon and access restrictions should also apply to assets in tier 0 to ensure only clean sources are accessing them, including the restriction to the use of non-critical functions from these servers such as checking email or browsing the internet. Organizations should deploy a privileged access management solution within the server environment. The PAM solution must include password rotation, an approval request flow process, auditing logs, session recording, and even remote RDP or SSH launchers where credentials are hidden.

> **Tip**
> To take this a step further, restrict the use of non-critical functions such checking email or browsing the internet. Implement application control policies through Windows Defender Application Control to prevent unauthorized software from running. You can also limit access to systems by funneling traffic through SSH proxies from a PAM solution.

Tier 1

Tier 1 is your middle tier and contains systems such as business servers, file servers, web application servers, and database servers. Administrators with access to tier 1 will be able to control servers in both tier 1 and tier 2. These servers need to be protected with similar precautions as the ones outlined for tier 0. When architecting the organizational structure of the tiered model, create child **Organizational Units** (**OU**) nested under the tier 1 parent and label them by business unit, application name, or function. Group policy can be used to define restricted groups that explicitly grant access permissions to security groups created and named to fit the labeling schema. Group members have access rights to RDP and only log on interactively to these defined tier 1 servers and not all servers in the tier 1 hierarchy. This provides more granularity and levels of organization. It may be necessary to restrict the use of non-critical functions from these servers such as checking emails or browsing the internet. Certain precautions need to be taken in the event an account becomes compromised. A best practice is to implement a PAM solution where an administrator is required to check out a different account to access these systems altogether. Once the account is checked back in, the password is immediately rotated. This creates a separation of privileges.

Tier 2

Tier 2 (bottom level) will contain more common devices seen in the everyday workplace. This includes end user workstations, laptops, printers, and virtual desktops. This tier is used by your level 1 support desk and field IT employees. Tier 2 administrators should only be allowed to log on to assets that are in tier 2 or lower if they exist. In *Chapter 7, Identity and Access Management*, we'll discuss implementing access management in more detail, including a discussion around local administrative access to workstations. Depending on your environment, the approach may differ, as there are unique considerations for each environment.

72　Server Infrastructure Management

The following screenshot shows an example of an OU structure that is recommended to support the tiered model approach. As you can see, in tier 0, there are separate OUs for admin accounts and server objects. This helps when creating policies that are either user targeted or computer targeted:

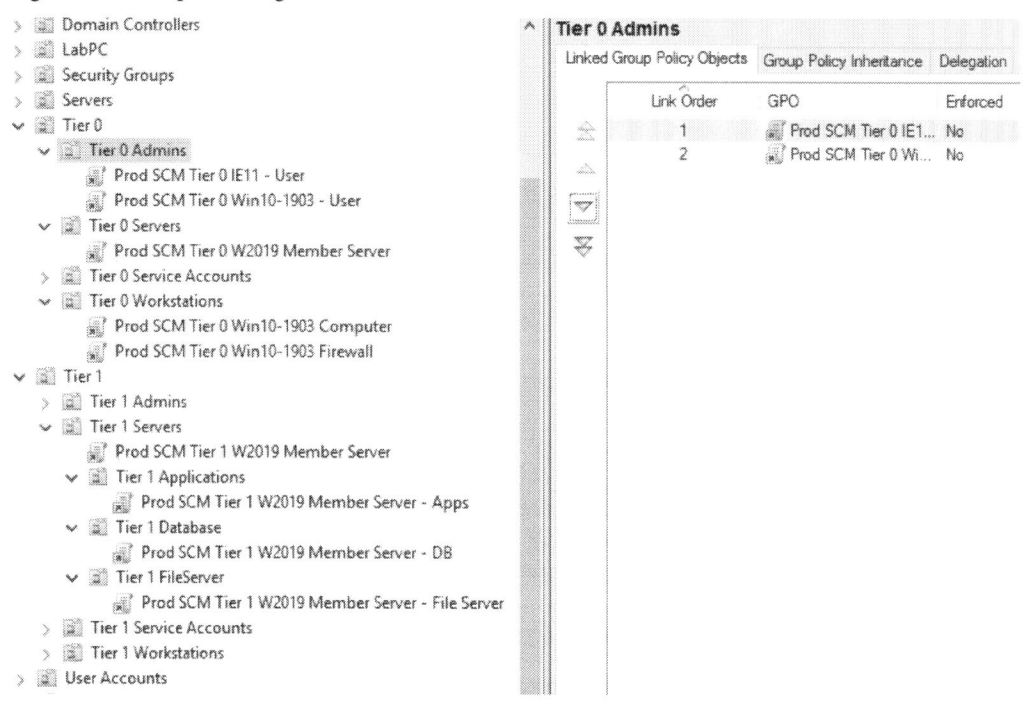

Figure 3.5 – An example OU structure of a tiered model approach

Now, let's look at some important things to consider.

Important considerations

Regardless of how many tiers are in the access model, there are important considerations worth discussing. Coupled with the tiered approach, each consideration – individually or combined – can add a substantial layer of security to your Windows systems. Let's take a look:

- For RDP and interactive logon scenarios, the source should be restricted to a **privileged access workstation** (**PAW**) or isolated management environment requiring a form of biometric or multifactor authentication.

- Network restrictions should be considered in tier 0 access scenarios by locking down incoming RDP connections and other management ports to sources from known VNETs, subnets, and workstations.

- When designing your tiered solution, be mindful and think about built-in security groups with escalated permissions such as Enterprise Admins, Domain Admins, Schema Admins, and Server Operators, to name a few.

- Local accounts can also become a problem if they're not managed properly and are an easy way for someone to create a backdoor without your knowledge. A PAM solution with discovery alert rules can be used to notify security teams when these accounts are created. If you're leveraging local accounts in an Active Directory domain, you can also implement Microsoft's **Local Admin Password Solution** (**LAPS**) to rotate passwords.

- Implement fine-grained password policies per tier to enforce stricter password requirements for administrative accounts.

- Leverage security baselines and group policy to further restrict access using defined restricted groups. Lock down logon types where credentials are exposed such as remote desktop or RunAs (interactive) so that they only come from trusted sources such as a PAW.

By using services from the Azure cloud, privileged access workstations can be deployed using a virtualized desktop service such as Windows Virtual Desktop or Citrix. Azure also has PaaS offerings available to cater for this scenario, such as the Azure Bastion service. Azure Bastion allows you to securely RDP or SSH directly to virtual machines over SSL, eliminating the need to expose your servers directly to the internet. This can all be done directly in the Azure portal, with no additional infrastructure. For on-premises installations, an **enhanced security administrative environment** (**ESAE**) can be used to administer the production forest.

Enhanced security administrative environment

The next design we will review is the ESAE administrative forest model. At a high level, you will set up a separate Active Directory forest that will be used for administrative purposes only. In this forest, you will build your user accounts and groups that will be provided with privileged access in the production user forest to complete any administrative tasks. To enable cross-forest access, one-way trust is created from the production user forest to the administrative forest. This allows the privileged administrator accounts to manage the production user forest. With this approach, you can completely isolate your privileged accounts from your standard user accounts, reducing the risk of compromise with elevated access within your production environment. This architecture, which is outlined in the following diagram, is also used by Microsoft's cybersecurity professional services teams to protect its customers:

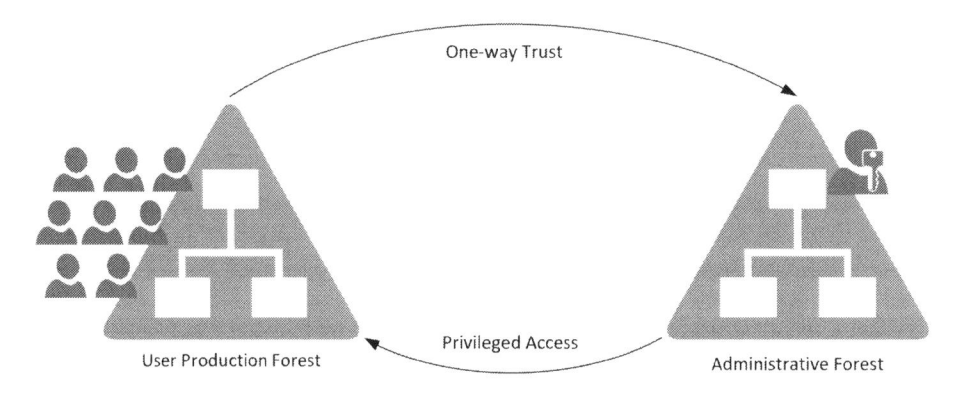

Figure 3.6 – The ESAE model

There is a lot more involved in setting up these models for your environment. To review additional details on both the tiered model and ESAE model for privileged access security, visit `https://docs.microsoft.com/en-us/windows-server/identity/securing-privileged-access/securing-privileged-access-reference-material`.

> **Tip**
> Both models require time and investment to implement correctly. It is easy to fall back and apply elevated access to standard users and over permission accounts to meet deadlines and so on. Don't fall into this trap! Ensure you spend time implementing these models correctly from the ground up and clearly define the account provisioning process. Enforcing these models will help ensure success with your security and hardening.

Now, let's recap and talk about access management best practices.

Access management best practices

Securing access to your environment can be a long and complex journey with many considerations to keep in mind. Security is an ever-evolving space due to the complexity and frequency of cyberattacks. New tools and services are regularly becoming available for organizations to help drive their business and are for those that simply don't have the resources, funds, or capabilities to deploy the solutions needed to protect them. Here is a high-level list of best practices to keep in mind when thinking about the scope of privileged access for your Windows servers and business services:

- Enforcing **multi-factor authentication** (**MFA**) should be at the top of the list. Require MFA for all cloud-based accounts using Azure MFA or another provider. For on-premise servers, you can install Azure MFA Server and have finer control over MFA methods.
- Deploy a **Privileged Access Management** (**PAM**) solution.
- Use just-in-time access to assign permissions dynamically and avoid permanent assignment for your privileged accounts. Helpful services include Azure **Privileged Identity Management** (**PIM**) coupled with Azure Security Center just-in-time access.
- Have an effective account provisioning and deprovision process. Automate disabling accounts when employees leave the company.
- Frequently audit privileged accounts in your environment.
- Limit the number of administrators. Always consider job role and function when provisioning administrative accounts and ensure the principal of least privilege applies.
- Separate administrative accounts with regular user's accounts. This will help mitigate credential exposure if the administrator's workstation becomes compromised.
- Limit access to email and internet browsing when applicable from privileged systems.
- Enforce strict fine-grained password policies on administrative accounts.
- Limit the amount of emergency "backdoor" accounts and monitor their usage.
- Ensure any changes to the environment go through an approval process by a change advisory board. This can include access to highly sensitive systems.

Go here for additional information on securing privileged access: `https://docs.microsoft.com/en-us/windows-server/identity/securing-privileged-access/securing-privileged-access`.

Now that you have an understanding of the different models used for access to Windows workstations and servers, next, we will discuss the tools used to help manage them. Although some are common, it is important to be aware of their utility when building baselines and hardening Windows.

Understanding Windows Server management tools

There are many tools available for Windows Server that are useful for both managing and securing the infrastructure. Management technologies were traditionally developed for on-premises deployments, but now, with cloud-based SaaS offerings, it seems the available solutions are growing exponentially. Microsoft offers solutions for enterprise-grade management through its **System Center** suite of tools such as **Operations Manager (SCOM)** and **Configuration Manager (SCCM)**. There are also third-party paid solutions from companies such as ConnectWise, SolarWinds, and CA Technologies, to name a few. Each offers a different feature set, depending on your management needs and varying price points. In this section, we will review the more common built-in tools available in Windows Server, including Server Manager, Event Viewer, and Windows Server update services for patch management. Then, we will discuss Windows Admin Center and how it can be used to help transition workloads into the Azure cloud.

Introducing Server Manager

Server Manager was introduced in Server 2008. It provides a centralized management tool for servers and can support up to 100 remote servers. The number of remote servers will vary, depending on their workload system performance of the server running it. Server Manager can also be installed on a workstation computer with **Remote Server Administration Tools (RSAT)**. To remotely manage servers, remote management must be enabled through Server Manager or with PowerShell. This is enabled by default in Windows 2012 and later. A list of tasks that can be completed through Server Manager include the following:

- Create, edit, or add custom server groups or pools of servers and clusters.
- Install, uninstall, or make changes to roles and features on both the local and remote servers.

- Open management tools such as Computer Management, Windows PowerShell, Registry Editor, and other MMC tools.
- Start and stop services, identify events, and collect performance data for analysis.
- Restart servers.
- Export settings to be imported on another system.

To add remote servers to Server Manager from the Dashboard view, right-click **All Servers** and choose **Add Servers**. Once servers have been added, all the roles that are capable of being managed will be added to the left-hand column. These roles are now available for management from a centralized point. Creating a server group will create a link on the left column for quick access to different sets of servers. The following screenshot shows the **MyServers** server group:

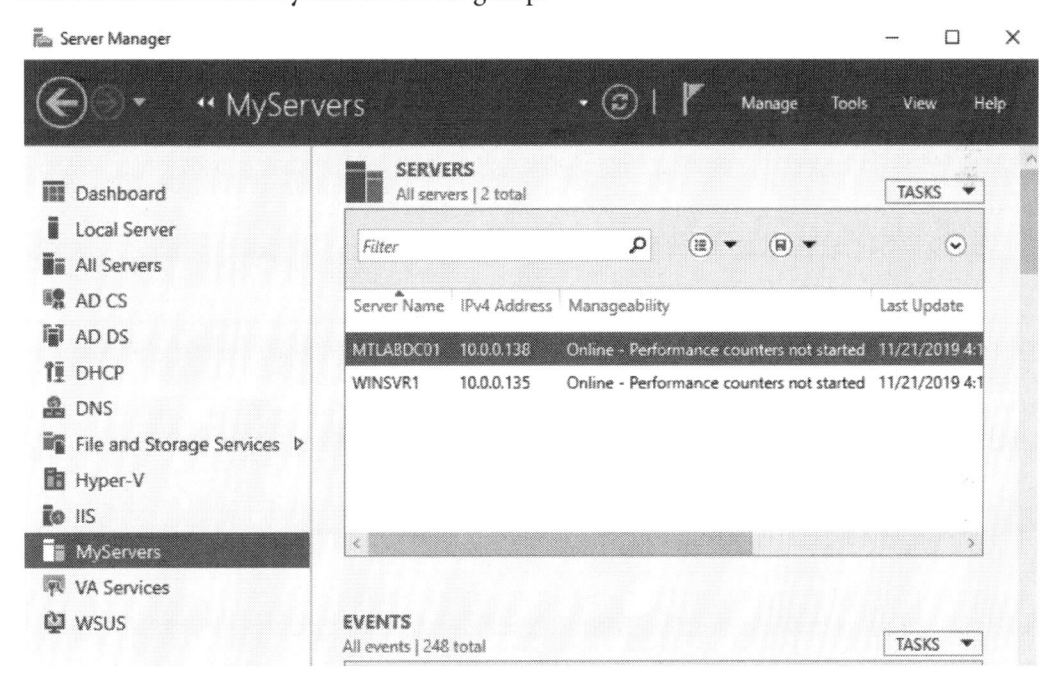

Figure 3.7 – A custom server group named MyServers, useful for quick access

Server Manager is a great place to view events, services, and performance from a single application. Events can be viewed and configured from every page except the dashboard. Certain event logs such as application logs are selected by default and include Critical, Error, and Warning severity levels, but they can be customized to fit your needs. The thumbnail alerts can be configured to include other events, and different severities can be included in alert highlighting. Only critical events are highlighted by default.

Using the Best Practices Analyzer (BPA)

The **Best Practices Analyzer** (**BPA**) tool is used to help reduce vulnerabilities by scanning the configured roles and comparing your configurations to what experts believe to be best practice guidelines. BPA can be executed from Server Manager as well as through Windows PowerShell. After the scan completes, the results can be viewed. These show whether a role is compliant with these best practices. The summary outlines the problem in detail, as well as list the impact and resolution steps. This can be seen in the following screenshot:

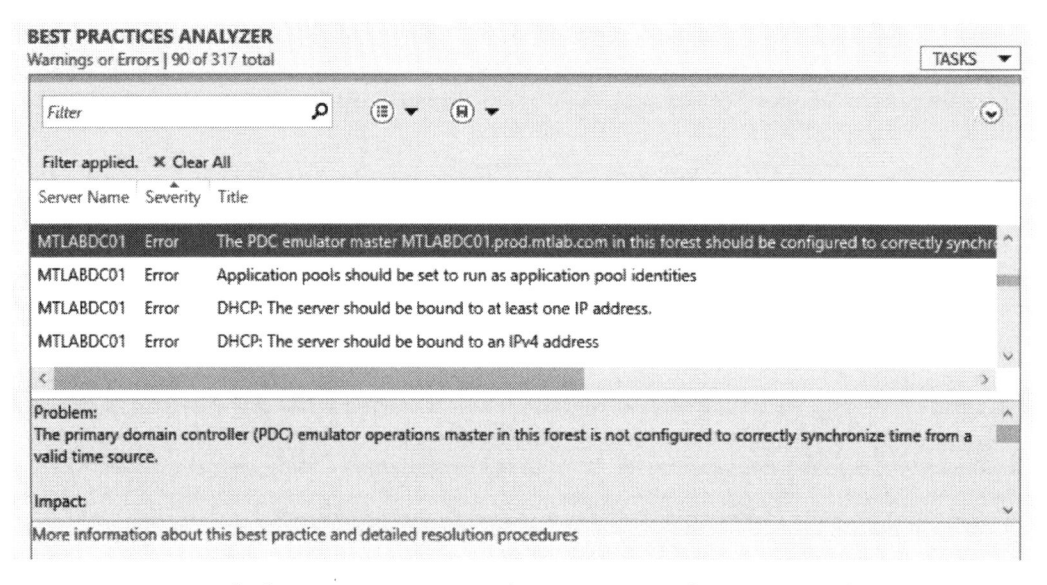

Fig 3.8 – Results from a BPA scan on Windows Server 2016 showing misconfigurations

For more information, please go to `https://docs.microsoft.com/en-us/windows-server/administration/server-manager/run-best-practices-analyzer-scans-and-manage-scan-results`.

Next, we'll look at using Event Viewer and examine common event IDs.

Looking at Event Viewer

Event Viewer is used to view log files from applications, including security and system-related events. Events are separated into error, warning, and informational events, which can also be useful for troubleshooting performance issues. PowerShell can be used to query events and Event Viewer can be used to view logs from remote computers. Event Viewer can be opened by using Windows Search and typing in Event Viewer. Once opened, to view logs from a remote computer, right-click on **Event Viewer (local)** at the top of the tree and choose **Connect to Another Computer…**.

Event Viewer can also be used for automating actions. Using **Attach a Task to this Event** action, a basic scheduled task can be created and run based on a specific event.

> **Tip**
>
> Event Viewer is very important for monitoring Windows events from a security perspective. Security professionals should pay close attention to sources from login activities, application crashes, network firewall rule changes, clearing of event logs, audit policy changes, and group policy changes.

Security-specific logs can be found in **Windows Logs > Security**. The following screenshot shows Event ID 4624, which indicates a successful logon. This Event ID contains a lot of information, including the **Logon Type**, account information, and network information about the user who has logged on:

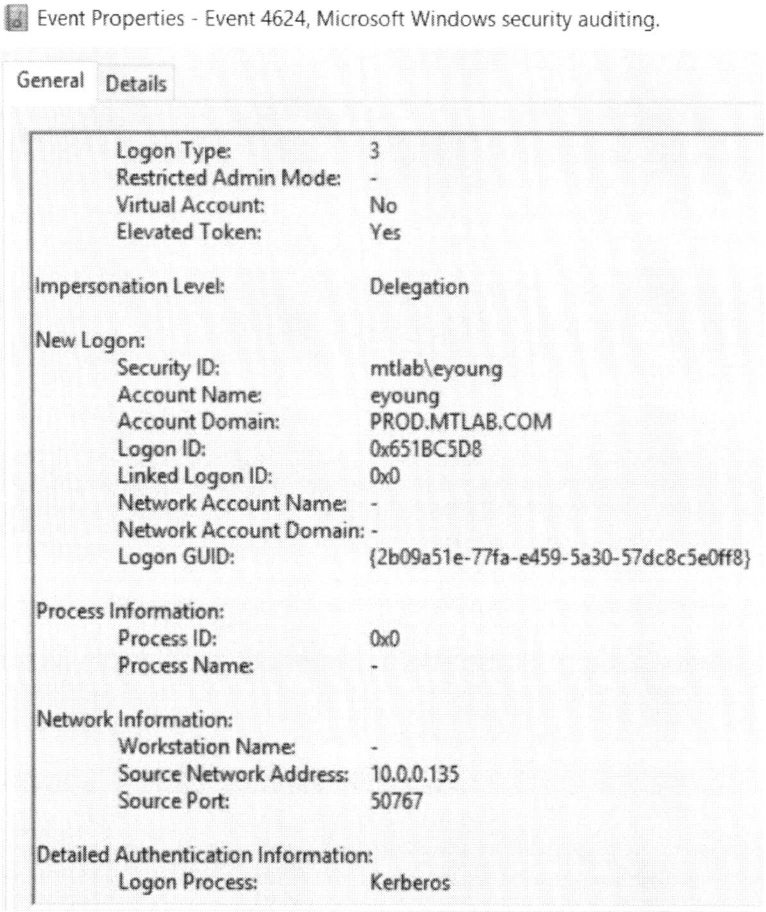

```
Event Properties - Event 4624, Microsoft Windows security auditing.

General  Details

    Logon Type:                3
    Restricted Admin Mode:     -
    Virtual Account:           No
    Elevated Token:            Yes

Impersonation Level:           Delegation

New Logon:
    Security ID:               mtlab\eyoung
    Account Name:              eyoung
    Account Domain:            PROD.MTLAB.COM
    Logon ID:                  0x651BC5D8
    Linked Logon ID:           0x0
    Network Account Name:      -
    Network Account Domain:    -
    Logon GUID:                {2b09a51e-77fa-e459-5a30-57dc8c5e0ff8}

Process Information:
    Process ID:                0x0
    Process Name:              -

Network Information:
    Workstation Name:          -
    Source Network Address:    10.0.0.135
    Source Port:               50767

Detailed Authentication Information:
    Logon Process:             Kerberos
```

Figure 3.9 – Event 4624, successful logon in Event Viewer

There are common security events to look for under **Windows Logs > Security** that could indicate an attacker attempting to grant access rights or access the system. While these event IDs are normal and typically do not indicate an attack, in the event a compromise was recognized, they are useful to mention and can help build a picture around the attack's timing and provide additional details during analysis:

- `4625`: Audit Failure Logon
- `4624`: Audit Success Logon
- `4648`: Login with explicit credentials
- `4735`: Security-Enabled local group was changed
- `4728`, `4732`, and `4756`: Member added to a security group
- `4740`: Account Lockout
- `1102`:Log Clear may indicate an evasive tactic by an attacker

Event ID `4624` includes a logon type field, which is useful for identifying how an account has logged into the system. The following table demonstrates the different logon types that are associated with Event ID `4624`:

Logon Type	Description
2	Interactive Logon (the user is physically at the device)
3	Network (Logon occurred elsewhere)
4	Batch (typically a scheduled task)
5	Service (system services)
7	Unlock (logged in from the lock screen)
8	Network Clear Text (logon with clear text or basic authentication)
9	New Credentials (typically with run as different user)
10	Remote Interactive (typically with remote desktop or terminal services)
11	Cached Interactive (cached credentials were used)

Figure 3.10 – Logon types for Event ID 4624

Windows Defender Event Viewer logs are useful for security monitoring and can be found under **Applications and Services Log > Microsoft > Windows > Windows Defender**. Interesting event IDs, including those for canceling or pausing malware protection scans, could indicate a malicious actor, prevalence of malware, or warrant further investigation.

> **Important note**
> Further reading on Windows Defender antivirus event IDs can be found at `https://docs.microsoft.com/en-us/windows/security/threat-protection/windows-defender-antivirus/troubleshoot-windows-defender-antivirus`.

From an operational perspective, especially when a **security operations center** (**SOC**) needs to monitor many systems, looking at Event IDs on servers individually isn't the most effective method. It is recommended to incorporate a **security information and event management** (**SIEM**) solution to better track and analyze event logs. Examples of a SIEM solution include Microsoft's security monitoring tools such as Azure Sentinel, Defender Advanced Threat Protection, Cloud App Security, and Azure Security Center or third-party tools such as Splunk, which can be used for log repositories and analysis. We'll cover SIEM tools and security monitoring in more detail in *Chapter 11, Security Monitoring and Reporting*, and *Chapter 12, Security Operations*.

Next, let's look at how to leverage Windows Server Update Services to manage security updates and patch vulnerabilities in the operating system.

Using Windows Server Update Services

Windows Server Update Services (**WSUS**) is used to keep standard security patch levels across your servers. In some instances, maintaining the same patch level is critical for applications to run, and relying on the standalone Windows Updates service doesn't suffice for this level of control. WSUS allows you to approve updates and choose when to deploy them. In a simple WSUS architecture, the WSUS downstream server talks to the Microsoft Update upstream server to act as the intermediary. Using a centralized console allows administrators to download critical updates, security patches, rollups, service packs, feature packs, Microsoft product updates, and antivirus definition files. Computers can be grouped together and targeted for a deployment.

For most deployments, WSUS requires minimal processing power on the host computer to operate and a single WSUS instance can host upward of 100,000 clients. For environments greater than 100,000 clients, multiple WSUS servers can be deployed by using a load balancer frontend. A single SQL server database will need to be deployed and shared by each WSUS instance if you're using a single centralized WSUS management solution to serve multiple locations and branch offices.

From a firewall perspective, clients connect to WSUS over HTTP/TCP port 8530. It is recommended to secure communications by deploying a custom SSL for clients to connect HTTPS/TCP over port 8531. IIS is required if you wish to use WSUS in both scenarios:

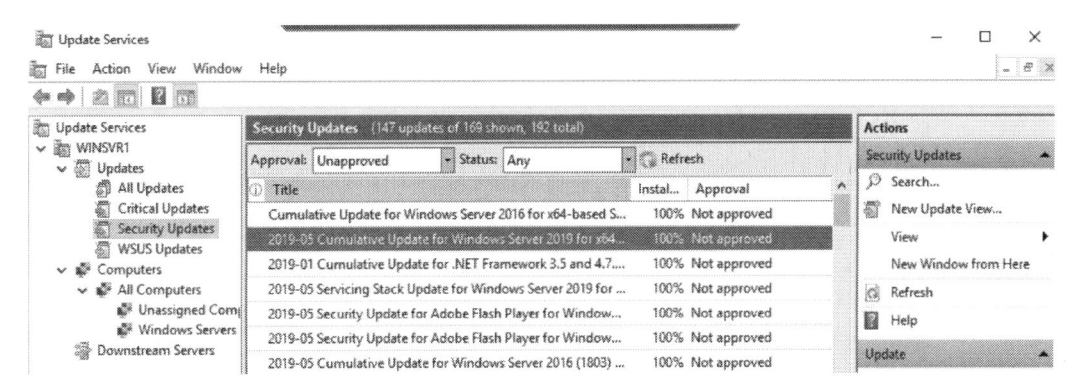

Figure 3.11 – List of security updates available for approval in the WSUS management console

Windows Defender Antivirus is the AV solution built into Windows 10 and Windows Server 2016 and later. If you're using WSUS, definition updates need to be scoped and downloaded from Microsoft Updates. Administering definition updates works similarly to Windows Updates and will require approval before your endpoints receive them. Consider creating automatic approvals for antivirus definition updates to ease the administrative overhead required to manage WSUS. Automatic Approvals allow you to automatically approve the installation for new updates for specified groups of systems.

WSUS can also deploy third-party updates for commonly used software such as Adobe Reader. Combining WSUS with a Configuration Manager software update point allows you to create a third-party software update catalog. Here, you can subscribe to a partner catalog that's connected to various software vendors that have partnered with Microsoft for releasing updates to their products. We will cover Configuration Manager in more detail in *Chapter 4, End User Device Management*, and *Chapter 8, Administration and Remote Management*. WSUS can be enhanced further by leveraging a cloud solution called Azure Automation Update Management. Update Management can manage updates for Windows and Linux systems hosted in Azure and on-premises directly with the Azure portal. This service supports Windows server downward to 2008 R2 and will be covered in more detail later in this chapter and in *Chapter 10, Keeping Your Windows Server Secure*.

As discussed in *Chapter 1, Fundamentals of Windows Security*, here are some helpful links for staying up to date on security updates:

- Microsoft Security Update Guide: https://portal.msrc.microsoft.com/en-us/security-guidance.

    Patch Tuesday Dashboard: https://patchtuesdaydashboard.com/.

- Information about CVE: https://cve.mitre.org/about/index.html.

In the next section, we will look at Windows Admin Center, a recently released tool that can help manage your servers.

Introducing Windows Admin Center

Windows Admin Center was released in April 2018 and provides an alternative to classic MMC and other remote management tools. Windows Admin Center is a browser-based tool that can be installed on Windows 10 or Windows Server 2016+. It supports the management of servers down to 2008R2 but may have limited functionality. No agents are required, and the UI frontend is fully built on WMI with PowerShell over WinRM to execute operations. To support down-level servers, **Windows Management Framework** (**WMF**) 5.1 is required. More information, including how to install MSI, can be downloaded from `https://aka.ms/WindowsAdminCenter`.

> **Tip**
> Windows Admin Center runs in HTML 5 and requires Microsoft Edge or Google Chrome browser to run on Windows Server. It cannot be installed directly on a domain controller.

Windows Admin Center's tools include Active Directory, DHCP, DNS, Firewall, Remote Desktop, Roles and Features, Scheduled Tasks, and Updates, to name a few. Many more features are available through extensions, including support for third-party developers.

Windows Admin Center can be used to manage on-premises and IaaS servers. It is included for free with your Windows Server license. A real piece of added value is that it allows you to shift on-premises workloads to Azure directly from the UI. With the appropriate tenant details and permissions, you can deploy and configure the Azure services directly through Windows Admin Center without having to open the Azure portal.

The Azure services available through Windows Admin Center include the following:

- Azure Site Recovery
- Azure Backup
- Azure File Sync
- Azure Monitor
- Azure Update Management
- Azure Active Directory Authentication

Windows Admin Center can be fully integrated with Azure Active Directory for authentication and supports MFA. The following screenshot shows the overview pane of Windows Admin Center:

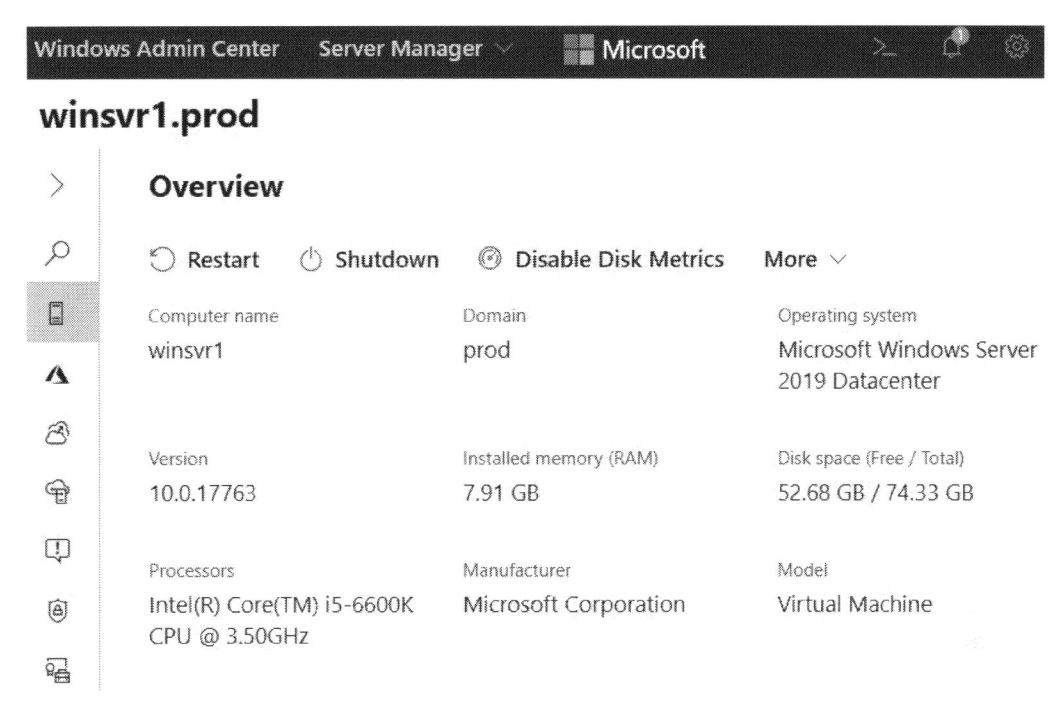

Fig 3.12 – Overview page of Windows Admin Center in Google Chrome

Next, let's look at Azure services that are useful for managing Windows Server environments.

Using Azure services to manage Windows servers

As discussed in the *Understanding Windows Server management tools* section, Windows Admin Center exposes Azure cloud services that can provide additional benefits for managing Windows servers. It is recommended that you start moving workloads to the cloud not only as part of your digital transformation, but also as a security initiative. Azure Active Directory roles and **role-based access control** (**RBAC**) allow for a fine-grained level of access provisioning over the management plane. In the next section, you will learn about the Azure services that are available for managing Windows servers for both IaaS and on-premises deployments. We will cover the following topics:

- The Azure portal and Marketplace
- RBAC
- Azure Resource Manager

- Azure Backup
- Azure Update Management
- Azure Site Recovery

The Azure portal and Marketplace

Simply put, the Azure portal is the user interface that's used to manage resources in the Azure cloud. Most operations can be performed directly through the Azure portal, but some advanced configurations will require the Azure **Command-Line Interface** (**CLI**), Azure PowerShell, or direct calls to the Graph API. Microsoft is doing a great job of adding many operations only supported by these command-line tools directly to the user interface in the portal. Follow these steps to access the portal:

1. Open a browser and navigate to `https://portal.azure.com`.
2. Sign in with your Azure account username and password.
3. If you don't have an Azure account, click **Create one!** to set one up.

To view and access your virtual servers within the Azure portal, simply click on **Virtual Machines**. You will be provided with the **Virtual machines** management page:

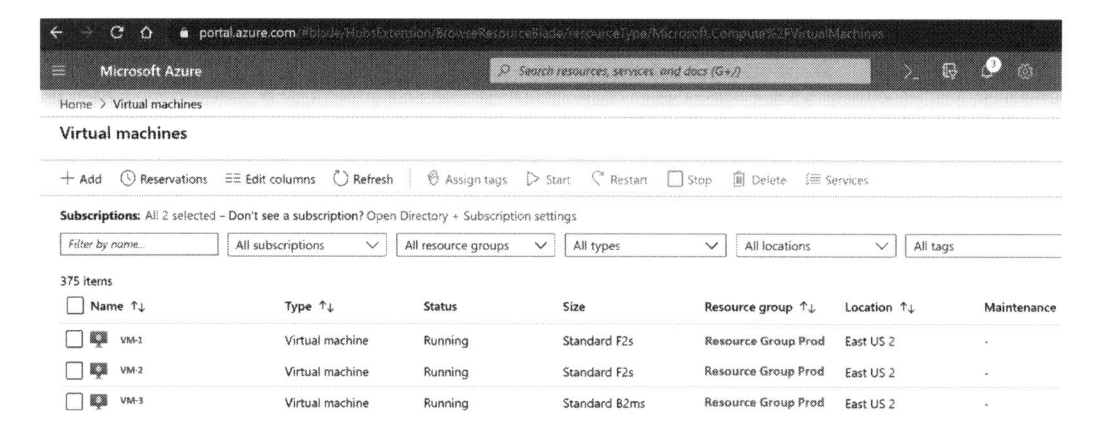

Fig 3.13 – Microsoft Azure portal Virtual machines page

We won't be going into detail around navigating the Azure portal, but we do want to call it out as an important tool for not only managing Windows servers, but also all cloud resources. For detailed instructions on customizing its look and feel, as well as creating custom dashboards and setting favorites, you can visit `https://docs.microsoft.com/en-us/azure/azure-portal/azure-portal-overview`.

Using the Azure Marketplace

The Azure Marketplace is the storefront in Azure where you purchase resources and solutions and deploy them directly to your tenant. There are many offerings available, from custom VM images, to databases, networking solutions, IoT, DevOps, and more. It can be accessed from the Azure portal or by going to https://azuremarketplace.microsoft.com/en-us/marketplace/.

In respect to Windows Server, the marketplace is useful for deploying pre-built images, which can be done in just a few clicks directly from the portal. You can use the Azure Marketplace to customize and create a Windows Server instance and then capture the customizations in a JSON template. By using this JSON, multiple servers can now be deployed at scale with all your custom configurations:

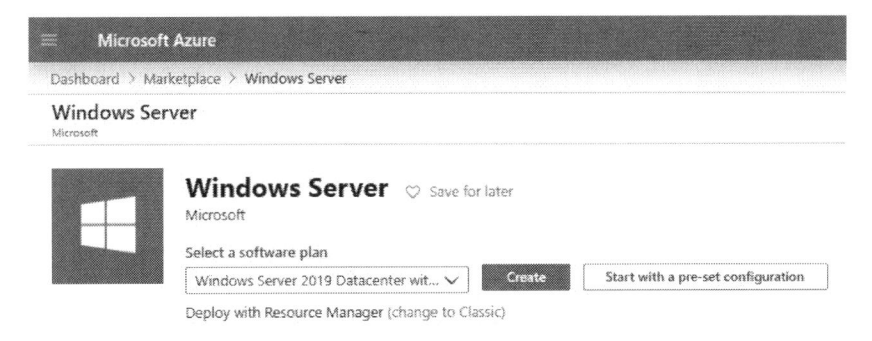

Figure 3.14 – Windows Server purchasing option from the Azure Marketplace in the Azure portal

With Azure Active Directory roles and role-based access controls, resource creation is typically locked down for Global Administrators or roles with contributor rights.

Next, we'll look at how to lock down access to Azure resources by implementing RBAC. We will also learn how to create a custom role using PowerShell and JSON.

Implementing role-based access control

RBAC in Azure is used to authorize access to resources through role assignments. A role assignment consists of a user, group, or service principal that has a set of permissions assigned. Those permissions are then scoped to a subscription, resource group, or resource. Permissions are inherited from parent scopes, so if a role assignment is set on the resource group level, all resources nested under that resource group will be in scope of the role assignment. When assigning permissions, RBAC takes an additive model. If the user is assigned to multiple roles, the least restrictive role won't take effect and will be assigned any additional rights for each additional role. Explicit Deny assignments must be applied to determine which set of actions are not allowed; otherwise, access is granted.

There are four main roles in Azure RBAC, and these are the standard levels of roles that can be applied to a scope. These are owner, contributor, user access administrator, and reader. Only the owner and user access administrator roles have permission to grant access rights for other users. Each role has the concept of action types such as **Actions**, **NotActions**, **DataActions**, and **NotDataActions**. When building a role definition, Actions refers to the management operations of the resource and controls things such as access, where **DataActions** refers to the underlying data operations such as read blobs in a container. Azure offers over 70 additional built-in RBAC roles that are preconfigured for specific use cases as they pertain to certain resources. Using JSON, you can export a built-in RBAC role and build custom roles to fit your needs. For more information regarding the role definition structure, go to https://docs.microsoft.com/en-us/azure/role-based-access-control/role-definitions.

In the following example, we will edit the Virtual Machine Contributor role and make a custom RBAC that contains all the VM contributor role permissions, including **DataAction**, to administratively log in to virtual machines. Let's get started:

1. Open PowerShell as an Administrator and install the Azure module. Choose *[A] Yes to All* when asked to install from an untrusted repository. Then, connect to Azure using the `Connect-AzAccount` cmdlet and retrieve your subscription ID. Take a note of the subscription ID; you will need this later:

    ```
    Install-Module -Name Az
    Connect-AzAccount
    Get-AzSubscription | Select ID
    ```

2. Enter your credentials at the password prompt and perform MFA to connect to your Azure tenant.

3. The first step is to export the built-in Virtual Machine Contributor role as the JSON template to build the custom role. We will export the role definition as JSON using the `Get-AzRoleDefinition` cmdlet:

    ```
    Get-AzRoleDefinition -Name "Virtual Machine Contributor"
        | ConvertTo-Json | Out-File "C:\MyFolder\VMContributor.json"
    ```

4. Open the **VMContributor.json** file we exported previously using a code editor of your choice, such as Notepad++, Code Writer, or even basic Notepad. We will need to make some modifications and save the file as a JSON, ready to be reimported.

5. On *line 2*, change the value of `"Name"` to `Administrative Virtual Machine Contributor`:

   ```
   "Name": "Administrative Virtual Machine Contributor"
   ```

6. On *line 4*, change the value of `"IsCustom"` to `true`:

   ```
   "IsCustom": true,
   ```

7. Modify `"Description"` on *line 5* so that it reads as follows:

   ```
   "Description": Lets you manage virtual machines, but not
   access to them, and not to the virtual network or storage
   account they are connected to.  Allow administrator
   login.",
   ```

8. To allow administrative login, we will need to add the ARM resource provider operation called `Microsoft.AAD` for the **DataAction** action type and the `Microsoft.Compute/virtualMachines/login/action` and `Microsoft.Compute/virtualMachines/loginAsAdmin/action` operations.

9. On *line 50* in the JSON, add these two lines:

   ```
   "Microsoft.Compute/virtualMachines/login/action",
   "Microsoft.Compute/virtualMachines/loginAsAdmin/action"
   ```

10. Next, we need to populate the `"AssignableScopes"` section. If you exported the built-in role, the / root value will be prepopulated, but this is only applicable to built-in roles. Assignable scopes can be scoped to multiple subscriptions, management groups, resource groups, or resources. In this example, we are going to use the subscription ID of our tenant. The subscription ID can be found using the PowerShell cmdlet, as we saw earlier, or through the Azure portal UI and typing "subscriptions" in the search field. Modify *line 57* so that it includes the subscription ID:

    ```
    "AssignableScopes": [
    "/subscriptions/8c24xxxa2-xxxx-47xx-3d-8929345de830"
    ]
    ```

11. Finally, save the edited JSON file. We will now import it using the `New-AzRoleDefinition` cmdlet:

```
New-AzRoleDefinition -InputFile "C:\MyFolder\
VMContributor.Json"
```

If its creation was successful, the custom role will be seen from the **Access control (IAM)** blade in your Azure subscription:

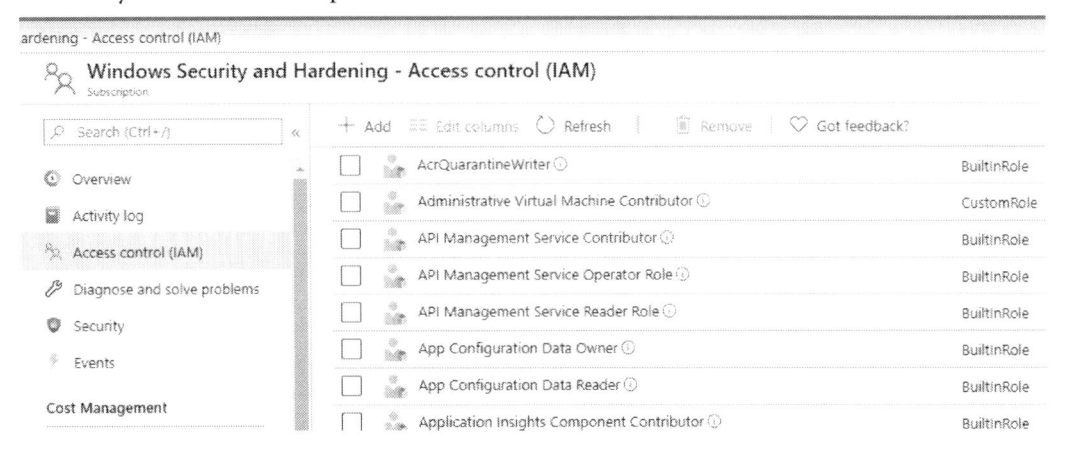

Figure 3.15 – Successful creation of the Administrative Virtual Machine Contributor role in the Azure portal

For more information about the resource provider operations that are available, visit this link: https://docs.microsoft.com/en-us/azure/role-based-access-control/resource-provider-operations.

For more information about JSON, visit this link: https://www.w3schools.com/whatis/whatis_json.asp.

Next, we'll take a look at the current management plane for Azure resources, which is called Azure Resource Manager.

Azure Resource Manager

It is important to be aware of Azure Resource Manager if you're working with Azure cloud to deploy Windows servers and other infrastructure. Currently, Azure Resource Manager is defined as a highly resilient management plane for all services that run in Azure. Any controls used that directly affect the management and security of resources is done through Azure Resource Manager. Azure Resource Manager, or ARM for short, can be manipulated directly using the Azure portal, Azure PowerShell, Azure CLI, or through APIs and custom tools developed with a **software development kit** (**SDK**). Custom templates written in JSON can be created and declaratively deploy resources repeatedly, at scale, and tracked directly in the Azure portal. More information about creating Azure Resource Manager templates, including the sections that make up the JSON, can be found at `https://docs.microsoft.com/en-us/azure/azure-resource-manager/template-deployment-overview`.

> **Tip**
> Additional information, including key terminology, benefits, and a descriptive understanding of the scope of the management plane, can be found at `https://docs.microsoft.com/en-us/azure/azure-resource-manager/resource-group-overview`.

In the next section, we will talk about using Azure Backup for creating backups of our servers.

Understanding Azure Backup

Azure Backup is a cloud service that can be used to replace an on-premises backup solution or used as an automatic storage management tool for hybrid scenarios where data is stored both on-premises and in the cloud. It requires zero infrastructure, has unlimited scaling capabilities, provides application-consistent backups, and data is encrypted both in transit and at rest. Azure Backup offers unlimited data transfers ingress and egress from Azure at no additional cost. There are **locally redundant** (**LRS**) and **geo-redundant** (**GRS**) storage options available, depending on your high availability needs. There is no time limit regarding data retention, and you can store up to 9,999 recovery points.

> **Important Note**
> For additional information on the Azure Backup service, go to `https://docs.microsoft.com/bs-latn-ba/azure/backup/backup-overview`.

In Windows Admin Center. you can take advantage of the built-in management and monitoring tools all from within the Backup dashboard.

Azure Backup's requirements include the following:

- A valid subscription
- Resource Group
- Recovery Services Vault
- Agent Deployment

Azure Backup includes Application- and Crash-consistent backups:

- **Application-Consistent Backup**: Use Windows VSS writers to create the backup and capture memory content and pending I/O operations. When recovering a VM using an app-consistent snapshot, there is no data loss.
- **Crash-Consistent Backup**: This occurs if an Azure VM shuts down during the time of a backup. Only disk data at the time of the backup is captured and a recovery doesn't guarantee data consistency.

These two options can be seen in the following screenshot:

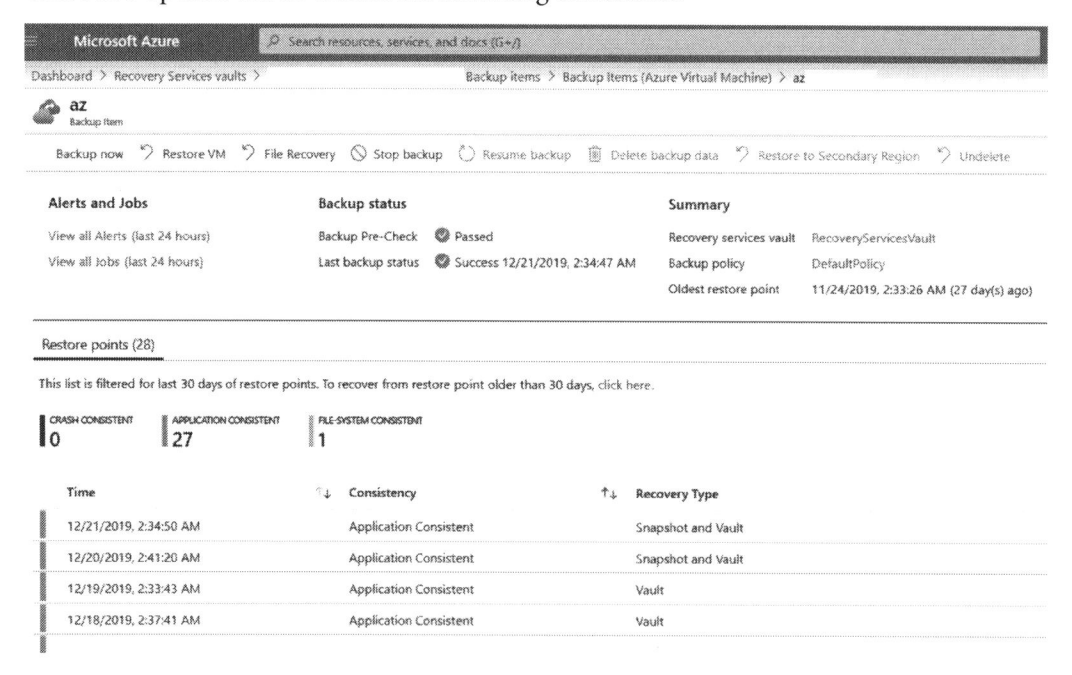

Fig 3.16 – Restore points of a Windows Azure VM with Application-Consistent restore points

Securing Azure Backup

For on-premises backups, encryption is done using a customer-specified passphrase. Once in transit, data is encrypted using AES256 and sent over HTTPS to Azure. For Azure VMs, data at rest is encrypted using **Storage Service Encryption** (**SSE**) and protected by HTTPS in transit while never leaving Azure. Azure Backup can also back up VMs that are encrypted using Azure Disk Encryption.

> **Tip**
> For customer specified passphrases, **DO NOT** lose the encryption passphrase. It is required to restore backups. Microsoft **CANNOT** recover this for you.

Backup data contains highly critical information and needs to be properly secured from unauthorized access. Access can be managed using Azure RBAC. Authentication also takes place through Azure Active Directory and monitoring is supported using Log Analytics. Let's highlight the built-in RBAC roles for Azure Backup:

- **Backup Contributor** has permissions to create and manage backups but cannot grant access or delete Recovery Services vaults.
- **Backup Operator** has similar permissions to the contributor except for removing backups and changing policies.
- **Backup Reader** can view all backup operations for monitoring purposes only.

For hybrid scenarios, additional security features are available, such as configuring retention periods, notifications for changes, and the ability to create security pins.

Another security feature for backups is soft delete. Soft delete is a feature that retains backups for 14 days after a deletion action and allows recovery without data loss at no additional cost. While this feature is enabled by default, you can permanently delete soft deleted backup items immediately or disable the feature altogether.

> **Important note**
> More information about Azure Backup RBAC can be found at `https://docs.microsoft.com/en-us/azure/backup/backup-rbac-rs-vault`.

In the next section, we will discuss using Azure Update Management to deploy updates to our servers.

Introducing Azure Update Management

As described earlier in *Using Windows Server Update Services*, Update Management is the Azure cloud-based solution to managing system updates for Windows. Update Management is available for the cloud and on-premises deployments.

The requirements to deploy Azure Update Management are as follows:

- Azure Subscription
- New or existing resource group
- Log Analytics workspace
- Azure Automation account
- Deployment of the **Microsoft Monitoring Agent (MMA)**
- Microsoft Update or WSUS configured on your systems

Update Management can be deployed using Windows Admin Center by following the onboarding steps directly in the portal. For information about onboarding multiple VMs from the Azure portal, go to `https://docs.microsoft.com/en-us/azure/automation/automation-onboard-solutions-from-browse`. The following is a screenshot of Update Management from the Azure portal automation account:

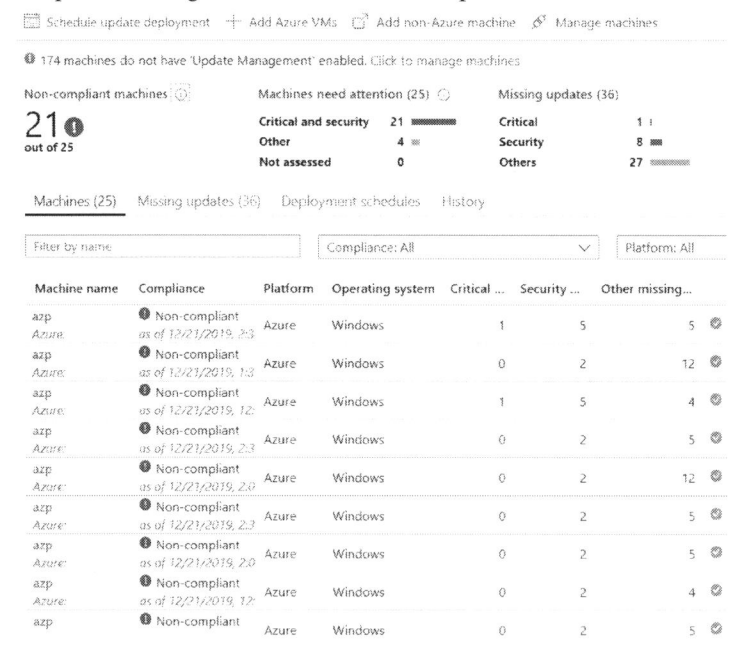

Figure 3.17 – Update Management dashboard, which shows the update compliance of individual Windows servers

The compliance comparison for the servers listed in the Update Management page will be compared to your WSUS server or directly to Windows Update services. Machines can be added by clicking on **Add Azure VMs** at the top of the page. For Non-Azure servers, the Microsoft Monitoring Agent can be deployed and configured to use the Update Management Log Analytics workspace during setup or when onboarded with Windows Admin Center. The following screenshot shows the missing updates tab, which lists all missing updates from your systems and includes columns that display details about the update name, classification, machines missing updates, operating system, and a KB information hyperlink:

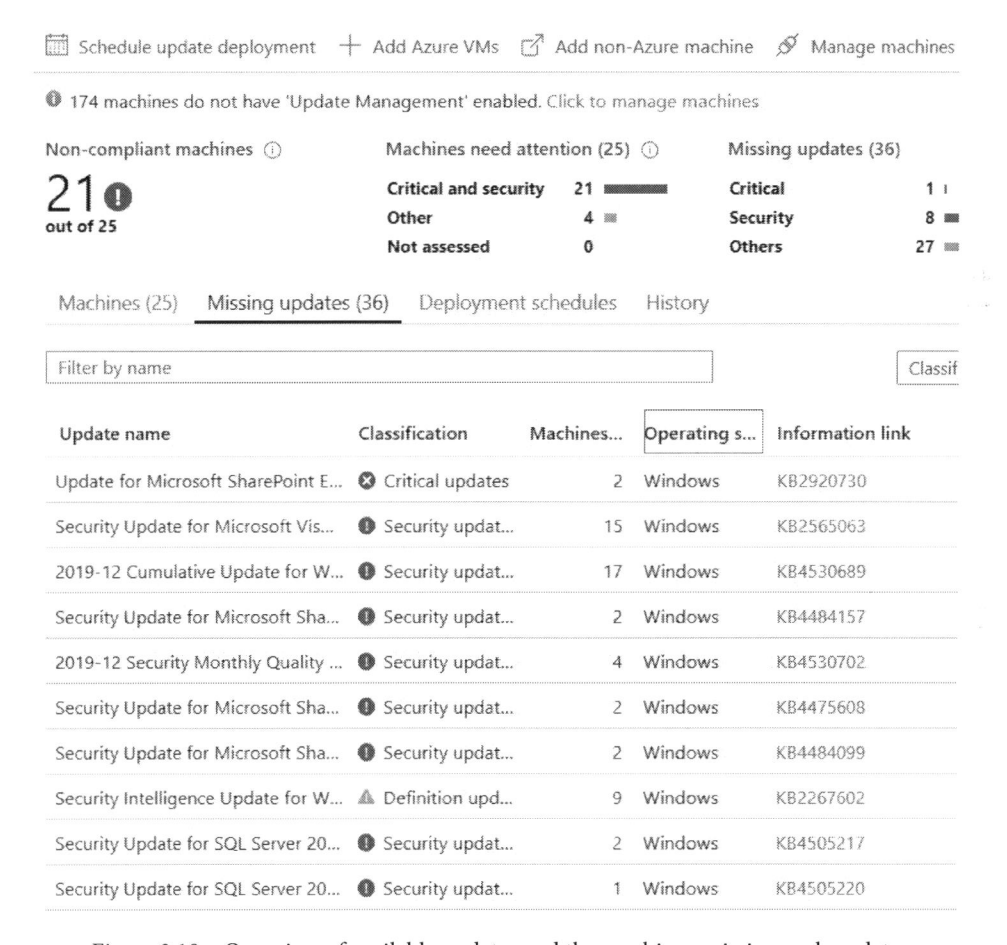

Figure 3.18 – Overview of available updates and the machines missing each update

Update deployments using update groups can be scheduled using the **Schedule Update Deployment** option at the top of the toolbar. Update groups can be created by using dynamic queries based on resource groups, locations, and tags, or you can explicitly select the machines you wish to include. There is a dropdown to scope which classification of update to deploy, as well as options to include or exclude specific KBs. The schedule settings allow you to set a one-time or recurring deployment. Additional options include setting a maintenance window time and several options for reboot behaviors.

The deployment status can be monitored with alerts using Azure Monitor. Action groups allow notifications via email/SMS/push/voice and can even trigger a webhook or Azure Automation runbook.

For additional information about the Update Management solution in Azure, go to `https://docs.microsoft.com/en-us/azure/automation/automation-update-management`.

The following are the Windows operating systems supported by Azure Update Management:

- Windows Server 2019
- Windows Server 2016
- Windows Server 2012 and R2
- Windows Server 2008 R2

> **Tip**
> Windows Clients and Windows 2016 Nano Server are not supported at this time.

We will cover how to set up and configure Azure Update Management in more detail in *Chapter 10, Keeping Your Windows Server Secure*.

Next, we'll look at **Azure Site Recovery** (**ASR**). Azure Site Recovery can be used as a disaster recovery scenario or as a tool to move systems in Azure.

Leveraging Azure Site Recovery

Azure Site Recovery is a business continuity and disaster recovery solution built into Azure for all types of workloads. The solution covers both Azure and on-premises Windows servers and VMs. **Azure Site Recovery (ASR)** consists of two major components:

- **Site Recovery Services**: Used for the replication of virtual machines and workloads from a primary to a secondary region in Azure.
- **Backup Services**: Azure Backup service for data backup and recovery.

For more information on Azure Site Recovery, visit this link:

https://docs.microsoft.com/en-us/azure/site-recovery/site-recovery-overview

When building a **business continuity (BC)** and **disaster recovery (DR)** strategy, most organizations outline **recovery time objectives (RTOs)** and **recovery point objectives (RPOs)** for business-critical services and applications. By using the Azure Site Recovery service, these workloads and virtual machines are replicated from primary to secondary sites. If a regional outage occurs in Azure, you can initiate a failover to the secondary region to meet the RTO/RPO objectives of the business continuity plan. Let's take a look at these in more detail:

- **Recovery Time Objective (RTO)**: The established duration of time for each business process in which services must be restored to meet SLAs.
- **Recovery Point Objective (RPO)**: The maximum amount of data that could be lost during a major outage. For example, if the RPO is 24 hours and the last backup was completed 6 hours ago at the time of an outage, there is 18 hours of time until the business will suffer a significant volume of data loss, as defined by the business objective's RPO.

ASR supports building customized recovery plans that allow you to strategically plan what services, VMs, and critical infrastructure fail over and when. Using PowerShell and Azure Automation, many tasks during the failover/recovery process can be automated. ASR also supports testing the failover through recovery plans. Using the overview dashboard, organizations can monitor the site recovery and backup of resources that are scoped for the Azure Site Recovery service:

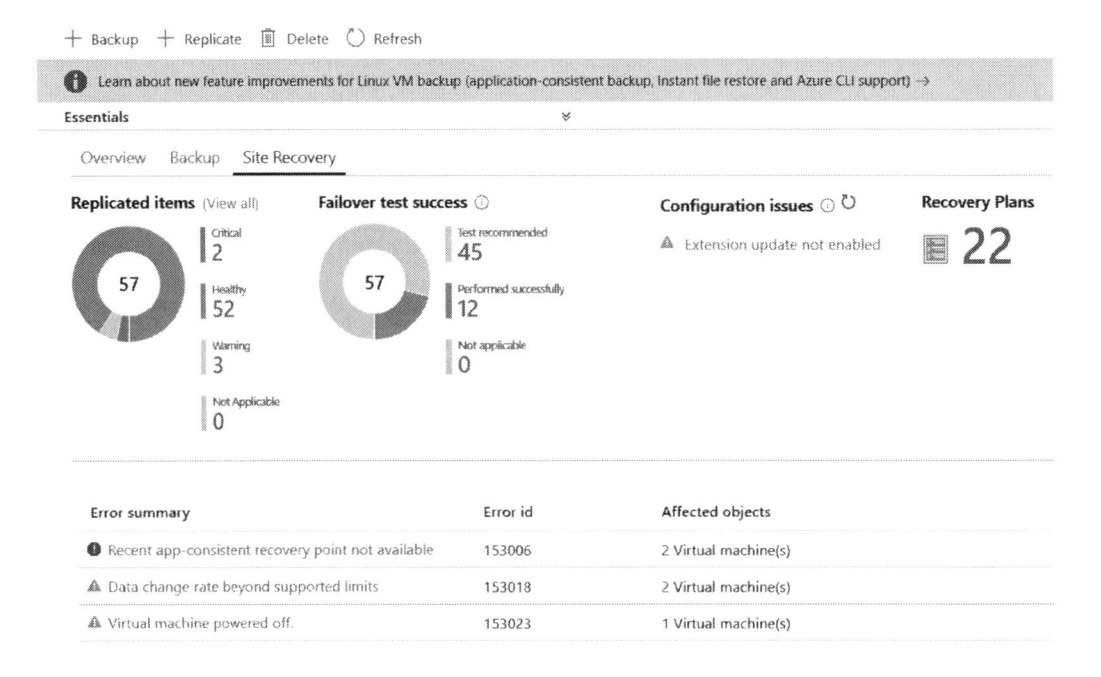

Figure 3.19 - Site Recovery dashboard view, which shows an overview of configured recovery services

> **Tip**
> Azure Site Recovery is a great solution for migrating on-premises machines to Azure using the same steps that were defined for disaster recovery, but without the failback! For more information, go to https://docs.microsoft.com/en-us/azure/site-recovery/migrate-tutorial-on-premises-azure.

There is an overwhelming number of tools and services available in Azure that support the management of your Windows infrastructure and Azure environment. Unfortunately, we won't be able to cover them all in this book, but you can view a comprehensive list of all Azure resources here: https://azure.microsoft.com/en-us/services/.

Summary

In this chapter, we provided an overview of the traditional on-premise data center and the most current model available, known as the cloud. Within the cloud model, we covered the three primary services, known as IaaS, PaaS, and SaaS, and then finished this section with an overview of the hybrid model. Next, we reviewed secure access management as it relates to both physical and user access to Windows servers and infrastructure. We then covered privileged access models with best practices for secure access management.

The following section covered Windows Server management tools, including Server Manager, Event Viewer, WSUS, and Windows Admin Center. The final section of this chapter moved on to Azure services for managing Windows servers. In this section, we provided details about the Azure portal and Marketplace, Azure RBAC, Azure Resource Manager, Azure Backup, Azure Update Management, and Azure Site Recovery. While we quickly scratched the surface of many available tools, we hope the acknowledgement of these services may spark an interest in you to research further. These concepts may eventually lead to these services being implemented in your own environment, which will increase your overall security posture.

In the next chapter, we will shift our focus away from the server infrastructure to end user device management. This chapter will cover the evolution of device management and the tools that have been used over the years. We will then cover these tools in more detail, specifically the ones regarding device imaging and Windows autopilot, Microsoft Endpoint Configuration Manager (formerly System Center Configuration Manager), and Intune.

4
End User Device Management

The device management model has been static for many years within enterprises. Before the advancement of some of the currently utilized enterprise device management tools, companies were challenged with efficiently deploying a consistently configured device to their users.

Companies may have utilized out-of-the-box images with the layering of Group Policy or even scripts to pre-configure specific settings for users. For many, this evolved into standalone imaging tools that allowed the organization to capture a pre-configured image or baseline that could be pushed out to new devices as part of a deployment. Traditionally, these methods were extremely time-consuming and resource-intense on organizations but still serve a valuable purpose for securing and hardening your Windows systems. In this chapter, we're going to cover the tools used to build and deploy a secured hardened image. We will provide an overview of the latest deployment model, known as the Windows Autopilot service. Then, we will cover two major enterprise device management models. It is important to understand the available features of each model as a properly hardened Windows system may include configurations enforced by one or both solutions. The following main topics will be covered:

- Device management evolution
- Device imaging and Windows Autopilot

- Microsoft Endpoint Configuration Manager (formerly SCCM)
- Intune **mobile device management** (**MDM**)
- Introducing Microsoft Endpoint Manager

Technical requirements

In this chapter, we will be referencing the following tools and services. If you wish to follow along, you can review the licensing requirements and download them from the links that follow:

- Windows Assessment and Deployment Kit:

    https://docs.microsoft.com/en-us/windows-hardware/get-started/adk-install

- Windows Deployment Services (Windows Server roles and features)
- Microsoft Deployment Toolkit:

    https://docs.microsoft.com/en-us/configmgr/mdt/

Additionally, we will be covering the following tools that require additional licensing:

- **Microsoft Endpoint Configuration Manager** (**MECM**/SCCM):

    https://www.microsoft.com/en-us/cloud-platform/system-center-pricing

- Microsoft Intune licensing:

    https://docs.microsoft.com/en-us/intune/fundamentals/licenses

- Windows Autopilot licensing:

    https://docs.microsoft.com/en-us/windows/deployment/windows-autopilot/windows-autopilot-requirements

> **Tip**
> Most Intune licenses also cover the use of System Center Configuration Manager and don't require a standalone purchase.

Device management evolution

Using a device management model, many large organizations have adopted **Microsoft Endpoint Configuration Manager** (**MECM**), formally known as **System Center Configuration Manager** (**SCCM**), which has been the standard for many years. Configuration Manager is a fully mature device management solution also used for image building and deployment. To operate effectively, an Configuration Manager hierarchy requires resources and the deployment of infrastructure either on-premises or in IaaS. As new PC hardware is purchased and new Windows builds are released, a lengthy and complex life cycle process to support the new requirements typically follows. This traditional model can make organizations less agile regarding staying up to date with the latest updates and security trends. Recently, we have seen disruption to this model and a shift that is changing the dynamics of device management. Throughout the book, we may refer to Configuration Manager as MECM, SCCM, and ConfigMgr. All are common acronyms used to reference Configuration Manager.

In recent years, this shift has come with the adoption of MDM tools that evolved with the growth of iOS and Android. This growth has shown two parallel environments within enterprises. One for phones and tablets, and the other for desktops and laptops. This generates a lot of overhead and a unique skill set to support, manage, and operate two separate environments. It also adds overhead to your security strategy as both your platforms need to meet the security requirements of your policies. Validating security within multiple environments can create challenges and adds its own complexity.

A major advantage of using an MDM solution is a shift from primarily an imaging model to an out-of-the-box approach. The ability to take your device out of the box, turn it on, and receive your policies, configurations, and security settings layered on top of your original OS is a game changer. This approach has been well-received and adopted for corporate-owned iOS and Android devices. With the release of Windows 10, Microsoft has followed suit and enabled the ability to enroll Windows into an MDM tool, allowing a shift away from traditional imaging and the overhead it brings. More recently, Windows 10 with Intune also allows the merging of two separate enterprise tools into one unified management approach for your device management program with Intune and SCCM co-management.

As the model continues to evolve, we are slowly seeing a transition to unified endpoint management. Unified endpoint management is essentially bringing together the management of all endpoint devices into one management solution, as shown in the following diagram:

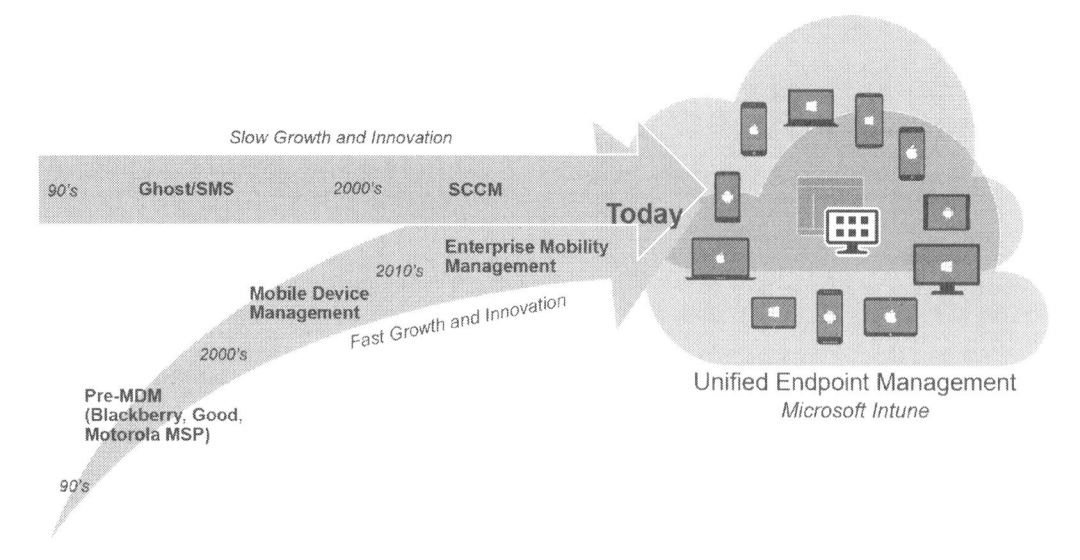

Figure 4.1 – The evolution of device management

For most organizations, this shift isn't going to happen overnight, but the good news is Microsoft has built a solid foundation and avenue to make the journey from the old to the new a reality. In the next section, we are going to discuss the classic device imaging model. Although it's been around for a while, device imaging is still tried and true and an important component for hardening your Windows systems with your security baselines.

Device Imaging and Windows Autopilot

It is strongly recommended to update your Windows clients to the latest version of Windows 10 as soon as possible. Windows 10 is rich with security features, a great productivity tool for your users, and is optimized for modern management, including support for a **bring your own device (BYOD)** scenario. The BYOD trend promises to significantly reduce cost and resource overhead for the IT department. While this is an effective approach in some scenarios, it still raises challenges from both a security aspect and the support and operational perspectives. Depending on the application payload and the customization of your line of business apps, it may not be suitable to offer BYOD. Factors that may influence this decision include compliance requirements, the complexity of application configurations, and delivery such as bandwidth requirements for large application payloads.

From a security perspective, you will not have as fine-grained control of the layering of security policies and configurations and there may be other privacy and legal concerns if corporate data resides on users' personal devices. Until apps become more modernized and built with the appropriate app protection policy SDKs for modern management, it'll likely be necessary to enforce restrictions at the device level with security baselines, hardened images, and Group Policy or MDM. There can be a clear advantage to maintaining hardened images in an enterprise scenario when these factors are taken into consideration. Nevertheless, MDM technologies such as Intune combined with the Windows Autopilot service have made image maintenance much lighter. After the baseline hardened image has been applied, Intune and Windows Autopilot can be used to layer additional security baselines and device configurations and to deliver the latest applications. The decision of determining where these settings are applied depends on your deployment scenario, environment, and compliance requirements. As we discuss device imaging, we will cover the core tools used to build and deploy images.

First, let's discuss the upgrade options if moving to Windows 10 or a version of Windows Server 2016 or later, known as an in-place upgrade or migration. Task sequence deployments are commonly used when upgrading multiple assets. They are a set of XML instructions that define a series of events placed in an order to help automate the installation process. Task sequences are created using tools such as MDT and sequence and orchestrate the installation of the device drivers, operating system, scripts, and software installations:

- **In-place upgrades**: In this option, Windows is upgraded from the source version to the desired version. Applications, settings, and user data are retained. Typically, these upgrades are managed by deploying task sequences using Windows Deployment Services or **Microsoft Endpoint Configuration Manager** (**MECM**). In this upgrade option, a new operating system is installed on top of the existing one. This can cause some inconsistencies and challenges due to the over-layering of the operating system and setting translations. For a list of supported upgrade paths, visit this link:

    ```
    https://docs.microsoft.com/en-us/windows/deployment/
    upgrade/windows-10-upgrade-paths
    ```

- **Migration**: In this option, Windows is completely reinstalled in this scenario and can be migrated from basically any operating system. Enterprise tools are used to manage migrations using task sequence deployments, similar to in-place upgrades. Applications, settings, and user data will need to be accounted for separately in this upgrade option as they will be deleted in the migration. Use tools such as the **User State Migration Tool (USMT)** or Windows Easy Transfer for migrating application and user data. For an overview of USMT, visit this link:

    ```
    https://docs.microsoft.com/en-us/windows/deployment/usmt/usmt-overview
    ```

There are many modern methods available to securely back up and restore user data and add value to tried and true migration techniques. In addition to using USMT, organizations can empower users to take ownership of their data and use cloud storage such as OneDrive for Business.

> **Tip**
> Many organizations have already adopted some form of cloud storage. If your company is a Microsoft shop, OneDrive for Business should be the preferred cloud storage tool to provide a more integrated solution with a reduced footprint in vendor management and support. The following provides additional information on OneDrive safeguards from Microsoft: `https://support.office.com/en-us/article/how-onedrive-safeguards-your-data-in-the-cloud-23c6ea94-3608-48d7-8bf0-80e142edd1e1`.

This is a great potential training opportunity to teach users good data backup practices. OneDrive for Business also has enhanced security controls for company-owned data, with the ability to restrict external sharing and apply information protection policies such as data labeling and classification. Once users have backed up their data, the migration path for Windows 10 can be used, and the user's data will be available for download directly from OneDrive via the desktop app or web portal. This also helps to set the stage moving forward in a break-fix scenario. End users will be less reliant on their specific device and be productive much faster with less worry if a replacement is needed. Organizations can keep track of how users are handling OneDrive data by using the activity list from the security and compliance center. It provides an audit trail of file interactions such as mass deletions and external sharing activity that may be flagged as risky. The following screenshot is the result of an alert that was generated for an unusual amount of file deletions. When viewing the details of the alert, you can see the amount of deleted actions that occurred in a short time period:

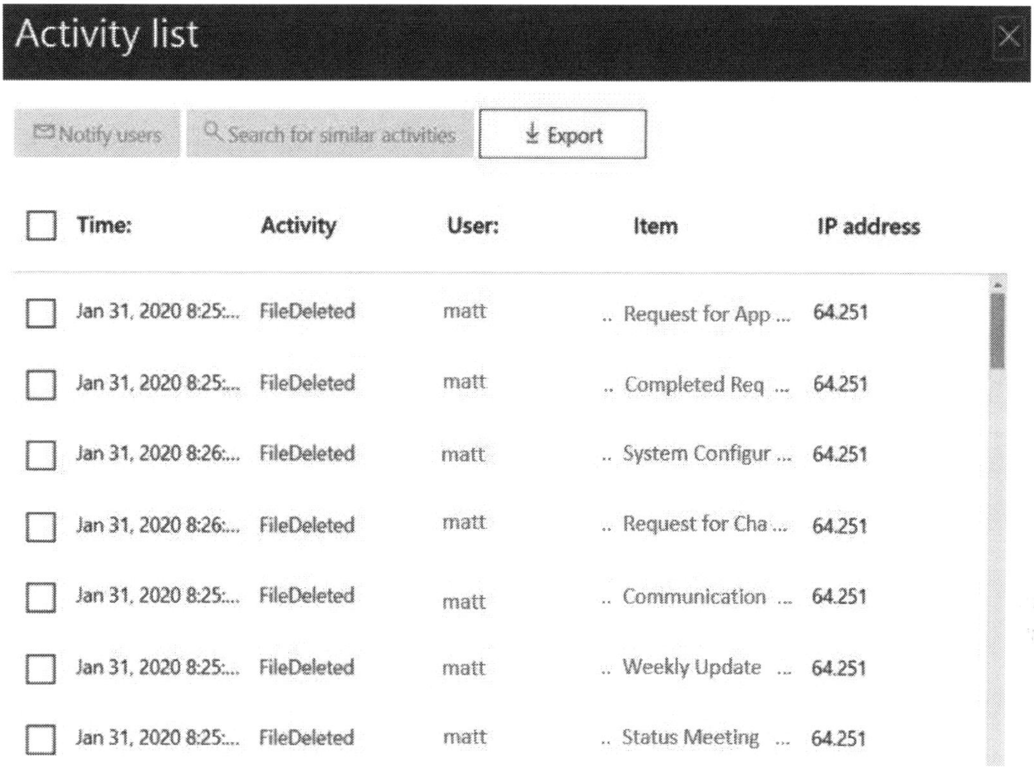

Figure 4.2 – Office 365 Security and Compliance activity list for file deletions from OneDrive

> **Tip**
> Use the redirect and move known Windows folders to OneDrive Group Policy. This can help ensure users' data is backed up prior to migration. To read more about this policy, visit this link: `https://docs.microsoft.com/en-us/onedrive/redirect-known-folders`.

Another feature available in **Azure Active Directory** (**AAD**) that's useful for migrating user data is known as Enterprise State Roaming. Enterprise State Roaming can manage specific settings such as theme, language preferences, and even mouse settings. Enterprise State Roaming's capabilities allow these settings to roam from device to device without manually backing them up. This can be enabled from a single setting in Azure Active Directory for all users or scoped to selected members. The following screenshot is the **Enterprise State Roaming** pane under **Devices** in Azure Active Directory:

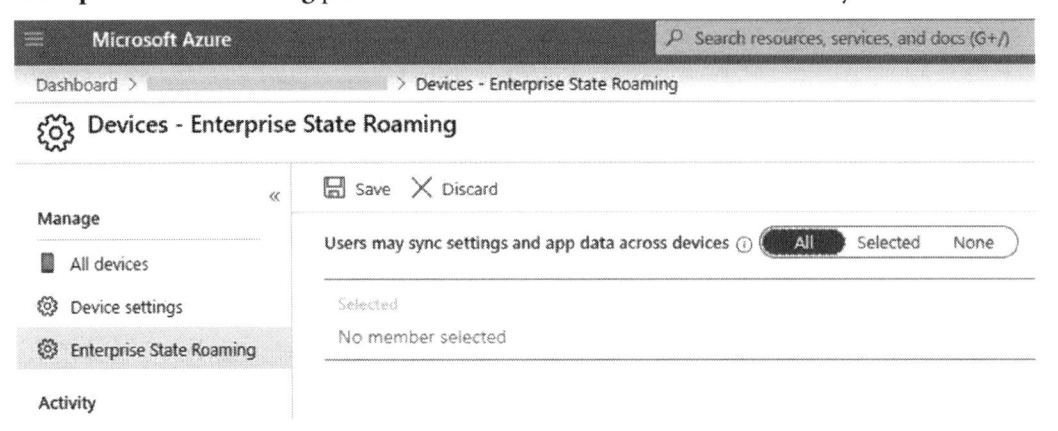

Figure 4.3 – Enable Enterprise State Roaming in Azure Active Directory

When **Enterprise State Roaming** is enabled, the user's settings are backed up to Azure, where the data is encrypted and decrypted using Azure Rights Management and Azure Information Protection. The data is retained indefinitely, determined stale by Microsoft, or after a user's Azure AD account has been deleted. Enterprise State Roaming uses the **sync settings** from the *Windows Settings>Accounts>Sync your settings* menu. In the screenshot that follows you can see that Enterprise State Roaming is disabled as Sync settings is configured to **Off**. This means it's being managed by the organization through an MDM policy:

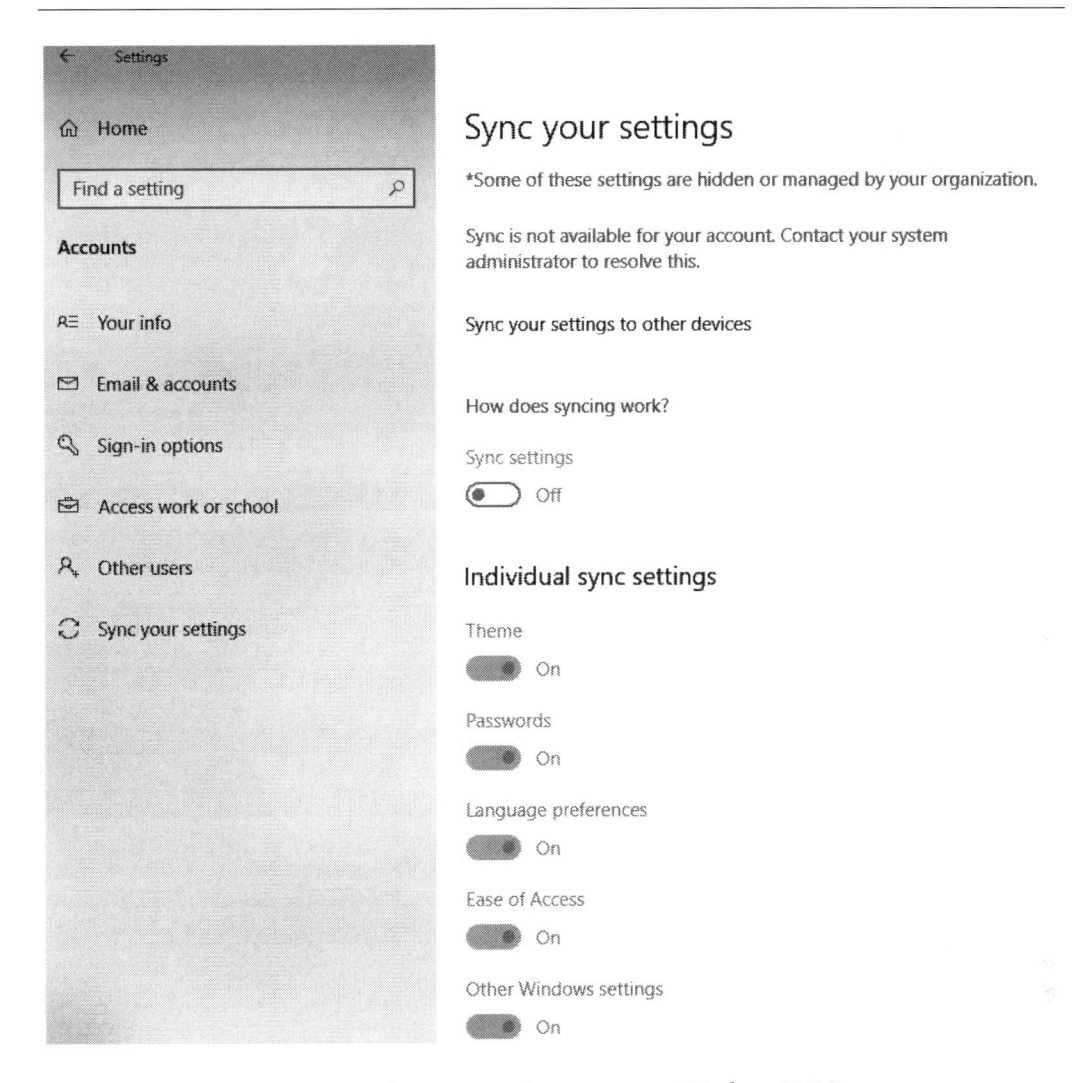

Figure 4.4 – Sync your settings menu on a Windows 10 PC

> **Tip**
> Be mindful setting Enterprise State Roaming in BYOD scenarios. Setting this policy with MDM or GPO will override any personal settings and can potentially have unwanted effects on users' personal devices.

We just covered the in-place and migration upgrade paths for the Windows operating system. We touched upon techniques that can be helpful when taking a modern approach to a Windows 10 upgrade by using OneDrive for Business and Enterprise State Roaming for Azure Active Directory joined devices. When combined with traditional methods, they can significantly help to simplify your upgrade deployments in a secure and cost-effective way. Next, let's discuss the tools used to build and deploy a hardened image. The topics we will cover include the following:

- Windows Assessment and Deployment Kit
- Windows Configuration Designer
- **Microsoft Deployment Toolkit (MDT)**
- **Windows Deployment Services (WDS)**
- MDT and Configuration Manager
- Windows Autopilot

Windows Assessment and Deployment Kit (Windows ADK)

Windows Assessment and Deployment Kit (Windows ADK) contains all the tools that are used to create custom images. We will discuss this first as it is a prerequisite for **Microsoft Deployment Toolkit (MDT)**. Here is a list of what Windows ADK can do and why it's used:

- Creates custom boot images or WIM files using the **Windows Preinstallation Environment (WinPE)**. WinPE is used for deployment and recovery and can later leverage a **Preboot Execution Environment (PXE)** or boot from USB.
- Creates an unattended (XML) Windows Setup answer file. The answer file is used to automate the selection of options during the Windows setup process. Unattend XML can apply custom configurations and security features such as setting registry keys, disabling Windows features, and running custom scripts.
- Backs up user data using USMT for migration or break-fix scenarios.
- Creates a reference hardened image used for deployment.
- Creates a **Provisioning Package (PPKG)** using **Windows Configuration Designer (WCD)**. This can be applied after an image and can enforce security settings; automate Azure AD Join; and add certificates, applications, and network configurations such as Wi-Fi.

Let's look at WCD, which is helpful for configuring shared devices, or a smaller subset of devices that may not require building and maintaining an image.

Windows Configuration Designer

WCD is an installation option of Windows ADK. Using a PPKG file is useful for automating the application of custom configurations and security settings. PPKG packages are useful for smaller organizations that may not have the resources to build and maintain images. **PPKG** are small files that can apply your baselines directly to an out-of-the-box or OEM Windows 10. Additional settings available in WCD include the following:

- Bulk MDM enrollment and Azure AD join
- Certificate enrollment
- Network profiles such as Wi-Fi and proxies
- Security restrictions such as password, device lock, encryption settings, update settings, and other privacy settings
- Customizations such as start tiles

> **Important note**
> To bulk enroll devices into Azure AD and Intune for a shared device scenario, a device enrollment manager account is used.

Device enrollment managers are configured under the **Devices** section in the Intune management portal. The following screenshot is a view of the Intune device settings overview, where you can add or remove these accounts for enrolling large quantities of devices:

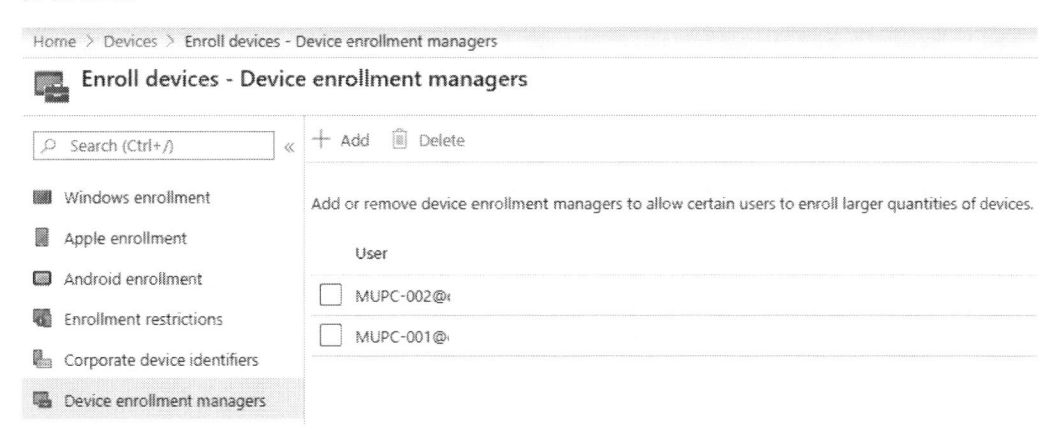

Figure 4.5 – Device enrollment managers in Microsoft Endpoint Manager

WCD has a built-in security feature that requires Azure AD join tokens to be renewed every 30 days. New PPKG packages will need to be created once that time expires in order to use the device enrollment manager for Azure AD Join. In the following screenshot, you can see the **Bulk AAD Token** option. Clicking on **Get Bulk Token** brings up an **Azure Active Directory** (**AAD**) login page where you will use one of the device enrollment manager accounts to acquire the AAD token:

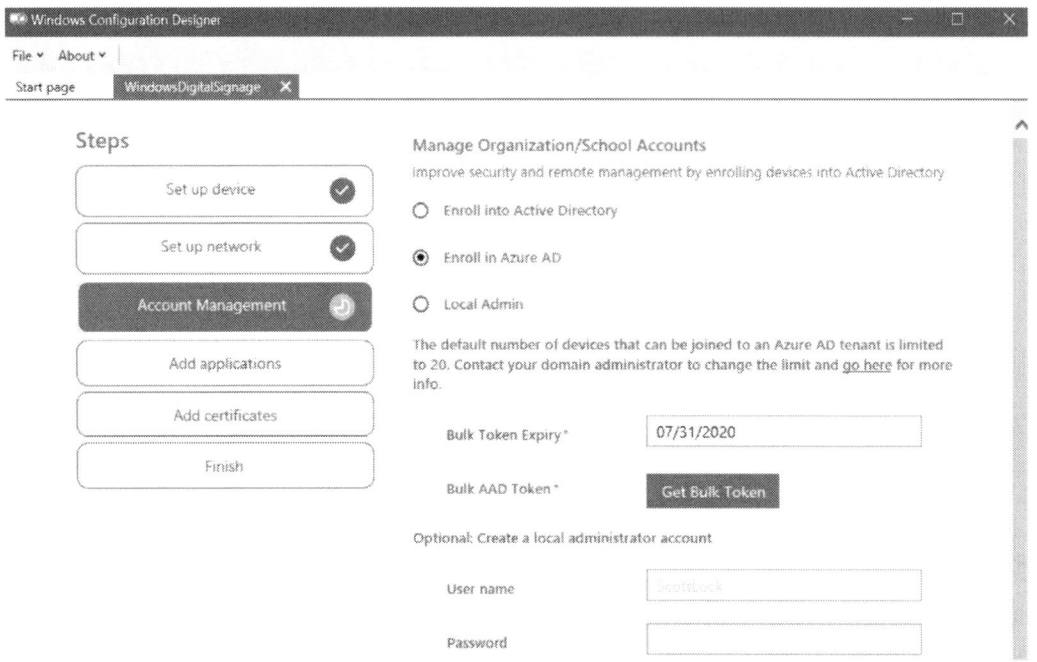

Figure 4.6 – Windows Configuration Designer Get Bulk Token option for Azure AD Join

For a full list of what can be configured in WCD, visit this link:

https://docs.microsoft.com/en-us/windows/configuration/provisioning-packages/provisioning-packages

Now that we have covered the WCD tool, let's discuss **Microsoft Deployment Toolkit** (**MDT**). MDT is the recommended tool for building custom images and offers the greatest flexibility for applying baselines and for bulk deployments.

Microsoft Deployment Toolkit

MDT is an enterprise standard for building boot images or custom reference images for **Light Touch Installation** (**LTI**) deployments. MDT creates boot media for standalone or network-based deployments as well as **Zero touch Installation** (**ZTI**) for **Microsoft Endpoint Configuration Manager** (**SCCM**). It is also a centralized place for building custom task sequences, maintaining security configurations, device settings, and for **sysprepping** a reference image to capture it.

> **Tip**
> System preparation or (**Sysprep**) is the process of preparing Windows to capture a reference image that can be used across multiple devices. Sysprep can be opened from *C:\Windows\System32\Sysprep* and is typically used to generalize Windows to remove PC-specific information.

MDT helps to reduce the complexity of using the standalone Windows ADK (which is a pre-requisite to using MDT). The following are additional security features of MDT to consider when creating a hardened image:

- The ability to apply local Group Policy Objects
- The ability to enable BitLocker in the WinPE environment (offline BitLocker)
- Customizable WindowsRE (recovery environment)
- The ability to add local administrators to devices
- The ability to add or remove Windows Server roles and features
- Support for UEFI
- USMT support to automate the backup of user data and settings

For a full feature list visit:

```
https://docs.microsoft.com/en-us/windows/deployment/deploy-windows-mdt/key-features-in-mdt
```

114   End User Device Management

The following screenshot is a task sequence in Microsoft Deployment Toolkit. It is the step-by-step set of instructions used during the **LTI** process to deploy the operating system and install applications and customizations:

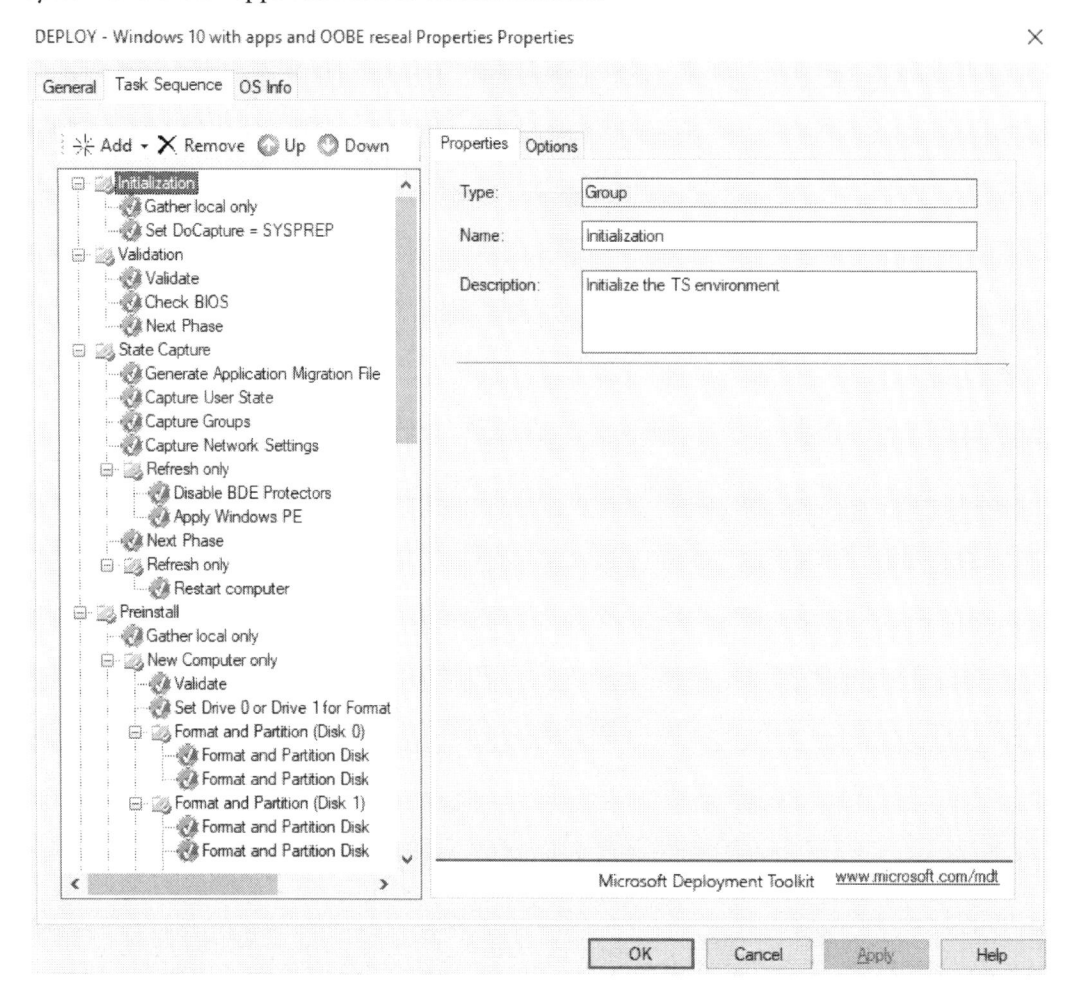

Figure 4.7 – Custom MDT task sequence

MDT can deploy custom images over an Active Directory network with deployment share replication using DFS-R. For information on configuring an MDT deployment environment and DFS-R replication, visit this link:

```
https://docs.microsoft.com/en-us/windows/deployment/deploy-
windows-mdt/deploy-a-windows-10-image-using-mdt
```

MDT is free to install from Microsoft. For the latest downloads and documentation, visit this link:

https://docs.microsoft.com/en-us/configmgr/mdt/index?redirectedfrom=MSDN

Now that we have covered the MDT tool, let's discuss two ways we can deploy our custom images. First, we will cover **Windows Deployment Services (WDS)**.

Windows Deployment Services

WDS is a feature of Windows Server used to deliver custom or MDT **Lite Touch Installation** (**LTI**) images over PXE. To use **Preboot Execution Environment** (**PXE**) requires a DHCP server role and a TFTP server on your network to retrieve the boot images.

Ways to secure your images with **Windows Deployment Services (WDS)**:

1. Set a UDP port range to limit communication protocols used to connect to WDS.
2. Require *F12* to enter PXE boot.
3. Use Active Directory authentication by specifying a domain controller to use for authentication and authorize your WDS through DHCP.
4. Use NTSF permissions on boot images and security groups on image groups to lock them down. `Read` and `Execute` are the only required permissions to deploy images.
5. Require administrative approval to PXE from unmanaged AD computer objects using the pending devices snap-in.
6. Specify the format of the computer name and **organizational unit (OU)** placement of the computer object in Active Directory. If necessary, use a staging OU that requires an administrator to move the PC object once the image is validated. This is also helpful so as to not overwrite an already active and existing PC object.

WDS is a common method used by organizations to deploy images. It typically requires its own standalone server and requires additional management. Now, let's look at Configuration Manager, which is another common solution used to deploy images. It supports MDT tasks sequences and doesn't require additional infrastructure if already being used to manage your windows systems.

MDT and Configuration Manager

Configuration Manager can be extremely helpful in deploying images in a medium-to-large organization. MDT task sequences can be built in Configuration Manager and targeted to a collection of resources. Collections are groups of users or devices for targeted deployments. Images can be directly deployed to clients with the Configuration Manager agent, USB media, or with PXE using an SCCM distribution point with PXE support.

New PCs can be pre-staged by MAC address in Configuration Manager and associated with the source PC prior to image deployment. Using a backup, task sequence data is stored on the site server with the State Migration Point role installed. Then, a Windows 10 task sequence can be deployed to the new PC and user data is automatically restored based on the association created.

For more information about creating task sequences with MDT using Configuration Manager, visit this link: `https://docs.microsoft.com/en-us/windows/deployment/deploy-windows-cm/create-a-task-sequence-with-configuration-manager-and-mdt`

The following are ways to protect your task sequences in Configuration Manager:

- Use security scopes and built-in security roles to define what objects administrators have access to. Security scopes can include boot images, driver packages, collection software updates, and applications, to name a few.
- Target only the collections necessary to receive your deployment.
- If leveraging PXE or media-based deployments, password-protect the task sequence.
- Modify the default permissions on deployment shares. This could be used to safeguard a user from accidentally kicking off a re-image if they unknowingly enter PXE.

WDS and MDT with Configuration Manager are common examples of how organizations deploy Windows images. Let's discuss a different approach to PC deployment, known as Windows Autopilot. Here, we will cover how the Autopilot service can be used to securely deploy PCs directly from the manufacturer with or without a custom image. This option can save a significant amount of time, free up resources, and even alter the PC life cycle as it's known today.

Windows Autopilot

Windows Autopilot is used to automate and customize the device setup, deployment, and life cycle of a Windows 10 PC and minimizes the effort needed by IT staff. This is a change of process compared with the traditional PC life cycle model by leveraging the power of the cloud and the Windows Autopilot service. From a supply chain perspective, organizations can order hardware directly from an OEM or retail vendor where devices are registered into your organization and shipped directly to the end user. All the user needs are credentials and a network connection, and the entire device provisioning process can be fully automated into a business-ready state.

To use Windows Autopilot, you will need a supported version of Windows 10, **Azure Active Directory** (**AAD**), and Intune licenses. Windows Autopilot also supports hybrid domain join. For more information about the Windows Autopilot requirements, visit this link:

```
https://docs.microsoft.com/en-us/windows/deployment/windows-autopilot/windows-autopilot-requirements
```

Windows Autopilot can be used for a cost savings initiative as well as to decrease the downtime seen in the traditional break-fix model with features such as Autopilot reset. The management of devices is simplified too through Azure AD Join, with automatic enrollment into Intune. Through an assigned Autopilot device profile, **out-of-box experience** (**OOBE**) settings can be customized and autoselected for the user. Registering the hardware to the Windows Autopilot service through your AAD tenant locks down the device's association to your organization. This helps to protect against theft and resale if the PC comes back online.

The Windows Autopilot cycle happens in three steps:

1. Devices are registered to your organization by the IT department or through an OEM or vendor.
2. Device profiles or Autopilot profiles are created and assigned to the devices.
3. The device is powered on, connected to a network, and checks the Windows Autopilot deployment service for registration.

Windows Autopilot supports a few different deployment scenarios, including the following two modes:

- **User-driven mode** is designed for the user self-service model requiring minimal IT interaction. A device can be shipped directly to the user, powered on, connected to a network, and fully provisioned by making a few selections in the **Out-of-Box Experience (OOBE)** menu.
- **Self-deploying mode** is useful for shared devices, kiosks, or digital signage. In self-deploying mode, all that is needed is an active network connection. Autopilot will join Azure Active Directory and apply all the security policies, configurations, and applications through an enrollment status page. Once complete, the desktop can be logged onto for use.

> Tip
> In the self-deploying scenario, the device is not associated with a user. Self-deploying mode requires Windows 10 1903 or later and a minimum of TPM 2.0.

White glove OOBE is available in Windows 10 1903 and later and allows the IT department to pre-provision a device like user-driven mode. White glove allows a technician to set up the device before to a business-ready state prior to handing it over to the user. This helps minimize the wait time before the user can be productive.

Windows Autopilot supports a device reset scenario, which is helpful for asset transfers to other associates. With Autopilot reset, a device is restored back its original settings and previous users' settings and data are removed. The asset can then be assigned to a new employee without having to re-image the PC.

> Tip
> Autopilot reset can be initiated locally and remotely with Windows version 1809 or later.

To recap, you have just learned about the different tools used to create and deploy images in addition to some of the security practices used to keep them from being tampered with. We also covered Windows Autopilot and the value-add to automate the deployment of a device to an end user. In the next section, we are going to discuss unified endpoint management and the enterprise solutions used to manage our end user devices.

Microsoft Endpoint Configuration Manager

Microsoft Endpoint Configuration Manager or System Center Configuration Manager is a world-class enterprise device management solution for workstations, laptops, and Windows servers. Its robust set of tools and centralized management are invaluable for ensuring device security and configurations are compliant. It is highly scalable and can deploy not only operating systems, but can control the application life cycle, as well as managing security updates, security baselines, antivirus, telemetry, and compliance policies with a robust set of reporting built in.

The Configuration Manager infrastructure is typically a hierarchy of servers with different configured roles and consists of a **Central Administration Site** (**CAS**) with additional primary or secondary sites based on the organization's scale. Depending on the size and geolocation of users and devices, there may also be multiple management points and distribution points for hosting content. Your entire ecosystem of devices can be controlled from a single administrative console. Windows servers and workstations are pushed an agent installation that creates the connection point to Configuration Manager.

Software Center is the name of the user-facing application installed on client machines that allows users to request and install applications, install software updates, and configure options such as active hours and power management policies. If the organization contains many remote employees that never connect to your corporate network or VPN, clients can be managed directly over the internet using an Azure **Platform as a Service** (**PaaS**) resource known as a cloud management gateway or through internet-based client management directly to internet-facing site systems. Content can also be stored in Azure Storage using the cloud management gateway. Renamed from System Center Configuration Manager in version 1910, Configuration Manager integrates with many other Microsoft cloud-based management solutions. These services include Intune for the co-management of devices, Desktop Analytics for reporting and telemetry, and Windows Autopilot for simplifying the deployment life cycle. Together, they create a suite of tools known as Microsoft Endpoint Manager. When using Configuration Manager to centrally manage and secure your devices, it's important to understand key concepts. In the next few sections, we will be covering the following topics:

- Securely deploying clients for Configuration Manager
- Client collections, settings, and communications

Let's have a look at them.

Securely deploying clients for Configuration Manager

There are a few different methods available for client deployment and we will provide an overview of each along with a list of best practices to ensure the site only accepts approved and trusted clients. Microsoft Docs has a great write-up that can be found at this link on best practices for client deployments of Configuration Manager:

https://docs.microsoft.com/en-us/configmgr/core/clients/deploy/plan/best-practices-for-client-deployment

Let's take a look at several different methods used to deploy clients today:

- Group Policy installation is supported for Windows only. Using a GPO, clients can be deployed to computer objects during the next policy processing without the need for a discovery cycle within the Configuration Manager console. GPO processes typically every 90 minutes or can be forced by running `gpupdate /force` from Command Prompt on the target system. The installation bootstrapper and commands are configured in the software installation node in GPMC under **Computer Configuration** > **Policies** > **Software Settings**, as shown in the following screenshot:

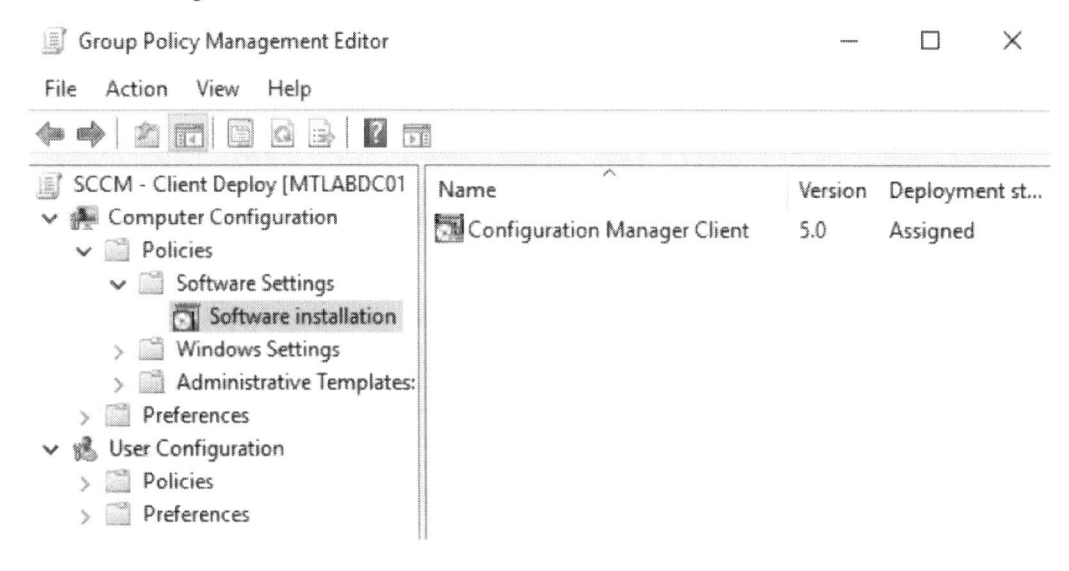

Figure 4.8 – Software installation Group Policy used to bootstrap the Configuration Manager agent

- Software update-based installation uses Group Policy to configure a software update point and can be used for both new installations and client upgrades. Software update-based installations use the software updates feature of Configuration Manager and will require a server with the **Software Update (SUP)** site system role installed. For more information about installing a software update point, view this link:

    `https://docs.microsoft.com/en-us/configmgr/sum/get-started/install-a-software-update-point`

- **Logon Script Installations** can install the Configuration Manager client using the `CCMSetup.exe` file located in the **Program Files/Microsoft Configuration Manager/Client** directory. To use the login script method, ensure the targeted computers have read access to the deployment share configured in the script. If the Active Directory schema hasn't been extended for Configuration Manager, then a management point and source directory must be specified in the installation command. For more information on extending the schema in Active Directory to publish site system information, visit this link:

    `https://docs.microsoft.com/en-us/configmgr/core/plan-design/network/extend-the-active-directory-schema`

- Client push installation methods can be used to deploy clients on computers that are discovered by site discovery within Configuration Manager. The site can be configured to automatically use client push for discovered computers or by using the Client push installation wizard on specific collections of resources.

- OS image installation is an option if using a reference image. The client can be preinstalled on the reference image.

- Manual or package installations are useful for boots-on-the-ground installations or for targeting a collection of devices for client upgrade scenarios.

- Intune installations for MDM Managed Devices can be used for devices that are managed by Intune. **CCMSetup.msi** is deployed as an app and uses AAD for authentication. Depending on your infrastructure requirements and the number of remote workers, `ccmsetup` can be customized for both intranet- and internet-based management. Each scenario requires different setup commands and additional requirements are needed if using a Cloud Management Gateway and enabling co-management. The following screenshot shows an example of the Intune app installation properties of the `ccmsetup.msi` bootstrapper:

Figure 4.9 – Microsoft Endpoint Manager view of the ConfigMgr client in Intune

For more information about configuring Configuration Manager to use Azure AD for authentication and the Cloud Management Gateway, visit this link:

```
https://docs.microsoft.com/en-us/configmgr/core/clients/
deploy/deploy-clients-cmg-azure
```

Regardless of the method used for deploying agents, there are a few security best practices outlined by Microsoft, as follows:

- Use PKI certificates for clients that communicate with IIS Site Systems by using HTTPS.
- If managing computers in Active Directory, only auto-approve clients from trusted domains.

If deploying the agent during OS imaging, remove the certificates before Sysprep to ensure clients don't impersonate each other.

- Use a trusted root key to validate management points for your clients.
- Always update software update points to include the latest agent version.
- Disable WINS lookup to ensure only Active Directory Domain Services is used to find valid management points.

To view the full list in detail of security best practices from Microsoft, visit this link:

`https://docs.microsoft.com/en-us/configmgr/core/clients/deploy/plan/security-and-privacy-for-clients`

Now that we have covered the methods used to securely deploy the clients, in the next sub-section, we will discuss how to secure settings and communications to your site systems.

Client collections, settings, and communications

It's important to understand the health and status of your clients as this can indicate potential security concerns. If a production client is active but not sending a heartbeat back to the central management point, then the client may have lost its ability to receive configurations or patches or be unable to be remediated in the event of a security incident. The activity status of clients may also be used for maintaining an inventory. Devices that are still active in a production environment likely contain sensitive data and we need to ensure they are actively managed and organized by IT.

In Configuration Manager, resources are managed by being placed into collections known as user and device collections. Several collections are pre-configured out of the box and custom ones are built by specifying sets of rules, or through WQL queries (SQL for WMI) to find resources. For more information about creating queries in Configuration Manager, visit this link:

`https://docs.microsoft.com/en-us/configmgr/core/servers/manage/create-queries`

Sub-collections are created by specifying a limiting collection. This limits the scope of resources that can be included in a sub-collection to those in the limiting collection. To secure collections, apply role-based administrative controls to dictate which sets of resources administrators have access to perform operations against. Role-based administration can also apply to the site scope and is helpful to give permissions to administrators that perform different functions and manage different sets of resources within the site. There are many built-in security roles and they can be assigned to individual users or Active Directory security groups. For example, the Application Administrator built-in security role grants permission to author and deploy applications. The Software Update Manager role grants permission to define and deploy software updates. Role-based administration is also helpful for hierarchies with multiple sites that have different administrators managing them to provide a separation of duties. To assign security roles, go to **Administration**, **Security**, **Administrative Users**. For more information about collections in Configuration Manager, visit this link:

`https://docs.microsoft.com/en-us/configmgr/core/clients/manage/collections/introduction-to-collections`

For more information about role-based administration in Configuration Manager, visit this link:

`https://docs.microsoft.com/en-us/mem/configmgr/core/understand/fundamentals-of-role-based-administration`

Once you have decided on a secure method of client deployment and outlined collections for your devices, you will need to define the settings the agents will use to communicate with the site systems. Next, let's look at the client settings options, as well as device actions that can be taken on individual clients.

Client settings

Custom client settings are used to specify agent configurations such as caching settings, policy polling, compliance settings, and customizations in Software Center such as company branding. Client settings can be deployed to different collections and multiple client setting policies can exist. When client settings are assigned, they are given a priority or weight variable to dictate which settings take precedence. The default custom client setting is set to 1000. In the following screenshot, you can see all the different configurable client settings:

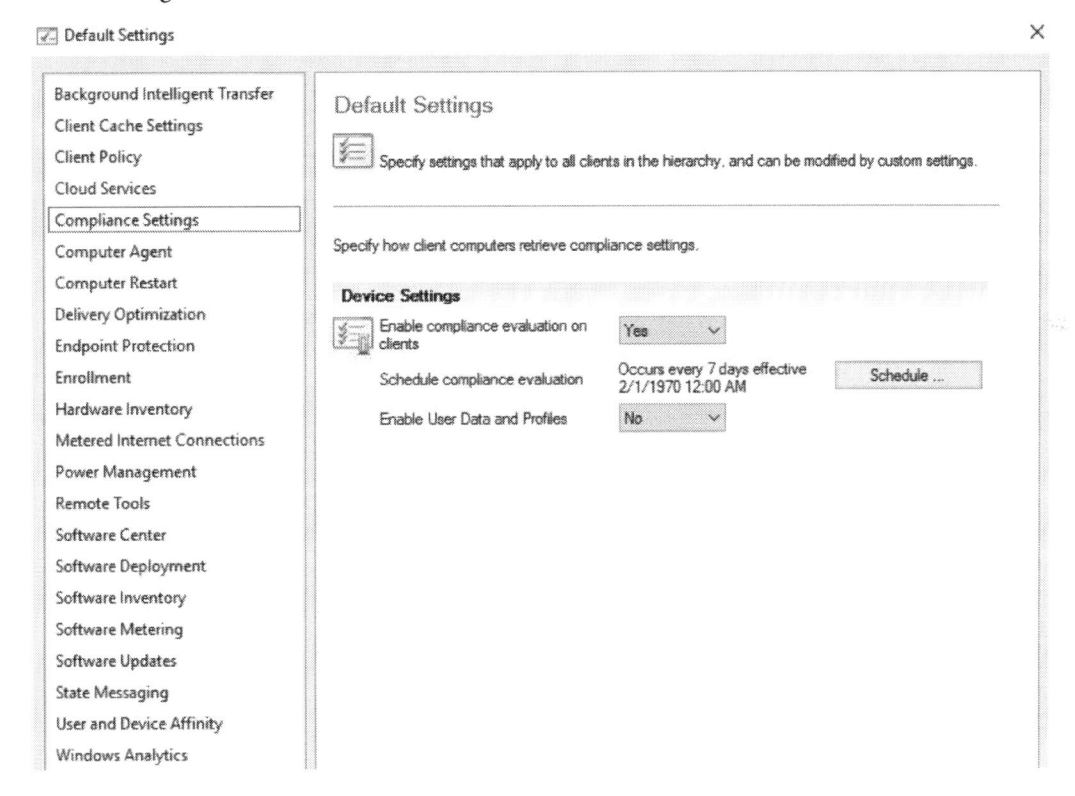

Figure 4.10 – Default client settings in Configuration Manager

Client settings can be configured under **Administration** > **Client Settings,** and include both device and user-based client settings.

In addition to setting custom client settings, Configuration Manager also has many device actions that can be performed directly on the client. This is helpful if a policy request needs to be made sooner than the next polling interval as configured in the settings. The following screenshot shows some of the available menu options for device actions:

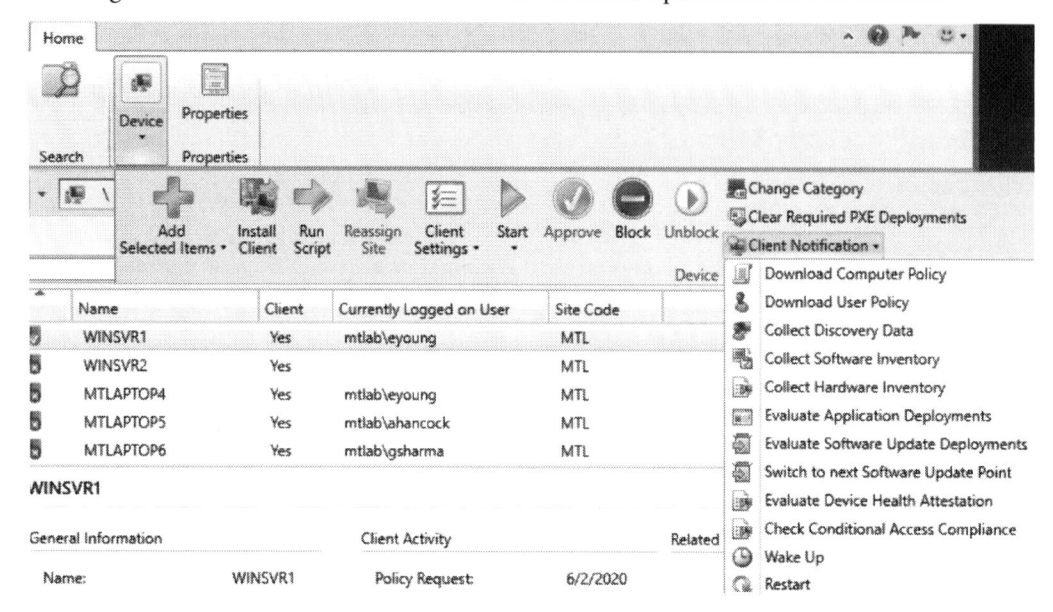

Figure 4.11 – A list of device management actions as seen from the Device node

In addition to the remote actions for policy polling under client notifications, there are other actions too. Using the **Client Settings** dropdown will show you a view of all client settings applied to a device. The **Start** dropdown will allow you to initiate a remote desktop session if configured. Another useful option under **Start** is the **resource explorer**. Resource explorer is the system information view, like `msinfo32.exe` but for a remote device. This is helpful for viewing hardware inventory or software inventory specific to an individual device. You can even run a script directly against the device using **Run Script**, or block it if it's deemed out of compliance.

For more details on client management operations, visit this link:

`https://docs.microsoft.com/en-us/configmgr/core/clients/manage/manage-clients`

Now that we have covered configuring collections and client settings, let's discuss how clients communicate with the central administration site.

Client communication

Clients communicate with different site system roles such as **Management Points** (**MP**) and **Distribution Points** (**DP**) using the most secure method available. An **MP** site system provides location information to clients, such as the location of DP, and delivers policy data. The **DP** site system role contains source files such as applications, software updates, and PC images and is where the client downloads content from. Client authentication uses HTTP or HTTPS and is only required when connecting to a DP to request content. When initiating communication to a management point, authorization occurs for both the device and the user.

Typically, clients have an enterprise PKI certificate issued through a certificate services auto-enrollment policy to prove its identity to the MP or DP. Client authentication can also use Azure Active Directory for user and device authentication. In the following screenshot, the Configuration Manager control panel applet displays the client certificate as using PKI:

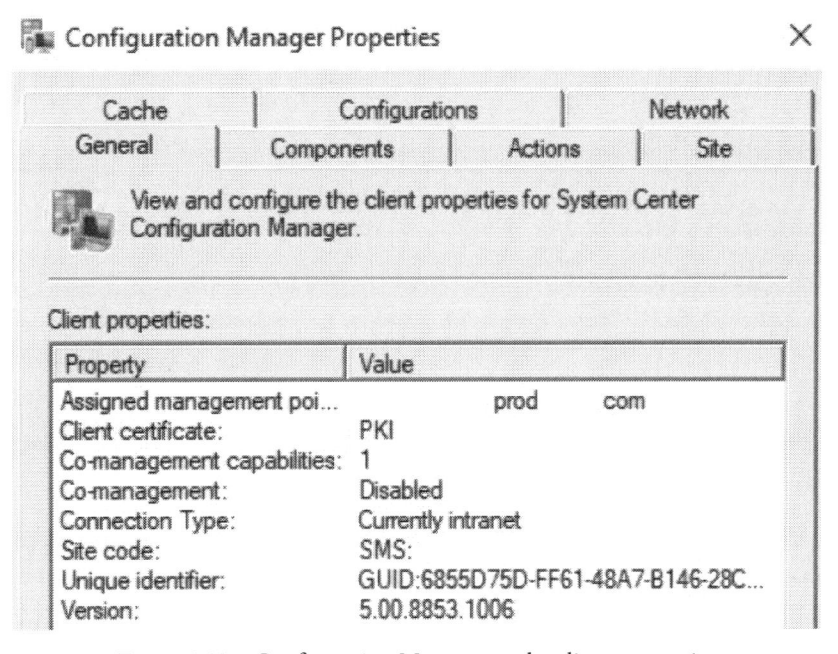

Figure 4.12 – Configuration Manager applet client properties

To read more about PKI certificate requirements, visit this link:

https://docs.microsoft.com/en-us/configmgr/core/plan-design/network/pki-certificate-requirements

To configure client communication settings for your Management Points and Distribution Points, go to **Administration, Site Configuration, Servers and Site System Roles**. Each site system you select will list all the installed site system roles that can be configured. Double-click them to open their properties. In the following screenshot, you can see the MP properties for this site server are requiring client communications to use HTTPS:

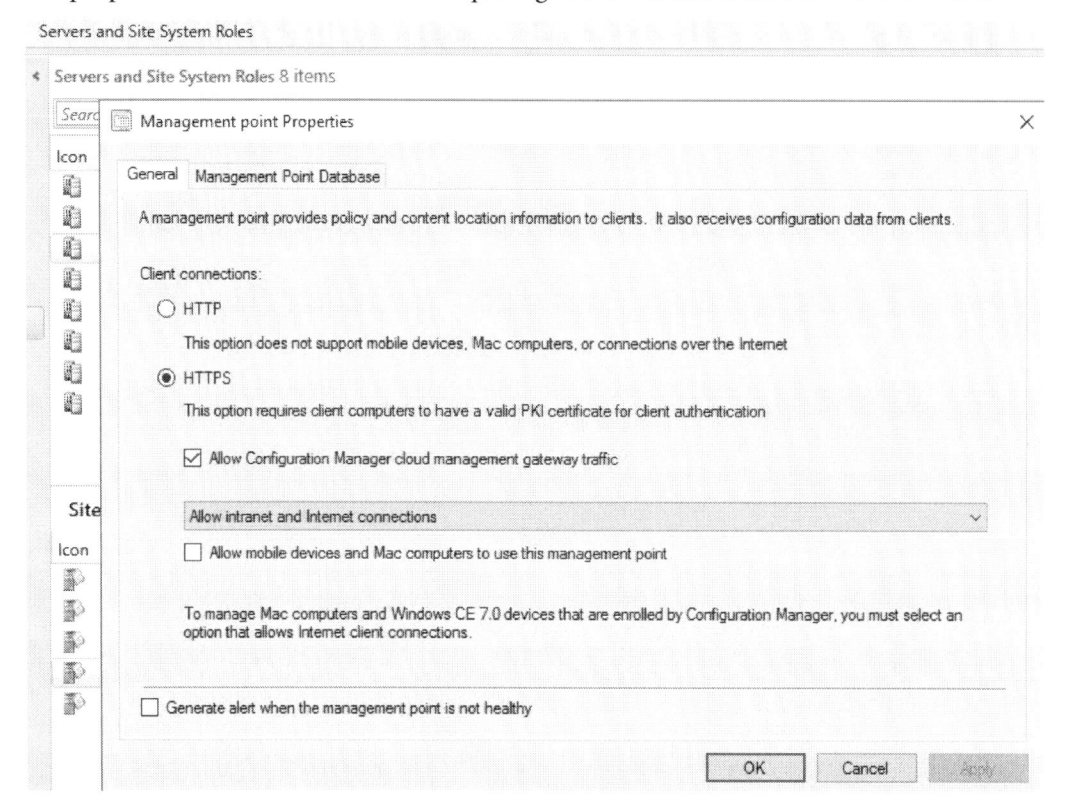

Figure 4.13 – MP client communication settings in Configuration Manager

We just covered the basics of deploying client settings and how clients securely communicate with the hierarchy. Much of the power of Configuration Manager comes from its ability to monitor clients and enforce compliance. We will cover different compliance settings and policies later, in *Chapter 8, Administration and Remote Management*. Next, let's look at Mobile Device Management for Windows 10 with Intune. Used together, Intune and Configuration Manager are collectively known as co-management. Co-management offers even greater flexibility by combining options from both solutions.

Intune Mobile Device Management (MDM)

Microsoft Intune is an Azure-based device management solution that integrates with many Microsoft services and is a standard for **Mobile Device Management** (**MDM**) and **Mobile Application Management** (**MAM**). Intune can manage and secure not only Windows devices, but macOS, iPadOS, and mobile devices built on iOS and Android. It is a single solution to enforce your security baselines by applying device configuration profiles, device restrictions, security policies, application and protection policies, and many more depending on the platform in scope.

Intune can be integrated with Configuration Manager for co-management or you can choose to be 100% Intune. Using compliance policies, security teams can define rules and settings that must be properly configured on your devices in order to meet compliance requirements. In conjunction with conditional access, organizations can assess the risk of a device and choose actions based on this condition such as blocking access or require **Multi-Factor Authentication** (**MFA**) when a device (or user) does not satisfy the compliance requirements. Next, we will cover the following topics as they relate to features in Intune:

- **Configuration Service Provider (CSP)**
- MDM versus MAM
- Windows enrollment methods

Let's discuss how Intune manages the configuration of your MDM enrolled devices using Configuration Service Providers or CSPs.

Configuration Service Provider

An MDM CSP is the layer that MDM providers use to configure custom settings on mobile devices. Specifically, Windows 10 uses the **Open Mobile Alliance Uniform Resource Identifier (OMA-URI)** to identify and configure these settings. Configurations for CSPs typically leverage the **Synchronization Markup Language (SyncML)** in XML format using the **Open Mobile Alliance Device Management** protocol **(OMA-DM)**. Just like traditional Group Policy, the CSP acts as a median to configure settings such as a registry key, for example. It is important to mention CSPs, as this is what MDM uses to expose configurations on your devices compared to using traditional domain Group Policy.

CSPs are typically represented in a tree-like format. In the diagram that follows, the root node is listed first followed by rounded elements and rectangular elements. The rounded elements are the different nodes and the rectangular elements represent different settings that require a value. The first element after the root dictates the name of the CSP and the first rectangular element is the setting that requires a value. When put together, they formulate the full URI path. The following diagram demonstrates the tree view of a CSP:

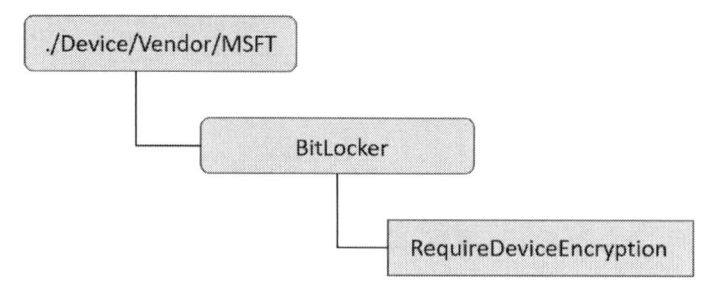

Figure 4.14 – CSP diagram for the BitLocker RequireDeviceEncryption setting

For this CSP, MSFT (Microsoft) is the vendor root and BitLocker is the CSP node. The full URI path for the CSP would be as follows in the XML format:

`./Vendor/MSFT/BitLocker/RequireDeviceEncryption`

Setting the Data integer to 0 In the SyncML XML format will disable this policy:

```xml
<SyncML>
    <SyncBody>
        <Replace>
            <CmdID>$CmdID$</CmdID>
            <Item>
                <Target>
                    <LocURI>./Device/Vendor/MSFT/BitLocker/RequireStorageCardEncryption</LocURI>
                </Target>
                <Meta>
                    <Format xmlns='syncml:metinf'>int</Format>
                </Meta>
                <Data>0</Data>
            </Item>
        </Replace>
    </SyncBody>
</SyncML>
```

Documentation on the BitLocker CSP can be found here:

https://docs.microsoft.com/en-us/windows/client-management/mdm/bitlocker-csp

CSPs can be manually configured using custom profiles in Intune. Many CSPs are already built into Intune (including the preceding BitLocker example) and should be set using the Windows 10 device restriction profiles over a custom OMA-URI path when applicable. The following screenshot shows configuring a custom profile OMA-URI for configuring a **Reset Password** link on the Windows 10 login page for `Self-Service Password Reset`:

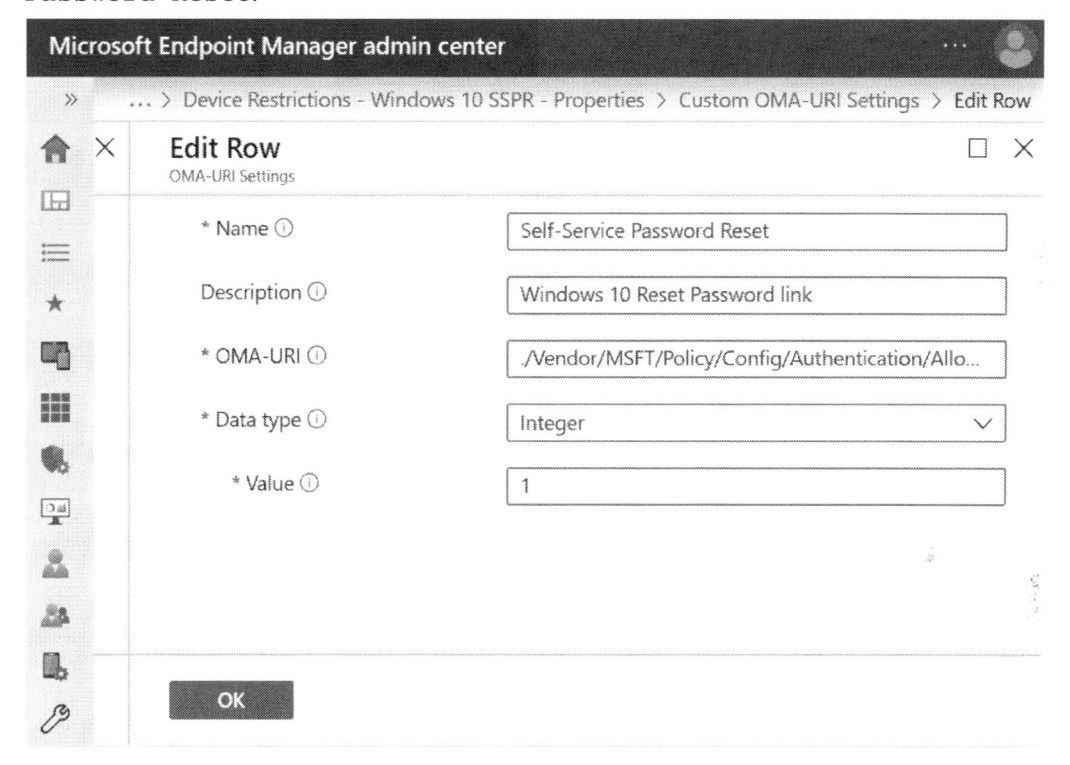

Figure 4.15 – Custom OMA-URI setting in Intune to enable the Self-Service Password Reset link

For a full list of the configuration service providers reference, visit this link:

https://docs.microsoft.com/en-us/windows/client-management/mdm/configuration-service-provider-reference

Now that we have discussed how Intune uses CSPs to apply settings to your devices, let's look at the difference between **Mobile Device Management** (**MDM**) and **Mobile Application Management** (**MAM**).

Mobile Device Management versus Mobile Application Management

In the managed device or MDM scenario, devices are enrolled in Intune to become fully managed at the device level. A Windows 10 MDM managed device can be layered with certain device restrictions using configuration profiles that include the following examples of settings:

- PIN requirements for unlocking your device
- Custom configurations for CSPs not included in the user interface
- VPN configurations and settings
- Certificates
- Wi-Fi settings
- Line of business applications and other apps
- Compliance policies such as a minimum required Windows version
- Security baselines and administrative templates (ADMX).

A fully managed device also allows device-specific remote actions such as force policy synchronization and a device wipe with organizational data removal. Using MDM, Intune also provides a comprehensive set of inventory and reporting data for managed devices. Unlike MDM, managed apps or MAM uses protection policies that are applied directly to the applications themselves. Protection policies can be applied to custom line of business apps and popular store apps that have been integrated with the Intune SDK to support Intune application protection policies. MAM can be used in conjunction with MDM as an additional security layer. While many device actions are unavailable in MAM, certain remote actions can be used to selectively wipe only the company data that is stored in the app. An example of a policy that can be applied with MAM includes requiring a PIN on app launch or blocking jailbroken or rooted devices. Application protection policies assigned to Windows 10 devices are known as **Windows Information Protection (WIP)**. Using MAM and WIP, policies are assigned to either protect or exempt applications and help to create a separation of corporate and personal data without the need to switch apps. An enlightened or protected app can be configured to protect enterprise data from being copied to a non-protected app. This level of protection can also be applied to data transfers with USB or other removable media. Using an information rights management system such as **Azure Rights Management (Azure RMS)**, data is encrypted by WIP and only authorized employees can open it.

Next, let's discuss the two types of enrollment methods used for Windows devices to come under Intune management.

Windows enrollment methods

There are two main types of enrollment methods for Windows and they are user self-enrollment and administrator-based enrollment. If licensed for Azure Active Directory Premium as well as Intune, organizations can configure automatic enrollment into Intune with Azure Active Directory join.

User self-enrollment scenarios:

- Windows Autopilot in user-driven mode
- Intune enrollment only (MDM only)
- Azure AD Join with auto enrollment
- **Bring your own device (BYOD)**

Administrator enrollment scenarios:

- Windows Autopilot using self-deploying mode or White glove
- Bulk enrollment
- Device enrollment manager to enroll devices such as kiosks or shared PCs
- Configuration Manager enrollment

Additional information about Windows enrollment methods can be found at this link:

```
https://docs.microsoft.com/en-us/intune/enrollment/windows-enrollment-methods
```

We just covered the basic framework of how Intune is used to manage and enroll your devices. We walked through how Intune layers settings on your device using CSPs, as well as the differences between MDM and MAM. Finally, we covered the two types of Windows enrollment methods used to bring your devices into Intune management. In the next section, we will discuss the Microsoft Endpoint Manager admin center, which is now the centralized hub for Intune. This admin center is the single pane of glass for Intune device management.

Introducing Microsoft Endpoint Manager

Microsoft Endpoint Manager Admin Center (**EMAC**) is the unified endpoint management solution that brings Intune, Configuration Manager, co-management, Windows Autopilot, and MDATP into one console. EMAC adds the power of cloud analytics to these standalone technologies and offers unified reporting views to gain insights into the compliance of your Windows devices from both Intune and Configuration Manager telemetry. Using software updates, Windows updates for business policies can be scheduled and assigned from the Microsoft Endpoint Manager console. The Microsoft Endpoint Manager admin center login page can be found at this link:

`https://devicemanagement.microsoft.com`

The following screenshot shows the status of all device configuration profiles as pushed to devices:

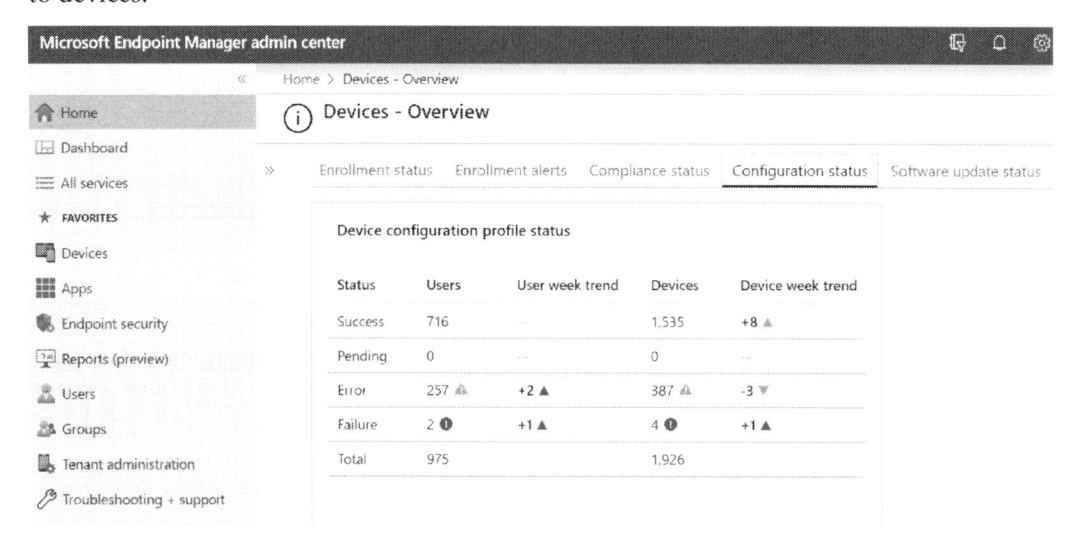

Status	Users	User week trend	Devices	Device week trend
Success	716	...	1,535	+8 ▲
Pending	0	...	0	...
Error	257 ▲	+2 ▲	387 ▲	-3 ▼
Failure	2 ⓘ	+1 ▲	4 ⓘ	+1 ▲
Total	975		1,926	

Figure 4.16 – Device configuration status overview from Microsoft Endpoint Manager

Recently rebranded, EMAC is the place to perform all remote actions for Intune enrolled devices. A valuable security feature available in EMAC for Intune enrolled devices is the ability to take immediate actions on devices that are compromised. In the following screenshot, you can see many options available for remote actions:

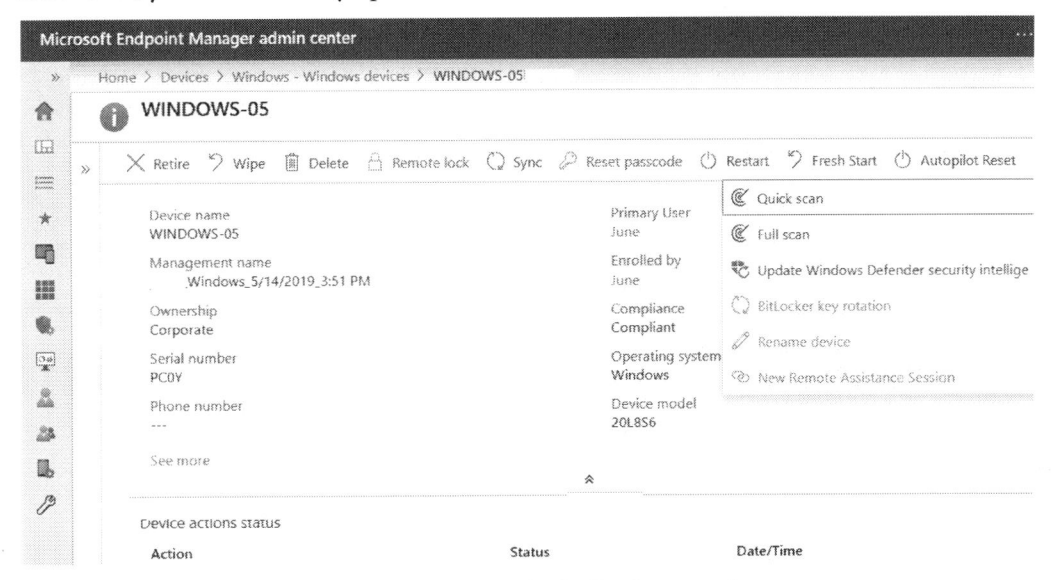

Figure 4.17 – Device actions in the Devices overview pane

This can help ensure that if a device is compromised, lost, or stolen, it can be immediately remediated, protecting both your user and your company.

Available immediate device actions include the following:

- **Retire** will remove managed app data.
- **Wipe** restores the device to the factory Windows OS.
- **Delete** removes the device from Intune management.
- **Sync** forces the device to check in to the admin console.
- **Restart** forces a device to restart.
- **Fresh Start** removes any apps (pre-installed OEM) installed on a Windows 10 PC.

- **Autopilot Reset** reapplies a device's original settings, bringing it back to a business-ready state.
- **Quick Scan / Full Scan** will run Defender antivirus scans.
- **Update Windows Defender security intelligence** will update the Defender malware definitions.

The **Reports** blade in EMAC allows organizations to quickly pull compliance reports with filtering options that are exportable to CSV. In the following screenshot, we pulled a Windows 10 compliance report for all Intune enrolled devices that are compliant, not compliant, or in the grace period. Using these reports, security or compliance admins can open tickets with the support teams to action these devices. The following screenshot displays an example of a device compliance graph in the reporting node of Endpoint Manager:

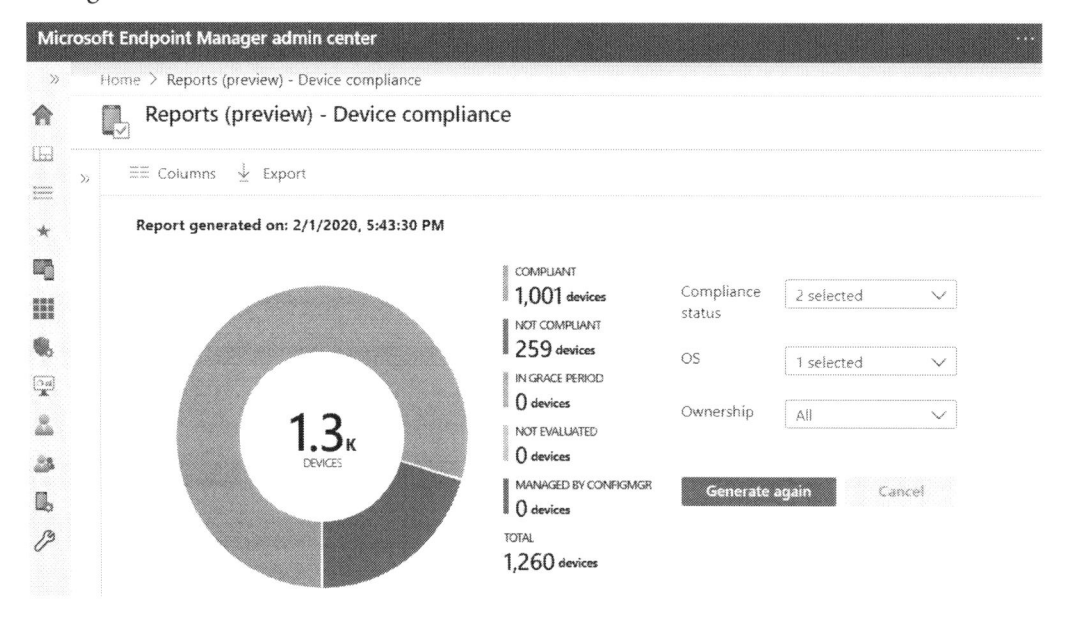

Figure 4.18 – Device Compliance report from the Microsoft Endpoint Manager admin console

Reports also have a **Trends** blade that displays a graphical view of compliance over time. The following screenshot shows the compliance of devices over the last 60 days in a visual area graph:

Figure 4.19 – The Trends blade will show a graph with a 60-day trend of device compliance

The Microsoft EMAC also allows you to easily search for AAD users and groups, similar to the Azure portal.

Summary

In this chapter, we covered end user device management with a focus on the importance of security as it relates to end user device management. In short, you simply cannot efficiently and securely manage your end user devices without a well-rounded management solution to ensure and enforce compliance. We introduced the chapter with a brief overview of the evolution of device management and the shift from traditional management tools to where we are today. We then shifted our focus toward device imaging and Windows Autopilot by discussing in-place upgrades and migrations. That section then covered Windows Assessment and Deployment Kit, Windows Configuration Designer, **Microsoft Deployment Toolkit (MDT)**, **Windows Deployment Services (WDS)**, MDT and Configuration Manager, and finally, Windows Autopilot.

The next section covered Microsoft Endpoint Configuration Manager, which was formerly known as SCCM. Within that section, we reviewed how to securely deploy clients for configuration. Following on from that, we reviewed Intune MDM, which covered the configuration service provider, MDM versus MAM, and Windows enrollment methods. We then finished off the chapter with an overview of the Microsoft Endpoint Manager admin center, which is essentially a unified endpoint management solution.

In the next chapter, we will cover hardware and virtualization. The chapter will review the importance of ensuring both your hardware and virtualized machines adhere to the same level of security that you implement on the Windows OS.

Section 2: Applying Security and Hardening

This section will provide you with the knowledge you need to apply all the recommended security settings. This will ensure your Windows environment is as hardened and secure as possible.

This section includes the following chapters:

- *Chapter 5, Hardware and Virtualization*
- *Chapter 6, Networking Fundamentals for Hardening Windows*
- *Chapter 7, Identity and Access Management*
- *Chapter 8, Administration and Remote Management*
- *Chapter 9, Keeping Your Windows Client Secure*
- *Chapter 10, Keeping Your Windows Server Secure*

5
Hardware and Virtualization

In this chapter, we will cover the importance of hardware and virtualization as it relates to security. These items can be easily overlooked but are critical components of the overall strategy for securing your Windows systems. As you purchase hardware, you need to consider the process that exists for the supply chain. Who is manufacturing the hardware and how do we trust that the components that build the final product are clean and free from vulnerabilities? How do we validate that no additional components have been added that could compromise our security and privacy? As we are aware, most of the manufacturing process occurs oversees and we have no visibility into the supply chain process other than receiving a product that's ready to turn on and use. We also need to take into consideration the existence of hardware vulnerabilities that become extremely difficult to manage. Ensuring your hardware is current and secure is just as important as protecting your OS. Vulnerabilities such as Meltdown and Spectre are prime examples of this. You can learn more about Meltdown and Spectre by reading this article: `https://www.us-cert.gov/ncas/alerts/TA18-004A`.

In addition to the underlying physical hardware is the hardening and securing of virtualized infrastructure that's used to deploy your data center and virtual workstations for users. Chances are most of you have some form of virtualization deployment within your environment. Moving from a decentralized management model to a centralized model for your systems could allow a single point of compromise to morph into a major compromise of many systems within your virtual infrastructure. For this reason, it is critical that you take the time to understand the hardware being used within your environment and ensure it is protected correctly and is secured. A weakness within your hardware is a vulnerability to the running OS on that hardware and all the investment you've spent on hardening the OS becomes obsolete.

Throughout this chapter, we will provide the awareness needed to ensure you know the best protection for your hardware and virtualized infrastructure for protecting your Windows OS is available. As you read through this chapter, you will learn more about the following topics:

- Physical servers and virtualization
- Introduction to hardware certification
- BIOS and UEFI, TPM 2.0, and Secure Boot
- Advanced protection with **Virtualization-Based Security** (**VBS**)
- Hardware security recommendations and best practices

Technical requirements

For the *Physical devices and virtualization* section, you will need a Windows 10 OS running with the supported hardware listed throughout to set up Hyper-V on Windows 10. You will also need access to an Azure subscription to set up a VM within Azure: `https://portal.azure.com/`.

For the remainder of this chapter, each section will have baseline requirements needed in order for you to turn on specific hardware-based security features and will include links to more information.

Physical servers and virtualization

Today, your organization will most likely have physical devices for both your data center and end users. In your data center, your servers will be running some form of Windows Server on top of the physical hardware layer and your end user devices will be running a version of Windows OS on top of the hardware layer. This adds an additional layer of concern as it relates to security. Within the physical device, your OS requires interaction with the hardware and your data will, at times, be in use on hardware components such as the CPU and RAM, which will be in clear text. The same will apply to the hard drive, which will contain your OS and any personal data stored locally when data is at rest. If no action is taken regarding your storage devices, your data will be in clear text and easily readable. Understanding the physical layer of your devices and what can be done to help better protect them is a critical step in protecting your Windows OS.

In addition to running a single OS on a physical device comes the concept of virtualization. Virtualization, in its simplest form, allows you to take a physical server and install multiple isolated **virtual machines** (**VMs**) with their own OSes and applications running on them. This allows greater efficiency and workloads with your current hardware and resources. There is a high chance that your organization has a combination of physical devices and a virtualized infrastructure within your data center. Prior to data center virtualization, you were required to deploy a physical server for each app/service you wanted to deploy (most likely more than one physical server for enterprise grade setups to support the separation of roles and **high availability** (**HA**) scenarios). This was a manageable process in the early days of server compute data centers but as more demand came along with the extremely fast pace of technology and the need for more apps, the ability to deploy physical servers quickly became very challenging and expensive.

Fortunately, the advancement of data center virtualization became available and the ability to deploy multiple OSes on a single piece of server hardware has been a game changer within the enterprise. In the following diagram, the physical server deployment underlying hardware only has one operating system, while the virtualized deployment has many sharing the same hardware host:

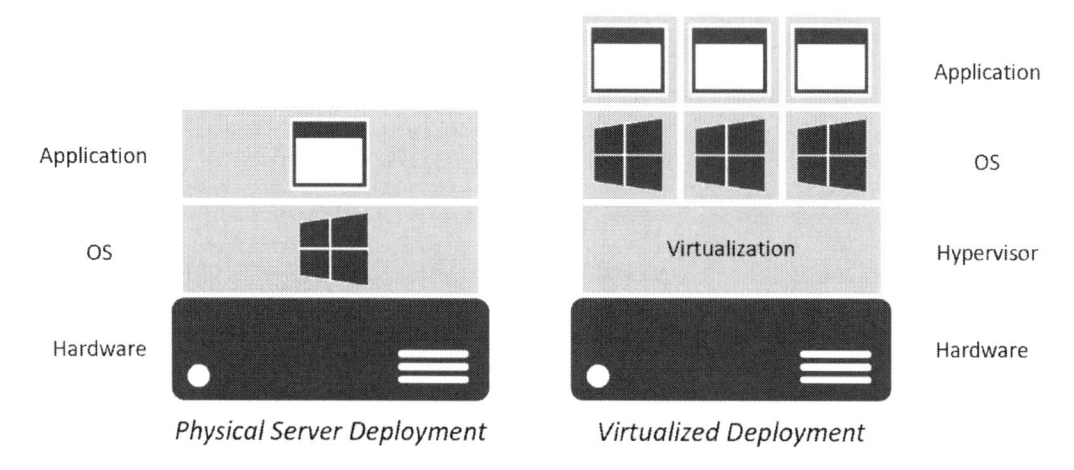

Figure 5.1 – Physical server deployments versus virtualized deployment

Within the end user world, virtualization has also been widely adopted. Physical devices are a primary driver for the most part, but virtualization of the desktop has allowed companies to overcome many challenges as it relates to quickly deploying desktops to contractors/vendors and offshore employees. Virtualization also provides access to legacy apps that may not be supported on the latest OS and provides additional desktops to users for development and testing. It is also a great scenario for part-time workers or those who only need limited access intermittently. Virtualization provides ample opportunity with great flexibility, but we must remember that it runs on a physical device and the same physical security concerns (and then some) exist when it comes to protecting Windows.

Microsoft virtualization

Let's take a quick look at what virtualization technologies Microsoft provides for both the Windows Server environment and end user desktop.

Hyper-V

For a traditional on-premise deployment, Microsoft has its Hyper-V technology, which is a hypervisor-based virtualization platform. Like other enterprise-grade platforms, Hyper-V allows you to manage, deploy, and run multiple VMs on a single piece of hardware, thus allowing better use of your hardware resources. The following requirements are needed to run the Hyper-V platform:

- Hyper-V Virtual Machine Management Service
- The virtualization WMI provider
- The **virtual machine bus** (**VMbus**)
- **Virtualization service provider** (**VSP**)
- **Virtual infrastructure driver** (**VID**)

The following tools can be used for managing the Hyper-V environment:

- Hyper-V Manager
- Hyper-V module for Windows PowerShell
- Virtual Machine Connection (sometimes called VMConnect)
- Windows PowerShell Direct
- System Center Virtual Machine Manager

For further information about Hyper-V, visit this link:

`https://docs.microsoft.com/en-us/windows-server/virtualization/hyper-v/hyper-v-technology-overview`.

Hyper-V can be run on both Windows Server and Windows Desktop, with the latest versions being Windows Server 2019 and Windows 10. There are differences between some of the features with Hyper-V on Windows Server and the Windows Desktop version. The primary differences are that Hyper-V on Windows Server is designed for more of an enterprise-grade deployment, thus allowing the migration of VMs between hosts and access to enterprise-grade storage for improved VM performance.

On the other hand, Hyper-V for Windows Desktop allows users to spin up multiple VMs for testing purposes, development purposes, and to run older versions of a client OS. Windows Server also supports advanced hardware protection features using TPM attestation with Guarded Fabric and Shielded VMs.

Hyper-V supports multiple versions of Windows Server, Windows Desktop, Linux OS, and Linux and Free BSD.

> **Tip**
> To view a list of supported operating systems that can run on Hyper-V, visit this link: `https://docs.microsoft.com/en-us/windows-server/virtualization/hyper-v/supported-windows-guest-operating-systems-for-hyper-v-on-windows`.

In order to get started with Hyper-V on Windows Server, you will need the following as a minimum:

- 64-bit processor with **second-level address translation** (**SLAT**).
- VM Monitor Mode extensions.
- At least 4 GB of RAM. This will increase the more VMs you would like to run concurrently.
- Virtualization support turned on in the BIOS or UEFI:

    a) Hardware-assisted virtualization.

    b) Hardware-enforced **Data Execution Prevention (DEP)**:

    -- Intel: XD bit (execute disable bit).

    --AMD: NX bit (no execute bit).

In addition to the basic requirements for Hyper-V, you will want to ensure you enable Guarded Fabric and Shielded VMs for best protection and security. In short, Guarded Fabric is the infrastructure component used to enable and protect Shielded VMs from being compromised. Shielding a VM allows it to only be run on an approved host and prevents unauthorized access within the environment, offline, or outside of the protected environment. Shielded VMs first became available in Hyper-V 2016 and require the following features:

- UEFI 2.3.1 (ensure boot is configured to use UEFI)
- TPM v2.0
- IOMMU and SLAT
- Secure boot enabled

You will need to be using generation 2 VMs and will require a minimum Windows Server 2012 OS in order to enable the Shielded VM feature.

> **Tip**
> More information on Guarded Fabric and Shielded VMs can be found at this link: `https://docs.microsoft.com/en-us/windows-server/security/guarded-fabric-shielded-vm/guarded-fabric-and-shielded-vms`.

Getting started with Hyper-V on your Windows 10 OS is a pretty painless task. The feature is free to enable, and you will only need licenses for the respective OS you would like to run.

The minimum requirements needed to enable Hyper-V on Windows 10 are as follows:

- Windows 10 Enterprise, Pro, or Education
- 64-bit processor with SLAT
- CPU support for VM Monitor Mode Extension (VT-c on Intel CPUs)
- Minimum of 4 GB memory
- Enabled in BIOS: Virtualization Technology and Hardware Enforced Data Execution Prevention

Before you enable this feature, verify the hardware is compatible by opening PowerShell or Command Prompt, type `systeminfo`, and press *Enter*. Scroll down to the Hyper-V requirements and verify **Yes** is listed next to all items.

To view the additional Windows 10 requirements to run Hyper-V, visit the following informational link: `https://docs.microsoft.com/en-us/virtualization/hyper-v-on-windows/reference/hyper-v-requirements`.

To install Hyper-V through the Windows UI, follow these instructions:

1. On your supported Windows 10 device, go to **Search** and type `Turn Windows features on or off`.
2. Select **Turn Windows features on or off** to open the **Windows Features** window.
3. Search for `Hyper-V` and select it. Ensure all sub-options are selected.

4. Click **OK** and click **Restart Now** when prompted to reboot your device, as follows:

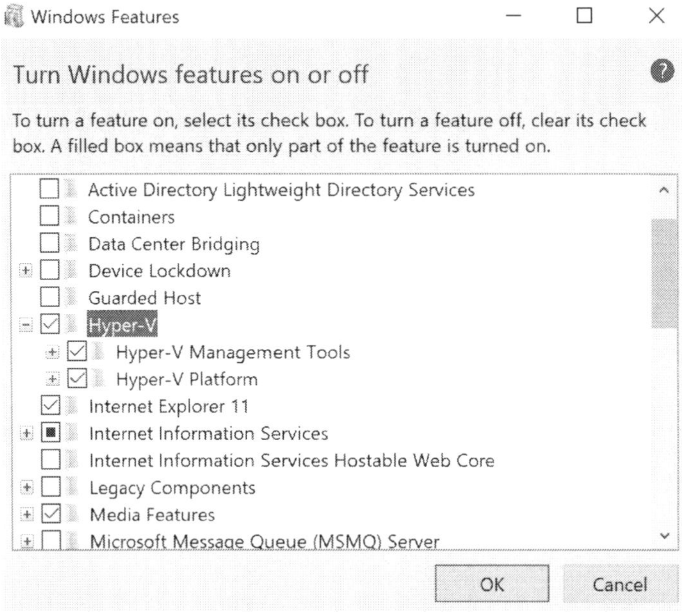

Figure 5.2 – Turning the Hyper-V feature on or off in Windows Features

> **Tip**
> For additional methods to enable Hyper-V, visit the following link:
> `https://docs.microsoft.com/en-us/virtualization/hyper-v-on-windows/quick-start/enable-hyper-v`.

Now that Hyper-V is enabled, you can start creating VMs on your Windows 10 device and set up your own lab to implement and test the recommendations being provided in this book.

For more information on setting up your first VM, follow the instructions provided here: `https://docs.microsoft.com/en-us/virtualization/hyper-v-on-windows/quick-start/quick-create-virtual-machine`. You will need a license to run any Windows VMs that you have set up.

> **Tip**
> The following link is for the installation documentation for Hyper-V on Windows Server. This deployment is more involved and will require multiple physical devices in order to be set up and secured correctly: `https://docs.microsoft.com/en-us/windows-server/virtualization/hyper-v/get-started/install-the-hyper-v-role-on-windows-server`.

Azure virtual machines

Microsoft's Azure cloud **Infrastructure as a Service (IaaS)** offering allows us to set up and consume VMs on-demand with no underlying infrastructure required from the customer. To create a VM within Azure, follow these steps:

1. Log into the Azure portal at `https://portal.azure.com`.
2. Click on the **Portal** menu in the top left (if the menu is hidden).
3. Select **All services** and choose **Compute**.

Here, you will see all the compute services, including virtual machines. You can either click on the **Virtual Machines** option to be directed to the Virtual Machines portal or you can hover over **Virtual Machines** to view additional information and options:

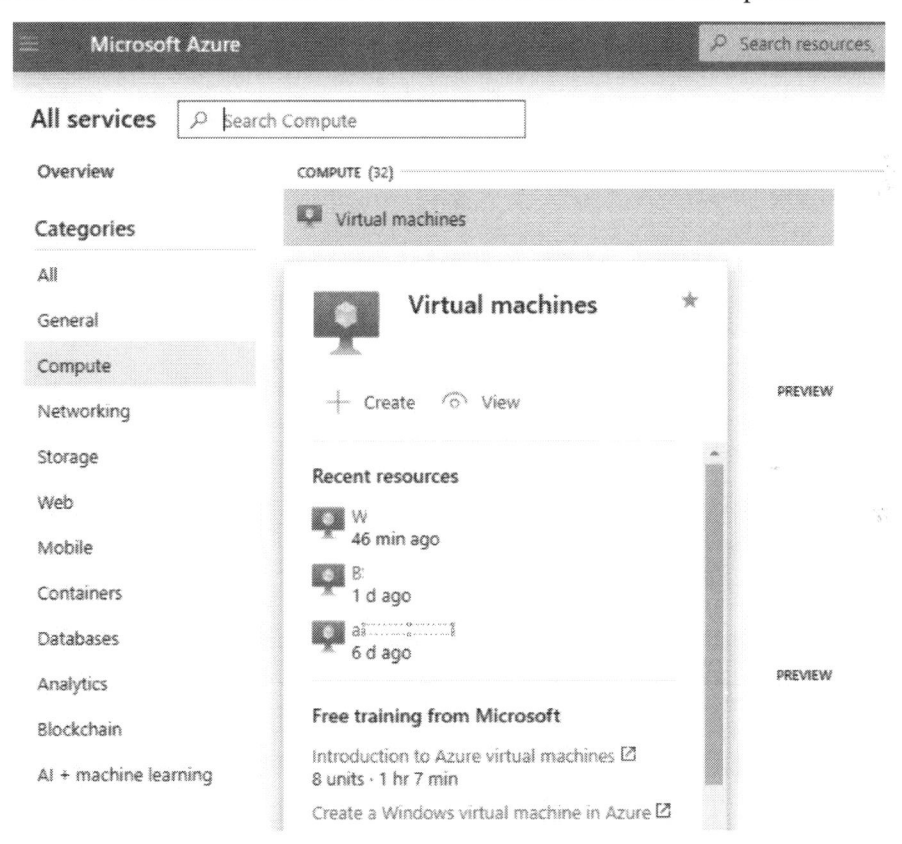

Figure 5.3 – Virtual machine tool tip in the All services section of Microsoft Azure

In addition to the Virtual Machines management portal, the Azure Marketplace has pre-defined images provided by Microsoft available to deploy. To view the available images within the Marketplace, follow these steps:

1. Search for *Marketplace* within the top search menu and choose **Marketplace**.
2. Select **Compute** in the **Categories** blade.
3. Search for *Windows* to view all the available Windows images:

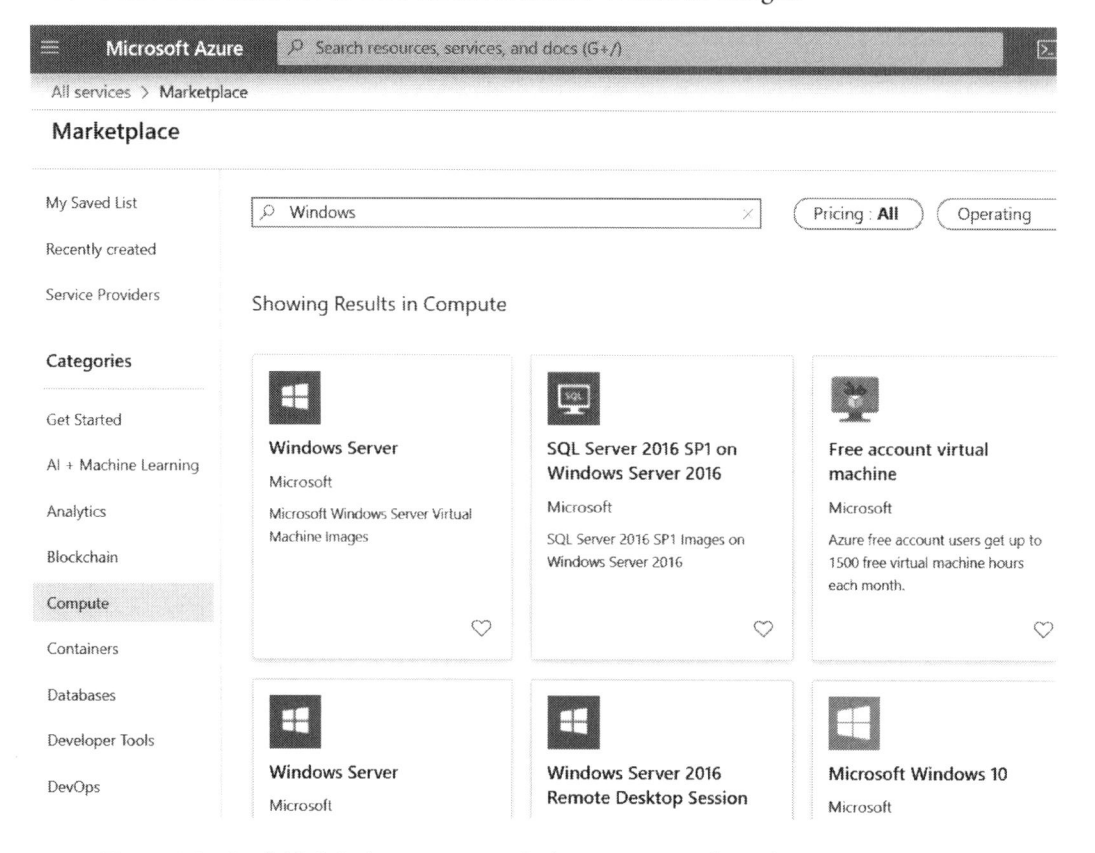

Figure 5.4 – Available Windows images to deploy using ARM from the Azure Marketplace

For more information about Windows VMs running in Azure, visit this link: `https://docs.microsoft.com/en-us/azure/virtual-machines/windows/overview`.

We recommend that you use Azure to deploy and test security configurations for Window Server and desktop for topics that are covered in this book.

Windows Virtual Desktop

Another option available for virtualization in Azure is Windows Virtual Desktop. This PaaS offering from Microsoft provides both desktop and app virtualization within the Azure cloud. The following features are provided with the Windows Virtual Desktop service:

- Multi-session Windows 10 hosts for non-persistent and persistent virtual machines.
- Desktop and application virtualization with MSIX support and app attach for app streaming.
- FSLogix profile containers using AzureNet App files for highly available streaming profiles.
- Office 365 ProPlus and OneDrive are fully compatible.
- Support for Windows 7 virtual desktops.
- Unified management portal to manage user sessions, published applications, and persistent and multi-session hosts.

Take a look at the following link to learn more about the Windows Virtual Desktop service running in Azure:

`https://docs.microsoft.com/en-us/azure/virtual-desktop/overview`.

> **Tip**
> Windows Virtual Desktop can be thought of as an end user cloud offering, similar to the Citrix Cloud service.

Next, we'll look at the security concerns that affect the underlying hardware of our systems.

Hardware security concerns

Protecting the hardware of your systems is a critical task and one that may not have been at the forefront of your security priorities in the past. Over the years, we have invested heavily on the software side of security but recently, the impact of hardware vulnerabilities has shown the criticality of ensuring your hardware is protected from exploits, thus requiring more attention in this area to address the risks.

The following are some of the risks with hardware that must be addressed:

- Hardware vulnerabilities, including the following:
  - Rootkits embedded in the BIOS and UEFI
  - Side channel attacks toward CPUs
  - Kernel-level exploits
  - Firmware attacks
  - Memory vulnerabilities
- Insider threats such as those with physical access to hardware and privileged access to your environment.
- Referencing back to the NIST Cybersecurity Framework, Supply Chain Risk Management was added to the latest version 1.1 in 2018. NIST references the following cyber supply chain risks to be aware of:
  - Any insertion of counterfeit items as part of the supply chain process.
  - The production of items that have not been approved.
  - Tampering with any items within the process.
  - Theft of any items.
  - The insertion of malicious software and hardware at any time during the process.
  - Manufacturing and development practices not maintaining expected standards during the supply chain process.

You can view additional information about the Cyber Supply Chain Risk Management project and the risks at this link:

`https://csrc.nist.gov/Projects/Supply-Chain-Risk-Management`.

> **Tip**
> NIST Cyber Supply Chain Best Practices: `https://csrc.nist.gov/CSRC/media/Projects/Supply-Chain-Risk-Management/documents/briefings/Workshop-Brief-on-Cyber-Supply-Chain-Best-Practices.pdf`.

Now that we've covered various security concerns and common scenarios that can cause exposure to risk, let's look at the concerns for the virtualized environment.

Virtualization security concerns

Now we have moved into a world where we have centralized hundreds and thousands of standalone workloads into significantly less hardware with the advancement of virtualization, it is just as critical that we ensure our virtualized infrastructure is protected correctly. A breach of a virtualized host could mean a compromise in hundreds of servers over a single physical server in the traditional model.

The following are some of the risks with virtualization that must be addressed:

- Everything listed in the *Hardware security concerns* section. Your virtualized infrastructure will be running on the same hardware.
- Hypervisor threats.
- Virtual machine escape or the ability to interact with the physical host operating system or hypervisor directly from a virtual machine.
- Non-segregation of resources, network, data, and so on.
- VM sprawl and allowing the business or non-IT users deploy VMs as needed.
- Non-encrypted storage, physical drives, virtual disk files, network traffic, and so on.

Although there are security tools and configurations that help ensure the security of your VMs and the data within them, you may want to consider physical separation of specific functions within your virtualized infrastructure. For example, the management plane, the production environment, the **demilitarized zone** (**DMZ**), and maybe highly confidential databases should be separated. Ensure the separation of these functions includes the physical host, network, and storage. This will help safeguard against the aforementioned risks. The following diagram shows a representation of using virtualization and isolation to separate different functions within an infrastructure deployment:

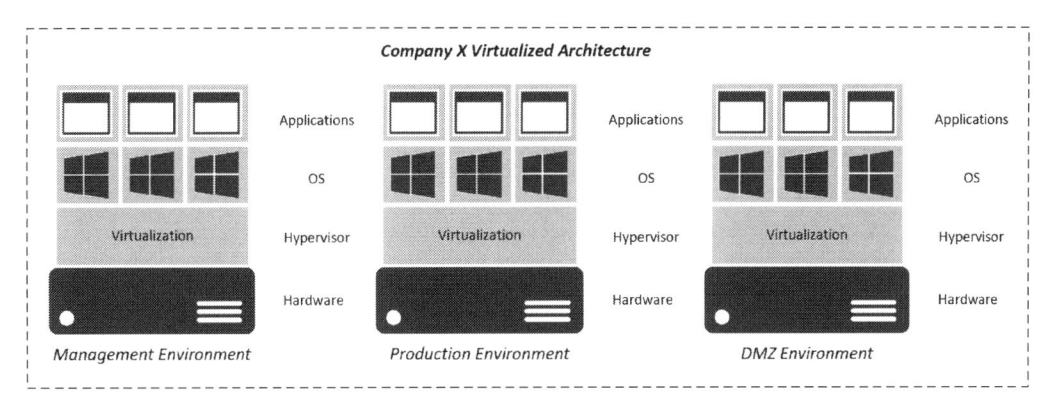

Figure 5.5 – Architecture of separating core functions on its own hardware

> **Tip**
> Microsoft docs has a writeup on Hyper-V security in Windows Server that can be found at this link: `https://docs.microsoft.com/en-us/windows-server/virtualization/hyper-v/plan/plan-hyper-v-security-in-windows-server`.

Cloud hardware and virtualization

As you move your workloads to the cloud, you will, at a minimum, subscribe to an IaaS service. Because of the dynamic changes with the cloud offering, you will no longer have any responsibilities regarding the hardware layer and the virtualized hypervisor layer. This will shift your effort from needing to implement any best practices being recommended in this chapter to validating that the provider has these best practices implemented and in place. With Microsoft Azure, Microsoft is only responsible for implementing the security requirements for both the hardware and virtualized hypervisor layer of the services being provided to you. This does not include any additional security hardening on the software layer, including the OS – this will be your responsibility. You will need to work with Microsoft (or your cloud provider) to provide evidence that they have implemented the best security practices with their cloud hardware and virtualization offerings. This is where you need to ensure Microsoft (or your cloud provider) provide responses to a security survey if they don't already have one available and request audits, penetration tests, and security assessments.

As we go through the remainder of this chapter, you will be provided with an overview of the hardware security components and recommendations to ensure your systems are as secure as possible. Although not always feasible based on hardware life cycle programs, it is recommended that you keep your hardware as current as possible and ensure the latest updates for any BIOS/UEFI, firmware, and drivers are applied, especially if there are any publicly known vulnerabilities.

Introduction to hardware certification

Ensuring your hardware is certified is a critical process of the overall security program. As you purchase new servers, PCs, storage, and peripherals, it is critical you validate that the hardware is compatible with your deployed systems. Using non-compliant hardware could make your hardware vulnerable to a compromise or the additional hardware components could even have a compromise already embedded in them.

An example would be allowing the use of USB drives on your devices. Users receiving a free USB drive don't realize that the drive itself could be infected and that, once inserted into your device, it could compromise your entire organization. Because of this, it is critical you only allow pre-certified USB drives that are encrypted and provided by the organization to be used by employees. Any data that is copied from a USB drive to a company device must require encryption. Another concern, as mentioned previously, is the supply chain process. Ensuring the vendor has certified the hardware for Windows significantly reduces the risk the hardware could be pre-infected with vulnerabilities. This doesn't necessarily mean it will be 100% guaranteed, but your risk is reduced significantly.

Purchasing and procurement teams are a critical component in validating the hardware you purchase has been through an appropriate certification process. These teams will help during the supply chain process to ensure vendors are compliant with your requirements, ensure contracts are maintained as promised, and maintain vendor relationships. You will need to work closely with procurement as they work through the **request for proposal** (**RFP**) and requirements for hardware-related requests. To ensure the procurement process is optimized, guidelines from technical and security experts should be clearly defined. One important point to call out is that you should be careful with going cheap on your hardware purchases. There is always a drive to bring costs down but opting for hardware that is cheaper than certified hardware could be a costly mistake. It may prove more cost-effective to get a contract with a vendor, standardize on hardware, and purchase a warranty program. There's a good saying in life: you get what you pay for!

> **Tip**
> Auditing, including vendor management, will be covered in more detail in *Chapter 13, Testing and Auditing*. This chapter will cover vendor management as it relates to compliance with your suppliers.

In addition to verifying the supply chain process is clean, you will want to ensure you are using hardware that has been certified and approved by Microsoft to run the Windows OS. Microsoft has a very well-defined Windows Hardware Compatibility Program for vendors to follow to ensure they are maintaining the highest standards of security and compatibility for running Windows. Using any hardware outside of this compatibility list could render your Windows OS unstable, and even more importantly, create security gaps within your systems.

> **Tip**
> Information about the Windows Hardware Compatibility Program can be found at this link: `https://docs.microsoft.com/en-us/windows-hardware/design/compatibility/`.

To view the Windows Hardware Compatibility List, browse to `https://partner.microsoft.com/en-us/dashboard/hardware/search/cpl`, type in a product name, and click *Search*. You will be provided with a list of compatible hardware based on your search. The following example returned all the items with laptop in their name:

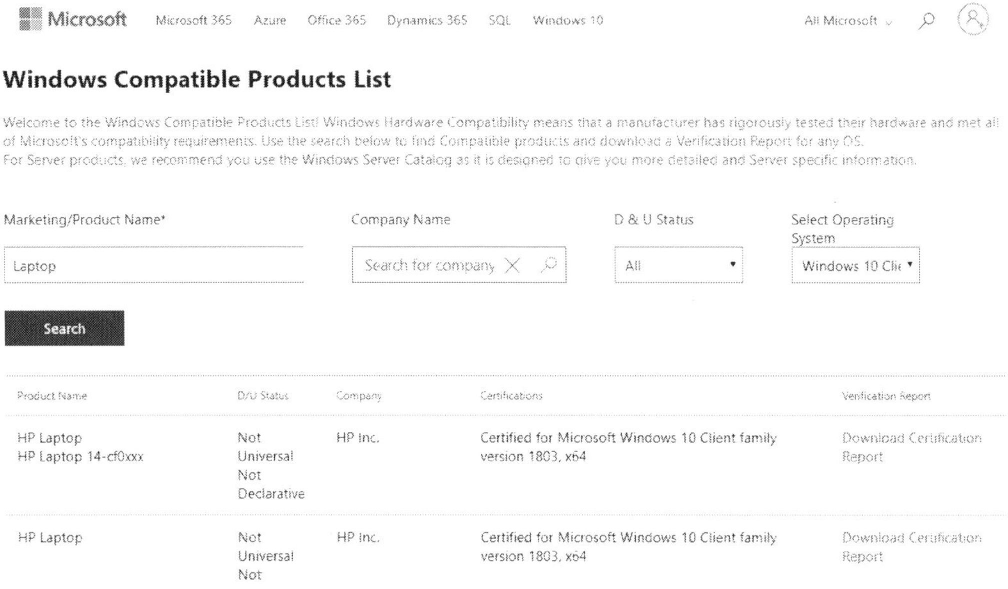

Figure 5.6 – Windows Compatible Products List for hardware compatibility

There is an additional portal where you can view certified products specific to Windows Server within the Windows Server Catalog. To view supported hardware for Windows Server, browse to `https://www.windowsservercatalog.com/`. Within the landing page, go to the **Hardware** section and click on the version of Server or specific product category that you would like to view. As you browse through the items, you will see which specific version is supported by Microsoft, along with the badges that were awarded for certification. Hyper-V 2016 and 2019 are also supported for any hardware that has been awarded the Windows Server 2016 and 2019 certified badges:

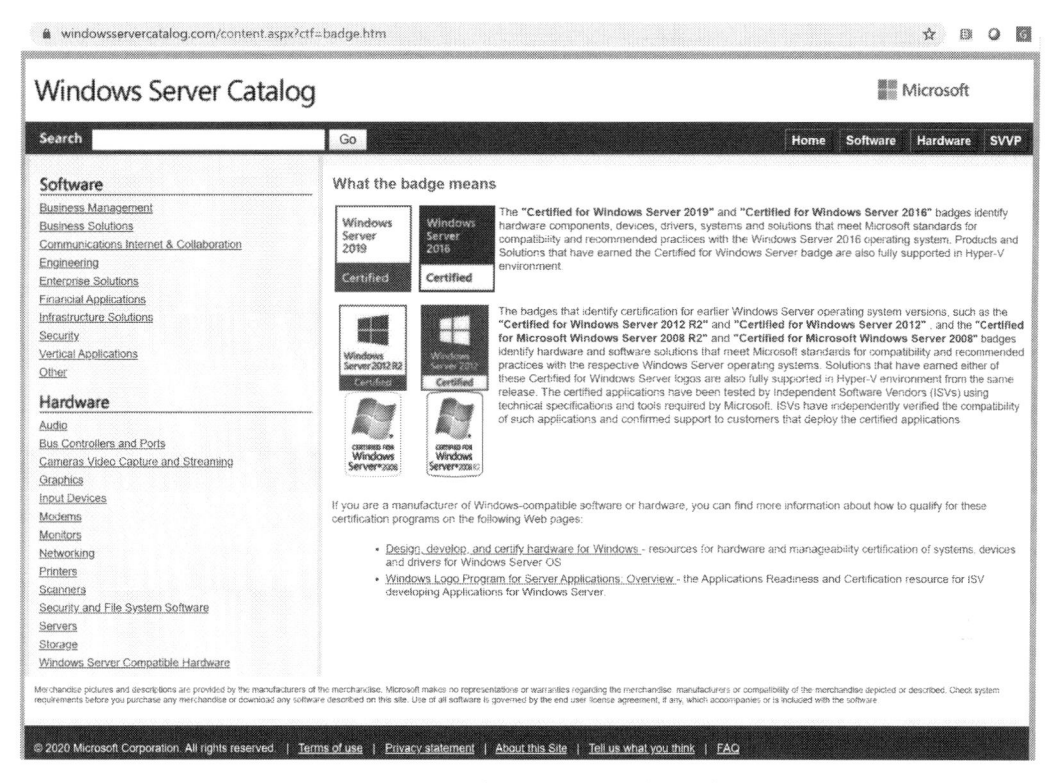

Figure 5.7 – Windows Server Catalog badges

As you read through this section, you probably realized there is a lot more due diligence needed before you go out and purchase any hardware. Although there is an incredible ecosystem of hardware that supports Windows, you will want to ensure that the hardware you are purchasing is the latest and supports the most current versions of Windows Server and Windows 10. The most current hardware will provide more enhanced features over older hardware. The following sections will cover the hardware security features that need to be enabled on your hardware. In the next section, we will review the BIOS, UEFI, Secure Boot, and TPM components.

BIOS and UEFI, TPM 2.0, and Secure Boot

BIOS, also known as the **Basic Input/Output System**, is loaded directly onto a PC motherboard. Its purpose is to initialize the physical hardware, go through a series of processes, and eventually boot into Windows. Just like the operating system or PC software, the BIOS in your systems can become outdated and vulnerable to unauthorized modification. Furthermore, the BIOS initializes privileged hardware processes with greater rights than the operating system itself. Malware not only targets the OS, but other mechanisms in the boot process, including the boot loader and hypervisor used for virtualization. It's important to have a system of authorized update mechanisms for updating the BIOS and ensure it's only configured and signed by an authentic source such as the device manufacturer. In order to maintain the integrity of the BIOS and mitigate risks from malware such as bootkits, digital signature verification should be used for updates and include a manual rollback and recovery process.

> **Tip**
>
> A bootkit is a manipulation of the Master Boot Record, which allows malicious software to load prior to the operating system and remain active after the OS loads.

According to the NIST BIOS Protection Guidelines, organizations should have an authenticated BIOS update mechanism using the **Root of Trust for Update** (**RTU**) measurement with approved digital signature algorithms for verification, as specified in NIST FIPS 186-3, Digital Signature Standard. The updated standard (186-4) can be found at this link:

`https://nvlpubs.nist.gov/nistpubs/FIPS/NIST.FIPS.186-4.pdf`.

The NIST security guidelines for protecting BIOS are specified in four system BIOS functionalities and state the following:

- Use an authenticated BIOS update mechanism with digital signatures to validate the integrity of updates.
- Secure the local update process with system passwords, physical locks, or only allow BIOS updates through a local update process with physical IT presence.
- Use integrity protection features to prevent modifications to BIOS.
- Implement non-bypassability features to ensure only the authenticated update mechanism is used.

To read more about the NIST security guidelines for protecting BIOS, visit this link:

`https://nvlpubs.nist.gov/nistpubs/Legacy/SP/nistspecialpublication800-147.pdf`.

Unified Extensible Firmware Interface

UEFI is also a form of BIOS and is now standard on most manufactured hardware. BIOS and UEFI (BIOS) have a similar boot process regarding the initializing flow but with some differences. UEFI does not rely on a boot sector to copy a Master Boot Record and uses what's known as a boot manager to determine what to boot. The traditional BIOS runs 16-bit code and leverages only the Master Boot Record, which presents limitations such as support for drives larger than 2 TB. UEFI uses the **GUID Partition Table** (**GPT**) and supports 32-bit or 64-bit code processes in "protected mode" before transferring control over to the OS during the **runtime** (**RT**) processes. The higher bit support has more space that allows for friendlier UIs and faster boot times. UEFI incorporates security technologies such as Secure Boot and additionally supports booting over the network or from flash memory.

Like the BIOS, the first phase in the UEFI boot process is known as the **Security Phase** (**SEC**). This acts as a core root of trust (or boot block in BIOS) to validate the integrity of the code and other firmware components before moving to the rest of the boot process. One of the biggest security advantages of using UEFI over BIOS is the ability to validate boot loaders by checking its digital signature using Secure Boot. If a boot loader has been replaced by malicious code, it won't be allowed to execute based on an invalid or revoked digital signature. This check starts the entire **trusted boot** process, which secures the boot chain all the way until Windows loads.

There are many types of security features built into the UEFI setup and they will vary by vendor. Some of the more common security features found in the UEFI setup are as follows:

- Password settings that include setting a supervisor password and lock settings preventing users from making changes without entering the supervisor password. You can also require a password at unattended boot, at restart, and even at the boot device list.
- Fingerprint settings to use biometrics during pre-desktop authentication as an alternative or in conjunction with entering a supervisor password.
- Security Chip settings for the **Trusted Platform Module** (**TPM**).
- UEFI BIOS Update settings to add protection regarding BIOS updates, including rollbacks.

- Memory Protection for execution prevention against virus and worm attacks that create memory buffer overflows.
- Virtualization settings to enable or disable virtualized hardware support such as Intel VT-x or AMD-V.
- I/O Port Access to enable or disable the use of devices such as wireless, Bluetooth, USB, cameras, microphones, and so on.
- Internal device access tamper detection of the physical covers of storage devices.
- Anti-theft to enable a "lo-jack" for your PC using a third-party provider.
- Secure Boot settings.
- Intel **Software Guard Extensions** (**SGX**) for hardware-based isolation of application code in memory.
- Device Guard, which is a feature set that consists of **Configurable Code Integrity** (**CCI**), VSM Protected Code Integrity, and Secure Boot. Device Guard features set the foundation for **Virtualization-Based Security** (**VBS**), which we will discuss in more detail later.

UEFI Secure Boot

Secure Boot is a hardware-based security feature available in the UEFI environment that ensures only trusted software and firmware can execute in the boot chain. Each software, driver firmware, and OS boot loader (Windows Boot Manager) has a digital signature or hash that is validated by referencing signature keys stored in the Secure Boot database. Secure Boot consists of a **platform key** (**PK**) created by the OEM that creates the trust to the **key exchange key** (**KEK**) with a public/private key pair. The KEK has public signing keys and is used to modify or add signatures to the **whitelist** (**DB**) or **revoked signature** (**DBX**) database to accommodate for new releases of Windows and known bad signatures for revocation purposes. These "allow" or "deny" databases are used for validation against the certificates, keys, or image hashes of boot loaders, firmware, and drivers. For example, if malware such as a bootkit invalidates the boot loader, then UEFI checks the secure boot database and won't allow the operating system to boot when the signature doesn't exist or is blacklisted. This is important to note because rootkits are typically low-level and hide themselves from the operating system, making them undetectable by most antivirus software:

BIOS and UEFI, TPM 2.0, and Secure Boot   161

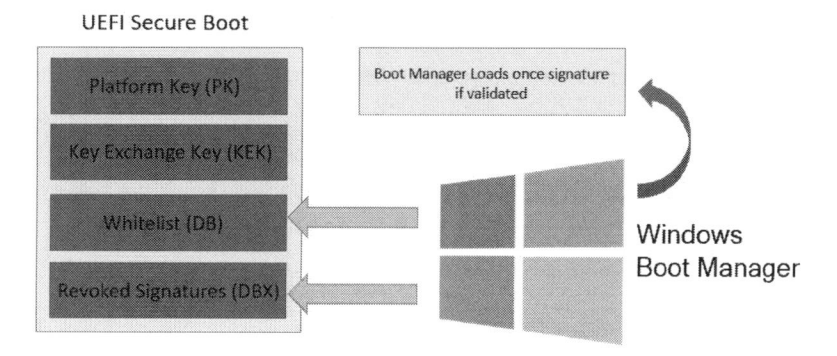

Figure 5.8 – Sample flow of Secure Boot validating the signature of Windows Boot Manager

Follow these steps to learn how to configure Secure Boot in UEFI BIOS:

1. Boot into UEFI Setup. Typically, pressing *F12* or *F10* during startup will load a boot device list where you can choose this setup.

> **Tip**
> If you're logged into Windows 10, hold down *Shift* and choose **Restart** to be presented with **Advanced Options** to boot into UEFI.

2. Secure Boot settings are typically found under the **Security** tab.
3. Change Secure Boot to **Enabled**, as shown in the following screenshot:

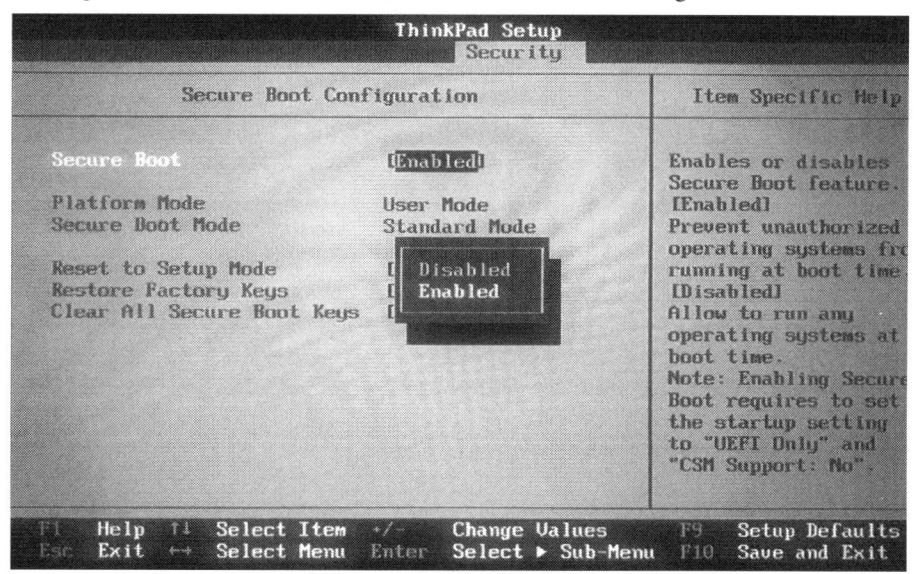

Figure 5.9 – Secure Boot configuration on a Lenovo ThinkPad workstation

Next, we'll look at the features of the TPM security chip that is embedded in the hardware

Trusted Platform Module (TPM 2.0)

A **Trusted Platform Module** or **TPM** provides hardware-based security typically in the form of a tamper-resistant chip built directly onto a motherboard. A TPM helps by providing a hardware layer separated from the memory and operating system. Its main purpose is to perform cryptographic functions in isolation and is often considered the hardware Root of Trust. TPMs primarily deal with the encryption and decryption of security keys and are passive, so they do not rely on the operating system to process instructions. Each TPM chip has its own unique RSA private key that's imprinted directly to the chip itself. This private key is never exposed to another external process, so only allow the decryption of TPM encrypted keys to be handled from the same TPM chip.

The TPM also has built-in protection against dictionary attacks, which are used to guess the authorization value for gaining access to protected keys. This is known as a TPM lockout and in Windows 10, a maximum count threshold of 32 is set with a 10-minute healing time to prevent tampering. TPM lockout settings can be managed using Group Policy and are located under `Computer Configuration\Administrative Templates\System\Trusted Platform Module Services`.

For more information about managing TPM lockout in Windows 10 and Server 2016 and later, visit this link:

`https://docs.microsoft.com/en-us/windows/security/information-protection/tpm/manage-tpm-lockout`.

Windows computers containing a TPM provide enhanced security features that can be leveraged for the following types of functions:

- Encryption, decryption, and other cryptographic functions
- Key storage and generation
- Integrity validation (security such as Secure Boot for firmware and boot loaders)
- Strong user and device authentication technologies (Windows Hello for Business and Virtual Smart Cards)
- Antimalware boot measurements for start state integrity checks
- Virtualized-based security features such as Windows Device Guard and Credential Guard
- BitLocker drive encryption
- Health attestation services for both local and remote attestation

In some use cases, such as Bitlocker drive encryption, a USB drive can act as a TPM alternative and must be present for the computer to start Windows. This is known as a TPM startup key and allows the use of BitLocker without a physically compatible TPM chip. Together, in conjunction with a TPM chip or PIN, this enables a form of BitLocker two-factor authentication.

Unlike in earlier versions of Windows, Windows 10 handles most of the provisioning of the TPM and reduces the need for manual configuration. For more information on how Windows 10 uses the TPM, visit this link:

https://docs.microsoft.com/en-us/windows/security/information-protection/tpm/how-windows-uses-the-tpm.

TPM 2.0 and Windows 10 support a feature known as the Health Attestation service. This allows MDM services such as Intune to collect telemetry data from Windows 10 managed devices in your organization for remote device health attestation reports. The state of your device's health attestation can be used with risk-based conditional access and block access to resources if certain compliance conditions aren't met. The additional level of analysis provides runtime protection of hardware after boot. The following screenshot shows a report of Windows Health Attestation telemetry from Microsoft Intune:

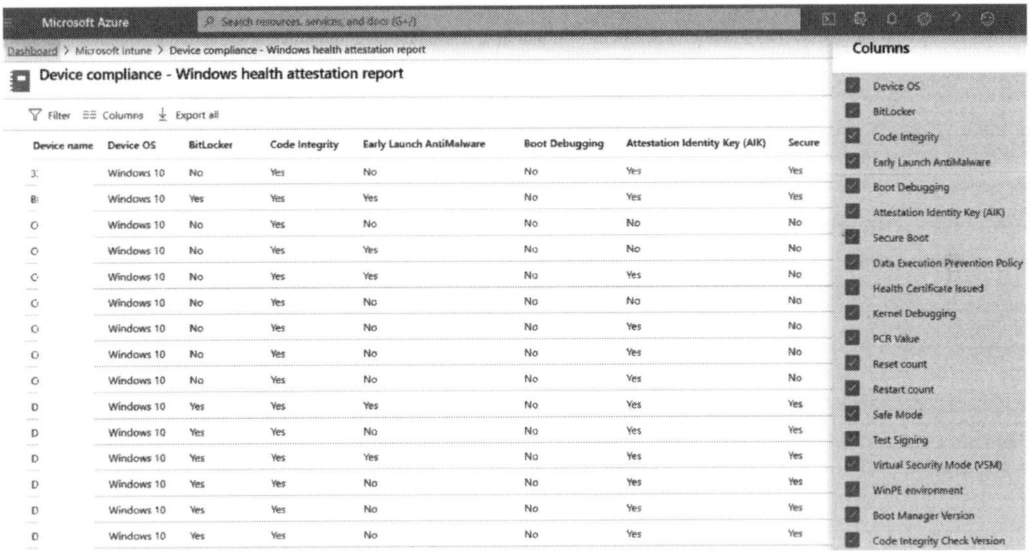

Figure 5.10 – Windows Health Attestation report from Intune

The TPM security chip is typically enabled in the **Security** tab of UEFI setup of processes such as Secure Boot:

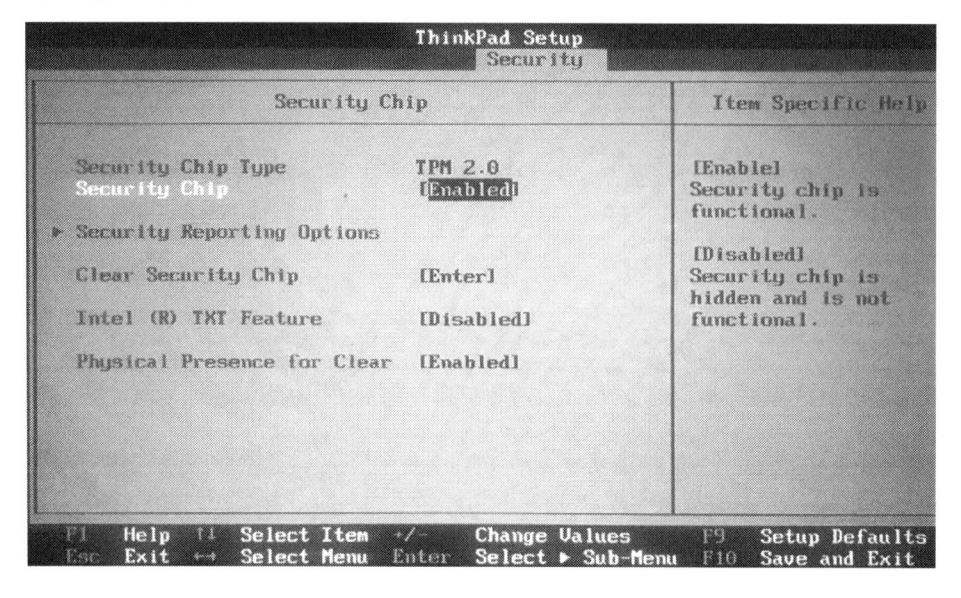

Figure 5.11 – TPM 2.0 enabled on a Lenovo ThinkPad workstation

To summarize, we just provided an overview of BIOS, UEFI, TPM, and Secure Boot. We discussed the security features of each, as well as the differences in BIOS compared with UEFI. We then discussed NIST recommended practices for securing BIOS and UEFI and the many functions of the Trusted Platform Module and how it's leveraged. In the next section, we are going to talk about advanced protection with **Virtualization-Based Security** (**VBS**) and how to enable features that are dependent on VBS such as Credential Guard and Device Guard.

Advanced protection with VBS

First available in Windows 10 and Windows Server 2016, VBS leverages physical hardware components and a Hyper-V hypervisor to create isolation or virtual secure mode for user and kernel operations. For a system to be considered VBS-capable, it needs to meet the following minimum hardware requirements:

- TPM 2.0
- UEFI SecureBoot Enabled
- Intel VT-x or AMD-v
- IOMMU (Intel VT-D, AMD-Vi) Input/Output memory management unit

- SLAT for Virtual Address Translation
- Windows **Hardware Lab Kit (HLK)** System Certified
- Device Servicing Program (Drivers and Firmware on Windows Update service)

For more detailed information around the hardware requirements for VBS, visit this link:

`https://docs.microsoft.com/en-us/windows-hardware/design/device-experiences/oem-vbs`.

VBS leverages hypervisors in order to create an isolated virtual secure mode to define virtual trust levels. The main hypervisor runs all the normal user mode operations, kernel mode code, and processes such as the Windows OS in **non-virtual secure mode**. The other hypervisor runs a secure isolated user and kernel mode in **virtual secure mode**. **User and kernel mode** code that run in the secure hypervisor can access normal mode operations, but not vice versa. For example, if malware infects the OS, it will remain contained to the OS and be inaccessible to virtual secure mode. This is mainly due to the features of **SLAT**, which stands for **Second Level Address Translation**.

The SLAT controlled by the hypervisor changes the page protections on the secured user and kernel mode processes to block access. Even kernel mode operations running on the main hypervisor in normal mode are blocked from accessing secure mode. Many available features of VBS are enabled by default in Windows 10 Enterprise and can be managed with Group Policy or Intune. The following diagram shows the level of separation that is accomplished through VBS security. Normal Windows operating processes occur on the left and are blocked from accessing secure mode on the right:

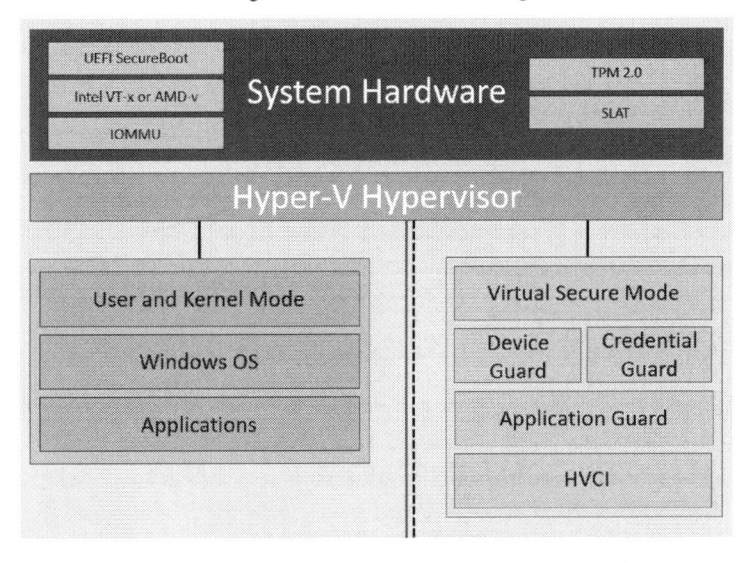

Figure 5.12 – A hypervisor isolates normal user and kernel modes

The following features are dependent on the VBS hardware requirements in order to be enabled:

- Credential Guard
- Device Guard with Windows Defender Application Control
- Windows Defender Application Guard (Microsoft Edge Sandbox)
- **Hypervisor-protected code integrity** (HVCI)

The following screenshot is from System Information on Windows and shows that virtualization-based security is running:

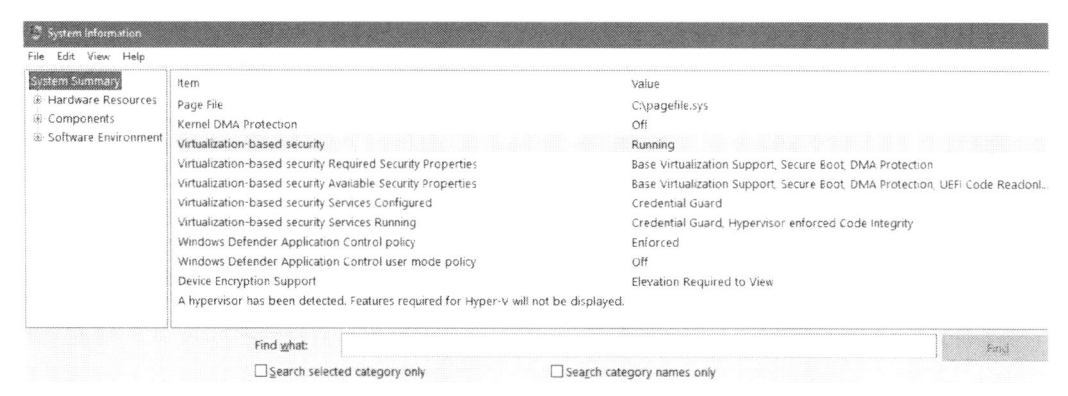

Figure 5.13 – MSinfo32.exe displaying VBS features on this system

Let's look at some of the features that leverage VBS. First, we will cover Credential Guard.

Credential Guard

Credential Guard helps protect user authentication and access tokens in the **Local Security Authority Subsystem** (**LSASS**) or `Lsass.exe` file from being stolen. Without Credential Guard enabled, derived credentials such as Kerberos tickets and password hashes are stored in memory without the secure isolated protection of a VBS hypervisor and are vulnerable to password stealing malware. With Credential Guard enabled, credentials are stored in a protected isolated process called `Lsaiso.exe`. LSAISO is only accessible by LSASS using secured **remote procedure calls** (**RPC**) and credentials stored in LSAISO are not exposed to processes outside of this protected container. This mitigates tools from stealing NTLM password hashes and Kerberos ticket-granting tickets stored in the memory thanks to virtual secure mode's isolation:

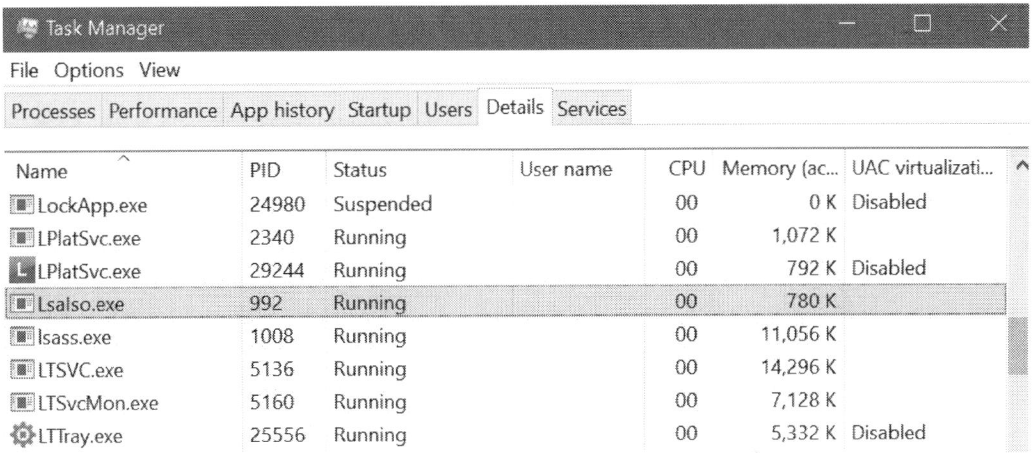
Task Manager
File Options View
Processes Performance App history Startup Users Details Services
Name PID Status User name CPU Memory (ac... UAC virtualizati...
LockApp.exe 24980 Suspended 00 0 K Disabled
LPlatSvc.exe 2340 Running 00 1,072 K
LPlatSvc.exe 29244 Running 00 792 K Disabled
LsaIso.exe 992 Running 00 780 K
lsass.exe 1008 Running 00 11,056 K
LTSVC.exe 5136 Running 00 14,296 K
LTSvcMon.exe 5160 Running 00 7,128 K
LTTray.exe 25556 Running 00 5,332 K Disabled

Figure 5.14 – LsaIso.exe process running in Task Manager

The following are the types of attacks that Credential Guard helps protect us against:

- **Pass-the-Hash** (**PtH**) is where an attacker can bypass entering a user's credentials by passing a captured password hash as an alternative authentication method.
- **Pass-the-Ticket** (**PtT**) is similar to PtH but where an attacker authenticates by using a Kerberos ticket instead of the user's password.

> **Tip**
> With Credential Guard enabled, single sign-on does not work with NTLMv1, MS-CHAPv2, Digest, and CredSSP authentication methods, and applications will prompt for credentials. It is also recommended to use certificate-based authentication for Wi-Fi and VPN using PEAP-TLS and EAP-TLS.

If you're considering enabling Credential Guard, it is recommended to read about the important considerations mentioned in the preceding information tip before turning it on. More information can be found at this link:

`https://docs.microsoft.com/en-us/windows/security/identity-protection/credential-guard/credential-guard-considerations.`

Next, we'll look at how to enable Credential Guard. We will use both Intune and Group Policy to do so.

Enabling Credential Guard with MDM (Intune)

To enable Credential Guard from Intune, follow these steps:

1. Log into Microsoft Endpoint Manager at `https://devicemanagement.microsoft.com`.
2. Choose the **Devices** blade and select **Configuration Profiles** under **Policy**.
3. Create a profile.
4. Give it a descriptive name such as `Endpoint Protection - Windows Credential Guard`.
5. Choose **Windows 10 and later** as the platform.
6. Choose **Endpoint Protection** as the profile type.
7. Select **Microsoft Defender Credential Guard**.
8. Select the dropdown and choose to enable with or without UEFI lock.
9. Click **OK**.
10. When back on the **Overview** page, choose **Assignment**.
11. Select a security group to assign the policy to, as shown in the following screenshot:

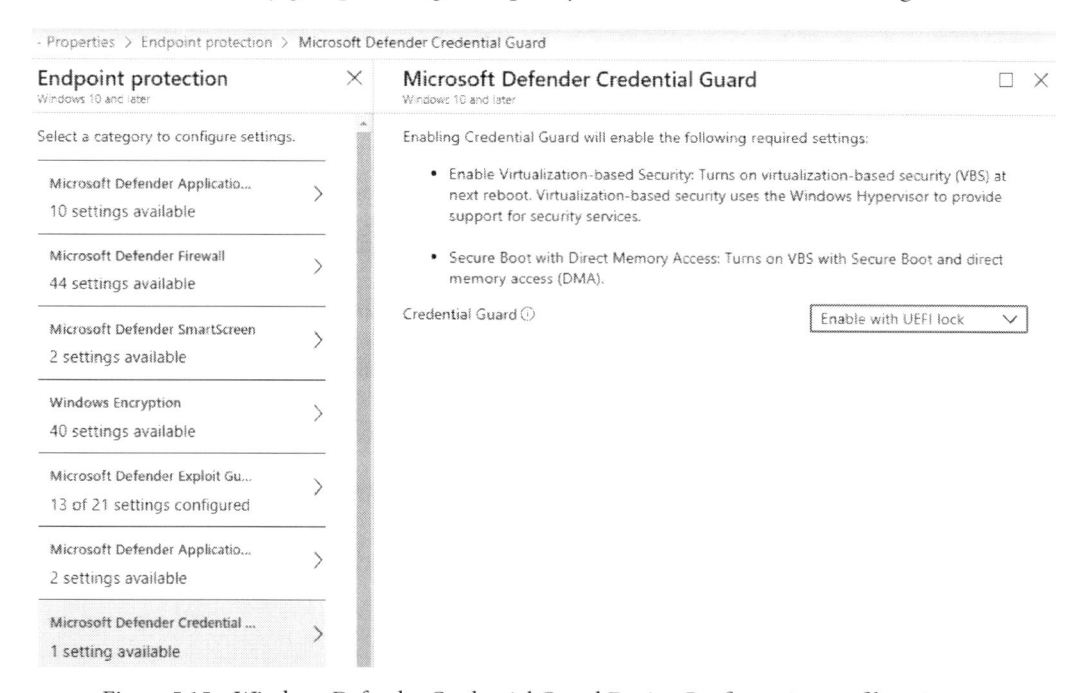

Figure 5.15 – Windows Defender Credential Guard Device Configuration profile in Intune

> **Tip**
> Note that enabling Credential Guard with Intune will also enable VBS and Secure Boot with **Direct Memory Access (DMA)**.

Enable with UEFI Lock (recommended) ensures that Credential Guard cannot be remotely disabled. If you need to disable it remotely, choose **Enable without UEFI lock**.

Now, we'll look at how to do this with Group Policy. As a best practice, we always recommend deploying Group Policy in a test environment before deploying it into a production.

Enabling Credential Guard with Group Policy

To enable Credential Guard with Group Policy, follow these steps:

1. Open the **Group Policy Management Console (GPMC)** and create a new policy scoped to the OU where the devices you wish to apply the settings to are.
2. Give it a friendly name such as `Windows 10 and Server 2019 - Credential Guard`.
3. Go to **Computer Configuration > Policies > Administrative Templates > System > Device Guard**.
4. Open **Turn on Virtualization Based Security** and choose **Enabled** (radio button).

5. Modify the following dropdowns, as shown in the following screenshot:

    – Select Platform Security Level: **Secure Boot and DMA Protection**

    – Credential Guard Configuration: **Enabled with or without UEFI lock**:

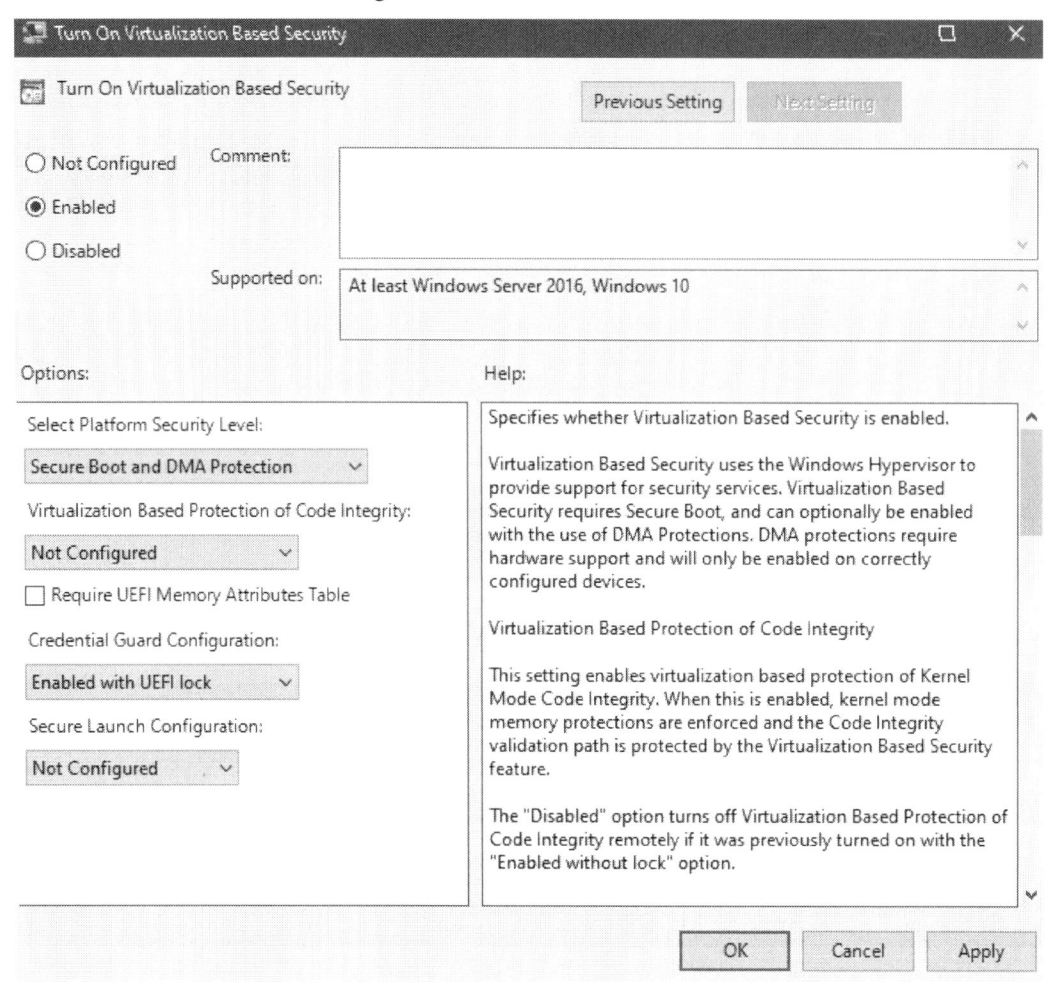

Figure 5.16 – Virtualization-Based Security Group Policy settings

6. Close GPMC.

For more information about how Windows Defender Credential Guard works, visit this link:

https://docs.microsoft.com/en-us/windows/security/identity-protection/credential-guard/credential-guard-how-it-works.

Device Guard

Device Guard is the combination of Virtualization-Based Security features, UEFI Secure Boot, and application control policies, which are used to determine what applications can run on your Windows systems. Application control policies are enforced using Microsoft **Windows Defender Application Control** (**WDAC**) (for Windows). WDAC policies are binary files that contain the instructions for whitelisting applications, file paths, COM objects, and can even enforce script signing. Windows Defender Application Control is built around the zero-trust model (discussed in *Chapter 1, Fundamentals of Windows Security*) and when a policy is enabled, applications need to be explicitly whitelisted in order to run, otherwise they will be blocked. Unlike AppLocker, WDAC enforces policies at the device level and cannot be granularly assigned to specific users and groups. Microsoft recommends a combination of WDAC and AppLocker if you need to be granular with policy configurations. When WDAC is combined with Hypervisor Protected Code Integrity and UEFI SecureBoot, it is known as Device Guard.

WDAC can be deployed without enabling VBS, but it does not provide virtual secure mode isolation to prevent WDAC policies being tampered with. Used together, Device Guard helps protect both user and kernel mode operations with this secure virtualized isolation. Device Guard and, more specifically, Windows Defender Application Control can be enabled with Group Policy, Intune, or Configuration Manager.

Enabling Device Guard and Windows Defender Application Control with Group Policy

To enable Device Guard with Group Policy, modify the **Turn on Virtualization Based Security** policy we created with Credential Guard and enable **Virtualization Based Protection of Code Integrity** (with or without a UEFI lock):

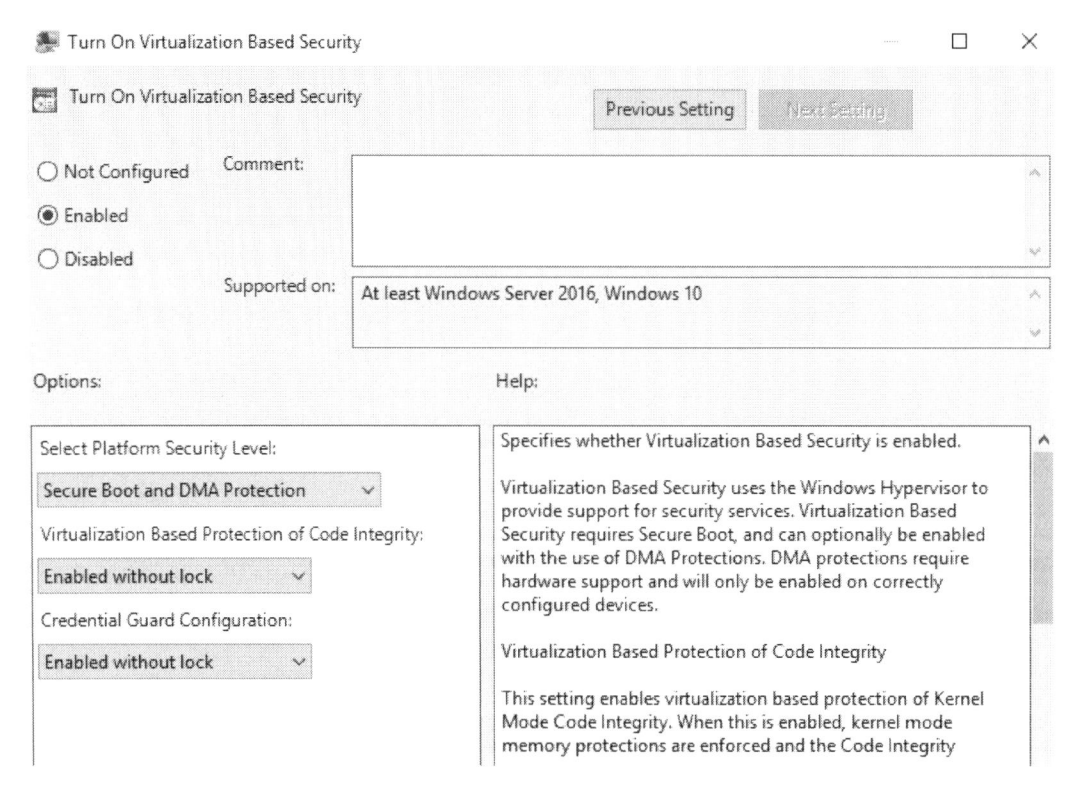

Figure 5.17 – Virtualization-Based Protection of Code Integrity Group Policy

Policies are built and defined in XML format and converted into binary with PowerShell. After your policies have been converted into binary, they need to be stored in a deployment share that can be read by computers in your Active Directory domain if you're using Group Policy. After the policy has been saved, an additional GPO needs to be configured. Follow these steps to learn how:

1. In **GPMC**, create a new policy or modify the existing **Credential Guard** policy.
2. Go to **Computer Configuration** > **Policies** > **Administrative Templates** > **System** > **Device Guard**.

3. Open **Deploy Code Integrity Policy** and **Enable** it.
4. Enter the UNC path to the .bin file located on the deployment share.
5. Click **OK**.

The following screenshot shows the Code Integrity policy file path for the Deploy Code Integrity Policy Group Policy preference:

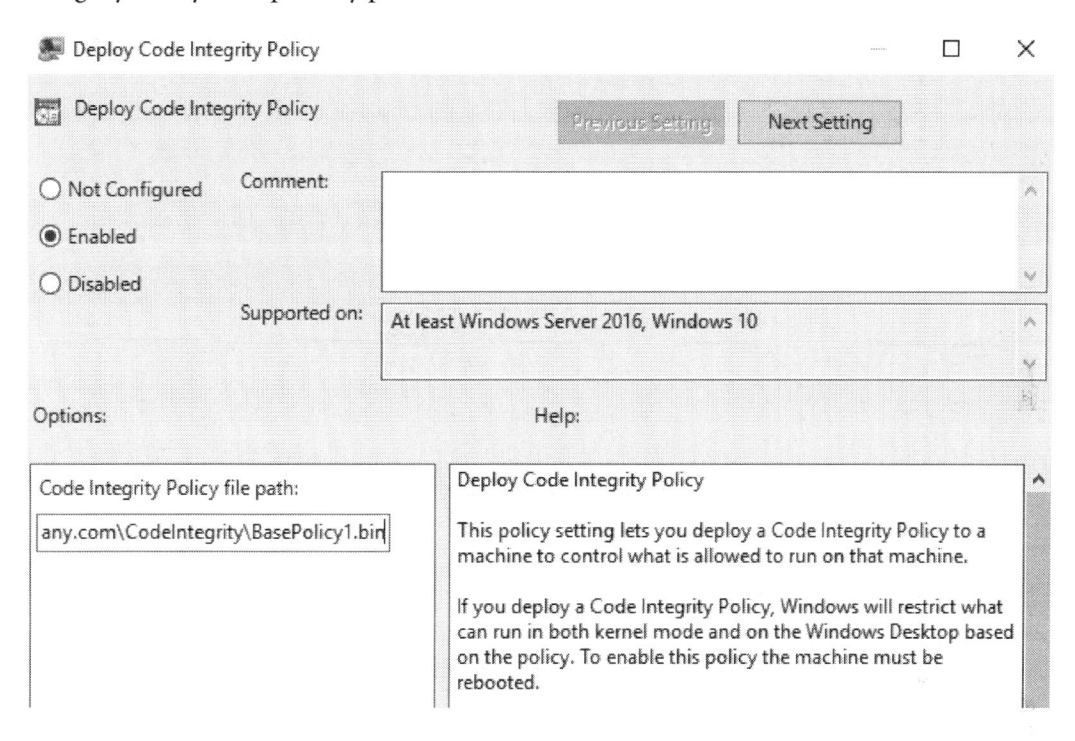

Figure 5.18 – Deploy Code Integrity Policy Group Policy

For more detailed information about deploying Windows Defender Application Control policies with Group Policy, visit this link:

`https://docs.microsoft.com/en-us/windows/security/threat-protection/windows-defender-application-control/deploy-windows-defender-application-control-policies-using-group-policy`

To enable basic enforcement of WDAC policies in Intune, create a new **Endpoint Protection** device configuration profile, as follows:

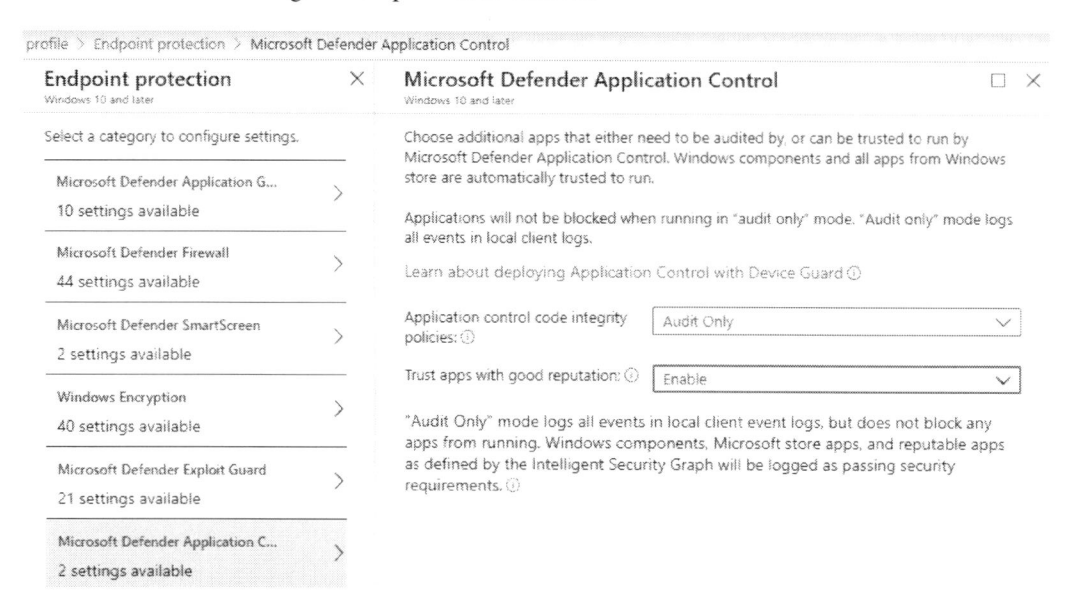

Figure 5.19 – Windows Defender Application Control Device Configuration profile in Intune

Using the UI-based Endpoint Protection profile is limited to what you can set for WDAC and does not support supplemental policies. Use the *ApplicationControl* **Configuration Service Provider** (**CSP**) with a custom profile for fine-grained control over WDAC policies. More information about the ApplicationControl CSP can be found at this link:

https://docs.microsoft.com/en-us/windows/client-management/mdm/applicationcontrol-csp.

> **Tip**
> Deploy a Microsoft Defender Application Control policy in audit mode first to understand the effects it will have on your Windows devices. Once enabled, policies log to Event Viewer under `Applications` and `Services\Microsoft\Windows\CodeIntegrity\Operational`. WDAC events can also be queried with KQL language using the Advanced Hunting feature of Microsoft Defender ATP.

Now that we have covered Device Guard, let's discuss how VBS can protect browser-level exploits with Windows Defender Application Guard.

Windows Defender Application Guard

Windows Defender Application Guard is designed to leverage the Virtual Secure Mode hypervisor isolation of VBS to protect against browser-based attacks through containerization of the Edge browser. Currently, WDAG has built-in support for Microsoft Edge browser, but extends these features to Google Chrome and Firefox through browser extensions. This allows untrusted sites that are opened in Chrome or Firefox to be redirected to a protected Edge browsing session:

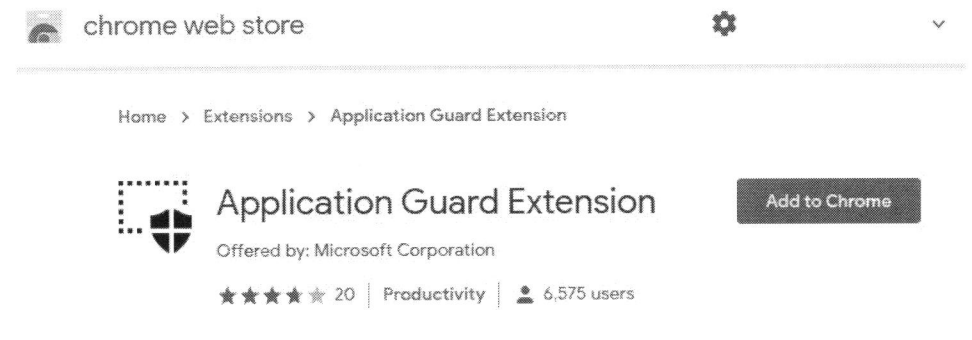

Figure 5.20 – Application Guard Extension available in the Google Chrome web store

> **Tip**
> When enabling the extension or deploying it through Intune, a Win32 component will need to be installed to activate Application Guard. A restart will be required.

Application Guard protects users from sites that aren't defined as trusted in a network isolation policy. Whenever a site is opened that's not in this policy, a new containerized browsing session is opened leveraging the virtual secure mode of VBS and isolating this session from user and kernel mode attacks on the underlying system.

A few examples of attacks Application Guard protects against are as follows:

- Zero-day and unpatched vulnerabilities exploited from a website
- Drive-by attacks where malicious code is injected into a website
- **Cross-site scripting** (**XSS**) attacks and other web-based malware

Application Guard can be enabled through **Group Policy**, **Intune**, or **Configuration Manager**, as follows:

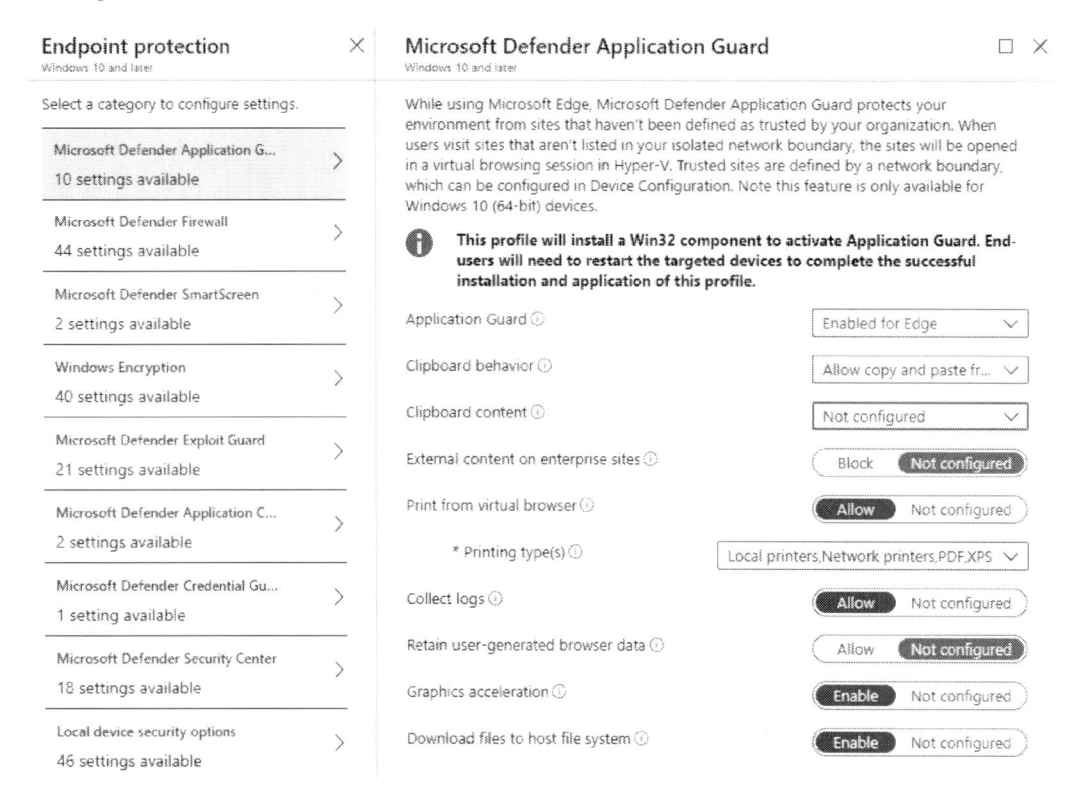

Figure 5.21 – Windows Defender Application Guard Device Configuration profile

The following screenshot shows how to configure network boundaries using the Network boundary profile type in Intune:

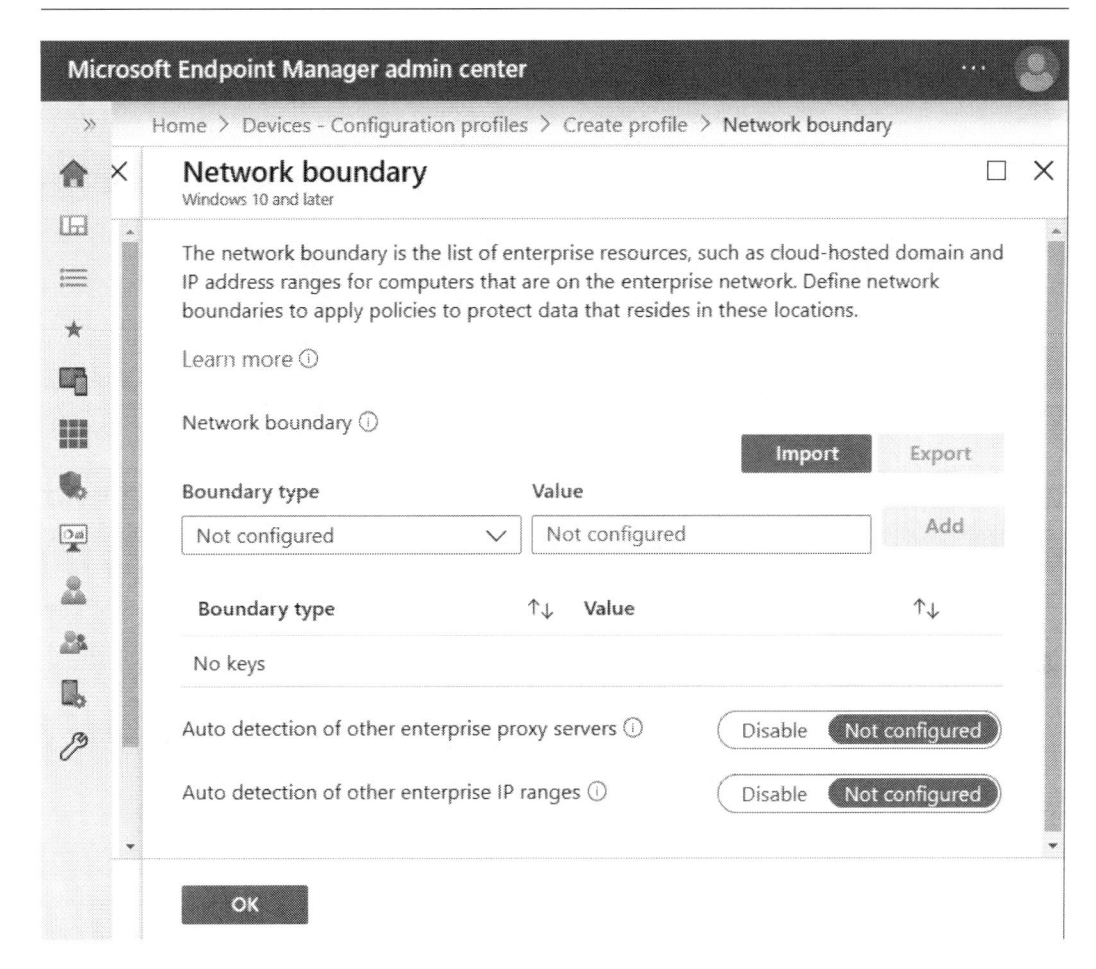

Figure 5.22 – Network boundary profile for configuring a trusted network boundary in Intune

Next, we'll look at Hypervisor-Protected Code Integrity and how it's used to enhance Windows Defender Application Control.

Hypervisor-Protected Code Integrity

Earlier in this chapter, we covered **Windows Defender Application Control (WDAC)** code integrity policies designed to whitelist what applications, drivers, and file paths can run. Hypervisor-protected code integrity adds an additional protection layer on top of this by taking these code integrity policies and expanding them into the virtualization-based security features of hypervisor isolation. This helps to ensure that WDAC policies remain resilient against tampering. HVCI is not only applicable to a single system running on physical hardware but can also protect generation 2 virtual machines with a Hyper-V host in Server 2016 or later.

HVCI is the key component of the Memory Integrity functionality of the Core Isolation security features in Windows system security. This helps to ensure that that the code integrity service used to validate the signatures of drivers and kernel mode processes are contained with hypervisor isolation, thus making them protected from being tampered with by malicious code:

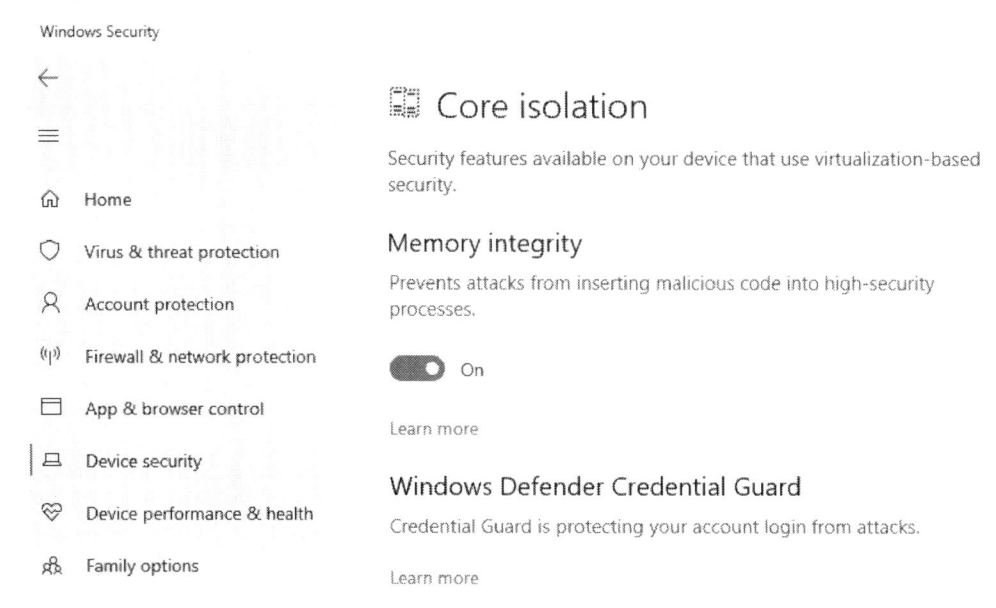

Figure 5.23 – Memory integrity feature enabled in Core isolation for VBS security features in Windows Security

> **Tip**
> While most modern systems have the hardware and drivers to fully support HVCI, it is important to point out that **ALL** drivers must be HVCI compatible; otherwise, it can result in blue screens or system failures.

To view the list of baseline protections that are required for both VBS and HVCI, visit this link:

https://docs.microsoft.com/en-us/windows/security/threat-protection/device-guard/requirements-and-deployment-planning-guidelines-for-virtualization-based-protection-of-code-integrity.

Enabling HVCI

If you followed the previous section to enable Windows Defender Application Control and Device Guard, then HVCI has inadvertently been enabled. To recap from earlier, do the following:

1. Open **GPMC** and create a new GPO or modify an existing one.
2. Go to **Computer Configuration > Policies > Administrative Templates > System > Device Guard**.
3. Open **Turn on Virtualization Based Security** and choose **Enabled** (radio button).
4. Ensure the dropdown under **Virtualization Based Protection of Code Integrity** is set to **Enabled** with or without a UEFI lock, as follows:

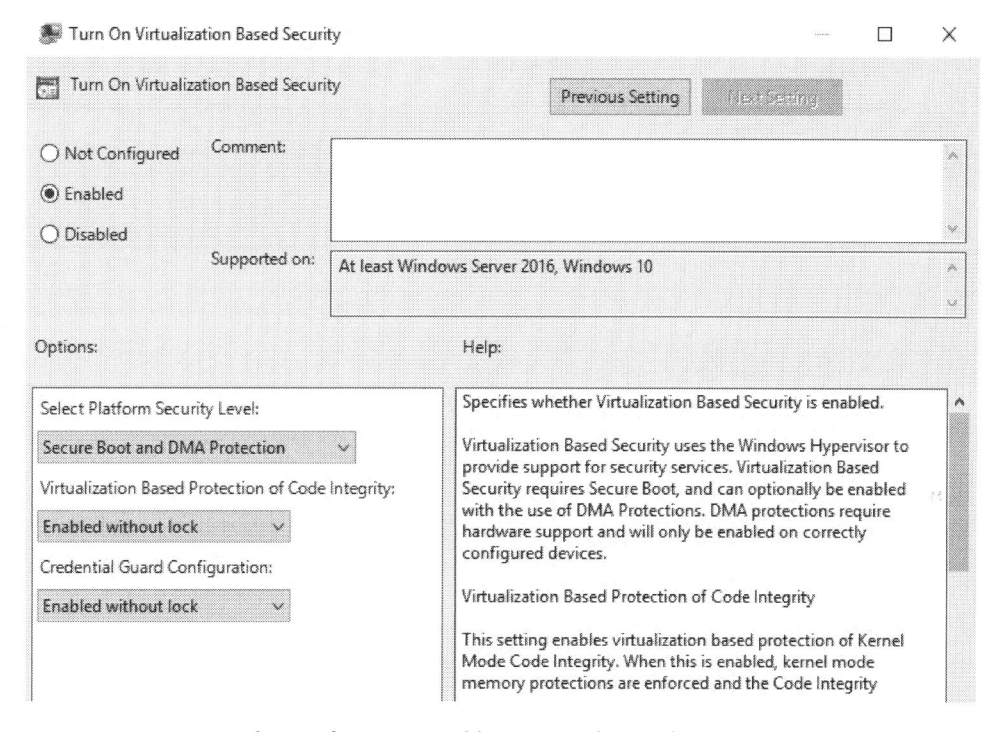

Figure 5.24 – Group Policy preference to enable HVCI and Virtualization-Based Security features

HVCI can also be validated by running `msinfo32.exe` in an elevated PowerShell window. Look for **Virtualization-based security Services Running** that lists **Hypervisor-enforced Code Integrity**, as shown in the following screenshot:

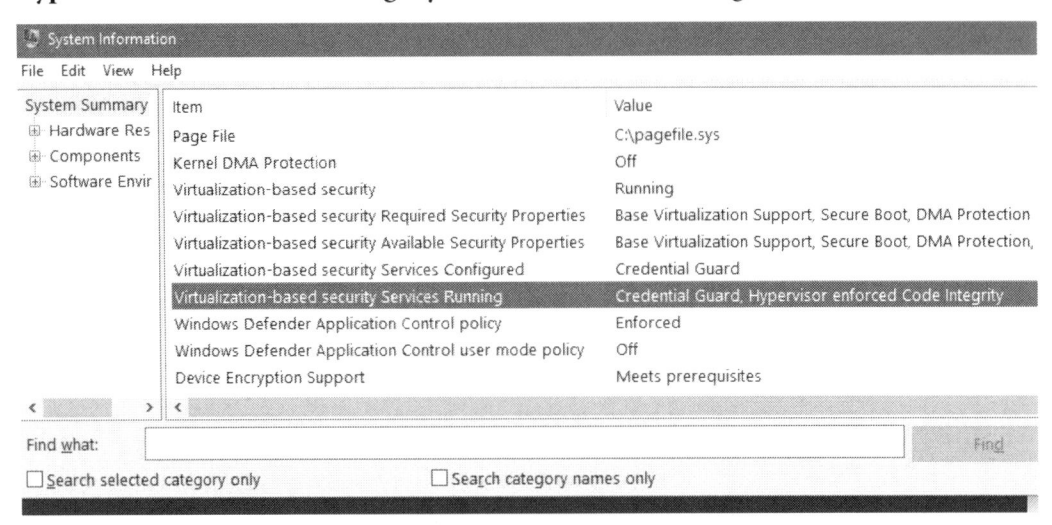

Figure 5.25 – System Information system summary showing that VBS services are running and configured for HVCI

Next, we'll have a look at System Guard.

Windows Defender System Guard

System Guard is a collective of hardware protection features (such as Secure Boot) that ensure the integrity of your system is protected on boot as well as after Windows is running. Using local attestation through **Root of Trust Management** (**RTM**) measurements and through remote attestation, RTM measurements can be sent for analysis to an MDM solution such as Intune or Configuration Manager. If a PC is determined to be untrustworthy, remote action can be taken to isolate the device. This helps to protect the system after boot through analysis and monitoring of these measurements. System Guard, by design, is aligned with the zero-trust security model and assumes that all processes could be compromised.

System Guard uses **Dynamic Root of Trust measurement** (**DRTM**) with a process known as Secure Launch to dynamically protect and add management flexibility over the **Static RTM** (**SRTM**) that's typically used for local attestation of boot processes. As we discussed earlier, the **security phase** (**SEC**) in UEFI is loaded at the start of boot and begins the Trusted Boot process. In order to achieve compliance with an SRTM, each piece of code in the entire boot process must be validated from start to finish against a whitelist of known trusted measurements. Due to the large number of hardware vendors, executables, libraries, BIOS versions, code updates, and length of code, support for scaling this whitelist is difficult. Also, SRTM does not protect the runtime after load operations and requires trust be maintained through the entire boot process. Dynamic root of trust measurement and the Secure Launch technology of System Guard help overcome these challenges.

DRTM simplifies SRTM management by allowing for the boot process (sometimes unvalidated) to be executed and immediately controlled by being forced into a secure Launch Code container. This launch code is known good code that's used to continue the boot process and is independent of specific hardware configurations. This dynamic measurement allows for more flexibility, and code that's not added to SRTM measurements can boot the system before Secure Launch takes control. The system can maintain a Trusted Computing Base standard without you having to reset the entire TPM and validate the entire boot chain end to end. **Trusted Computing Group** (**TCG**) has defined a **Trusted Computing Base** (**TCB**) as what protects the system and enforces computer security policy.

For more information on the DRTM specification, visit this link:

`https://trustedcomputinggroup.org/wp-content/uploads/DRTM-Specification-Overview_June2013.pdf`.

> **Tip**
> Only TPM2.0 supports System Guard Secure Launch and remote attestation. To enable System Guard Secure Launch, all requirements for Device Guard, Credential Guard, and VBS must be met.

We have just covered many of the hardware-based security features that are used to protect your systems all the way through the boot process. Now, we'll recap this chapter by providing a list of security recommendations.

Hardware security recommendations and best practices

When looking at the security of hardware, it's important to keep these considerations in mind:

- Only purchase hardware that has been through a proper hardware certification program. The Windows Hardware Compatibility Program Certification process is a great resource to help ensure the hardware is reliable and compatible for Windows.

- Have a good secure system for upgrading Firmware/BIOS and ensure the proper protections are enabled to ensure only approved sources can update them.

- Purchase physical hardware with a minimum of TPM 2.0 in order to leverage the advanced cryptographic functionality it offers. Most new hardware-based security features require it.

- Turn on Virtualization-Based Security as soon as possible and enable Credential Guard, Device Guard, and Application Guard to put the power of your hardware into action.

Summary

In this chapter, we provided an overview of the hardware-based security features used to protect Windows from the boot chain, the OS layer, and for virtualization of the OS. We covered hardware concerns in terms of vulnerabilities such as rootkits and bootkits and the importance of the supply chain to ensure your organization purchases hardware that has been properly certified. Next, we covered BIOS, Secure Boot, and TPM and how these hardware components are the framework for hardware backed VBS. We talked about the latest advanced protection features using VBS such as Credential Guard, Device Guard, Windows Defender Application Control, and Hypervisor-Protected Code Integrity, as well as how to enable them using MDM or through Group Policy.

Finally, we finished by discussing how System Guard uses dynamic root of trust measurements and remote attestation to help protect your systems from the boot process into runtime.

In the next chapter, we will discuss networking and the fundamentals that play a large role in securing your Windows systems. We will discuss physical hardware components used in the network infrastructure and the Windows Defender Firewall software, including configurations with Intune, Group Policy, and Configuration Manager. We will enable a feature of Windows Defender known as Windows Defender Exploit Guard-Network Protection, which acts as a proxy to protect us against social engineering and phishing attacks. Finally, we will provide an overview of Azure network solutions that are used to secure Windows systems inside an Azure virtual network.

6
Network Fundamentals for Hardening Windows

In this chapter, we will cover the importance of networking for the overall security and hardening of your Windows systems. Network security has traditionally been at the heart of security for users over the years, but this has shifted recently. Network security hasn't become any less important, but with the shift to the cloud and the more we decentralize our users from traditional office space, the strategy for securing our users has needed to change. Our security strategies have needed to shift from a strong focus on network perimeter security to device-level and identity focused security. This is for the simple reason that devices are no longer sitting within your corporate office anymore; they travel everywhere and connect to any network they can find.

Even though the workforce has become more decentralized and services are moving to the cloud, there is still a need to maintain the same level of network security within your offices and on-premises data centers. In addition, you will need to implement more advanced security at the desktop level and adopt a strategy for the security of your virtual networks and cloud data center. With this comes complexity, and it's important to have the right tools and skillsets that support the strategic vision, deployment, and maintenance of your network tools and solutions.

Throughout this chapter, we will cover security fundamentals to raise awareness of the supporting network infrastructure for your Windows environment. We will then review some of the network security tools available, including the software-based Windows Defender Firewall and Advanced Security features. Finally, we will cover Azure network security solutions that protect and allow access to your Windows virtual machines. This chapter includes the following topics:

- Network security fundamentals
- Understanding Windows Network Security
- Windows Defender Firewall and Advanced Security
- Azure network security solutions for Windows VMs

Technical requirements

In order to complete the exercises in this chapter, we recommend the following requirements. For Windows Defender Exploit Guard Network Protection, the minimum requirements are as follows:

- A Windows 2016 Active Directory domain with Group Policy
- Domain Admin rights or equal permissions to create Group Policy objects for the scoped OU of the target systems
- A Windows 10 Pro or Enterprise workstation domain-joined and/or Intune enrolled

To complete the Azure Security Center just-in-time exercise and Azure Bastion, you will need the following minimum requirements:

- An Azure tenant with a virtual network, subnet, and resource group
- An available IP range inside your virtual network that can accommodate a /27 CIDR
- A Windows 10 or Server 1909 data center virtual machine with a public IP
- Azure Security Center Standard (or a free 30-day trial)

Network security fundamentals

Networking can be a very challenging task for technology teams. Networks can be very sensitive and commonly take the blame for most outages, without people even knowing the true root cause of an issue. This is simply because most of our data traverses over a network, so it's critical that it performs optimally. If it doesn't, it can bring a business to its knees because of how dependent we have become on the network. In addition to the already challenging task of managing a network comes network security. Ensuring that the data we send/receive is secure, no perpetrators are accessing our network who shouldn't be, preventing traffic that isn't welcome, and ensuring confidential data is isolated are some of the challenges faced with network security.

As we mentioned previously, this shift in security is mainly due to the evolution of device access and cloud technologies that have forced us to change our strategies. Although this has shifted the core from a network security perimeter-focused strategy, network security has never been more important than it is today. Additional advanced security features are now required to secure and harden both the device and the cloud technologies used.

Before we review some of the core network security technologies, it's important that we review and cover the **Open Systems Interconnection** (**OSI**) and **TCP/IP** (also known as the internet protocol suite) models. These models have been built to allow an open standard/framework to be referenced. The OSI model is a framework that is used as more of a guideline that provides a standard for network communications. It provides a great reference that allows us to understand the flow of network traffic from one endpoint to the other and serves as a great troubleshooting tool for us to understand where any breakdowns or failures may be occurring. The TCP/IP model is comprised of open standard protocols for network communication and has become more adopted for use over the OSI model.

The following diagram provides a comparison of both the OSI model and TCP/IP model, along with examples of what falls within each of the layers. Understanding where communication is failing within the network will significantly help a security expert with any investigative and/or troubleshooting tasks:

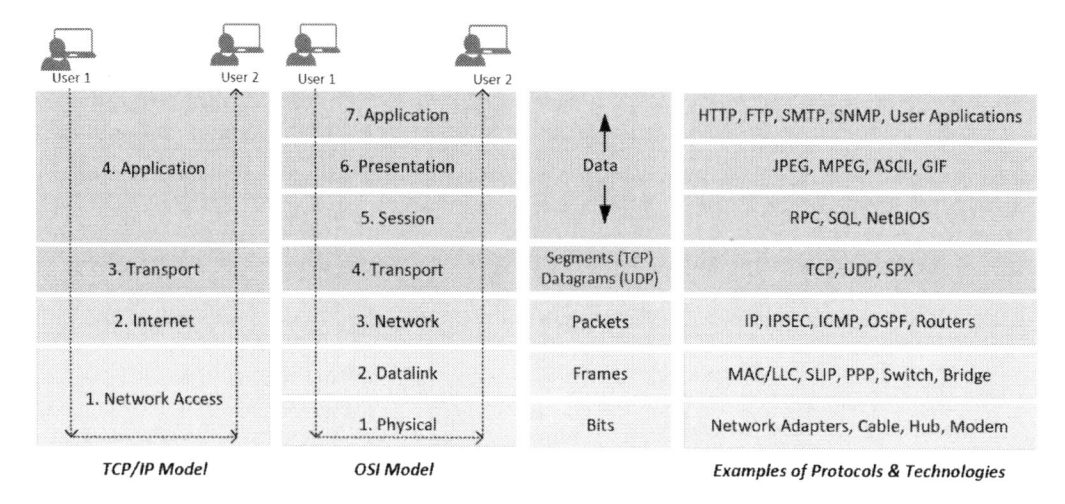

TCP/IP Model	OSI Model		Examples of Protocols & Technologies
4. Application	7. Application	Data	HTTP, FTP, SMTP, SNMP, User Applications
	6. Presentation		JPEG, MPEG, ASCII, GIF
	5. Session		RPC, SQL, NetBIOS
3. Transport	4. Transport	Segments (TCP) / Datagrams (UDP)	TCP, UDP, SPX
2. Internet	3. Network	Packets	IP, IPSEC, ICMP, OSPF, Routers
1. Network Access	2. Datalink	Frames	MAC/LLC, SLIP, PPP, Switch, Bridge
	1. Physical	Bits	Network Adapters, Cable, Hub, Modem

Figure 6.1 – The OSI and TCP/IP models

In addition to being familiar with the OSI and TCP/IP models, knowing the more common ports is somewhat an expectation of any network or security professional. As you build out and architect your solutions and integrate your technologies, knowing which ports are used by which protocols allows more intelligent decisions so that you can provide better security.

> **Tip**
> When building network security groups or firewall rules, a best practice is to limit communications from known sources using only the required ports needed to create the connections.

In addition, when troubleshooting cyberattacks, being able to quickly identify the type of traffic and which ports are being used may speed up your ability to mitigate an attack. The following is a list of some of the more common ports and the protocols/services that use them:

Port #	Service
20-21	FTP
22	SSH
23	Telnet
25	SMTP
53	DNS
69	TFTP
80	HTTP
88	Kerberos
110	POP3
115	SFTP
123	NTP
137-139	NETBIOS
143	IMAP
161-162	SNMP
179	BGP
389	LDAP
443	HTTPS
464	Kerberos
636	LDAPS
993	IMAPS
995	POP3S
989-990	FTPS
1433-1434	SQL
1512	WINS
3306	MYSQL
3389	RDP

Figure 6.2 – Common ports and services

> **Tip**
> The **Internet Assigned Numbers Authority (IANA)** website provides a list of all registered service names and port numbers: https://www.iana.org/assignments/service-names-port-numbers/service-names-port-numbers.xhtml.

There are many components involved in a network architecture and the topology can be extremely complex. The following technologies are considered more critical for your enterprise deployment as they relate to your network security and should be implemented to protect your Windows environment:

- Routers and switches using VLANs
- A next-generation type firewall
- A **Virtual Private Network (VPN)** to encrypt connections
- **Intrusion Detection Systems (IDS)/Intrusion Prevention Systems (IPS)** to proactively detect and prevent threats
- Wi-Fi with a minimum of WPA2-Enterprise security
- **Network Access Control (NAC)** to better manage endpoint access to your network
- A proxy/web content filter to prevent malicious websites
- Next-generation antivirus and anti-malware tools for more intelligent protection
- **Data Loss Prevention (DLP)** to prevent the loss of sensitive data
- Email/spam filtering to protect users against spamming, phishing, and so on
- **Security Information and Event Management (SIEM)** to help you detect abnormal activity
- DNSSEC to protect your DNS services
- **Public Key Infrastructure (PKI)** to provide digital certificates for encryption

From a network device management perspective, the following are important:

- Ensure you keep the software of your network devices current
- Enable auditing on the devices
- Integrate authentication using LDAP
- Leverage a PAM solution
- Disable or prevent local account access and change default usernames/passwords
- Ensure the management of devices is encrypted (SSH)
- Isolate the management network
- Don't allow management from the internet

For a more detailed review on securing network infrastructure devices, the Department of Homeland Security has a Security Tips reference: https://www.us-cert.gov/ncas/tips/ST18-001.

These technologies are very involved and, in most cases, require specialized skillsets to implement and manage them daily. Some of these technologies are both hardware- and software-based. Hardware-based technologies are typically the rack-mounted gear in your **main distribution frame** (**MDF**) and primarily protect your facilities and data centers.

Software-based technologies protect the OS, end users, and provide protection for virtual networks. An example would be your computer's firewall. Ensure you deploy the latest next-generation hardware or virtual-based firewalls at your data center locations (including the cloud) and physical offices and enable the software-based firewalls on your Windows OS for additional protection. Software-based technologies are becoming more critical for end user devices due to the shift from centralized offices to a dispersed and remote workforce.

The Microsoft technology stack offers many solutions that can be compared to other networking vendor offerings as an alternative or as a compliment. As a security professional, it is important you are aware of and understand each of the technologies referenced earlier for the best protection within your organization. Throughout the remainder of this chapter, we will review the Microsoft-specific network technologies that provide the best protection for Windows devices.

Understanding Windows Network Security

In this section, we will review the core networking functions of Windows 10 and Windows Server. Having familiarity with these components is a must for any security professional when managing and troubleshooting Windows devices. It's also recommended that you apply the baseline recommendations that can be applied to the network and ensure your system is hardened correctly.

Network baselining

Referencing back to *Chapter 2, Building a Baseline*, you will want to ensure that your network-specific hardening components have been configured based on the recommendations. There are many network-related settings for Windows and implementing the baseline recommendations is the more practical approach compared to building your own standards from scratch. As an example, referencing back to the Microsoft security baseline and the baseline settings within the `MS Security Baseline Windows 10 v1909 and Server v1909.xlsx` spreadsheet, simply filtering for the network keyword in the **Security Template** worksheet provides 40 settings:

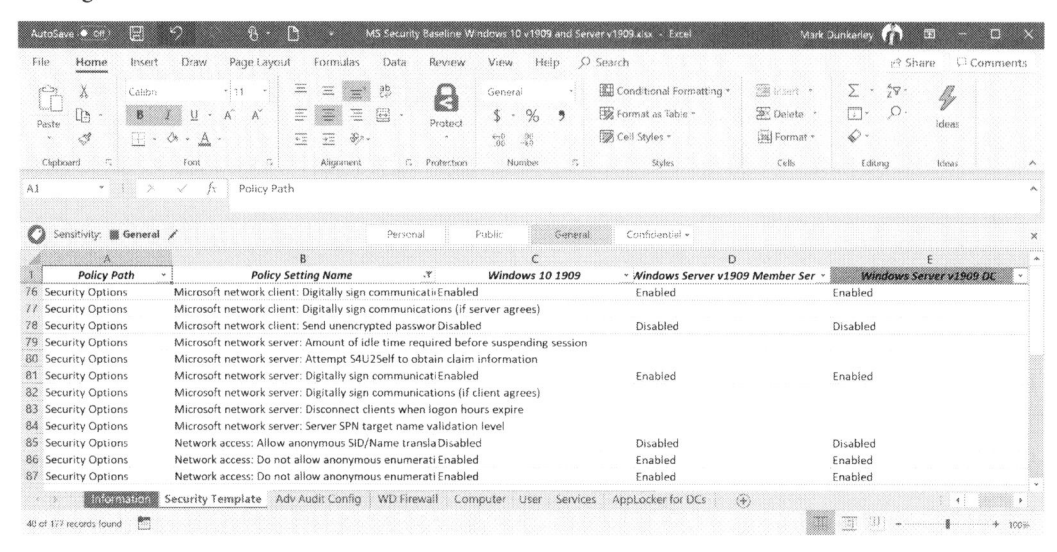

Figure 6.3 – Network-specific configurations within the Microsoft security baselines

The preceding settings will need to be enabled via Group Policy or your device management tool in order to ensure enforcement and consistency. Unless you only have a few devices or servers to manage, individually configuring these settings is not realistic.

> **Tip**
> As a reminder, be extremely cautious when enabling any new settings and, more specifically, network settings on any devices or servers. They can be very disruptive to production if they're not tested correctly.

Windows 10

Next, we will review the **Network & Internet** management console within your Windows 10 device. To access the **Network & Internet** management console, type `Network` within the search option and click on **Network status**. You will be presented with the **Network & Internet** management console, as shown in the following screenshot:

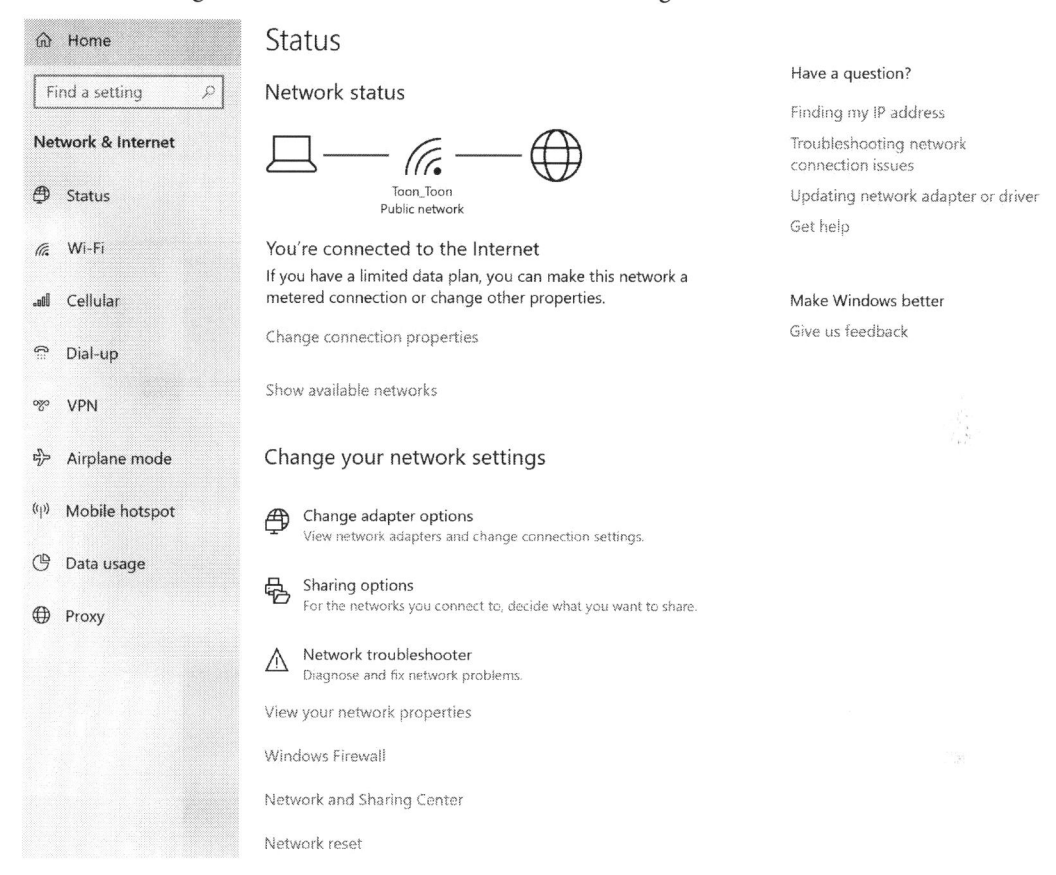

Figure 6.4 – Windows 10 Network & Internet management console

In the **Network & Internet** management console, you will have access to all the network components on your Windows 10 device. Here, you can view your current network status and additional settings such as **Windows Firewall**, **Network and Sharing Center**, adapter-specific settings (**Wi-Fi, Cellular, VPN,** and **Ethernet**), **Data usage, Proxy** settings, **Network reset** functions, and much more.

In addition to these settings, you can also view your network connections and active adapters on your device by searching for Network once again within the search option and then clicking on **View Network Connections**. You will be presented with the following screen:

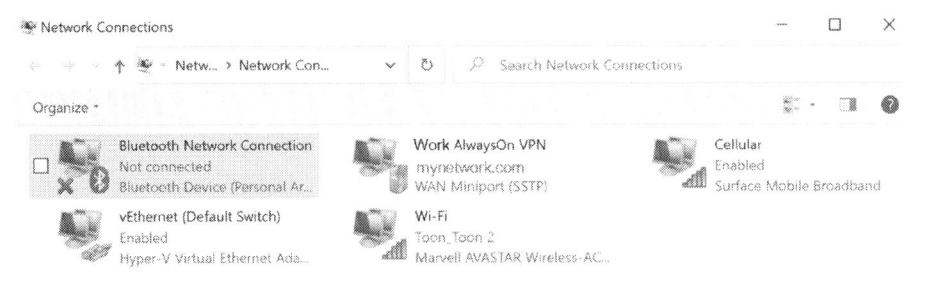

Figure 6.5 – Windows 10 Network Connections

Here, you can view your network settings for any connected adapters by right-clicking one and clicking **Status**. You will be able to view settings such as **IPv4/6 connectivity**, **Media State**, **speed**, and more specific details such as the **IP**, **MAC**, **Default Gateway**, **DHCP**, and **DNS** addresses.

The following technologies are considered more critical for your end user devices and need to be set up correctly to ensure a safer environment for your users.

Wireless Local Area Network (WLAN)/Wi-Fi

WLAN technology is a necessity within the world of technology today. Almost every laptop and mobile device will have some form of Wi-Fi connectivity available for use. As with all technologies, there are threats, and the same applies to Wi-Fi. Unfortunately, Wi-Fi is much more susceptible to vulnerabilities than **Local Area Network** (**LAN**) technologies due to the information being transmitted over the air and not through a cable, which is much more difficult to breach. There are many threats when it comes to Wi-Fi, and some of the more known ones include rogue access points or networks, man-in-the-middle attacks, and unauthorized access to insecure WLAN systems.

Securing your corporate Wi-Fi is not a small task and will require very skilled network engineers to architect and implement correctly, especially with enterprise-grade security for the best protection. Here are a few important tips for Wi-Fi security and your Windows 10 devices:

- Do *not* use **Wired Equivalent Privacy** (**WEP**)
- Enable enterprise-grade authentication – WPA2-Enterprise with EAP-TLS: https://docs.microsoft.com/en-us/windows/win32/nativewifi/wpa2-enterprise-with-tls-profile-sample.

- Ensure any guest networks are isolated from production networks and ensure all guest access is protected. If using guest SSID with a password, implement a process to rotate the password regularly.

- Ensure the WLAN infrastructure is kept current and up to date.

For a more comprehensive list regarding how to secure your enterprise-grade wireless infrastructure, both the Department of Homeland Security and NIST have guides available for reference:

- Department of Homeland Security: `https://www.us-cert.gov/ncas/tips/ST18-247`

- NIST: `https://nvlpubs.nist.gov/nistpubs/Legacy/SP/nistspecialpublication800-97.pdf`

Always be cautious when using open Wi-Fi in public places because of the ongoing threats from attackers. We don't know how well other Wi-Fi networks have been configured, and vulnerabilities may exist within their networks. When travelling, use cellular data to connect to the internet if it's an option or ensure you connect to VPN once you're connected to any public Wi-Fi. Make sure you provide security awareness to your users and advise them about the risks of public Wi-Fi and what they should be doing to protect themselves.

> **Tip**
> Your home is just as vulnerable to threats regarding Wi-Fi and even more so as we connect more devices (IoT) within our home to it. Educate your users and provide them with the awareness needed to protect themselves from the ongoing threat landscape. The Department of Homeland Security provides home network security tips here: `https://www.us-cert.gov/ncas/tips/ST15-002`.

Let's take a look at Bluetooth technology and discuss a few recommendations to ensure secure Bluetooth connections.

Bluetooth

Your Windows 10 device most likely has Bluetooth as a connectivity option since most user devices do today. Although an extremely convenient technology, it also comes with many flaws. There are many Bluetooth threats today that you should be familiar with. Some include **Bluejacking**, **Bluesnarfing**, and **Bluebugging**. The best protection against Bluetooth is to disable it and prevent your users from using it. Unfortunately, this may not be a reality for most, so it is important to understand the technology and the risks associated with it. To help you understand Bluetooth and the risk it entails, NIST has published a *Guide to Bluetooth Security*, also known as *NIST Special Publication 800-121 Revision 2*: `https://nvlpubs.nist.gov/nistpubs/SpecialPublications/NIST.SP.800-121r2.pdf`.

The *Guide to Bluetooth Security* is an extremely comprehensive document that provides you with all the knowledge needed to secure your Windows devices using Bluetooth, including a security recommendation checklist. In addition, the following three recommendations are provided in the guide to help you improve your Bluetooth security:

- Ensure the strongest Bluetooth security mode is enforced for all users where Bluetooth is enabled and allowed to be used. Depending on the version of Bluetooth, there are different modes and security levels within the modes that determine how secure the Bluetooth communication is. For example, for Bluetooth v4.1, Security Mode 4 using Level 4 is recommended. For Bluetooth v2.1 - v4.0, Security Mode 4 using Level 3 is recommended and for anything older than Bluetooth v2.1, Security Mode 3 is recommended. Security Mode 1 is least restrictive and is not recommended.

- Ensure Bluetooth is listed and referenced in the company security policies and that the device settings have been modified to reflect these policies.

- Ensure any users enabled to use Bluetooth are fully aware of security issues with Bluetooth and their responsibilities while using it.

Now that we have covered Wi-Fi and Bluetooth connections, let's discuss VPNs and their use in organizations to connect to internal resources.

Virtual Private Networks (VPNs)

The more remote the workforce has become, the more we have relied on VPN connectivity. A VPN is essentially a technology that allows users to connect to their corporate network over an encrypted secure connection on the internet. A VPN allows a user to be anywhere at any time to access corporate data securely. As part of your policies and remote strategy, it is critical that you ensure users are connecting to a VPN when remote. Connecting your work device (or any device) to open Wi-Fi connections in public places creates a significant risk. When connecting to any network outside of your corporate office, a VPN should be connected to ensure a secure working session. VPNs have been around a long time and are a tool you have most likely used at some point during your working career. One primary challenge with a VPN is that it requires user interaction to connect once logged into your device. For the most secure working environment, a VPN should automatically connect once connected to a network on your corporate network. Microsoft has a technology known as **Always On VPN**. Always On VPN can be configured in Windows 10 as a VPN profile that will automatically connect to your corporate network whenever you are remote. This is a great technology and works very well! In order to use the Always On VPN technology with Windows 10, you need several components for the infrastructure to support it. The following documentation provides more details on the Always On VPN configuration for Windows 10 clients: `https://docs.microsoft.com/en-us/windows-server/remote/remote-access/vpn/vpn-device-tunnel-config`.

Additional "Always On" VPN solutions are also available from Palo Alto Networks through their GlobalProtect client and Cisco's AnyConnect. There is also an option within Windows 10 to leverage the built-in VPN client to connect to other third-party VPN services or providers. Take a look at the following link to learn how to set up a VPN connection from your Windows 10 device: `https://support.microsoft.com/en-us/help/20510/windows-10-connect-to-vpn`.

> **Tip**
> For personal use, you may want to consider a VPN service for your devices when you're away from home and are in cafes or public places. There are many options to choose from and using a VPN service will provide a much secure working environment for your personal services and data.

Next, we'll look at the network security components in Windows Server, as well as the roles and features that can be enabled as components of a network infrastructure.

Windows Server

For Windows Server 2019, the same applies to accessing the **Network & Internet** settings. When you search for Network, you will be presented with **Settings**. Click on **Settings** and then select **Network & Internet** to access your network-specific settings:

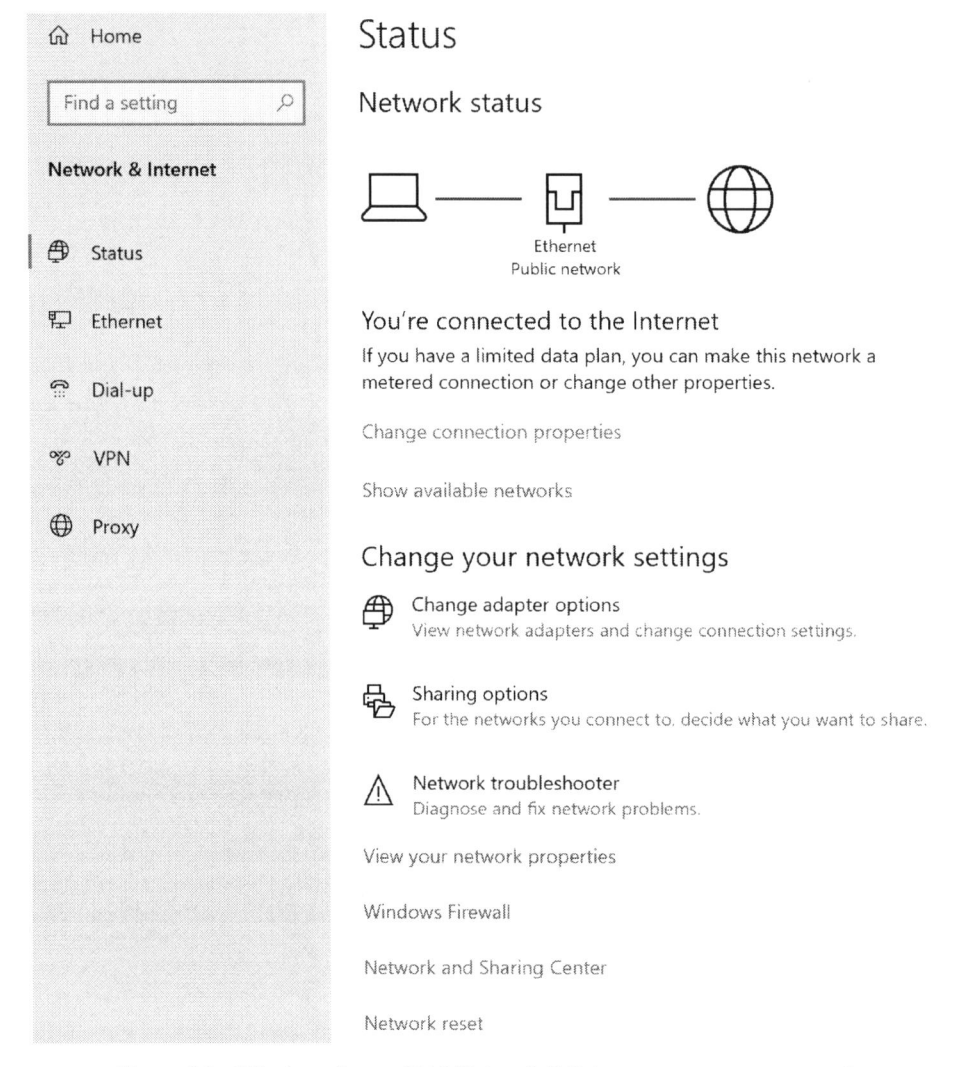

Figure 6.6 – Windows Server 2019 Network & Internet management console

With Windows Server, you will notice that you won't have any of the wireless technologies listed as you should only be using a physical connection for any network connectivity to your Windows servers. Like the Windows 10 settings, the **Network & Internet** management console for Windows Server will provide access to all the network components on your Windows Server. Without going into detail about each of these items, you can view your current network status and properties, **Windows Firewall**, **Network and Sharing Center**, adapter-specific settings (**VPN**, **Ethernet**, and so on), **Proxy** settings, **Network reset** functions, and much more.

Local Area Network (LAN)/Ethernet

Your server should only be connected using Ethernet for network access and any necessary internet access. Ethernet is much more secure than Wi-Fi and provides greater reliability. In addition to using Ethernet, ensure your servers are on a separate network segment from your user segment. Separation should go as far as segments for highly confidential data, the **demilitarized zone** (**DMZ**), and traffic that flows to databases. To accomplish this, you will need to implement VLANs for your LAN and ensure your servers are on a separate and secure VLAN.

Server roles and features

In addition to the base OS for Windows Server, there are server roles and features. There are many available roles and features that will provide separate services for your enterprise. A few of the more common ones include **Active Directory** (**AD**) **Domain Services**, **Web Server** (**IIS**), and **SMTP Server**, to name a few.

To access these roles and features, search for `Server Manager` within the search option and click on it. Once **Server Manager** is open, ensure you are within the dashboard and click **Add Roles and Features**. Here, you can add your desired network-related **Server Roles** and **Features**:

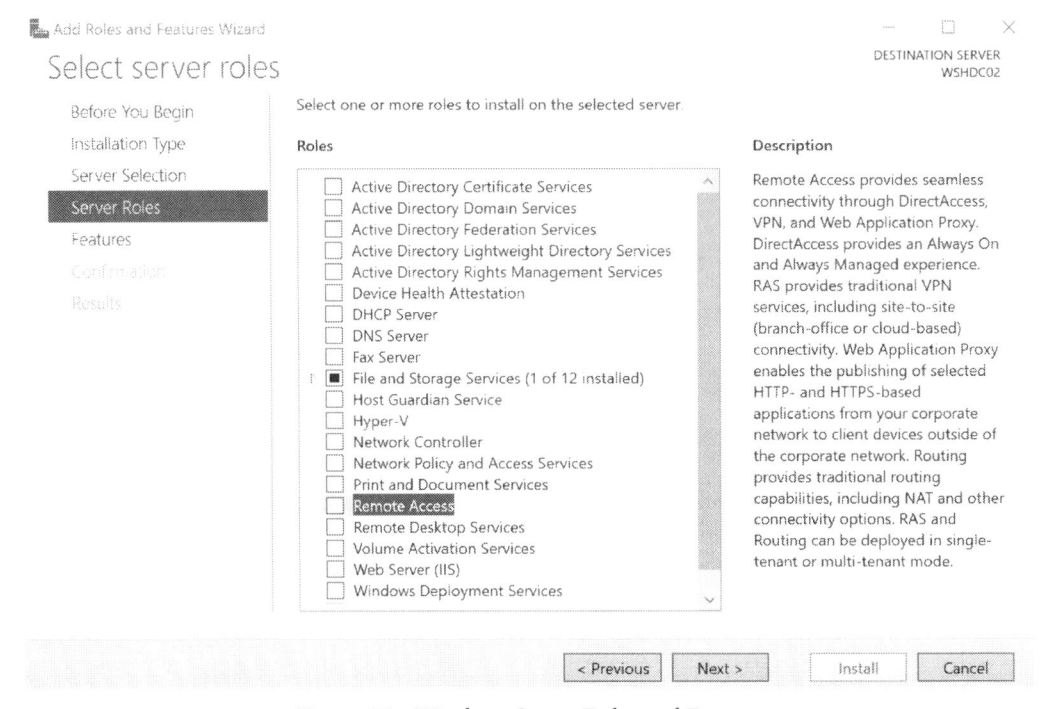

Figure 6.7 – Windows Server Roles and Features

There are many roles and features available that support network-specific functions. Some of them include the following:

- DNS Server
- DHCP Server
- Active Directory Certificate Services
- Network Policy and Access Services
- Remote Access
- Network Load Balancing
- SMTP Server
- SNMP Service

To implement the Windows 10 Always On VPN, the following needs to be deployed within your server environment:

- Active Directory Domain Services
- DNS Server
- Network Policy and Access Services (NPS-RADIUS)
- Active Directory Certificate Services (CA)
- Remote Access (Direct Access and VPN-RAS)

Networking and Hyper-V

As discussed in the previous chapter, virtualization has become prevalent within enterprises but brings a lot of additional risk compared to a traditional physical server deployment model. The same applies to the network layer within the Hyper-V architecture. Ensuring the network is set up correctly and following best practices is a must. The most concerning risk within the network layer is allowing services to use the same network segment or VLAN. Network isolation is critical within the virtualization architecture and must be implemented for the best security.

The following documentation provides an overview of networking within Hyper-V so that you are familiar with the basics as they relate to Hyper-V: `https://docs.microsoft.com/en-us/windows-server/virtualization/hyper-v/plan/plan-hyper-v-networking-in-windows-server`.

There is also this reference for Hyper-V security for Windows Server, which should be reviewed: `https://docs.microsoft.com/en-us/windows-server/virtualization/hyper-v/plan/plan-hyper-v-security-in-windows-server`. Within this reference, the network-specific security items include the following:

- Use a secure network for both host management and VMs.
- Use separate networks and dedicated physical adapters for the physical hosts.
- Use a separate secure network to access virtual hard disk files and VM configurations.
- Use a separate secure network for any VM migrations and ensure encryption is enabled.
- For VMs, ensure the virtual NICs are connected to the correct virtual switch and are configured with the correct security settings.

Now that we have reviewed the network components of Windows Server and tips for securing Hyper-V, let's take a look at some of the tools that are helpful when troubleshooting network-related issues.

Network troubleshooting

As a security professional, you are going to need to be familiar with troubleshooting and investigative work. Chances are, the network layer will be involved as part of your troubleshooting and investigative work at some point. Microsoft initially had its own tool that was able to capture and analyze network traffic, known as Microsoft Network Monitor 3.4, which was then replaced with **Microsoft Message Analyzer** (**MMA**). Unfortunately, MMA has recently been retired. Currently, Microsoft has no plans to replace MMA. Fortunately, there are alternatives and, most likely, the tools referenced here are already being used by your network and security staff today. A couple of widely adopted tools that allow the inspection and analysis of network traffic are as follows:

- Wireshark: `https://www.wireshark.org/`
- Telerik Fiddler: `https://www.telerik.com/fiddler`

In this section, we reviewed some of the basic Windows Network Security implementations for Windows 10, Windows Server, and Hyper-V. We also resurfaced the topic of baselining for network-specific hardening within your environment. Next, we will move on and look at advanced network security features within Windows that fall within the Windows Defender technology feature set. Some of the items that will be covered include configuring a firewall rule with Group Policy, Windows Defender Exploit Guard Network Protection, and how to configure Windows Defender Exploit Guard Network Protection using Group Policy.

Windows Defender Firewall and Advanced Security

Windows 10 Firewall is a software-based firewall that's enabled out of the box and used to allow or block connections to your PC. To view the basic firewall settings, including their statuses, open **Windows Security** from the **Settings** app and select **Firewall & Network Protection**. There are local security settings you can change from here, including configurations specific to each network profile, such as blocking incoming connections, allowing an app through the firewall, and restoring the default firewall settings.

The three network profile types in Windows Firewall are **domain**, **private**, and **guest/public**, as follows:

- **Domain Profile** settings are defined by the domain profile and are set systemically using Group Policy or from network devices located on the corporate network. Local policy settings are typically overwritten if they're managed systemically.
- **Private Profile** is used for home network or **small office home networks** (**SOHOs**) where a domain controller may not be present. A private profile can be configured by a local security policy and by default, incoming connections to apps are blocked if they are not on the list of allowed apps.

> **Tip**
> If an app is blocked, you can view the event log or firewall log for more details. Event ID 5031 in **Windows Logs/Security** will show you if the firewall blocked an incoming connection from an application.

- **Public Profile** is used for guest or public networks. Network discovery is turned off by default in Windows 10 for this profile, which blocks file and print sharing. Incoming connections are set identical to the private profile where apps are blocked that are not on the list of allowed apps.

Clicking on **Advanced Settings** and elevating user account control with an administrative account will open **Windows Defender Firewall with Advanced Security**. With Advanced Security, you can control inbound rules, outbound rules, and connection security rules. Here, you have complete control over all packets, both ingress and egress. The inbound/outbound rules can specify specific ports, programs, or use custom settings that may include a combination of ports, programs, and physical network adapters. Windows Defender Firewall already comes configured with a set of predefined rules. These rules cannot be directly modified, but they can be enabled or disabled.

> **Tip**
> A green checkbox next to the rule name means that it is enforced. If many modifications are needed in addition to the predefined rules, this is a good use case for you to build them into your hardened image.

A connection security rule is used to define the conditions in which a connection can connect to another system. An example of a connection security rule would be to specify a required method of authentication needed to establish a connection. If the source and destination systems in the scope of the connection security rule do not meet the conditions, then the connection is denied. Connection security rules can be defined to require and/or request authentication, both inbound and outbound, and include settings for common authentication methods such as using certificates or Kerberos and NTLMv2 for computer and user authentication.

> **Important note**
> An important difference between firewall rules and connection security rules is that, simply put, firewall rules are used to allow or deny traffic.

Connection security rules are used to secure the communications between the source and destination using IPsec and define the authentication conditions. Typically, advanced connection security rules are managed through third-party devices or software and are managed systemically.

The last part of this Windows Defender Firewall with Advanced Security overview that's worth mentioning is the monitoring section. Within the monitoring pane is a high-level overview of the status of each of the network profiles. It also has helpful links so that you can view active firewall rules, active connection security rules, security associations, and logging settings.

Typically, Windows Defender does a good job of allowing applications through the firewall that are known and trusted. In some scenarios, such as with a home-grown custom line of business app, you may need to push a firewall rule to allow the app. This can be easily accomplished using Group Policy. Let's look at how to use Group Policy to configure a line of business app through Windows Firewall.

Configuring a firewall rule with Group Policy

Let's assume there is a line of business app called `BusinessApp.exe` that runs under the *C:\Program Files (x86)\MyLOBApp* path and we need to allow inbound/outbound connections over the domain profile only. This will ensure that connectivity will work only while connected to the corporate network. Follow these steps to allow the app through the firewall with Group Policy:

1. Open the **Group Policy Management** snap-in from your management workstation and create a new GPO linked to an OU that contains the computer systems you wish to target.

2. Give it a friendly name such as `Windows Defender Firewall - Connection Rules`, right-click it, and choose **Edit**.

3. Navigate to **Computer Configuration** > **Policies** > **Windows Settings** > **Security Settings** > **Windows Firewall with Advanced Security**, expand it, and then expand it again.

4. Right-click **Inbound Rules** and choose **New Rule** to open **New Inbound Rule Wizard**.

5. Select **Program**, click **Next**, and select the radio button next to **This program path**.

6. Enter the path of the executable file for the custom LOB app from the install directory; for example, `%ProgramFiles% (x86)\MyLOBApp\BusinessApp.exe`. Click **Next**.

7. Select **Allow the connection on Action** menu.

8. Select the domain profile only and click **Next**.

9. Give it a friendly name such as `Allow BusinessApp` and click **Finish**.

10. Repeat the same process, but for **Outbound Rules**.

The following screenshot shows the applications allowed in the **Inbound Rules** of Windows Defender Firewall after a Group Policy refresh:

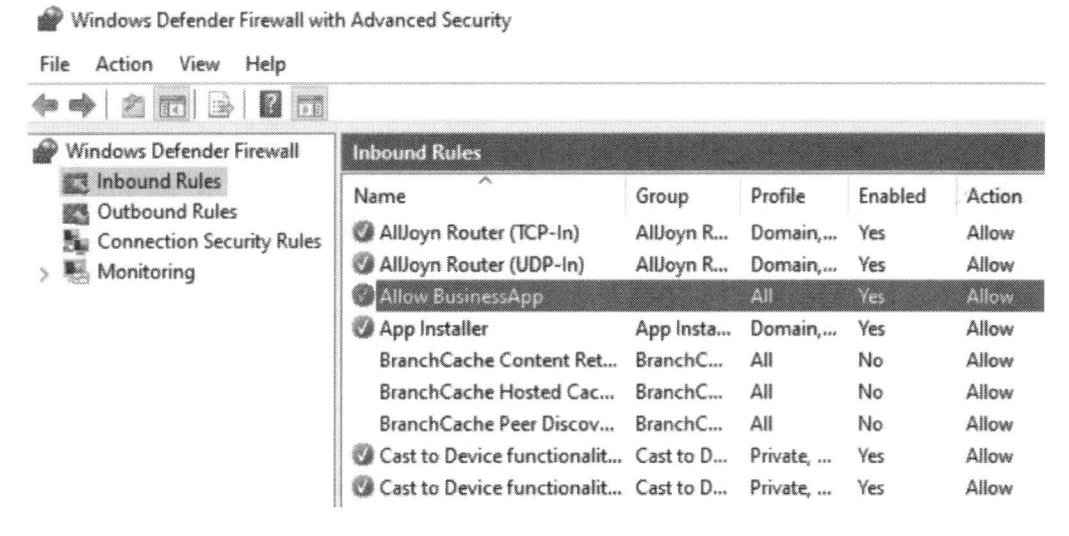

Figure 6.8 – Inbound Rules in Windows Defender Firewall with Advanced Security

> **Tip**
> Configuring firewall rules through Group Policy does not support environmental variables used to resolve the context of the current user. This can cause some challenges if non-administrative users are being prompted to allow an app through the firewall that is running from the `%APPDATA%` or `%USERPROFILE%` locations.

Windows Defender Firewall rules can also be configured using an Intune Device Configuration profile. Choose the **Endpoint protection** profile type for Windows 10 and later:

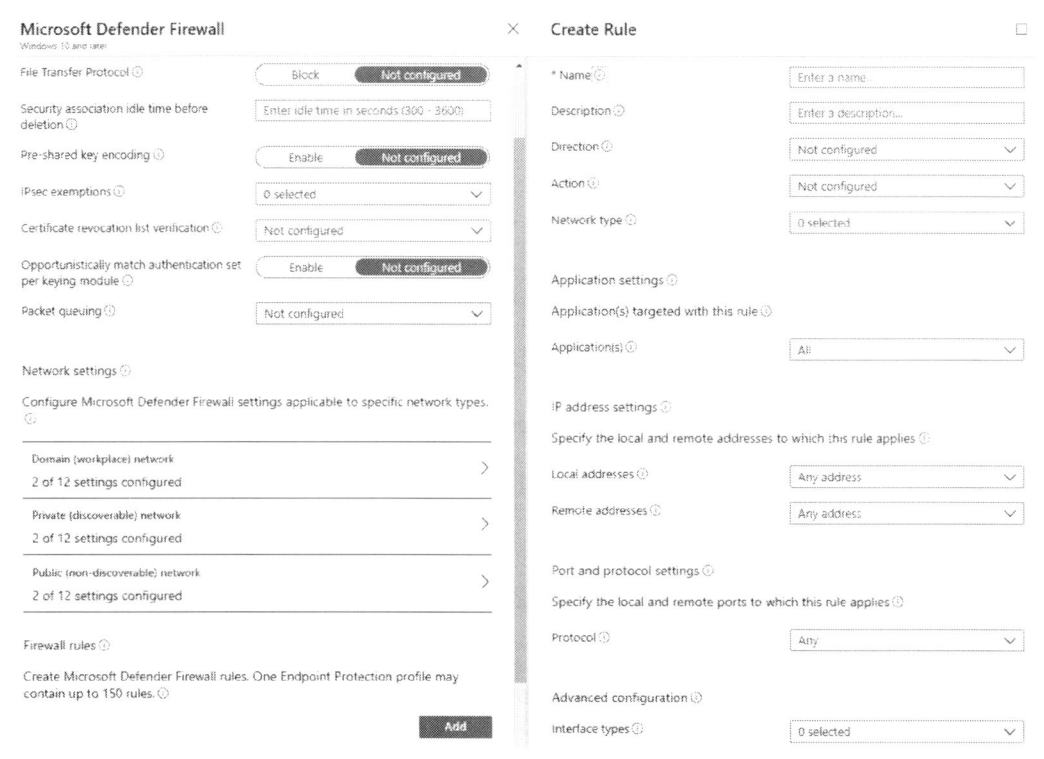

Figure 6.9 – Microsoft Defender Firewall device configuration profile in Intune

Next, we'll look at Windows Defender Exploit Guard Network Protection and how to configure it with Group Policy.

Windows Defender Exploit Guard Network Protection

Network Protection is a security feature that can be enabled through the Exploit Guard functionality of Windows Defender. Network Protection helps to reduce attacks such as phishing, social engineering, and malicious browser redirects. Its protection covers all major browsers, including Microsoft Edge, Google Chrome, and Mozilla Firefox. If you're a Microsoft Defender Advanced Threat Protection customer, Network Protection sends telemetry data to the ATP service for advanced investigation. At a high level, the feature works by protecting your PC from known low-reputation IP and URL sources by blocking the outbound connections. When a connection is blocked, a toast notification from the Action Center informs the user of the blocked connection and allows customizable actions such as a phone number for IT support or adding an email button.

The list of IPs and URLs used for revocation are maintained by Microsoft's threat intelligence service. Network Protection is a great feature for small- or medium-sized businesses or those looking to get away from third-party proxy services and the administration required to maintain a network with them.

> **Tip**
> If Network Protection is alerting you of false positives, Microsoft recommends opening a support case so that their threat team can investigate.

In the following screenshot, **Kusto Query Language** (**KQL**) is being used to query the Windows Defender ATP logs for Exploit Guard Network Protection events:

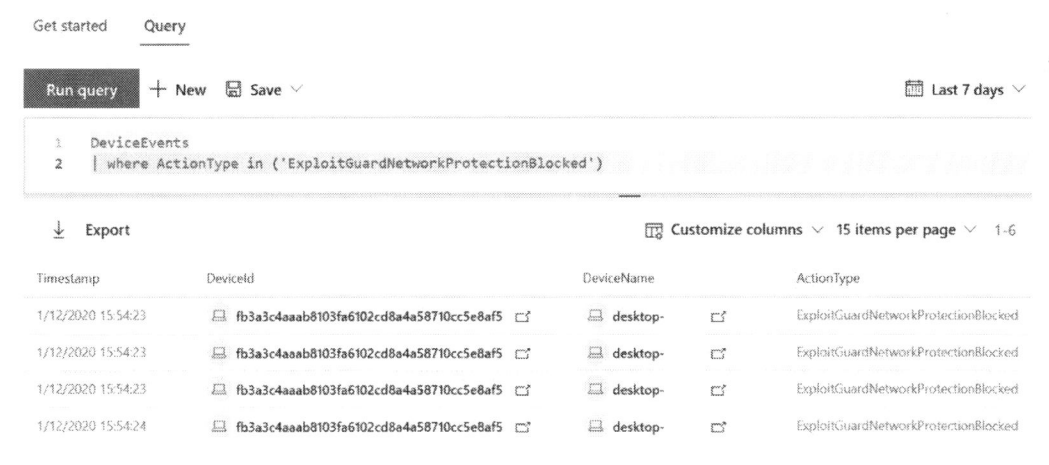

Figure 6.10 – An advanced hunting Kusto query in the Microsoft Defender ATP portal to show blocked actions for the Network Protection feature

For the user to be alerted about a blocked connection, their notifications must be enabled. In addition to toast notifications, a badge is also visible after the fact in the Action Center. Some of the customizations available include options to set the company's name, contact phone number, website, and skype ID.

When a blocked connection is detected, the action is logged and sent to the Microsoft Defender ATP portal or can be viewed by creating a custom view locally in Event Viewer as seen in the following screenshot:

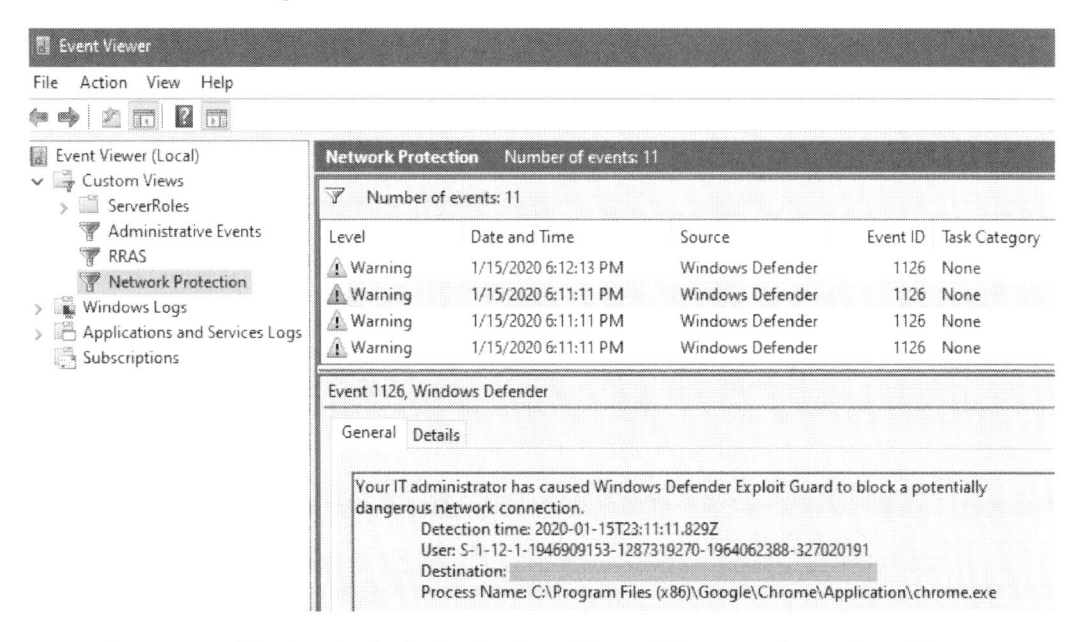

Figure 6.11 – Windows Defender Exploit Guard Network Protection logs in Event Viewer

For information about how to create a custom view using XML for Network Protection, visit this link:

`https://docs.microsoft.com/en-us/windows/security/threat-protection/microsoft-defender-atp/event-views`.

To enable Network Protection through Group Policy, you will need the Exploit Guard ADMX and ADML files. For information about managing a central store and the latest downloads for administrative templates, visit this link: `https://support.microsoft.com/en-us/help/3087759/how-to-create-and-manage-the-central-store-for-group-policy-administra`.

Configuring Windows Defender Exploit Guard Network Protection using Group Policy

In this section, we will configure Network Protection so that we can block connections and customize the toast notifications presented to users when they visit a low-reputation IP or URL. To complete this exercise, the Exploit Guard ADMX and ADML files must be imported into `C:\Windows\PolicyDefinitions` or to your Group Policy central store. Follow these steps to enable Network Protection using Group Policy:

1. Open the **Group Policy Management** snap-in console from a management workstation and create a new GPO linked to an OU that contains the computer systems you wish to target.

2. Give it a friendly name such as `Windows Defender Exploit Guard - Network Protection`, right-click it, and choose **Edit**.

3. Navigate to **Computer Configuration > Policies > Administrative Templates > Windows Components > Windows Defender Antivirus > Windows Defender Exploit Guard > Network Protection**.

4. Open the **Prevent users and apps from accessing dangerous websites** policy setting and set it to **Enabled**.

5. To set the customized toast notifications, go to **Computer Configuration > Policies > Administrative Templates > Windows Components > Windows Security > Enterprise Customization**.

6. Choose **Configure Customized Notifications** and set it to **Enabled**.

7. Choose **Configure customized contact information** and set it to **Enabled**.

8. Open **Specify contact company name** and set it to **Enabled** and enter a company name.

9. Choose **Specify contact phone number or Skype ID** and set it to **Enabled**. Enter the phone number of your support line.

10. Choose **Specify contact website** and set it to **Enabled**. Enter your IT or support website.

As shown in the following screenshot, the Windows toast notification displays a blocked connection warning with the customized branding, as specified in the GPO:

Figure 6.12 – Windows Security notification for a blocked connection

> **Tip**
> If a user suppresses notifications, they will not receive any notice that a connection has been blocked. Network Protection can be deployed in **Audit** mode if you wish to evaluate this behavior before enabling the feature.

In the previous sections, we covered Windows Defender Firewall with Advanced Security, including how to create custom inbound/outbound rules using Group Policy. We looked at the device configuration profile in Intune, as well setting Defender Firewall for MDM enrolled devices. Next, we enabled a feature of Windows Defender Exploit Guard known as Network Protection, which is used to help protect end users from low-reputation IPs and URLs. In the next few sections, we'll shift focus and discuss Azure cloud solutions that can be used to provide network security to your Windows virtual machine endpoints in Azure.

Introducing Azure network security

When protecting your Windows resources in Azure, there are a few types of cloud offerings that can be used to filter activity and ensure only trusted and legitimate traffic can reach your virtual machines. Foundationally speaking, Azure networking consists of a virtual network containing an address space. Just like traditional networking concepts, the virtual network or "VNET" can then further be divided into segments called subnets, where resources such as Windows virtual machines are assigned to a designated space. Azure resources inside the same VNET are typically allowed to communicate with each other. Resources are also to able communicate with other PaaS services outside of the VNET, such as Azure App Service or Azure Cosmos DB, using service endpoints. With a feature known as VNET peering, other VNETs can be connected and allow cross-VNET communication. Using a combination of **user-defined routing** (UDR), **network security groups** (NSG), Azure firewalls, and **network virtual appliances** (NVA) allows you to ensure that communications are locked down to allow only the necessary traffic to reach resources in your VNET.

> **Tip**
> When creating a new VNET, outbound connectivity to the internet is allowed by default.

In this section, we are going to focus on network security access control using a feature known as **Network Security Groups** (NSGs).

Network Security Groups (NSGs)

An NSG is an Azure resource that acts as a stateful firewall for evaluating inbound and outbound traffic. It is used to allow or deny traffic through a set of weighted security rules that are evaluated based on a priority integer value. A stateful firewall in Azure uses a five-tuple hash value to determine whether the traffic is based on source, destination, IP, ports, or protocols and then evaluates it against the inbound/outbound NSG security rules. NSG resources can be associated with subnets or virtual network interfaces. As a best practice, it is recommended that NSGs are applied at the subnet level over direct assignment to a network interface. This helps minimize the amount of NSGs for simplification purposes. A security rule inside an NSG has the following properties:

- **Name**, which is used to identify it; for example, *AllowRDP*.
- **Priority** between 100 and 4,096, which is used as the weight during evaluation.
- **Source or Destination**. This can be *ANY*, an individual IP, a range specified in CIDR notation, or a service tag.

- **Protocol** support for TCP, UDP, ICMP, or *Any*.
- **Direction** (inbound or outbound).
- **Port range**.
- **Action**, such as *allow* or *deny*.

> Tip
> When assigning a priority, it is recommended to assign them in intervals of 50 or 100 to ensure there is plenty of space to insert rules in the future.

Service tags

The destination value for a security rule can also be an Azure service tag. Service tags are available to help simplify the creation and maintenance of security rules instead of manually specifying and maintaining IP ranges for common connection points such as the internet. This is helpful when defining rules for connections to the internet or to an Azure service such as an Azure load balancer. Microsoft will maintain the connection information for these services. Examples of service tags in Azure include values such as **VirtualNetwork**, **Storage**, **SQL**, or **Internet**. The full list of available virtual network service tags can be found at this link:

`https://docs.microsoft.com/en-us/azure/virtual-network/service-tags-overview`.

> Tip
> Security rules can also be augmented security rules that contain a comma-separated list of IP ranges in CIDR notation instead of you having to create separate rules for each IP block.

Introducing Azure network security   213

The following screenshot shows the NSG inbound security rules. You can see the service tags depicted as **Internet** and **VirtualNetwork** in the **Source** and **Destination** sections:

Home > Network security groups > NSG-Identity-Prod

NSG-Identity-Prod
Network security group

→ Move   🗑 Delete   ↻ Refresh

Resource group (change) : RG-Identity-Prod   Custom security rules : 2 inbound, 0 outbound
Location   : East US 2   Associated with   : 1 subnets, 0 network interfaces
Subscription (change)   : Windows Security and Hardening
Subscription ID   : 8c24c8a   a30
Tags (change)   : Click here to add tags

Inbound security rules

Priority	Name	Port	Protocol	Source	Destination	Action
1001	⚠ IBA_RDP_3389	3389	TCP	Internet	VirtualNetwork	⊘ Allow
1050	IBA_RDP_65001	65001	TCP	Internet	VirtualNetwork	⊘ Allow
65000	AllowVnetInBound	Any	Any	VirtualNetwork	VirtualNetwork	⊘ Allow
65001	AllowAzureLoadBalancerInBound	Any	Any	AzureLoadBalancer	Any	⊘ Allow
65500	DenyAllInBound	Any	Any	Any	Any	⊗ Deny

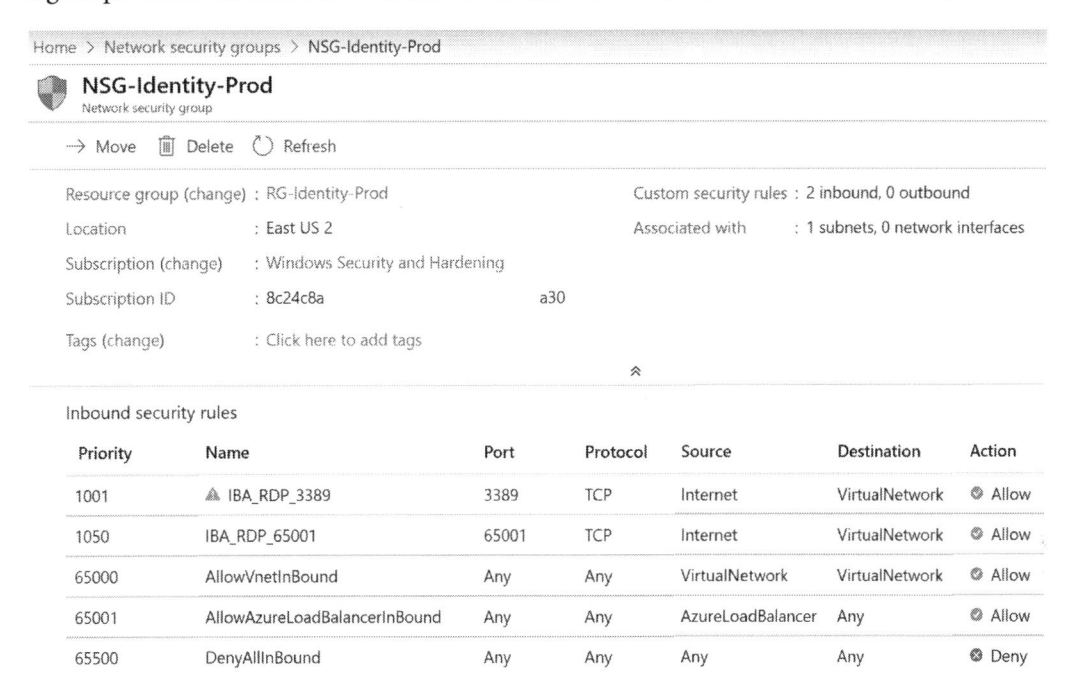

Figure 6.13 – NSG inbound security rules in Azure

Application Security Groups (ASGs)

ASGs are an additional enhancement for simplifying NSG rules as they allow you to create your own groups or 'service tags' of applications that can be specified inside a security rule, similar to a service tag. For example, let's say you have a few shared backend app servers and DB servers. As the business requirements evolve, there may be a need to leverage these resources to service other business functions that are housed in different subnets. By grouping these resources together and creating an ASG, you can specify the source as this grouping in the NSG rule and you don't have to granularly define each component moving forward.

Creating a network security group in Azure

One common method when deploying new infrastructure to Azure is to leverage a jump box server as a part of the management plane over other resources. Although we strongly recommend against using a jump box for an extended period, we want to demonstrate how to create an NSG rule on the jump box subnet to allow RDP traffic over the internet using a non-common port. Using a non-common port will help deter malicious actors actively looking for connections listening on `3389` (RDP) over the internet.

This demo assumes the following has already been configured:

- A resource group, Azure VNET, and a subnet
- A Windows virtual machine with a public IP

We are going to create a new NSG and define two new inbound security rules. One will use `3389` to allow modifications to be made to the VM resources using the default RDP port, while the other will allow port TCP `65001` over the internet to accommodate connections after the port change. We will then create an inbound firewall rule for TCP port `65001` in Defender Firewall on the virtual machine host and change the listening port for RDP through the registry. Let's get started:

1. Log into the Azure portal at `https://portal.azure.com`.
2. Search for `Network Security Groups` and select it.
3. Click **Add** or **Create network security group** if none have been created.
4. Choose the subscription and then select the resource group that contains your Windows virtual machine. Give it a friendly name such as `NSG-Identity-Prod`. In our example, we are creating an NSG for a subnet that contains domain controllers.
5. Select the region that your subnet resides in and choose **Review + Create**. Then, select **Create** after the validation passes. Go to the resource after the deployment completes.

NSGs have predefined security rules out of the box and cannot be deleted. Their priority is specifically set high and they allow plenty of space for custom security rules to be defined with lower integer values. The maximum integer for a custom defined security rule is 4096.

1. Click on **Inbound security rules** under **Settings**.
2. Click **Add** to create a new inbound rule with the following settings:

    Source: Service Tag

    Source service tag: Internet

    Source port ranges: *

    Destination: VirtualNetwork

    Destination port ranges: 3389

    Protocol: TCP

    Action: Allow

    Priority: 1001

    Name: IBA_RDP_3389

3. Click **Add** to create the rule.
4. Repeat these steps to create the inbound allow rule for the custom TCP port 65001, but with the following changes:

    Destination port ranges: 65001.

    Priority: 1050.

    Name: IBA_RDP_65001. This is short for inbound allow, remote desktop protocol, and port number 65001.

5. Click **Add** to create the second rule.

Notice the warning symbol in the following screenshot next to the inbound allow rule for `3389`. Azure does a good job of warning you that a common port is open to the internet:

Inbound security rules

Priority	Name	Port	Protocol	Source	Destination	Action
1001	⚠ IBA_RDP_3389	3389	TCP	Internet	VirtualNetwork	Allow
1050	IBA_RDP_65001	65001	TCP	Internet	VirtualNetwork	Allow
65000	AllowVnetInBound	Any	Any	VirtualNetwork	VirtualNetwork	Allow
65001	AllowAzureLoadBalancerInBound	Any	Any	AzureLoadBalancer	Any	Allow
65500	DenyAllInBound	Any	Any	Any	Any	Deny

Figure 6.14 – Inbound security rules inside an NSG in Azure

Now, let's associate the NSG with a subnet:

1. Click on **Subnets** in **Settings**.
2. Choose **Associate**, select a Virtual network from the dropdown, and select the subnet that contains your Windows VMs. Click **OK**.

Now that we have created the NSG rules and associated them with a subnet, we can remote into the Windows VM and modify the settings to change the RDP listening ports to `65001`. Follow these steps to do so:

1. Find the VM by searching for it by name in the Azure portal. On the **Overview** tab, click **Connect** to download the RDP file and connect over public IP with the default RDP port of `3389`.
2. Log into the VM using the administrative account you used when creating the virtual machine to load the desktop.
3. Once at the desktop, search for `Windows Defender Firewall with Advanced Security` to open the advanced menu. Click on **Inbound Rules**.
4. Click **New Rule** and create a new inbound rule.
5. Select **Port** as the rule type to create and click **Next**. Select **TCP** and enter `65001` in the box to specify **Specific local ports** and click **Next**.
6. Keep the default of **Allow the connection** selected and click **Next**.
7. Keep all three profiles selected and click **Next**.
8. Give the rule a friendly name such as `Remote Desktop - IBA 65001` and click **Finish**.

9. Open the registry editor (regedit), go to the *HKEY_LOCAL_MACHINE\System\CurrentControlSet\Control\Terminal Server\WinStations\RDP-Tcp* registry subkey, and look for the DWORD **PortNumber**.

10. Open the DWORD **PortNumber**, choose **Decimal**, and modify the port number so that it states 65001. Click **OK**.

11. Restart the virtual machine.

12. Validate that the port number change worked by connecting to the VM with RDP by specifying the IP and port; for example, 40.70.223.4:65001.

When clicking **Connect** from the virtual machine **Overview** page, be sure to change the port number to 65001 to reference the custom port we configured. The following screenshot shows the **Connect to virtual machine** menu that appears after clicking **Connect**:

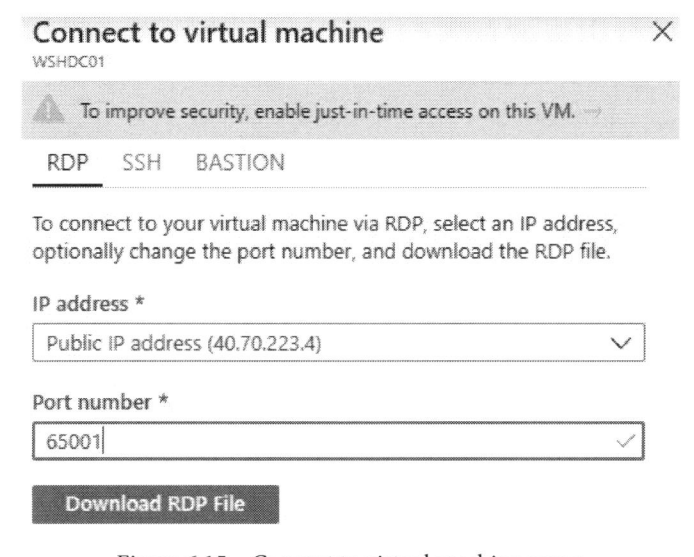

Figure 6.15 – Connect to virtual machine menu

To recap, we just created a new NSG with two inbound rules to allow TCP ports 3389 and 65001 to accommodate RDP traffic. Then, we modified the default RDP listening port on the virtual machine host to TCP 65001 and created a new inbound allow firewall rule in Windows Defender Firewall to allow TCP 65001.

Summary

In this chapter, we started by looking at network security fundamentals and covered the OSI and TCP/IP models, reviewed common ports and protocols, and looked at the important technologies needed to help with network security. Next, we covered Windows network security, which started with network baselining for your Windows devices. This section then covered the Windows 10 network management pane before moving on to securing WLAN/Wi-Fi, Bluetooth, and VPN, including Microsoft's Always On VPN. The following section covered the Windows Server **network management** pane, including LAN and Ethernet best practices for your servers, and provided an overview of the server roles and features. The final sections overviewed Hyper-V networking and security before finishing off with network troubleshooting tools.

Following Windows network security, we covered Windows Defender Firewall and Advanced Security, which provided steps you can follow to configure your firewalls with Group Policy; a detailed overview of Windows Defender Exploit Guard Network Protection; and how to configure Windows Defender Exploit Guard Network Protection. The final topic of this chapter was Azure network security solutions for Windows VMs. Here, we covered NSGs, ASGs, and steps on how to create a network security group in Azure.

In the next chapter, we will review identity and access management and its importance in Windows management. We will look at account and access management and review many of the components involved in the life cycle of accounts and the types of access needed. Then, we will review authentication technologies and provide recommendations on how you should be using these authentication protocols in today's world. We will finish with a review of conditional access and identity protection.

7
Identity and Access Management

In this chapter, we will be reviewing identity and access management in depth, as well as their importance within an enterprise today. With the shift to a decentralized user environment and everything moving to the cloud, identity has become extremely critical and the need to protect our user identities has never been more important. Since users can now access their corporate information from anywhere over the internet, a simple breach of their identity could allow an intruder to log in and access the user's information and any data they have access to within the environment. Because of this, we need to revisit the traditional method of using a username and password and add enhanced protection to our identity and access model, which will be covered in more detail in this chapter.

In today's world, the use of passwords is becoming obsolete. Because of ongoing major breaches and the advancement of technology, our passwords have most likely already been breached and are sitting on the dark web for sale. In addition, there is a chance that the password you use has either been re-used on other accounts or there is some small variation in the re-used password. What does this mean? Essentially, someone with your password will be able to start accessing all your accounts if there is no additional security added. We are already seeing user accounts within services that haven't been breached being hacked because hackers are reusing usernames and passwords from other services to try and gain access. This type of attack is known as credential stuffing and, unfortunately, it is working!

In this chapter, we will provide an overview of identity and access management and all the components required to build a robust program. We will then cover account and access management, followed by authentication and **Multi-Factor Authentication** (**MFA**), and discuss what is next with authentication by considering a passwordless world. The end goal of your authentication strategy? To get to a passwordless world! We will finish off the chapter with some extremely powerful Microsoft cloud technologies to better protect your identities—Conditional Access and Identity Protection.

This chapter will include the following topics:

- Identity and access management overview
- Implementing account and access management
- Understanding authentication, MFA, and going passwordless
- Using Conditional Access and Identity Protection

Technical requirements

In this chapter, we will refer to identity management solutions, such as **Microsoft Identity Manager** (**MIM**). We will also provide overviews of different access and identity management services within Azure, and they require varying levels of licenses and requirements. It is encouraged that you research the specific licensing requirements for each solution independently if they fit your needs. At a minimum, you can follow along with the referenced solutions using the following:

- An Azure **Active Directory** (**AD**) tenant with subscription owner and global administrator rights: `https://portal.azure.com/`
- Azure AD Premium P2: `https://azure.microsoft.com/en-us/pricing/details/active-directory/`
- An Azure Security Center standard subscription: `https://azure.microsoft.com/en-us/pricing/details/security-center/`

Now, let's look at an overview of identity and access management.

Identity and access management overview

Identity and access management has never been as important as it is today. Identity can be somewhat considered as the foundation for security within your organization. Although there are other methods of compromising data, simply gaining access to a user or administrative account can be destructive. If an intruder compromises an account, they now acquire the same account level of access across all systems and data. All this can take place without anyone being alerted. It is very important that you are rigid with your identity and access policies. The role of **least-privilege** is a must! This is a role where no access is added to your account until needed based on your job function. We cover this in more detail in the *Authorization* section of this chapter. Essentially, if you don't need access, you don't get it. In addition, ensuring that you separate user accounts from administrative accounts is critical. There should never be elevated or privileged permissions added to your regular user accounts where general day-to-day tasks are performed. As already stated, passwords have become obsolete and do not provide the level of security needed today. You need to start implementing MFA as soon as possible, along with more modern technologies to protect your users and your organization's data.

Let's look at the foundation or framework of what comprises a solid identity and access management program. If you have studied for your CISSP certification, or some other security-related exam, you will be familiar with the term **Identification, Authentication, Authorization, and Accountability (IAAA)** or just **Authentication, Authorization, and Accountability (AAA)**. (Here, we will use IAAA to emphasize identity as the first component of the process because, without an identity, the proceeding components cannot exist.)

Identity

The identity portion for your access relates to something that identifies who you are. In simple terms, it is a unique identifier that you enter to let the system know it is you who is trying to access it. A simple example could be a username, an email address, or an employee ID number. Traditionally, within a Windows environment, you may be familiar with sAMAccountName, which was essentially a username that only worked within your corporate network. Using this outside your corporate network was not possible as there was no unique identifying factor that accompanied the username on places such as the internet. Today, you will need to adopt the **userPrincipalName** (**UPN**) method for your identity in order to support internet- and cloud-based technologies. The UPN appends a domain that you own to the end of your username to provide a unique identity no matter where you are and how you access it. An example of a UPN identity could be user@windowssecurityandhardening.com.

Authentication

After you have entered your identity, you will typically be presented with some form of authentication to validate that you are the person who should be gaining access to the system. The most common form of this is entering a password. As part of authentication, there are four different methods to authenticate your identity that are worth mentioning:

- **Type 1** is something you know. This is currently the most common and widely adopted method of authentication. Some examples include a password, PIN, or passphrase.

  > **Tip**
  > An example of a password could be `W!nd0ws10`, while a similar passphrase could be `W!nd0ws $ecure 10`. Typically, passphrases can contain spaces, are longer, and are easier to remember than a password.

- **Type 2** is something you have. This authentication method consists of something you have with you in order to confirm it is you. Some examples include a hard token, a soft token on your phone, or a smart card. With Microsoft, the Authenticator app is an example of this.

- **Type 3** is something that you are. This authentication method is commonly known as biometrics or something physical that is used to authenticate you. Some examples of something that you are include your fingerprints and facial or iris scans. On Microsoft, Windows Hello falls under this category of authentication.

- **Type 4** is location-based. This authentication method may not be as commonly used but can be extremely powerful with the advancement of cloud compute and AI technologies. Authenticating based on location allows you to authenticate users based on a defined geolocation. Think of a company that only conducts business within the United States. Why would they expect anyone to access their servers from outside the United States? Anyone accessing them from outside the United States can be expected to be an intruder and should be blocked. On Microsoft, Conditional Access can provide this level of authentication.

Next, let's look at authorizing your identity against the system to gain access to data.

Authorization

Once you have been authenticated into your environment or system, you will need to access the data or systems you have been authorized to access. Authorization is a method in which permissions have been added to your identity to allow access to some information or a system. Just because you have been authenticated, it doesn't mean you are authorized to access data or a system. This is where the principle of **least-privilege** comes into play and as a best practice, there should be no authorization added to a new identity by default. Authorization isn't an easy task, especially as an organization grows. Ensuring that someone only has access to what they are authorized to do can be a full-time role, especially ensuring that the authorization is updated and removed as roles change. To better help with authorization, you need to ensure you have a well-defined access model in place and tools such as identity management, AD for centralized user and group management, and most importantly, **Role-Based Access Control** (**RBAC**) to define your users' authorization based on their job functions.

Now that the identity has been authenticated and authorized to your system, let's look at what accountability is in terms of the actions and data accessed inside an environment.

Accountability

The last function is known as accountability, also referred to as accounting. This is the function that allows us to ensure that an identity or user is not abusing their rights or the authorization provided. Here, we need to ensure that we track all the activities of our users and ensure auditing is in place to hold anyone accountable for any misuse of their identity and access. This is also a critical process as part of any investigative and forensic work that is carried out for attempted breaches or compromised accounts. Knowing exactly where an account has been authenticated and what data it has accessed must be captured and audited for historical purposes.

As you can see, the full scope of an identity and access management program will take great effort and time to implement correctly. With the identity of your users being at the forefront and essentially serving as the key to your data and systems, organizations must implement a well-rounded and robust identity and access management program. As we discussed earlier in this book, ensure your policies and standards have leadership support to ensure your program is effective.

> **Tip**
> As a start, to assist with password management practices, it is highly recommended that you provide a form of a password manager to your users. It is also recommended that you educate your users about identity protection services. There are many services available and you can view the service as insurance coverage for your identity. It is worth the investment!

To finish off this section, we wanted to remind you of the importance of physical access security. We also touched on this in *Chapter 3, Server Infrastructure Management,* in the *Physical and user access security* section. Ensuring that an intruder can't easily walk into your site is not only critical to your data, but also to the safety of your employees. Nothing is more important than human safety! Referring back to the NIST cybersecurity framework, there is a specific category and subcategory to ensure you implement the minimum recommended guidelines for physical security, as shown:

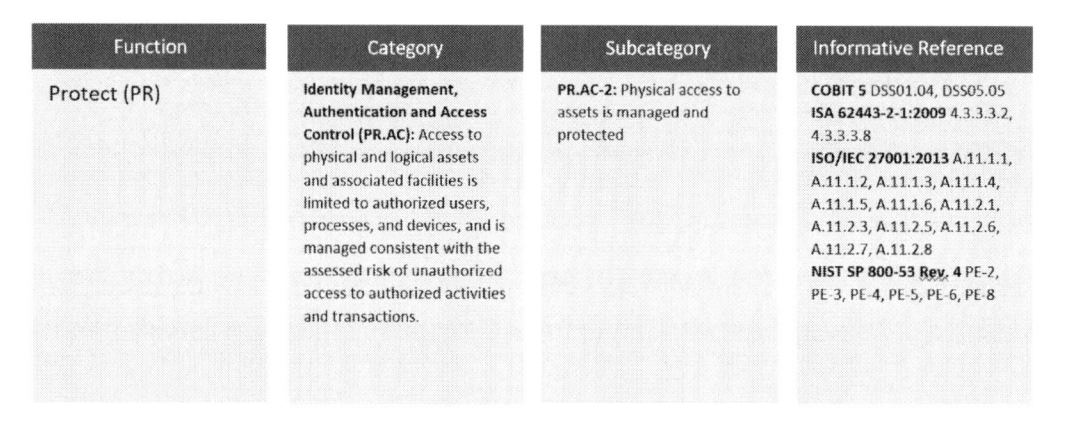

Function	Category	Subcategory	Informative Reference
Protect (PR)	**Identity Management, Authentication and Access Control (PR.AC):** Access to physical and logical assets and associated facilities is limited to authorized users, processes, and devices, and is managed consistent with the assessed risk of unauthorized access to authorized activities and transactions.	**PR.AC-2:** Physical access to assets is managed and protected	**COBIT 5** DSS01.04, DSS05.05 **ISA 62443-2-1:2009** 4.3.3.3.2, 4.3.3.3.8 **ISO/IEC 27001:2013** A.11.1.1, A.11.1.2, A.11.1.3, A.11.1.4, A.11.1.5, A.11.1.6, A.11.2.1, A.11.2.3, A.11.2.5, A.11.2.6, A.11.2.7, A.11.2.8 **NIST SP 800-53 Rev. 4** PE-2, PE-3, PE-4, PE-5, PE-6, PE-8

Figure 7.1 – The NIST cybersecurity framework's physical access to assets guidelines

The following link gives you access to *NIST Special Publication 800-53 (Rev. 4)*, referenced in the preceding figure:

https://nvd.nist.gov/800-53/Rev4/family/Physical%20and%20Environmental%20Protection

Next, we will review account and access management and what is involved in the identity management life cycle.

Implementing account and access management

One of the most important tasks with your identity and access management program is the management of accounts and the access they have. There is a whole life cycle process that relates to account and access management and may involve multiple teams to make the process a success. There's also a chance that multiple systems and tools are involved in the life cycle, including manual human processes that have room for error and increase vulnerability due to poor housekeeping. The account and access management life cycle is a complex process and has only become more challenging with the ongoing expansion of more apps, as well as the shift to the cloud. A typical account and access management program may involve resources from HR, the identity and security teams, technical operations teams, hiring managers, and potentially others.

To ensure success with your account and management program, it is critical that you have well-defined policies in place that enforce the correct standards and procedures that must be followed. This process is critical as part of this life cycle. Any mismanagement of this process could result in significant damage to your organization. Some examples of this include applying incorrect permissions to a user account, not disabling a disgruntled employee's account who was dismissed, or not managing and auditing your privileged accounts, to name a few. One item to help with any mismanagement or even manual errors is to implement automation. The more you can automate, the fewer errors will occur. There will always be a need for manual processes, whether it be the initial input of user data, physical validation that the information is correct, or applying an end date to a user, but the more you can reduce any manual intervention, the less error-prone it will be.

Every organization is structured differently, but for the most part, you will likely have accounts categorized by **Full-Time Employee** (FTE), contractor, vendor, guest, or service accounts. For each of these categories, you will need separate policies and procedures for their management. Your FTE accounts will most likely be managed differently to your contractor accounts, as well as your vendor and guest accounts. Ensuring all these accounts are managed correctly will require the ongoing management and auditing of your accounts and their access. This will require close collaboration between HR, the identity and security teams, and the hiring or reporting managers of these accounts. In the next few subsections, we will cover the following topics:

- HR and identity management
- Integrating directory services
- Using local administrative accounts
- Managing Azure external user access (**Business-to-Business (B2B)**)

- Understanding the Azure cloud administrative roles
- Implementing privileged access management security tools
- Using Azure RBAC

> **Tip**
> Never use shared accounts within your environment. All users who access your environment should have an account assigned that identifies them. Without an assigned identity, you have no accountability.

Let's look at a typical account and access life cycle scenario that starts with HR as the source of authority for the identity.

HR and identity management

Your identity management life cycle needs to start somewhere, and that is most likely with your HR department. This is where your employees start their journey within your organization. Once an employee has accepted a position, their digital profile is created. HR software is very specialized and is typically independent of the core IT identity services. Within an HR system, you can expect to manage your personal information, time off, payroll, performance, employees you manage, and learning, as well as view internal job opportunities, and much more. The big challenge with your HR system is efficiently integrating the application into your core identity services.

> **Tip**
> There are many HR platforms available on the market today. Microsoft also has a product for an HR management suite known as Dynamics 365 Human Resources. Other products you may be familiar with include SAP SuccessFactors, Workday, and Oracle PeopleSoft.

When you look at your core identity services, you are most likely going to have an AD deployment in your on-premise environment that's even synchronized to Azure AD if you have already begun your cloud journey. One of the challenges of AD within a traditional deployment is the limitation on delivering a well-rounded identity service beyond the basics. Having the ability for employees to request contractor accounts, manage their own AD groups, update members and profile information, use a self-service portal, and provide advanced ID management and full life cycle management of identities and automation are not native features of AD. Because of this, there is a need for an identity management solution to sit between your HR source and AD to provide the required efficiency.

From a Microsoft standpoint, this solution is known as MIM, which is the latest edition of **Forefront Identity Manager** (**FIM**). MIM is an extremely powerful management tool and serves as a critical component of the overall identity life cycle and supports your organization's identity and access processes. MIM deployments can be highly complex depending on the level of customizations needed. To learn more about MIM and its capabilities, visit `https://docs.microsoft.com/en-us/microsoft-identity-manager/microsoft-identity-manager-2016`.

> **Tip**
> Ensure you have set up secure automated integration from your HR system into your identity management system. In addition, your HR system will contain **Personal Identifiable Information** (**PII**), so it is critical that you work closely with the HR team to ensure the data is correctly secured and encrypted any time it leaves the HR system.

As cloud adoption strengthens, an ideal scenario would be to directly integrate your HR system with a cloud identity provider, such as Azure AD. Unfortunately, many organizations have compliance requirements to keep identities and passwords on-premises and many applications still rely on AD for authentication and as the identity provider. Because of this, a hybrid deployment from on-premises to the cloud is commonly seen within your identity architecture.

Next, we will review the available Microsoft directory service technology to support your identity life cycle.

Integrating directory services

Beyond an HR system with integration into your identity management solution or MIM is **AD**. AD is an on-premise hierarchical directory that stores objects, such as user accounts, passwords, user information, computer objects, security groups, and much more. This is where the identity of your users will be active and enabled for accessing the IT systems within your environment.

Referring back to the overall identity life cycle, once an object has been established in MIM, based on the HR feed, it will then provision an account in AD for the user. The MIM object isn't the account that the user will use but is typically set up as the authoritative source to the AD object. What this means is if the MIM object is set to be termed because the HR system sent a term instruction, the AD object will be disabled. Depending on your configuration, re-enabling the account directly within AD will eventually revert it to a disabled state since MIM is authoritative. This is extremely powerful and exactly how the process should work. It also helps prevent anyone with access to AD from creating and enabling accounts that they shouldn't. All requests should filter through MIM, or other identity management tools, for better control and accountability as they serve as the centralized place for all identity and access requests.

> **Tip**
> Protecting your active identities is critical and AD needs to be at the core of this protection. The following is Microsoft's best practices for securing AD: `https://docs.microsoft.com/en-us/windows-server/identity/ad-ds/plan/security-best-practices/best-practices-for-securing-active-directory`

With a shift to the cloud, a copy of these identities needs to be synchronized to Azure AD to support the identity and authentication requirements of the modern world. To support this, a synchronization tool is needed between your on-premises AD environment and the cloud identity provider or Azure AD. This will enable the hybrid identity of your organization. Microsoft has a tool known as Azure AD Connect that provides synchronization for all or any selected objects or **Organizational Units** (**OUs**) from your AD into Azure AD. With Azure AD Connect, you can provide a single identity for your user to access both on-premises resources as well as cloud-based resources.

One important decision to make around Azure AD Connect is the method of authentication for your users to sign in. Since Azure AD only syncs a copy of your identity, you need to determine how to manage your passwords within the cloud. Azure AD Connect provides the option to sync the hash (known as password hash sync), pass-through authentication back to on-premises to authenticate, or leverage federated authentication, such as **Active Directory Federation Services** (**AD FS**) or a supported third-party system. In order to take advantage of Microsoft's advanced cloud security identity features, you will need to enable password hash sync.

> **Tip**
> Microsoft does not sync the actual passwords of your user accounts. For optimal security of your user passwords, a hash of the password with a per-user salt is synced to Azure AD.

Azure AD is Microsoft's enterprise cloud identity provider, providing the next generation of identity management and security for your users. Some examples of services that a user will log into using their Azure AD account are Exchange Online, OneDrive for Business, and so on. The user will not know the difference between the traditional AD account versus the Azure AD account. This is optimal for the user experience.

In its simplest form, this completes the life cycle of a user's identity from the system of record up to the cloud. The life cycle provided can be applied using any identity service or vendor and the following workflow should be referenced for the life cycle and process of your identities:

HR > Identity management system > Traditional directory service > Identity synchronization > Modern directory services

It's also critical to ensure the off-boarding process works correctly throughout this life cycle. If properly configured, when HR initiates a termination, the account should be disabled throughout all directories. Any failures in this process could allow a user to access resources after they have left the organization, which is a serious security concern.

> **Tip**
> Make sure you are fully aware of synchronization times within each of your identity systems. Terminating a user within HR can take time to synchronize downstream through your systems. For immediate action, you may need to manually intervene to ensure identities are correctly disabled in a timely fashion.

In addition to your identity life cycle is your group management strategy. Ensure you constantly audit group memberships and understand what services, applications, and data your users have access to. Ensure users don't have access to groups that they shouldn't and as users change roles, it is critical they are removed from groups that they no longer need access to. Group management must be part of your identity life cycle and the correct processes and procedures are critical to ensure they are managed correctly.

The following diagram illustrates a high-level architecture of what your identity life cycle may look like:

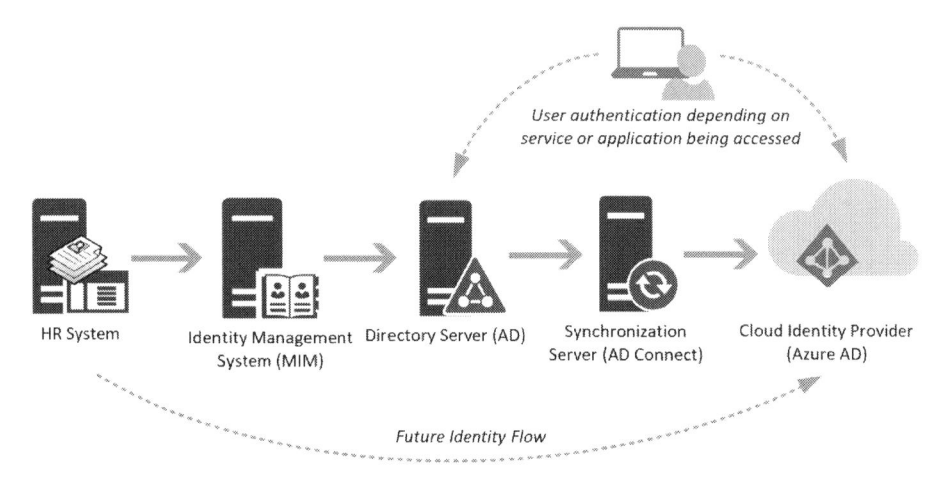

Figure 7.2 – The identity life cycle architecture example

The account life cycle can be very complex, and mismanagement of this process can easily open up opportunities for vulnerabilities with your Windows devices. Some best practices with this architecture include working closely with your HR team, ensuring all traffic, feeds, and integrations are encrypted, minimizing the number of privileged identities, and enforcing MFA on all accounts. Be sure to enable auditing to hold accountability and add safeguards to ensure the identity portal is secure and not accessible over the internet if possible.

Next, let's look at local administrative accounts and how to reduce the vulnerabilities associated with them.

Using local administrative accounts

There are a few different schools of thought when it comes to local administrator accounts on devices. One is simply not to allow them and is the obvious, more secure choice. Any means of elevated access should be managed by either AD group membership or through Azure AD roles. These accounts should also have strict password requirements, managed with a **Privileged Access Management** (**PAM**) solution, and should not be local to the device. On the other hand, there may be legitimate reasons as to why these local accounts exist. Perhaps the help desk leverages these accounts to remotely install an application. They may exist as a failsafe if systems don't frequently connect to a domain controller and are prone to trust relationship errors. They can even be useful in a scenario where an Azure AD-joined device is un-joined and there is no account available to log in locally.

Another common scenario where local administrators exist is when users claim they need this access to perform their job functions. While this may prove true in some scenarios, this is not generally the case. Many times, the user just doesn't want to be inconvenienced if they need to install an app or run some process that requires a call to the support desk. To combat this, many organizations incorporate a form of approval for temporary admin access. This can be accomplished either through temporary security group membership in AD or through a software center package with a scheduled task to remove them after a specified amount of time. In our experience, unless the user absolutely must have administrative rights and is willing to get documented approval from their supervisor, we advise against doing this. In addition, we recommend that if a user must have a local administrative account, it should be a separate account to their regular identity, have stricter password requirements, and be managed by IT, where access can be revoked or the password changed at any time. Imagine two common attack scenarios.

In *scenario one*, the user unknowingly downloads a macro-enabled Excel spreadsheet that invokes a PowerShell command. The command enumerates all local users and mapped drives, can now run processes in the user's context, and attempts to install a keylogging application. If the user's normal identity has local administrative access, then the malicious macro inherits these permissions and can complete the installation. Now, the keylogging application sends keystrokes and all harvested data back to a remote server in another country.

In *scenario two*, the user requests a unique local admin account but sets an identical password. A malicious actor has infiltrated the network and uses a technique known as **Link-Local Multicast Name Resolution Poisoning** (**LLMNRP**) with NetBIOS name service spoofing to trick a response to the computer. As a result, the user's system is redirected to fake services that wait for mistyped network shares or system addresses that do not resolve in the local host's file or DNS. The credentials and the user's hash are then harvested by displaying a fake password prompt to what looks to be a legitimate login page. Now, using the recovered credentials, the actor can enumerate other accounts on the system and, through trial and error, attempt to crack the local admin account or gain other access using credential stuffing. Even worse, if this system is connected to the domain, they can further query the domain controller and enumerate users, systems, and groups and continue to further move laterally.

These are just two common examples. The following are a few recommendations to better manage local admin accounts:

- For domain-joined systems, implement a system known as a **Local Admin Password Solution** (**LAPS**) to rotate local administrative account passwords if they must exist. For more information, including a link to download the LAPS solution, visit `https://www.microsoft.com/en-us/download/details.aspx?id=46899`.

- Use a PAM solution from reviewed vendors, such as Thycotic or BeyondTrust, to manage the local administrative accounts on your workstations. These vendors offer robust solutions, can manage multiple account types, and have reporting and auditing functionalities built into them.

- If you are using Windows Autopilot, set the user account type to **standard** in the Autopilot profile. This will allow the user to enroll a device onto Azure AD and Intune but remain a standard user.

- For Azure AD-joined devices, leverage the additional local administrators on the Azure AD-joined devices setting in **Device Settings**, also known as **the Device Administrators** Azure AD role.

> **Tip**
> Using the **Device Administrators** Azure AD role is a convenient way to add accounts as local administrators, but be mindful that this will make them an administrator for all Azure AD-joined devices.

Next, let's look at external or guest accounts, which are commonly referred to as B2B.

Managing Azure external user access (B2B)

Azure AD B2B is a game-changer within the enterprise identity space. When looking back at the traditional model with AD and on-premises applications, providing access to external partners was far from an easy task. For most, setting up an identity within their local directory server was probably standard practice. This meant needing to create and manage the life cycle of external accounts within your environment, far from a secure model. Others may have set up AD FS or third-party federation applications to support the ability to allow the external party to use their own ID. The issue with this is the involvement, complexity, and effort to set up the federation between external vendors. The more external vendors you work with, the more integrations you will need to set up and systems to manage.

Azure AD B2B allows you to simply invite an external or guest user into your Azure environment and provide them access to your applications and services. Once invited into your organization, the external user then authenticates with their current work identity and password to access approved applications. There is no need to provision new accounts or add any additional infrastructure to support collaboration with your external users. The best part of this process is the user's identity is managed and maintained by their hosting organization, which is a significant improvement over past models. Once the external user is termed within their hosting environment, they can no longer access your environment. From a security and auditing perspective, this is a major advantage.

You can learn more about Azure AD B2B from `https://docs.microsoft.com/en-us/azure/active-directory/b2b/what-is-b2b`.

To view and access the external user settings, log into `https://portal.azure.com`, click on the portal menu at the top left, and choose **Azure Active Directory**. Select **User Settings** and click on **Manage external collaboration settings**. Here, you can configure the external collaboration settings. The settings in the following screenshot are a good place to start to secure your external collaboration settings:

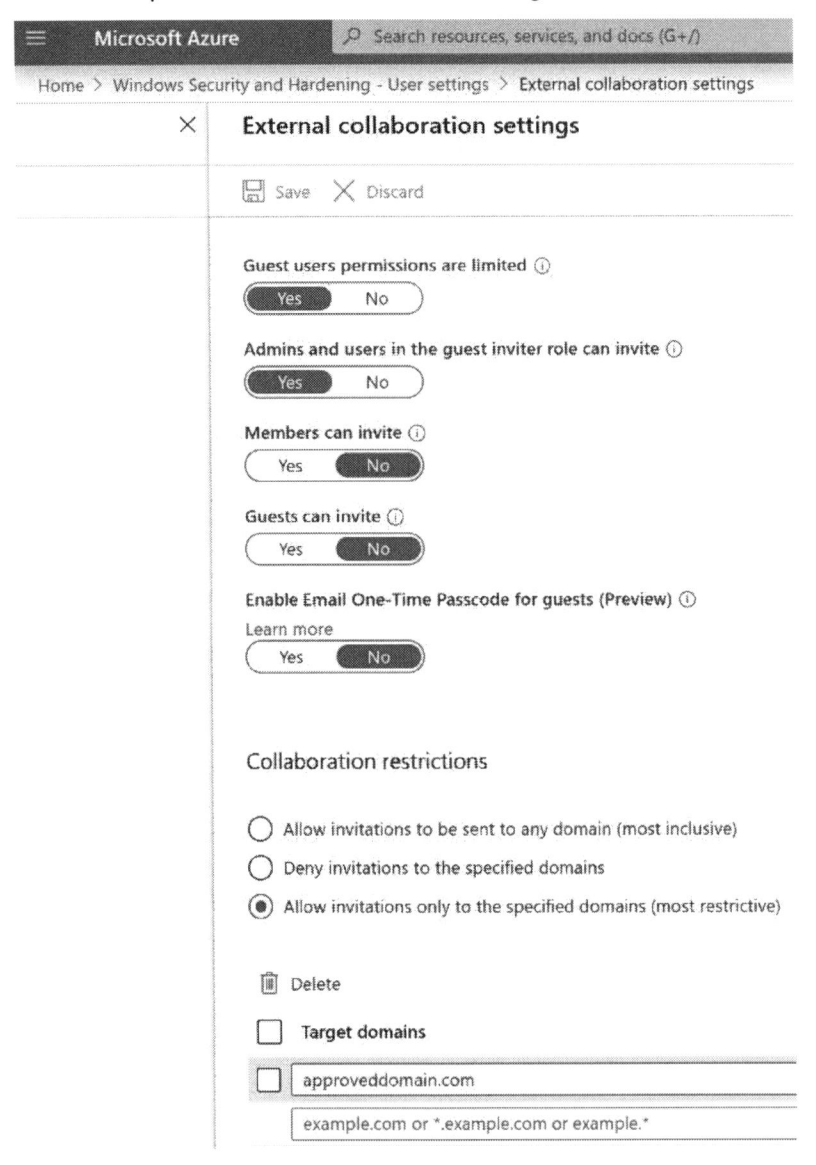

Figure 7.3 – The Azure AD external user settings

To invite a new external user into your organization, go back to the Azure AD management screen and click on **Users**, then click on **New Guest User**. You will be asked to provide information, such as **Name**, **Email address**, **First name**, **Last name**, **Personal message**, **Groups**, **Roles**, **Usage location**, **Job title**, and **Department**. By default, the user will not have access to anything other than the Office 365 portal. Once this information is entered, click on **Invite**.

The external user will receive a welcome email, as in the following screenshot, to accept the invitation and gain access to your environment using their business email:

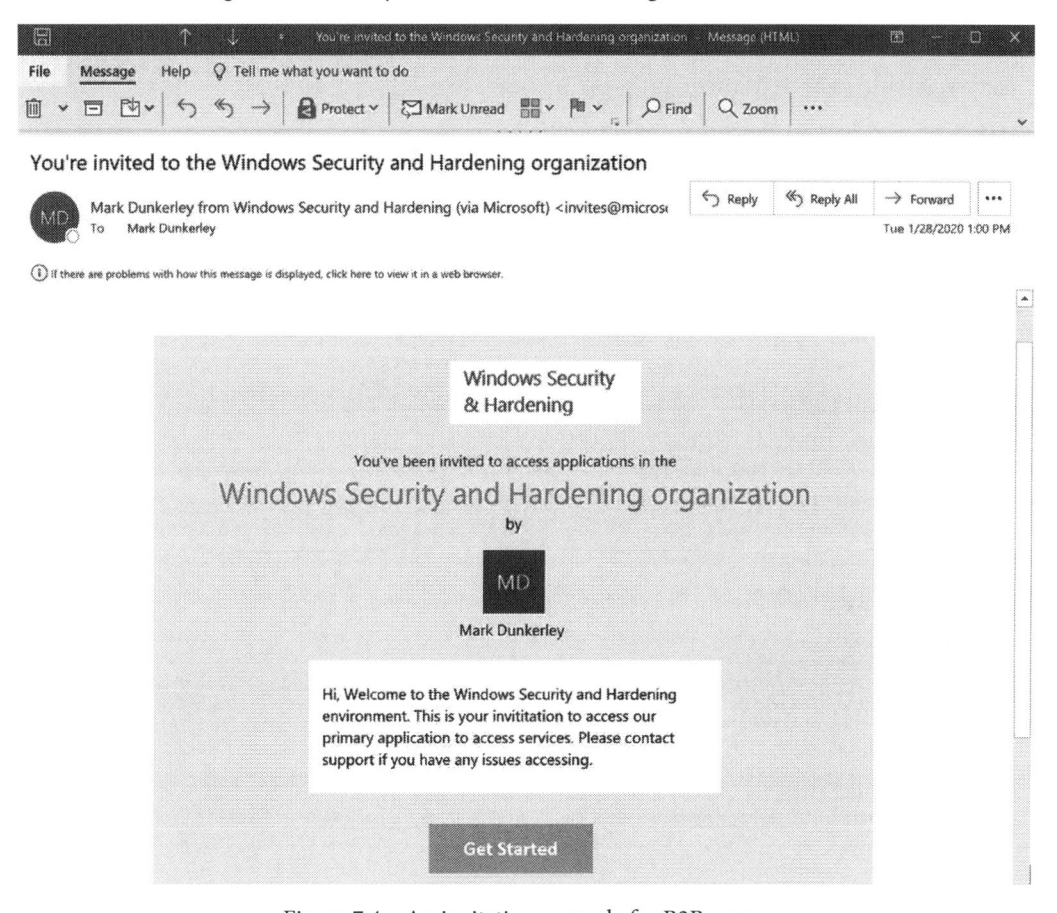

Figure 7.4 – An invitation example for B2B access

Microsoft has both B2B and B2C as part of its guest access services. You can visit https://docs.microsoft.com/en-us/azure/active-directory/b2b/compare-with-b2c to view the differences.

The Azure AD B2B model is extremely powerful and allows you to move away from old methods of needing to provision accounts within your environment. The model is very simple and, from a security and auditing perspective, is a step in the right direction.

> **Tip**
> To enforce additional security on your external and guest users, use a conditional access policy to enforce MFA.

Next, let's discuss the different types of administrative roles available on the Azure cloud. It's important to cover these roles as they directly relate to your Windows systems due to their control over the management plane in which Windows is administered.

Understanding the Azure cloud administrative roles

Administrative role permissions are worth discussing as they can have a direct impact on your Windows workstations and servers that run in the cloud. An example of this is that an Office administrative role may have permission to add or remove licenses. If an Intune license is removed, then the user will be kicked out of Intune management. Another example could be an Intune administrator that can perform actions such as adding or removing apps and configurations, as well as accidentally initiating remote actions, such as wiping or deleting a device. It is important that these permissions are only assigned as needed and limited. There are many types of cloud-based administrative roles that serve different purposes, and although they are named similarly, they can perform different types of actions. Let's break them down into a few categories, which include the following:

- The Office 365 admin and Azure AD roles
- Intune roles
- Security and compliance admins

Let's look at these different types of admin roles.

The Office 365 admin and Azure AD roles

These administrative roles are mainly available to be assigned in the **Microsoft 365 (M365)** admin center and are commonly used to assign permissions that administer many of the SaaS offerings from Microsoft, such as SharePoint or Teams. Most of the M365 admin roles will overlap with the Azure AD roles and an assignment in either portal will be honored. Some examples of Office 365 admin roles include the following:

- SharePoint admin
- Exchange admin
- Teams admin
- PowerBI admin

> **Tip**
> The M365 admin center has a useful feature called **Compare Roles**. Select up to three roles to compare their permissions.

The following screenshot shows the **Compare roles** page:

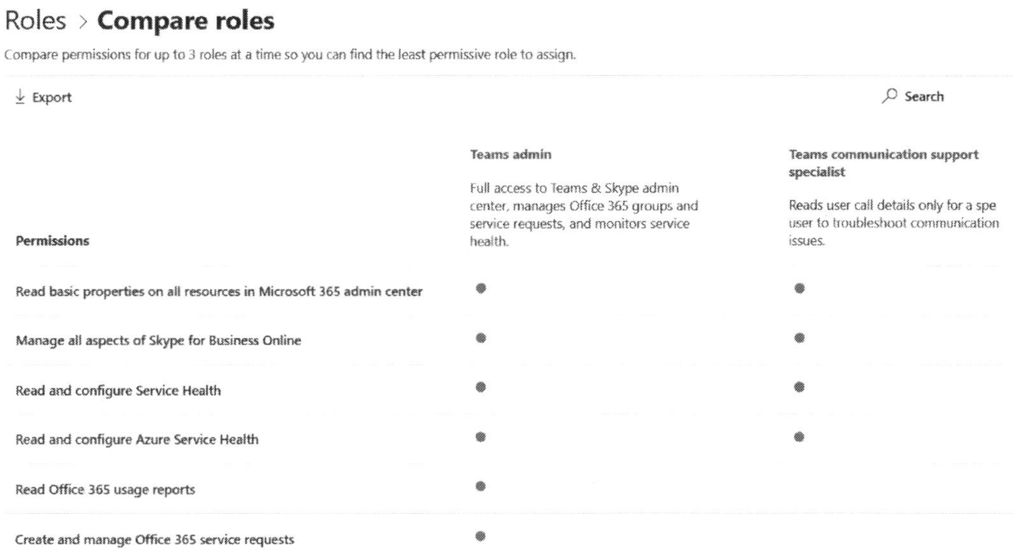

Permissions	Teams admin Full access to Teams & Skype admin center, manages Office 365 groups and service requests, and monitors service health.	Teams communication support specialist Reads user call details only for a spe user to troubleshoot communication issues.
Read basic properties on all resources in Microsoft 365 admin center	●	●
Manage all aspects of Skype for Business Online	●	●
Read and configure Service Health	●	●
Read and configure Azure Service Health	●	●
Read Office 365 usage reports	●	
Create and manage Office 365 service requests	●	

Figure 7.5 – The M365 admin center Compare roles page

Like Office 365 admin roles, the Azure AD roles are used to grant access to Azure AD and other Microsoft services. They also contain additional roles specific to managing Azure AD directories and B2C identities.

Next, let's look at the roles that are specific to managing aspects of the Intune service.

Using Intune roles

You can use Intune roles to limit access to specific functions inside Intune and to create custom roles. Intune administrator is the only built-in role available to M365 and Azure AD roles and grants full administrative access. Use the Microsoft Endpoint Manager admin center to granularly assign permissions using the built-in roles. The following screenshot shows some of the built-in roles available for assignment:

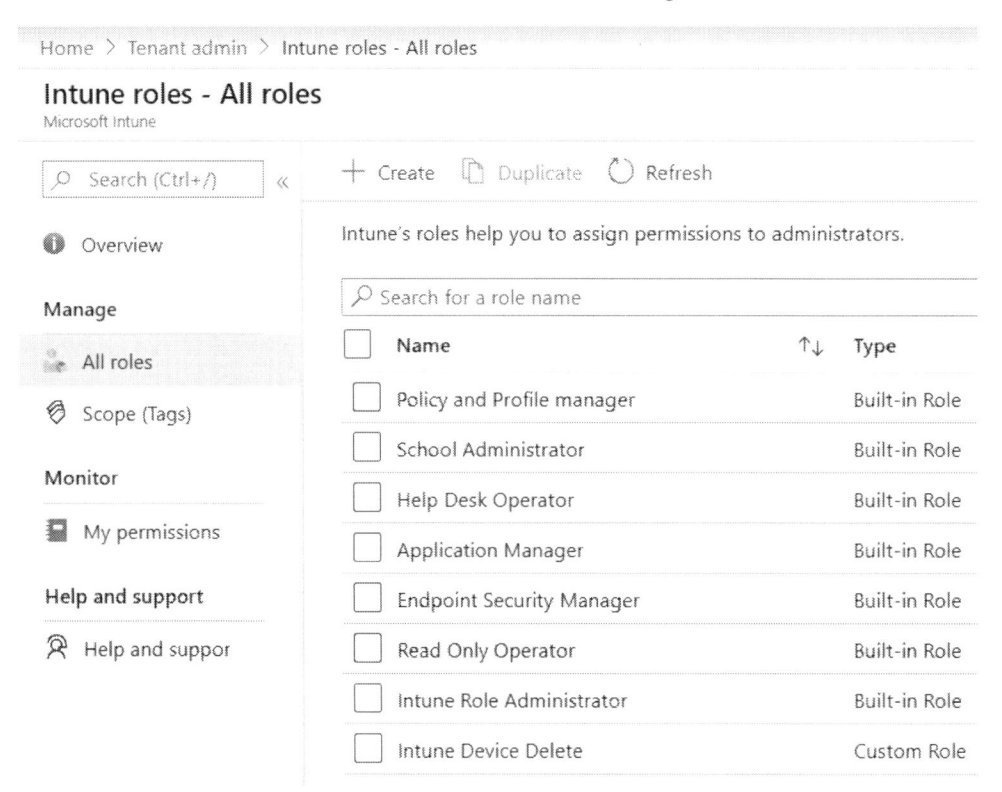

Figure 7.6 – Intune roles within the Microsoft Endpoint Manager admin center

Next, let's look at the **Security & Compliance** administrative roles.

Security and compliance admins

The security and compliance admin roles contain permissions that are specific to compliance and document forensic tasks, such as data loss prevention, litigation holds, and eDiscovery. While they don't have a direct impact on Windows systems and subsystems, admins with these assigned roles can view classified documents, OneDrive files, email content, and where these files move to. These types of permissions are often exploited for corporate espionage. The following screenshot shows the security and compliance roles:

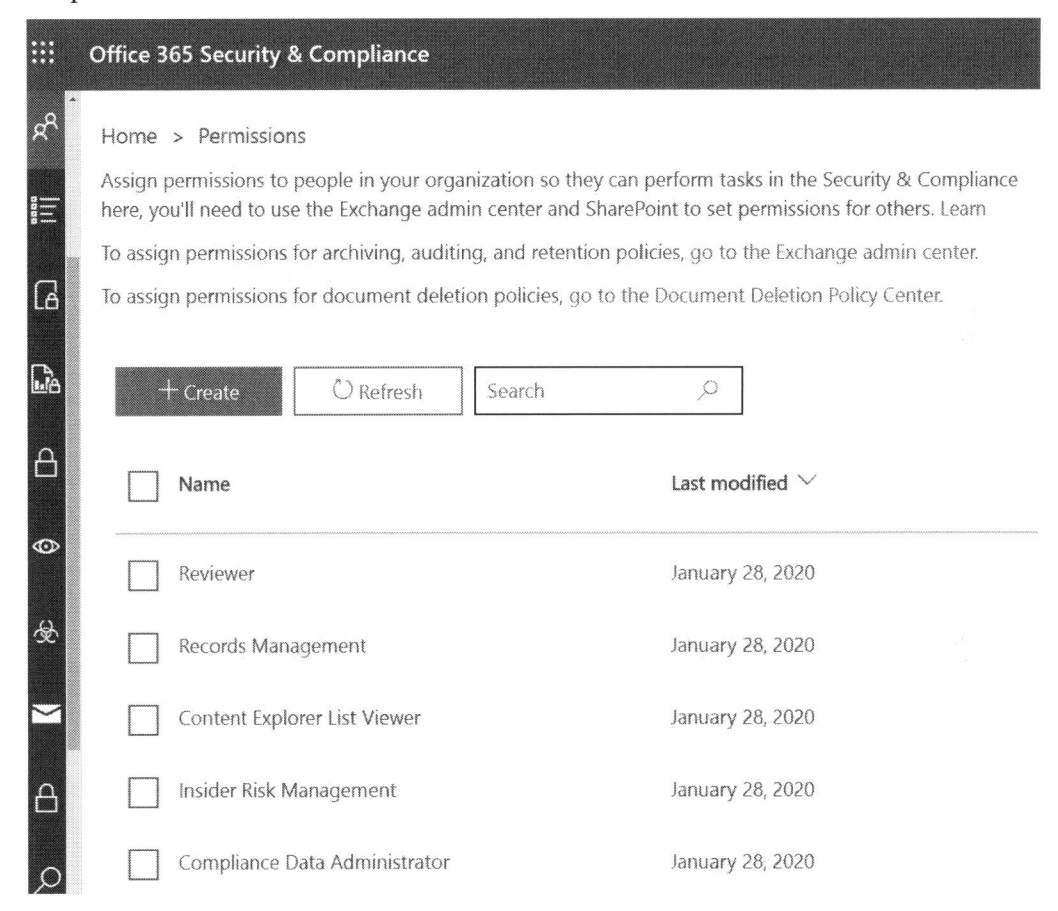

Figure 7.7 – The Office 365 security and compliance roles

Now that we have identified different types of privileged roles, including Office 365 and Azure AD admin roles, let's look at how you can protect access to your Windows systems using PAM and other identity management tools.

Implementing PAM security tools (PAM, PIM, and JIT)

When referencing the topic of privileged access security in terms of securing access to a Windows server, we can think of it as the action of accessing a server with an account or service with elevated rights. This account can be used interactively with remote desktops with tools such as PowerShell, or as a service account leveraged to run an underlying system service or scheduled task. We would not want anybody to have access to use these accounts or even apply elevated permissions to a user account granting rights to perform highly privileged actions on systems in the environment. Let's look at three ways to secure access using PAM, **Privileged Identity Management** (PIM), and **Just-In-Time** (JIT) solutions.

Using PAM

A PAM solution can be critical in helping organizations secure access to systems, meet compliance, and monitor the privileged accounts used in their environment. Privileged access can be defined when an administrator or account accesses a sensitive system and, therefore, directly exposes it to a higher risk of attack due to the ability to perform privileged actions. With an ever-growing threat landscape and a seemingly unlimited amount of attack vectors, implementing a PAM solution can provide a huge benefit in strengthening your company's security posture. PAM also helps organizations maintain compliance and avoid penalties from compliance violations if access is regularly audited. By implementing a PAM solution coupled with a JIT request approval process, the risk of compromise is greatly reduced. The core principle of JIT access uses a workflow approval process that provides temporary access or grants escalated permissions when needed. It helps eliminate the need for free-standing privileged accounts. A free-standing account always exists in the environment, whether it is actively in use or not, and can make great attack targets for malicious actors.

When choosing a PAM solution, look for the following core sets of features:

- Account discovery for all systems, devices, and applications, which includes, but is not limited to, Windows, Linux, Unix, Cisco devices, and other networking equipment
- The ability to manage local accounts and service accounts and restart services when needed to minimize the impact
- Credential management capabilities, including password rotation, a workflow approval process, and auditing trails
- Password rotation for stale passwords of free-standing (always-existing) privileged accounts

- The ability to provide access to systems using tools, such as web password fillers and **Remote Desktop Protocol (RDP) Secure Shell (SSH)** launchers, that never expose credentials
- Discovery alert rules to notify the security team if new backdoor accounts were created without approval
- Automation workflows for privileged execution using scripted tasks
- Monitoring and auditing capabilities through remote session recording, command logging, and analytics
- The capability to link to an **IT Service Management (ITSM)** tool or change management process
- SIEM integration for leveraging **Security Operations Center (SOC)** services
- Third-party access leveraging **Single Sign-On (SSO)** and MFA

SaaS solutions are becoming a popular option in the PAM space. Depending on your use case for PAM, a SaaS solution can offer a lighter footprint and eliminate the need to deploy extensive infrastructure

Next, let's enhance the PAM solution and look at JIT access.

Connecting with JIT access

JIT access is used to provide an account with the permissions needed to perform its operations for a limited time and then remove unnecessary access after the time expires. While PAM is a means to control access to accounts, JIT adds an additional layer to help mitigate any risks from "free-standing" or always-available accounts. Typically, access is granted through an approval process with a set of policies that defines who can request the defined role. With this, JIT helps enforce the principle of least-privilege. Many PAM vendors have a JIT solution built into their product, these days. Azure offers two solutions that have a similar feature set, as described previously, called Azure PIM and Azure Security Center JIT access. Azure JIT is available through Azure Security. Azure JIT provides JIT access by policing the inbound traffic ports used for the remote management of your virtual machines by a set of rules enforced through network security groups. By using an approval workflow through Azure Security Center, when access is granted, the locked-down ports are opened.

> **Tip**
>
> *Chapter 6, Network Fundamentals for Hardening Windows*, includes a walkthrough to configure Azure Security Center JIT access, but further reading can also be found at `https://docs.microsoft.com/en-us/azure/security-center/security-center-just-in-time`.

While Azure Security Center JIT access protects access through network rules, let's look at Azure PIM to provide temporary access to admin roles through eligibility.

Enabling admins with Azure AD PIM

Azure PIM is a service that allows you to control access to resources and services in Azure at the identity level. Let's consider an example of the VP of sales for a company to explain "privileged" identity. This VP may be considered high profile, but in the context of PIM, it's unlikely that they have any elevated access permissions to IT services and resources. A service desk employee, on the other hand, who may be an offshore resource or an hourly based employee, may have been over-provisioned and assigned a contributor role to your subscription at some point to perform a function. They may also have local administrator rights to Azure devices and/or server operator group membership in AD.

This service desk employee's account would be considered a privileged identity. Not only is the principle of least-privilege thrown out the window in this example, waiting for regular auditing of account permissions to flag this account as a high risk to remove privileges could occur too late, and your organization might be at risk if this account is compromised. Implementing Azure PIM helps balance these security risks while still allowing your employees to perform their duties safely. In fact, a key benefit of PIM is detecting which users are assigned privileged roles as a built-in auditing capability. PIM is built around the concept of eligibility by leveraging "eligible" admins as opposed to permanent admins. A permanent admin is a user who always has the privileges needed to perform their required actions. An eligible admin is a role that requires a user to activate their eligibility when they need to perform an elevated function. As far as permissions are concerned, both a permanent and an eligible admin can have the same rights, but the eligible admin doesn't need these permissions all the time.

For more information on the Azure PIM service, go to `https://docs.microsoft.com/en-us/azure/active-directory/privileged-identity-management/pim-configure`.

Implementing account and access management   243

In the following example, we are going to set up an eligible admin in Azure PIM for the Intune administrator Azure AD role. We will require justification and a ticket number reference and we will need to specify a maximum time that the role can be active for. Then, we need approval to activate it.

Azure AD Premium P2 is required to use and manage Azure PIM:

`https://docs.microsoft.com/en-us/azure/active-directory/privileged-identity-management/pim-getting-started`

Take the following steps to enable Azure PIM:

1. Log in to the Azure portal at `https://portal.azure.com`.
2. Search for **Azure AD Privileged Identity Management** and select it.
3. Select **Azure AD Roles** from the **Manage** section.
4. Select **Settings** under **Manage**.
5. First, we will modify the Intune service administrator role. Select **Roles**, and then find and select **Intune Service Administrator**.
6. Change the maximum activation duration (in hours) to 2. Enable **Notifications**, **Incident/Request ticket**, and **Require Approval**.
7. Scroll down and click on **Select approvers** and choose your account or an approver. Choosing at least two approvers is recommended.
8. Click **Save**.

> **Tip**
> **Enable Multi-Factor authentication** is grayed out for this role, but some roles require it to be enabled. Make sure you check the other role settings and enable MFA when requesting activation.

9. Now, let's make a user an eligible admin for this role. Click on **Azure AD Roles – Settings** in the breadcrumb navigation to go backward. Select **Members** under **Manage**.
10. Click on **Add Member**.
11. Choose **Select a role**, select **Intune Service Administrator**, and click on **Select**.
12. Choose **Select members** and find an eligible user, then click on **Select**.
13. Click on **OK**.

By default, it will add the user as an eligible activation to the Azure AD role. When the user logs in to the Azure portal, they can search for Azure AD PIM and choose the Azure AD roles. It will display a list of eligible and current active roles. The following screenshot shows the activation screen:

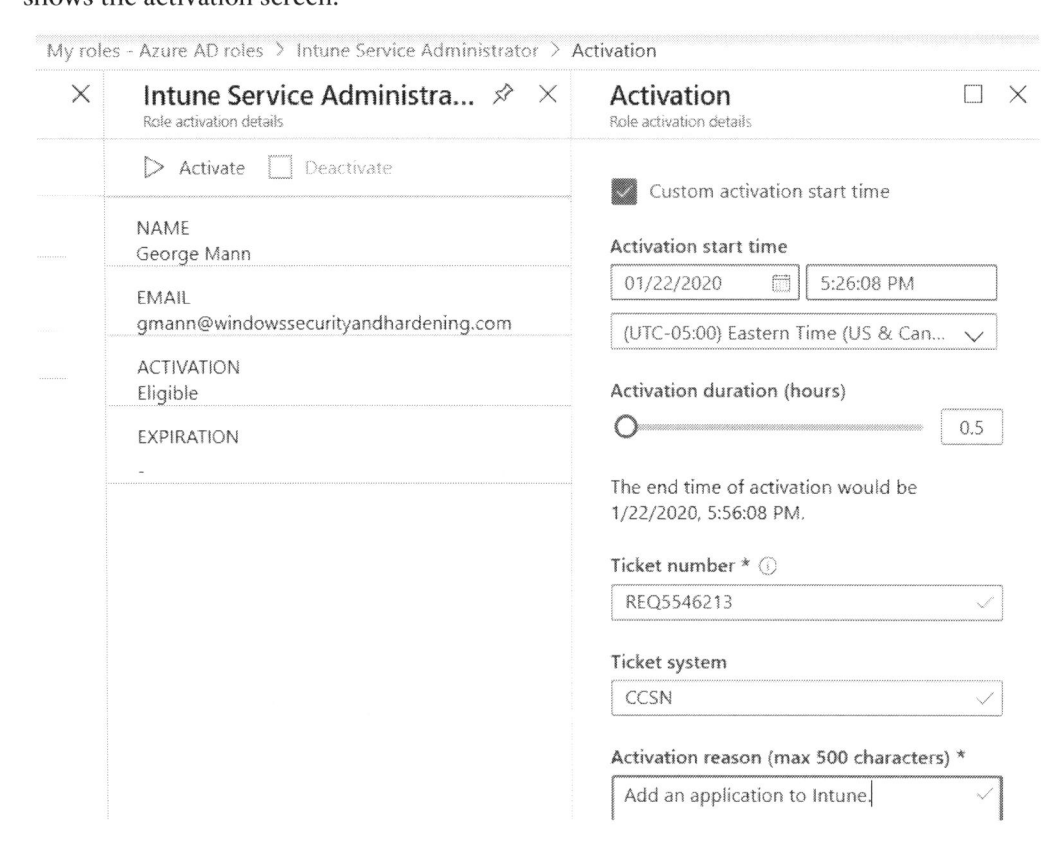

Figure 7.8 – Activate a user as an Intune service administrator

This is a very basic example of how Azure PIM can be used to protect your Windows systems. PIM also extends beyond Azure AD roles to Azure RBAC for managing resources. Discovery is also useful for finding and auditing all permanent and eligible privileged roles in your subscription.

> **Tip**
> Azure PIM also supports external users to collaborate on Azure resources using B2B. For more information about B2B, visit `https://docs.microsoft.com/en-us/azure/active-directory/privileged-identity-management/pim-resource-roles-external-users`.

Next, let's look at Azure RBAC and provide an overview of how it's used for authorization

Using Azure RBAC

Once the account is set up and active, authorization will need to be added, depending on how many systems, services, applications, or access to third-party environments are needed. RBAC is the best solution to solve this challenge, but in most cases, you are not able to implement it 100% because of the constant growth and change. RBAC in Azure is used for the authorization of access to Azure resources by using role assignments. An example of an Azure resource could be anything from a virtual machine, a virtual network interface, Azure Firewall, or a load balancer, to name a few. RBAC roles are assigned actions based on resource providers and are typically assigned to a scope for granularity. Azure already has many built-in roles, and custom roles can be built using them as a template. To read the official documentation on RBAC for Azure resources, visit https://docs.microsoft.com/en-us/azure/role-based-access-control/.

> Tip
> We covered creating a custom RBAC role in *Chapter 3, Server Infrastructure Management*.

In this section, we covered various topics regarding identity and access management. To recap, we covered the account life cycle, beginning with the source of authority from HR to ensuring proper controls are in place to disable accounts when employees leave the company. Next, we discussed local administrator accounts and accounts that allow collaboration from external vendors, known as B2B. Finally, we discussed cloud-based administrative roles in Azure and Office 365 and finished discussing access management solutions, such as PAM, PIM, and JIT, before ending with RBAC. Next, let's look at the methods used for authentication, as well as how best to protect these methods and provide a good and secure experience for your end users.

Understanding authentication, MFA, and going passwordless

In this section, we will review authentication as you are familiar with it today. We will also look at MFA and its importance in today's technical world. We will finish with a review of what we can expect the next generation of authentication to look like with no more passwords. As already stated, a compromise of credentials is one of the most common methods of a breach today. Our current authentication models are outdated and need updating. The traditional method of entering a username and password is simply not acceptable and you need to make changes to improve. If you don't have a strategy in place to improve your authentication posture, add it to your top three security priorities. We need to assume that our account information and passwords have already been breached. If they haven't, it's only a matter of time before they are!

Looking at a traditional on-premises deployment, authentication methods consist of Kerberos, Integrated Windows Authentication, Digest Authentication, NTLM authentication, or TLS/SSL, depending on what you are accessing from your device and how you are accessing it. Modern authentication within Azure AD uses an access security token with claims, OAuth 2.0, and SAML, depending on what you are accessing and how it's been configured. Using a hybrid model will include all of these protocols as part of your authentication process, depending on what is being accessed and where the service is being provided.

> **Tip**
> For your on-premises deployment of AD, it is highly recommended that you enforce secure LDAP. By default, LDAP traffic is not encrypted and could easily be viewed by an attacker within your network.

Let's look at password management and recommendations for how to manage passwords.

Securing your passwords

Since passwords are still relevant and will be for a while, it is important to review your current policies and it could be time to make some changes based on newer recommendations. Your current password policies may consist of what has always been recommended as standard. This includes changing them every 90 days, using 8 characters as a minimum, and ensuring complexity. Now, security research has suggested new recommendations based on advances in cracking tools, password leaks on the dark web, predictable passwords as a result of frequent change, and users writing them down due to complexity. The following current recommendations are now widely recommended to counter these challenges:

- Consider using passphrases over passwords.
- Use a minimum of 12 characters. The more the better.
- Remove the periodic requirements to change passwords and only change them in the event of account compromise.
- Don't use common passwords.
- Reduce complexity rules to allow passphrases to be easier to remember.

In your Windows AD environment, you can configure your password policy natively using Group Policy if you only require one policy for your domain. If there is a requirement to deploy additional password polices, then a fine-grained password policy can be configured and allows multiple password policies per domain. An example of this would be to enable a stronger password requirement for privileged accounts.

> **Tip**
> You can only apply a fine-grained password policy against global security groups or user objects. In addition, to use fine-grained password policies, the domain functional level must use Windows Server 2008 or newer.

Take the following steps to implement a password policy using Group Policy:

1. To change the password policy using Group Policy, open the **Group Policy Management** snap-in from your management workstation.

2. Right-click on **Default Domain Policy**, select **Edit**, then browse to **Computer Configuration** | **Policies** | **Windows Settings** | **Security Settings** | **Account Policies** | **Password Policy**. In the following screenshot, you can see where to configure your domain password policy:

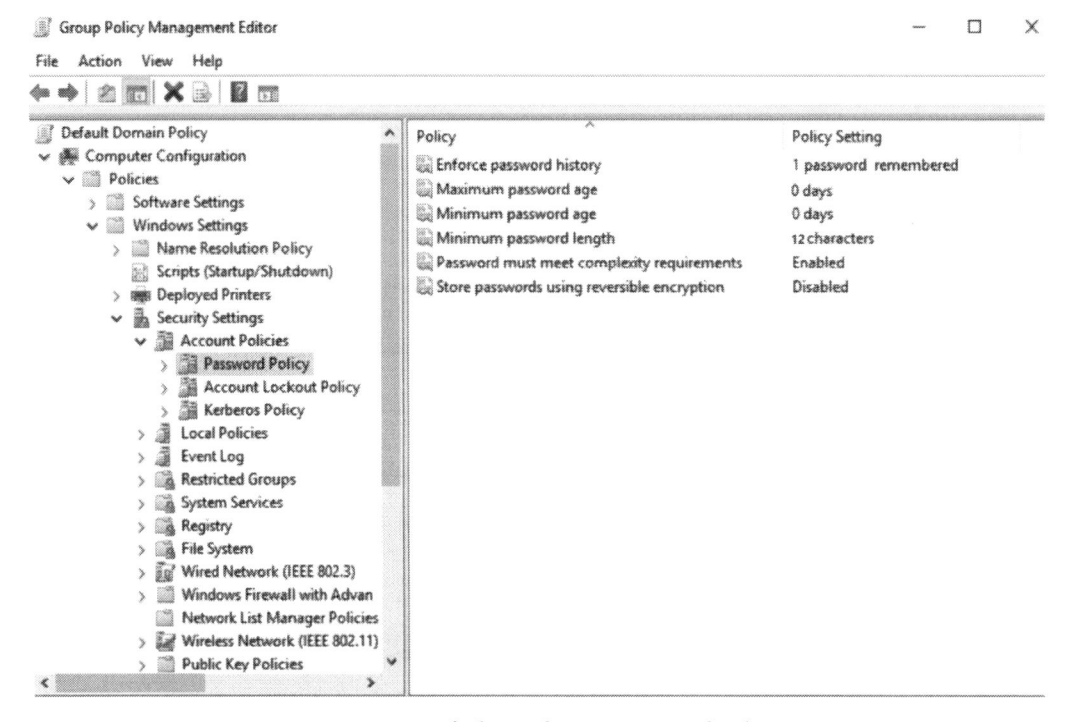

Figure 7.9 – Default AD domain password policy

Use the following steps to implement more than one password policy using a fine-grained password policy:

1. To use fine-grained password policies, log in to your domain controller (Windows 2012 or newer) with the appropriate permissions.

2. Search for **Active Directory Administrative Center** and click on **domain (local)**, then double-click on **System** and double-click on **Password Settings Container**.

3. Right-click on the main screen and select **New**, then click on **Password Settings**.

Understanding authentication, MFA, and going passwordless   249

4. Fill out the requirements for your password policy and select the groups of users that the policy will apply against, then click **OK**. The following screenshot shows the new policy screen:

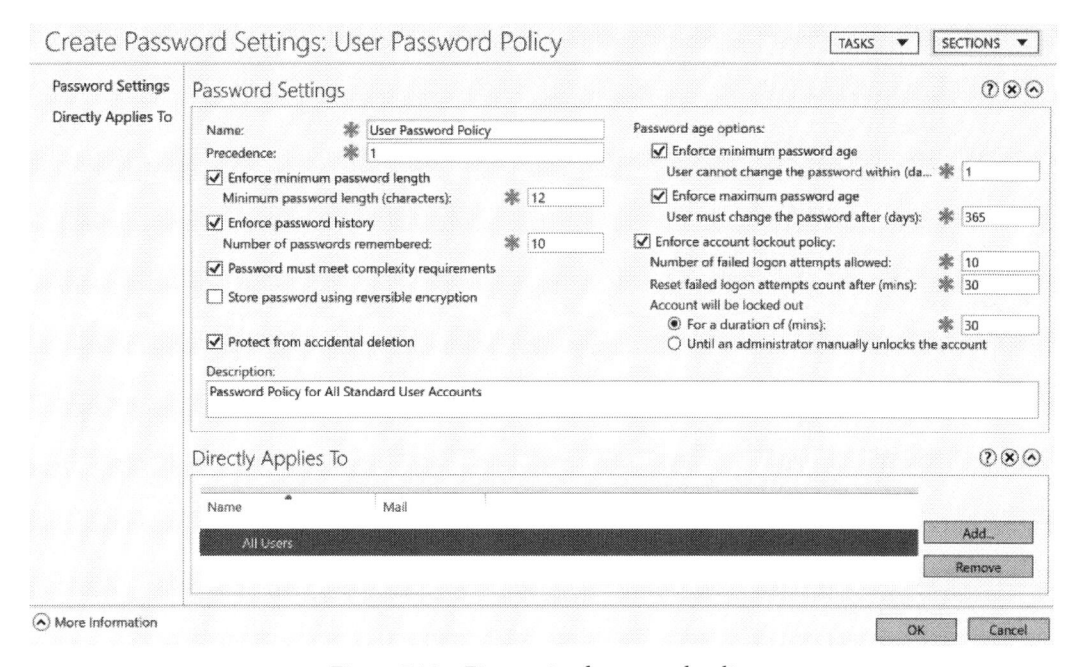

Figure 7.10 – Fine-grained password policy

For your Azure password policy, your options to modify are limited. By default, any account created in Azure can use a password between 8 to 256 characters, requires complexity, expires every 90 days, receives a notification after 14 days of setting it, doesn't allow the last used password to be used again, and locks a user out after 10 incorrect attempts. There are two sections to configure your Azure passwords. The first section is for setting the password expiration and the number of days that the user will be notified before expiration. To modify these settings, follow these steps:

1. Log in to `https://portal.office.com` with the correct permissions.
2. Click on the menu at the top left. Click on **Admin | Show All | Settings**. Click on the **Settings** sub-menu, then on **Security & Privacy | Password expiration policy**.
3. Select **Set user passwords to expire after a number of days** to configure the two options. These policies apply to any accounts created directly in Azure AD.

The second section is the **Password Protection** section to prevent users from using easily guessed passwords and to customize the lockout settings for your tenant. To modify these settings, follow these steps:

1. Log in to `https://portal.azure.com/` with the correct permissions.
2. Click on the menu at the top left. Click on **Azure Active Directory | Security | Authentication Methods | Password Protection**.
3. Here, you can modify the lockout threshold and the lockout duration in seconds, enable a custom banned list, enable password protection on a Windows Server AD, and change the password protection mode to **Enforced** or **Audit**.

The following article provides instructions to deploy Azure AD password protection on-premises:

`https://docs.microsoft.com/en-us/azure/active-directory/authentication/howto-password-ban-bad-on-premises-deploy`

Next, let's look at configuring **Self-Service Password Reset** (**SSPR**) as a self-help tool for your users.

Introducing SSPR

SSPR is a feature of Azure AD that allows users to self-set, reset/change, or unlock their passwords. This feature is only free for cloud identities looking for password change functionality. If syncing from an on-premises AD, then M365 Business or Azure AD Premium P1 or greater is required. For this discussion, let's assume we have hybrid users that have an on-premises AD identity synchronized to Azure AD.

In this section, we are going to cover how to enable SSPR, as well as how to configure a link on the Windows login page in the event that a user cannot get into their device. This can considerably minimize support calls and save the worker's time if they forget their password or device PIN. To do this themself from the end user's perspective, all that is required is an internet connection and an alternative method of authentication, depending on the SSPR configuration. To enable SSPR and set up the authentication and registration methods, follow these steps:

1. Log in to the Azure portal at `https://portal.azure.com`.
2. Go to **Azure Active Directory | Users | Password Reset** and choose **All** (or **Selected** to test), then click **Save**.

> **Tip**
> You only can choose one security group if you are using the **Selected** option to enable SSPR. Keep this in mind if you're thinking about rolling this out.

3. Choose **Authentication methods** under the **Manage** menu. Select **1** for the number of methods required to reset and select **Mobile app code** and **Mobile phone** as the methods available to users. Click **Save**.

4. Choose **Registration** under the **Manage** menu. Leave **Yes** selected to require users to register when signing in and leave the default value of **180** days to require re-confirmation of their authentication information.

> **Tip**
> This is an important setting worth noting if you're using regular user identities as service accounts. If SSPR is scoped to **All users**, then any service account will be required to re-confirm their verification methods every 180 days and can cause a process to stop as a result. The best practice is to use service principals as service accounts in Azure.

5. Choose **Customization** under the **Manage** menu. Choose **Yes** to customize the help desk link and enter an email or URL to your service desk.

6. Choose **On-Premises integration** under the **Manage** menu. In order to configure password writeback, Azure AD Connect must be set up with the password writeback configuration. Choose **Yes** and select **No** for the option to allow users to unlock accounts without resetting their password.

The following screenshot shows the password writeback to on-premises AD setup option on the self-service password reset page:

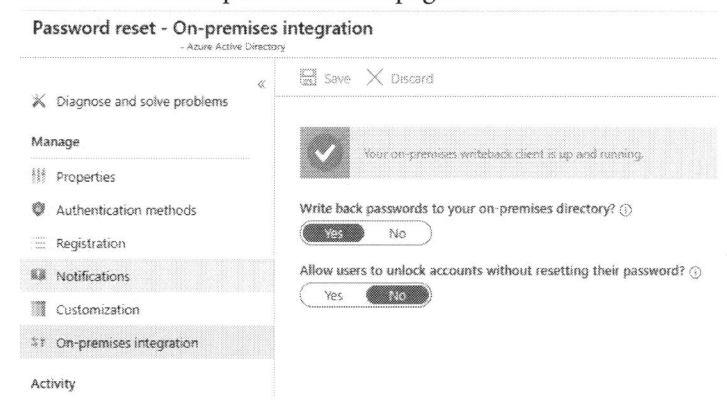

Figure 7.11 – On-premises AD integration

For more information about how to configure password writeback with Azure AD Connect, visit `https://docs.microsoft.com/en-us/azure/active-directory/authentication/howto-sspr-writeback`.

Once the self-service password reset has been configured, users can go directly to `https://aka.ms/sspr` to reset their passwords.

After they enter their user ID and enter the characters for the CAPTCHA, they will be asked to verify their identity with an alternative method, as shown:

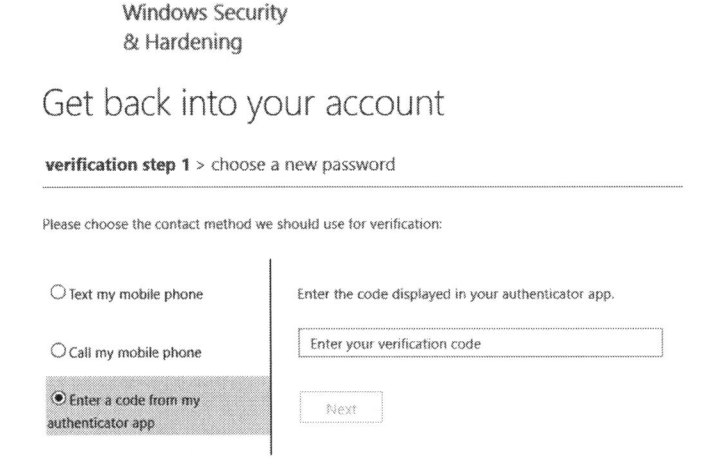

Figure 7.12 – The self-service password reset portal asking for additional security verification

Now that we have enabled SSPR, we will show you how to implement the **Reset password** link on the Windows 10 login screen.

Implementing SSPR for Windows 10 login

There are a few prerequisites and limitations to keep in mind before enabling the **Reset password** link on the Windows 10 login screen. This next walkthrough is going to assume that your workstations are all Windows 10 Azure AD-joined and Intune-managed. We will be using a custom OMA-URI setting on Intune device restriction profiles to deploy the **configuration service provider (CSP)**.

For more information around the limitations and restrictions of using the **Reset password** link for Windows 10 clients, visit https://docs.microsoft.com/en-us/azure/active-directory/authentication/howto-sspr-windows.

To enable the **Password Reset** link on the Windows 10 login page, follow these steps:

1. Log in to the Microsoft Endpoint Manager admin center at https://devicemanagement.microsoft.com.

2. Click on **Devices** and choose **Configuration profiles** under **Policy**. Create a new profile.

3. Give it a friendly name, such as Device Restriction - Windows 10 SSPR, and a description. Select **Windows 10 and later** for **Platform** and choose **Custom** for **Profile type**.

4. Click on **Add** to add a new OMA-URI setting with the following configurations:

    Name: Self-Service Password Reset

    Description: Windows 10 Reset Password link

    OMA-URI: ./Vendor/MSFT/Policy/Config/Authentication/AllowAadPasswordReset

    Data Type: Integer

    Value: 1

5. Click on **OK** and select **Create**. Click on **Assignments** and choose a security group or specific users or devices.

The following screenshot shows the `Reset password` link that takes the user to the Azure AD SSPR web page:

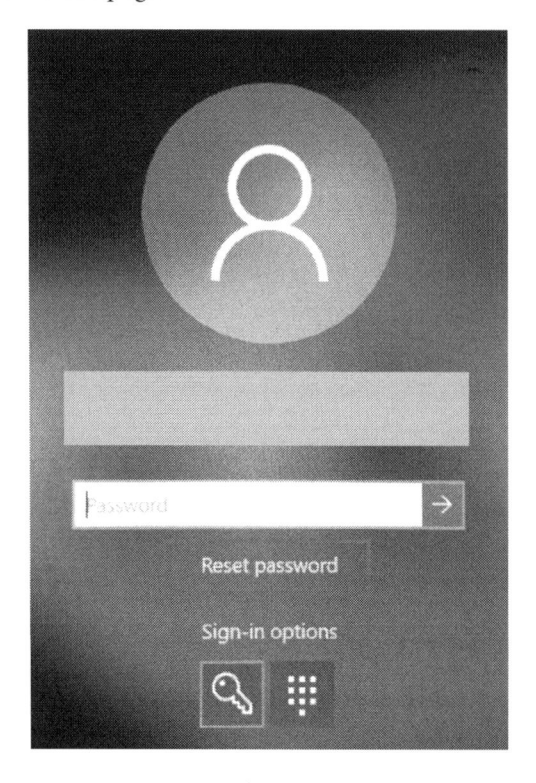

Figure 7.13 – The Windows 10 Reset password link

We just covered passwords and the best practices for password management. Next, let's look at one way to eliminate the need for users to enter passwords multiple times, creating a better and more secure user experience with **Azure AD Seamless SSO**.

Using Azure AD Seamless SSO

Organizations whose devices are not fully Azure AD-joined can still leverage Azure AD authentication for domain-joined systems using **Azure AD Seamless SSO**. With Azure AD Seamless SSO, users' passwords are validated using either Azure AD pass-through authentication or Azure AD password hash synchronization. Both can provide a seamless SSO experience for users to access apps, such as Office 365, SaaS, and other line-of-business apps, without requiring additional login. First, let's clarify the difference between pass-through authentication and password hash synchronization.

Azure AD pass-through authentication allows a synchronized password between on-premises and the cloud. Passwords are validated directly against a Windows Server AD. Choose pass-through authentication if you wish to enforce on-premises security and password policies and do not want passwords to be stored with the Azure AD authentication service.

Azure AD password hash synchronization synchronizes the stored on-premises password hash to the Azure AD authentication service using Azure AD Connect. Authentication takes place against Azure AD, not against on-premises AD. Whenever a password is changed on-premises, the password is synced (within 2 minutes) to Azure AD. If password writeback is configured, then a user can change the password from the cloud and sync it back on-premises. If using password hash synchronization, any on-premises password complexity policy will override any policies configured in the cloud. Any on-premises expiration policy will not be honored in the cloud and if a user's password expires on-premises, cloud services will not be interrupted.

> **Tip**
> Currently, a policy called `EnforceCloudPasswordPolicyForPasswordSyncedUsers` is in public preview, as well as a feature to synchronize temporary passwords with the ability to force a password reset on the next login.

Next, let's consider seamless sign-on. Not only can the user use the same password to log in to cloud applications, but with a few additional configurations, they can now also silently sign in to apps, such as the Office 365 web portal, without having to re-enter their credentials. In the Azure AD pass-through authentication architecture, the Azure AD Connect agent allows the passing of Kerberos tickets to and from the domain up to the cloud to provide an authentication mechanism. To view the status of Azure AD Connect, as well as the agent status, follow these steps:

1. Log in to the Azure portal at `https://portal.azure.com`.
2. Choose **Azure Active Directory** and select **Azure AD Connect** from the **Manage** section.
3. Under the **User Sign-In** section, **Pass-through authentication status** should be set to `Enabled`. You can click on it to view its status, IP address, and any warnings issued for the authentication agent.

256　Identity and Access Management

If you are leveraging Azure AD pass-through authentication, there is one additional step that is needed for your endpoint to leverage the feature using Group Policy. There are two Azure AD URLs that need to be added to your computer's intranet zone that will allow successful Kerberos pass-through. Take a look at these steps:

1. Add the URLs to **User Configuration** > **Administrative Templates** > **Windows Components** > **Internet Explorer** > **Internet Control Panel** > **Security Page** > **Site to Zone Assignment List**.

2. Set this policy to `enabled` and add the following URLs with a value of 1. Anything with a value of 1 is placed into the intranet zone:

   `https://autologon.microsoftazuread-sso.com`

   `https://aadg.windows.net.nsatc.net`

   The following screenshot shows the added URLs with a value of 1:

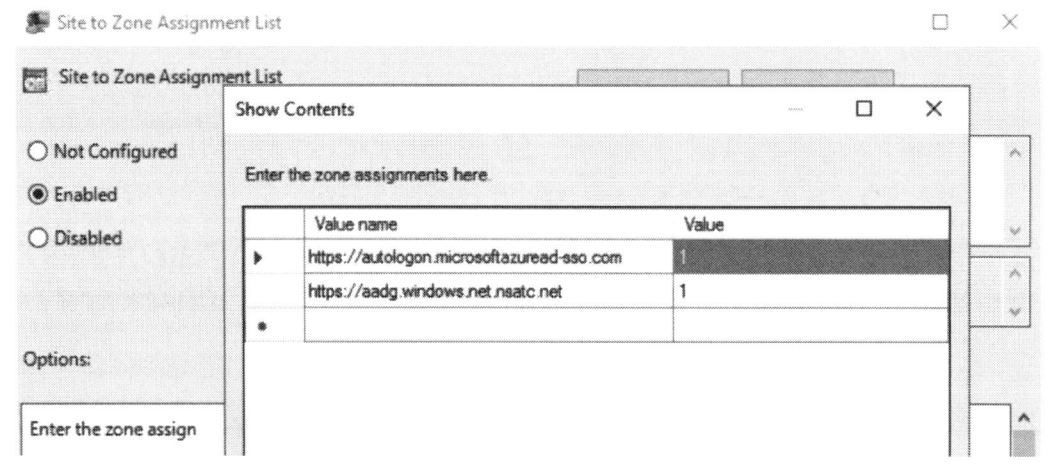

Figure 7.14 – The site-to-zone assignment list for trusted sites

The Microsoft documentation has a full write-up on SSO deployments and can be reviewed at `https://docs.microsoft.com/en-us/azure/active-directory/manage-apps/plan-sso-deployment`.

Next, let's look at how we can configure Azure SSO for other applications to leverage an Azure AD identity and authentication.

Configuring Azure SSO

You are probably already aware of SSO and most likely have it deployed within your environment today. Having SSO in your environment provides significant improvement and security over your account management. Without SSO, users would need usernames and passwords for every application and service they need access to. Not only is this a bad experience for the user but from an administration and operations perspective, it becomes unmanageable. The downside is that one account now has access to many applications and services with SSO, which is why it is important to ensure you provide strong access and management policies with your user accounts. Applying technologies such as MFA and location-based access will help with these scenarios.

The modern version of SSO from Microsoft is currently known as **Azure AD SSO**. Azure SSO allows you to integrate your Azure identity into any SaaS, on-premises, or custom-developed app that supports standard SSO protocols, such as the **Security Assertion Markup Language** (**SAML**). The on-premises version of Azure SSO that you may be familiar with is AD FS. AD FS has served a great purpose in the traditional world for federation and SSO, but the infrastructure needed to support and maintain deployment can become very complex. Shifting this service to Azure requires no infrastructure to support SSO and integrating SSO has become very simple, with minimum configuration and clicks needed. In addition to the standard SSO integration, Azure SSO builds on Azure AD with the ability to use all the advanced and security features for your enterprise app deployments.

A simple SSO setup with an external enterprise app using SAML can be configured by taking the following steps:

1. Log in to `https://portal.azure.com`.
2. Search for **Enterprise Applications** and navigate to the management console.
3. Click on **All applications** on the left, then click on **New Application**.
4. For the purposes of this demonstration, we will select **Non-gallery application** (there are also many featured applications that you can select to set up SSO with those apps).
5. Enter a name for the app and click on **Add**. Once you click on **Add**, you will be directed to the new app.
6. Click on **Single sign-on** from the left-side menu, then click on **SAML**.
7. Next, you will be prompted to enter your SAML information. If you are using a third-party SaaS app, it will need to provide you with the basic SAML configuration and you will need to provide it with the SAML signing certificates.

The following screenshot is of the SAML SSO configuration page:

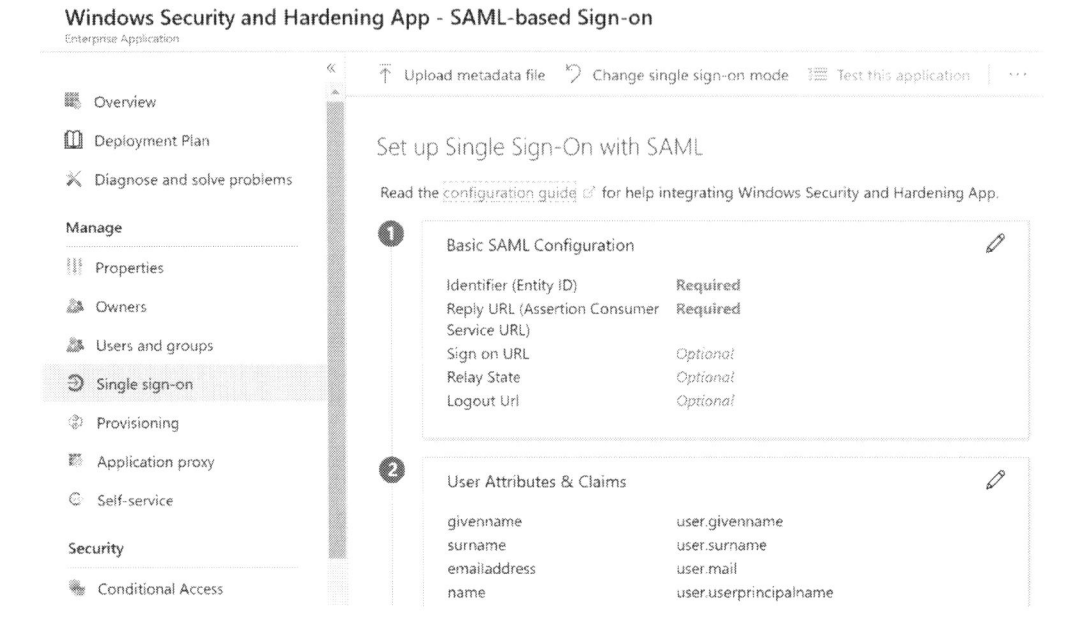

Figure 7.15 – The Azure Enterprise app with the Azure SSO SAML configuration screen

If you look at the left-side menu in the preceding screenshot, you will see that you have the ability to configure who can access the app with the **Users and groups** option and you can apply Conditional Access policies, audit logs, and much more to ensure access to your Enterprise applications are hardened and secured.

Next, let's look at how to enable MFA.

Configuring MFA

One of the more important technologies in this book that we would recommend you deploy immediately if not already enabled is MFA. Passwords have become obsolete, especially used as the only factor for authentication. If you aren't using MFA with your Azure subscription, then make doing so a priority now. The benefit of using MFA in Azure is that you can complement it with Conditional Access policies or Azure AD Identity Protection. Complementing MFA with these technologies means you don't have to force the user to use MFA all the time, but instead, you can apply rules or risk-based conditions that would enforce the need for MFA to be prompted. This provides a very powerful, secure deployment and, at the same time, eases the technology onto your users without causing too much disruption.

Understanding authentication, MFA, and going passwordless   259

> **Tip**
> Azure MFA is included in the free Azure AD license, but in order to take advantage of the advanced features of MFA, you will need to increase your license. The following link provides an overview of the different license types:
> `https://azure.microsoft.com/en-us/pricing/details/active-directory/`

To access the Azure MFA settings, follow these steps:

1. Log in to `https://portal.azure.com/`.
2. Click on the portal menu at the top left and choose **Azure Active Directory**.
3. Select **Security** and choose **MFA**. You will see the following screen:

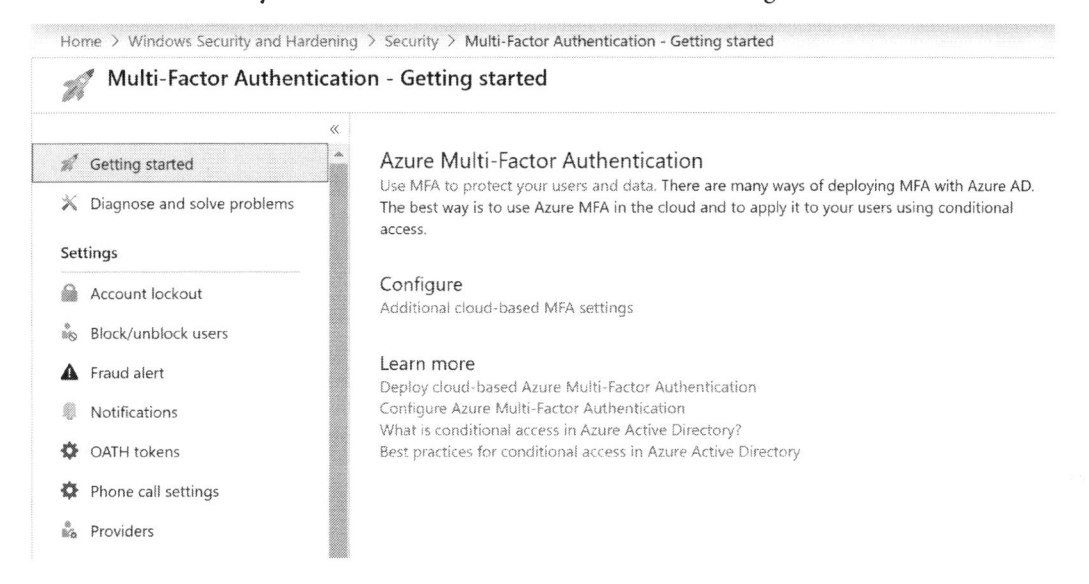

Figure 7.16 – The Azure MFA settings

> **Tip**
> From the **Getting started** screen, click on **Additional cloud-based MFA settings** to add/remove the specific verification options you would like your users to use.

You can find additional details on the configurations shown in the preceding screenshot at `https://docs.microsoft.com/en-us/azure/active-directory/authentication/howto-mfa-mfasettings`.

There are several authentication methods currently available on Azure AD. They include the following:

- Using the Microsoft Authenticator app on your Apple or Android device:

    --Verification code provided on the app (renews every 30 seconds)

    --A push notification where you click on **Approve** when prompted

- A verification code provided to a hardware token
- A call to your cell phone where you will need to press #
- A text message to your phone with a verification code

There are three supported methods in which MFA can be required for your users:

- Enabled at the user level, which will require MFA every time the user authenticates. This option takes precedence over the other two methods, so it may not be the most practical one to use. This option is more fitting for privileged accounts.
- Enabled using Conditional Access policies, allowing the use of advanced criteria such as the location, device state, device compliance, approved applications, assigned roles, and so on. This requires the Azure AD Premium license to be enabled on the user's device.
- Enabled using Identity Protection, applied when any detected sign-in attempt or user risk occurs. This also requires the Azure AD Premium license to be enabled on the user's device.

You can enable user-level MFA by using the following steps:

1. Log in to `https://portal.azure.com`.
2. Click on the portal menu at the top left, then click on **Azure Active Directory**.
3. Click on **Users**, then put a checkmark next to the user you would like to enable MFA for.
4. Click on **Multi-Factor Authentication** and a new window will open.

5. Put a checkmark next to the user you would like to enable, then click on **Enable**, as in the following screenshot:

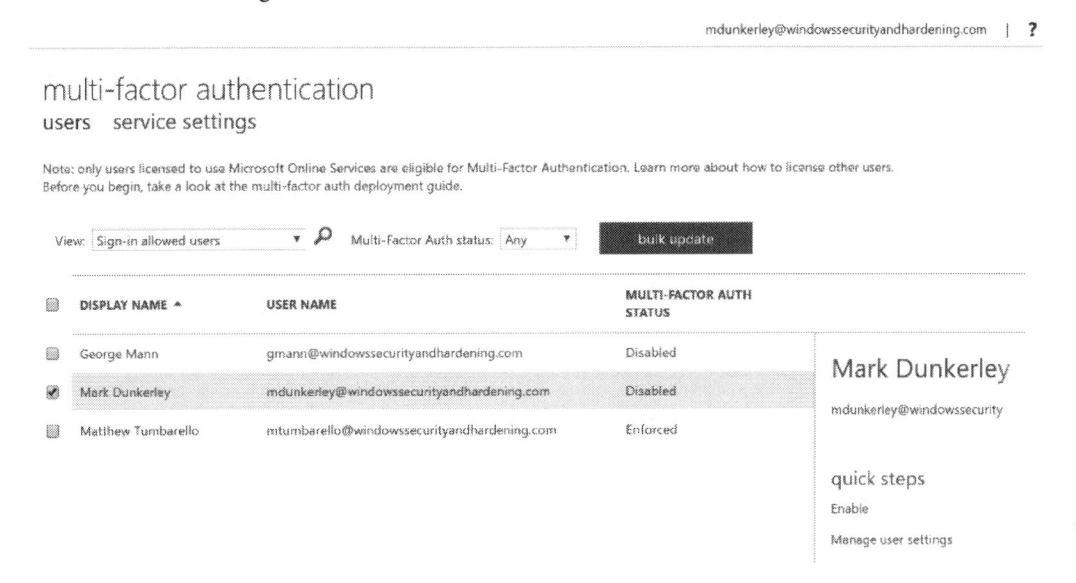

Figure 7.17 – Enabling MFA for a user

6. Click on **enable multi-factor auth** on the pop-up window, then click **close**.

When the user you enabled accesses the portal for the first time, they will be required to set up MFA for their account. If the user is using the free version of an MFA license, they will only see the mobile app option:

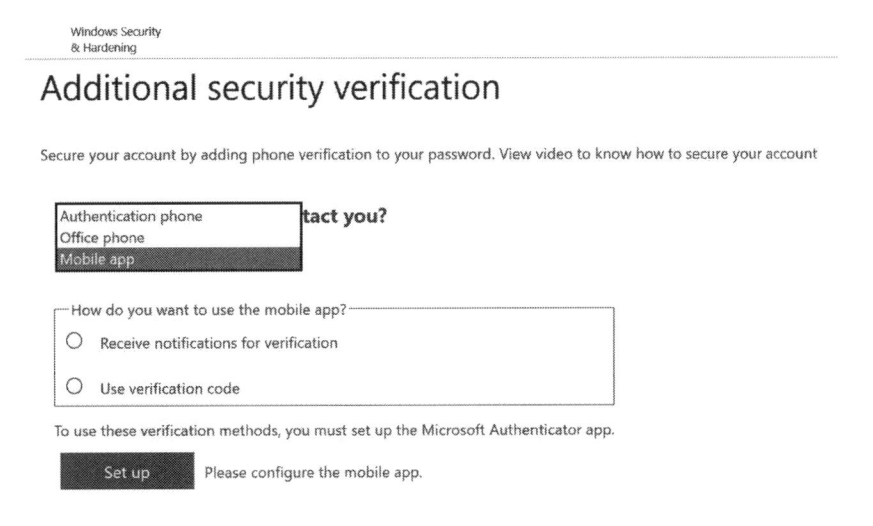

Figure 7.18 – Setting up MFA for the first time

> **Tip**
> Microsoft no longer supports the MFA server as of July 1st, 2019. In order to protect your on-premises infrastructure with MFA, you will need to review the third-party options or ensure you have PAM in place for the best protection.

Next, let's look at using a form of biometric authentication to log in to your Windows devices, known as Windows Hello.

Introducing Windows Hello

Windows Hello is Microsoft's biometric or PIN authentication feature for your Windows 10 devices. This technology replaces the traditional password authentication methods that have always been used on Windows devices. Windows Hello works with a Microsoft account, an AD account, or an Azure AD account. Support is also in progress to support an identity provider service or a reliable party service that supports **Fast ID Online (FIDO)** v2.0. Windows Hello provides two options for biometric authentication on supported hardware, and the biometric data and PIN are only stored on the local device and are not available externally. This is a significant security enhancement that helps ensure an attacker isn't able to get a copy of your biometric data. The two options for Windows Hello biometrics are as follows:

- Facial recognition
- Fingerprint recognition

Next, let's look at what it means to go passwordless.

Understanding going passwordless

Passwordless is the future and Microsoft's making a big push in this direction as an authentication strategy. The technology is already available, and you can go passwordless today. Unfortunately, it may not be easy to get to a passwordless world straight away, but you do need to understand and begin this journey sooner rather than later. The methods that are used to provide a passwordless world are currently much more secure for your users.

With the elimination of passwords, authentication is improved by using something you already have, such as a phone or a security key, in addition to something you are or know, such as biometrics or a PIN. Microsoft supports passwordless authentications with Windows Hello for Business, the Microsoft Authenticator app, or a FIDO2 security key.

Understanding authentication, MFA, and going passwordless

> **Tip**
> FIDO is an alliance that works toward improving today's authentication challenges with passwords. They are looking to provide simpler and secure authentication methods using open standards. You can view additional information about this at `https://fidoalliance.org/`.

To enable passwordless in Azure, follow these steps:

1. Log in to `https://portal.azure.com`.
2. Click on the portal menu at the top left and choose **Azure Active Directory**.
3. Click on **Security**, then choose **Authentication methods**.
4. Click on **Authentication methods - Authentication method policy**. Here, you can configure FIDO2 or the Microsoft Authenticator app for passwordless sign-in.

The following screenshot shows the configuration screen for passwordless:

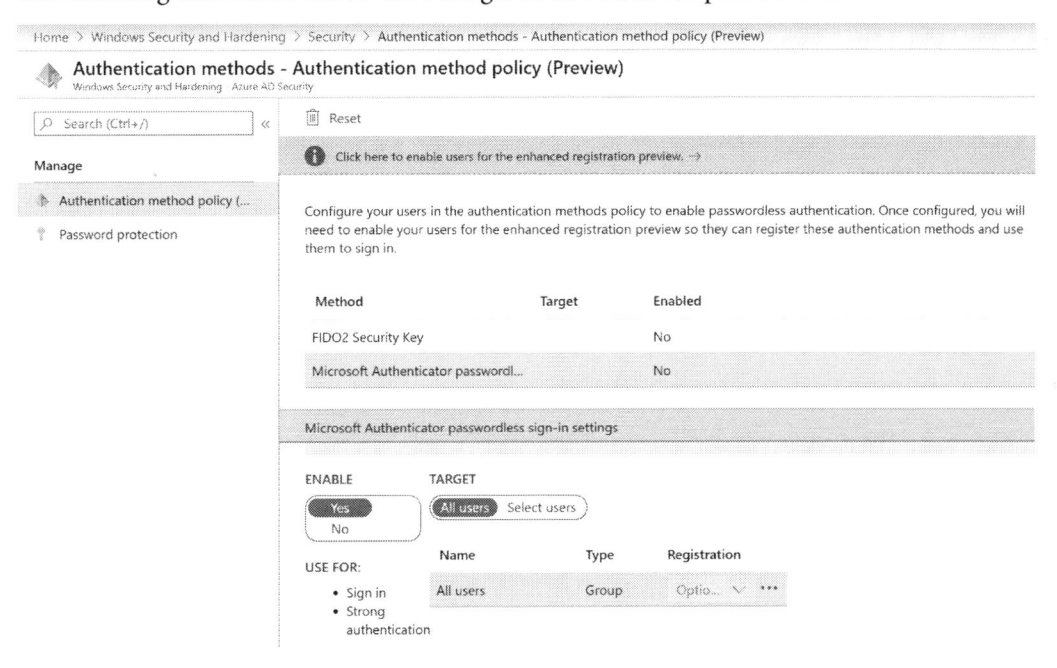

Figure 7.19 – Enabling passwordless in Azure portal

As you can see from the screenshot, passwordless is in preview at the time of writing, and is not generally available with full support.

The final section we will cover in this chapter is Conditional Access and Identity Protection, leveraging the power of the cloud for much more advanced identity technology.

Using Conditional Access and Identity Protection

Conditional Access is an Azure cloud policy tool that enforces compliance based on conditions for your users. The Conditional Access policies allow you to specify criteria against your users that will trigger specific requirements or exceptions based on the location, device platform or type, application, group membership, and much more. For example, if a user is not on a trusted device and is trying to access their email via Exchange Online, they will be required to use MFA. This is a simple example, but the possibilities of this scenario are extensive and allow increased security. Conditional Access is a necessity within the cloud world, and you need to use it. If not, prioritize and enable it immediately.

You can learn more about Conditional Access at `https://docs.microsoft.com/en-us/azure/active-directory/conditional-access/overview`.

The following is a list of several use cases to get you started today with Conditional Access:

- Require MFA for your admins (privileged roles).
- Require compliant mobile devices before allowing access to company resources.
- Enable MFA for all guest users.
- Block all legacy authentication protocols.
- Allow users on trusted company devices to access resources without MFA.
- Block any access outside a specific region—for example, a United States-based company could block any connection from everywhere outside the United States.
- Enforce MFA on any app that contains PII, whether on a trusted device or not.
- Only allow specific applications to be accessed from trusted devices.

To set up a Conditional Access policy, follow these steps:

1. Log in to `https://portal.azure.com`.
2. Click on the portal menu at the top left and choose **Azure Active Directory**. Click on **Security**, then **Conditional Access**, then click on **New Policy**.

> **Tip**
> By default, Microsoft enables security defaults, which are a set of standard security features that Microsoft enforces. To set up your own Conditional Access policies, you will need to disable this by going to the portal menu at the top left. Click on **Azure Active Directory** | **Properties** | **Manage Security Defaults**. Change this setting to **No**, then click **Save**.

The following screenshot shows where you will need to set up your new Conditional Access policy:

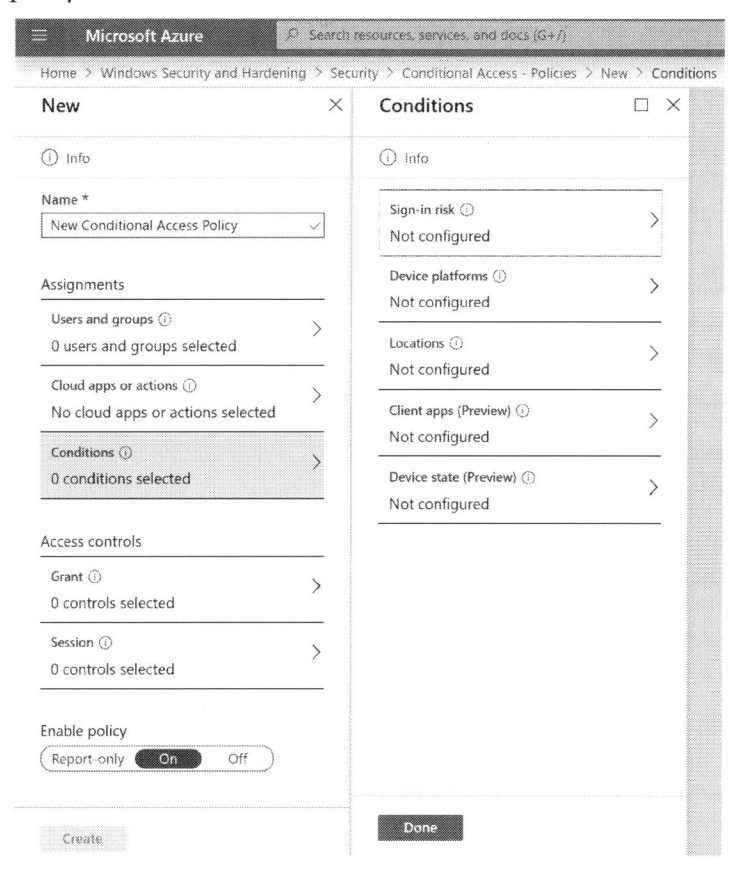

Figure 7.20 – New Conditional Access policy

Within the new policy, configure your assignments and the following configurations:

Users and groups is where you can include and/or exclude users and groups.

Cloud apps or actions is where you can include or exclude apps as part of the policy, as well as any user-specific actions.

Conditions is where you configure specific conditions for the policy. These include **Sign-in risk**, **Device platforms**, **Locations** (using IP ranges or countries/regions), **Client apps**, and **Device state**.

3. Next, you will configure your access controls:

   Grant is where you can grant or block access. If you grant access, you can select multiple requirements to comply with—for example, requiring MFA and devices to be marked as compliant.

   Session applies session limits to cloud apps.

4. Finally, select **Report-only** to review the policy or select **On** to enable, then click on **Done** to complete the policy setup.

> **Tip**
> Ensure you thoroughly test the Conditional Access policy before enabling it for the organization. There are scenarios where you could lock yourself out or cause major disruption to your users if you don't test and validate.

To add an additional layer of security, you could also add a location condition to block anyone from accessing the organization outside of a specific country. To do this, you can build locations within the **Named locations** option within the Conditional Access policy and add a new location based on IP ranges or country/region.

> **Tip**
> MFA does not work with legacy protocols, so it is highly recommended and important that you block legacy authentication to prevent a breach with any apps still using any legacy protocol. Some examples include POP, IMAP, and SMTP. The following guide provides the steps to block authentication:
>
> ```
> https://docs.microsoft.com/en-us/azure/active-directory/conditional-access/block-legacy-authentication
> ```

Azure Identity Protection, like Conditional Access, is an Azure cloud-based security tool. With the advancement of the cloud and its collective customers, Microsoft currently analyzes 6.5 trillion signals per day to help better protect its customers and support services like Identity Protection. Identity Protection provides security for your users with any identity-based risks. Detection and remediation of these risks can be automated for quick protection. There are two types of identity-based risks used. User risks try to determine whether an account has been compromised and sign-in risks try to determine whether the authentication request is from the real owner. Risk is identified by atypical travel, anonymous IP addresses, unfamiliar sign-in properties, malware-linked IP address, leaked credentials, and Azure AD threat intelligence.

> **Tip**
> To learn more about the risks, visit https://docs.microsoft.com/en-us/azure/active-directory/identity-protection/concept-identity-protection-risks.

To access Identity Protection and enable the policies, go to the portal menu at the top left. Click on **Azure Active Directory**, choose **Security**, and click on **Identity Protection** to access the Identity Protection features. Within this management console, you can enable **User risk policy**, Sign-in risk policy, and **MFA registration policy** (required to protect against sign-in risks unless you block access). To enable the user risk policy, select **User risk policy** from the left and configure each of the following options:

- **Users**: Decides who will be included or excluded from the policy
- **Conditions**: Where you select the user risk level (**Low and above**, **Medium and above**, or **High**)
- **Access**: To block or allow access and require password change if allowed
- **Estimated impact**: To provide an overview of the percentage that the user's policy will apply to

Once configured, change the policy to **On** and click **Save**. The following screenshot shows the **User risk policy** configuration screen:

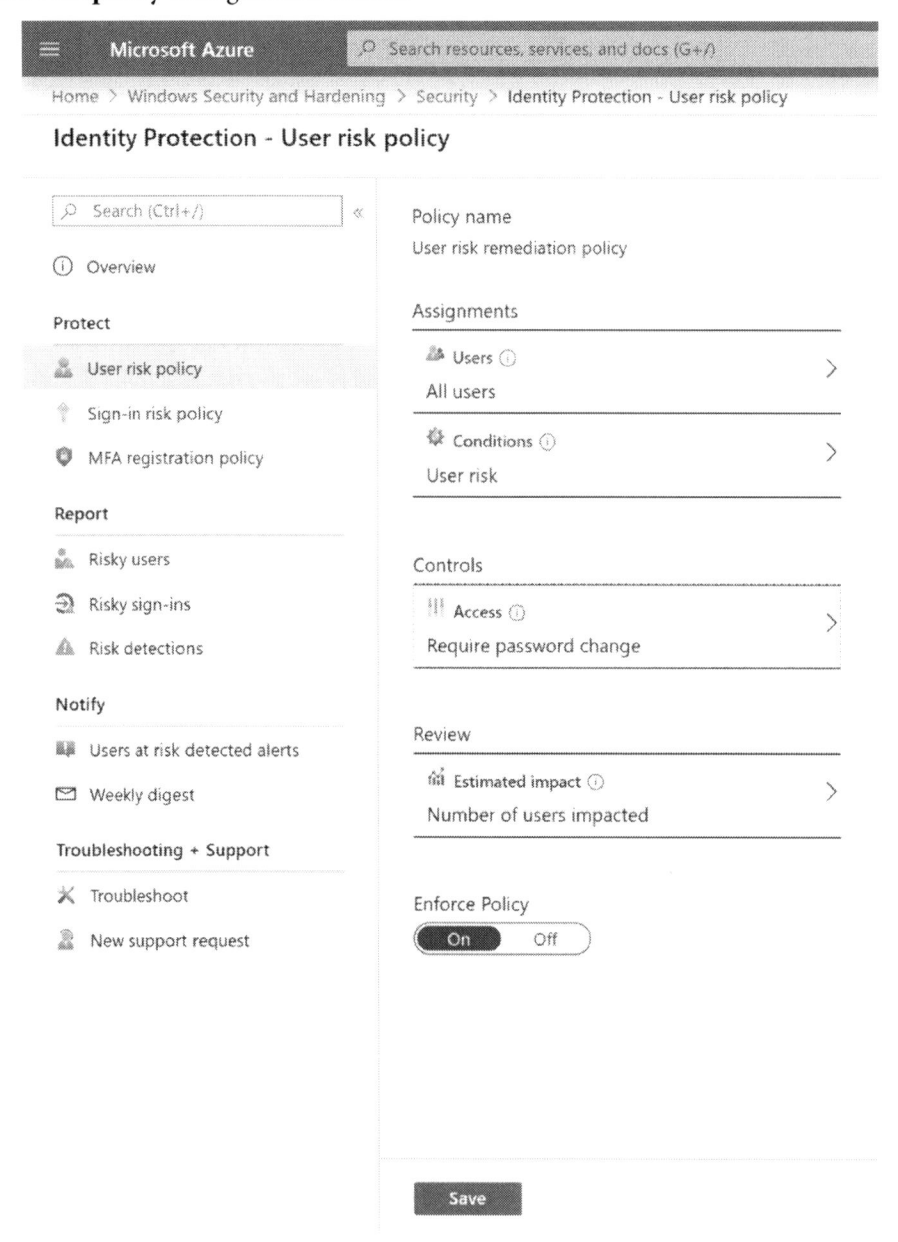

Figure 7.21 – Enabling the user risk policy

Complete the preceding steps again for the sign-in risk policy and ensure you enable the MFA registration policy as well.

> **Tip**
> The recommendation from Microsoft is to set the user risk policy to high and the sign-in risk policy to medium and above.

Summary

In this chapter, we extensively covered identity and access management and its importance to ensure you provide the best protection for your users and Windows devices. We started with an overview, covering the foundation of **IAAA** and what each component of it is. We then reviewed account and access management, which covered the life cycle of identity management, as well as external access and privileged access.

Next, we covered authentication methods, including password management, **SSPR**, and different **SSO** methods. The remainder of this section included a review of MFA and Windows Hello and an overview of the future of a passwordless world. We finished this chapter by covering some new advanced cloud authentication tools, known as Conditional Access and Identity Protection.

In the next chapter, we will be looking at the administration and remote management of your Windows environment. In this chapter, we will review device administration, modern device management, security baseline enforcement, and remote management.

8
Administration and Remote Management

In this chapter, we will be covering the administration and remote management of Windows devices within an organization. The administration of your devices is a very important task and one that needs ongoing interaction and support to stay current. The foundation of your Windows administration will be developed from your established framework and baselines, as discussed in *Chapter 2, Building a Baseline*. However, just as important are your policies, standards, and procedures, which should have already been built to direct how you administer your Windows environment. With that, the administration of your devices should become a much simpler task of execution to meet the defined requirements that have been created and agreed upon.

When it comes to remote management, ensuring a secure and locked down model is a must. Support staff who have remote access to your Windows devices are privileged users that have elevated rights to administer your servers and workstations. Because of this, ensuring a rigid structure for your remote management is essential. Any misconfiguration or open back door could allow an attacker to gain easy access to your environment and data. One simple example is if you exposed your server's **Remote Desktop Protocol (RDP)** access directly to the open internet. This configuration can be highly prone to attacks.

Both your administrative and remote management strategies need to be well defined and implemented based on your standards, policies, and baselines. In order to enforce these baselines, let's look at ways to accomplish this by reviewing the following topics:

- Understanding device administration
- Enforcing policies with **Mobile Device Management (MDM)**
- Building security baselines
- Connecting securely to servers remotely
- Introducing PowerShell and security

Technical requirements

This chapter will cover a range of technologies including several step-by-step instructions. To follow along, you will need the following technical requirements as a minimum:

- Configuration Manager
- An Intune subscription
- Permissions to modify Group Policy
- The Microsoft Security Compliance Toolkit
- The `Convert-GPOtoCI` PowerShell script: https://github.com/SamMRoberts/Convert-GPOtoCI
- Azure Security Center standard
- Azure Bastion

Check out the following video to see the Code in Action: `https://bit.ly/2D7BJFB`

Understanding device administration

Without device administration, the task of ensuring your devices are secured and hardened is unrealistic. Unless you manage a very small number of devices, you are going to need some form of device administration to ensure your devices are set up to meet compliance policies and are secured when they are handed over to your employees. Even after the devices have been handed over, you are going to need to continuously push changes to these devices. Without effective administration, your organization will be putting itself in an extremely vulnerable situation.

We covered the concepts and Microsoft tools used to manage both your end user devices and Windows servers in detail in *Chapter 3, Server Infrastructure Management*, and *Chapter 4, End User Device Management*. This chapter will expand on those tools, and you will learn how to administer your devices along with enforcing the predefined baselines your company has agreed upon to ensure your devices are within compliance. First, let's look at how your devices are joined to your environment, as each provides different methods of administration, especially as we move into a cloud-first world.

The following section will provide an overview of what domain join, hybrid, and Azure AD joined are and the differences between them.

Differences between domain join, hybrid, and Azure AD joined devices

Domain join is the traditional model and allows the central administration of your corporate end user devices and Windows servers in an on-premises scenario. When joining your device to a Domain, you are joining that device or server to your Active Directory Domain. Once joined, you can use **Group Policy Objects (GPOs)** to configure and enforce your policies based on your defined baselines. For your end user devices, you will most likely supplement Group Policy with an additional management tool such as Configuration Manager. This method has served as a very mature and reliable model.

If you want to take the approach of moving to a cloud-only world to administer your devices, then you will need to **Azure Active Directory** (**Azure AD**) or (**AAD**) join your devices. This method directly joins your device to the cloud environment and Azure AD, where you can manage and administer your devices using Intune. This model also supports the ability to use co-management with Microsoft Endpoint Configuration Manager. Moving to the cloud model provides a far more powerful and robust deployment, allowing the improved provisioning of your devices and increased flexibility for your users. Azure AD joined devices will require you to log in with your Azure AD cloud credentials, which can be synced from an on-premises AD.

> **Tip**
> There is also the concept of Azure AD registered devices, which supports the use case of **Bring Your Own Device** (**BYOD**). This allows Windows 10, iOS, Android, and macOS devices access to your corporate resources without being required to sign in to your device with your work account.

Many organizations may face a dependency that still exists with on-premises infrastructure. To provide the ability to take a step into the Azure cloud there's the option of hybrid Azure AD join devices. With this method, your devices will still be joined to your on-premises AD but will also register in Azure AD. This allows management using Group Policy, Configuration Manager, or the option to use co-management with Microsoft Intune. Windows 7, 8.1, and 10 and Windows Server 2008/R2, 2012/R2, 2016, and 2019 all support this method.

The following diagram shows these three different options for your devices:

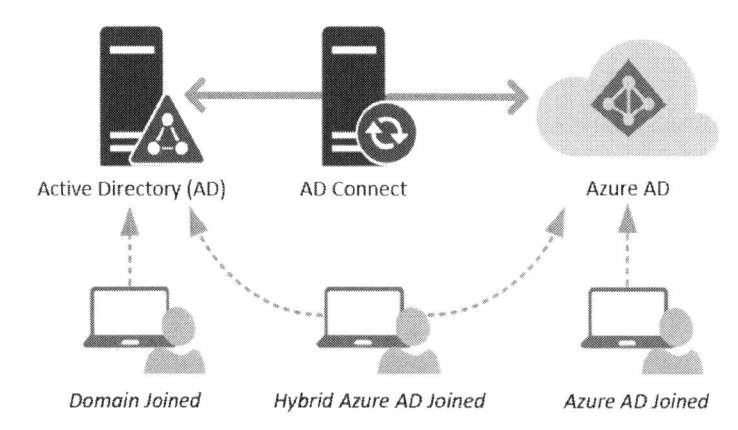

Figure 8.1 – Domain, Hybrid, and Azure AD joined examples

In the next section, we will provide details on how to enforce policies with MDM using Configuration Manager and Intune.

Enforcing policies with MDM

When a device becomes fully Azure AD joined, it opens new opportunities to layer and enforce security policies. Unlike domain-joined or hybrid-joined devices, a fully Azure AD joined device is not part of an on-premises domain, it never connects to a domain controller, and it does not receive Group Policy. Many organizations have years worth of GPOs that they rely on to harden their Windows systems and the question now becomes how to move and enforce these policies with MDM. The answer is to use Configuration Manager, Intune, or a combination of the two with co-management. Unfortunately, there is no clear lift-and-shift path, and part of the challenge is the auditing and evaluation of what currently exists.

In this section, we are going to learn about creating and enforcing policies with MDM. We will walk through how to build, assign, and enforce compliance settings such as configuration items and configuration baselines in Configuration Manager and how to report on them. Then, we will take a similar approach with Intune to create device configuration profiles and assign compliance policies to be used for device compliance evaluation.

Creating compliance settings with Configuration Manager

To view all of the compliance settings inside of Configuration Manager, navigate to **Assets and Compliance** > **Overview** > **Compliance Settings**. These settings are used to enforce your Windows baselines to ensure they are securely hardened and in compliance with your policies. Some of the available compliance settings include the following:

- **Configuration Items** that contain settings for computers or mobile devices. You can create your own custom Configuration Items or download and import them from a vendor.
- **Configuration Baselines** contain the Configuration Items that you want to deploy to a collection in order to evaluate compliance. Deployments can be put into a monitor or remediate mode.
- **User Data and Profiles** manage the user's settings for folder redirection, offline files, and roaming profiles.
- **OneDrive for Business Profiles** is used to configure the OneDrive for Business settings for Windows clients such as known folder redirection.

- **Compliance Policies** are where you create policies that can be used in conjunction with conditional access. Compliance policies can be created for devices without the Configuration Manager client.

- **Conditional Access** settings manage conditional access to company resources.

> **Tip**
> Most conditional access settings will be moving to the Microsoft Endpoint Manager Admin Center at `https://devicemanagement.microsoft.com`. Later versions of the Configuration Manager current branch now direct you to use this portal.

- **Company Resource Access** allows you to create VPN, Wi-Fi, and certificate profiles to deploy to your devices.

- **Microsoft Edge Browser Profiles** contain custom settings to create an Edge Browser policy in Windows 10.

Let's look at what Configuration Items are and how they are used to evaluate settings on Windows 10 devices and servers.

Introduction to Configuration Items

A Configuration Item contains a list of settings and compliance rules that are used for evaluation. When creating a new Configuration Item, you can specify whether the targeted devices are with or without the Configuration Manager client, and then select the supported platforms to choose between different versions of the **operating system** (**OS**). Depending on the platform that is selected, different options will be available to choose from. Selecting *Windows Desktops and Servers (custom)* will provide the greatest flexibility when creating your settings. Each setting is given a name, description, and a setting type to determine the detection method for where this setting exists on the PC.

Some of the available setting types in a Configuration Item include the following:

- An Active Directory query
- An assembly
- A filesystem
- IIS Metabase
- A registry key and registry value
- Using a custom script

- A SQL query
- An XPath query

The following screenshot shows a Configuration Item using an integer registry value as the setting type for the detection method. The specific hive, key path, and value name are all specified:

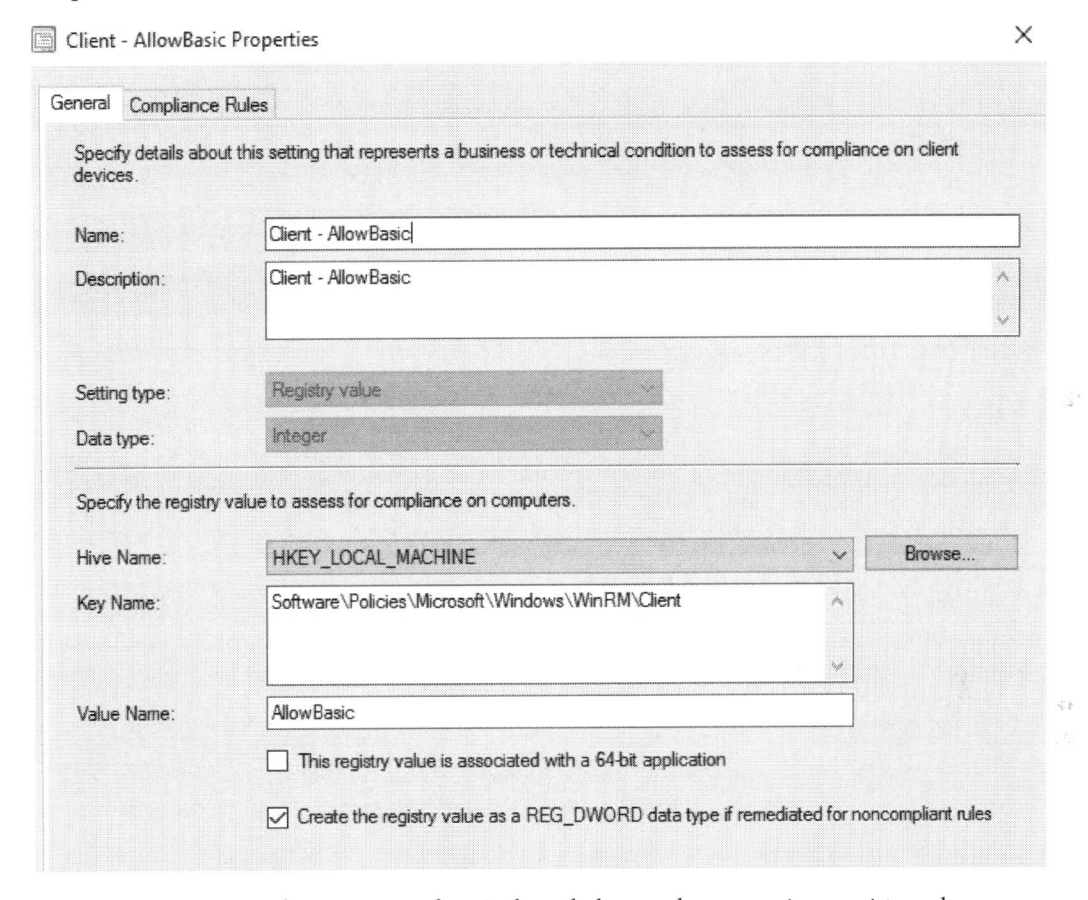

Figure 8.2 – Configuration Item for Windows desktop and servers using a registry value

> **Tip**
> The checkbox for **Create the registry value as a REG_DWORD data type if remediated for noncompliant rules** is selected. This allows the REG_DWORD data type to be created if the Configuration Baseline is set to remediate noncompliant rules.

278　Administration and Remote Management

The **Compliance Rules** tab in the Configuration Item setting is where you can specify the conditions that determine whether the device is compliant. Each setting can have more than one compliance rule.

The following screenshot shows a compliance rule with the condition that says the value name must be set to zero to be compliant. Choose the **Remediate noncompliant rules when supported** checkbox to force this setting onto the PC if found to be noncompliant:

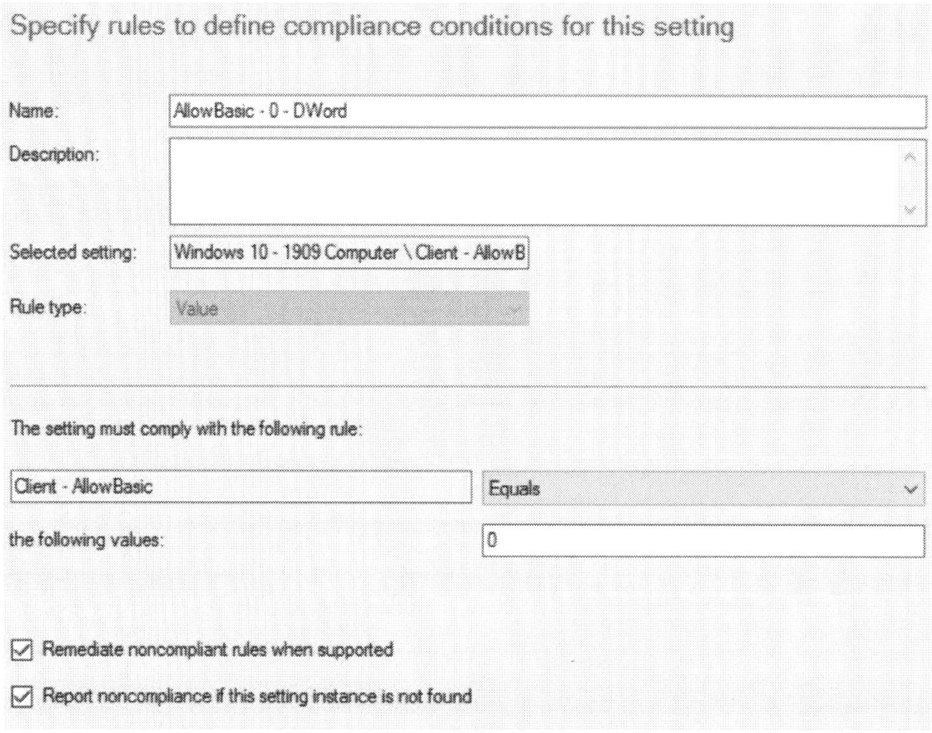

Figure 8.3 – Compliance rule options for a Configuration Item

Creating Configuration Items can be compared to creating and organizing GPOs. One example is a Configuration Item for Google Chrome policy settings. You can specify the different policies and set their values using registry keys with a Configuration Item and then assign that Configuration Item to a Configuration Baseline to report on compliance and take any remediation actions. Later in this chapter, in the *Creating a Configuration Baseline from a GPO* section, we will walk through exporting a prebuilt GPO and creating a Configuration Item from its settings.

Let's walk through how you create a Configuration Item in Configuration Manager.

Creating a Configuration Item

Follow these steps to create a new Configuration Item. We will be building a Configuration Item to apply a Google Chrome policy to disable the password manager:

1. In the Configuration Manager console, go to **Assets and Compliance**, choose **Compliance Settings**, and select **Configuration Items**. Click on the **Create Configuration Item** button in the toolbar.

2. Give it a friendly name, for example, `Google Chrome - Computer`. Enter a description and choose **Windows Desktops and Servers (custom)** under the settings for devices managed with the Configuration Manager client.

3. Keep all versions selected in the **Supported Platforms** section as they are.

4. Choose **New** in **Specify settings for this operating system** and set the following options:

   Name: `Chrome - PasswordManagerEnabled`

   Description: `Disable the Google Chrome password manager`

   Setting type: `Registry Value`

   Data type: `Integer`

   Hive Name: `HKEY_LOCAL_MACHINE`

   Key Name: `Software\Policies\Google\Chrome`

   Value Name: `PasswordManagerEnabled`

5. Select the **Create the registry value as a REG_DWORD data type if remediated for noncompliant rules** option.

6. Click on the **Compliance Rules** tab and choose **New**. Set the following options in the **Specify rules to define compliance conditions for this setting** menu:

   Name: `PasswordManagerEnabled - 0 - Dword`

7. In the **Setting must comply with the following rule** section, choose **Equals** from the drop-down list and enter the value of `0`.

8. Select both options to **Remediate noncompliant rules when supported** and **Report noncompliance if this setting instance is not found**.

9. Choose **Information** for **Noncompliance severity for reports**.

10. Choose **OK** and then **OK** again. Click on **Next** to see your compliance rule.

11. Click on **Next** to view the summary and create the Configuration Item.

The following screenshot shows the **Google Chrome - Computer** Configuration Item we created among many other Configuration Items. You can double-click on it to open the properties to add new settings or edits made:

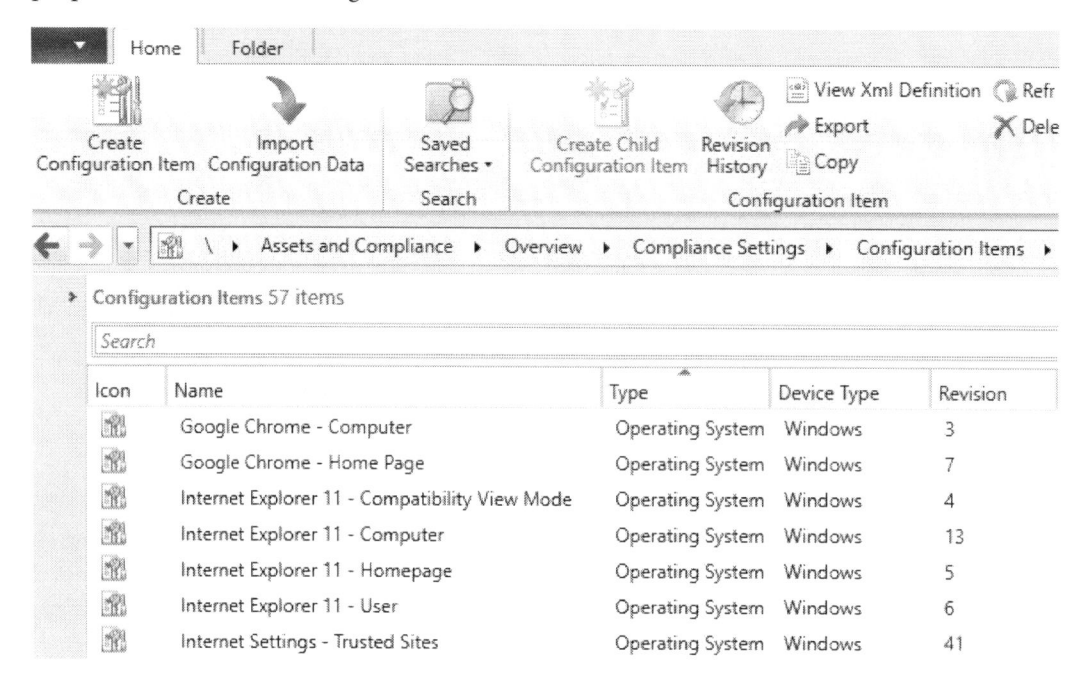

Icon	Name	Type	Device Type	Revision
	Google Chrome - Computer	Operating System	Windows	3
	Google Chrome - Home Page	Operating System	Windows	7
	Internet Explorer 11 - Compatibility View Mode	Operating System	Windows	4
	Internet Explorer 11 - Computer	Operating System	Windows	13
	Internet Explorer 11 - Homepage	Operating System	Windows	5
	Internet Explorer 11 - User	Operating System	Windows	6
	Internet Settings - Trusted Sites	Operating System	Windows	41

Figure 8.4 – Configuration Items in Configuration Manager

Now that we have covered how to create a Configuration Item, let's look at building a Configuration Baseline using this Configuration Item to remediate any noncompliant configurations.

Building a Configuration Baseline

A Configuration Baseline can contain single or multiple Configuration Items, other baselines, or software updates that are used for evaluation. A Configuration Baseline is assigned to collections where each device downloads it and assesses it against its current configuration. The following screenshot is the Configuration Manager applet from the control panel on a workstation. It shows all of the Configuration Baselines and the **Compliance** status for each baseline:

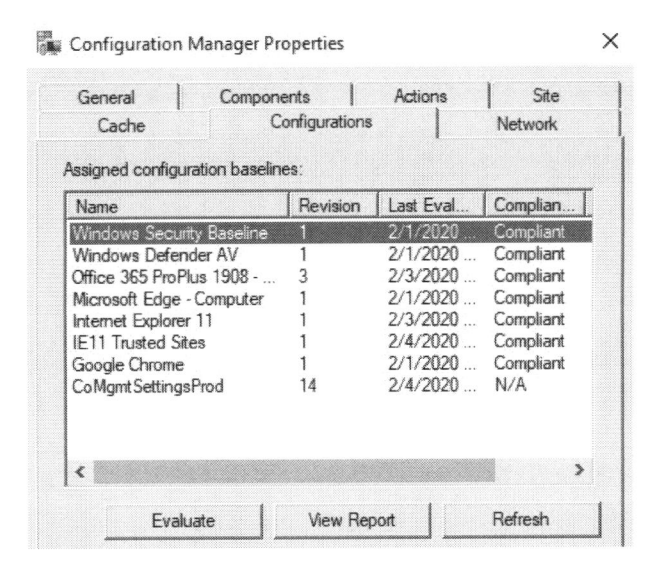

Figure 8.5 – Configuration Baselines in the Configuration Manager control panel applet

To create a Configuration Baseline using the Configuration Item we created for the Google Chrome password manager in **Create a Configuration Item**, follow these steps:

1. In the Configuration Manager console, go to **Assets and Compliance**, **Compliance Settings** and choose **Configuration Baselines**. Click on **Create Configuration Baseline** from the top toolbar.

2. In the **Create Configuration Baseline** dialog box, enter the following settings:

    Name: Google Chrome

    Description: Google Chrome computer policies

3. Click on **Add** and choose **Configuration Item**.

4. In **the Add Configuration Items** dialog box, find the **Google Chrome – Computer** Configuration Item that we created earlier. Select it and then click on **Add**. Select **OK**.

5. Click on **OK** to commit the changes.

> **Tip**
> The **Always apply this baseline even for co-managed clients** checkbox is important to note. Selecting this option will force the baseline to evaluate the device, even if the device configuration workload is configured to Intune in the co-management settings.

Next, let's look at deploying this policy to a collection of devices. Follow these steps to deploy the baseline:

1. Select **Google Chrome Configuration Baseline**, and click on **Deploy** in the toolbar to open the Deployment menu.
2. Select the checkboxes for **Remediate noncompliant rules when supported** and **Allow remediation outside the maintenance window**.
3. Click on **Browse** next to **Select the collection for this Configuration Baseline deployment**.
4. Click on the drop down and choose **Device collections**. Then, select the collection you wish to target. In this example, we have a device collection called `All Workstations` that targets all Windows workstations. Click on **OK**. We strongly encourage you to test a smaller collection first before scheduling a larger rollout.
5. Under **Schedule**, keep **Simple schedule** selected and change the **Run every** option to 3 days. Click on **OK**.

> **Tip**
> For non-mission critical baselines, we find that between 1 and 3 days is a good middle ground for policy evaluations. Keep in mind that the shorter the time interval, the more network traffic and strain is placed on the site server and its services.

In the following screenshot, you can see the menu options for **Deploy Configuration Baselines**:

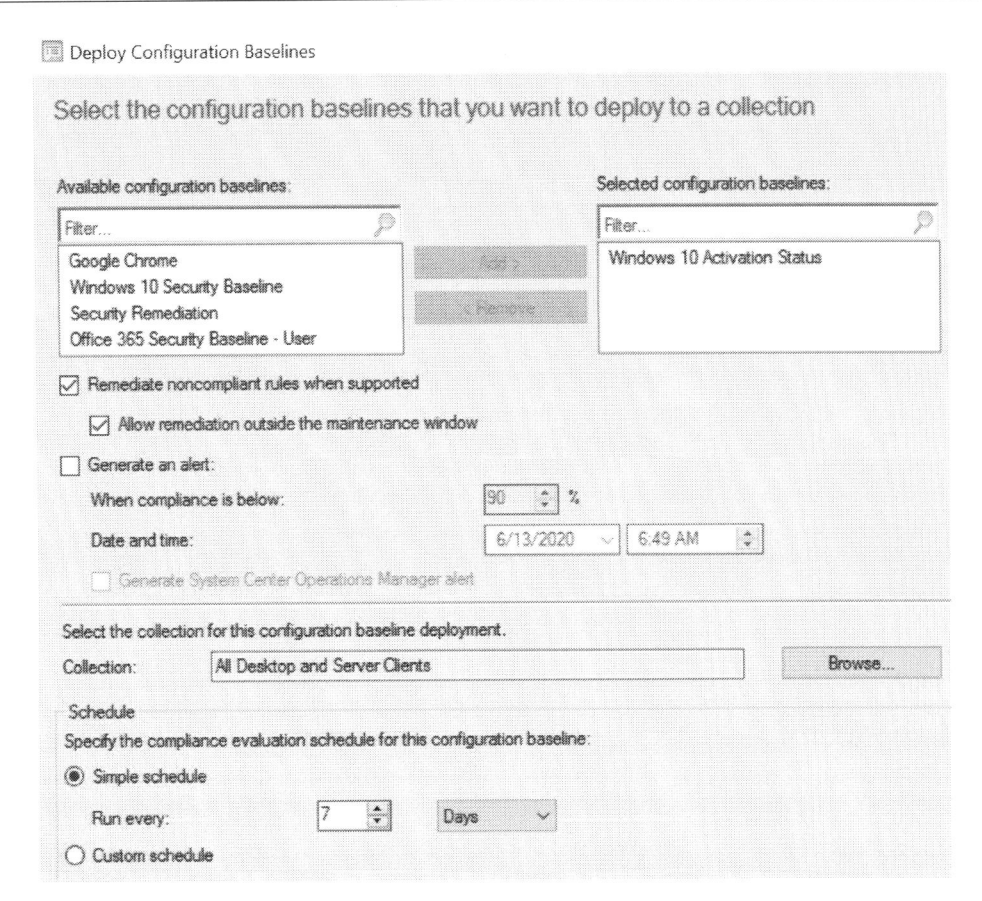

Figure 8.6 – The Deploy Configuration Baselines menu in Configuration Manager

Now that we have deployed a Configuration Baseline, let's look at how to run reports to view device compliance.

Reporting on a Configuration Baseline

Configuration Manager is filled with built-in or "canned" reports. Let's look at a high-level view of the overall compliance of the Configuration Baseline we just deployed. Follow these steps to run the **Summary compliance of a Configuration Baseline for a collection** report:

1. In the Configuration Manager console, go to **Monitoring**, click on **Reporting**, and choose **Reports**. Expand the **Reports** folder in the left-hand navigation to view the expanded tree view.

2. Select the **Compliance and Settings Management** folder and choose the **Summary compliance of a Configuration Baseline for a collection** report to open the menu.

3. Click on **Values** next to the Configuration Baseline name and select the **Google Chrome baseline** that we created earlier.

4. Click on **Values** next to **Collection**, and choose a collection that you wish to report on. In this case, we will choose the collection we deployed earlier.

5. Click on **View Report** to open the report.

The following screenshot shows the compliance status of the Google Chrome baseline. Click on the disk icon in the toolbar to view the export options, such as **export to CSV**:

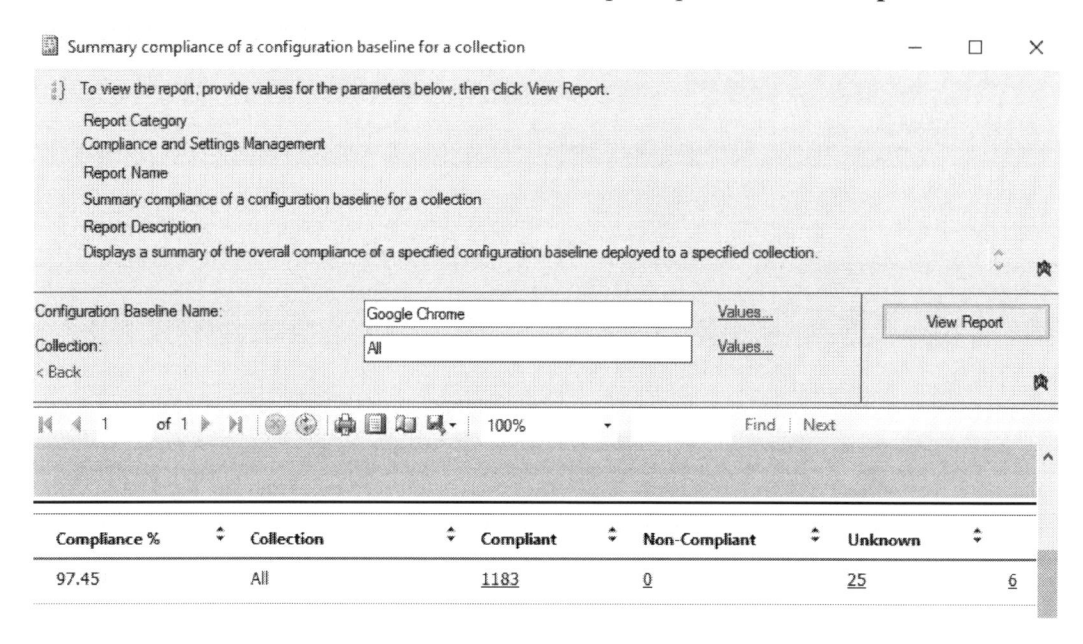

Figure 8.7 – Compliance report for a Configuration Baseline

We just learned how to create a Configuration Item, building and deploying a Configuration Baseline, and how to report on compliance. Next, let's take a look at assigning Endpoint Protection policies with Configuration Manager.

Assigning Endpoint Protection

Configuration Manager can manage Endpoint Protection policies for Windows Defender ATP and Windows Firewall. If you are using co-management, check where your workload settings are set in the co-management settings to determine whether you are using Intune or Configuration Manager to configure Endpoint Protection. With **Assets and Compliance** > **Endpoint Protection**, you can create the following types of policies:

- **Antimalware** policies are used to determine the actions taken by Endpoint Protection and include setting actions for the following:

    --Scheduled scans.

    --Scan settings.

    --Default actions for how Endpoint Protection responds to detected threats.

    --Real-time protection settings.

    --Exclusion settings.

    --Advanced settings such as notifications and when to delete quarantined files.

    --Threat overrides for custom remediation actions.

    --Cloud protection services allow the collection and sending of information regarding detected malware to Microsoft for analysis.

    --Security intelligence updates.

- **Windows Defender Firewall** policies are used to enable Windows Defender Firewall for domain, private, and/or public profiles. You can choose to block all incoming connections on each and notify the user when Windows Defender Firewall blocks a new program.

- **A Windows Defender ATP policy** is used to onboard or offboard devices to the Microsoft Defender **Advanced Threat Protection** (**ATP**) service. You will need to generate a configuration file from the Microsoft Defender ATP portal to deploy to your devices.

- **Windows Defender Exploit Guard** policies allow you to manage the settings around attack surface reduction, controlled folder access, exploit protection, and network protection.

- **Windows Defender Application Guard** policies set the protection used by Hyper-V virtualization, which protects your end users by opening untrusted sites in an isolated container with Microsoft Edge.

- **Windows Defender Application Control** is a set of policies that dictates which trusted executable files, system files, file paths, and drivers can run on Windows 10 devices.

If you are using the Windows Defender ATP service, machines will need to be onboarded with an onboarding package. We will cover onboarding Windows devices to the Defender ATP service in *Chapter 9*, *Keeping Your Windows Client Secure*. Next, let's dive into Intune and learn how to create and enforce policies with **Mobile Device Management** (**MDM**).

Creating Policies with Intune

A great benefit of managed devices is the ability to set compliance requirements that must be met to ensure security settings are in place and the device is compliant. When a Windows device is evaluated, Intune leverages Azure AD to keep a compliance status. This status, coupled with conditional access, allows administrators to block or apply restrictions on devices until they meet the rule requirements set by the policies.

The following screenshot is the device compliance overview of a managed Intune device. There are six separate compliance policies assigned to this device used in the compliance evaluation:

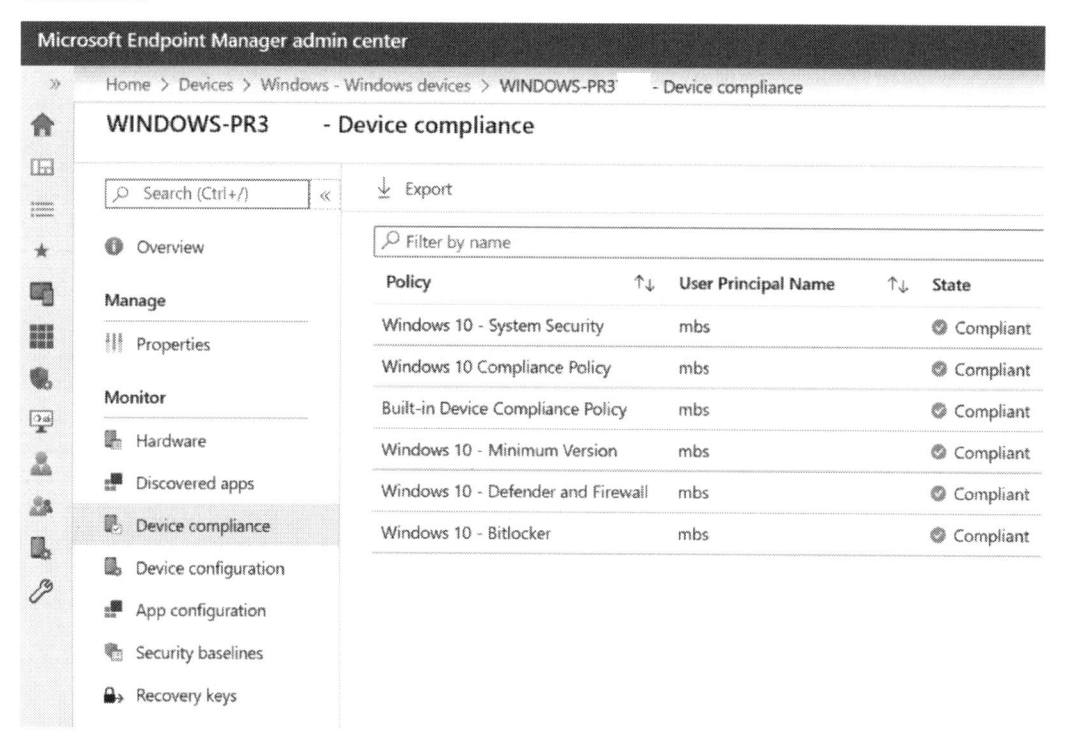

Figure 8.8 – Device compliance state of an Intune managed device

There are three actions that can be configured for devices that are noncompliant, and they are as follows:

- Mark a device noncompliant.
- Send an email to the end user.
- Remotely lock the noncompliant device.

The **Device compliance** evaluation status can then be used as an access condition for a conditional access policy; for example, a conditional access policy to all users that says access to SharePoint Online requires multi-factor authentication or a compliant device. If the user's device falls out of compliance, then they must use multi-factor authentication to access SharePoint Online even if on a company-issued device.

We recommend configuring Windows 10 compliance policies for the following evaluations:

- Device Health Attestation evaluation rules requiring BitLocker, Secure Boot, and Code Integrity
- Minimum OS version
- Block simple passwords
- Require a **Trusted Platform Module** (**TPM**) to be present
- Require the Microsoft Defender AV solution to be enabled and require real-time protection
- Require a machine risk score to be medium or lower from the Microsoft Defender ATP service

> **Tip**
> Co-management customers can also leverage Configuration Manager compliance as an evaluation condition for devices.

Let's look at how to create and assign a device compliance policy that checks for a minimum Windows 10 OS version.

Configuring a device compliance policy

To create a device compliance policy that checks for a minimum OS version, follow these steps. We will set Windows 10, version 1909 (OS build 18363.628), as the required minimum to meet compliance:

1. Log in to `https://devicemanagement.microsoft.com`.
2. Choose **Devices** and select **Compliance Policies** from the **Policy** section.
3. Click on **Create Policy** from the toolbar and provide these inputs:

   Name: `Windows 10 - Minimum Version`

   Description: `Windows 10 Version compliance`

   Platform: Windows 10 and later
4. Click on **Settings** and choose **Device Properties**. In the **Minimum OS version**, enter `10.0.18363.628` and click on **OK**.
5. Click on **OK** again and select **Actions for noncompliance**.
6. Let's leave **Mark device noncompliant** as the action, but note that this is where you can add **Send email to user** as an additional action.
7. Click on **Create** to build the policy.
8. Select your policy from the list of compliance policies. In the **Manage** section, choose **Assignments**, and select the Azure AD user security group you wish to target.

The assignment status on your compliance policy can be viewed directly in the overview of the policy itself. The following diagram shows the assignment status of devices assigned the policy:

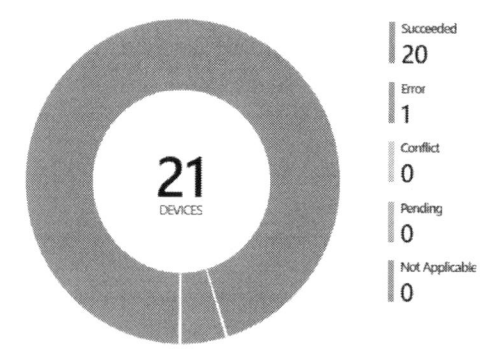

Figure 8.9 – Policy assignment status overview of an Intune compliance policy

Next, let's look at device configuration profiles in Intune and some of the settings that can be applied to Intune managed devices.

Configuring a device configuration profile

Device configuration profiles are where the majority of settings are configured for device security and personalization settings. Examples of the profile types that can be configured include the following:

- Administrative Templates for ADMX-backed policies such as Group Policy preferences that exist today
- Device restriction profiles that contain security features such as password settings, privacy, and personalizations
- Delivery optimization to control the bandwidth and caching for Windows Update for Business
- Device firmware settings for vendors that support the **Device Firmware Configuration Interface (DFCI)** in UEFI
- Endpoint Protection to configure features of Microsoft Defender such as Firewall, SmartScreen, Exploit Guard, and Encryption
- Trusted, SCEP, and PKCS certificate deployments
- VPN configurations
- Custom profiles for deploying OMA-URIs that have yet to be implemented in the UI

These are only a few of the available options for Windows 10 and later device platforms, and Microsoft is doing a great job of constantly exposing new features to the UI.

Like compliance profiles, device profiles are assigned directly to Azure AD user or device groups. Profiles that use the Windows 10 and later platforms option also allow the use of applicability rules. Here, they can define a criterion that a device must meet for the settings to apply. Currently, these rules support the property values of the OS version or edition. The following screenshot demonstrates an applicability rule to only assign the profile if the device version is between Windows 10, version 1809 and 1909:

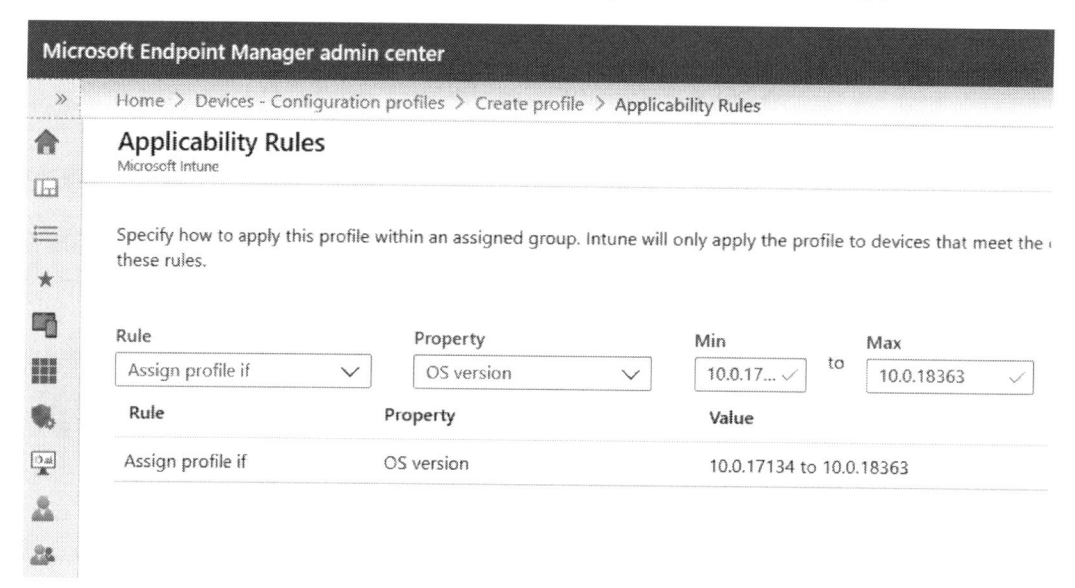

Figure 8.10 – Applicability Rules in Intune device configuration profile settings

> **Tip**
> For co-management customers, device configuration profiles will not apply to your devices unless the device configuration workload is configured for Intune. This setting can be found in Configuration Manager co-management settings.

Co-management workload settings can be found in Configuration Manager by going to **Administration** > **Cloud Services** and selecting **Co-management**. The `CoMgmtSettingsProd` Configuration Item has a **Workloads** tab with sliders for different workloads.

For more information about how to switch Configuration Manager workloads to Intune, refer to `https://docs.microsoft.com/en-us/configmgr/comanage/how-to-switch-workloads`.

Next, let's look at where to deploy custom PowerShell scripts to your devices.

Deploying PowerShell scripts

The PowerShell scripts node can be found under the **Devices** > **Policy** section. In order to use PowerShell scripts, devices must be enrolled in Intune and joined to Azure AD. On the local device, the PowerShell scripts function relies on the Intune Management Extension service to check for and run scripts. It can be found in the `Services` app. For devices that are under co-management, be sure to set the app-specific workload to `Intune`. For more information about PowerShell scripts in Intune, refer to `https://docs.microsoft.com/en-us/mem/intune/apps/intune-management-extension`.

Next, let's take a look at how to use the Administrative Templates device configuration profile type and security baselines.

Using Administrative Templates

Included in device configurations for Windows 10 and later platforms is the Administrative Templates profile type. These Windows settings are familiar to the GPO settings available in Active Directory, but they are delivered through Intune. Administrative Templates include policies for Windows, Office, and Microsoft Edge.

Assignments are applied to both user and device groups depending on whether the policy is scoped to user-specific or computer-specific settings. Currently, not all the Group Policy Administrative Templates are available yet, and legacy settings for older versions of Windows have purposely been omitted.

When browsing through Administrative Templates, use the familiar path of a group policy setting to find the appropriate path in Intune. For example, in the following screenshot, polices found traditionally in `Computer Configuration \ Administrative Templates \ Windows Components \ Windows Remote Management` can be found by using the same path starting **with Windows Components**:

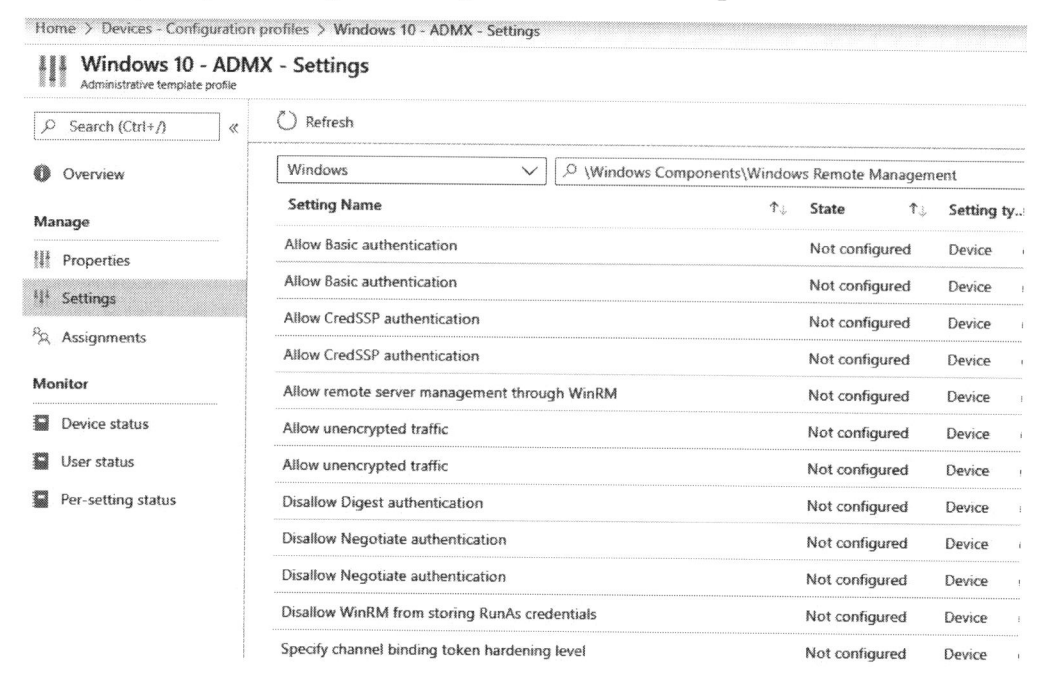

Figure 8.11 – Administrative Templates device configuration profile in Intune

Administrative Templates are great as they provide a match to commonly used GPO policies. Like Group Policy, manually configuring each setting to meet your baselines can be a tedious task. In order to help alleviate some of the administrative overhead of manually setting policies there are security baselines in Intune. Next, let's look at enforcing Intune security baselines.

Enforcing Intune security baselines

Available in Intune are preconfigured groups of Microsoft's recommended Windows 10 security settings known as security baselines. They can be thought of as the cloud equivalent to the recommended security baselines available in the Windows Security Compliance Toolkit. Security baselines can be targeted at both groups of users and devices for Windows 10 and later platforms. Whenever an updated version of a recommended baseline is released by Microsoft, you can compare the new release to your current baseline. When you are ready to append your baselines to the newly released policies, a new profile is not needed. All you need to do is change the instance version to deploy the updated policies.

Intune security baselines provide recommendations for Windows 10 MDM, Microsoft Defender ATP, and Microsoft Edge. With built-in monitoring, you can get insights about how compliant your devices are to the security configurations you set for them. The security baseline posture overview shows how many devices match the baseline, do not match, are misconfigured, or are not applicable compared to the scope of the policy assignment.

In this example, we are going to create a Microsoft Defender ATP baseline using Intune. Follow these steps:

1. Go to the Microsoft Endpoint Manager at `https://devicemanagement.microsoft.com`.
2. Log in with an account that has Intune administrative rights.
3. Go to **Endpoint Security**.
4. Choose **Security baselines**.
5. Select the **Microsoft Defender ATP** baseline.
6. Select **Create Profile**.
7. Give it a friendly name such as `Windows 10 MDATP Baseline`.
8. Microsoft already preconfigures its recommended settings based on its security analysis. Click on **Next** to accept the defaults or make any modifications to fit your custom baseline policies.

The following screenshot shows the Microsoft Defender ATP configuration settings that are available when creating a security baseline policy in Intune:

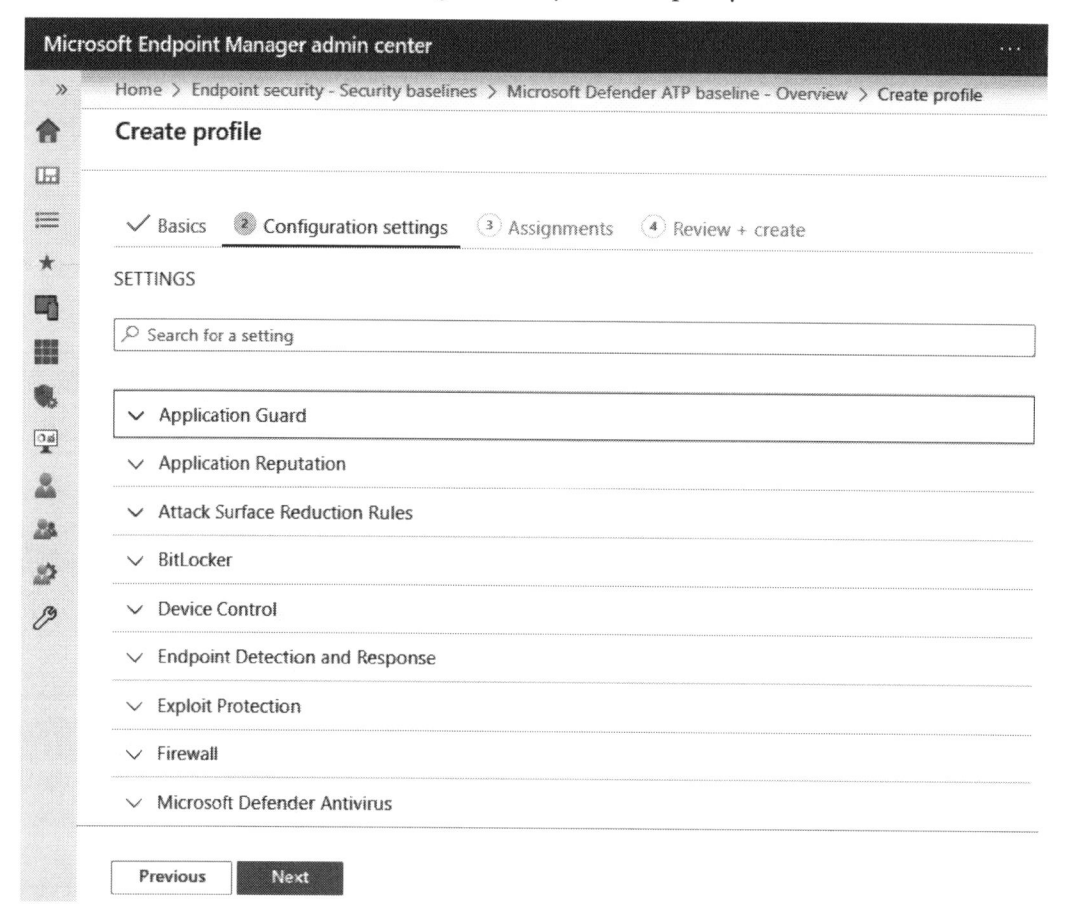

Figure 8.12 – Example of Intune security baseline configuration

9. On the **Assignments** page, decide which selected groups to include or exclude.
10. **Review + Create**.

To recap, we just covered creating compliance policies and applying configurations to your devices both with Configuration Manager and Intune. We learned about creating Configuration Items and assigning them to Configuration Baselines for evaluation and how to report on them. Then, we looked at applying device configuration profiles in Intune including Administrative Templates and Microsoft-recommended Intune security baselines. Next, let's look at using the Microsoft Security Compliance Toolkit to build your baseline policies and analyze them with the Policy Analyzer tool.

Building security baselines

Security baselining is the practice of implementing a minimum set of standards and configurations within your environment. More specifically, it involves capturing a minimum configuration for your Windows devices. Building a baseline provides a minimum defined standard that will help ensure a more secure environment as you deploy systems and devices within an organization. We covered building standards for security baselines in *Chapter 2*, *Building a Baseline*. However, here, we want to focus specifically on Windows using the Microsoft Security Compliance Toolkit to create, apply, and analyze your Windows baselines.

Using the Microsoft Security Compliance Toolkit

We will be using the recommended baselines from the Microsoft Security Compliance Toolkit to build our policies. When downloading the toolkit, the following options are available for selection from the Microsoft download site:

- Windows 10 security baselines
- Windows Server security baselines
- Microsoft Office security baselines
- Microsoft Edge security baselines
- Policy Analyzer and **Local Group Policy Object** (**LGPO**) tools

For more information about the tools that are included, refer to `https://docs.microsoft.com/en-us/windows/security/threat-protection/security-compliance-toolkit-10`.

A direct download to the toolkit can be found at `https://www.microsoft.com/en-us/download/details.aspx?id=55319`.

The following describes what's included in the security baselines ZIP file(s):

- The **documentation** folder includes an `Announcement.xml` file that summarizes recommendations along with a *What's New* section. It also includes `PolicyRules` files that are useful when running the Policy Analyzer tool and Excel files that list the configurations and settings in spreadsheets.
- The `GP Reports` folder lists the outputs of each GPO in HTML format.
- The `GPOs` folder contains the **globally unique identifiers** (**GUID**) for each GPO setting.

- The `Scripts` folder contains helpful scripts that can be used to map the GPO GUIDs to friendly names or to import baselines into Active Directory.
- The `Templates` folder includes `ADMX` and `ADML` files for group policies that are referenced in the new baselines and might not be included in the latest available download of Administrative Templates.

Let's look at the Policy Analyzer tool and explore how we can use it to compare the GPOs from the toolkit to the current local registry and policy settings.

Comparing policies with Policy Analyzer

The Policy Analyzer tool is useful for comparing GPOs against other GPOs, the local policy settings on the computer, and the local registry. If you have downloaded the Microsoft Security Compliance Toolkit already, ensure you have selected `PolicyAnalyzer.zip` and `Windows 10 Version 1909 and Windows Server version 1909 Security Baseline.zip` at a minimum. Extract them if you wish to follow along.

Let's compare the out-of-box Windows 10 settings to the Windows 10 1909 computer security baseline by following these steps:

1. Open **PolicyAnalyzer.exe** as an **Administrator**.
2. Click on **Add**, choose **File**, and select **Add files from GPO(s)….**
3. Open the directory where you extracted the Windows 10 security baselines, and select the folder with the GUID for the **MSFT Windows 10 1909** – computer policy.

> **Tip**
> There are many GUIDs inside the GPO folder of the extracted baseline. Clicking on the `gpreport.xml` file will display the friendly name.

4. In the **Policy File Import** menu, click on **Import**. Give it a friendly name such as `MSFT Windows 10 1909 - Computer`, and click on **Save**.
5. This will bring you back to the main menu of **Policy Analyzer**. Ensure the policy you imported is selected and select the **Compare Local Registry** option. Click on the **View/Compare** button to bring up the **Policy Viewer**.

The column headings are straightforward and provide an overview of the policy group or registry key as well as the policy setting. If you click on a row, detailed information will be presented about the policy in a **Details** pane. Here are a few notes to keep in mind about the menu options:

- Selecting **View** > **Show only Differences** will display all of the differences between the recommended baseline and what's currently set in the local registry.

- Selecting **View** > **Show only Conflicts** will display settings that differ from the recommended baseline to the current setting. These will be highlighted in yellow.

- Selecting **Export** > **Export table to Excel** will export only the table with differences or conflicts.

- Selecting **Export** > **Export all data to Excel** will include the **Details** pane explanation.

The following screenshot shows the Policy Viewer output after clicking on the **View/Compare** option. Anything highlighted in yellow is a conflict between the GPO and the current setting in the local registry:

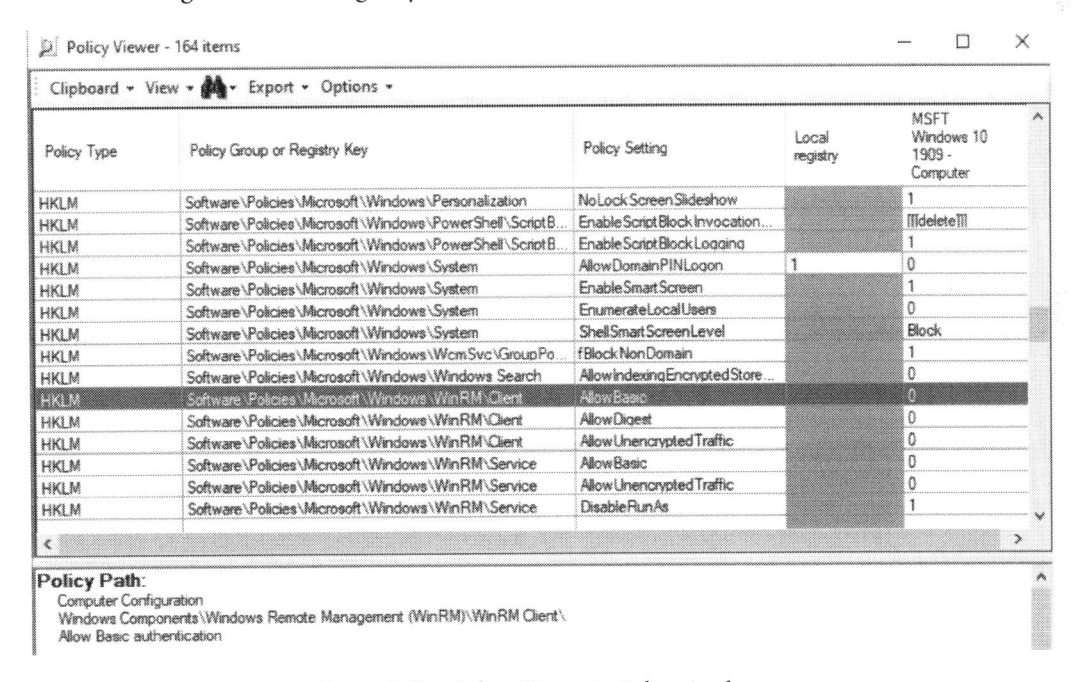

Figure 8.13 – Policy Viewer in Policy Analyzer

Next, let's demonstrate how to take the Windows 10 Computer recommended baseline and create and assign a GPO to an **Organizational Unit** (**OU**) in Active Directory.

Creating a GPO from the baseline recommendation

Let's create a GPO from the Windows 10 1909 Computer baseline. To do this, we will need to connect to a workstation that can edit Group Policy and has access to the downloaded Windows 10 baseline files from the toolkit. Open the **Group Policy Management** console, and follow these steps:

1. Select an **Organizational Unit (OU)** that contains the systems you wish to target. Right-click on it and choose **Create a GPO in this domain, and Link it here...**.
2. Give it a friendly name such as `Windows 10 - 1909 Computer`.
3. Click on the **Group Policy Objects** folder and find the policy that you created earlier. Right-click on it and choose **Import Settings**.
4. Click on **Next** a few times until you get to the **Backup location** where you can choose a backup folder. Browse to the GPOs folder inside the downloaded and extracted baseline: `Windows 10 Version 1909 and Windows Server Version 1909 Security Baseline.zip`. Click on **Next** and then select **MSFT Windows 10 1909 – Computer** from the list of backed-up GPOs.
5. Click on **Next** until you get to the **Migrating References** menu, and select **Copying them identically from the source**. Click on **Next** and then **Finish**.

If the Group Policy imported successfully, it will show **GPO: Windows 10 -1909 Computer...Succeeded**. Now that the policy is imported, let's modify the default settings to change the behavior of the elevation prompt for standard users and set to prompt for credentials on elevation:

1. Right-click on the GPO and choose **Edit**. Navigate to `Computer Configuration > Window Settings > Security Settings > Local Policies > Security Options`. Find the **User Account Control: Behavior of the elevation prompt for standard users** policy and double-click on it. Change the drop down to **Prompt for credentials on the secure desktop**. Click on **OK**.

This setting will allow us to open the Command Prompt window as an administrator if we are logged on as a standard user. If we left this policy, the user would receive a blocked notice and would need to contact the IT administrator.

> **Tip**
> Right-click on the **GPO** and choose **Save Report** to export a handy HTML of all the settings that will be applied.

Let's connect to a workstation that is targeted by the new policy to validate it. Follow these steps to run a **Resultant Set of Policies** (**RSOP**) and use Policy Analyzer to compare the baseline GPO to the applied settings:

1. Open Command Prompt and run `gpupdate /force` to check for policy updates.
2. Next, open Command Prompt as an administrator and type in `gpresult /r /scope computer`. If the **GPO** was applied, you should see the **Windows 10 1909 – Computer** policy listed like in the following screenshot of **Applied Group Policy Objects**:

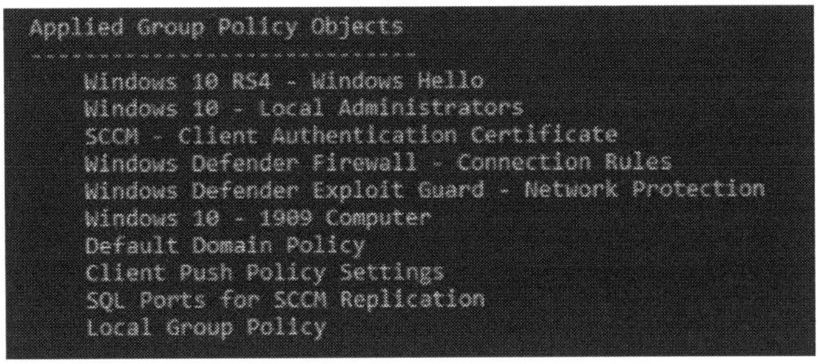

Figure 8.14 – RSOP of Applied Group Policy Objects

3. Now that we have confirmed the policy was applied, open `PolicyAnalyzer.exe` as an administrator on the workstation.
4. Select the **MSFT Windows 10 1909 – Computer** policy definition we created earlier, and then select **Compare local registry**. Click on **View / Compare**.
5. Click on **View**, then choose **Show only Conflicts**. Note the conflicts from the policy that we modified before running the RSOP.

The following screenshot shows a conflict between the recommended baseline policy and the modification we made to allow a prompt for credentials using a standard account. Also enabled on this PC is to allow a PIN to be used to log on to the domain:

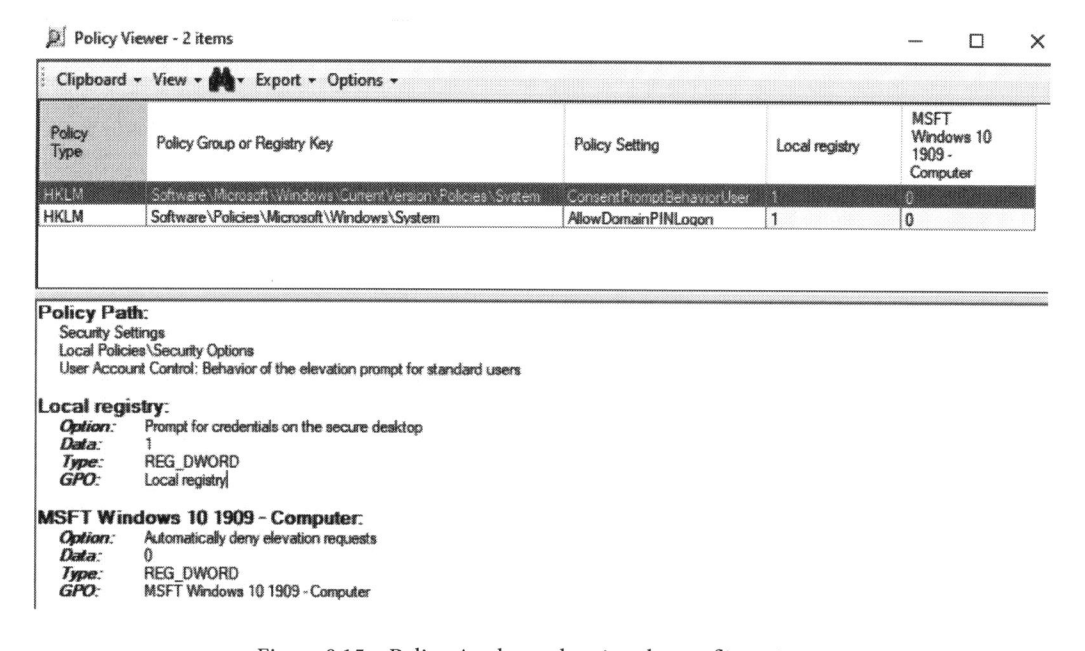

Figure 8.15 – Policy Analyzer showing the conflicts view

> **Tip**
> If choosing the **Local Policy** option, Policy Analyzer will automatically create a policy definition file to use for comparison later.

We strongly recommend that you test these settings out before deploying them in a production environment so that you can truly understand the effects they will have on your systems and your end user's experience.

Next, let's take a look at how you can use Configuration Manager to report compliance on your security baseline and even force remediation for noncompliance. This is extremely useful in co-management scenarios when devices are Azure AD joined and do not use Group Policy.

Creating a Configuration Baseline from a GPO

To create a Configuration Baseline from the settings of a GPO, we need to export the GPO and create a Configuration Item from the settings. For this task, we are going to be using the `Convert-GPOtoCI.ps1` PowerShell script from the `SamMRoberts` GitHub repository. To download the PowerShell script, go to https://github.com/SamMRoberts/Convert-GPOtoCI and click on **Clone or Download** to download the ZIP file. It is recommended that you read the `README.md` file for full usage instructions, including syntax. Follow these steps to import the GPO settings to a Configuration Item:

1. Extract the downloaded ZIP file to a system that has access to manage **Group Policy Objects** and connect to **Configuration Manager PowerShell**.

2. Open PowerShell as an administrator and go to the extracted directory by typing in `CD "PATH/TO/Extracted/Folder"` and replacing the PATH in quotes with the actual file path of the extracted script. Press *Enter*.

   We are going to target the **Windows 10 – 1909 Computer** policy that we created earlier. You will need the **Fully Qualified Domain Name** (**FQDN**) of your domain and the three-letter site code in order to create the Configuration Item. We will also be using the `-Remediate` option to allow the settings to be remediated if noncompliance is found.

3. In PowerShell, type in the following code and replace the parameters to fit your site and domain settings: `.\Convert-GPOtoCI.ps1 -GpoTarget "Windows 10-1909 Computer" -DomainTarget mydomain.prod.com -siteCode ABC -Remediate`.

4. If prompted, press *R* to run once.

   > **Tip**
   > Depending on the script execution policies, you may see a different security warning. To learn more about execution policies, please refer to https://docs.microsoft.com/en-us/powershell/module/microsoft.powershell.core/about/about_execution_policies.

The script will process the targeted GPO. As shown in the following screenshot, it found 86 keys and 100 values:

```
1  cd "C:\Convert-GPOtoCI-master"
2  .\Convert-GPOtoCI.ps1 -GpoTarget "Windows 10 - 1909 Computer" `
3      -DomainTarget "prod.mtlab.com" `
4      -SiteCode "MTL" `
5      -Remediate
```

```
PS C:\Convert-GPOtoCI-master> cd "C:\Convert-GPOtoCI-master"
.\Convert-GPOtoCI.ps1 -GpoTarget "Windows 10 - 1909 Computer" `
    -DomainTarget "prod.mtlab.com" `
    -SiteCode "MTL" `
    -Remediate
Querying for registry keys associated with Windows 10 - 1909 Computer...
    87 keys found.
    105 values found.
Creating Configuration Item...
Setting DCM Digest...
Complete

PS C:\Convert-GPOtoCI-master>
```

Figure 8.16 – Convert-GPOtoCI.ps1 PowerShell script creating a Configuration Item

5. Open the Configuration Manager console and navigate to **Assets and Compliance** > **Compliance Settings** > **Configuration Items**. You should see the **Windows 10 – 1909 Computer** Configuration Item that was created by running the script.

If you open the properties of the Configuration Item and click on the **Settings** tab, you can see all of the registry values that were imported, as follows:

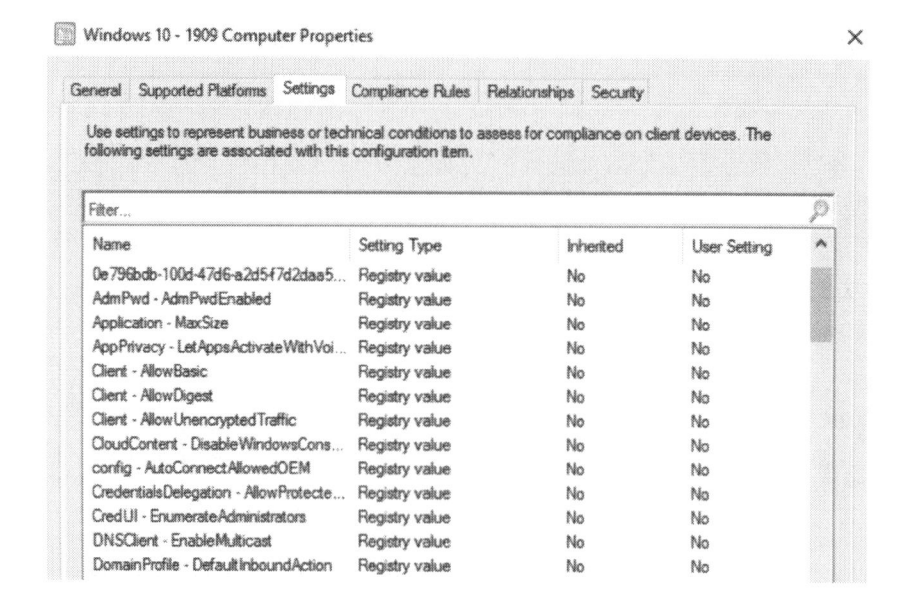

Name	Setting Type	Inherited	User Setting
0e796bdb-100d-47d6-a2d5-f7d2daa5...	Registry value	No	No
AdmPwd - AdmPwdEnabled	Registry value	No	No
Application - MaxSize	Registry value	No	No
AppPrivacy - LetAppsActivateWithVoi...	Registry value	No	No
Client - AllowBasic	Registry value	No	No
Client - AllowDigest	Registry value	No	No
Client - AllowUnencryptedTraffic	Registry value	No	No
CloudContent - DisableWindowsCons...	Registry value	No	No
config - AutoConnectAllowedOEM	Registry value	No	No
CredentialsDelegation - AllowProtecte...	Registry value	No	No
CredUI - EnumerateAdministrators	Registry value	No	No
DNSClient - EnableMulticast	Registry value	No	No
DomainProfile - DefaultInboundAction	Registry value	No	No

Figure 8.17 – The Settings tab of a Configuration Item

Click on the **Compliance Rules** tab and open a rule. You can see that **Remediate noncompliant rules when supported** and **Report noncompliance if this setting instance is not found** are both checked.

> **Tip**
> The severity of the noncompliant items can be changed by specifying the severity setting in the PowerShell command. The default value is `Information`.

Next, let's continue and assign this Configuration Item to a Configuration Baseline and validate the settings against our workstation.

6. Navigate to **Assets and Compliance** > **Compliance Settings** > **Configuration Baselines**, click on **Create** in the toolbar, and then select **Create a Configuration Baseline**.

7. Give it a friendly name such as `Windows 10 Security Baseline`. Give it a description.

8. Click on **Add** under the **Configuration data** and choose **Configuration Items**. Select the **Windows 10 – 1909 Computer** Configuration Item that was just created and click on **Add**. Choose **Ok**. Choose **OK** back in the **Create Configuration Baseline** menu to build it.

9. Select the security baseline and click on **Deploy** in the toolbar. We will leave the defaults as they are since the workstations being targeted are domain-joined, and we don't want to enforce policies from two sources. Click on **Browse** to select a collection to target. We clicked on the drop down to switch to **Device collections** and chose our **All Workstations** collection, which contains Windows 10 workstations. Click on **OK**.

10. Change the **Run every** schedule to `1` day. We will want to ensure this policy is being evaluated frequently. Click on **Ok**.

Let's head over to our workstation and check whether the baseline is being evaluated.

11. Open **Control Panel**, filter to **small items**, and choose the **Configuration Manager** control panel applet.

12. Click on the **Configurations** tab and check for the *Windows 10 Security Baseline*. Select it and click on **Evaluate**.

> **Tip**
> From the Configuration Manager control panel applet, choosing the **Actions** tab and running the **Machine Policy Retrieval & Evaluation Cycle** will force the PC to check Configuration Manager and download any new policies.

As shown in the following screenshot, the baseline policy is reporting as **Non-Compliant**:

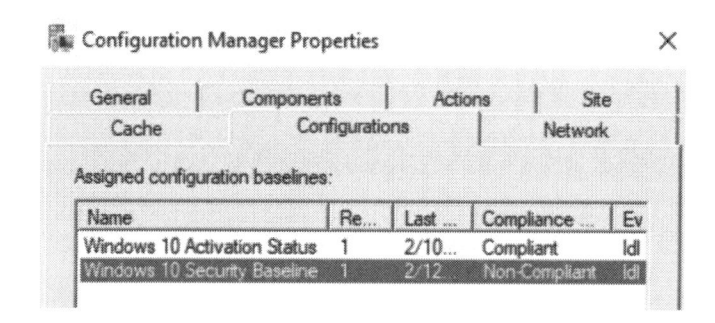

Figure 8.18 – Non-Compliant evaluation of a security baseline

13. Click on the **View Report** button to look at an HTML view of the conflicts.

The following screenshot shows the HTML compliance report comparing the local configured settings against the security baseline that was evaluated through Configuration Manager:

Summary:

Name	Revision	Type	Baseline Policy	Compliance State	Non-Compliance Severity	Discovery Failures	Non-Compliant Rules
Windows 10 Security Baseline	1	Baseline		Non-Compliant	Information	0	6
Windows 10 - 1909 Computer	2	Operating System Configuration Item	Required	Non-Compliant	Information	0	6

Details:

NAME: Windows 10 Security Baseline
TYPE: Baseline
REVISION: 1
COMPLIANCE STATE: Non-Compliant
NON-COMPLIANCE SEVERITY: Information
DESCRIPTION: Windows 10 1909 Computer Security Baseline

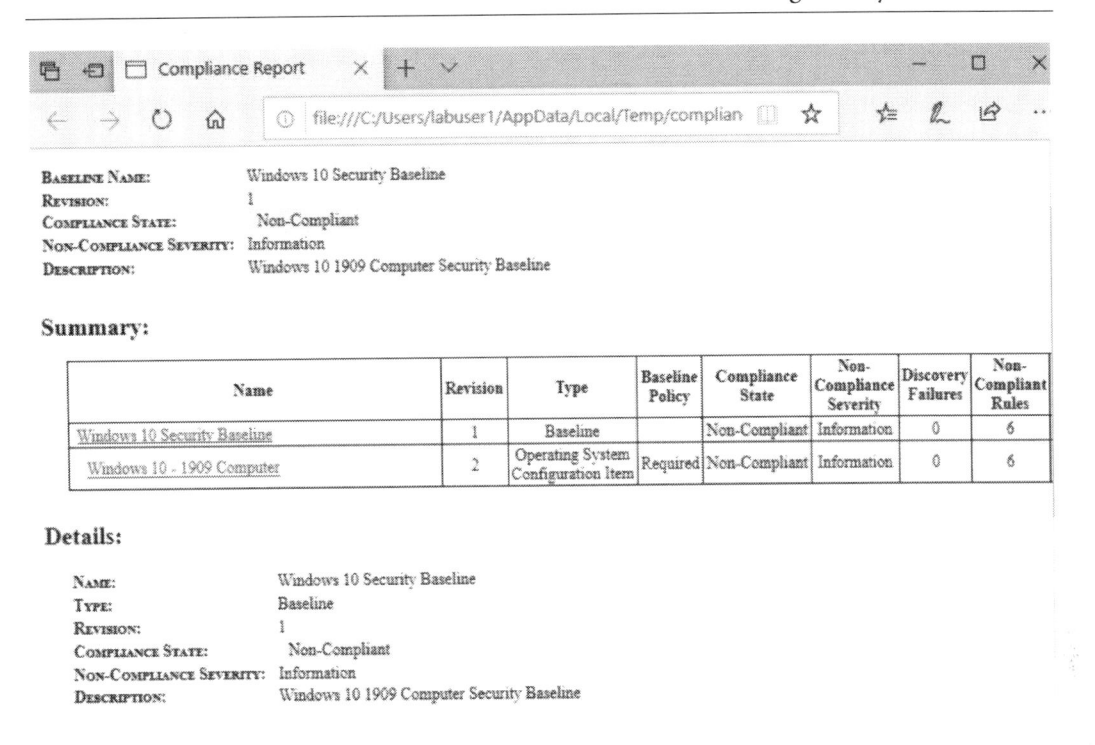

Figure 8.19 – HTML Compliance Report on the local workstation

During the import of the GPO to the Configuration Item, some settings might have a `null` value in the expression and may need to be manually updated for proper compliance to be reported. In the HTML compliance report, the **expression** column will display `Equals`, but there will be no value included. Typically, there are only a few settings and they can quickly be remediated by cross-checking the actual GPO, the registry key on the local device, and the compliance rule from the setting within the Configuration Item.

We have just covered how to use the Microsoft Security Compliance Toolkit to build security baselines. We learned how to use the Policy Analyzer tool to compare the Microsoft-recommended baselines to the current configurations on a Windows workstation. Next, we created a GPO from the baseline and deployed it to an OU in Active Directory. Finally, we imported the GPO to a Configuration Manager Configuration Item using the `SamMRoberts` GitHub PowerShell script that can be used in a security baseline for mitigation of noncompliant settings or reporting purposes.

Next, we will cover the best practices for securely connecting to servers remotely and provide an overview of two Azure services that ensure secure connectivity and **Just-in-Time (JIT)** access.

Connecting securely to servers remotely

There should be extra attention paid when setting up and configuring remote access to your environment. Remote access should be very strategic and the footprint extremely small. Access to your environment directly over the internet should be limited. This exposure poses significant risks and could easily allow an attacker to gain access to your servers. Ensure your standards cover a secure and locked-down remote management strategy, and limit or eliminate internet access to your servers. This section will provide more detail about several tools that you can use to enforce a secure remote access policy.

Remote management and support tools

Remote management is a critical task that is used to support both your end users and the infrastructure within your environment. There are many methods available to remotely manage and access your environment. Your support desk will have some form of remote management tools in place to access end user devices. Ensure whatever remote support tool is selected is thoroughly reviewed and provides a secure connection to your support staff. Additionally, ensure that no one can connect to your user's device without the user providing permission, as this could become a liability issue.

For your infrastructure, your support staff most likely leverages **Remote Desktop Protocol** (**RDP**) or PowerShell to manage your Microsoft servers and services. Just like support for your end users, there are many options available in which to access your servers for remote management. It is important, as an organization, that you define and enforce policies that specify exactly how your support staff handles these remote management tasks. Consider the following recommendations when building your remote access strategy:

- Never allow direct remote management from the internet:

    --Use a jump server or use VPN at a minimum.

    --Change the default RDP port from `3389`.

- Enforce strong access policies:

    --Ensure separate accounts are used to access servers.

    --Enforce multi-factor authentication.

- Enforce encryption and secure access for remote management and limit where connections can originate from.
- Minimize the number of support staff accessing your infrastructure and servers.
- Monitor and audit all access to your infrastructure and servers.

> **Tip**
> To limit interactive logons to servers, you can deploy **Remote Server Administration Tools (RSAT)** to administrative workstations: `https://docs.microsoft.com/en-us/windows-server/remote/remote-server-administration-tools`.

Next, we will review JIT access and Azure Bastion services to provide additional security within your remote access management strategy.

Using Azure Security Center Just-in-Time access

As a feature of **Azure Security Center** (**ASC**) standard, **JIT** access works by creating or modifying **Network Security Group** (**NSG**) and Firewall rules in Azure to protect access at the network layer. The ports that you wish to be available are configured in the JIT access configuration. When a user needs just-in-time access, they issue an access request through ASC. Once approved, ASC automatically adds an inbound rule opening the configured ports on the resources' NSG or firewall. The traffic is allowed for the duration of time specified in the request and once the time allotment expires, the NSG rules are returned to the previous **deny** state. For a user to use the request access functionality through JIT, a custom **role-based access control** (**RBAC**) role might need to be created and assigned directly to the user. It must contain these actions:

- `Microsoft.Security/locations/jitNetworkAccessPolicies/initiate/action`
- `Microsoft.Security/locations/jitNetworkAccessPolicies/*/read`
- `Microsoft.Compute/virtualMachines/read`
- `Microsoft.Network/networkInterfaces/*/read`

We covered creating a custom role in *Chapter 3, Server Infrastructure Management*, implementing role-based access control. To read more information about the resource policy providers specified earlier, visit `https://docs.microsoft.com/en-us/azure/role-based-access-control/resource-provider-operations`.

> **Tip**
> These policies must be scoped to the subscription or resource group in which the VM and network interface reside.

Further information about Azure Security Center JIT access can be found at https://docs.microsoft.com/en-us/azure/security-center/security-center-just-in-time.

Let's look at creating a JIT access rule to allow RDP over port 65001. In *Chapter 6, Network Fundamentals for Hardening Windows*, we covered modifying the default listening port for RDP to 65001 on a Windows Server 2019 host, in the *Creating a network security group in Azure* section. If you don't have Azure Security Center standard, you can enable a free 30-day trial and deploy the agents directly from the Security Center overview page in order to continue with the step-by-step instructions:

1. Open **Security Center** by searching for it in the Azure portal.
2. Click on **Just in time VM access** under **Advanced Cloud Defense**.
3. In the **Virtual Machines** section, click on **Recommended** to view VMs that are recommended for JIT VM access to be applied.

> **Tip**
> The **No Recommendation** tab lists VMs that may either not be running or are not part of an NSG.

4. Select the VM we previously modified when creating the custom RDP rule. Choose **Enable JIT on 1 VMs**.
5. On the JIT VM access configuration page, the default port rules are already created. Let's add a new rule to accommodate the custom port of 65001.

    JIT VM access configuration already has default rules for the following ports:

    --Port 22 is common for SSH.

    --Port 3389 is the default RDP port.

    --Port 5985 and 5896 are WinRM ports.

6. Click on **Add** and enter 65001 for the port number and choose **TCP** for the protocol. Leave **Max request time** at 3 hours. Click on **OK**.
7. Click on **Save**.

Let's take a look at the new configuration. In the Azure portal, navigate to the VM used to configure JIT and click on **Networking** under **Settings**. In the following screenshot, notice a new inbound augmented security rule, called `SecurityCenter-JITRule`, that has all the ports specified in the configuration. By default, the action is set to **Deny**:

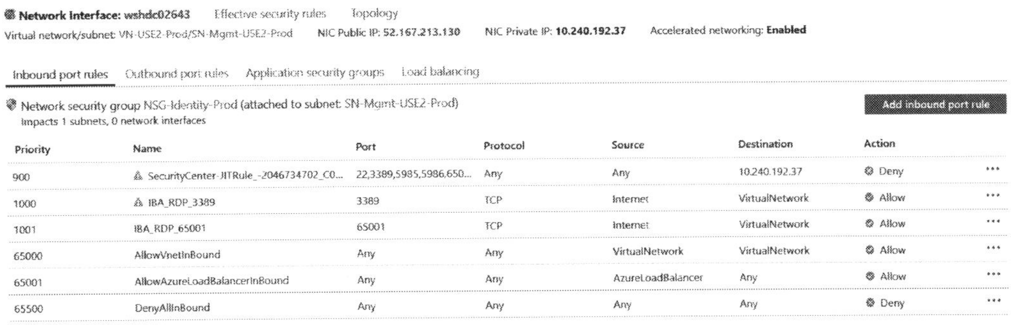

Priority	Name	Port	Protocol	Source	Destination	Action
900	SecurityCenter-JITRule_-2046734702_C0...	22,3389,5985,5986,650...	Any	Any	10.240.192.37	Deny
1000	IBA_RDP_3389	3389	TCP	Internet	VirtualNetwork	Allow
1001	IBA_RDP_65001	65001	TCP	Internet	VirtualNetwork	Allow
65000	AllowVnetInBound	Any	Any	VirtualNetwork	VirtualNetwork	Allow
65001	AllowAzureLoadBalancerInBound	Any	Any	AzureLoadBalancer	Any	Allow
65500	DenyAllInBound	Any	Any	Any	Any	Deny

Figure 8.20 – Networking settings for the network interface attached to a VM

> **Tip**
>
> Security Center JIT rules default to a priority of 4096, which is the highest integer value that you can set in a custom security rule. If custom rules were created to allow RDP previously, modify the priority of the new Security Center rule to be a lower integer, or delete the previous rules in order to use JIT effectively.

Once the JIT access rule has been configured, RDP will effectively be blocked. To request access, follow these steps:

8. Navigate to **Security Center** in the Azure portal.
9. Choose **Just in time VM access** under **Advanced Cloud Defense**.
10. Under the **Configured** tab, select the VM to RDP into, and choose the **Request Access** button.
11. Toggle the rule for port 65001 to **On**, and select **My IP** in the **Allow Source IP** column. We can leave the time range as 3 hours.
12. Enter a request justification and choose **Open Ports**.

The following screenshot shows the custom port rule we created. During the access request, you can specifically choose the ports you need for connectivity:

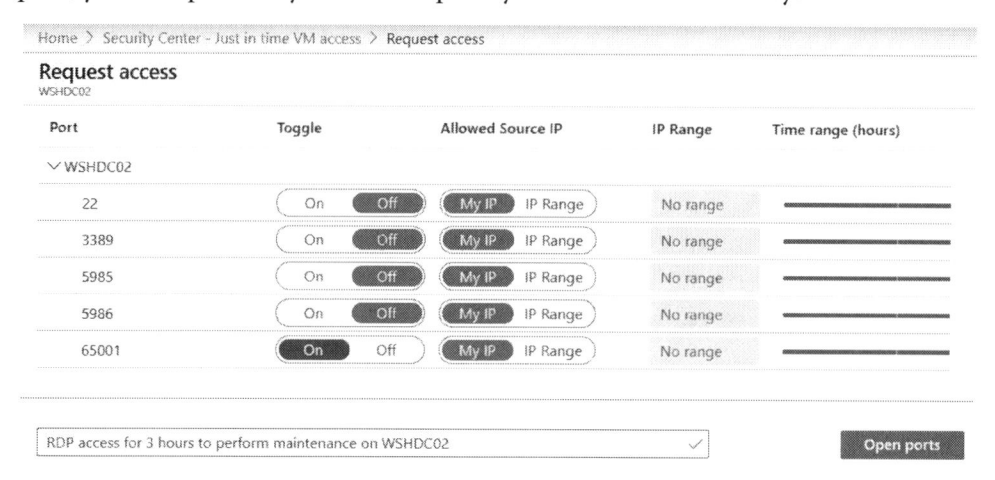

Figure 8.21 – Azure JIT port request

If the appropriate RBAC is applied to request access to a VM, the access request will be approved, as indicated in the **Last access** column of the following screenshot:

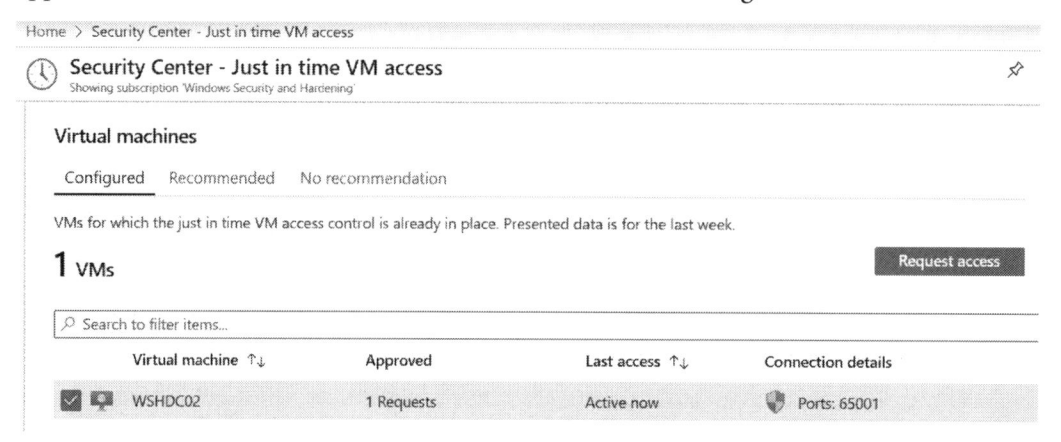

Figure 8.22 – JIT access rule over port 65001 showing as active

The RDP over port `65001` is now active. Browse back to the VM network interface inbound port rules. A new **Allow** rule has been added, similar to the following screenshot, using your public IP as the source:

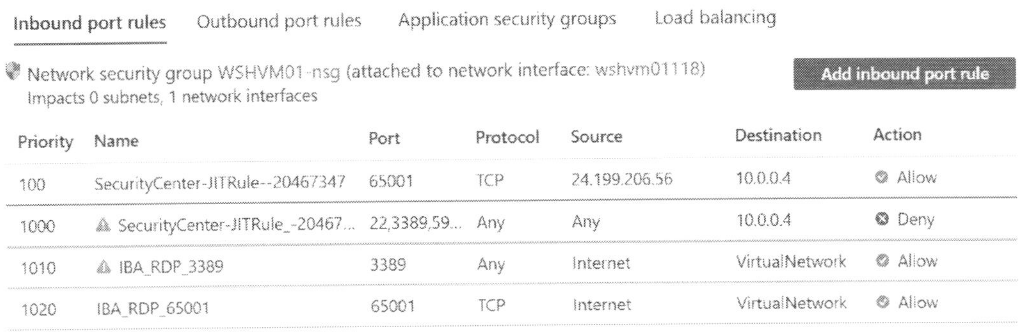

Priority	Name	Port	Protocol	Source	Destination	Action
100	SecurityCenter-JITRule--20467347	65001	TCP	24.199.206.56	10.0.0.4	Allow
1000	SecurityCenter-JITRule_-20467...	22,3389,59...	Any	Any	10.0.0.4	Deny
1010	IBA_RDP_3389	3389	Any	Internet	VirtualNetwork	Allow
1020	IBA_RDP_65001	65001	TCP	Internet	VirtualNetwork	Allow

Figure 8.23 – Network interface inbound port rules with an active ASC JIT rule

Following the approval of the ASC JIT rule, the source is configured from your public IP address. Network address translation in Azure allows the destination to the VM to be a private IP. In order to connect to this server with RDP, you may need to add the port number at the end of the IP address. In this example, `52.167.213.130:65001` would be used to create the connection and includes the custom port.

Next, let's look at using the Azure Bastion service to connect to a VM without having to expose it directly to the internet.

Connecting with Azure Bastion

Available in Azure as a PaaS service, **Azure Bastion** allows SSL-secured RDP or SSH connections into VMs directly from the Azure portal, eliminating the need for a jumpbox.

With Azure Bastion, you provision an isolated or *bastion* subnet directly inside your virtual network. This keeps all of the RDP or SSH traffic inside of your virtual network, so the protocols are not exposed over the internet. Now, VMs no longer require direct exposure to the internet with public IPs, which helps to protect these endpoints from threats such as port scanning. The Azure Bastion service always uses your resource's private IP address to create secured connections and significantly reduces the attack surface by minimizing what's exposed directly over the internet. Azure Bastion only supports RDP or SSH with HTML5 currently, but development is in the works to support other tools such as **Remote Desktop Connection** (**MSTSC**).

Let's look at configuring Azure Bastion. In order to enable the Azure Bastion service, a *bastion* subnet must be created inside your virtual network, named `AzureBastionSubnet`, with a minimum **Classless Inter-Domain Routing (CIDR)** range of `/27` before continuing. To create the Bastion resource and connect to a VM, follow these steps:

1. Log in to the Azure portal at `https://portal.azure.com`.
2. Search for `Bastions` and select **Bastions** under **Services**.
3. Click on **Create Bastion**.
4. Select your **Subscription**, and choose a **Resource group**. We selected the resource group our VNET was in.
5. Give it a friendly name and choose the region your resources are in.
6. Select your virtual network and choose **AzureBastionSubnet**.
7. Create a new IP address and give it a friendly name.
8. Click on **Review + Create**. Then, select **Create**.

> **Tip**
> Azure Bastion does not support customized TCP ports. If you are using the VM configured earlier, the RDP listening port must be changed back to `3389` or you will receive a bad connection error. Additionally, NSG rules will need an allow rule to open access to the default `3389` RDP port, and any JIT access rules need to be accounted for or connections may be blocked.

To connect to a VM with Azure Bastion, follow these steps:

1. Go to the **Virtual Machines** pane inside the Azure portal.
2. Search for your VM and select it in order to bring it up in the overview pane.
3. Click on **Bastion** under **Operations**.
4. Enter the VM's administrator username and password and click on **Connect**.

You may have to allow popups if your pop-up blocker is enabled. The following screenshot is the **Connect to virtual machine** menu. Select the **BASTION** tab to connect:

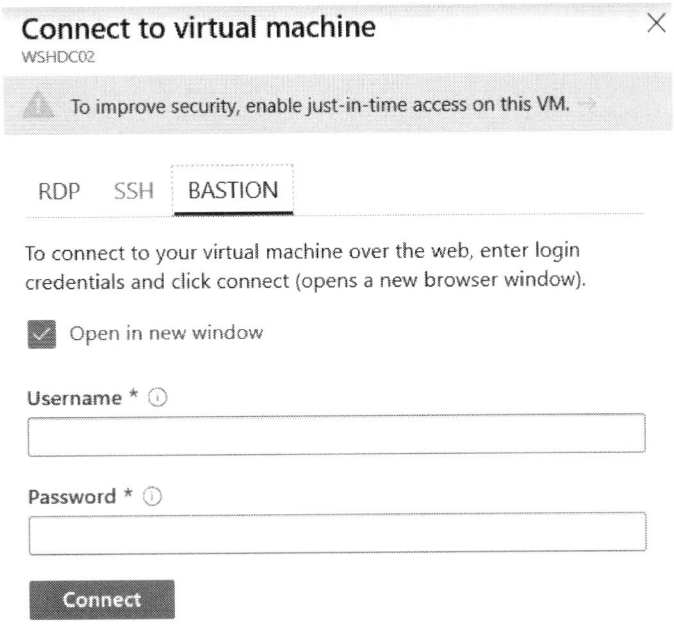

Figure 8.24 – The Connect to virtual machine menu from the Overview pane

Now that we have covered how to connect remotely to Windows servers with RDP, let's take a look at PowerShell. PowerShell has quickly become a standard for many administrative tasks, and there are a few security steps that should be taken to help secure its use.

Introducing PowerShell security

PowerShell has become one of the most popular tools in the sysadmin's toolbox in recent years. Its uses range from the ability to batch processes and build tools to automating repeatable tasks. There are many importable modules that allow interaction with a range of services such as Azure AD and Exchange Online. As a result, PowerShell can be exploited as an attack tool due to this flexibility. It has close interaction with various OS system-level components, such as **Windows Management Instrumentation (WMI)**, and can avoid detection as it's a commonly used process. Out of the box, there are limited security measures enabled for PowerShell, so let's discuss what we can do to help secure its use.

Configuring PowerShell logging

There are a few types of logging that can be enabled for PowerShell to start logging events for auditing purposes. Some of the logging options include the following:

- **PowerShell Transcription** allows Windows to capture the input and output of PowerShell commands in text-based transcripts. PowerShell Transcription can be enabled through the following Group Policy and registry setting:

    ```
    Computer Configuration / Policies / Administrative
    Templates / Windows Components / Windows PowerShell / Turn
    on PowerShell Transcription
    ```

    Enable the policy and specify an output directory. Documents are the default output directory if nothing else is specified:

    HKEY_LOCAL_MACHINE\SOFTWARE\Policies\Microsoft\Windows\PowerShell\Transcription

    EnableTranscription DWORD equals 1.

    OutputDirectory REG_SZ equals PATH TO DIRECTORY.

- **PowerShell Script Block Logging** enables the logging of all PowerShell script blocks in the Event Viewer. PowerShell Script Block Logging can be enabled through Group Policy, Intune Administrative Templates, or the registry:

    ```
    Computer Configuration / Policies / Administrative
    Templates / Windows Components / Windows PowerShell / Turn
    on PowerShell Script Block Logging
    ```

    Enable the policy and select **Log script block invocation start/stop events** for additional logging:

    HKEY_LOCAL_MACHINE\SOFTWARE\Policies\Microsoft\Windows\PowerShell\ScriptBlockLogging

    EnableScriptBlockLogging REG_DWORD equals 1.

    EnableScriptBlockInvocationLogging REG_DWORD equals 1.

Additionally, there are Group Policy settings to enable module logging. If enabled, the modules must be added to the list of module names in the policy setting, and anything after the pipeline for events of the specified modules will be captured in the Event Viewer.

If using Log Analytics in Azure, you can choose to collect events from the **Microsoft-Windows-PowerShell** logs under **Advanced settings** > **Data** in your Log Analytics workspace. This will allow you to configure alerts based on the events or forward them to a **Security Information and Event Management** (**SIEM**) solution for monitoring.

> **Tip**
> Consider expanding the Windows Event log size if enabling script block logging to avoid logs being overwritten too quickly.

Next, let's explore how to use the PowerShell constrained language mode for a restricted set of commands.

Using PowerShell Constrained Language Mode

The PowerShell Constrained Language Mode is used to lock down which "types" can be executed from within a PowerShell session. Some of the default restrictions of constrained language mode include the usage of most COM objects, using **Add-Type** to load arbitrary C# code or Win32 APIs, and .NET methods that are not of the allowed types. To view the list of allowed types along with a detailed definition of the constrained language mode, open PowerShell and run `Get-Help about_ConstrainedLanguage`.

The constrained language mode is designed to support **User Mode Code Integrity** (**UMCI**) policies though **Windows Defender Application Control** (**WDAC**) and Device Guard for enforcement. Specific scripts or even your code-signing authority can be added to the WDAC policy, which allows them to run in full language mode if constrained language is too restrictive. Alternatively, constrained language mode can be set by creating an environment variable via a GPO with a `__PSLockdownPolicy` value of 4. However, this can easily be circumvented if the user has the right to override these settings.

To check the current language mode of the execution context in PowerShell, run this command:

```
$ExecutionContext.SessionState.LanguageMode
```

To read more about the different types of language modes in PowerShell, refer to https://docs.microsoft.com/en-us/powershell/module/microsoft.powershell.core/about/about_language_modes?view=powershell-5.1.

Next, let's look at enabling script execution. For best practice, it's recommended that you only allow `RemoteSigned` scripts to be executed or even use the default restricted mode.

Enabling script execution

PowerShell execution policies determine which types of scripts can run on the system. While not directly used to deny users from running commands, execution policies are designed to help prevent the unintentional execution of scripts, and they can be circumvented by using the command line. A few examples of script execution policies include the following:

- **Restricted** is the default for Windows workstations and allows individual commands but prevents scripts from running.
- **Bypass** is where scripts and commands run freely without warning.
- **RemoteSigned** requires scripts to be signed by a trusted publisher to run if downloaded from the internet.
- **AllSigned** requires all scripts to be signed by a trusted publisher, including ones built locally. PowerShell will prompt you before allowing the script to run from unknown publishers.

To learn more about script execution policies in PowerShell, type in `Get-Help about_execution_policies`. It is recommended that you keep the default of **Restricted** enabled or use **RemoteSigned**. PowerShell script execution can be set using Group Policy, Intune Administrative Templates, or the registry. Use the following location for Group Policy or Intune:

- Navigate to **Computer Configuration** > **Administrative Templates** > **Windows Components** > **Windows PowerShell** > **Turn on Script Execution**
- Choose **Allow local scripts and remote signed scripts** to set the `MachinePolicy` scope to `RemoteSigned`.

You can list all of the execution policy modes for each scope by typing `get-executionpolicy -list` in PowerShell. The following screenshot shows five different scopes. If all scopes are set to `Undefined` except for one, then that is the current effective policy. If setting the script policy through a GPO, as in the following, that will remain the more effective scope:

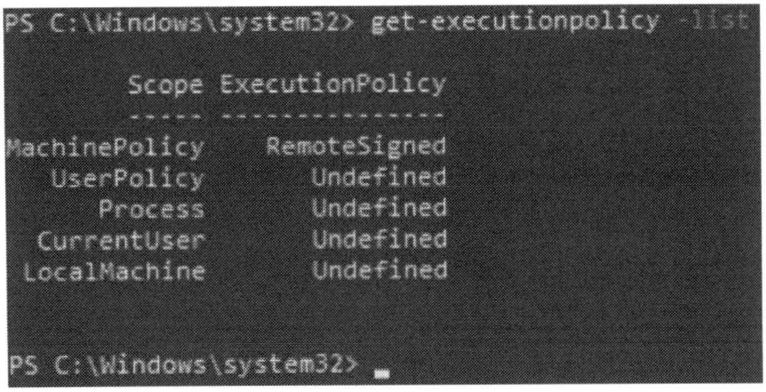

Figure 8.25 – Execution policy of a PowerShell session

To recap, we just covered PowerShell and how to enable transcription logging for monitoring events, discussed the constrained language mode, and covered the different types of execution policies for protecting your systems.

Summary

In this chapter, we covered what administration and remote management are and their importance for your Windows environment. We started with an overview of device administration and the different ways in which Windows devices can connect and register to your domain. We then learned how to enforce compliance and configured settings on your devices using MDM with Configuration Manager and Intune.

Next, we walked through building a Windows 10 security baseline using the Microsoft Security Compliance Toolkit. We discussed using the Policy Analyzer tool to compare settings and created a GPO from the recommended baseline and assigned it to an Active Directory OU. Then, we learned how to take existing GPOs and convert them into Configuration Manager Configuration Items to both remediate noncompliant settings or use monitor mode for reporting purposes. Finally, we reviewed remote management and provided details on how to deploy Azure Security Center JIT access and Azure Bastion. The chapter finished with several ways to secure and audit PowerShell events.

Moving on to *Chapter 9*, *Keeping Your Windows Client Secure*, we will cover Microsoft Defender ATP, learn how to onboard machines, and discuss deploying and configuring Windows Update for Business. Then, we will cover securing and hardening Windows with various configurations before finishing the chapter with Windows 10 privacy settings and the importance of data labeling and classification.

9
Keeping Your Windows Client Secure

In this chapter, you will learn about the best practices and techniques that are used to keep the Windows **operating system** (**OS**) secure. So far, we have covered many technologies that make up a robust and well-rounded security program. This includes administration and management tools, hardware security, network security, and an identity management program. This chapter, along with *Chapter 10, Keeping Your Windows Server Secure*, will cover the core of what this book is about, directly securing and hardening the OS that your users use.

Securing your Windows client is a critical task, and it is one that requires ongoing maintenance and operation in order to protect your devices as vulnerabilities continue to evolve and grow. In this chapter, we will cover how to keep your Windows devices up to date by deploying Windows Update for Business and securing your devices with advanced hardening configurations. Then, we will finish the chapter by discussing configuring Windows 10 privacy settings.

This chapter will include the following topics:

- Securing your Windows clients
- Introducing Windows Update for Business
- Advanced Windows hardening configurations
- Windows 10 privacy

Technical requirements

There are many walk-throughs throughout this chapter that will instruct you on how to enable different types of settings. In order to follow along, you must have an **Azure Active Directory** (**Azure AD**) tenant configured and administrative rights to manage resources in Azure. You will also need Active Directory Domain Services configured to follow along with the Group Policy guides. In addition, a few services that we cover will require licenses and infrastructure in order to follow the references in this chapter. They include the following:

- Microsoft Intune License
- Configuration Manager hierarchy

Let's start by learning how to secure your Windows clients.

Check out the following video to see the Code in Action: `https://bit.ly/2D7pVTJ`

Securing your Windows clients

It's important to keep up to date with your workstation OS because once a product is made end of life by Microsoft, they no longer invest time to release updates for these products. Extended support is available in some instances. However, generally, outdated OSes will only provide hackers more incentive to target these systems. If you aren't on Windows 10 already, start planning an upgrade as soon as possible!

Currently, there are no plans to increment the major build number to version 11 or 12. New builds (known as feature updates) are released at no charge to users if their license is valid. Depending on the edition, updates are released on servicing channels and can be configured through various means, including automatic updates through Windows Updates, Windows Update for Business, and **Windows Server Update Services** (**WSUS**), and they can be delivered and configured through tools such as Intune, Configuration Manager, or Azure Automation Update Management.

Windows as a Service (WaaS) is a concept that was first introduced with Windows 10. While this idea is multi-faceted, it typically revolves around Microsoft's continued effort to improve the deployment and servicing of Windows clients. Traditionally, a servicing strategy involves extensive IT effort along with the coordination of end users to schedule support time for tasks such as re-imaging, updating, and deploying PCs. This also limits the speed of which new features become available and slows the security update process that helps protect the organization and enable new technology for users. Key concepts to understand with Windows as a Service include the types of updates delivered as well as the servicing channels that determine "when" the updates will be available. This will be covered in more detail in the *Introducing Windows Update for Business* section.

> **Tip**
>
> You can learn more about Windows as a Service at `https://docs.microsoft.com/en-us/windows/deployment/update/waas-overview`.

First, let's take a look at Windows Update for Business and provide you with the information that is needed to configure Windows Updates with Intune.

Introducing Windows Update for Business

One of the major differences between **Windows Server Update Services** (**WSUS**) and Windows Update for Business is a direct connection from the computer endpoint to the Windows Update service when it's configured using the Windows Update for Business policies. Updates are no longer approved and deployed granularly according to "what" type or KB, as is the case with WSUS, but managed to the level of "when" they are deployed. **Windows Update for Business**, also sometimes referred to as **WufB**, can be configured by Intune or Group Policy. Let's take a look at a few key concepts to understand the types of updates delivered and the servicing channels that determine "when" updates will be available to devices:

- **Feature Updates** are released twice a year, usually around the end of Q1 and Q3. These are the major build releases in Windows, and they offer the latest updates in security features and UI enhancements.

- **Quality Updates** can be scoped to security and non-security-related fixes. Quality updates include critical updates, security patches, drivers, updates to the servicing stack (windows update service), and Windows product updates. Typically, these are the patches that are released on "Patch Tuesday."

- **Driver Updates** can be delivered through Windows Updates and toggled on or off.
- **Microsoft Product Updates** are updates targeted to Windows Apps and Office products.
- There are two types of release schedules available when configuring update policies, and they are as follows:
- **Semi-Annual Channel** is the "production" or regular servicing channel that receives feature updates twice per year.
- **Windows Insider Program** is for the release available prior to general availability. This allows organizations to test builds, validate compatibility, and send feedback to Microsoft before they are released into production.

Microsoft recommends using deployment rings to deploy Windows features and quality updates. This will allow you to specify groups of computers to deploy updates to and pilot updates before rolling them out to all your systems. A common scenario would be to separate your deployment rings by department. Depending on the number of devices, you can create an early adopter or pilot user group for each department and a production or general release ring. This will allow time for the pilot group to validate and report to the IT team that there are no issues. It's important when deciding on test groups that there is equal representation across the different business workloads and app personas that exist in your organization. One example of this could be to create groups for Finance, HR, and IT and choose 10-15 people who are willing to provide feedback and offer insights to their update experience. These groups should receive the update well in advance of others in their departments, and they should have a clear escalation point to IT so that it can be determined whether an update has broken a critical business app. Luckily, Intune Windows 10 Updates has a pause and rollback feature in case there are problems that need to be mitigated from the pilot phase discovery.

The following screenshot demonstrates the use of deployment rings to target subsets of user devices and incrementing the feature and quality update deferral periods:

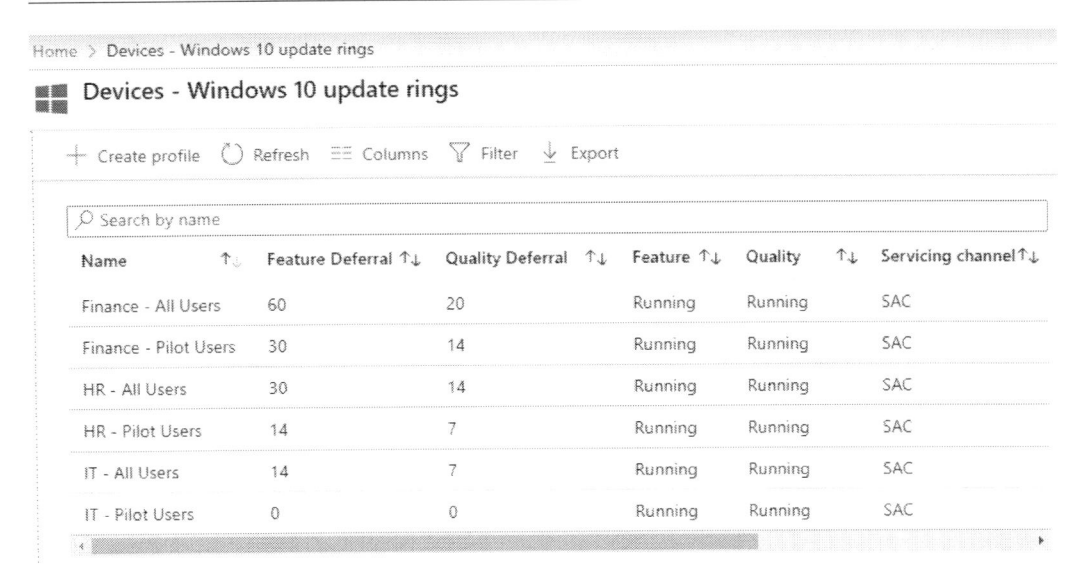

Figure 9.1 – Windows 10 update rings in Intune

For more information about building update deployment rings for Windows 10, visit `https://docs.microsoft.com/en-us/windows/deployment/update/waas-deployment-rings-windows-10-updates`.

Next, let's take a look at how to build and deploy Windows 10 update policies using Intune.

Configuring Windows updates in Intune

Follow these steps to configure Windows 10 update deferral periods, specify installation maintenance times, and set update deadlines:

1. Log in to the **Microsoft Endpoint Manager Admin Center** at `https://devicemanagement.microsoft.com`.

2. Click on **Devices** and choose **Windows 10 update rings**. Click on **+ Create profile**.

3. Give it a friendly name such as `Procurement - Pilot Users` and a description. Click on **Next**.

4. Set the **Update settings**, as shown in the following screenshot:

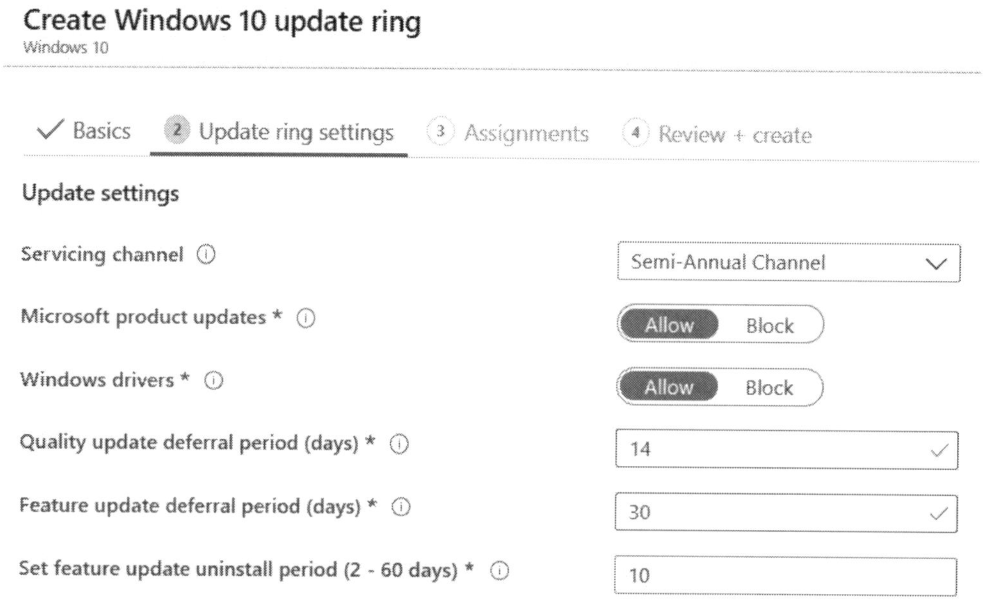

Figure 9.2 – Update settings in the Windows 10 update policy in Intune

5. In **User Experience Settings**, set the following values:

   Automatic Update Behavior: `Auto install and restart at maintenance time`

   Active hour start: `8 AM`

   Active Hours end: `5 PM`

   Restart checks: `Allow`

   Option to pause Windows updates: `Disable`

   Option to check for Windows updates: `Enable`

   Require the user's approval to restart outside of work hours: `Not Configured`

   Remind user prior to required auto-restart with dismissible reminder (hours): `4`

   Remind user prior to required auto-restart with permanent reminder (minutes): `30`

The **active hours** start and end periods determine the time during which updates will be suppressed. Using the **Auto install and restart at maintenance time** option will allow the PC to reboot during the maintenance window outside of the device's active hours setting.

For more information about managing device restarts and the different update behaviors, visit `https://docs.microsoft.com/en-us/windows/deployment/update/waas-restart`.

6. In the **Use deadline settings**, let's configure the number of days during which a user must install feature and quality updates before they are automatically applied:

   Deadline for feature updates: 7

   Deadline for quality updates: 3

   Grace period: 2

   Auto reboot before deadline: yes

   > **Tip**
   > New update behavior settings are frequently being added to Intune. Some of the settings are not available in all Windows 10 versions. Research which settings are available before deploying them to your users.

7. Click on **Next**. Choose a group to assign the policy to and click **Next**.
8. Click **Review + Create** and choose **Create** to build the policy.

Windows update policies can be assigned to both user and device groups. If your organization has many shared devices, then we recommend using device groups to avoid assignment conflicts that can occur from multiple users logging in to the same shared device. One strategy would be to use Azure Automation to dynamically populate device groups based on the user's primary device. Then, you can assign the policy to the device group but organize the deployment by users.

Managing update deployments

In the Microsoft Endpoint Manager admin center, go to **Devices** and choose **Windows 10 update rings**. Select the profile that was created earlier. In the Overview section, notice the toolbar and its available actions. Here, you can decide to pause both feature updates and quality updates. There is also an option to uninstall them if you need to roll back. If you use the **Pause** feature, updates are paused for up to 35 days. If you need to extend this, use the **Extend** feature.

The following screenshot shows all of these actions from within the deployment ring:

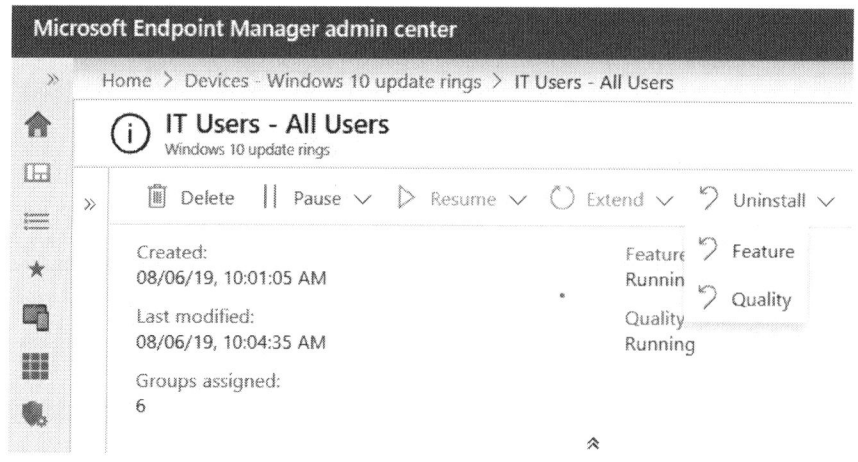

Figure 9.3 – Windows 10 update rings in Intune

Let's now take a look at the monitoring section.

Monitoring update deployments

Under the monitoring section, there are three built-in reports for the Device status, User status, and the End User update status to help monitor the profile settings. The Device status and the User status will display the deployment status of the Windows Update profile against the members of the groups to whom the profile was assigned. The end user update status will give you details about the current device's **Quality Update Version** and **Feature Update Version**. As you can see in the following screenshot, additional information is provided, listing the name of the device, the user, the last scan time, and the device's last check-in time:

Device	User	Update Status	Quality Update Version	Feature Update Version	Last Scan Time	Last Check-in Time
WINDOWS-1C4...	jcal...	Up to date	10.0.18363.592	Latest	2/17/20, 8:32 AM	2/18/20, 7:40 PM
WINDOWS-57C...	Syst...	Pending updates	10.0.18363.592	Latest	2/18/20, 7:18 AM	2/18/20, 10:39 AM
WINDOWS-D9B...	ede...	Up to date	10.0.18363.592	Latest	2/18/20, 7:46 AM	2/18/20, 12:13 PM
WINDOWS-IFAA...	tdi...	Pending updates	10.0.18363.592	Latest	2/18/20, 8:30 AM	2/18/20, 6:30 PM
WINDOWS-BM...	eva...	Up to date	10.0.18363.592	Latest	2/06/20, 7:06 AM	2/07/20, 9:45 AM
WINDOWS-M76...	bej...	Up to date	10.0.18363.535	Latest	2/05/20, 3:18 PM	2/12/20, 8:47 AM
WINDOWS-JV0...	bco...	Pending updates	10.0.18362.329	1903	9/20/19, 8:04 AM	2/18/20, 2:29 PM
WINDOWS-29I...	jgra...	Up to date	10.0.18362.476	1903	1/06/20, 2:12 PM	1/28/20, 10:08 AM

Figure 9.4 – End user update status in Windows 10 Update profile

While this provides a helpful overview of the current status of your quality and feature updates, the end user update status doesn't provide much in-depth information about the overall compliance of your updates, nor any troubleshooting information for failed installations. We recommended deploying the Update Compliance solution in Log Analytics.

The following diagram is from the `WaaSUpdateInsights` solution, which is available for free in Log Analytics. The solution will break down the rollout of security updates, feature updates, Defender AV signature updates, and **Delivery Optimization** (**DO**) settings:

LATEST SECURITY UPDATE DEPLOYMENT STATUS

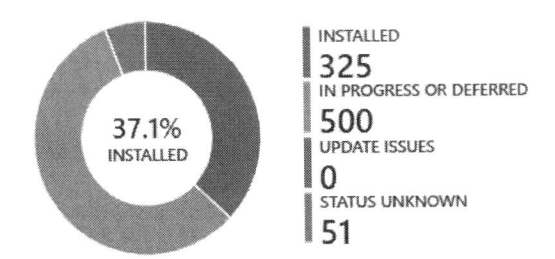

37.1% INSTALLED

INSTALLED
325
IN PROGRESS OR DEFERRED
500
UPDATE ISSUES
0
STATUS UNKNOWN
51

OS BUILD	VERSION	INSTALLED	IN PROGRESS OR DEFERRED	UPDATE ISSUES	STATUS UNKNOWN
18363.657	1909	304	165	0	10
18362.657	1903	14	298	0	25
17763.1039	1809	5	36	0	10
17134.1304	1803	2	0	0	3

Figure 9.5 – Security update deployment status in Update Compliance

Next, let's take a look at the advanced Windows hardening configurations to help protect your ecosystem of devices.

Advanced Windows hardening configurations

Next, let's look at the advanced Windows hardening configurations to deploy to your client workstations. These configurations will cover user authentication with biometrics and PINs, risk prevention by setting up Defender AV scan settings and SmartScreen filters, and the protection of user data with BitLocker Drive Encryption. We will also discuss how to mitigate common attack vectors, such as name resolution poisoning and **Man-in-the-Middle** (**MITM**) attacks, that can be overlooked in your default Windows baseline policies and put your systems at risk from an inside attack.

First, let's look at using Windows Hello for Business to replace passwords as an authentication mechanism.

Enabling Windows Hello for Business

Windows Hello for Business is a great first step in a passwordless journey and enables the use of biometric sensors or device PINs as an alternative way to log in to Windows. Windows Hello for Business is backed by an asymmetric public/private key pair or certificate-based authentication, which can be used to authenticate with Azure AD, on-premises AD, and other identity providers that support **Fast ID Online v2** (**FIDO**). When a user registers for Windows Hello for Business through a new device enrollment, or later on through the Windows settings app, the credentials are bound to the device, and the public key is mapped to an identity provider such as Azure AD. The validation of this pairing occurs through a two-step verification during the registration process. Keys can be generated either by a device's hardware **Trusted Platform Module** (**TPM**) or by software, and they can be configured in the deployment settings. Currently, Windows Hello for Business supports the following types of authentication mechanisms:

- Device PIN
- Fingerprint or face biometric authentication
- Phone sign-in when using Windows Hello for Business PIN on an Azure AD joined companion device

For more information about using Windows Hello biometrics in an enterprise, refer to `https://docs.microsoft.com/en-us/windows/security/identity-protection/hello-for-business/hello-biometrics-in-enterprise`.

For more information on *Why a PIN is better than a password*, visit `https://docs.microsoft.com/en-us/windows/security/identity-protection/hello-for-business/hello-why-pin-is-better-than-password`.

Let's use Intune to configure Windows Hello for Business and set PIN requirements using these steps:

1. Log in to `https://devicemanagement.microsoft.com`.
2. Choose **Devices** and select **Windows** under the **By platform** menu. Choose **Windows Enrollment** to edit the enrollment settings.

3. Select **Windows Hello for Business** under **General**. Change the dropdown, and **Configure Windows Hello for Business** to `Enabled`.

4. Click on **Save** to apply and assign the policy to all users.

The Windows enrollment settings in Microsoft Endpoint Admin Center are where you can configure options such as automatic enrollment to Intune with Azure AD join and configure autopilot profiles. Select **Windows Hello for Business** to configure the preceding settings:

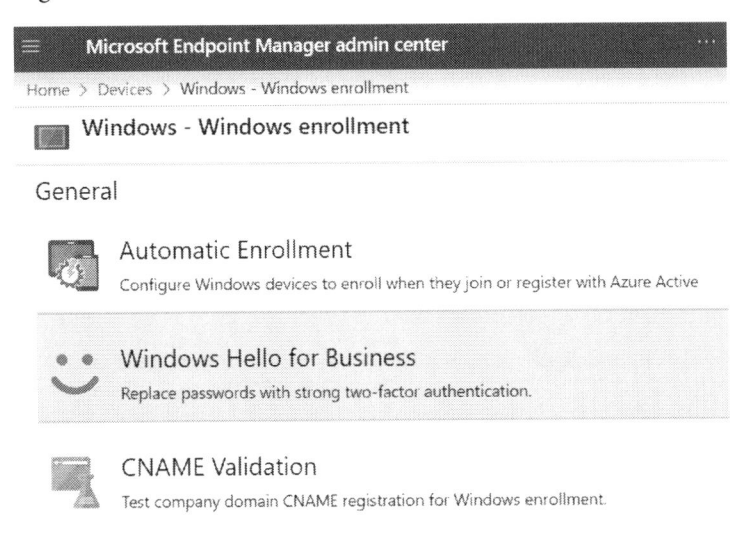

Figure 9.6 – Windows enrollment settings in Intune

The default settings are a good starting point and offer a balance of both security and usability for your users. Modify any settings as necessary to meet your baseline requirements.

When users enroll a new device or log in with their passwords after the settings have been applied, Windows will prompt them to configure a Windows Hello for Business login method. The available options will depend on whether the underlying hardware supports it. Users can also modify or configure additional sign-in methods using **Sign-in Options** from the **Settings** app, as shown in the following screenshot. If these settings have been set with Intune or Group Policy, users will see the message **Some of these settings are hidden or managed by your organization*:

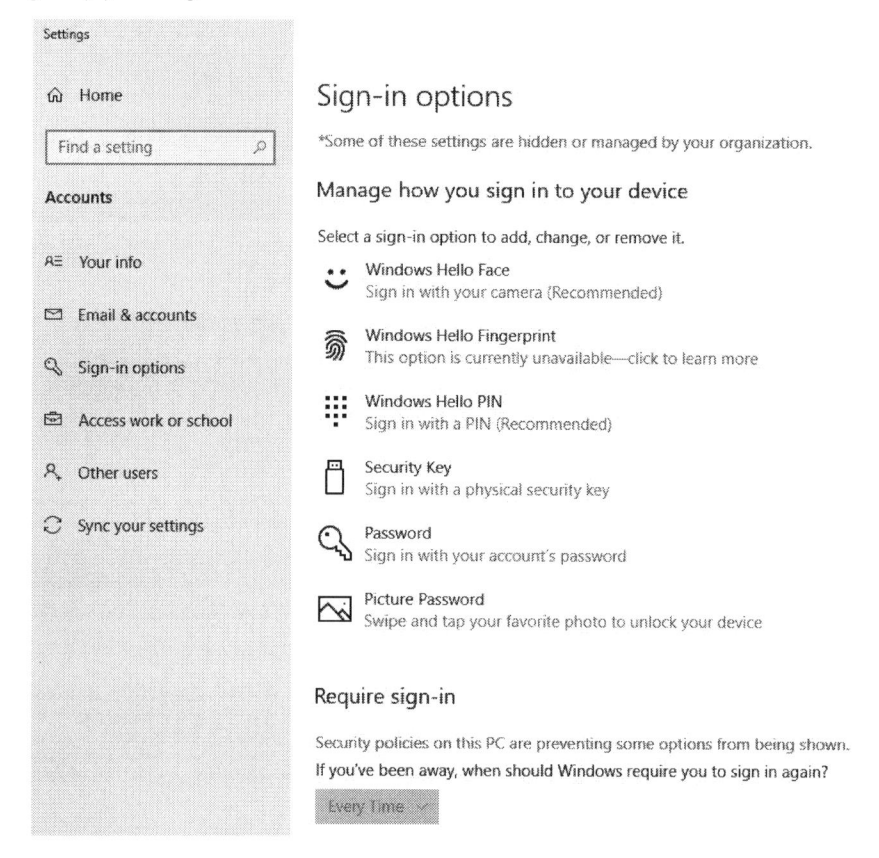

Figure 9.7 – Windows Hello for Business Sign-in options in the Settings app

Next, let's look at how to configure BitLocker encryption using Intune and leverage Azure AD to store recovery keys.

Managing BitLocker encryption

BitLocker encryption is a common technology used to encrypt device data on disk drives. Historically, BitLocker was deployed and managed using the **Microsoft BitLocker Administration and Monitoring (MBAM)** tool, which is part of the **Microsoft Desktop Optimization Pack (MDOP)**, through Group Policy administrative templates. The MBAM administrative interface is used to report compliance, manage configurations, and store recovery key information for organizations. MBAM can also integrate with Configuration Manager for native functionality directly from the Configuration Manager console. Microsoft recently announced that MBAM development ended in 2019 and its services will be deprecated in 2024: `https://docs.microsoft.com/en-us/windows/security/information-protection/bitlocker/bitlocker-management-for-enterprises`. It is strongly recommended that you start leveraging Azure AD and Intune to deploy and manage BitLocker Drive Encryption settings as soon as possible. For an in-depth overview of BitLocker Device Encryption in Windows 10, we recommend visiting `https://docs.microsoft.com/en-us/windows/security/information-protection/bitlocker/bitlocker-device-encryption-overview-windows-10`.

Using Intune and Azure AD, BitLocker can be managed using device configuration profiles, Intune security baselines, or by manually using the BitLocker **Configuration Service Provider (CSP)**. Follow these steps to enable BitLocker Device Encryption for Windows 10 devices using a device configuration profile and save your recovery keys to Azure AD:

1. Sign in to `https://devicemanagement.microsoft.com`.
2. Go to **Devices** and choose **Configuration Profiles** under **Policy**.
3. Create a profile and give it a friendly name, such as **Windows 10 - Bitlocker**. Enter a description and choose **Windows 10 and later** from the **Platform** dropdown.
4. Choose **Endpoint Protection** as the profile type and click on **Settings**. Choose `Windows Encryption`.

> **Tip**
> There are many available configurations for Windows encryption. By enabling BitLocker, a recommended set of minimum requirements is configured. Each organization may have its own unique encryption standards and policies.

5. Change **Encrypt Devices** to `Require`.
6. Change **Configure encryption methods** to `Enable`. Leave the default settings as they are.

7. Under the BitLocker OS drive settings, change **Additional authentication at startup** to `Require`.
8. Change **OS drive recovery** to `Enable`.
9. Change **Recovery options in the BitLocker setup wizard** to `Block`.
10. Change **Save BitLocker recovery information to Azure Active Directory** to `Enable`.

> **Important note**
> Make sure that you enable this setting to store your BitLocker keys in Azure AD.

11. Change **Store recovery information in Azure Active Directory before enabling BitLocker** to `Require`.
12. Change **Write access to fixed data drive not protected by BitLocker** to `Block`.
13. Change **Fixed drive recovery** to `Enable`.
14. Change **Recovery Options in the BitLocker setup wizard** to `Block`.
15. Change **Save BitLocker recovery Information to Azure Active Directory** to `Enable`.
16. Change **Store recovery information in Azure Active Directory before enabling BitLocker** to `Require`.
17. To enable BitLocker on removable drives such as USB, change **Write access to removable data drive not protected by BitLocker** to `Block`.
18. Choose **OK**, and then click on **Create** to build the profile. Click on **Assignments** under Manage, and select a device security group to assign the profile to.

Once the profile makes its way to the device after the next policy sync, the user is prompted via a toast notification to enable device encryption, which opens the BitLocker Drive Encryption wizard.

> **Tip**
> Changing the **Warning for other disk encryption** setting to `Block` will attempt to silently enable BitLocker; otherwise, the user will be asked. WARNING: Turning on BitLocker with another device encryption solution enabled can render the device unusable.

The BitLocker recovery key will be stored in Azure AD and is recoverable by both the end user and the Azure cloud device administrators. The following screenshot shows the **Recovery keys** option under the **Monitor** menu when you view information about a managed intune device:

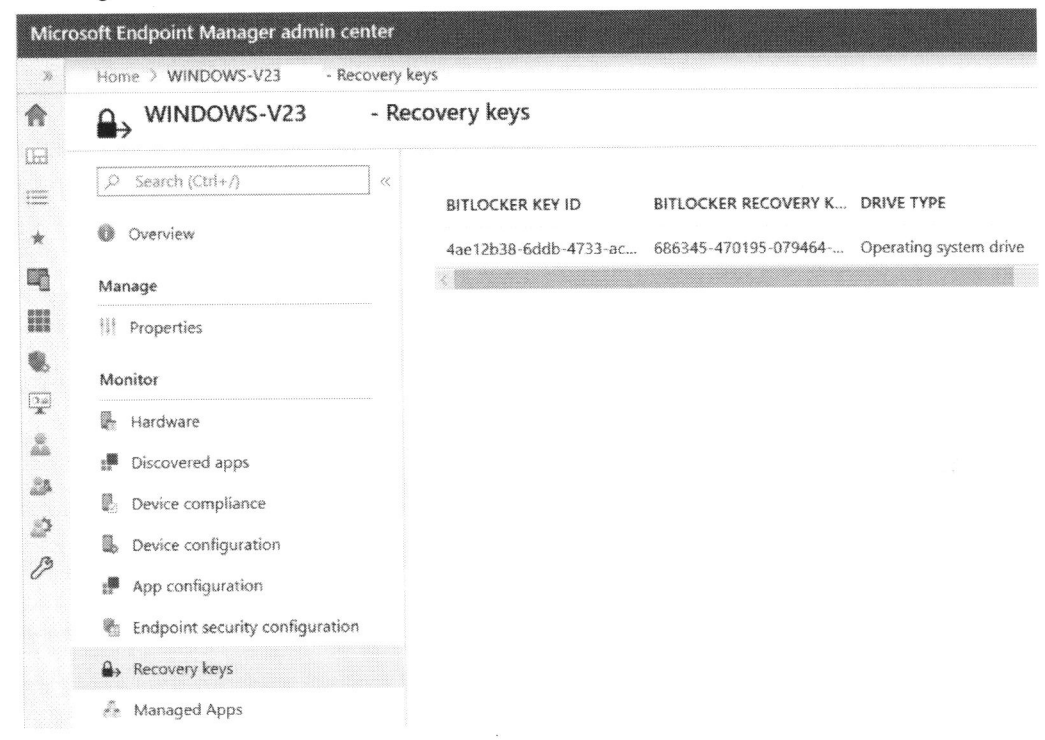

Figure 9.8 – Recovery keys in Microsoft Endpoint Manager admin center

End users can self-service their BitLocker recovery keys by logging in to https://myapps.microsoft.com and choosing their name (located in the top-right corner). Then, simply select **Profile** and then **Get BitLocker keys** next to your device name. A popup will display the PC name and recovery key, as shown in the following screenshot:

Figure 9.9 – Self-service recovery key from the apps Access Panel profile

Next, let's look at real-time protection settings by configuring the Windows Defender AV scan settings using Intune.

Configuring Windows Defender AV

Windows Defender is built into Windows 10 out of the box with a predefined set of configurations. By default, protection is enabled, and virus definition updates are delivered through the Windows Update service unless they are configured differently. Let's take a look at configuring real-time protection scan settings in order to optimize your Windows Defender protection. Follow these steps to create a device configuration profile in Intune to manage Defender AV settings. For more information about configuring Windows Defender AV scanning options, visit `https://docs.microsoft.com/en-us/windows/security/threat-protection/windows-defender-antivirus/configure-advanced-scan-types-windows-defender-antivirus`:

1. Sign in to `https://devicemanagement.microsoft.com`.

2. Click on **Devices**, choose **Windows**, and select **Configuration Profiles** under **Windows Policies**. Click on **Create Profile** to build a new device configuration profile.

3. Give it a friendly name, such as `Windows 10 - Defender Antivirus`, and a description. Choose `Windows 10 and later` as the **Platform type** and `Device restrictions` as the **Profile type**.

4. Choose `Microsoft Defender Antivirus`. The following table lists a recommended configuration baseline for your consideration:

Baseline Microsoft Defender Antivirus Scan Settings	
Real-time monitoring	Enable
Behavior monitoring	Enable
Network Inspection System (NIS)	Enable
Scan all downloads	Enable
Scan scripts loaded into Microsoft Web browsers	Enable
Security intelligence update interval (in hours)	8
Monitor file and program activity	Monitor all files
Days before deleting quarantine malware	7
CPU usage limit during a scan	50
Scan archive file	Enable
Scan incoming mail messages	Enable
Scan removable drives during a full scan	Enable
Scan mapped network drives during a full scan	Not Configured
Scan files opened from network folders	Enable
Cloud-delivered protection	Enable
File Blocking Level	Not configured
Time extension for file scanning by the cloud	0

Figure 9.10 – Defender AV scan recommendations for device configuration profiles

5. Click on **OK** and **OK** again, and choose **Create** to build the new profile.
6. Click on **Assignments** and select a device group to assign the profile to.

When configuring the profile, we skipped over a few configurations, one of which was to configure actions on detected malware threats. Many settings are only applicable to certain device platforms or when choosing **Not configured**, which will accept the default out-of-the-box settings.

Next, let's learn how to add some additional protection for websites and downloaded applications by configuring Microsoft Defender SmartScreen.

Enabling Microsoft Defender SmartScreen

Microsoft Defender SmartScreen is a protection feature that is used to help deter or block your users from visiting potentially malicious websites and running harmful files downloaded from the internet. SmartScreen cross-checks the potential website or file against a list of reported phishing sites and files downloaded by other Windows users. If the site or file in question is found, a warning notification will be presented to the user. SmartScreen for websites (previously known as SmartScreen filter) and downloaded files can be configured by Group Policy or MDM. The following screenshot shows a SmartScreen notification that is blocking the execution of a known malicious file:

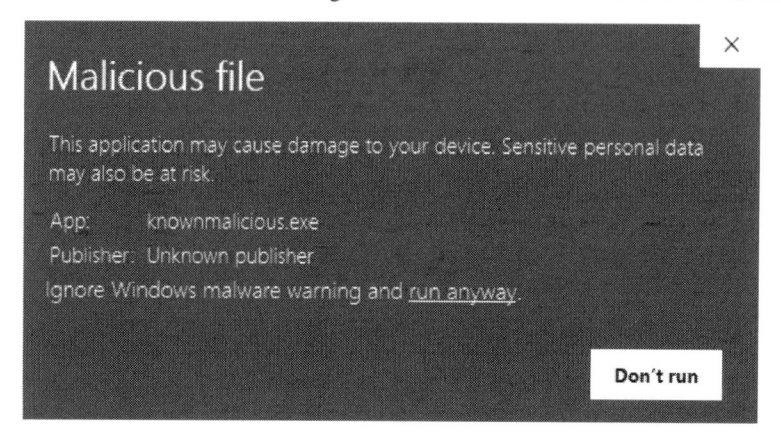

Figure 9.11 – Windows Defender SmartScreen blocking a malicious app

Let's configure Defender SmartScreen for both apps and websites using Intune by following these steps. You will be creating two separate profiles:

1. Sign in to `https://devicemanagement.microsoft.com`.

2. Click on **Devices**, choose **Windows**, and select `Configuration Profiles` under **Windows Policies**. Click on **Create Profile** to build a new device configuration profile.

3. Give it a friendly name, such as `Windows 10 - Defender SmartScreen`, and a description. Choose `Windows 10 and later` as the **Platform type** and `Endpoint Protection` as the **Profile type**.

4. Click on **Settings** and choose `Microsoft Defender SmartScreen`. Enable **SmartScreen for apps and files** and leave **Unverified files execution** as `Not Configured`.

5. Click on **OK** and **OK** again, and choose **Create** to build the profile.
6. Click on **Assignments** and select a security group of devices to which you want to assign the policy.
7. Repeat steps *1* to *3* to create a new profile. Choose a unique name such as `Windows 10 - Defender SmartScreen Web Filter`. Choose `Windows 10 and later` as the **Platform type** and `Device Restrictions` as the **Profile type**.
8. Select **Microsoft Defender SmartScreen**. Set **SmartScreen for Microsoft Edge** to `Require`, and choose `Block` for **Malicious Site Access**.
9. Click on **OK** and **OK** again, and choose `Create` to build the profile.
10. Click on **Assignments** and select a security group of devices to which you want to assign the policy.

The following screenshot is an example of a known malicious website being blocked:

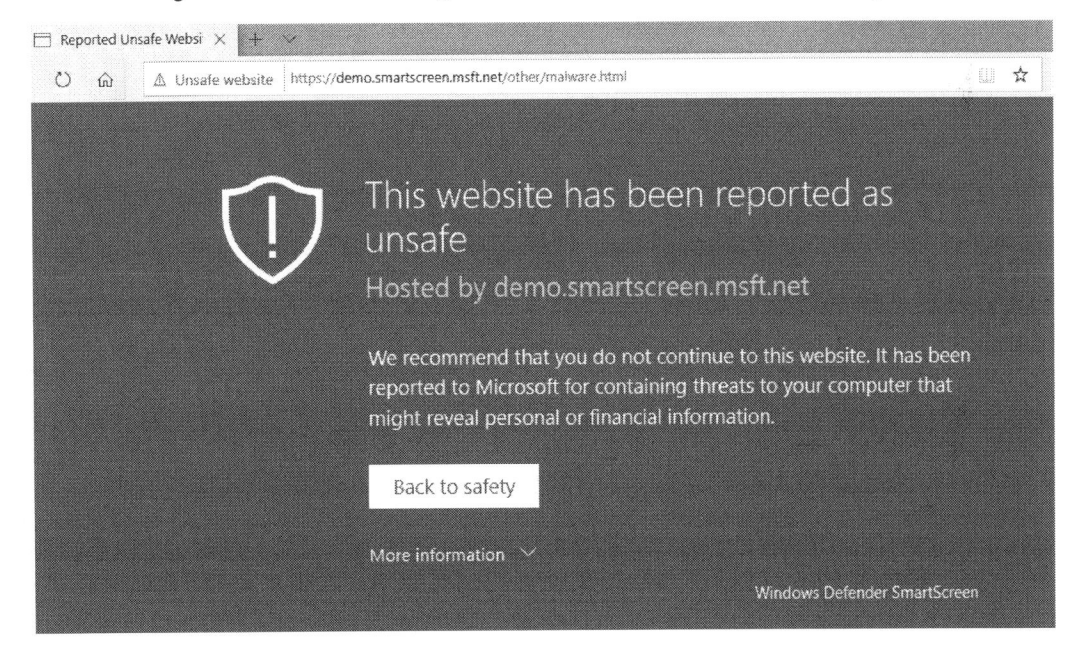

Figure 9.12 – Website blocked by the Microsoft Defender SmartScreen filter

We have now covered several great security features of Windows, including Windows Hello for Business, BitLocker encryption, Windows Defender AV, and configuring SmartScreen. Next, let's look at additional advanced hardening configurations to prevent intruders from intercepting communications that can lead to breached accounts.

Preventing name resolution poisoning

When a Windows system attempts to communicate using internet protocols such as TCP/IP, UDP/IP, or ICMP/IP, it must discover the IP address of the destination system in order to create the communication. To do this, Windows will attempt to use a local hosts file or send a DNS request in the hope that it finds the entry. It's when these methods fail that communications become prone to name poisoning exploits. If a request fails, the Windows system will attempt to send two additional types of requests over the local network to facilitate a response. They are known as **Link-Local Multicast Name Resolution** (**LLMNR**) or **NetBIOS Name Service** (**NBT-NS**) type requests. If you are using the popular Google Chrome browser, an additional service, known as a **Multicast Domain Name System** (**mDNS**), will also be enabled and prone to the same types of attacks.

If an attacker gains access to your network, they can set up fake services in order to trick clients into connecting to them by offering responses to these unanswered requests. The malicious services will present a fake login prompt that can trick the user into entering their credentials, which ultimately results in the capturing of password hashes. These hashes are harvested and can later be cracked by using various cracking techniques. Let's take a look at LLMNR first and learn how to disable it.

Link-Local Multicast Name Resolution

Using a tool such as Responder (`https://github.com/SpiderLabs/Responder`), an attacker can intercept multicast requests if they are not disabled on your devices. In the following screenshot, a poisoned answer was sent to a PC from a multicast request on the local network. An attacker can then coerce a user into entering their credentials into a false prompt that results in a captured password hash. The `LLMNR` protocol is enabled by default in Windows systems:

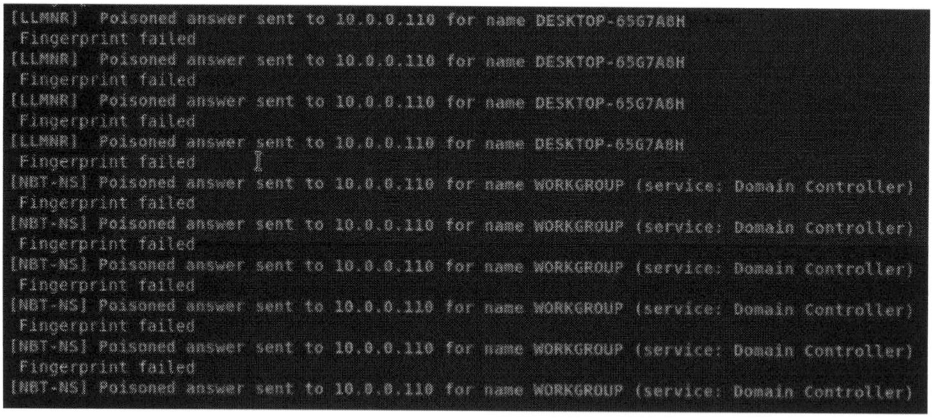

Figure 9.13 – Responder sending a poisoned LLMNR response to a client

The following screenshot shows a successful poisoning attack extracting the password hash:

Figure 9.14 – Successful capture of a password hash

LLMNR can be disabled using the following registry key:

- **HKEY_LOCAL_MACHINE\SOFTWARE\Policies\Microsoft\Windows NT\DNSClient**
- **EnableMulticast** REG_DWORD value of **0**

To disable LLMNR with Group Policy, follow these steps:

1. Open the Group Policy Management Console and create or modify an existing GPO.
2. Go to **Computer Configuration** > **Administrative Templates** > **Network** > **DNS Client**.
3. Open the **Turn off multicast name resolution** policy and set it to **Enabled**.

Once the policy has been applied, an attempt to poison the LLMNR protocol response has been rectified. The following screenshot shows no successful attempts to poison any responses to the target system:

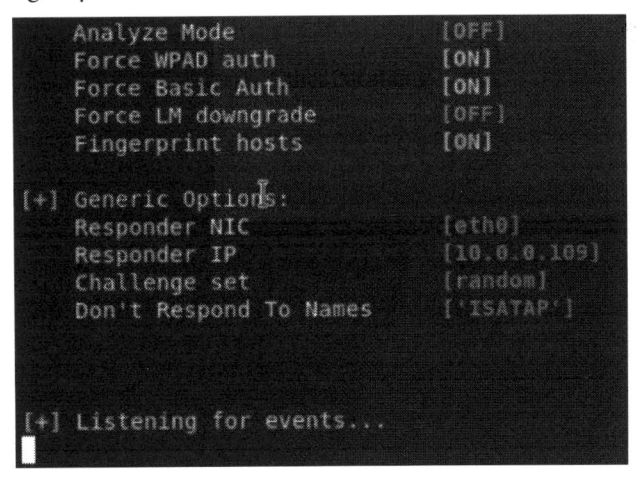

Figure 9.15 – No responses found using the LLMNR protocol

> **Tip**
> We strongly encourage that you understand the use of the LLMNR protocol and how it can adversely affect workstation communications before disabling it. Some organizations may need to consider additional network access controls and rely on strong password requirements as mitigation if this cannot be turned off.

Next, let's look at the NetBIOS name service and how to disable NetBIOS over TCP/IP for network interfaces.

NetBIOS Name Service (NBT-NS)

NBT-NS is another broadcast protocol over TCP/IP that, like LLMNR, is leveraged by the Windows system to find resources. It is enabled by default for all interfaces in Windows and can be exploited in a similar way to the LLMNR protocol. If the Windows system localhost's file or inquiry to DNS cannot resolve the request, then it will resort to using NBT-NS to find the resource. Any rogue system can then respond to these broadcast messages and send poisoned responses.

> **Tip**
> As previously mentioned for LLMNR, disabling NetBIOS can break communication with your systems if broadcast messages are being used to resolve NetBIOS queries. This should be understood carefully before disabling.

To view the NetBIOS settings of an adapter, open the **Network and Sharing Center** and click on **Change adapter settings**. Double-click on your Ethernet adapter, select **Internet Protocol Version 4 (TCP/IPv4)**, and choose **Properties**. Click on **Advanced** and choose the **WINS** tab. As you can see in the following screenshot, NetBIOS settings are set to default, which enables NetBIOS over TCP/IP:

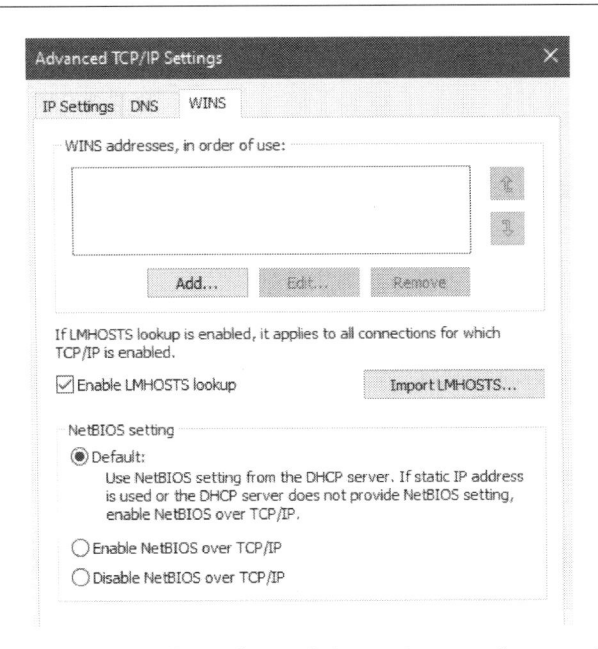

Figure 9.16 – The WINS tab in Advanced TCP/IP Settings of a network interface

Unfortunately, NBT-NS must be disabled on all interfaces on a system and cannot be accomplished using Group Policy alone. Let's look at how we can use a PowerShell discovery script and a Configuration Manager configuration item to detect and disable NetBIOS over TCP/IP for all interfaces:

1. Open the **Configuration Manager** console. Go to **Assets and Compliance** > **Compliance Settings** > **Configuration Items** and click on **Create Configuration Item**.

2. Give it a friendly name, such as `Disable NetBIOS Interfaces`, and click on **Next**.

3. Click on **Next** at the **Supported Platforms** menu options to keep the default settings:

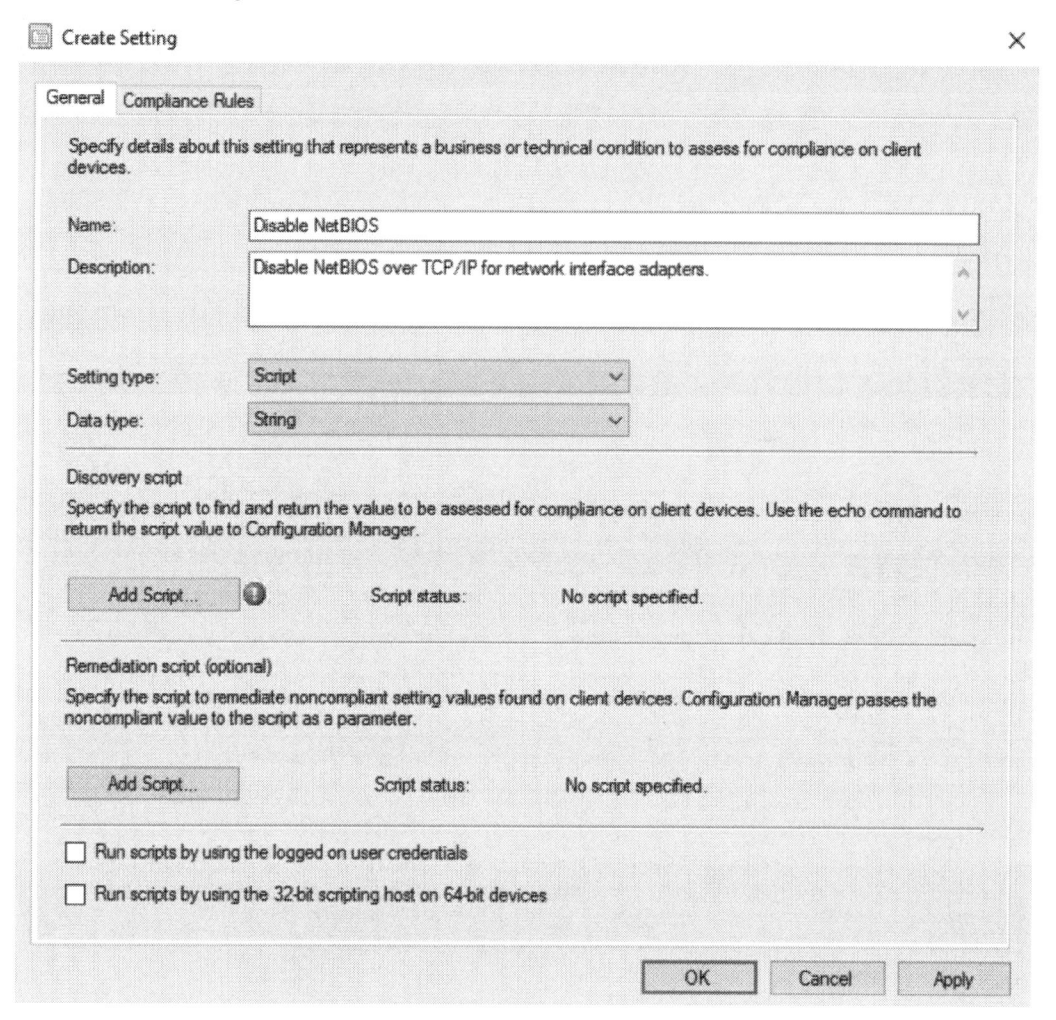

Figure 9.17 – Create Setting in a configuration item

4. Under **Discovery script**, select **Add Script...**.
5. Keep Windows PowerShell selected and let's build the discovery script.

The first section of the code will define the $NBTNS variable. We will use the `Get-ItemProperty` cmdlet to look in the following registry hive and enumerate all of the `TCPIP_GUID` keys that start with **tcpip** using a * wildcard. We want to look specifically at the `REG_DWORD` value of **NetbiosOptions**. In this location of the registry, there can be many entries depending on the number of network adapters used:

```
$NBTNS = Get-ItemProperty HKLM:\SYSTEM\CurrentControlSet\
Services\NetBT\Parameters\Interfaces\tcpip* -Name
NetbiosOptions
```

- The **NetbiosOptions** value of **0** is the default.
- The **NetbiosOptions** value of **1** is enabled.
- The **NetbiosOptions** value of **2** is disabled.

In the following screenshot, you can see the amount of unique TCPIP_GUID values to potentially look through:

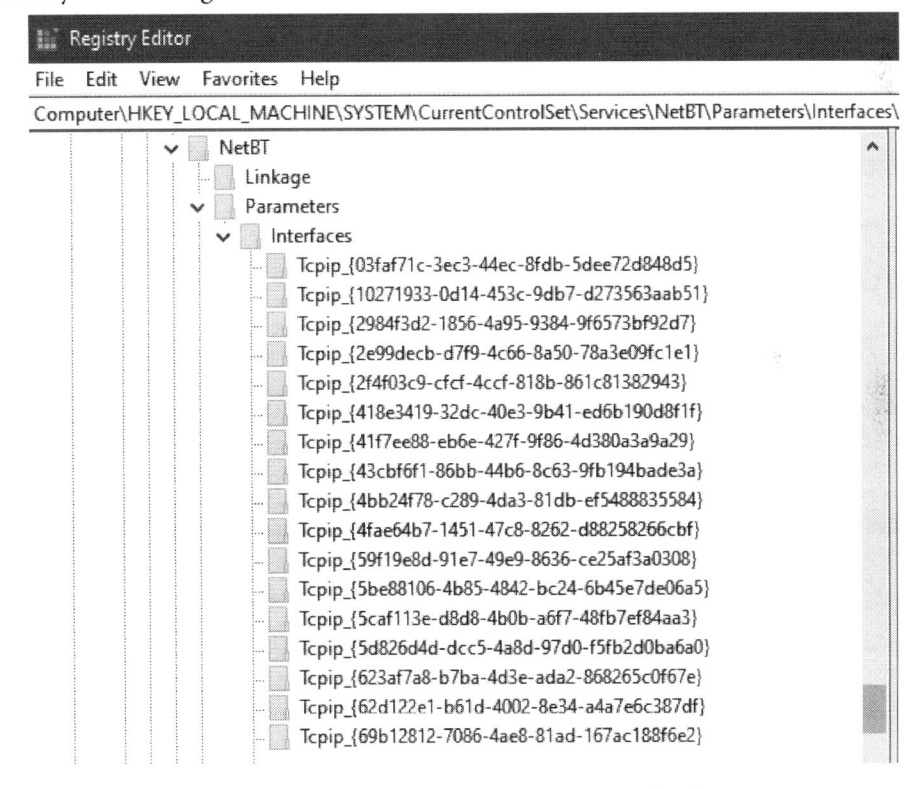

Figure 9.18 – TCPIP_GUID network adapters stored in the registry

Next, we will create an `IF` statement that says that if the value of **NetbiosOptions** does not equal 2, set the `$NTBNSCompliance` compliance variable to `No`. If it does equal 2, set it to `Yes`:

```
If (!($NBTNS.NetbiosOptions -eq "2")){ $NBTNSCompliance = "No" } Else { $NBTNSCompliance ="Yes" }
```

Now, we will print the output of `$NBTNSCompliance` so that Configuration Manager can use it for evaluating compliance, as shown in the following screenshot:

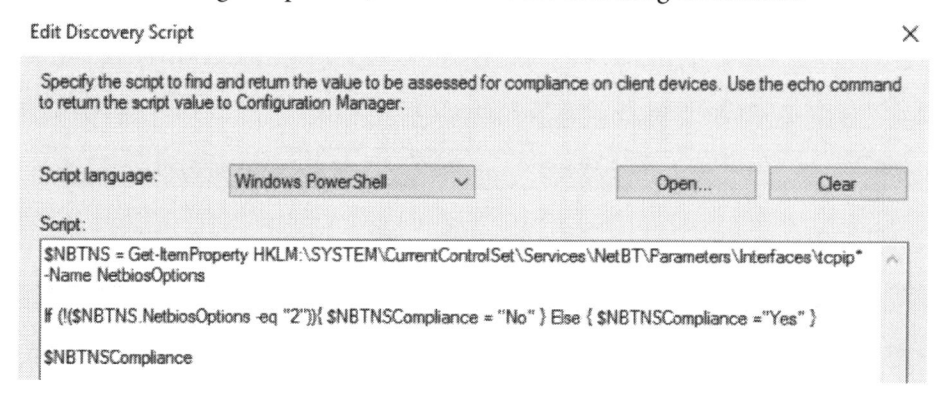

Figure 9.19 – Edit Discovery Script of a Configuration Item

Click on **OK**. Then, click on **Add Script** under *Remediation Script*. Keep Windows PowerShell as the script language.

In order to remediate each unique network adapter, we will use the `Set-ItemProperty` cmdlet to change all of the `NetbiosOptions REG_DWORD` values to 2 for each unique `TCPIP_GUID`:

```
Set-ItemProperty HKLM:\SYSTEM\CurrentControlSet\Services\NetBT\Parameters\Interfaces\tcpip* -Name NetbiosOptions -Value 2
```

The following screenshot shows the **Edit Remediation Script** dialog box with the script code used for this task:

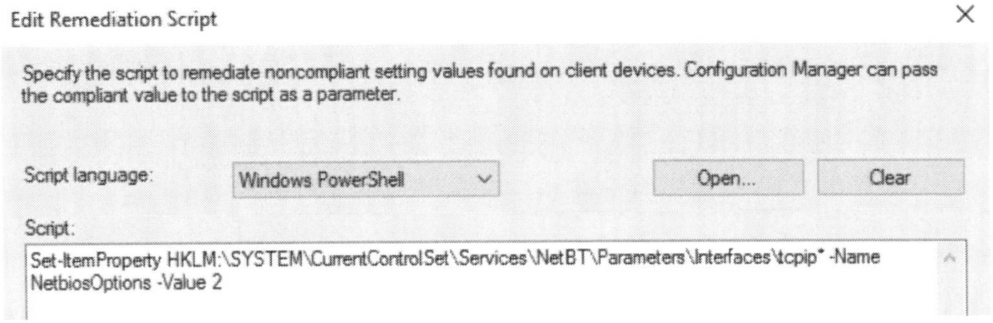

```
Edit Remediation Script                                                    X

Specify the script to remediate noncompliant setting values found on client devices. Configuration Manager can pass
the compliant value to the script as a parameter.

Script language:    Windows PowerShell    v       Open...        Clear

Script:
Set-ItemProperty HKLM:\SYSTEM\CurrentControlSet\Services\NetBT\Parameters\Interfaces\tcpip* -Name
NetbiosOptions -Value 2
```

Figure 9.20 – Edit Remediation Script in a configuration item

1. Click on **OK**, and then click on the **Compliance Rules** tab in the *Create Setting* dialog box. Click on **New** to create a new compliance rule.

2. Give it a friendly name, such as `Disable NetBIOS`. In **The setting must comply with the following rule**, leave **Equals** selected and enter `Yes` in the box.

3. Select both **Run the specified remediation script when this setting is noncompliant** and **Report noncompliance if this setting instance is not found**.

4. Choose `Information` for **Noncompliance severity for reports**. Click on **OK**, click on **OK** again, and choose **Next** back in the **Create Configuration Item Wizard**.

5. Click on **Next** a few times to complete the wizard and build the configuration item.

For this configuration item to be used in the evaluation of compliance and for remediation, create or assign it to an existing security baseline. We covered creating a security baseline in *Chapter 8, Administration and Remote Management*, specifically in the *Building a configuration baseline* section.

After the security baseline has been assigned and evaluated on a source system, we can confirm the configuration by checking the interface settings. The following screenshot shows that **Disable NetBIOS over TCP/IP** is selected in the **Advanced TCP/IP Settings** of this network adapter:

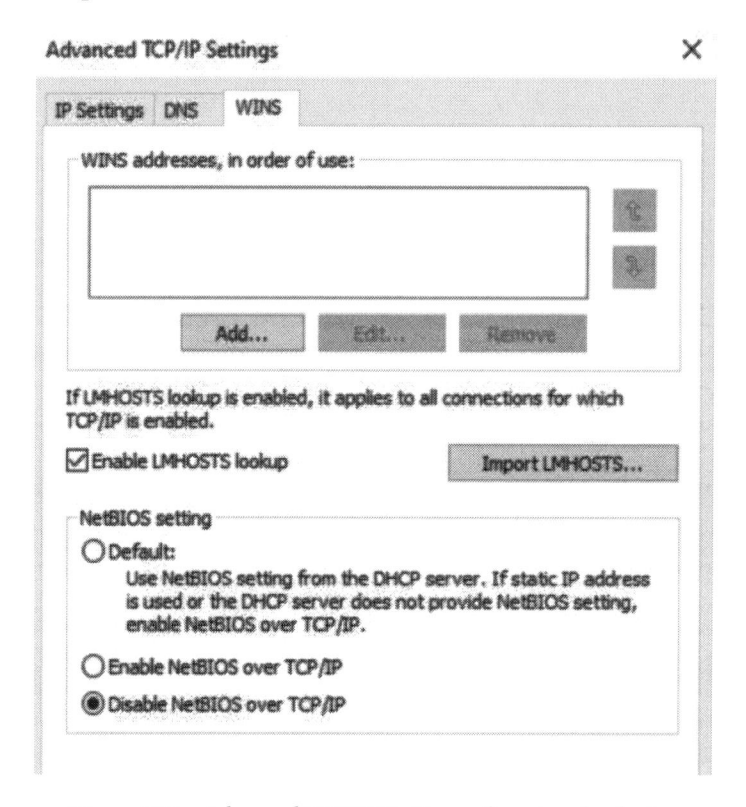

Figure 9.21 – Advanced TCP/IP Settings of a network adapter

Next, let's take a look at disabling a feature enabled with the Google Chrome browser, known as mDNS, which can similarly be exploited as an attack vector.

Disabling Google Chrome mDNS

The Google Chrome browser includes a built-in mDNS service known as Bonjour, which is used in its broadcasting technology for locating computers and streaming devices. The Google Chrome mDNS service is generally unnecessary in a corporate environment, although it is useful for consumers for streaming to home media devices or using Chrome's Google Cast. As we learned with the LLMNR protocol and NBT-NS earlier, mDNS is prone to the same types of request/response poisoning, which makes it an exploitable attack vector for someone inside your network. The following screenshot is the Google Cast functionality in the Chrome browser:

Cast tab

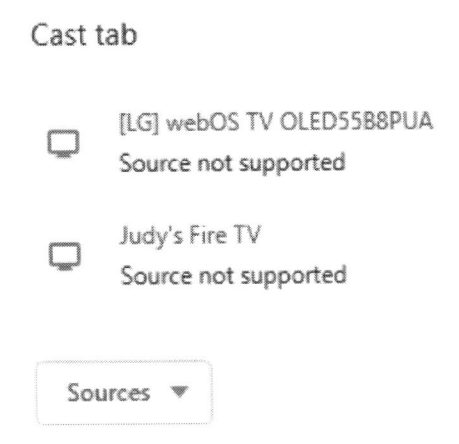

[LG] webOS TV OLED55B8PUA
Source not supported

Judy's Fire TV
Source not supported

Sources ▼

Figure 9.22 – Google Cast from the Chrome browser

It is recommended that you mitigate the risks associated with Google Chrome mDNS by disabling Google Cast and blocking the Google Chrome mDNS service with a firewall rule. Let's look at how to accomplish this.

When Google Chrome is installed, it creates an inbound firewall rule, with the display name **Google Chrome (mDNS-in)**, allowing communication on port UDP 5353 inbound for all profiles, as follows:

Name	Group	Profile	Enabled	Action
File and Printer Sharing (Spool...	File and Printer Sh...	Domain	No	Allow
File and Printer Sharing over S...	File and Printer Sh...	All	No	Allow
Google Chrome (mDNS-In)	Google Chrome	All	Yes	Allow
Groove Music	Groove Music	Domai...	Yes	Allow
HomeGroup In	HomeGroup	Private	No	Allow
HomeGroup In (PNRP)	HomeGroup	Private	No	Allow
iSCSI Service (TCP-In)	iSCSI Service	Private...	No	Allow
iSCSI Service (TCP-In)	iSCSI Service	Domain	No	Allow

Figure 9.23 – Windows Defender Firewall with Advanced Security Inbound Rules

With netstat and process monitor (ProcMon) logging enabled, using Google Cast will show that `chrome.exe` is leveraging communications over UDP 5353:

Figure 9.24 – The netstat output showing that chrome.exe is using UDP 5353

Unfortunately, just disabling this firewall rule will not work because, each time Google Chrome updates, the rule will be re-enabled. For this scenario, we can turn to a discovery/remediation script and use Configuration Manager as the compliance engine. Let's demonstrate how to do this using these steps:

1. Open the **Configuration Manager** console. Go to **Assets and Compliance** > **Compliance Settings** > **Configuration Items** and click on **Create Configuration Item**.

2. Give it a friendly name, such as `Google Chrome Security`, and click on **Next**.

3. Click on **Next** in **support platforms** to keep the default settings. Click on **New** in **Specify settings** and enter the following settings:

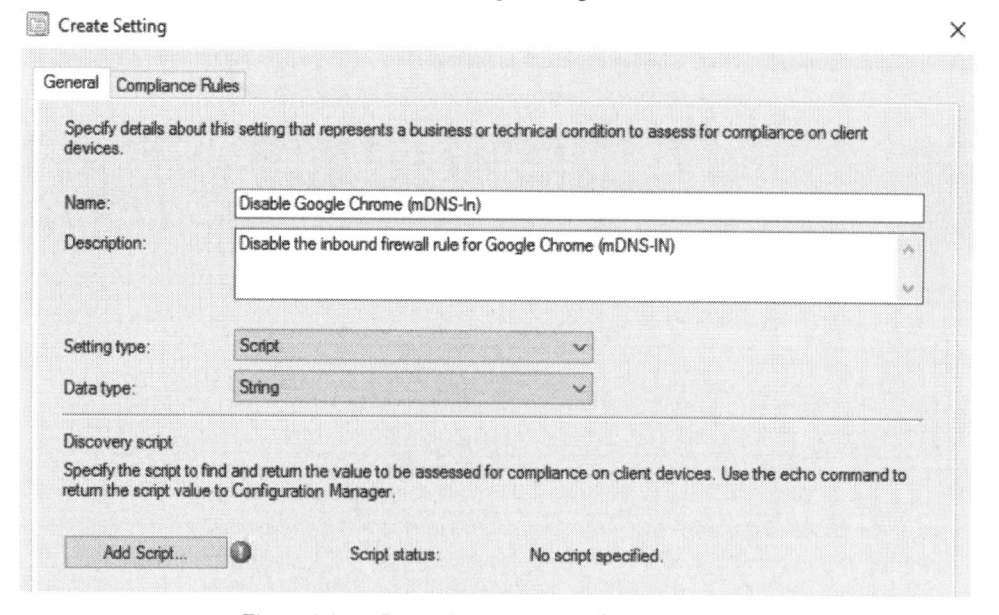

Figure 9.25 – Create Setting in a configuration item

4. Under **Discovery script**, select **Add Script…**.
5. Keep Windows PowerShell selected, and let's build the discovery script.

We will be using the `Get-NetFirewallRule` PowerShell cmdlet to find a rule that matches the display name of **Google Chrome (mDNS-In)**. Let's set the `$ChromeMDNS` variable and use the cmdlet to filter and return any results that match the display name:

```
$ChromeMDNS = (Get-NetFirewallRule | Where {$_.DisplayName -eq "Google Chrome (mDNS-In)"})
```

Next, we want to use an `IF` statement to determine whether the property dereference operator of the action on the `$ChromeMDNS` variable is set to `Allow`. Based on the return, we will use it to set a variable for compliance, called `$ChromeMDNSCompliance`. If the firewall rule is set to `allow`, set the compliance variable to `No`, or else set it to `yes`:

```
If ($ChromeMDNS.Action -eq "Allow"){ $ChromeMDNSCompliance = "No" } else { $ChromeMDNSCompliance = "Yes" }
```

Finally, print the output to be used for evaluating compliance:

```
$ChromeMDNSCompliance
```

The compliance evaluation shows the full code source in the **Edit Discovery Script** window:

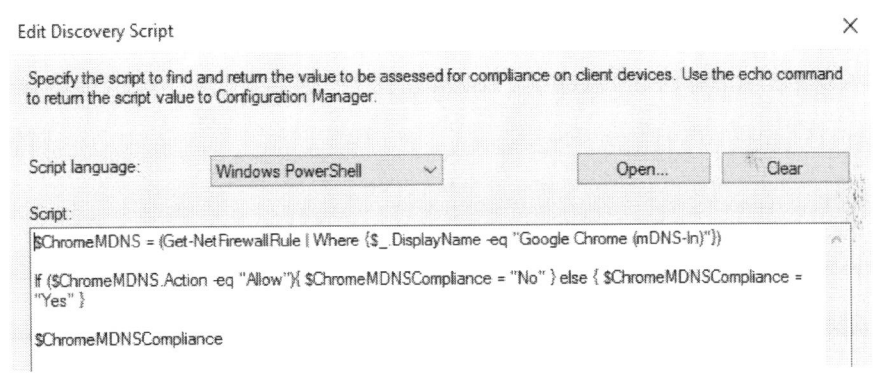

Figure 9.26 – The Edit Discovery Script window

1. Click on **OK**. Click on **Add Script** under **Remediation Script**. Keep Windows PowerShell as the script language.

We will leverage the `Set-NetFirewallRule` cmdlet to block any firewall rule that is found with the display name **Google Chrome (mDNS-In)**:

```
Set-NetFirewallRule -DisplayName "Google Chrome (mDNS-In)" -Enabled True -Action Block
```

2. Click on **OK** and then click on the **Compliance Rules** tab in the **Create Setting** dialog box. Click on **New** to create a new compliance rule.

3. Give it a friendly name such as `Disable Chrome mDNS-In`. In **The setting must comply with the following rule**, leave `Equals` selected and enter `Yes` in the box.

4. Select both **Run the specified remediation script when this setting is noncompliant** and **Report noncompliance if this setting instance is not found**.

5. Choose `Information` for **Noncompliance severity for reports**. Click on **OK** and click on **OK** again to get back to **Create Configuration Item Wizard**.

Next, we want to disable Google Cast. Google Chrome has ADMX-backed templates available that can be downloaded from the Enterprise standalone pack and imported into Group Policy. However, since we are building a configuration item, let's look at how to use the registry key and enforce compliance using a security baseline:

1. Click on **New** to create a new setting, and enter the information shown in the following screenshot:

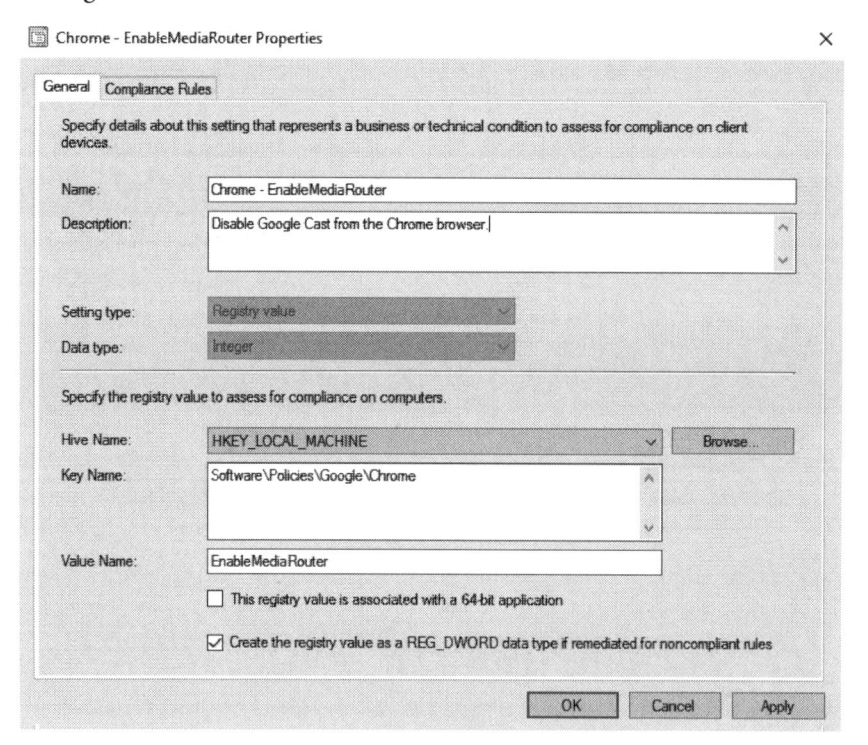

Figure 9.27 – The Create Setting window in a configuration item

2. Click on the **Compliance Rules** tab, and enter the settings displayed in the following screenshot:

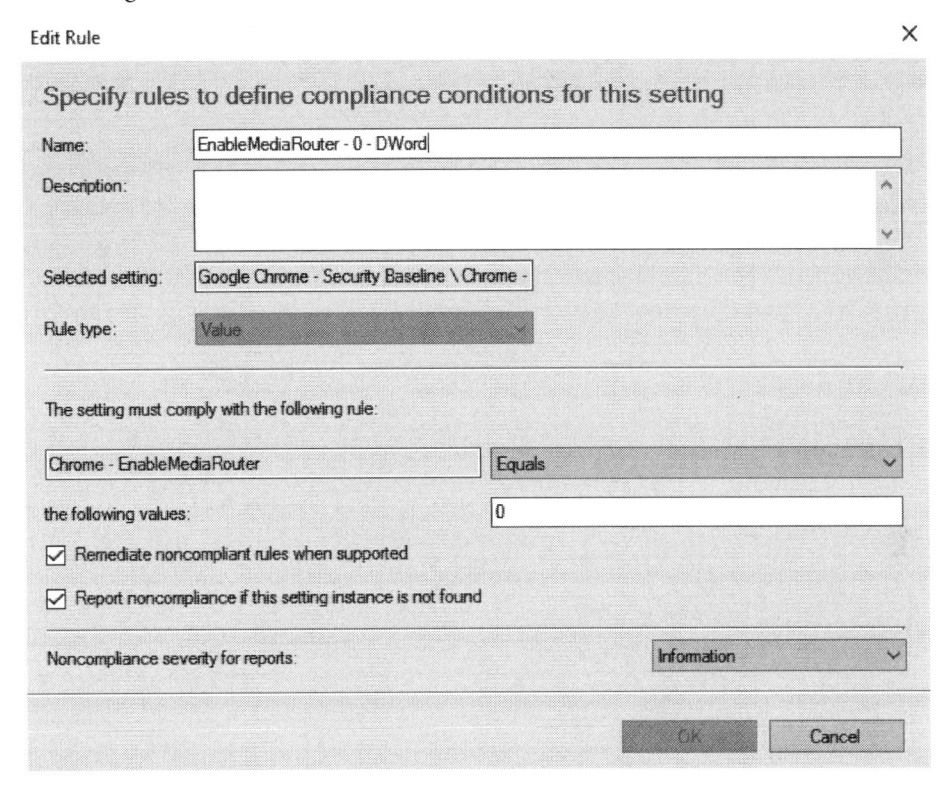

Figure 9.28 – Compliance Rule in a configuration item

3. Click on **OK**, click on **OK** again, and then choose **Next** back in **Create Configuration Item Wizard**.
4. Click on **Next** a few times to complete the wizard and build the configuration item.

Once the configuration item has been created, create or assign it to an existing security baseline where it will remediate for noncompliance. Once the setting is applied, the **Cast** option is removed from the browser and the firewall rule will be blocked, as shown in the following screenshot:

Figure 9.29 – Inbound Firewall Rules in Windows Defender Firewall

Next, let's take a look at how to prevent an MITM attack by disabling the **Web Proxy Autodiscovery Protocol** (**WPAD**).

Disabling the Web Proxy Autodiscovery Protocol (WPAD)

WPAD is used by the Windows system to find a configuration file called **wpad.dat**, which is used to determine the IP or server to proxy HTTP(S) web traffic. With WPAD enabled, an unknowing computer can broadcast a request to find a proxy either issued through DHCP or DNS. If no resolution is found, an attacker can poison the DNS response and effectively use their system as a web proxy to serve a modified wpad.dat file. Once an unknown victim's machine uses this fake proxy, all web traffic can be monitored through the fake service, including the ability to modify requests and responses using tools such as Burp Suite (MITM). If the attacker's malicious proxy server forces HTTP-NTLM authentication, it can entice users to supply credentials that can lead to captured passwords.

The following screenshot shows the default Windows 10 settings with WPAD enabled. This PC even has the Windows 10 recommended computer baseline applied:

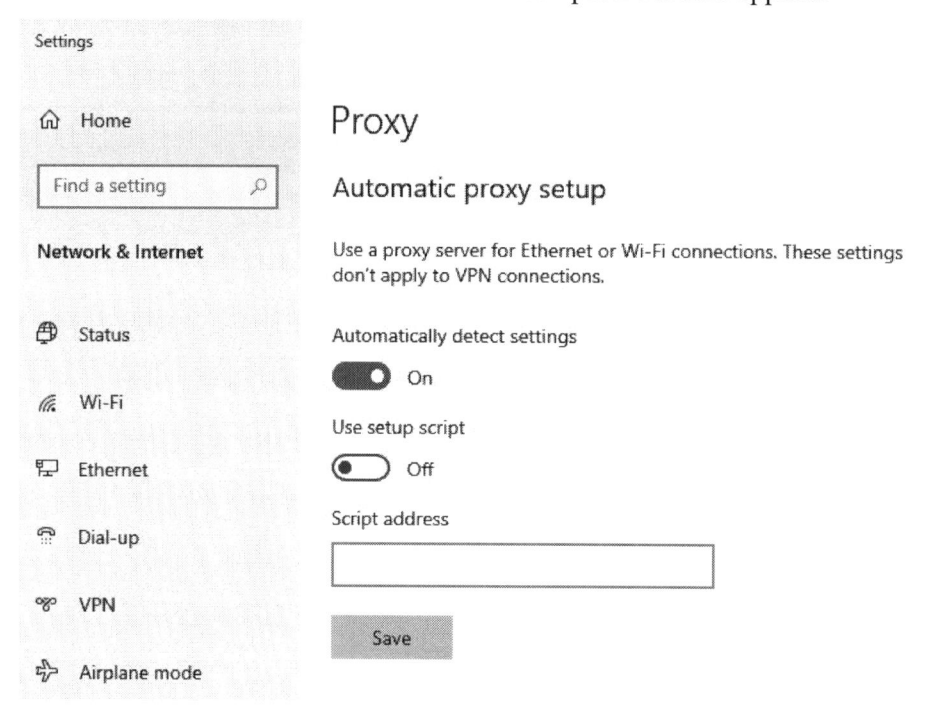

Figure 9.30 – Proxy settings

To disable WPAD, we recommend that you disable two services using Group Policy or registry settings:

- **WinHTTP Web Proxy Auto-Discovery Service** – `WinHttpAutoProxySvc`

Registry settings can be configured and enforced using both Group Policy and a security baseline in Configuration Manager. Set the following value to disable `WinHTTPAutoProxySvc`:

- **HKLM\SYSTEM\CurrentControlSet\Services\WinHTTPAutoProxySvc**
- **Start** `REG_DWORD` is 4 (this sets the start up mode to disabled)

Once the PC restarts, the service is stopped, and the start up type is set to disabled. Additionally, if a user tries to re-enable WPAD, the setting will not be enforced unless they physically start the service using administrative rights. The following screenshot shows the LAN settings in **Internet Properties** once the service has been disabled:

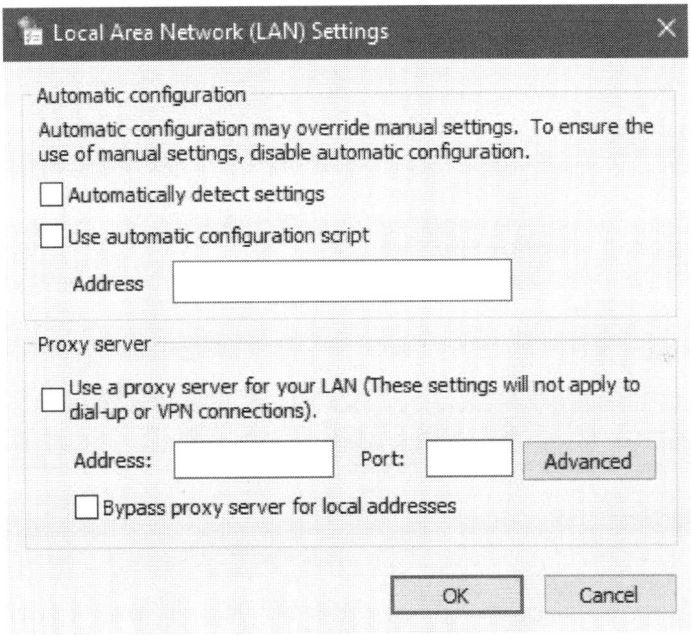

Figure 9.31 – Internet Properties > Local Area Network (LAN) Settings

So, we have just covered advanced configurations that are used to prevent attackers from poisoning responses to communications over the network. We covered multicast name resolution, NetBIOS-NS, multicast DNS, and WAPD. Next, let's look at how to configure a Microsoft Office security baseline.

Configuring Office security baselines

Another area that should be considered when hardening Windows is the office suite of applications. Microsoft Office is one of the most widely used sets of applications in Windows systems and is the target of many vulnerabilities. According to the cybersecurity firm Kaspersky, there has recently been a shift in focus for attackers with Microsoft Office as the preferred target in comparison to other attack surfaces, such as browsers, Flash, Java, and PDF file formats. Refer to the following article:

https://www.kaspersky.com/blog/ms-office-vulnerabilities-sas-2019/26415/

There are several different ways that Office security baselines can be applied. The Microsoft Security and Compliance Toolkit offers a recommended baseline included in its toolkit package for both computer-based and user-based policies. Security configurations can be enforced onto devices using the following:

- GPOs for AD domain-joined or hybrid Azure AD join
- The Administrative Templates device profile type for Intune and Azure AD joined devices
- Configuration Manager security baselines and LGPO packages
- User-based policies using only the Office cloud policy service for Office 365 ProPlus

The Office cloud policy service for Office 365 ProPlus is the most modern approach to deploying user-targeted office policies. There are some base requirements and limitations to using this service. The web interface, as shown here, is the administrative console used to create policies and build customized installations of Office for deployments:

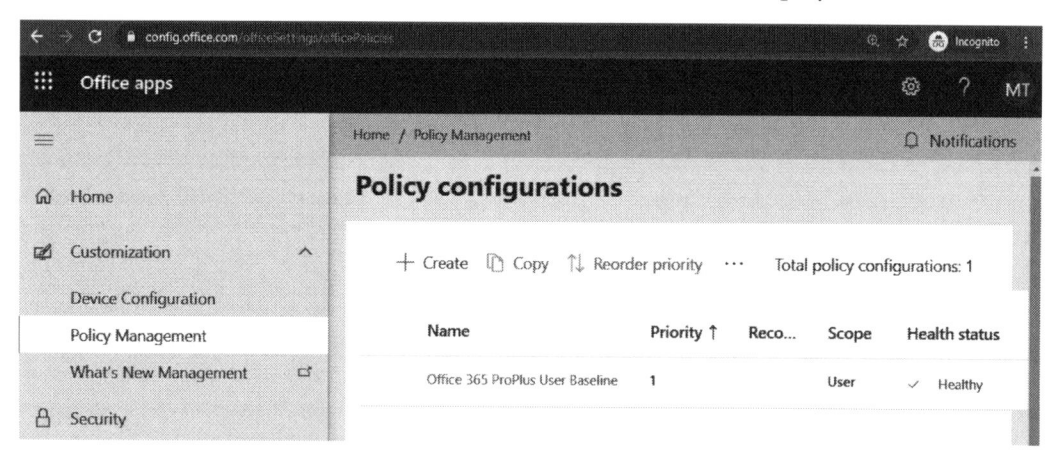

Figure 9.32 – Office cloud policy service admin center

For more information about the Office cloud policy service, including the minimum requirements to use it, refer to `https://docs.microsoft.com/en-us/deployoffice/overview-office-cloud-policy-service`.

Let's look at how to use the recommended Office security baselines from the Microsoft Security and Compliance Toolkit in order to create a Configuration Manager configuration baseline and deploy user-based policies with an LGPO package.

Deploying user-based office policies

This scenario works well for co-managed devices where workloads favor Configuration Manager:

1. Log in to your Configuration Manager site server or location with access to a deployment share for creating packages.

2. Download the `Office365-ProPlus-Sept2019-FINAL.zip` baseline or the latest available version from the Microsoft Security and Compliance Toolkit at the following link and extract it:

    `https://docs.microsoft.com/en-us/windows/security/threat-protection/security-compliance-toolkit-10`

3. Download `LGPO.zip` and extract it.

    The first step is to import the baseline into a GPO to act as a template. We can then make changes to and use this template as a reference point moving forward. Create a testing **Organizational Unit (OU)** so as not to apply these policies to any production objects. For this example, we created a TestGPO OU under **Workstations**.

4. Open the Group Policy Management Console and create a new GPO under a Test OU. Give it a descriptive name, such as `Office 365 ProPlus - User 1908`.

5. Find the newly created GPO under the **Group Policy Objects** folder, right-click on it, and choose `Import Settings`.

    We are going to want to find the extracted folder with the Office 365 security baseline that we downloaded earlier. Additionally, you may need to import the Office 365 ProPlus ADMX files to map the settings to the GPOs. Otherwise they will not have friendly names. Instructions on how to manage a Group Policy Central Store can be found here:

    `https://support.microsoft.com/en-us/help/3087759/how-to-create-and-manage-the-central-store-for-group-policy-administra`

A download link for the Office 365 ProPlus ADMX files can be found here:

https://www.microsoft.com/en-us/download/details.aspx?id=49030

1. Click on **Next** and **Next** again, and then click on **Browse** to find the location of the GPO's folder from the extracted Office 365 security baseline. Click on **Next**.

2. In the list of GPOs, select the **MSFT Office 365 ProPlus 1908 – User** policy and then click on **Next**. Click on **Next** again, and choose **Finish**. Finally, click on **OK** a few more times to finish the import wizard.

There are several other policy files included with the Office baselines, such as newly added configurations to supplement the standard default baseline. It is recommended that you review these policies and append the GPO you created if you wish to include them in the policy. Once all the changes have been added to the GPO, let's back it up and save it to the deployment share. We will be using the `.pol` file from the backup to apply user policy settings with the `LGPO.exe` tool via a deployment package.

3. Go to **Group Policy Object**, right-click on the GPO, and choose **Back up…**. Select the destination folder to back up the policy.

4. Create a new folder in the deployment share where you keep your applications and packages and give it a friendly name.

5. Navigate to the directory where you backed up the GPO and go to *{GUID}\DomainSysvol\GPO\User*. Copy the `registry.pol` file to the directory you created on the deployment share.

6. Find the `LGPO.exe` file extracted earlier from the LGPO download and copy it into the same folder as the `registry.pol` file in the deployment share.

> **Tip**
> We will be using this directory in the Configuration Manager package as our source files later. It's important to save the directory to a deployment share so that we can use the **Uniform Naming Convention** (UNC) network path as the source folder location.

Next, we are going to create a `.bat` file to kick off the unattended installation of LGPO. exe. For this, we will use Notepad:

1. Open **Notepad** and enter the following code. This will call the *LGPO.exe* tool and use the `/u` switch to install the *registry.pol* file user policies. `gpupdate /force` will apply them immediately:

   ```
   @echo off
   LGPO.exe /u %~dp0registry.pol
   gpupdate /force
   ```

2. Navigate to **File** > **Save As**, and change **Save as type** to `All files`. Enter `install.bat` in the filename and browse to the directory in the deployment share that has `LGPO.exe` and `Registry.pol`. Then, click on **Save**.

   Next, let's create a package in Configuration Manager for deployment.

3. In the Configuration Manager console, go to **Software Library** > **Application Management**, and choose **Packages**. Click on **Create Package**.

4. Give it a name, such as `Office 365 ProPlus - User Policy`, and a description.

5. Select **This package contains source files**. Click on **Browse** and choose **Browse** again. Enter the UNC path to the directory that you saved in the deployment share earlier. Click on **OK**.

6. Click on **Next**. Click on **Next** on **Program Type** and keep **Standard Program** selected.

7. In the **Standard Program** menu, enter a name such as `Install GPO`. Click on **Browse** in **Command Line**, and navigate to the deployment share directory with the `Install.bat` file created earlier and select it.

   > Tip
   > By default, the **Open** dialog box when browsing for a command line is scoped to **Executable files**. Make sure that you click on the drop-down list and select **All Files** to find the `.bat` file.

8. Enter the information displayed in the following screenshot for **Run**, **Program can Run**, and **Drive Mode**:

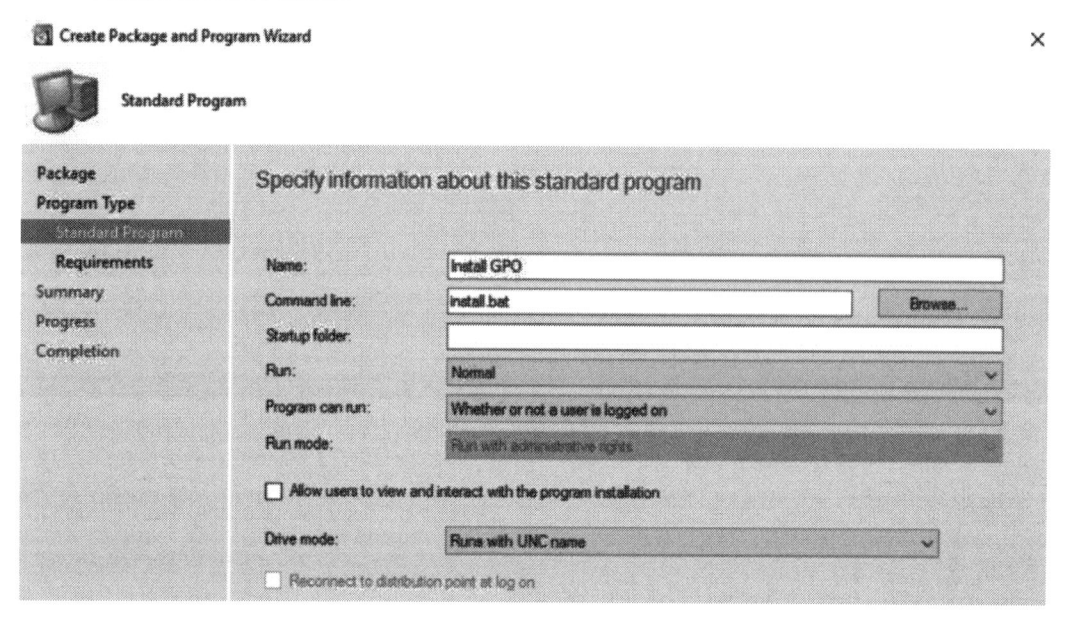

Figure 9.33 – Create Package and Program Wizard in Configuration Manager

9. Click on **Next**. Click on **Next** in the **Requirements** menu to keep the defaults as they are. This is to allow the program to run on any platform with an unknown disk space and a maximum allowed runtime (minutes) set to 120.

10. Click on **Next** in the **Summary** menu after confirming the settings. Click on **Close** in the completion screen.

11. Select the new package and click on **Deploy** from the toolbar.

12. Click on **Browse** and select a device collection. Click on **Next**.

13. In the **Content** menu, click on the **Add** dropdown, choose **Distribution Point Group**, and select a distribution point group to distribute content to. Click on **OK**. Then, click on **Next**.

14. In the **Deployment settings** menu, keep **Required** selected for **Purpose**. Select the **Allow clients on a metered Internet connection to download content after the installation deadline, which might incur additional costs** option.

15. In the **Scheduling** menu, select **Schedule when this deployment will become available**. Then, click on **New** in **Assignment Schedule** and click on **OK** to assign to the following schedule.

16. Click on the dropdown in **Rerun behavior** and choose **Always rerun program**. Click on **Next**.

17. In the **User Experience** menu, select **Allow users to run the program independently of assignments**. Click on **Next**.

18. Select **Download content from distribution point and run locally** for both deployment options in the **Distribution Points** menu. Click on **Next**.

19. Click on **Next** after confirming the settings. Click on **Close** in the **Completion menu**.

The following screenshot shows the package deployment in Software Center for one of the target workstations:

Figure 9.34 – Package installation in Software Center

Now that we have deployed the LGPO package for Office 365 User policies, we can create a configuration item and baseline to monitor the settings for our compliance reports. We cover the process of creating a configuration item from a GPO step by step in *Chapter 8*, *Administration and Remote Management*, in the *Creating a configuration baseline from a GPO* section.

After importing the template GPO into a configuration item, we built a baseline called `Office 365 Security Baseline - User` and deployed it in monitor mode to the workstations. When opening the Configuration Manager applet from the control panel on a workstation, you can see the evaluation condition against the LGPO package we deployed earlier in the following screenshot:

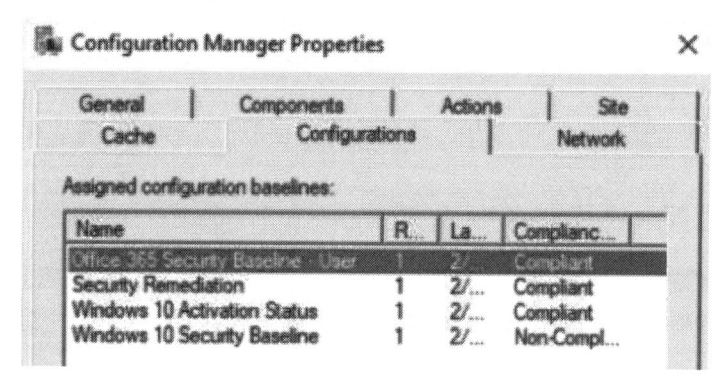

Figure 9.35 – The Configuration Manager applet from Control Panel

Now we have a reporting mechanism to use against the user policies. From a life cycle perspective for the user-based policies, use the GPO you created in the TestGPO earlier to act as a template. Any time a change is required, update the GPO and repeat the process here to deploy an updated package and an updated configuration item.

This process may seem tedious, but it works well for Azure AD joined devices where Group Policy is not applicable. If you are using Intune Administrative Templates, there is no way to bulk import all of the recommended Office security baselines at this time, and recreating the baseline would take a lot of time.

Hardening Google Chrome

The Google Chrome browser has quickly become one of the most popular browsers used in organizations today according to *statcounter global stats*:

https://gs.statcounter.com/

Not only is it quick and user friendly, but it also offers cross-platform compatibility and has a great set of built-in configurable security features. Google also offers an enterprise bundle that allows fine-grained control over security policies, add-on extensions, and customizations that can be controlled with Group Policy or by using Google Cloud Management. To download the Google Chrome Enterprise bundle, visit this link:

https://cloud.google.com/chrome-enterprise/browser/download

Included in the bundle is a set of ADMX and ADML files that can be imported into your Central Store for Group Policy management. The **Center for Internet Security (CIS)** readily releases benchmarks for the Google Chrome web browser, and it is recommended that you download and review these settings in detail. You can download the free benchmarks here: https://www.cisecurity.org/cis-benchmarks/

Let's now look at a few of the policies that should be considered for implementation immediately in order to harden Google Chrome using Group Policy. Once the ADMX and ADML files have been imported to the Central Store, navigate to **Computer Configuration** > **Administrative Templates** > **Google** > **Google Chrome**. Consider the following settings as a good starting baseline:

Policy	Setting	Comment
Ads setting for sites with Intrusive Ads	Enabled	Do not allow ads on sites with intrusive ads
Allow download restrictions	Enabled	Block dangerous downloads
Allow running plugins that are outdated	Disabled	
Ask where to save each file before downloading	Enabled	
Block third party cookies	Enabled	
Browser Sign-In Settings	Disabled	
Continue running backgrounds apps when Google Chrome is closed	Disabled	
Enable alternate error pages	Disabled	
Enable AutoFill for addresses	Disabled	
Enable AutoFill for credit cards	Disabled	
Enable component updates in Google Chrome	Enabled	
Enable Network Prediction	Enabled	Do not predict network actions on any network connection
Enable search suggestions	Disabled	
Enable third party software injection blocking	Enabled	
Enable URL-keyed anonymized data collection	Disabled	
Enabled WPAD optimization	Disabled	
Extend Flash Content setting to all content	Disabled	
Use built-in DNS client	Disabled	

Figure 9.36 – Recommended settings for Google Chrome security policy

Navigate deeper into the policy tree to **Google** > **Google Chrome** > **Content Settings**. Consider the following settings as part of the baseline:

Policy	Setting	Comment
Default Flash Setting	Enabled	Click to Play
Default Geolocation Setting	Enabled	Do not allow any site to track the user's physical location
Default Notification Setting	Enabled	Do not allow any site to show desktop notifications

Figure 9.37 – Recommended settings for Content Settings

The following table shows additional settings that are worth your consideration:

Location	Policy	Setting
Chrome / Google Cast	Enable Google Cast	Disabled
Chrome / Google Cast	Show the Google Cast toolbar icon	Disabled
Chrome / HTTP Authentication	Supported authentication schemes	Enabled (ntlm, negotiate)
Chrome / Password Manager	Enable saving passwords to the password manager	Disabled
Chrome / Printing	Enable Google Cloud Print Proxy	Disabled
Chrome / Printing	Enable submission of documents to Google Cloud Print	Disabled
Chrome / Proxy Server	Choose how to specify proxy server settings	Enabled (never use a proxy)
Update / Applications / Google Chrome	Update policy override	Enabled (Always allow updates)

Figure 9.38 – Additional recommended settings

We will now look at Chrome extensions.

Whitelisting extensions

Extensions are a popular way to enhance the functionality of Google Chrome. From a security perspective, they prove to be difficult to control or report on their use. This is because extensions aren't installed like a normal application running on your Windows systems. One example would be a VPN extension that a user installs to try and circumvent a firewall rule blocking access to a video streaming site. In order to control extensions, it's recommended that you set the following policies under **Google > Google Chrome > Extensions**:

Policy	Setting	Comment
Configure extension installation blacklist	Enabled	*
Configure extension installation whitelist	Enabled	Extension_ID

Figure 9.39 – Recommended extension policies for Google Chrome

By setting the **asterisk** (*) value in the **Configure extension installation blacklist** policy, you will effectively block all extensions unless they are specified in the **Configure extension installation whitelist** policy. An extension ID can be found by going to the Chrome web store here: https://chrome.google.com/webstore/category/extensions?hl=en-US

> Tip
> By configuring the blacklist policy, users will be prevented from installing any extensions that aren't whitelisted.

Find the extension you want to whitelist. The extension ID is the long string of characters at the end of the URL in the address bar. For example, the extension ID for Windows 10 accounts is `ppnbnpeolgkicgegkbkbjmhlideopiji`. In the following screenshot, you can see the extension ID in the address bar before the question mark at the end of the URL:

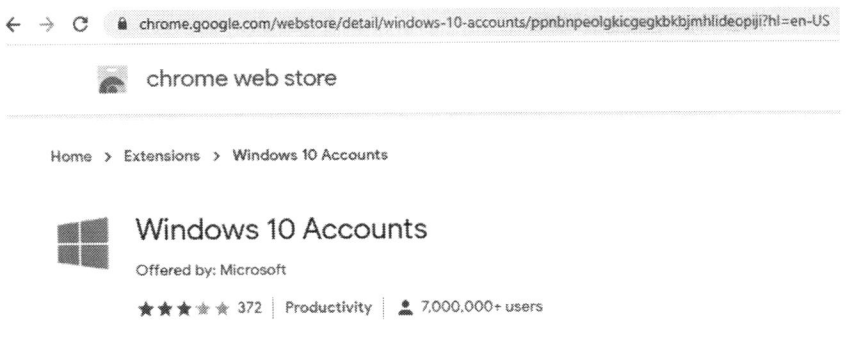

Figure 9.40 – Chrome web store for installing extensions

Next, let's take a look at how to lock down the registry and prevent user modification with Group Policy settings.

Preventing user access to the registry

Another area of consideration for hardening Windows is to restrict user access to the registry through Group Policy. This can help to prevent the unauthorized modification of the registry through the user's context, but it does not protect other administrative sources from making changes. You can prevent access to registry editing tools by using Group Policy and these steps:

1. Open the **Group Policy Management Editor** and create a new GPO within an OU that contains user accounts.

2. Give it a friendly name, such as **Windows 10 – Reg Lock**. Right-click on it and choose **Edit**.

3. Navigate to **User Configuration** > **Policies** > **Administrative Templates** > **System**. Select **Prevent access to registry editing tools**.

4. Choose **Enabled** and select **Yes** in the dropdown under **Disable regedit from running silently**.

5. Click on **OK** and close the **Group Policy Management Editor**.

The next time a user goes to open `regedit.exe`, even if the user is a local administrator, they will receive a message similar to the following screenshot:

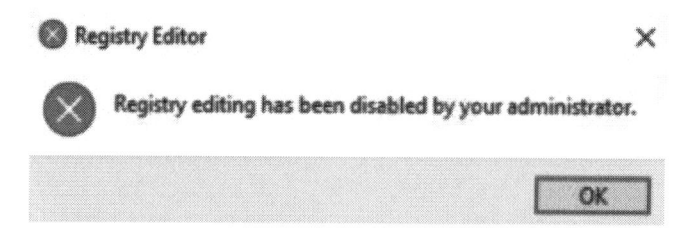

Figure 9.41 – Registry Editor disabled with Group Policy

This will also help to prevent any modification of the registry if malicious codes gain access to the user context and try to make registry modifications.

For the best security and to ensure that other applications do not modify your registry settings without approval, it is recommended that you use AppLocker or **Windows Defender Application Control** (**WDAC**) to whitelist an allowed list of applications. Next, let's take a look at WDAC and how it protects your system by policing what applications can run on your Windows systems.

Windows Defender Application Control

WDAC is used to create a whitelist of applications, file paths, and **Component Object Model** (**COM**) objects, and can enforce protections such as script signing - on processes to help protect your system from unauthorized applications. WDAC is built around the Zero Trust model in which applications and processes must prove their trustworthiness before they are able to execute. If the application, process, or path is not whitelisted, it will be blocked. Unlike AppLocker, WDAC enforces policies at the device level and cannot be assigned to specific users and groups. Additional protection can be used to complement WDAC when used in conjunction with the hypervisor isolation of **Virtualization Based Security** (**VBS**) and UEFI SecureBoot. Both technologies combined have been collectively referred to as *Device Guard*. WDAC can be deployed separately from VBS. However, without the isolation features that VBS offers, you don't get the full protection of user and kernel-mode operations. WDAC policies can be enabled with Group Policy, Intune, or Configuration Manager.

It is recommended that you thoroughly understand the effects that WDAC policies have on your systems. As mentioned earlier, they are designed with the Zero Trust concept and can block critical applications from running if the policy isn't configured carefully. Deploy a Microsoft Defender Application Control policy in audit mode first to understand the effects on your Windows devices. Once audit mode is enabled, you can view the WDAC logs from **Event Viewer** under *Applications and Services\Microsoft\Windows\CodeIntegrity\Operational*. WDAC events can also be queried with the **Kusto Query Language (KQL)** using **Advanced Hunting in Microsoft Defender ATP**.

If using Configuration Manager to deploy WDAC policies, you can choose to enable **Audit only** mode, as shown in the following screenshot:

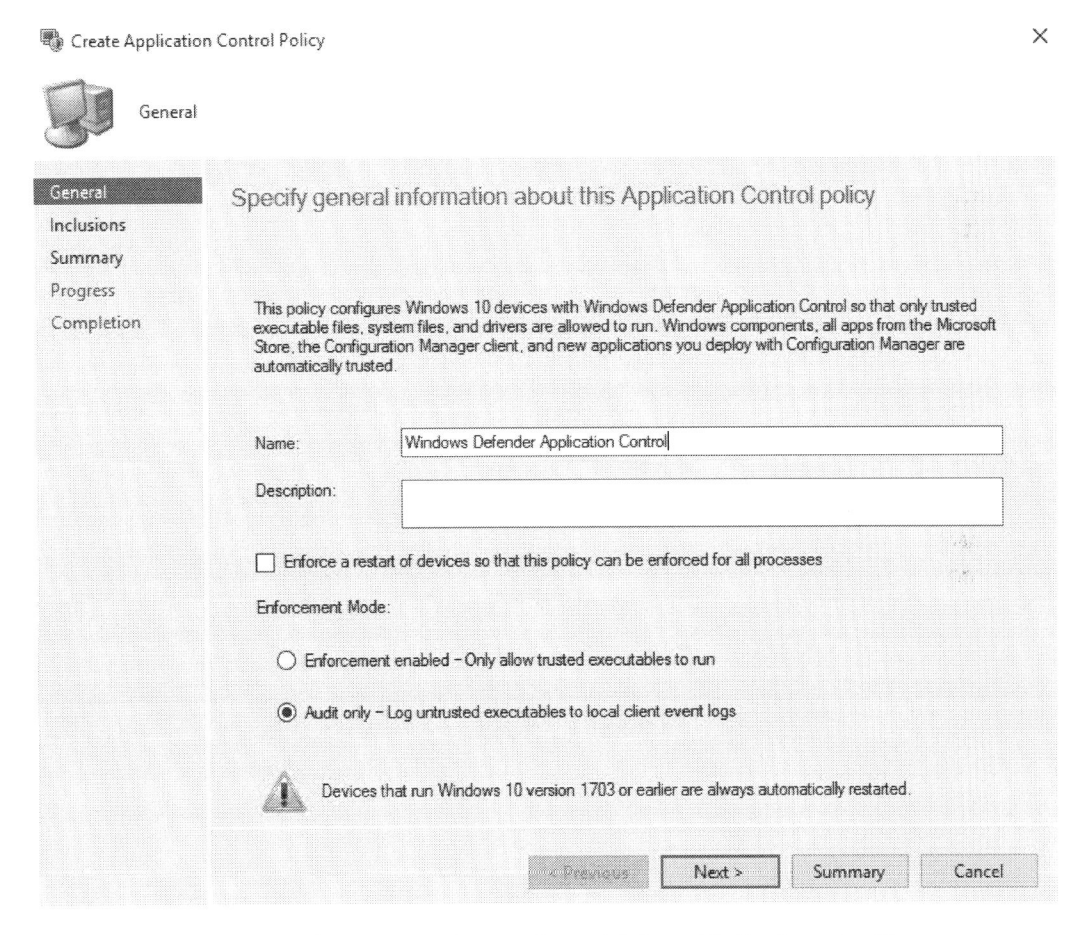

Figure 9.42 – Deploying an Application Control Policy with Configuration Manager

> **Tip**
> WDAC policies are built in XML format. They are configured using PowerShell and are converted into binary before they are deployed. Windows has preconfigured base policies that can be used to build your own XML definitions. To view the rules of these policies, use the `Get-CIPolicy` cmdlet. Example policies are stored in the following path: *%OSDrive%\Windows\schemas\CodeIntegrity\ExamplePolicies*

Considerations for WDAC or AppLocker

Both technologies are designed to support the policing of applications and files that can run on your Windows systems. The biggest difference between WDAC and AppLocker is that WDAC policies are always targeted at the device level and will affect all users that use the device. With AppLocker, policies can be enforced to specific users or groups of users. While WDAC is the preferred method of applying application control policies for Windows 10, Microsoft still recommends using AppLocker in combination with WDAC if you require a granular level of enforcement.

Configuring customized policies can be extremely time-consuming and may require careful consideration when planning for a deployment. Microsoft has created a lot of documentation regarding the deployment of WDAC policies that should be read in detail before starting an implementation on your Windows device. For more information, refer to https://docs.microsoft.com/en-us/windows/security/threat-protection/windows-defender-application-control/windows-defender-application-control.

Next, let's look at the different privacy settings in Windows 10 and learn how to configure them.

Windows 10 privacy

Windows 10 has many great features that provide an enhanced and connected experience for its users. As a result, there are many data- and privacy-related settings that are enabled by default that could pose a potential security risk for some organizations. While many of these features are great for consumer use, they may not be applicable to work organizations. Let's run through a few settings and look where to disable them if needed. To configure these privacy settings, we will leverage Intune device configuration profiles. All of the settings in the following table are available via a Windows 10, and later, platform using the **Device Restrictions** profile type.

This table is a compiled list of base recommendations:

Category	Setting Name	Configuration
App Store	Game DVR (desktop only)	Block
Cellular and Connectivity	Automatically connect to Wi-Fi Hotspots	Block
Cellular and Connectivity	Bluetooth Advertising	Block
General	Geolocation	Block
General	Device Discovery	Block
Locked Screen Experience	Cortana on locked screen	Block
Locked Screen Experience	Toast Notifications on locked screen	Block
Locked Screen Experience	Voice activate apps from locked screen	Disabled
Privacy	Privacy Experience	Block
Privacy	Input Personalization	Block
Privacy	Account Information	Block
Privacy	Contacts	Block
Privacy	Location	Block
Privacy	Feedback and diagnostics	Block
Privacy	Sync with devices	Block
Projection	Require PIN for pairing	Require
Windows Spotlight	Third-party suggestions in Windows Spotlight	Block
Windows Spotlight	Consumer Features	Block
Windows Spotlight	Windows Spotlight in action center	Block

Figure 9.43 – Recommended privacy settings in Intune

For a full list of settings that can be configured using Device Restriction profiles, including the preceding setting definitions, refer to `https://docs.microsoft.com/en-us/intune/configuration/device-restrictions-windows-10`.

Controlling the privacy settings for each app

Depending on your organization's privacy policies, configuring settings from the **Privacy** category in an Intune Device Restrictions profile allows you to configure which features are available for use on a per-app basis. Some of the available settings include the following:

- Account information
- Calendar
- Camera
- Contacts

- Email
- Location
- Microsoft
- Notifications

If using the **Privacy** category to configure these settings, you can use the **Per-app privacy exceptions** category to explicitly configure which applications are allowed access to use these features. Otherwise, all applications will be blocked.

Additional privacy settings

There are a few additional privacy settings for consideration that are not configurable with Device Restriction profiles. Let's look at how to set the following privacy options using custom profiles and Group Policy:

1. Disable the device advertising ID that lets apps make ads more interesting to you based on your app activity.
2. Disable any tailored experiences based on diagnostic data, which are used for personalized tips, ads, and recommendations that enhance Microsoft products and services for your needs.
3. Set the diagnostic data that is sent to Microsoft to **Basic Only**.
4. Disable the app launch tracking that enables Windows to track app launches in order to improve start and search results.

To disable the advertising ID and tailored experiences, create a custom profile Intune Device Configuration profile:

1. From the **Microsoft Endpoint Manager admin center**, click on **Devices** and select **Create Profile**.
2. Give it a friendly name, such as `Windows 10 - Custom Privacy Settings`, and give it a description. Choose `Windows 10 and later` as the **Platform** and `Custom` as the **Profile type**.
3. In the **Custom OMA-URI** settings, click on **Add** to create a new setting. Create these two configurations with the following settings:

To disable the advertising ID, create the OMA-URI setting, as shown in the following screenshot. Use this OMA-URI string: **./Device/Vendor/MSFT/Policy/Config/Privacy/DisableAdvertisingID**:

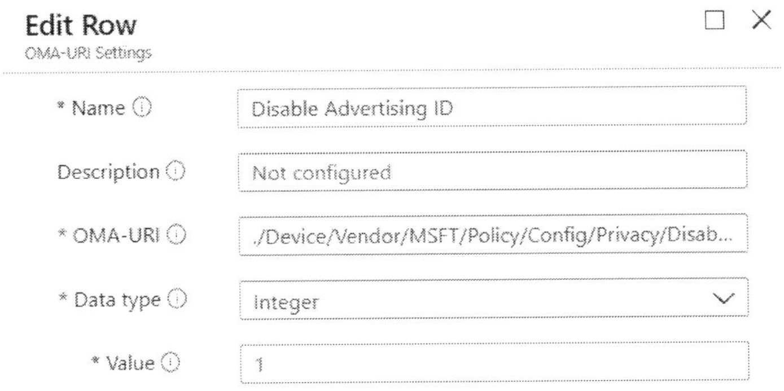

Figure 9.44 – Custom OMA-URI setting

Once this setting has been configured, click on **Add** to create an additional setting for **Tailored Experiences**. To disable **Tailored Experiences** from using diagnostic data, use the OMA-URI settings shown in the following screenshot. Use this OMA-URI string, `./User/Vendor/MSFT/Policy/Config/Experience/AllowTailoredExperiencesWithDiagnosticData`, as follows:

Figure 9.45 – Custom OMA-URI setting

After the row has been added, click on **Add** to create an additional setting to change the default level of diagnostic data sent to Microsoft. We recommend that you keep the default or, at least, allow the basic setting depending on your organization's privacy concerns. Allowing telemetry data to flow to Microsoft helps to improve their machine learning. To change the level of telemetry to basic, use the OMA-URI settings shown in the following screenshot. Use this `OMA-URI` string, `./Device/Vendor/MSFT/Policy/Config/System/AllowTelemetry`, as follows:

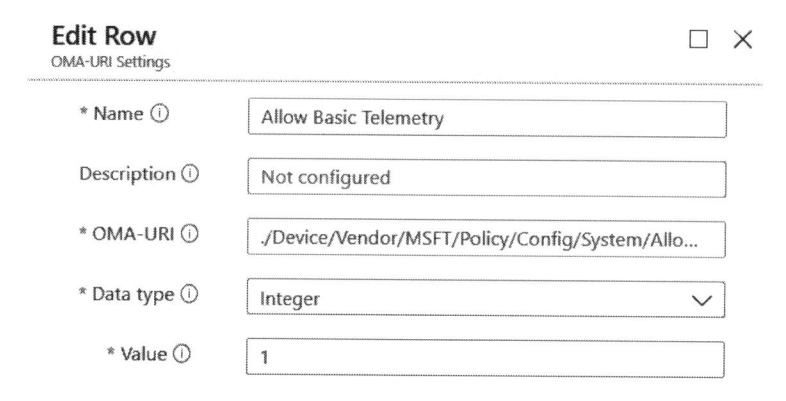

Figure 9.46 – Custom OMA-URI setting

> **Tip**
> When collecting telemetry in Log Analytics or another solution in Azure, be sure to configure and set **System/AllowDeviceNameInDiagnosticData** to an integer value of 1 in order to allow the device name to be sent. Otherwise, you will see a # in place of the device name.

Next, let's look at how to disable Windows track app launches in order to improve the start and search results. For this policy, we can use Group Policy or the registry.

If using Group Policy, set the following policy:

- **User Configuration** > **Administrative Templates** > **Windows Components** > **Edge UI**

  Enable the **Turn off tracking of app usage policy**.

To set this setting with the registry, modify the following registry key:

- **HKEY_CURRENT_USER\SOFTWARE\Policies\Microsoft\Windows\EdgeUI**

  Set the **DisableMFUTracking** `REG_DWORD` to `1`.

To check other available privacy settings, open the **Settings** app, and click on **Privacy**. You can see two of the settings we just disabled in the following screenshot that are under **General**:

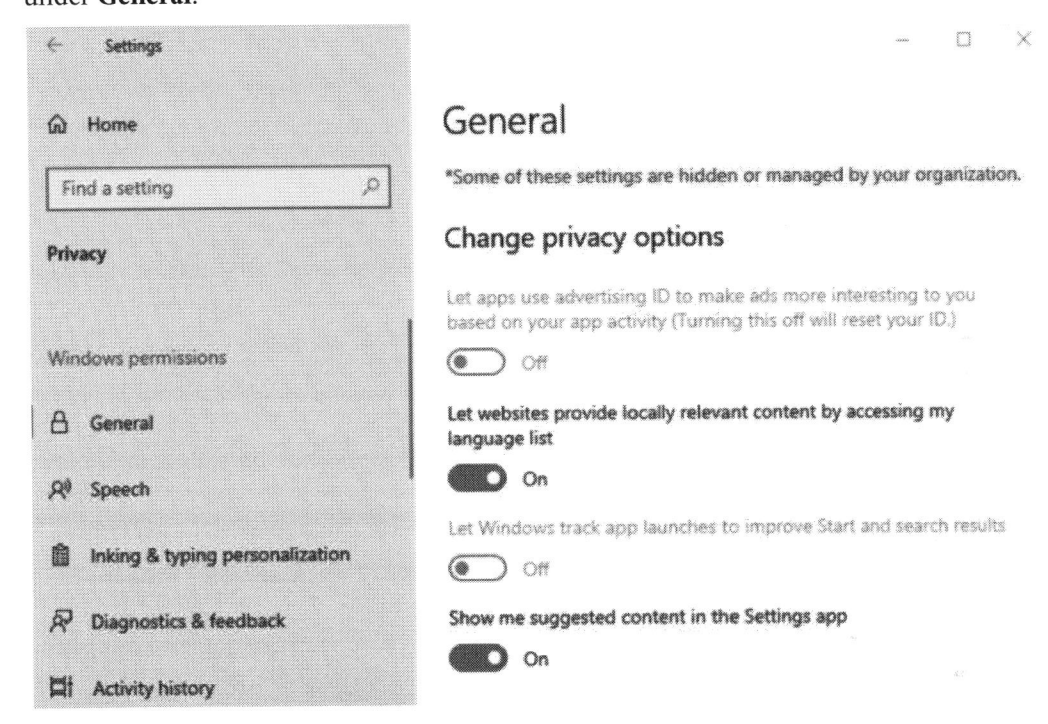

Figure 9.47 – General options in the Privacy settings

Let's now take a look at the privacy settings for the Microsoft Edge browser.

Privacy settings for Microsoft Edge

Microsoft has recently rebuilt Microsoft Edge based on the open source Chromium project. Its rebirthing, according to Microsoft, will help to realign the browser and contribute to the open source community to deliver improved compatibility across all browsers. As a result, many of the security policies we covered in the *Hardening Google Chrome* section apply to the Edge browser. To download the latest Microsoft Edge security baselines, visit this link:

```
https://docs.microsoft.com/en-us/windows/security/threat-protection/security-compliance-toolkit-10
```

Using the Administrative Templates device configuration profile in Intune, and following the guidance of the Security and Compliance Toolkit, you can build and assign an Edge security baseline directly in Intune that is completely customizable. You can also use the Microsoft recommended baseline settings by deploying the Microsoft Edge baseline profile in Intune Endpoint Security, as shown here, from the Microsoft Endpoint Manager admin center:

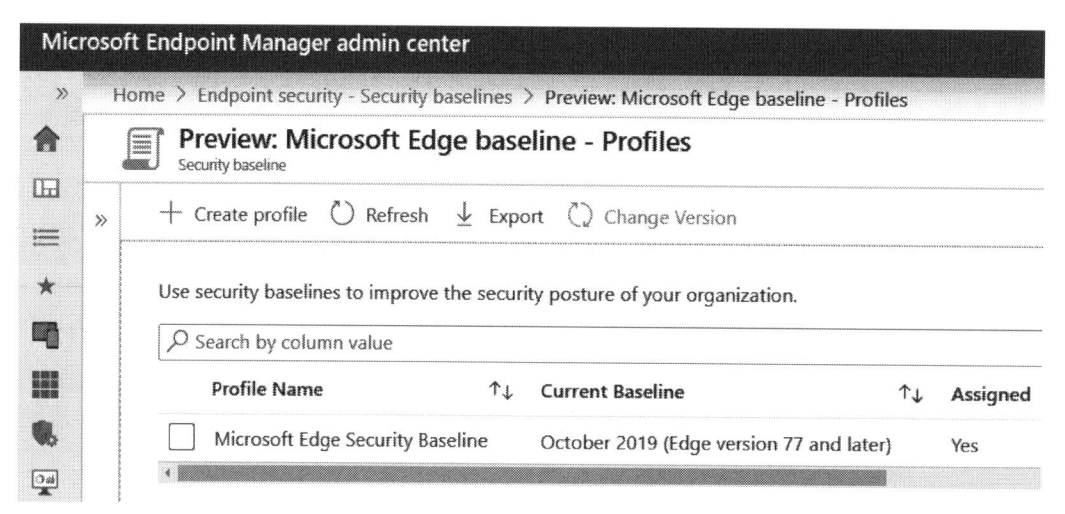

Figure 9.48 – Microsoft Edge baseline in Intune

All three policy options support the Chromium-based Edge browser. When attempting to change privacy settings in Edge, you will see the briefcase icon that displays the information tooltip, as shown in the following screenshot:

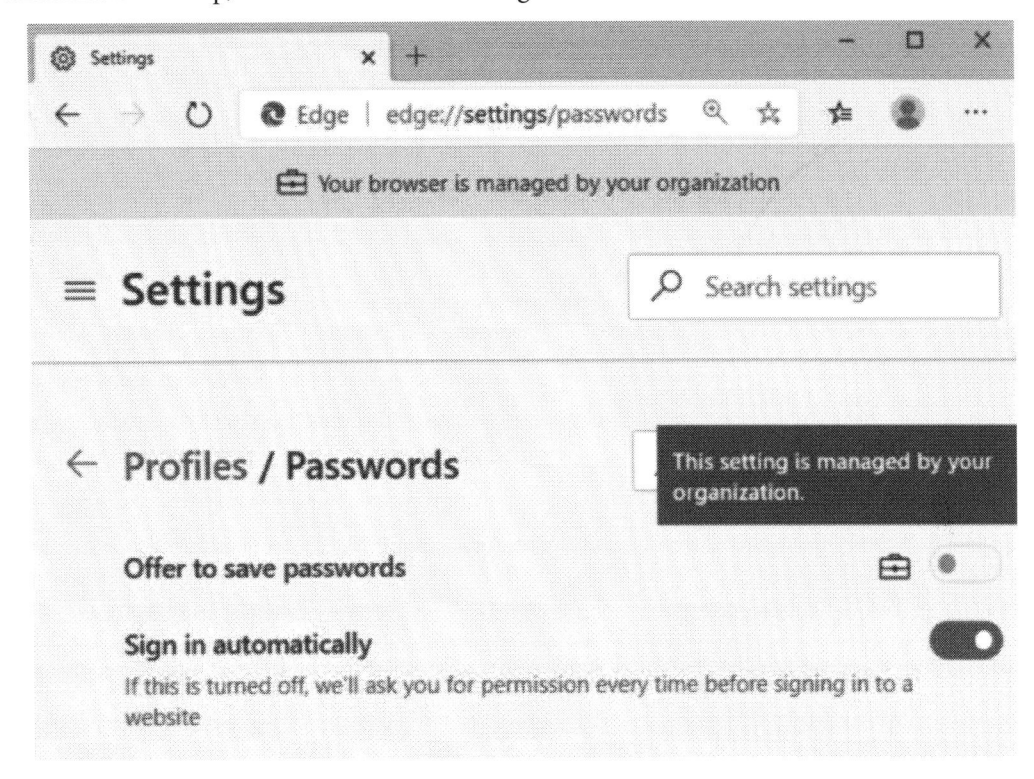

Figure 9.49 – Edge Chromium privacy settings

To download Microsoft Edge for business, visit this link:

https://www.microsoft.com/en-us/edge/business/download

Summary

In this chapter, we introduced securing end user Windows devices and some of the different Windows 10 versions available. We then covered the Microsoft Defender ATP service by providing a feature overview and guidance for onboarding machines. Following this, we discussed Windows 10 updates using the Windows Update for Business technology and how to configure deployment rings using Intune.

Next, we reviewed advanced Windows hardening configurations, which included technologies such as Windows Hello for biometric authentication, Windows encryption using BitLocker, how to configure Windows Defender AV real-time protection, and SmartScreen. Then, we discussed additional hardening tips to prevent name resolution poisoning and MITM over network communications. We also covered additional hardening tips by discussing Microsoft Office security baselines and hardening Google Chrome. Finally, we finished the chapter with Windows 10 privacy and data protection.

In the following chapter, you will learn how to keep your Windows server secure. We will introduce you to securing your Windows server and reviewing the roles and features within the Windows server. We will also be covering Microsoft Defender ATP and Windows updates before finishing the chapter with a discussion on how to harden your Windows server.

10
Keeping Your Windows Server Secure

Throughout this chapter, you will learn about the best practices and tools that you can use to keep your Windows server secure. As mentioned in *Chapter 9, Keeping Your Windows Client Secure,* this chapter will cover the core of what this book is about but for your Windows servers. Directly securing and hardening your Windows server OSes where your data, services, and applications live is a very important task. A breach of a server could lead to significant damage to your organization.

Your Windows servers serve as the core of your data and the applications for your users and customers. Protecting them requires well-defined standards and ongoing maintenance to ensure they stay protected. With Windows server, there are many built-in roles and features that allow additional functionality for your environment. Ensuring these are hardened is also just as critical. As a standard rule, none of your servers should be web-facing unless they are specifically providing a public web service, in which case those servers should be given extra attention and hardening.

This chapter will cover server protection through onboarding with Microsoft Defender ATP and delivering security updates with WSUS and Azure Update Management. Ensuring that your servers have the latest security updates and virus definition updates is a must. These two technologies are foundational for server security.

The *Hardening Windows Server* section will cover the technologies and configurations needed to round off Windows server security. This includes referencing back to pre-defined baselines, as shown in *Chapter 2, Building a Baseline*, enforcing these settings using Group Policy, and enabling disk encryption with Azure Disk Encryption. Finally, we will cover advanced application control by deploying Windows Defender Application Control polices. This chapter includes the following topics:

- Windows server versions
- Installing Windows server roles and features
- Configuring Windows updates
- Connecting to Microsoft Defender ATP
- Hardening Windows server
- Deploying Windows Defender Application Control

Technical requirements

This chapter will provide instructions that will allow you to enable security features in Windows server and configure Group Policy. In order to follow along, you will need basic knowledge of PowerShell, access to server roles that need to be installed, and be able to modify Group Policy in your domain environment and deploy resources in Azure. The following products and tools will be referenced:

- Windows Server 2019 Core and Desktop versions
- **Windows Server Update Services (WSUS)**
- Azure Subscription with Contributor Rights: `https://azure.microsoft.com/en-us/free/`
- PowerShell, including the Azure PowerShell Az module: `https://docs.microsoft.com/en-us/powershell/azure/new-azureps-module-az?view=azps-4.1.0`

Check out the following video to see the Code in Action: `https://bit.ly/31HVNZ9`

Windows Server versions

This book focuses on Windows Server 2016 and 2019. Most versions of Windows Server 2012 are under support until 2023, and support for Windows Server 2008 versions has ended. It is important to be familiar with the Microsoft life cycle of your server's OSes. The following URL provides the most current Window server release information: `https://docs.microsoft.com/en-us/windows-server/get-started/windows-server-release-info`

To view the life cycle for a specific Windows server version, go to this link:

`https://support.microsoft.com/en-us/lifecycle/search/1163`

> **Important note**
> Microsoft also has a **Semi-Annual Channel** (**SAC**) option, in addition to a **Long-Term Servicing Channel** (**LTSC**). The SAC version releases feature updates twice a year to allow customers to adopt changes faster. The latest SAC version, at the time of writing, is Windows server version 1909.

Windows Server 2019 has Standard and Datacenter versions. The Datacenter version provides additional enhancements over the Standard version. In addition to the available editions, there are a few different installation options available:

- **Desktop Experience** is the traditional deployment of Windows server and includes a **Graphical User Interface** (**GUI**). This option is only available in the LTSC version.

- **Server Core** only includes the required server role and doesn't include the GUI. This option is available for both the SAC and LTSC versions.

- **Nano Server** was introduced in Server 2016, has an even smaller footprint than Server Core, and can only be administered remotely. It only supports 64-bit applications, tools, and agents. A couple of examples include using Nano Server for **Internet Information Services** (**IIS**) or a DNS server. This option is only available in the SAC version.

As a best practice, we recommend using the most minimal installation option to reduce the footprint of the server and minimize the attack surface. Deploying a server without a GUI and limiting logon types to remote administration is a significant security improvement and should be considered where possible.

Windows Server 2019 includes the following new security highlights:

- Windows Defender ATP
- Windows Defender ATP Exploit Guard
- Security with **Software-Defined Networking (SDN)**
- Improvements with **Shielded Virtual Machines (VMs)**
- HTTP/2 to provide a safer web experience and faster browsing
- Encrypted networks

The following URL provides a list of all the new features of Windows Server 2019: `https://docs.microsoft.com/en-us/windows-server/get-started-19/whats-new-19`

In *Chapter 2, Building a Baseline*, we provided a minimum set of policy recommendations within the *Policies* sub-section of the *Policies, Standards, Procedures, and Guidelines* section. By completing this chapter, you will be able to cross-reference back to those policy items to see where there are gaps. The importance of building your policy to reference against it is critical to hardening your servers throughout your environment.

Next, will we review Windows server's roles and features and highlight the security-specific roles available that will help you secure your environment.

Installing Windows Server roles and features

Roles and features add additional functionality to your environment. As you add roles, it is critical that hardening is also taken into consideration and understood. For example, hardening a **Domain Controller (DC)** will be different to that of an IIS web server. There will be some base similarities, but you need to understand what each of these roles and features provide and how to best secure them if they are to be enabled. Any mishandling could provide an opportunity for a hacker to exploit or infiltrate your environment.

The following roles are features in Windows Server 2019 that are available to help with securing and hardening your environment:

- Active Directory Certificate Services
- Active Directory Domain Services
- Active Directory Federation Services
- Active Directory Rights Management Services
- Device Health Attestation

- Host Guardian Service
- Network Policy and Access Services
- Remote Access
- Remote Desktop Services
- Windows Server Update Services
- BitLocker Drive Encryption
- BitLocker Network Unlock
- Group Policy Management
- **Remote Server Administration Tools (RSAT)**
- Windows Defender Features (installed by default)
- Windows PowerShell (installed by default)

The following URL provides a complete list of all Windows Server 2019 roles and features available for deployment: https://docs.microsoft.com/en-us/windows-server/get-started-19/editions-comparison-19

Reducing the Windows Server footprint

Any opportunity where unnecessary roles and features can be reduced, or actions that can be enforced to limit the amount of direct interaction with the server, should be taken. For example, if Windows Server Core has a role for Active Directory Domain Services, it is recommended to deploy it using Server Core. Once deployed as a Core version, this role can be fully managed through remote tools such as **PowerShell, RSAT** or **Windows Admin Center**. This significantly reduces your threat footprint. Most of the roles and features included with the **Desktop Experience** are also supported by Server Core.

The following URL provides a complete list of all Windows Server Core roles and features available for deployment:

https://docs.microsoft.com/en-us/windows-server/administration/server-core/server-core-roles-and-services

Installing Nano Server 2019

Nano Server is the newest installation option and has fewer roles to choose from but is the most secure option. Nano Server can only be managed remotely using tools such as **PowerShell**, **Windows Remote Management (WinRM)**, and **Windows Management Instrumentation (WMI)**.

The following URL provides a complete list of all Nano Server roles and features available for deployment:

https://docs.microsoft.com/en-us/windows-server/get-started/deploy-nano-server

Hardening server roles and features should be included in your baselines and will differ, depending on the roles you have installed. These differences are provided in the CIS Benchmarks and Windows Security baselines that we covered in *Chapter 2, Building a Baseline*. CIS provides specific benchmarks that include specifics for Microsoft IIS Server and Microsoft SQL Server, in addition to many others. The Windows Security baselines provide hardening recommendations for domain controllers, in addition to the foundational Windows server baseline. Each server will have unique use cases with different datasets that need to be identified and protected correctly.

Let's walk through the installation of the **Windows Server Update Services** (**WSUS**) on a Windows Server 2019 Core edition. To install it, complete the following steps:

1. Create your *Windows Server 2019 Core machine* with your defined baseline and configure it with your standard build document; for example, domain join and apply updates.

2. Log in to your Windows Core machine. You will be presented with the command prompt. Type `PowerShell` to open PowerShell.

3. Type `Install-WindowsFeature UpdateServices` and hit *Enter*.

4. The installation will take a few minutes. Once complete, you will see the following screen:

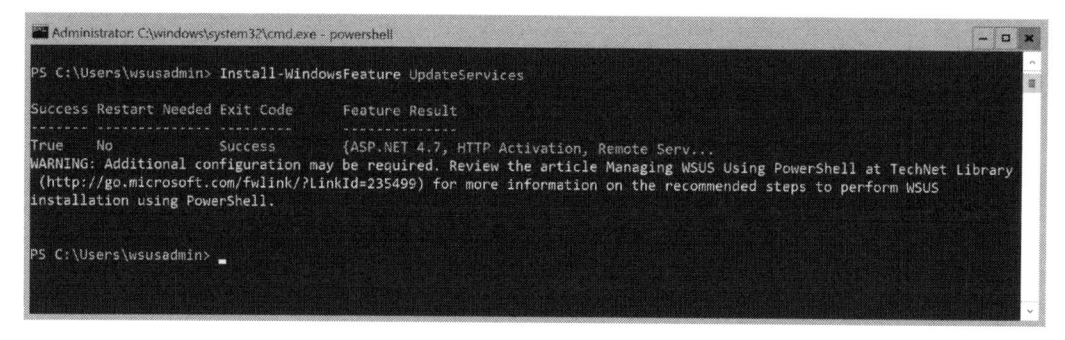

Figure 10.1 – Installing the WSUS Windows feature in Server Core

That completes the base installation of the WSUS feature on the Windows Core server, which wasn't difficult at all. We will complete the configuration in the next section, *Configuring Windows updates*.

We have just provided an overview of the Windows server roles and features and the importance of reducing the footprint by using Server Core or Nano Server where applicable. Next, we will look at configuring Windows updates using Windows Server Update Services and Azure Update Management.

Configuring Windows updates

To manage Windows updates for your servers, Microsoft has a well-known tool named **Windows Server Update Services** (**WSUS**). For your traditional and IaaS environments, WSUS provides the tools needed to deploy and update your servers as updates are released. Due to moving into the cloud world with Azure, Microsoft now has an Update Management solution as part of Azure Automation. Update Management allows you to manage your servers, both Windows and Linux, within your cloud and on-premises environments. An overview of WSUS was provided in *Chapter 3, Server Infrastructure Management* within the *Using Windows Server Update Services* subsection of the *Understanding Windows Server management tools* section.

Implementing Windows Server Update Services (WSUS)

First, we will review WSUS and how to use it as a follow-up from installing the feature within Windows Server Core earlier in this chapter. Before we access the management console, we will need to run through a few tasks to complete its setup. Let's get started:

1. Log back in to your Windows Core WSUS server and type `PowerShell` to open PowerShell.
2. Type each of the following commands one at a time to complete the setup process:

   ```
   New-Item -Path "C:\" -Name "WSUS" -ItemType "directory"
   CD "C:\Program Files\Update Services\Tools"
   .\wsusutil.exe postinstall CONTENT_DIR=C:\ "WSUS"
   ```

> **Tip**
>
> The following guide provides instructions on how to configure and enable SSL for your WSUS environment: `https://docs.microsoft.com/en-us/windows-server/administration/windows-server-update-services/deploy/2-configure-wsus#25-secure-wsus-with-the-secure-sockets-layer-protocol`

To configure WSUS on the Windows Server Core server, we will need to access a Windows client or server to install the WSUS management tools. To install the WSUS management tools on a Windows 2019 Server, complete the following steps:

1. Log on to a Windows server used for management and open **Server Manager**.
2. Click on **Manage** and then click **Add Roles and Features**.
3. Click **Next**, click **Next**, click **Next**, and finally, click **Next** (leave everything with the default settings until you get to **Features**).
4. Scroll down to **Remote Server Administration Tools** and expand the menu, expand the **Role Administration Tools** menu, and then select **Windows Server Updates Services Tools**.
5. Click **Next**, click **Install**, and then click **Close** once complete.

Next, we will connect to the Windows Server Core WSUS server and configure it:

1. On the management server, search for and open *Windows Server Update Services*.
2. Click **Connect to Server** to open the dialog box, as shown in the following screenshot:

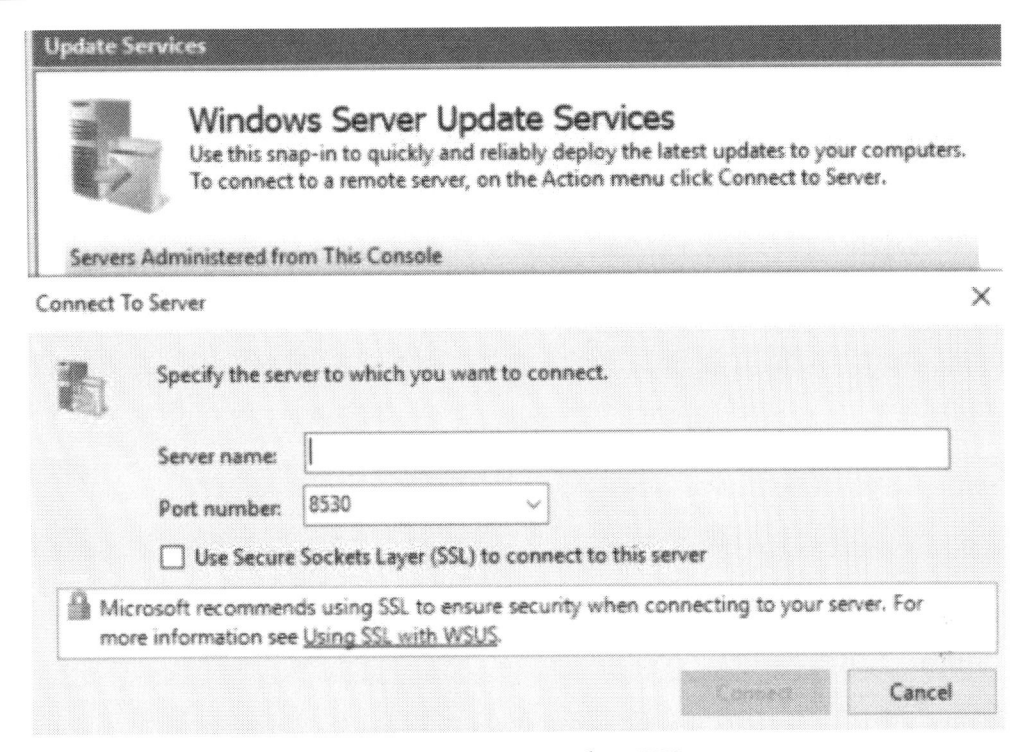

Figure 10.2 – Connecting to the WSUS server

3. Enter the *Windows Server Core name* or *IP* that was configured, leave the port as 8530 if SSL is not set up (it is recommended to set up SSL), and then click **Connect**.

4. In the WSUS Configuration Wizard, click **Next**, and then **Next** again. If this is your first WSUS server, select **Synchronize from Microsoft Update** and then click **Next**.

5. If you're using a proxy, select **Use a Proxy** and then enter the required information. If not, leave this *unchecked* and click **Next**. Then, click **Start Connecting** (this step may take a while to complete).

6. Once complete, click **Next**, select the *Languages* needed, and click **Next**.

7. Select all the products you need to update and click **Next**.

8. Select **Classification of Updates** to download it. At a minimum, select **Critical Updates** and **Security Updates**. Then, click **Next**.

9. Select **Synchronize automatically** and schedule your *first sync (Outside of Business hours)*. Select how many times you wish to sync per day and click **Next**.

10. Select **Begin initial synchronization** and click **Next**. Click **Finish** to view the management console. This can be seen in the following screenshot:

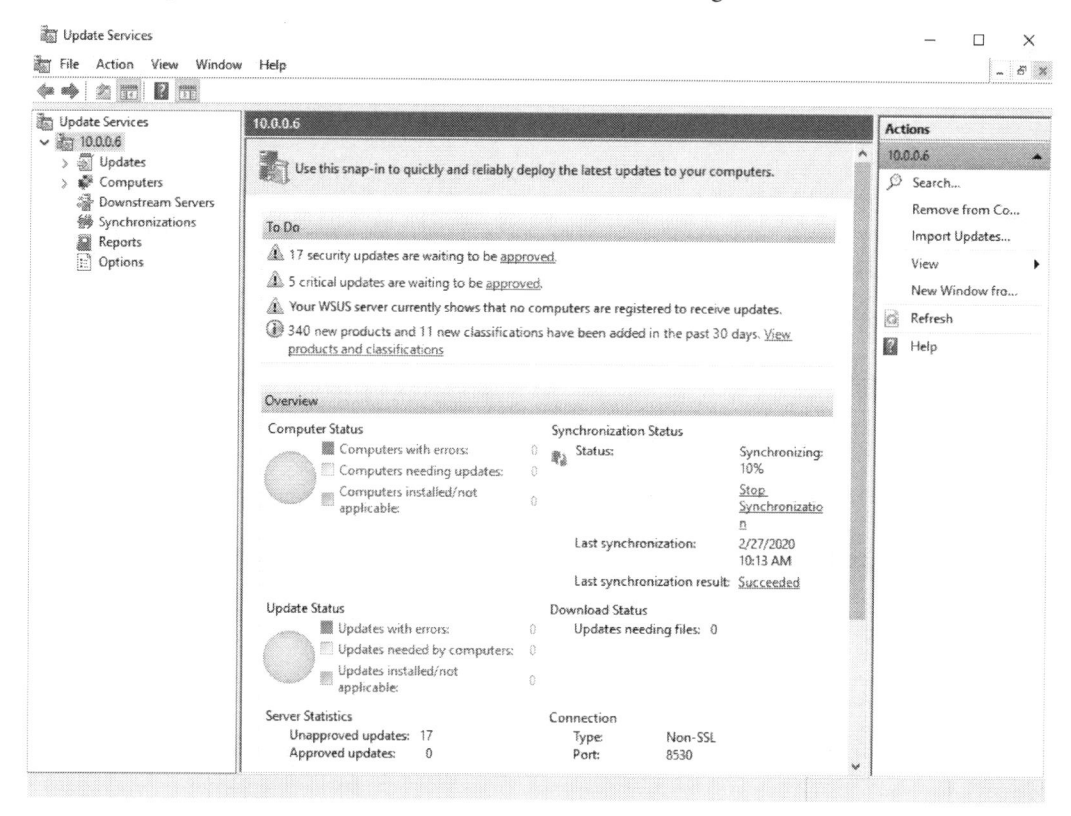

Figure 10.3 – WSUS Management Console

Additional configurations, including modifying the configured settings during setup, can be viewed by clicking on **Options** within the management console.

Next, we will work through the configurations needed to update your clients. First, we will create a computer group that can be used to test updates. You can create as many groups as needed to organize your servers. To create a group, navigate and expand the **Computers** menu, right-click **All Computers**, and then click **Add Computer Group…**. Name your group and then click **Add**.

Now, we will configure WSUS so that it uses Group Policy in order to efficiently manage the autoconfiguration of the servers. To do this, go to **Options** within the management console and then click on **Computers**. Change the option to **Use Group Policy or registry settings on computers** and then click **OK**.

Now, we are ready to configure Group Policy so that it instructs your Windows servers where to connect to (WSUS server) for Windows updates, along with additional configuration for the servers:

1. Access your *Group Policy Management Console* and create a new GPO or use a current one.
2. Edit the GPO, browse to **Computer Configuration, Policies, Administrative Templates, Windows Components**, and select **Windows Updates**.
3. Enable the following three settings:

   Configure Automatic Updates: Configure this to the preference of your organization.

   Specify intranet Microsoft update service location: Add your WSUS server to (in the format of `http://servername:8530` for HTTP and `:8531` for HTTPS) both the **Set the intranet update service for detecting updates** and **Set the intranet statistics server** fields.

   Enable client-side targeting: This is the group name you created within the WSUS management console for testing or to organize your clients if needed.

   The following screenshot shows the three settings you need to configure within GPO to force WSUS to be the update server for your Windows servers:

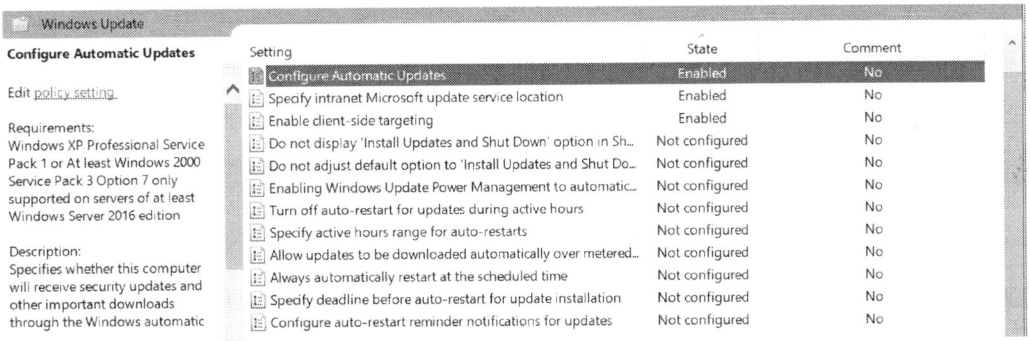

Figure 10.4 – Group Policy configuration

Now that the servers have been configured to connect to the WSUS server, the last step is to approve and push the updates to the clients.

4. From the WSUS management console, browse to **Updates** and click **Updates needed by computers** on the main screen. Select all the available updates that need to be deployed, right-click, and then click **Approve** to open the **Approve Updates** dialog box, as follows:

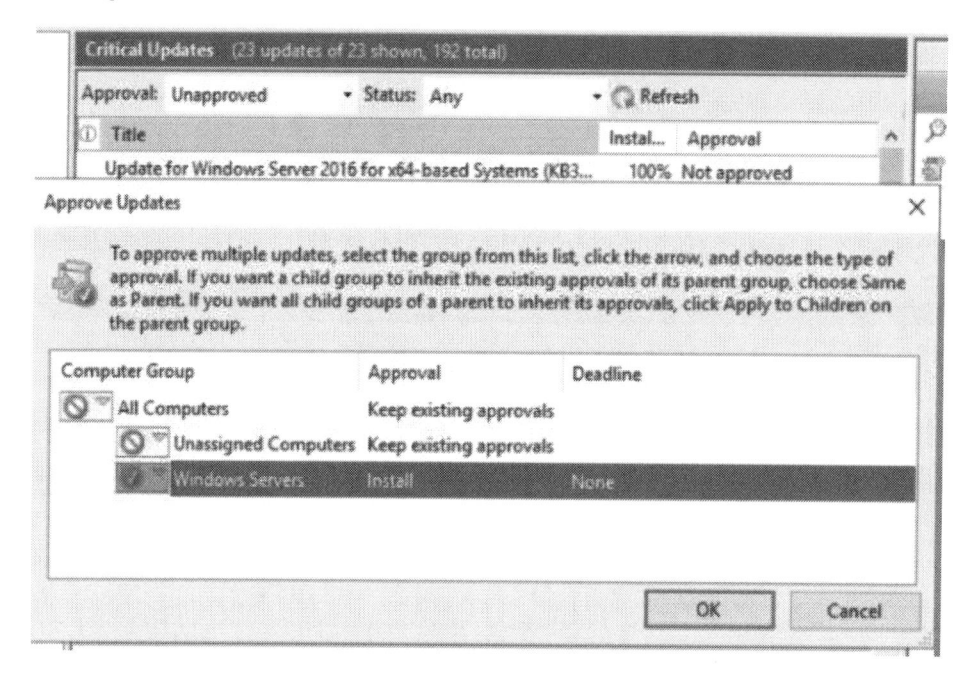

Figure 10.5 – Approving WSUS updates for installation

5. Click the group you would like to deploy to (your test group, if it's the first time you're installing the patch), select **Approved for Install**, and click **OK**. The updates will be installed at the scheduled time you configured within Group Policy.

Automatic approval rules can be specified if desired. Different automatic approval rules can be configured based on your groups, and deadlines can be applied to force the installation according to a specific time period. Automatic approval rules can reduce the administrative overhead of managing a WSUS environment and ultimately save time. Good candidates for automatic approval rules include critical security updates or antivirus definition updates. When creating a rule, you can specify the properties and conditions for an update to determine whether it passes the approval rule. These properties include the specific classification (such as critical updates, drivers, feature packs, and definition updates), a specific product, and the ability to set a deadline for installation following approval.

A good use case for automatic approval rules would be to deploy critical updates automatically to a group of servers to validate the fact that updates don't break business processes and then manually deploy them to the rest of your systems.

To set up automatic approvals, browse to **Options** within the WSUS management console and click on **Automatic Approvals** to set up and configure your automatic rules.

Next, we will review the *Azure Update Management* solution. Azure Update Management can be used to expand WSUS capabilities to the cloud and includes support for Linux servers and Windows, both on-premises and in Azure. In addition, Azure Update Management is provided as a service within Azure and can eliminate the need for additional server infrastructure to run WSUS.

Deploying Azure Update Management

In order to use Azure Update Management, you are going to need the following:

- **Log Analytics Workspace**, to collect and analyze the data.
- **Azure Automation Account**, to be able to configure Azure Update Management.

To get started, you'll need to create a Log Analytics and Azure Automation Account, if you don't already have one:

1. Log in to `https://portal.azure.com` and search for **Automation Accounts**.
2. Click **Add** and enter *Name, Subscription and Resource Group,* and *Location*.
3. Choose **Yes** to create an *Azure Run As account* and click **Create**, as shown in the following screenshot:

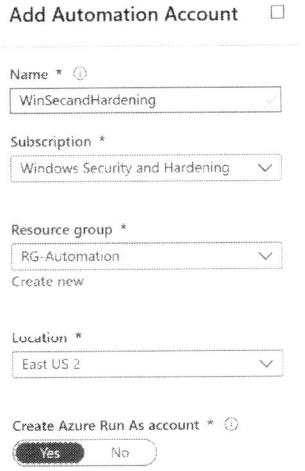

Figure 10.6 – Adding an automation account in Azure

4. Once the automation account has been created, click on it to access it.

5. Click on **Update Management** within the *Log Analytics Workspace* section, click the drop-down menu, select **Create New Workspace** if you don't already have one to use, and click **Enable**.

6. Once complete, click back on **Update Management** in the blade column to get to the management screen, as follows:

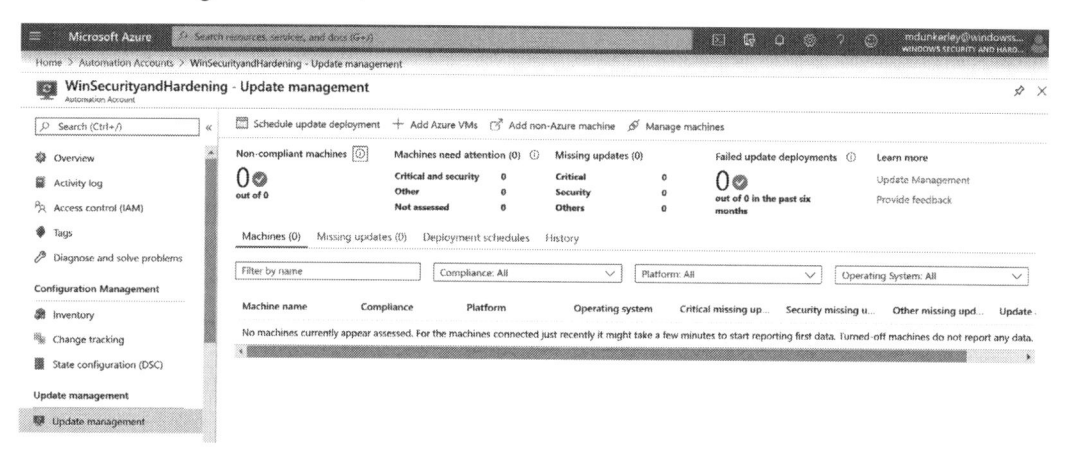

Figure 10.7 – Azure Update Management console

Now that Update Management is set up, we can enable a VM. To enable a VM within Azure, you have two options:

- **From within the VM settings in Azure**, click on **Update Management** and then click **Enable**.

- **From within the Update Management console**, click on **Add Azure VMs**. Select the VMs you would like to enable and then click **Enable**.

Once enabled, it can take up to 6 hours for the data to become available. Once available, you will see the updates that have been installed, those that are missing, and so on, as shown here:

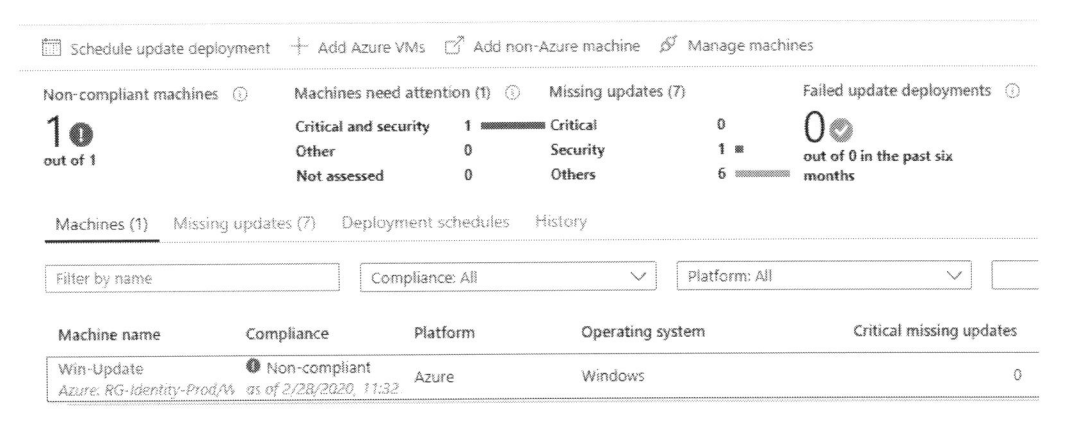

Figure 10.8 – Azure Update Management console with statistics

> **Tip**
> The following article provides troubleshooting advice for Update Management: https://docs.microsoft.com/en-us/azure/automation/troubleshoot/update-management

To add non-Azure VMs, you will need to install an agent on the machines. This will allow them to connect to Azure Log Analytics so they can be managed for updates. To do this, complete the following steps:

1. Open the *Log Analytics workspace* connected to your Automation Account.
2. In the **Overview** section, click **Windows, Linux and other sources** under **Connect a data source**.

3. Within **Connected Sources, Windows Servers**, download the 32- or 64-bit Windows agent and make note of the *Workspace ID and Key*:

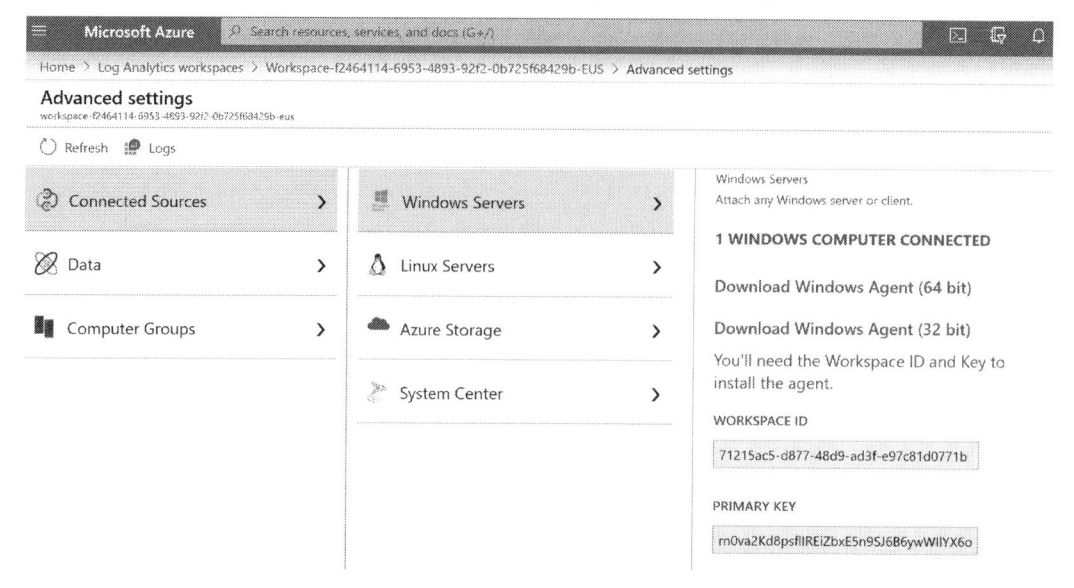

Figure 10.9 – Log Analytics agent download

4. Log on to Windows Server and install the downloaded agent.

5. Once Windows Server checks into Azure, you may need to enable **Update Management**. To do this, browse back to the Update Management console within your Automation Account and click **Manage Machines**.

To deploy updates to your servers, you will need to set up a *Deployment Schedule*. To set up a Deployment Schedule, complete the following steps:

6. Open Update Management from **Automation Accounts** and click on **Schedule update deployment**.

7. Complete the set up by providing the required information to create your new update deployment, as shown in the following screenshot:

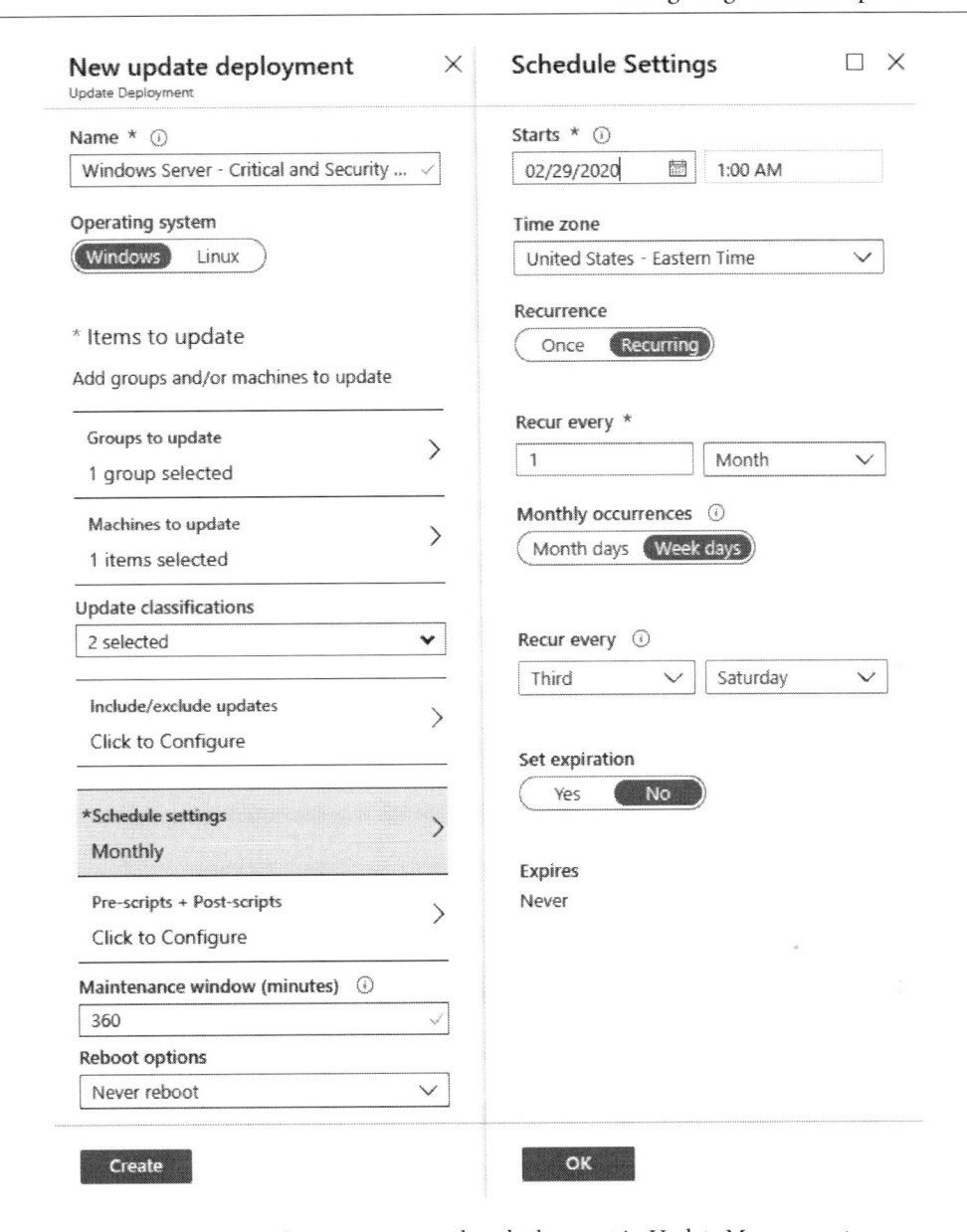

Figure 10.10 – Creating a new update deployment in Update Management

8. Click **Create** once you're finished.

Once your schedule has been deployed, updates will deploy to the clients, and the Update Management console will inform you once your servers are compliant. This can be seen in the following screenshot:

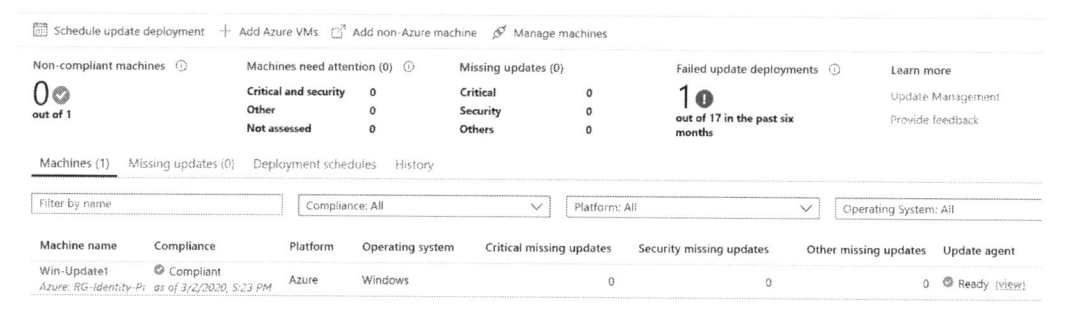

Figure 10.11 – Azure Update Management console with a compliant server

> **Tip**
>
> You will want to schedule a frequent update deployment schedule for definition updates if you have Windows Defender deployed.

To learn more about Update Management and understand the additional options, take a look at this document repository: https://docs.microsoft.com/en-us/azure/automation/automation-update-management

We have just provided two different options for deploying security updates using WSUS and Azure Update Management. Next, we will look at onboarding servers to Microsoft Defender ATP to take advantage of the advanced threat protection services.

Connecting to Microsoft Defender ATP

Microsoft Defender ATP was initially designed to support the Windows 10 OS, but now has extended support to include versions of Windows server. This includes servers that use Windows Defender Antivirus, as well as System Center Endpoint Protection. The following servers support onboarding to the Microsoft Defender ATP service:

- Windows Server 2008 R2 SP1
- Windows Server 2012 R2
- Windows Server 2016

- Windows Server, version 1803
- Windows Server 2019

The official Microsoft documentation for Microsoft Defender ATP, including an overview of its features, can be found at this link:

https://docs.microsoft.com/en-us/windows/security/threat-protection/microsoft-defender-atp/microsoft-defender-advanced-threat-protection

There are two methods supported that allow you to onboard Windows Server 2016 and lower. You can automatically onboard with **Azure Security Center** (**ASC**) using an Azure VM extension or deploy and configure the Microsoft Monitoring Agent to report data to Microsoft Defender ATP. If you use the Azure Security Center option, there will be additional cost considerations as the Log Analytics workspace you configure must be using the Security Center Standard tier. Azure Security Center is a great automated option if your VMs are hosted in Azure and if auto provisioning is enabled to enroll VMs to ASC.

Now, let's look at how to onboard Windows Server 2019 with Group Policy, as well as Configuration Manager.

Onboarding with Group Policy

In order to use Group Policy to onboard Windows Server 2019, download the onboarding package from the Microsoft Defender Security Center portal. Follow these steps to create the GPO to onboard machines:

1. Log in to the **Microsoft Defender Security Center** portal at https://securitycenter.windows.com.
2. Choose **Settings** and select **Onboarding** from the **Machine management** section.
3. Choose **Windows Server 1803 and 2019** for your OS and select **Group Policy** from the **Deployment Method**. Then, click **Download Package**.

Create a network share somewhere in the domain that has been given read-only access by the machines being targeted for ATP onboarding and extract the package's content. Inside the ZIP file will be a `.cmd` file named `WindowsDefenderATPOnboardingScript.cmd`, as shown in the following screenshot:

Figure 10.12 – Windows Defender ATP onboarding package extracted

4. Open **Group Policy Management Editor**, create a new policy, and link it to the OU where the Windows server objects in the scope reside. Give it a friendly name, such as `Windows Server - Defender ATP Onboarding`.

5. Go to **Computer Configuration** >**Preferences** > **Control Panel Settings** and right-click **Scheduled Tasks**. Select **New** and choose **Immediate Task (At least Windows 7)**. Give it a friendly name such as `Defender ATP Onboarding`.

6. Under **Security Options**, select **Change User or Group** and type in `SYSTEM`. Click **Check Names** and choose **OK**.

7. Select the radio button next to **Run whether user is logged on or not**.

8. Choose **Run with highest privileges**, as shown in the following screenshot:

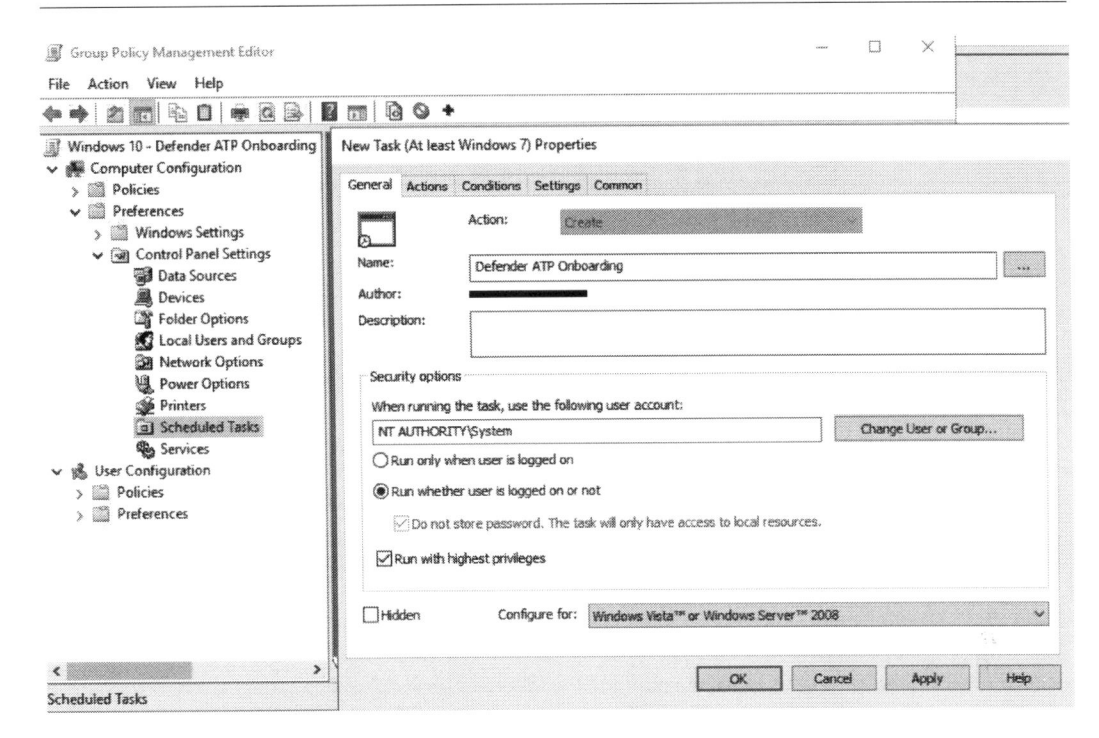

Figure 10.13 – Creating a scheduled task with Group Policy

9. In the **Actions** tab, click **New** and validate that **Start a program** is selected.

10. Go to the path where you extracted the `WindowsDefenderATPOnboardingScript.cmd` file. Hold *Shift*, right-click, and choose **copy as path**. Paste the path into the **Program/Script** field and click **OK**. Click **OK** again to commit the change.

The **New Action** settings should appear as follows:

Figure 10.14 – Configuring a new action for a scheduled task

Once the scheduled task has been configured, you will see it appear in the **Scheduled Tasks** section of the GPO:

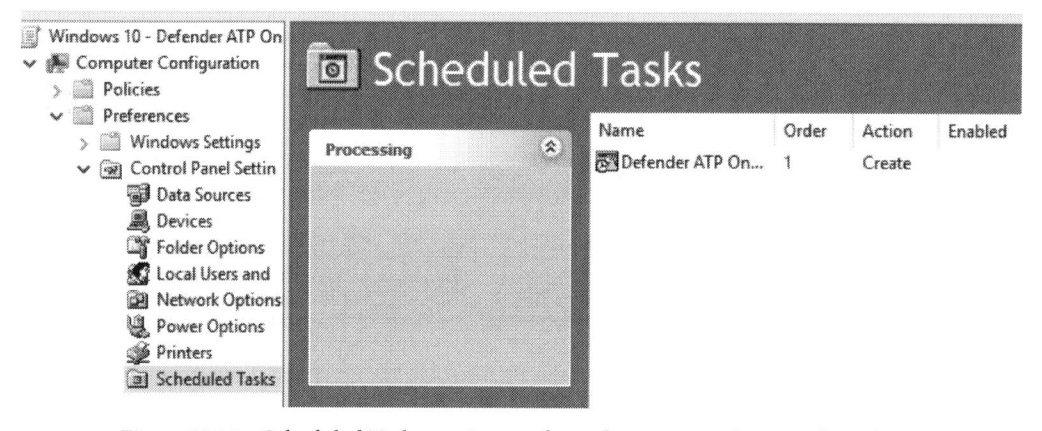

Figure 10.15 – Scheduled Tasks section configured to run in a Group Policy object

11. Close any open GMPC windows.

There is no method available for monitoring deployments using Group Policy for your machines. Typically, machines onboard within 24 hours, but it can take several days for telemetry data to flow. To view the machine's status, go to the Microsoft Defender Security Center portal at `https://securitycenter.windows.com`, click **Machines** from the navigation panel list and search for the hostname of a recently onboarded machine in the search bar, as follows:

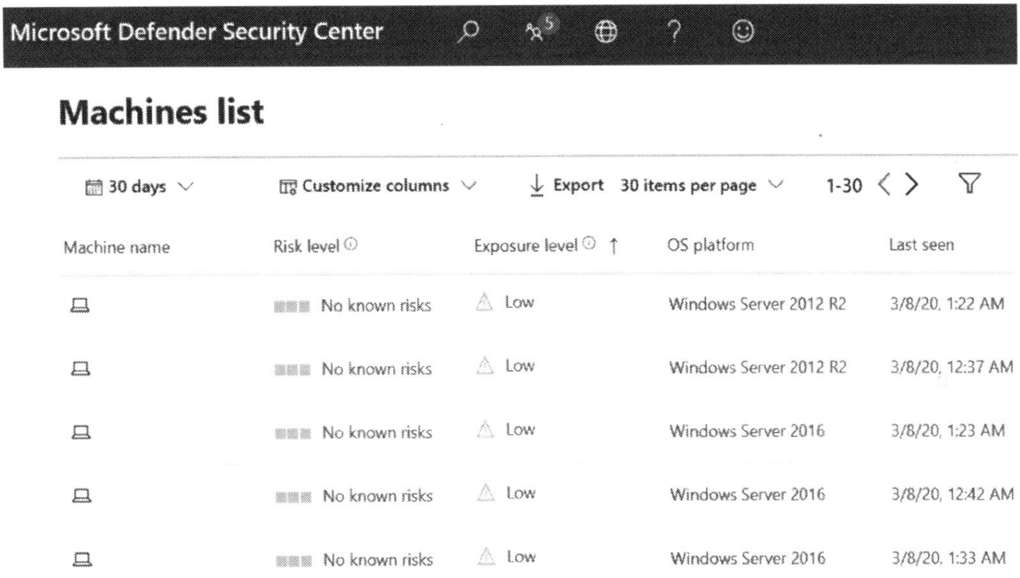

Figure 10.16 – Windows Server machines reporting to Defender Security Center

Next, let's look at how to use Microsoft Defender ATP policies in Configuration Manager to onboard Windows Server.

Onboarding with Configuration Manager

As mentioned previously in the *Onboarding with Group Policy* section, you will need to download and extract the Configuration Manager-specific package from the Microsoft Defender Security Center portal. To deploy the onboarding package, you will need to use the Microsoft Defender ATP policies node of **Assets and Compliance** by following these steps:

1. Log in to the **Microsoft Defender Security Center** portal at `https://securitycenter.windows.com`.
2. Choose **Settings** and select **Onboarding** in the **Machine management** section.

398 Keeping Your Windows Server Secure

3. Choose **Windows Server 1803 and 2019** for the OS and select **System Center Configuration Manager** from the **Deployment Method** section. Choose **Download Package**.

4. Extract the ZIP package to a deployment share used by SCCM to deploy apps and packages and open the System Center Configuration Manager console on the Site server. In these instructions, we are using version `1906`.

5. Go to **Assets and Compliance**, expand **Endpoint Protection**, choose **Microsoft Defender ATP Policies**, and click **Create Microsoft Defender ATP Policy**. The **Create Microsoft Defender ATP Policy Wizard** window will open, as shown in the following screenshot:

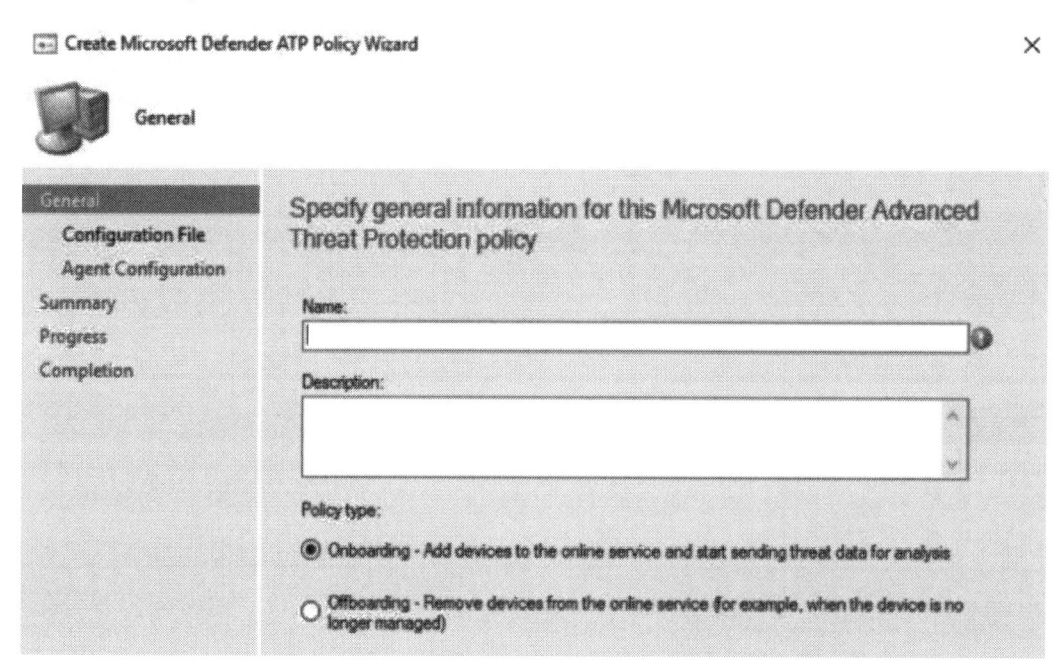

Figure 10.17 – Creating a Defender ATP policy in Configuration Manager

6. Enter a friendly **Name**, **Description**, and choose **Onboarding** as the policy type. Then, click **Next**.

7. Select **Browse** and select the extracted **WindowsDefenderATP.onboarding** file you extracted earlier. Notice that the **Organization ID** of your Microsoft Defender ATP subscription **auto-fills**. Click **Next**, as follows:

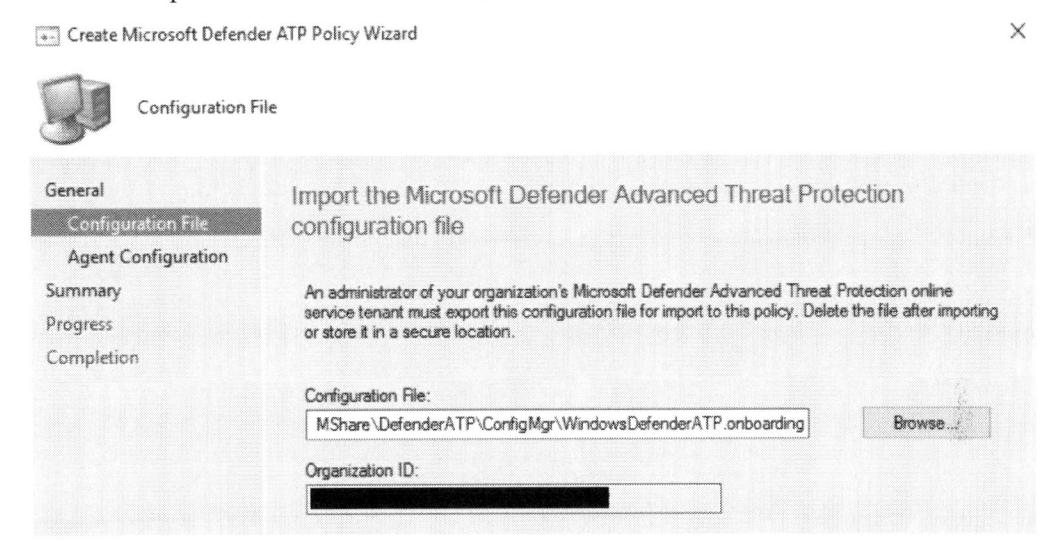

Figure 10.18 – Importing the Defender ATP configuration file

8. Leave the defaults configured on the **Agent Configuration** menu. Click **Next**.

9. Click **Next** again to finish the Microsoft Defender ATP Policy Wizard and click **Close**.

10. Right-click the policy and click **Deploy**. Choose a collection that will target your Windows 2019 servers.

We just covered how to onboard Windows servers to the Microsoft Defender ATP service using both Group Policy and Configuration Manager. Next, we will review the Windows server hardening configurations that are available and cover how to use Azure Disk Encryption to encrypt VMs.

Hardening Windows Server

Ensuring your Windows servers are properly hardened is critical to maintaining a good security posture and minimizing the attack surface. A best practice for Windows server is to only enable the roles and services required to perform necessary functions and to lock down the network to only allow the required ports and sources to communicate. Next, we will look at implementing a security baseline. We will cover how to implement the Microsoft Security and Compliance toolkit recommended baseline for member servers, discuss network access controls and the various logon types used to access servers, configure inactivity timeouts for interactive sessions, and configure account lockout policies. Finally, we will discuss implementing a fine-grained password policy in order to enforce strict requirements to highly privileged accounts and securing the logon process before learning about how to use Azure Disk Encryption to encrypt data on VMs that live in Azure.

Implementing a security baseline

With any good security program, it's important to have a foundation that consists of clearly defined policies, standards, procedures, and guidelines and ensure they are in place and enforced. Security baselines are more than just a set of configurations that apply to devices. They can encompass an entire program that includes collaboration with many teams, as well as support and backing from leadership stakeholders. In *Chapter 2, Building a Baseline*, we covered these concepts and discussed their importance, and provided an overview of the different frameworks seen today. We also discussed using baseline controls from **Center for Internet Security** (**CIS**) and Microsoft to build the specific configurations that apply to your Windows servers.

Next, we will look at implementing the Windows Server 2019 Member server baseline from the Security and Compliance Toolkit and apply it with Group Policy. In addition, we will cover enforcing additional recommendations, as specified in the CIS benchmarks. To download the CIS benchmark for Windows Server 2019, visit this link:

`https://www.cisecurity.org/cis-benchmarks/`

> **Tip**
> We strongly recommend downloading and reviewing the CIS Windows server benchmarks and comparing them to the Microsoft recommendations.

To download the Microsoft Security and Compliance Toolkit baselines, visit this link and choose the Windows 10 Version 1909 and Window server Version 1909 Security `Baseline.zip` files:

`https://www.microsoft.com/en-us/download/details.aspx?id=55319`

On a workstation that has access to modify Group Policy, extract the downloaded ZIP file. To import the Member server baseline, follow these steps:

1. Open **Group Policy Management Editor**. Create a GPO that is linked to an OU that contains Member servers. Give it a friendly name such as `Tier 0 W2019 Member Server`.

2. Click on the **Group Policy Objects** folder and find the GPO you created previously. Right-click and choose **Import Settings**.

3. Click **Next** twice and choose **Browse**. Navigate to the GPO folder of the extracted ZIP file and click **OK**. Then, click **Next**.

4. Select the **MSFT Windows Server 1909 – Member Server** policy and click **Next**. Click **Next** again. Click **Next** on **Migrating References** to copy them identically from the source. Then, click **Finish**.

5. Click **OK** to finish importing the policy settings.

The documentation folder from the extracted ZIP file contains an Excel spreadsheet of all the policy settings and descriptions of them. The GP reports folder contains HTML extracts of the GPO if you need to review them in a reader-friendly format.

In order to report compliance on the security baseline, you can use a management tool such as Configuration Manager and monitor the settings. We covered how to do this in *Chapter 8, Administration and Remote Management*, in the *Creating a configuration baseline from a GPO* section.

Microsoft used to support a tool called **Security Compliance Manager** (**SCM**). It was used to compare GPO-based security configurations and provide recommendations for baselines on Windows servers. Unfortunately, this tool has been retired and many organizations have started using other means to manage these configurations. One popular option is **Windows PowerShell Desired State Configuration** (**DSC**). DSC is useful for maintaining a configuration base for resources to help ensure that systems remain in the state outlined in the configuration. For more information about PowerShell DSC, visit this link:

`https://docs.microsoft.com/en-us/powershell/scripting/dsc/overview/overview?view=powershell-7`

If your servers are running in Azure, there is a VM extension that supports **Azure Desired State Configuration** (**DSC**). More information about Azure DSC can be found here:

https://docs.microsoft.com/en-us/azure/virtual-machines/extensions/dsc-overview

Next, let's look at enforcing and modifying some of the preconfigured Microsoft recommended baselines, as outlined by the CIS benchmarks.

Controlling User Rights Assignment

User Rights Assignment policies define the ways a user or service can log on and interact with a server. They apply locally to each server and include authorizing a user to log on, as well as the permissions that they can control access to. User Rights Assignment policies can be found under **Computer Configuration** > **Windows Settings** > **Security Settings** > **Local Policies** > **User Rights Assignment**. According to the CIS benchmark for Windows Server 2019, the policy configurations in the following table are recommended in addition to the default Microsoft Security Baseline:

Policy	Policy Setting
Adjust memory quotas for a process	Administrators, LOCAL SERVICE, NETWORK SERVICE
Allow log on through Remote Desktop Services	Administrators, Remote Desktop Users
Change the system time	Administrators, LOCAL SERVICE
Change the time zone	Administrators, LOCAL SERVICE
Deny log on as a batch job	Guests
Deny log on as a service	Guests
Deny log on locally	Guests
Deny log on through Remote Desktop Services	Guests, Local Account
Shut down the system	Administrators

Figure 10.19 – Recommended User Rights Assignment settings

Once the User Rights Assignment policies have been set, the built-in local security groups can be managed by using Restricted Groups. This will allow you to specify what domain-based security groups will be members of the built-in local security groups on each server. To modify a Restricted Groups Group Policy and add a domain group called `T0-Operators` to the Administrators group, follow these steps. You will need to be editing a Group Policy object to do so:

1. Go to **Computer Configuration** > **Windows Settings** > **Security Settings** > **Restricted Groups.** Then, right-click and choose **Add Group**.

2. Click on **Browse** and search for the `T0-Operators` group. Click **Check Names**. Once the group is found, click **OK**. Click **OK** again on the **Add Group** menu.

3. On the **Properties** menu, click **Add** next to the `"This group is a member of"` selection. Click **Browse**, type in `Administrators`, and choose **Check Names**. Click **OK**.

4. Click **OK** on the **Properties** menu to commit the changes, as shown in the following screenshot:

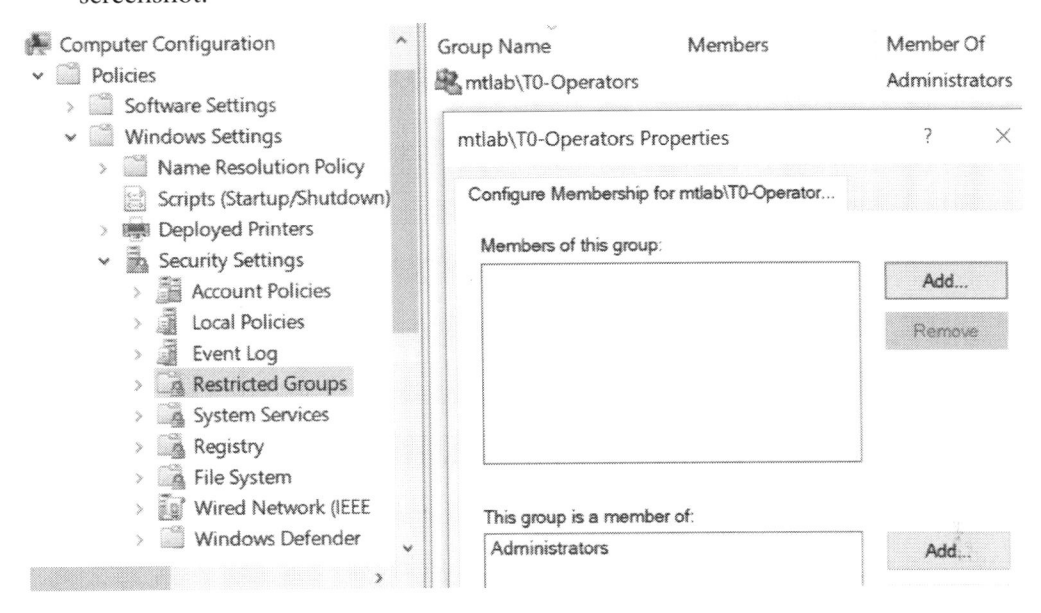

Figure 10.20 – Modifying a Restricted Groups Group Policy

After Group policy has had a chance to process, you will see that the group has been added to the Built-in Administrators group in Local Users and Groups on the server, as shown in the following screenshot:

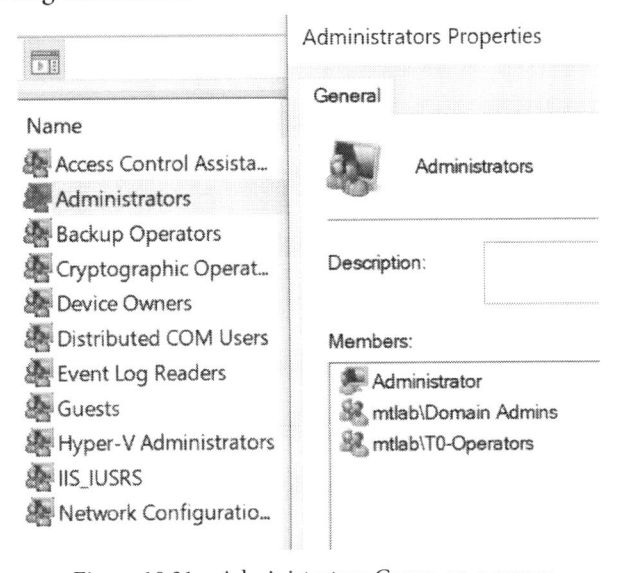

Figure 10.21 – Administrators Group on a server

> **Tip**
> If a user is added manually to a built-in group and is not a member of the domain group or added through the Restricted Groups policy, they will be removed on the next policy sync.

Next, we'll look at configuring Accounts security settings.

Configuring Accounts settings

It's important for a good security and access strategy to implement policies around the types of accounts that are available to log in to your servers. Identity and Access Management is a critical piece to the overall security framework, and we want to ensure that this is locked down in the local policy settings. Accounts policies can be found under **Computer Configuration > Windows Settings > Security Settings > Local Policies, Security Options.** We recommend setting the following policies compared to the Microsoft baselines:

Policy	Policy Setting
Accounts: Administrator account status	Disabled
Accounts: Block Microsoft Accounts	Users can't add or log on with Microsoft Accounts
Accounts: Guest account status	Disabled
Accounts: Rename administrator account	Choose another name and change description
Accounts: Rename guest account	Choose another name and change description

Figure 10.22 – Recommended Accounts policy settings for local policies

> **Tip**
> Be mindful when disabling the Administrator account. If the member server and domain controller lose the connection to authenticate securely, there may be no local account available to log in with.

Next, we'll look at configuring Interactive Logon security settings.

Configuring Interactive Logon

An interactive logon is when a user logs into a server using a Local or Domain account by supplying credentials or using a smart card or form of biometrics. In an interactive logon scenario, the user may have physical access to the server or remotely through terminal services and **Remote Desktop Services (RDS)**. The latter is known as remote interactive. Interactive Logon policies can be set under **Computer Configuration > Windows Settings > Security Settings > Local Policies > Security Options**. The settings shown in the following table are additional recommendations compared to the Microsoft baselines:

Policy	Policy Setting
Interactive logon: Do not display last username	Enabled
Interactive logon: Do not require CTRL+ALT+DEL	Disabled
Interactive logon: Message text for users attempting to log on	Include a legal notice or a warning about the fact that accessing systems are being monitored.
Interactive logon: Message title for users attempting to log on	Include a title for the legal notice
Interactive logon: Number of previous logons to cache (in case domain controller is not available)	4 or fewer. (Default is 10)
Interactive logon: Prompt user to change password before expiration	Between 5 and 14 days
Interactive logon: Require Domain Controller authentication to unlock workstation	Enabled

Figure 10.23 – Recommended settings for Interactive Logon scenarios

Next, we'll look at configuring a Remote Desktop Protocol timeout limit. This will help ensure that any idle account will be disconnected from your servers, thus increasing security as well as freeing up system resources.

Setting Remote Desktop Protocol session time limits

Setting the **Remote Desktop Protocol (RDP)** session time limits keeps idle users from tying up resources. This helps prevent password lockouts, especially if a **Privileged Access Management (PAM)** solution has been deployed with password rotation functionality. It can also free up available sessions for servers not configured with an RDS license that can only handle a few concurrent sessions. Remote desktop session time limits can be set under **Computer Configuration > Policies > Administrative Templates > Windows Component > Remote Desktop Services > Remote Desktop Session Host > Session Time Limits**. The recommendations shown in the following table are in addition to the Microsoft baseline:

Policy	Policy Setting
Set time limit for active but idle Remote Desktop Services sessions	Enabled: 15 minutes or less
Set time limit for disconnected sessions	Enabled: 1 minute

Figure 10.24 – Session time limits for Remote Desktop Protocol

Additionally, you can force users' sessions to log off instead of disconnecting. To do this, set the **End session when time limits are reached** policy to **Enabled**.

Next, we'll look at configuring account policies such as an account lockout policy and a password policy for the domain.

Configuring account policies

Typically, account policies are applied at the domain level in the default domain policy. There can only be one account policy defined in each domain. If any other policy is created in a down level OU and not linked to the root of the domain, it will only affect the local accounts on the member servers. When deploying Active Directory Domain Services, there are default values that are configured in the default domain policy. Let's look at the default values, as well as additional recommendations not set in the default domain policy.

The following screenshot shows the recommendations for a **Password Policy**:

Policy	Setting
Enforce password history	24 passwords remembered
Maximum password age	365 days
Minimum password age	1 day
Minimum password length	14 characters
Password must meet complexity requirements	Enabled
Store passwords using reversible encryption	Disabled

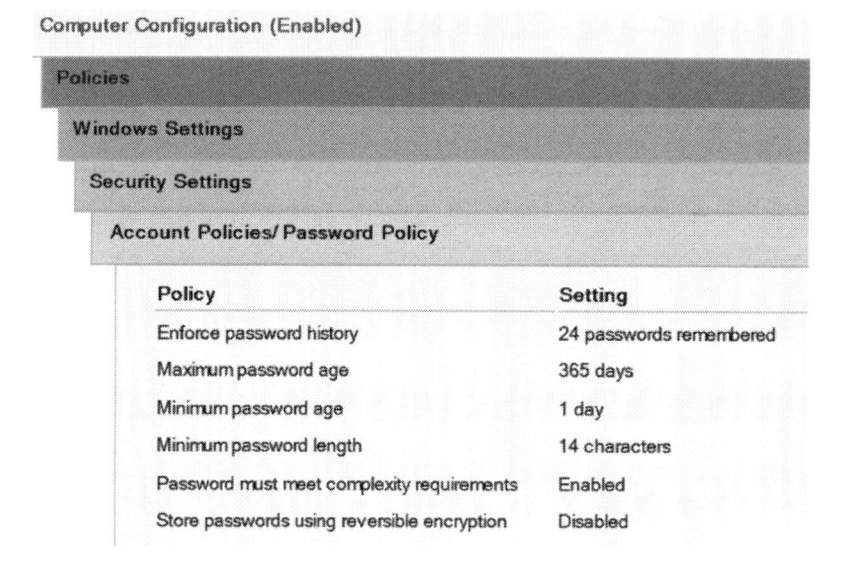

Figure 10.25 – Default domain policy – Password Policy

From the preceding screenshot, we can see the following:

- **Maximum password age**: 365 days
- **Minimum password length**: 14 characters

> Tip
> Based on recent research, data, and recommendations from NIST, Microsoft, and others, the latest password recommendations are to remove periodic password change requirements and to only change a password in case of potential threat or compromise.

Now, let's look at modifying the **Account Lockout Policy**. The recommended settings can be seen in the following screenshot:

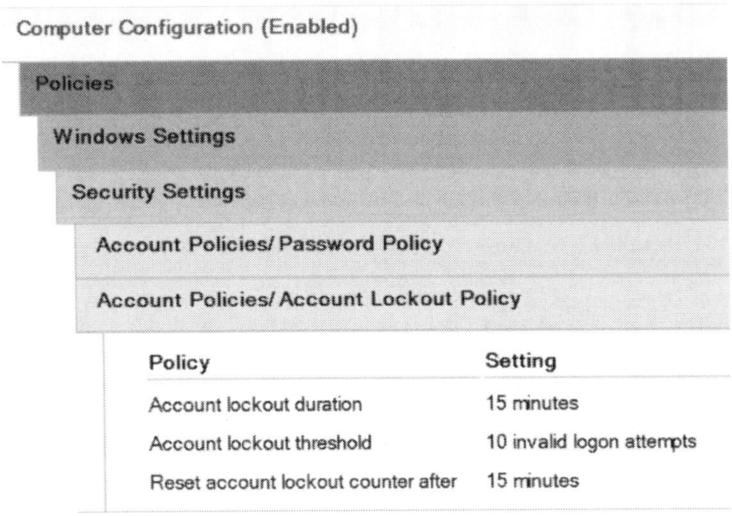

```
Computer Configuration (Enabled)
  Policies
    Windows Settings
      Security Settings
        Account Policies/ Password Policy
        Account Policies/ Account Lockout Policy
```

Policy	Setting
Account lockout duration	15 minutes
Account lockout threshold	10 invalid logon attempts
Reset account lockout counter after	15 minutes

Figure 10.26 – Recommended Account Lockout Policy

From the preceding screenshot, we can see the following:

- **Account lockout duration**: 15 minutes

Leaving this setting as 0 will require an administrator to manually unlock an account if it's locked out, leading to increased calls to the support desk. Setting a duration can also help mitigate a potential **denial of service (DoS)** attack.

- **Account lockout threshold**: 10 invalid logon attempts

Setting a lockout threshold helps to prevent successful brute-force attacks by triggering an account lockout. The account will remain locked out for the duration set.

- **Reset account lockout counter after**: 15 minutes

This setting determines how long before the threshold resets back to 0. Keep this setting aligned with the lockout duration. The default settings could be vulnerable to DoS attacks and can lock out users in your environment permanently until they're manually unlocked by an administrator.

If setting one password policy for your domain isn't enough to meet your compliance needs, domain administrators can use **fine-grained password policies** or **Password Settings Object** (**PSOs**) to more granularly apply a password policy. Let's look at implementing PSOs.

Implementing fine-grained password policies

In addition to the default domain policy, if there is a requirement to deploy additional password polices, then a fine-grained password policy can be configured. Examples of this would be to enable stronger password requirements for your privileged accounts compared to your standard user accounts, in addition to a separate one for your service accounts. FGPPs are set in PSOs and not Group Policy. Unlike the default domain policy, PSOs are applied directly to users or security groups. We covered how to implement PSOs in detail in *Chapter 7, Identity and Access Management*, in the *Securing your passwords* section.

To configure a PSO, open **Active Directory Administrative Center** and click on **Tree** view. Expand the domain, go to **System container**, and find **Password Settings Container**. Click **New**, **Password Settings** under **Tasks** to create a new PSO. The following screenshot shows a password policy targeted at the Domain Admin security group:

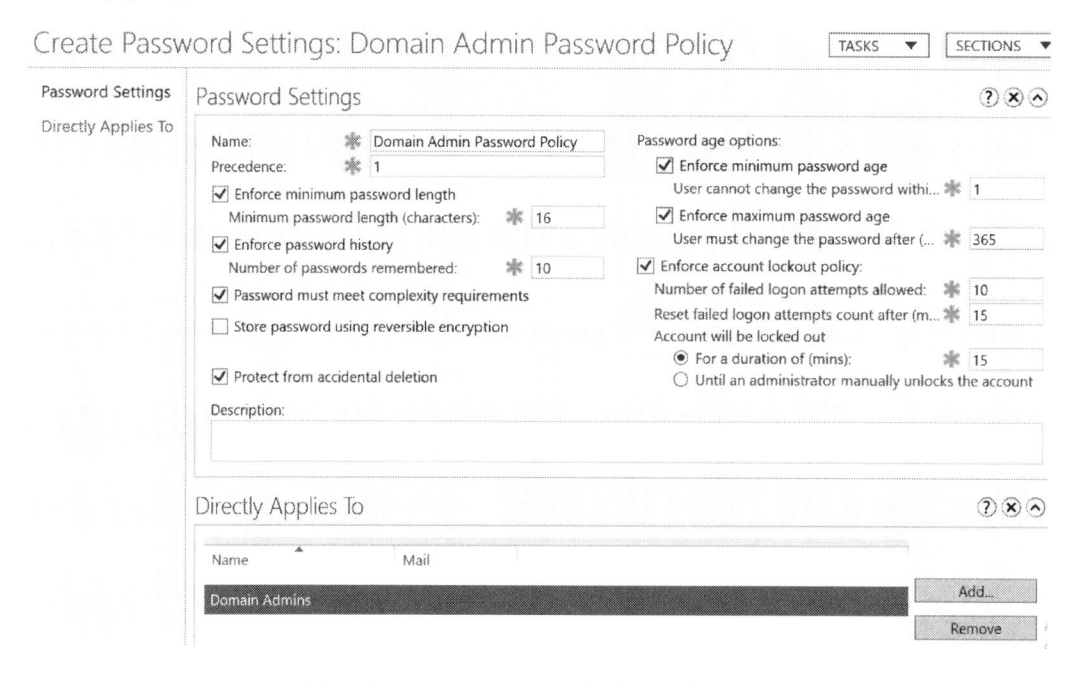

Figure 10.27 – Fine-grained password policy in Active Directory

We just covered how to implement security settings related to account policies, interactive logons, and password settings. Next, we'll look at how to secure the logon process and lock screen for Windows Server.

Securing the logon process

Securing the logon process can help to reduce risk by limiting the amount of information that is available when logging on. Securing these settings will eliminate the enumeration of users, hide account details, and limit interaction with networks on the login screen. The following table shows the additional recommendations not enforced in the Microsoft baseline:

Policy	Policy Setting
Block user from showing account details on sign-in	Enabled
Do not display network selection UI	Enabled
Do not enumerate connected users on domain-joined computers	Enabled
Turn off app notifications on the lock screen	Enabled
Turn off picture password sign-in	Enabled
Turn on convenience PIN sign-in	Disabled

Figure 10.28 – Recommended login processes

> **Important note**
> When using picture password sign-in or a convenience PIN, the domain password is cached in the system vault.

Many of these settings are disabled by default and not configured in Group Policy. It's best to enforce them to ensure that a user with administrative access does not modify the default settings. Next, we will discuss how to encrypt server disks using Azure Disk Encryption and how to store keys in Azure Key Vault for recovery key management.

Using Azure Disk Encryption

Historically, both Windows PCs and Windows servers have leveraged BitLocker Drive Encryption and on-premises management solutions such as **Microsoft BitLocker Administration and Monitoring** (**MBAM**) to handle the storage and administration of recovery keys. BitLocker settings are typically configured and managed with Group Policy and PowerShell. For Windows Server 2012 and later, BitLocker Drive Encryption can also be enabled through the Add Roles and Features Wizard of Server Manager. Recently, Microsoft has announced that MBAM will no longer be developed and has offered extended support up until 2024. Due to the end of life of MBAM, it is strongly recommended to move your BitLocker administration workloads to Azure.

For Windows server virtual machines in Azure, disk encryption can be accomplished by using Azure Disk Encryption. Azure Disk Encryption is for Windows VMs and provides BitLocker encryption for both OS and data disks. It uses Azure Key Vault to store secrets and keys and securely wraps encryption secrets using a **key encryption key** (**KEK**). For Windows Server 2012 version 1511 or later, the XTS-AES 256-bit encryption method is used. Let's look at how to create an Azure Key Vault. Then, we can use it to hold **BitLocker Encryption Keys** (**BEK**) for drive recovery.

Creating an Azure Key Vault

To create an Azure Key Vault, we will be using the Azure PowerShell Az module. Information about the Az module, including installation instructions, can be found at this link:

https://docs.microsoft.com/en-us/powershell/azure/new-azureps-module-az?view=azps-3.6.1

Open PowerShell as an administrator and install and import the Azure Az module by following these steps:

1. Type `Connect-AzAccount`, press *Enter*, and input your username and password. Then, accept the MFA challenge.

   We will be using an existing resource group called `RG-Identity-Prod` to create the Key Vault. If you do not have a resource group, you will need to create one.

2. Use the following cmdlet to create a Key Vault named *Prod-KeyVault-USE2* and set the `-EnabledForDiskEncryption` flag:

   ```
   New-AzKeyvault -name "Prod-KeyVault-USE2"
   -ResourceGroupName "RG-Identity-Prod" -Location "eastus2"
   -EnabledForDiskEncryption
   ```

If the command completed successfully, the Key Vault can be viewed inside the g from the Azure portal, as shown in the following screenshot:

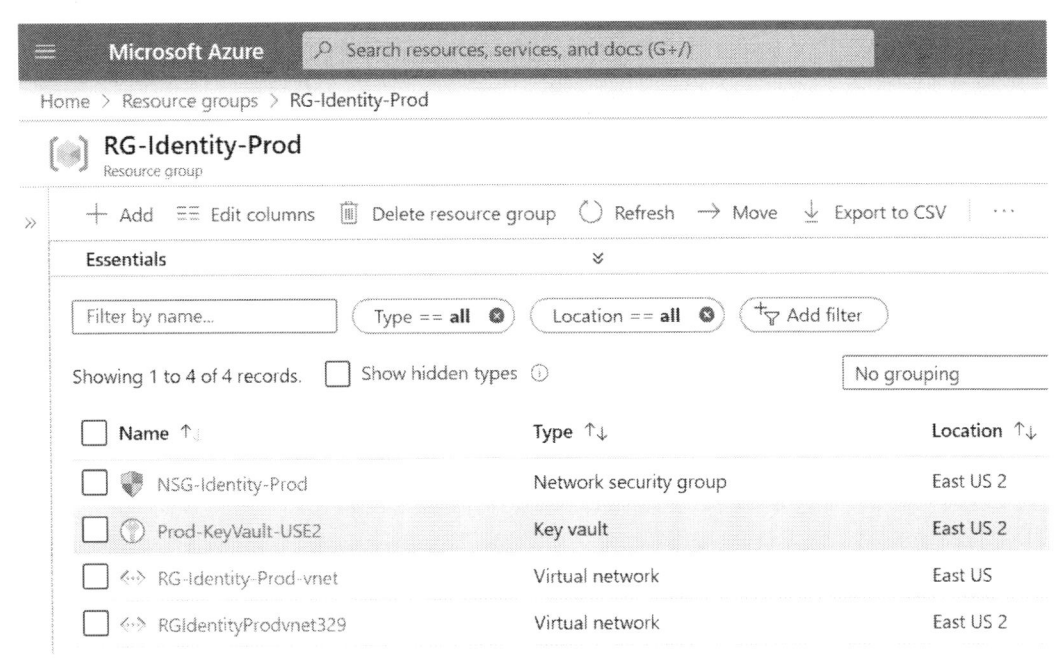

Figure 10.29 – Resources inside a resource group from the Azure portal

Next, we'll create a KEK. This key will be used to wrap encryption secrets before writing them to the vault. This adds an additional layer of protection for encryption keys.

Creating a key encryption key (KEK)

Using the same PowerShell Az module, create a new KEK by following these steps when using the `Add-AzKeyVaultKey` cmdlet.

Type in the following cmdlet to create a KEK named *IdentityKEK* for the Key Vault we created previously:

```
Add-AzKeyVaultKey -name "IdentityKEK" -VaultName "Prod-KeyVault-USE2" -Destination "Software"
```

> **Tip**
> Azure Key Vault supports RSA encryption. Currently, **Hardware Security Modules** (**HSMs**) are only supported in the premium pricing tier for Azure Key Vault.

Next, we'll enable the virtual machine disk encryption extension on a VM named `WSHUSE2DC01` in the `RG-Identity-Prod` resource group using the KEK and Key Vault we created previously.

Enabling Azure Disk Encryption on a virtual machine

To enable Azure Disk Encryption, we will be leveraging the same PowerShell Az module that we used previously. To follow along with these steps, open PowerShell ISE as an administrator and connect to Azure using the `Connect-AzAccount` cmdlet:

1. First, let's define the variables for the resource group, Key Vault, KEK, and VM name. Then, we will run `Set-AzVMDiskEncryptionExtension` to encrypt all disks, sign the secret with the KEK, and store it in the Key Vault:

    ```
    $Rg = "RG-Identity-Prod"
    $KeyVault = Get-AzKeyVault -VaultName "Prod-KeyVault-USE2" -ResourceGroupName $Rg
    $VaultKEK = Get-AzKeyVaultKey -VaultName "Prod-KeyVault-USE2" -Name "IdentityKEK"
    $WinVM = "WSHUSE2DC01"
    ```

2. Next, run the `Set-AzVMDiskEncryptionExtension` cmdlet with the following flags and variables:

    ```
    Set-AzVMDiskEncryptionExtension -ResourceGroupName $Rg
    -VMName $WinVM -DiskEncryptionKeyVaultUrl $KeyVault.
    VaultUri -DiskEncryptionKeyVaultId $KeyVault.
    ResourceId -KeyEncryptionKeyVaultId $KeyVault.ResourceId
    -KeyEncryptionKeyUrl $vaultKEK.Id -SkipVmBackup
    -VolumeType All
    ```

3. Click **Yes** if prompted by the **Enable AzureDiskEncryption on the VM prompt** warning stating that encryption may take 10-15 minutes and may prompt the virtual machine to reboot:

Figure 10.30 – Enable AzureDiskEncryption on the VM warning prompt

4. Once the process is complete, an output will be returned with an `IsSuccessStatusCode` that should read **True**. This can be seen in the following screenshot:

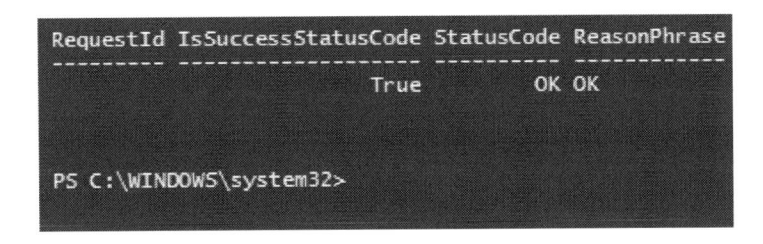

Figure 10.31 – PowerShell output showing Success status code

To validate the fact that encryption has been enabled, log in to the Azure portal and open the **VM overview** pane. In the **Extensions** blade, the **AzureDiskEncryption** extension will have a status of **Provisioning Succeeded**. If you click on the **Disks** option under **Settings**, encryption should be **Enabled**.

Finally, if you open the Key Vault, the **BitLocker Encryption Key** (**BEK**) will be stored under the **Secrets** blade, under **Settings**, as shown in the following screenshot:

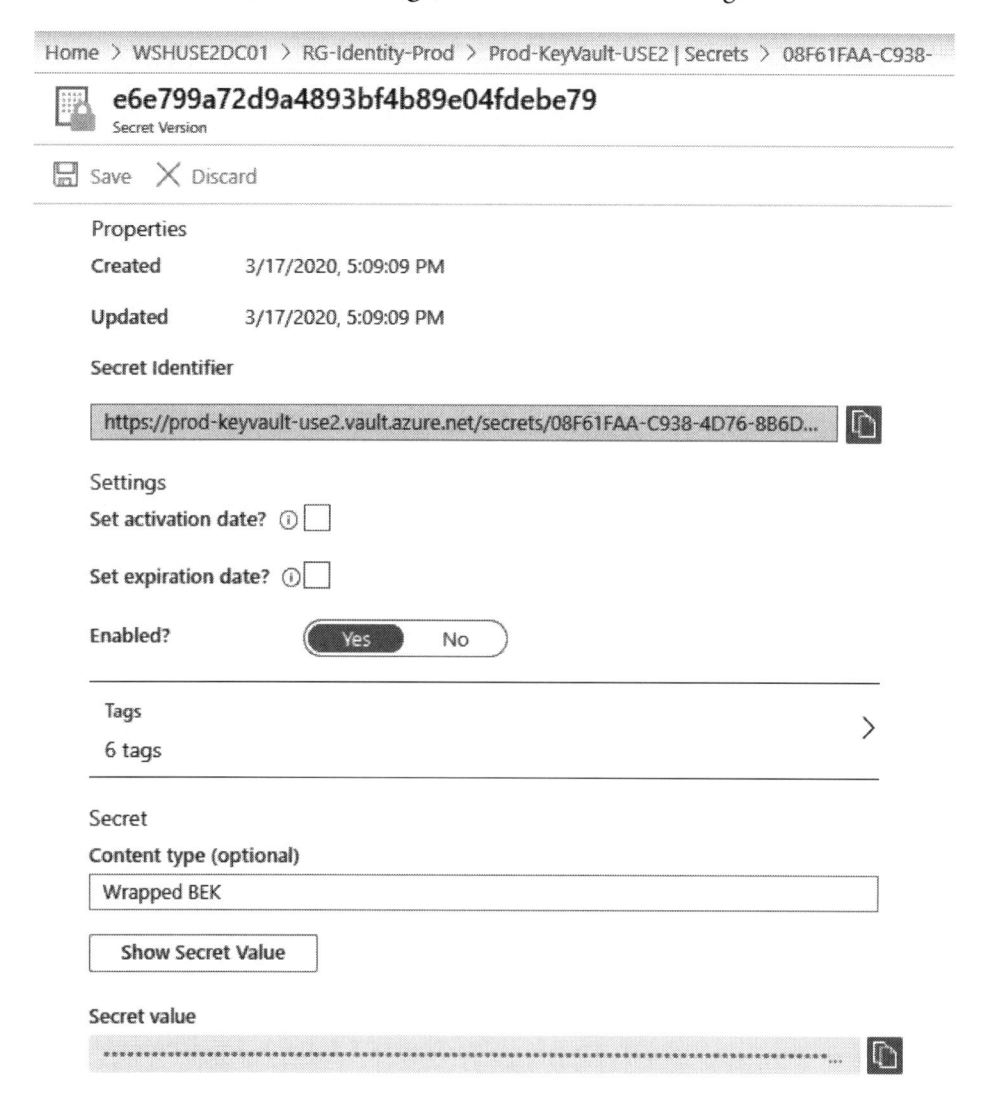

Figure 10.32 – Encryption secret stored in Azure Key Vault

For more information about Azure Disk Encryption, visit this link:

```
https://docs.microsoft.com/en-us/azure/virtual-machines/windows/disk-encryption-overview
```

Now that we have covered enabling Azure Disk Encryption and using Key Vault to store recovery keys, we'll look at creating a code integrity policy. Using **Windows Defender Application Control** (**WDAC**), you can deploy a code integrity policy whitelist that controls what applications can run on your servers. This greatly reduces the attack surface by denying unknown processes.

Deploying Windows Defender Application Control

WDAC adheres to a zero-trust model and only allows whitelisted, digitally signed software to run on Windows systems. WDAC uses a **Configurable Code Integrity** (**CCI**) policy to act as the whitelist configuration. When combining WDAC with virtualization-based security hypervisor isolation and UEFI Secure Boot, the technology is collectively known as Device Guard. Windows Defender Application Control can be managed with Group Policy, Configuration Manager, and Intune and can be configured with PowerShell. The Audit-only enforcement mode logs events to Event Viewer for analysis before enforcing the policy on endpoints.

> **Tip**
> It's extremely important to understand the effects of deploying a WDAC policy in your environment. We strongly encourage you to read the Microsoft Policy Design guide and build a strategy that fits your environment's needs before deploying a policy. Information about designing a policy can be found at this link: `https://docs.microsoft.com/en-us/windows/security/threat-protection/windows-defender-application-control/understand-windows-defender-application-control-policy-design-decisions`

When creating a WDAC policy, the whitelisting rules that can be defined are based on the following conditions:

- Attributes of a code-signing certificate
- Attributes of an app's binaries that come from metadata (original filename, version, or hash)
- The apps' reputation, as defined by Microsoft Intelligent Security Graph
- The process that launched the app or the path where the process or file is located

If your organization has customized line-of-business applications, Microsoft recommends signing the application and avoiding using the hash from the app's binaries. Otherwise, the CCI policy will need to be updated each time the app receives updates.

Application and catalog signing can be accomplished using the following methods:

- An internal digital certificate or **Public Key Infrastructure (PKI)**
- Employing a third-party signing authority such as Entrust, DigiCert, or GlobalSign
- The Windows Defender Device Guard signing portal through the Microsoft Store for Business

In a well-controlled environment with good application management, a reference system can be used to build a WDAC template policy. Once the policy has been built and tested on the referenced system, it can be deployed to other systems in audit mode and analyzed further. After this discovery has taken place, all the audited policies can be merged, set to enforced, and deployed to the environment.

Now, let's look at how to build a reference policy from a clean Windows server source. We will deploy the default Windows base policy in audit mode. Follow these steps:

1. In File Explorer, create a new directory on the root of the OS drive called **WDAC**.
2. Go to `C:\Windows\schemas\CodeIntegrity\ExamplePolicies`. Copy the `DefaultWindows_Audit.xml` policy and paste it into the `C:\WDAC` directory. Rename it something friendly such as `WSHMemberSVR_CIPolicy.xml`.
3. Open **PowerShell ISE** as an administrator. Next, we are going to create a variable for the policy file called `$PolicyFile`, as follows:

    `$PolicyFile = "C:\WDAC\WSHMemberSVR_CIPolicy.xml"`

4. For version control, we need to assign a unique ID, name, and version using the `Set-CIPolicyIDInfo` and `Set-CIPolicyVersion` cmdlets. Then, we will run the following command:

```
$PolicyFile = "C:\WDAC\WSHMemberSVR_CIPolicy.xml"
Set-CIPolicyIDInfo -FilePath $PolicyFile -PolicyName
"WSHMemberSVR_CIPolicy"
Set-CIPolicyVersion -FilePath $PolicyFIle -Version
"1.0.0"
```

Open the XML file. The version number you set previously will be under `<VersionEx>`, while the policy name will be under the `PolicyInfo` setting provider. Toward the top of the XML policy is where the enforcement rules are defined. Let's set a few additional rules to enable the Microsoft Intelligent Security Graph and managed installer options. Information about the WDAC policy rules options can be found at this link:

https://docs.microsoft.com/en-us/windows/security/threat-protection/windows-defender-application-control/select-types-of-rules-to-create

5. Run the following command using the `Set-RuleOption` cmdlet to enable the option 13 and 14 rules:

```
$PolicyFile = "C:\WDAC\WSHMemberSVR_CIPolicy.xml"
Set-RuleOption -FilePath $PolicyFile -Option 13
Set-RuleOption -FilePath $PolicyFile -Option 14
```

6. Next, convert the policy file into a binary file using the `ConvertFrom-CIPolicy` cmdlet:

```
ConvertFrom-CIPolicy $PolicyFile "C:\WDAC\WSHMemberSVR_CIPolicy.bin"
```

In order to apply the policy, the .bin file will need to be placed on a network share that servers can access. Since we are building a reference WDAC policy, we can leave it in the path from the `ConvertFrom-CIPolicy` cmdlet.

7. Open **Local Group Policy Editor**, go to **Administrative Templates > System > Device Guard**, and select the **Deploy Windows Defender Application Control** policy.

8. Select **Enabled** and enter the `C:\WDAC\WSHMemberSVR_CIPolicy.bin` path. Click **OK**. Then, restart the server.

To see whether the `.bin` file has been applied, open **Event Viewer** and go to **Applications and Services** > **Microsoft** > **Windows** > **Device Guard** > **Operational**. Event ID `7010` will display if the policy was applied correctly, as shown in the following screenshot:

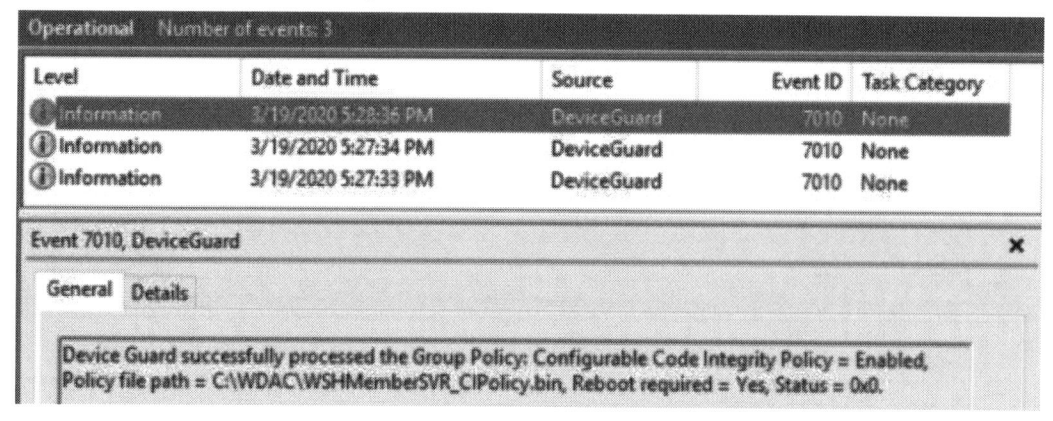

Figure 10.33 – Device Guard policy applied in Event Viewer

To view the audit events generated by the WDAC policies, go to **CodeIntegrity** > **Operational** under **Applications and Services**. This log file will show all the processes that tried to execute that were not specified in the WDAC policy. The **AppLocker** logs under **Applications and Services** will audit Windows Installer and script files:

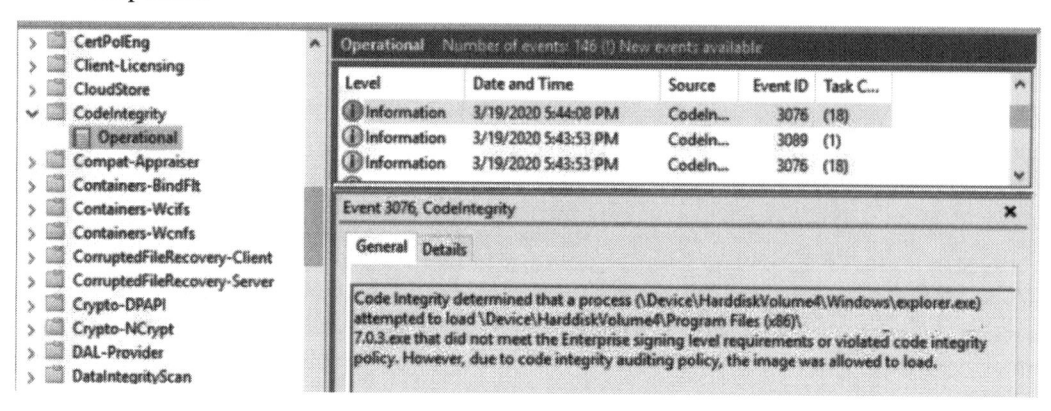

Figure 10.34 – CodeIntegrity Operational logs from Event Viewer

Once the policy has run in audit mode for some time, the audit logs can be reviewed, exported, and merged with the base policy. Now let's look at how to create a CI policy from the Event Viewer logs and merge it with the base policy using the `New-CIPolicy` cmdlet.

9. Run the following cmdlet to export the Event Viewer audit logs to a new CI policy:

   ```
   New-CIPolicy -Audit -Level Hash -FilePath "C:\WDAC\
   EventLog_Audit.xml" -UserPEs
   ```

10. Next, we will set a few variables to specify the policy paths and run the `Merge-CIPolicy` cmdlet to combine both the original and audit log policies:

    ```
    $BasePolicy = "C:\WDAC\WSHMemberSVR_CIPolicy.XML"
    $AuditCI = "C:\WDAC\EventLog_Audit.xml"
    $CombinedCI = "C:\WDAC\WSHMemberSVR_CIPolicy_v2.xml"
    Merge-CIPolicy -PolicyPaths $BasePolicy,$AuditCI
    -OutputFilePath $CombinedCI
    ```

11. Update the policy rule and version number in the XML file:

    ```
    $CombinedCI = "C:\WDAC\WSHMemberSVR_CIPolicy_v2.xml"
    Set-CIPolicyIDInfo -FilePath $CombinedCI -PolicyName
    "WSHMemberSVR_CIPolicy_v2"
    Set-CIPolicyVersion -FilePath $CombinedCI -Version
    "1.1.0"
    ```

12. Use the `ConvertFrom-CIPolicy` cmdlet to convert the merged policy into a binary file:

    ```
    $CombinedCI = "C:\WDAC\WSHMemberSVR_CIPolicy_v2.xml"
    $CombinedBIN = "C:\WDAC\WSHMemberSVR_CIPolicy_v2.bin"
    ConvertFrom-CIPolicy $CombinedCI "C:\WDAC\WSHMemberSVR_
    CIPolicy_v2.bin"
    ```

13. If you wish to audit the new policy before enforcing it, update the **local Group Policy setting** to the new .bin file. Restart the server.

    Depending on how strict you need the policy to be in order to lock down servers, a policy rule of the `FilePublisher` level and a fallback of the hash can be created for the entire OS drive. To do this, run the following cmdlet (assuming the OS disk is the drive letter *C*):

    ```
    $OSPolicyCI = "C:\WDAC\OSDrive_CI.xml"
    New-CIPolicy -ScanPath "C:\" -Level FilePublisher
    -Fallback Hash -UserPEs -FilePath $OSPolicyCI
    ```

> **Tip**
> Running the `New-CIPolicy` cmdlet on the OS drive to complete the scan will take some time.

14. Merge the policy rules and increment the version by following *steps 10-12*.

    Before enforcing the policy, it's recommended to set rule options 9, **Advanced Boot Options Menu**, and 10, **Boot Audit on Failure**. This way, if the WDAC policy blocks a driver during startup, Windows will continue to boot.

15. To enable the **Advanced Boot Options Menu** and **Boot Audit on Failure** rule options, run the following command:

    ```
    $CIPolicyPath = "C:\WDAC\WSHMemberSVR_CiPolicy_v3.xml"
    Set-RuleOption -FilePath $CIPolicyPath -Option 9
    Set-RuleOption -FilePath $CIPolicyPath -Option 10
    ```

16. Let's make a copy of the policy a backup and append `Enforced` to the end of the filename by running the following command. This will help us differentiate between the XML files:

    ```
    Copy $CIPolicyPath "C:\WDAC\WSHMemberSVR_CIEnforced.xml"
    ```

17. To set the policy to Enforced mode, run the following command:

    ```
    $EnforcedCI = "C:\WDAC\WSHMemberSVR_CIEnforced.xml"
    Set-RuleOption -FilePath $EnforcedCI -Option 3 -Delete
    ```

18. Convert the policy into binary format and increment the filename to keep the labeling consistent by following the steps in number *12*. Make sure you rename the variable so that it points to the copied XML file where we appended `Enforced` in the filename. For example, the `.bin` file could be `WSHMemberSVR_CIEnforced.bin`.

    Now, we are ready to test drive the WDAC policy in Enforced mode. It is recommended to slowly roll out the policy if possible or test it thoroughly before deploying it to live production systems. When comfortable, rule options 9 and 10 can be deleted to add additional protection.

19. To deploy the policy domain wide, copy the .bin file to a deployment share where your servers have access, such as an SCCM share.

20. Create a GPO and link it to an OU that contains the server systems you wish to scope. Follow steps *7-8* again and replace the local path with the UNC path to the file on the deployment share.

Once the policy is enabled, you can verify that it has been read by opening Event Viewer and going to **DeviceGuard** > **Operational** under Applications and Services. Event ID 7010 will show the .bin file and **Configurable Code Integrity policy** = **Enabled**, as shown in the following screenshot:

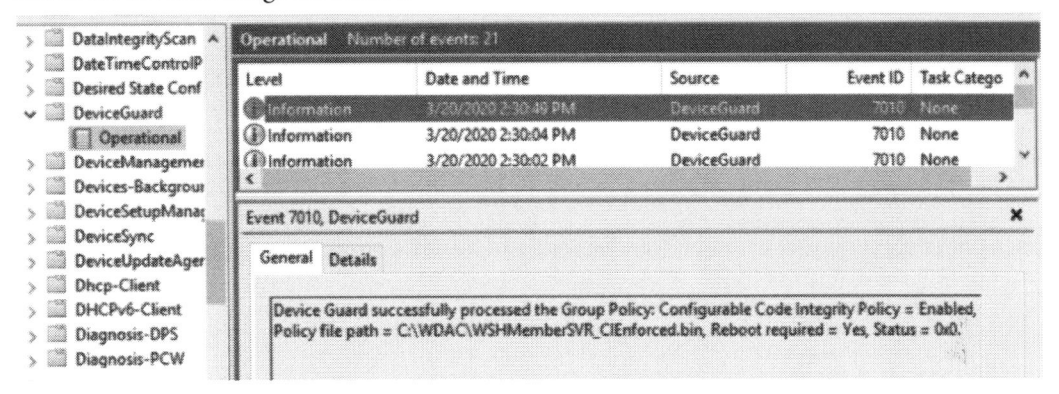

Figure 10.35 – Device Guard Operational logs in Event Viewer

The AppLocker logs under Applications and Services will show us whether applications have been blocked as a result of the WDAC policy:

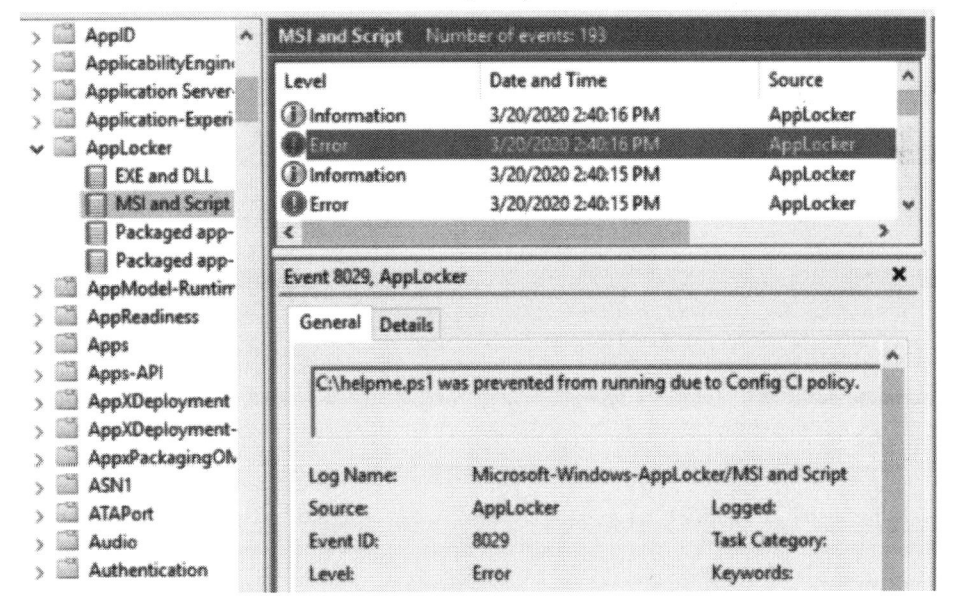

Figure 10.36 – AppLocker logs in Event Viewer

For more information regarding the full list of rules, system requirements, and tips for deployment planning, visit this link:

`https://docs.microsoft.com/en-us/windows/security/threat-protection/windows-defender-application-control/windows-defender-application-control`

Summary

In this chapter, we covered how to secure Windows Server. First, we reviewed different installation options for Windows Server and looked at security enhancements with Windows Server 2019. In the next section, we discussed different server roles and features and highlighted specific roles that could be used as part of your security strategy. Then, we moved on and look at the installation of WSUS on a Windows Server Core installation.

In the next section, we covered Windows updates and how to manage and deploy them using WSUS and Azure Update Management. Then, we reviewed threat protection with Microsoft Defender ATP – specifically, how to onboard your Windows server machines to the ATP service. Afterward, we discussed hardening Windows server and walked through implementing a baseline, reviewed CIS benchmark configurations for Microsoft defaults, and discussed enabling Azure Disk Encryption. Finally, we covered how to deploy a Windows Defender Application Control policy.

In the next chapter, we will cover security monitoring and reporting. Here, we will discuss the various features of the Windows Defender ATP solution, configure alerts with Azure Monitor, review Activity Logs, and cover how to onboard servers to Log Analytics workspaces and add protection with Azure Security Center.

Section 3: Protecting, Detecting, and Responding for Windows Environments

This section will describe the importance of continual assessment, monitoring, and security operations. You will learn about the different monitoring technologies that are used to detect and protect your environment, as well as how to gain insights from them.

This section includes the following chapters:

- *Chapter 11, Security Monitoring and Reporting*
- *Chapter 12, Security Operations*
- *Chapter 13, Testing and Auditing*
- *Chapter 14, Top 10 Recommendations and the Future*

11
Security Monitoring and Reporting

In this chapter, we will provide solutions for security monitoring and reporting within your environment. In previous chapters, we learned about what is needed to implement and enforce a secure environment for your users and Windows systems. Now that the baselines have been enforced and documented controls are in place, we need to ensure that monitoring and reporting programs are available to alert you of potential vulnerabilities or weaknesses within your environment. Next, we will review the different solutions used to capture telemetry and query data to provide insights and recommendations for keeping our environment secure.

First, we will review monitoring with **Microsoft Defender Advanced Threat Protection (MDATP)**. Within this section, we will cover areas such as investigating an alert, as well as provide an overview of the different dashboards used to report on threats and the overall exposure of your environment. Next, we will cover how to onboard Windows 10 devices and configure Intune compliance policies based on the MDATP machine risk score. Following this, we will look at deploying Log Analytics and installing solutions from the gallery to analyze telemetry data, as well as an overview of Azure Monitor.

Next, we will review **Azure Security Center** (**ASC**) and learn about the services it provides. We will look at the different tools available within ASC and how to onboard resources. Finally, we will discuss the benefits of using monitoring tools to create performance baselines. To recap, in this chapter, we will cover the following topics:

- Monitoring with MDATP
- Deploying Log Analytics
- Monitoring with Azure Monitor and activity logs
- Configuring ASC
- Creating performance baselines

Technical requirements

In order to follow along with the overviews in this chapter and complete the how-to instructions, the following requirements are recommended:

- An Azure subscription with contributor rights: https://azure.microsoft.com/en-us/free/
- MDATP licensing: https://docs.microsoft.com/en-us/windows/security/threat-protection/microsoft-defender-atp/minimum-requirements
- A Log Analytics workspace: https://docs.microsoft.com/en-us/azure/azure-monitor/learn/quick-create-workspace
- An Azure Automation account: https://docs.microsoft.com/en-us/azure/automation/automation-create-standalone-account
- ASC Standard: https://docs.microsoft.com/en-us/azure/security-center/security-center-pricing

Let's start by looking at how to monitor your Windows systems with MDATP

Monitoring with MDATP

Formerly known as Windows Defender, Microsoft Defender is the anti-malware solution that is shipped with Windows. It provides threat detection solutions for Windows desktops and servers, Linux, and macOS. Microsoft Defender, when combined with ATP, becomes the MDATP solution. MDATP not only allows organizations to detect threats, but also provides threat intelligence, analytics, and **Endpoint Detection and Response** (**EDR**), and includes automated investigations for the **Security Operations Center** (**SOC**) to follow up on alerts.

The capabilities of the MDATP solution can be broken down into the following areas:

- The **Threat & Vulnerability Management** feature discovers device vulnerability and misconfigurations using Microsoft Intelligent Security Graph. This provides real-time detection and response insights.
- **Attack surface reduction** is used to describe the technology for mitigation of potential attack surfaces using controls such as hardware-based isolation, application controls, exploit protection, network protection, and controlled folder access.
- **Next-generation protection** combines machine learning, analytics, and threat-resistance research from the cloud to offer near-real-time protection against new and emerging threats.
- **EDR** refers to the use of sensors to detect near-real-time events and to create alerts. EDR responses create incidents that can be tracked and actioned by the SOC.
- The **automated investigation and remediation** features are what MDATP uses to examine common alerts and known techniques to take immediate action on an alert.
- **Microsoft Threat Experts** is an additional service offering of proactive hunting with collaboration from Microsoft security experts directly from the MDATP portal.
- **Advanced Hunting** uses the **Kusto Query Language** (KQL) for query-based filtering and deep analysis of MDATP telemetry.

> **Tip**
> MDATP data can also be used when calculating a device's secure score. In order to use Secure Score, the telemetry needs to be enabled in **Advanced Features**.

Next, let's look at what investigating an alert looks like in the MDATP portal.

Investigating an alert

Selecting an alert will bring up the alert's details display. Here, you will see an overview of the malware, including the severity of the alert, the category, the techniques used, and the detection source. If you are leveraging the incident system of MDATP, you can open the incident page directly from the alert and assign it to a security analyst to investigate.

Microsoft leverages the **MITRE** enterprise framework to return results for the techniques used in the alert card. Clicking on the link listed under **Category** and **Technique**, as in the following screenshot, will bring up the relevant MITRE details page:

⚡ Alerts > ⚡ **Process hollowing detected**

⚡ Process hollowing detected
This alert is part of incident (528)

Automated investigation does not support OS

Actions ⌄

Severity:	Medium
Category:	Defense Evasion
Technique:	T1055: Process Injection, T1093: Process Hollowing, T1036: Masquerading
Detection source:	EDR
Detection technology:	Behavioral

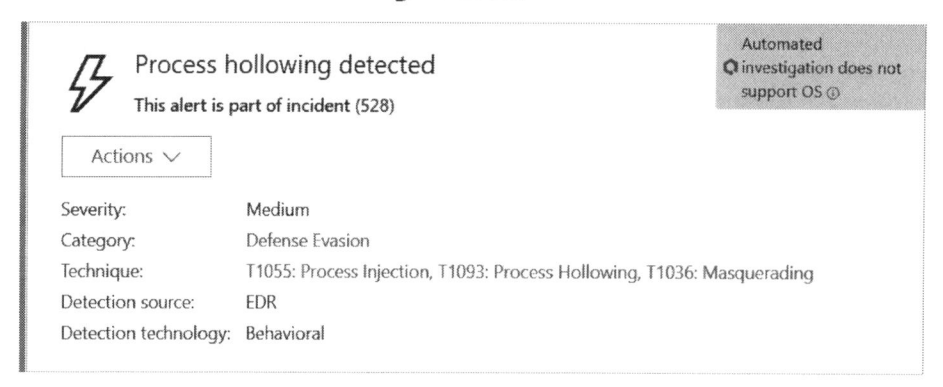

Figure 11.1 – Alert details in the MDATP portal

Clicking on the **Actions** dropdown allows you to perform tasks such as suppressing or classifying an alert, adding comments, and viewing the alert history. Let's look at an alert using **Alert process tree**.

In the following example, an EDR response was detected for a technique called **process hollowing**. Process hollowing occurs when a known process is loaded and placed in a suspended state. The process memory is containerized and injected with a malicious program so that it can run undetected. It avoids detection by tricking Windows into thinking that the original **trusted** process is what's running.

In the following alert tree, a file named `Payment Invoice.exe` attempted to load the `RegAsm.exe` assembly registration tool. The circular lightning bolt icon in the tree indicates the **alert evidence** and displays what process should be examined:

Alert process tree

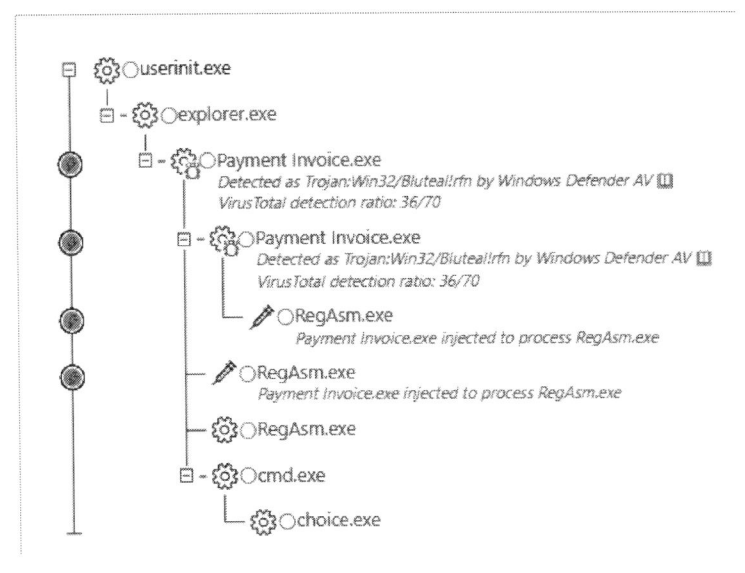

```
□ ⚙○userinit.exe
   │
   □ - ⚙○explorer.exe
      │
      □ - ⚙○Payment Invoice.exe
         │    Detected as Trojan:Win32/Bluteal!rfn by Windows Defender AV
         │    VirusTotal detection ratio: 36/70
         │
         □ - ⚙○Payment Invoice.exe
            │    Detected as Trojan:Win32/Bluteal!rfn by Windows Defender AV
            │    VirusTotal detection ratio: 36/70
            │
            └ ✎○RegAsm.exe
                 Payment Invoice.exe injected to process RegAsm.exe
         │
         ├ ✎○RegAsm.exe
         │    Payment Invoice.exe injected to process RegAsm.exe
         │
         ├ ⚙○RegAsm.exe
         │
         □ - ⚙○cmd.exe
            │
            └ ⚙○choice.exe
```

Figure 11.2 – An alert process tree in MDATP

Clicking on the **Payment Invoice.exe** process in the tree will open the **Investigate Files** details page. Here, you can gain insights into the process, which includes a malware detection confidence score and file prevalence in your environment and worldwide. MDATP also includes several actions to assist with immediate remediation if needed, as shown:

⊘ Stop and Quarantine File   + Add Indicator   ↓ Download file   ? Consult a threat expert   ▭ Action center

Figure 11.3 – Immediate actions available to perform against a file

430 Security Monitoring and Reporting

Using the incident graph on the alert's details page helps to visually understand the attack chain and where the compromise may have originated. You can click on each link in the graph to bring up the corresponding investigation pages. In this example, as shown in the following screenshot, a malware originated on one PC and spread to another using the Halloween.doc filename:

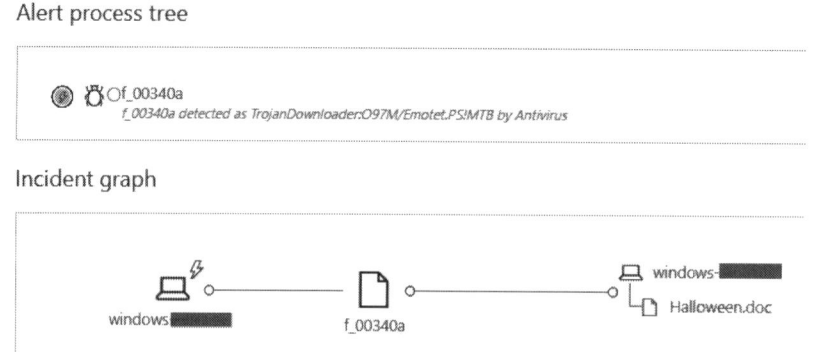

Figure 11.4 – An incident graph under the MDATP alert details

Next, let's look at an overview of some of the current dashboards currently available on MDATP.

The Threat analytics dashboard

The **Threat analytics** dashboard provides an overview of current threats and how devices in your organization are impacted. Each threat also provides an executive summary report that explains how each threat works:

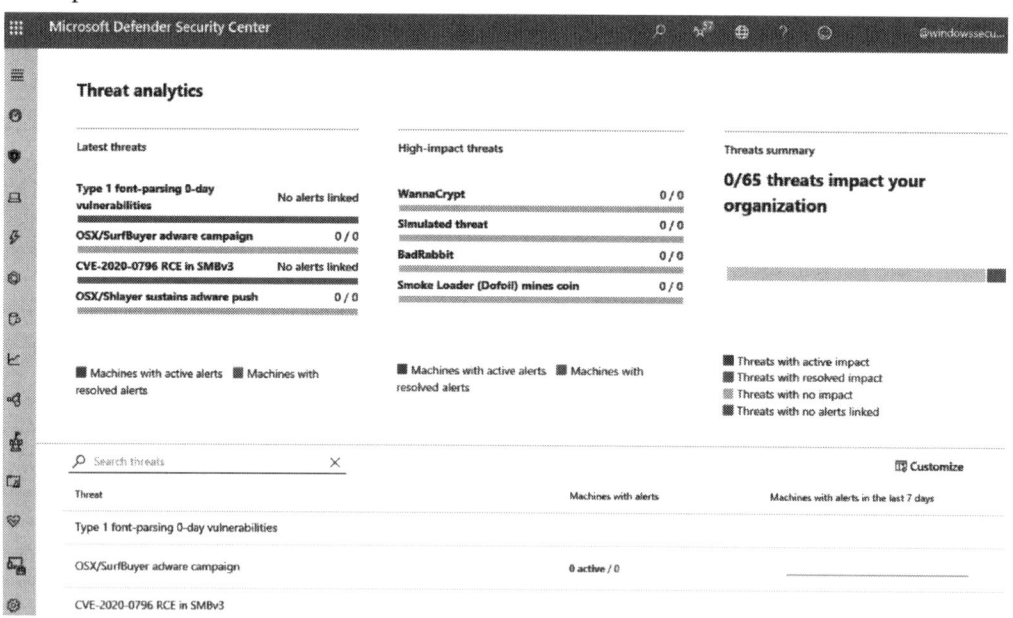

Figure 11.5 – The Threat analytics dashboard in MDATP

More information on the **Threat analytics** dashboard can be found at https://docs.microsoft.com/en-us/windows/security/threat-protection/microsoft-defender-atp/threat-analytics.

The Threat & Vulnerability Management dashboard

The **Threat & Vulnerability Management** dashboard displays an analysis of the EDR data and offers exposure and configuration scores based on recommended Microsoft security best practices. Selecting a security recommendation provides a description of the vulnerabilities. Choosing a category under **Organization configuration score,** such as **Application** or **Operating System**, provides tailored security recommendations for each category:

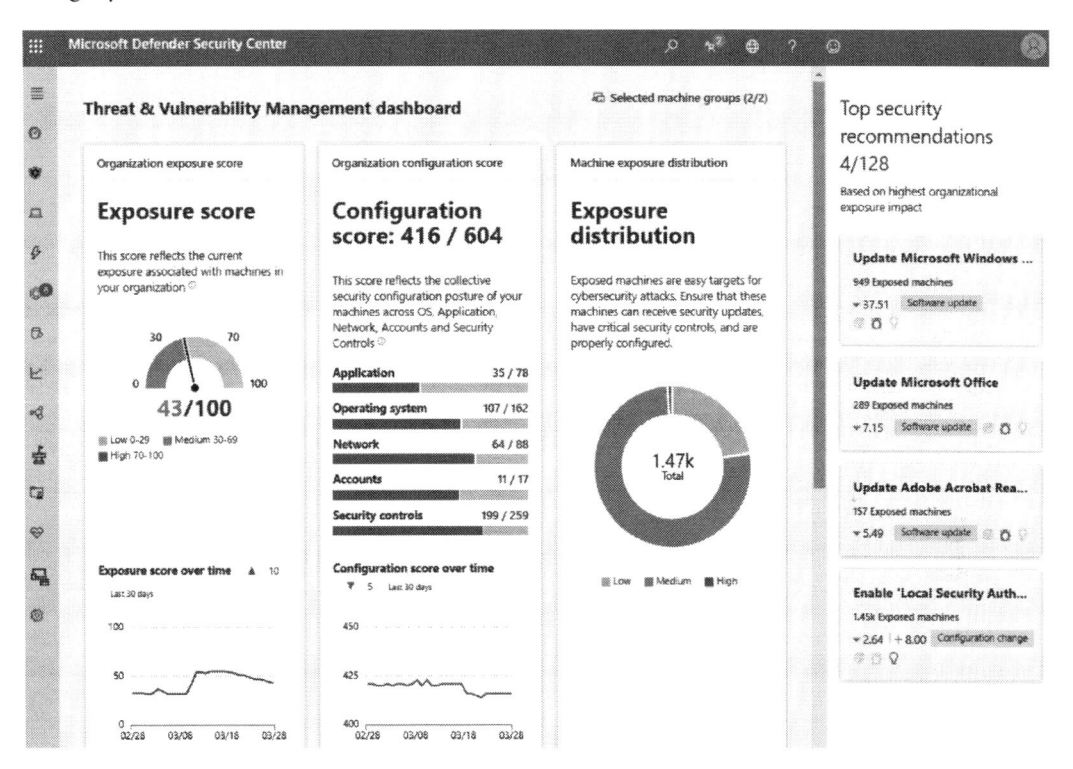

Figure 11.6 – The Threat & Vulnerability Management dashboard in MDATP

To learn more about the Threat & Vulnerability Management dashboard, visit https://docs.microsoft.com/en-us/windows/security/threat-protection/microsoft-defender-atp/tvm-dashboard-insights.

Machine health and compliance

The **Machine health and compliance** report allows you to visually see the health state of your devices from a sensor and antivirus definition status perspective:

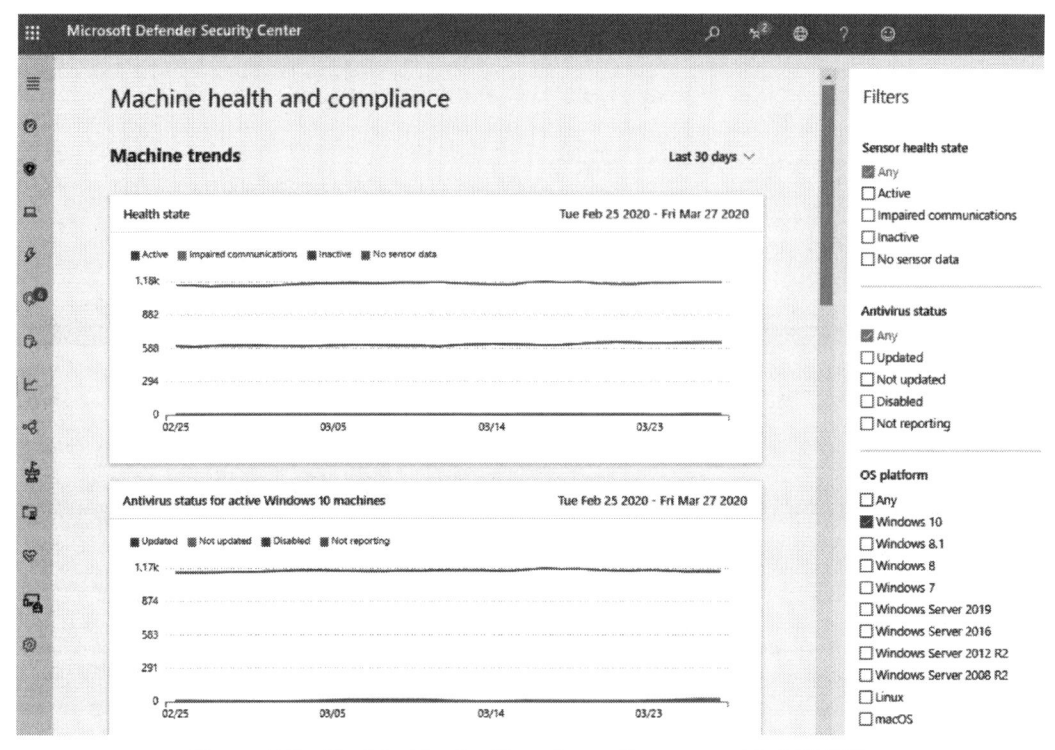

Figure 11.7 – The Machine health and compliance report in MDATP

For more information about the **Machine health and compliance** report in MDATP, visit `https://docs.microsoft.com/en-us/windows/security/threat-protection/microsoft-defender-atp/machine-reports`.

Software inventory report

MDATP also has a software inventory report, which includes the name of the product and the version, and calculates a weakness score and lists detected vulnerabilities for those versions. The software inventory report also leverages the EDR data as its discovery source for software.

More information about the software inventory report can be found at `https://docs.microsoft.com/en-us/windows/security/threat-protection/microsoft-defender-atp/tvm-software-inventory`.

Next, let's look at how to onboard a Windows 10 workstation to MDATP.

Onboarding workstations to the MDATP service

The deployment options for onboarding Windows 10 workstations support the following methods:

- Group Policy
- System Center Configuration Manager
- Intune (and other MDM providers)
- Local script

Depending on the preferred method, an onboarding configuration package needs to be downloaded from the MDATP portal. Let's look at deploying an onboarding package with Microsoft Intune by following these steps:

1. Log in to the MDATP portal by going to `https://securitycenter.windows.com`.

2. Go to **Settings** and choose **Onboarding** under the **Machine Management** section in the left navigation pane.

3. Select **Windows 10** for the operating system and choose **Mobile Device Management / Microsoft Intune** from the **Deployment Method** dropdown.

4. Choose **Download Package**, and then save the ZIP file and extract it.

5. Log in to the **Microsoft Endpoint Manager Admin Center** (**EMAC**) by going to `https://devicemanagement.microsoft.com`.

6. Select **Devices**, choose **Configuration Profiles**, and select **Create Profile** to build a new **Device Configuration** profile.

7. Enter a friendly name, such as `Microsoft Defender ATP Onboarding`, and give it a description. Select **Windows 10 and Later** for **Platform** and choose **Microsoft Defender ATP (Windows 10 Desktop)** for **Profile type**.

8. Choose **Onboard** from the MDATP client configuration package type.

9. Click on the folder icon to browse to the `WindowsDefenderATP.onboarding` file, which was part of the ZIP file extracted earlier from the MDATP portal. Click on **OK**.

The following screenshot shows the MDATP profile type for Windows 10 and later platforms:

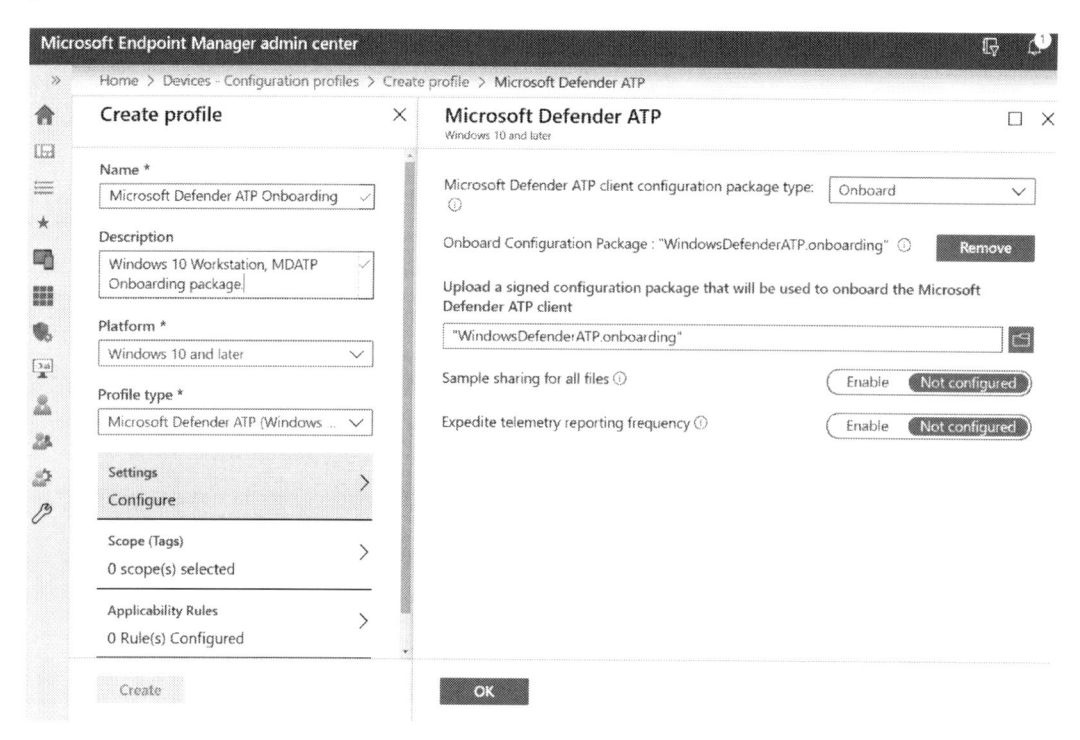

Figure 11.8 – MDATP onboarding device configuration profile in Intune

10. Click on **Create** to save your changes and create the profile. Click on the **Assignments** blade and choose a group to target for the deployment.

Machines will typically start to display in the portal within 24 to 48 hours.

To view machines from the MDATP portal, click on **Machines** in the navigation panel and search for a recently onboarded PC name in the search bar, then view the results, as demonstrated in the following screenshot:

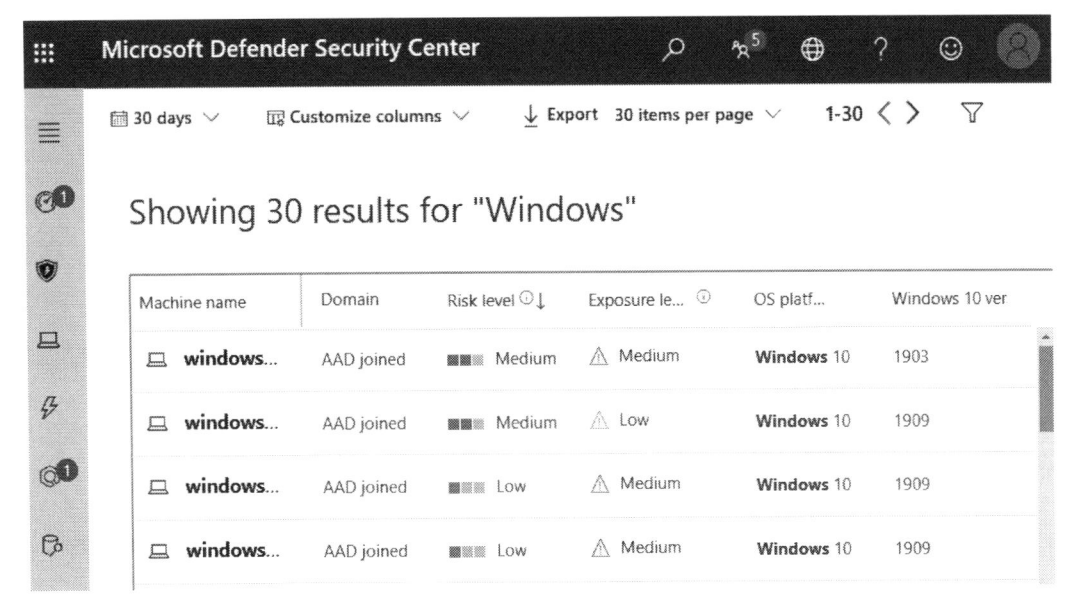

Figure 11.9 – Machine search result in the MDATP portal

Now that we have looked at onboarding machines, let's look at enabling the MDATP connector for Intune. This will allow you to use **Risk level** (as seen in the previous screenshot) to create a compliance policy that can later be used for device-based conditional access or reporting purposes.

Enabling the Microsoft Intune connection

Enabling an Intune connection to MDATP allows data to flow between both services and for you to use the device's **Risk level** information for evaluation compliance. To enable the connection, follow these steps:

1. Log in to the **Microsoft Defender Security Center** portal at `https://securitycenter.windows.com`.

2. Go to **Settings** and choose **Advanced features**. Switch the slider to **On** next to **Microsoft Intune Connection** and choose **Save Preferences**.

3. Log in to the MEMAC at `https://devicemanagement.microsoft.com`.

4. Choose **Endpoint Security** and select **Microsoft Defender ATP** under the **Setup** menu.

5. Turn **Connect Windows devices version 10.0.15063 and above to Microsoft Defender ATP** to the **On** setting. Click on **Save**.

The connection status to the MDATP service, as well as the last synchronized date, will be displayed in the MDATP setup, as in the following screenshot, after a browser refresh:

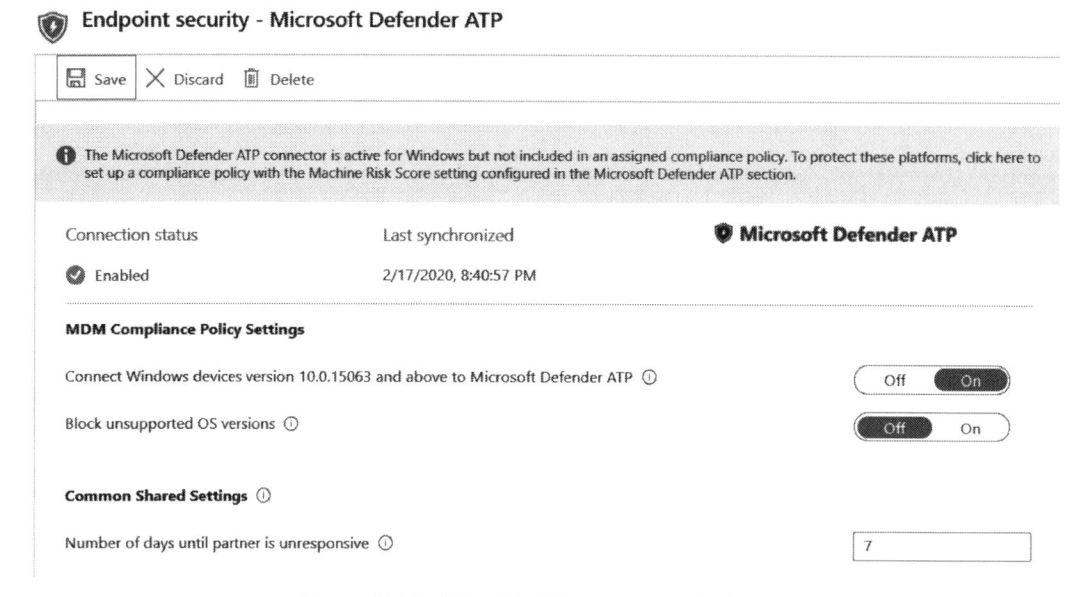

Figure 11.10 – The MDATP setup status in Intune

Now that we have enabled the connection from Intune to the MDATP service, let's create a compliance policy using the machine's risk score.

Creating a machine risk compliance policy

Creating a compliance policy will let you take advantage of the compliant device condition in Azure **Active Directory** (**AD**) Conditional Access. You can define policies that block access to cloud apps if a device doesn't meet the organization's risk level or you can require the use of **Multi-Factor Authorization** (**MFA**). To create a compliance policy based on the MDATP machine risk score, follow these steps:

1. From the MEMAC, go to **Devices** and choose **Compliance Policy**, and then click on **+ Create Policy**.

2. Enter a friendly name, such as `Windows 10 - MDATP Risk Score`, and give it a description. Choose **Windows 10 and Later** for **Platform**.

3. Under **Settings**, choose **Microsoft Defender ATP**. Click on the dropdown and choose **Medium** for **Require the device to be at or under the machine risk score**. Click on **OK**. Click **OK** again and then click **Create**.

The following screenshot shows the compliance policy settings for MDATP. The options are **Not Configured**, **Clear**, **Low**, **Medium**, and **High**:

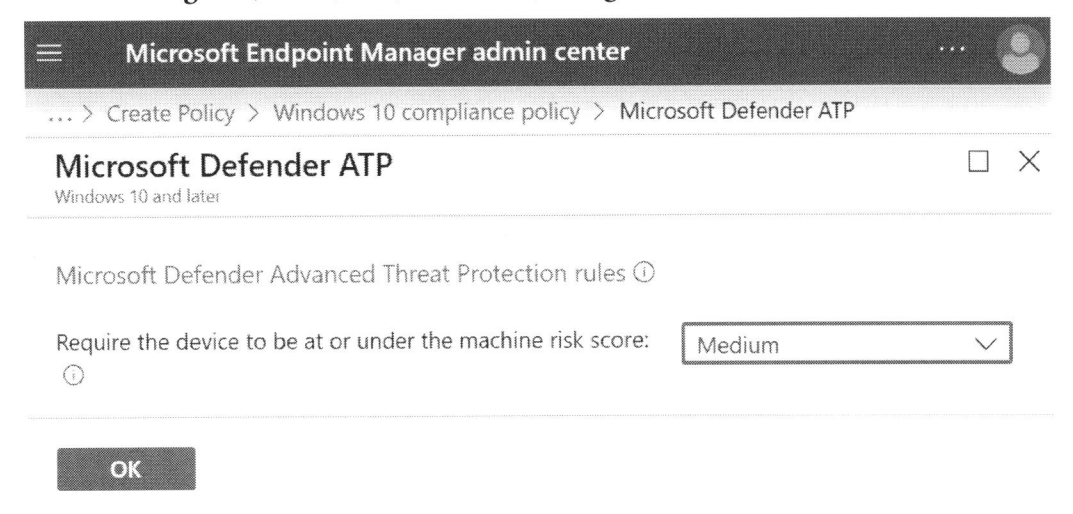

Figure 11.11 – The MDATP machine risk compliance policy settings

4. Choose **Assignments** and select a security group to target for the deployment.

> **Tip**
> The machine risk score is the maximum allowed score evaluated by MDATP. Anything that exceeds this score will be marked as non-compliant.

Now that the compliance policy has been enabled for evaluation, using the **Require device to be marked compliant** condition includes the machine risk score evaluation from MDATP. The following screenshot shows the **Grant** control of an Azure AD Conditional Access policy requiring both MFA and devices to be marked as compliant:

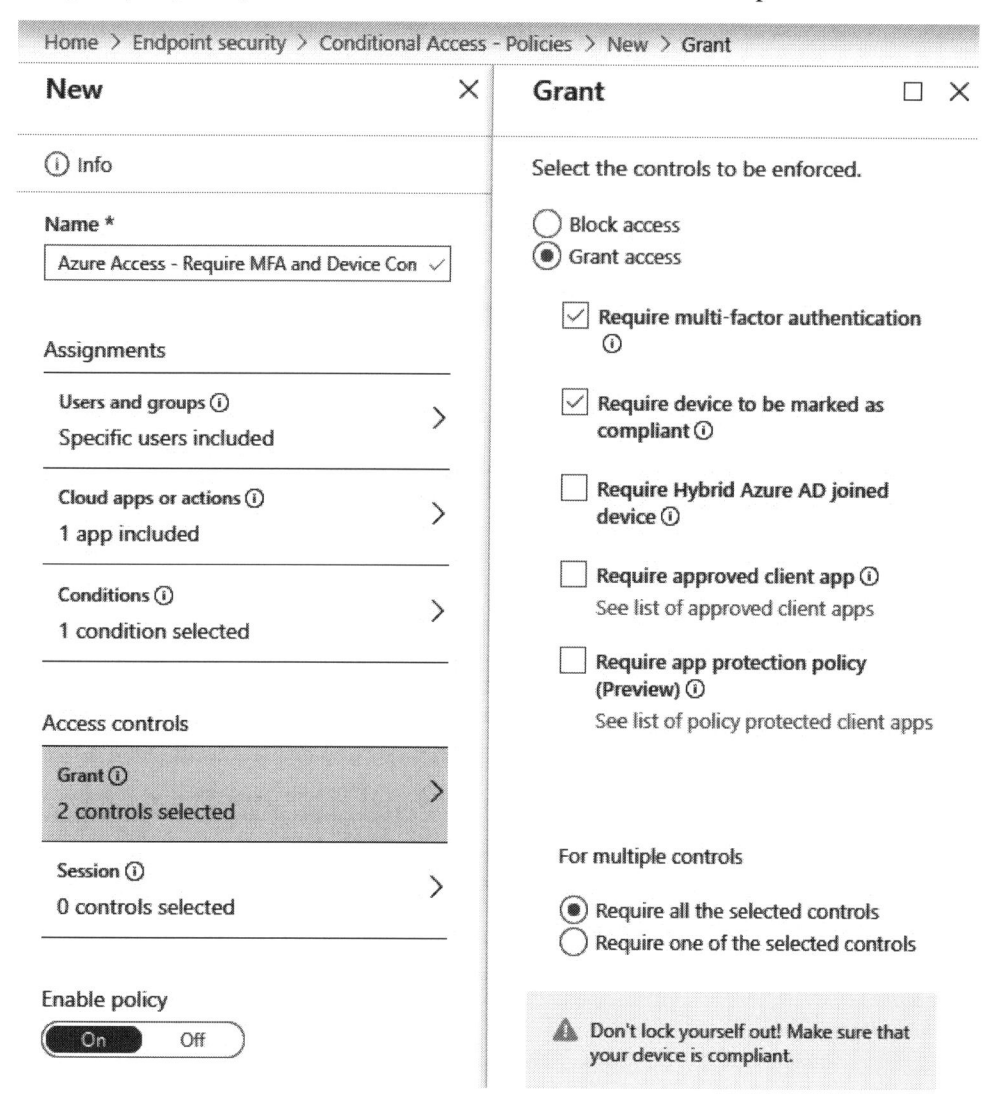

Figure 11.12 – The Azure AD Conditional Access policy access controls

> **Tip**
> To validate whether controls are in place, you can use the **What If** tool. When running **What If**, you can check what policies will apply. The **What If** tool can be found next to **+ New Policy** in the **Conditional Access - Policies** blade.

Enabling advanced features

MDATP allows many connections to other security products to further analyze the data collected. It's worth mentioning the **Advanced Features** settings and reviewing them to get more out of the MDATP service. By default, most of these settings are disabled. To view the available **Advanced Features** settings, go to **Settings | Advanced Features** in the MDATP portal.

We have just learned about how to use MDATP to analyze threats and investigate malware alerts. Let's now look at another solution in Azure that's used to collect and analyze telemetry data, known as Log Analytics.

Deploying Log Analytics

Log Analytics is a telemetry solution used to collect resource data for both your on-premises servers and for resources running in Azure. Data is stored in a workspace where it can be directly queried using KQL or visualized in the workspace summary by installing gallery solutions from the marketplace. Data from Log Analytics workspaces can be connected and used for analysis in other Azure services, such as ASC, Azure Monitor, and Azure Sentinel. Using this data allows IT professionals to analyze and create visualizations for effective monitoring and alerting using many different types of datasets. To use Log Analytics to collect telemetry data, you will need to deploy a Log Analytics workspace in Azure. We covered how to create a new Log Analytics workspace as part of setting up an Automation account in *Chapter 10*, *Keeping Your Windows Server Secure*, in the *Deploying Azure Update Management* section. You can use the Log Analytics workspace created in that chapter, or, if you don't have one created, you can create a new Log Analytics workspace by completing the following steps:

1. Log in to `https://portal.azure.com` and search for `Log Analytics workspaces`.
2. Click **Add** and enter the details for **Log Analytics Workspace name**, **Subscription**, **Resource Group**, **Location**, and **Pricing tier**.
3. Click **OK**.

The following screenshot shows a dashboard created for monitoring remote desktop sessions in a **Virtual Desktop Infrastructure (VDI)** environment. The underlying data is built off Log Analytics queries and by adding gallery solutions:

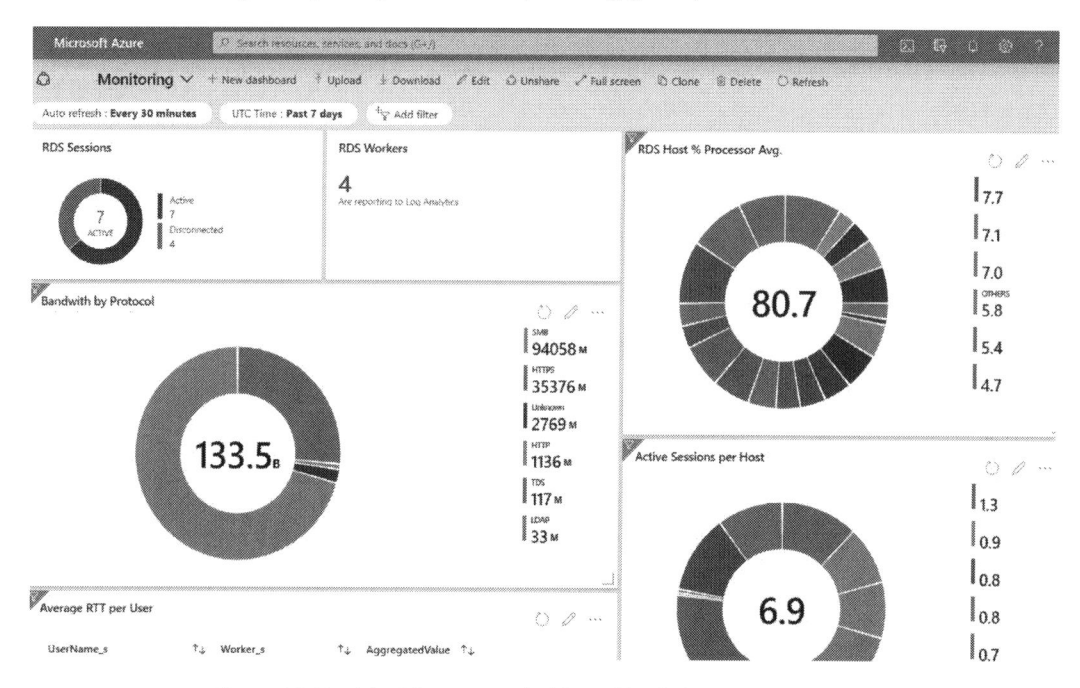

Figure 11.13 – The Monitoring dashboard built from Log Analytics

Telemetry data is gathered from your resources by installing the **Microsoft Monitoring Agent** (**MMA**). For virtual machines, the agent can be installed automatically if you are enabling automatic onboarding of servers to ASC. It can also be installed manually or with a virtual machine extension using **Azure Resource Manager** (**ARM**) templates or **PowerShell Desired State Configuration** (**DSC**). For on-premises resources, use a software management solution, such as Configuration Manager, to deploy the agent and configure the workspace ID and key.

> **Tip**
> The MMA can be configured for multiple workspaces using a multi-homed configuration.

For more information about connecting Windows servers to Log Analytics, visit `https://docs.microsoft.com/en-us/azure/azure-monitor/platform/agent-windows`.

Next, we will look at how to install gallery solutions onto a Log Analytics workspace and view them in the workspace summary.

Installing gallery solutions

Once the monitoring agent has been installed and data sources configured with the workspace ID and key, solutions can be installed to help analyze the data. To install a solution, follow these steps:

1. Log in to the Azure portal at `https://portal.azure.com`.
2. Open your Log Analytics workspace.
3. Choose **Workspace Summary** under **General**.
4. Click on **+ Add** in the toolbar to open up the marketplace.

There are many solutions available in the marketplace. Let's look at a few for monitoring your Windows computers.

Update Compliance for Windows 10

The **Update Compliance** solution in the marketplace is specifically for Windows 10 devices. It provides update deployment reports and configuration details for clients using **Windows Update for Business** (**WUfB**). If you are using Log Analytics to capture Windows 10 telemetry data, the **Update Compliance** solution will allow you to track and report the following information:

- Feature and quality updates
- The Windows Defender Antivirus status
- WUfB configurations
- The delivery optimization status

The following screenshot shows sample data analyzed by the **Update Compliance** solution:

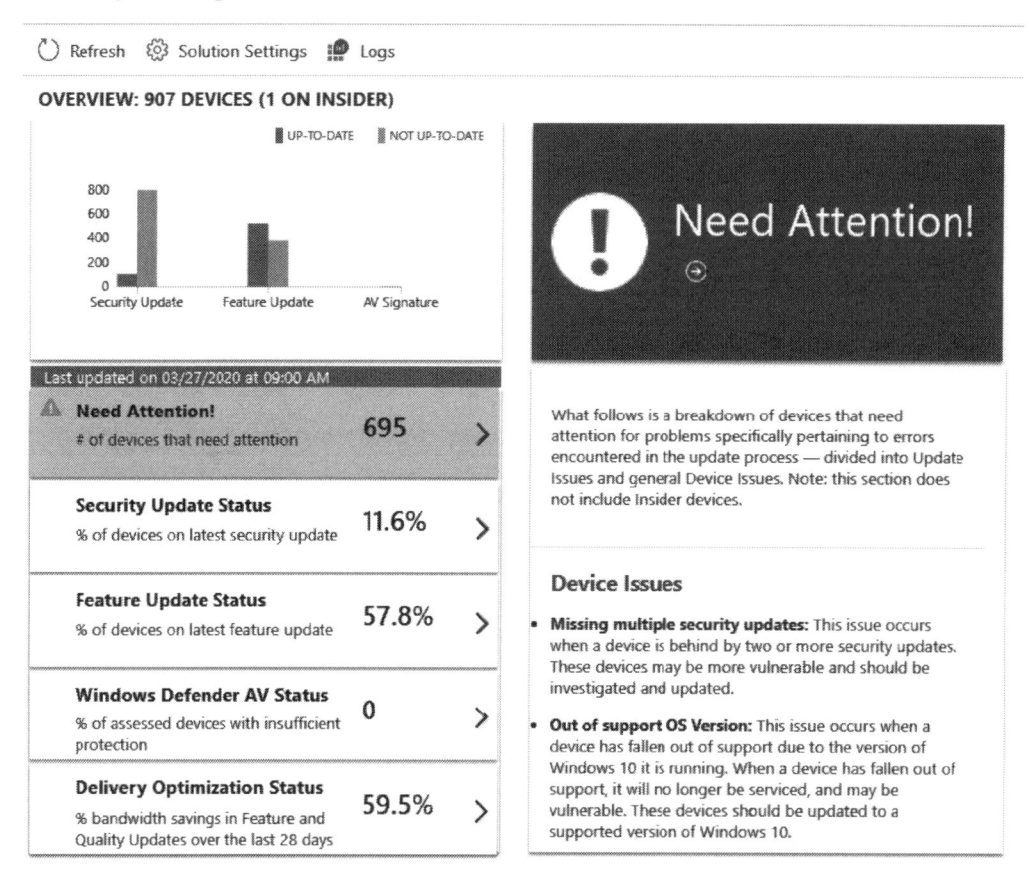

Figure 11.14 – The Update Compliance solution in Log Analytics

Clicking on each blade will provide more details about the status of your devices, including the status of update deployments and WUfB configurations.

> **Tip**
> To use the Windows Defender Antivirus status, cloud-delivered protection must be enabled on your devices. Information on how to enable this can be found at `https://docs.microsoft.com/en-us/windows/security/threat-protection/windows-defender-antivirus/enable-cloud-protection-windows-defender-antivirus`.

Once the **Update Compliance** solution is installed, a commercial ID will be generated in the solution settings. Let's look at how to use the key and deploy an Intune device configuration profile and configure the telemetry to report to **Update Compliance**.

Onboarding Windows workstations

From the Log Analytics workspace where the **Update Compliance** solution was installed, click on **Solutions** under **General** and choose the **WaaSUpdateInsights** solution name. From the **WaaSUpdateInsights** overview, choose **Update Compliance Settings** under **Settings**. Copy the **Commercial Id** key. Next, create two device configuration profiles. One profile will set the shared usage data value for telemetry and the other is a custom OMA-URI to configure the telemetry-specific settings. Now, follow these steps:

1. For the first profile, create a device restrictions profile with the following settings:

Name	Setting
Name	Device Restrictions - Telemetry
Description	Set the level of diagnostic Data
Platform	Windows 10 and later
Profile Type	Device Restrictions
Category	Reporting and Telemetry

    Figure 11.15 – Recommended settings for the device configuration profile

2. Configure the settings as in the following screenshot, setting **Share usage data** to **Enhanced**:

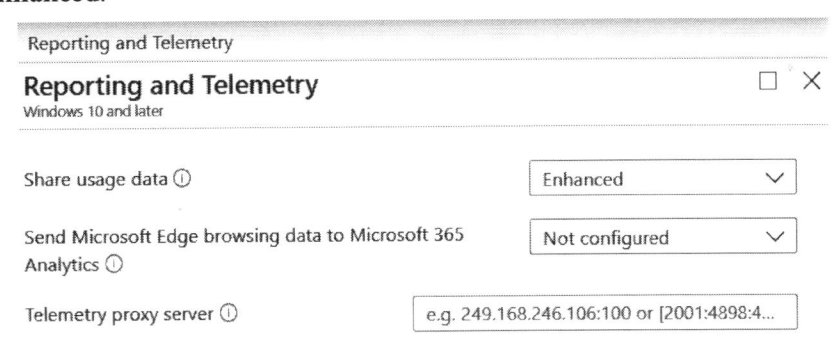

    Figure 11.16 – The Reporting and Telemetry setting in Intune

3. Save and assign the profile to users or device groups.

4. Next, create a new device configuration profile with the Custom profile type with the following settings:

Name	Setting
Name	Device Configuration – Update Compliance
Description	Telemetry configuration for Log Analytics
Platform	Windows 10 and later
Profile Type	Custom
Custom OMA-URI Settings	See values below

Figure 11.17 – The device configuration profile recommended settings in Intune

5. Add the OMA-URI settings with the following configurations. Replace the commercial ID with the key taken from the **Update Compliance** solution and set it as a string value. The rest are integer value types:

Name	OMA-URI	Value
CommercialID	./Vendor/MSFT/DMClient/Provider/MS DM Server/CommercialID	0cc3cdc7
AllowDeviceNameInDiagnosticData	./Vendor/MSFT/Policy/Config/System/AllowDeviceNameInDiagnosticData	1
ConfigureTelemetryOptInSettingsUX	./Vendor/MSFT/Policy/Config/System/ConfigureTelemetryOptInSettingsUx	1
LimitEnhancedDiagnosticDataWindowsAnalytics	./Vendor/MSFT/Policy/Config/System/LimitEnhancedDiagnosticDataWindowsAnalytics	1

Figure 11.18 – The OMA-URI settings for the telemetry policies

For more information, including descriptions and possible values for the **Policy Configuration Service Provider (CSP)** settings in the previous diagram, visit `https://docs.microsoft.com/en-us/windows/client-management/mdm/policy-csp-system`.

Allow 24 to 48 hours for the telemetry data to start to flow into the **Update Compliance** solution.

> **Tip**
> Windows Analytics has recently migrated to Desktop Analytics. While the **Update Compliance** solution is still useful for WUfB reporting, use Desktop Analytics if you are looking for all the Windows Analytics features. More information about the Desktop Analytics solution can be found at `https://docs.microsoft.com/en-us/configmgr/desktop-analytics/overview`.

For Windows servers, use the **Update Management** solution in Log Analytics with Azure Automation. There is a walkthrough showing how to enable and deploy the **Update Management** solution in *Chapter 10, Keeping Your Windows Server Secure*. Once this is configured, let's look at enabling an additional solution called **ChangeTracking**.

Deploying ChangeTracking

The **ChangeTracking** solution is useful for identifying and tracking configuration changes to software, files, and Windows services. Having the ability to identify when changes occur is useful from both a performance and security perspective. In order to use **ChangeTracking**, you will need to have both a Log Analytics workspace and an Azure Automation account. The **ChangeTracking** solution can be enabled through your Automation account, on the virtual machine directly, or added as a solution using the marketplace. The following screenshot shows an overview of **ChangeTracking** and displays the changes that occurred on the servers over 28 days:

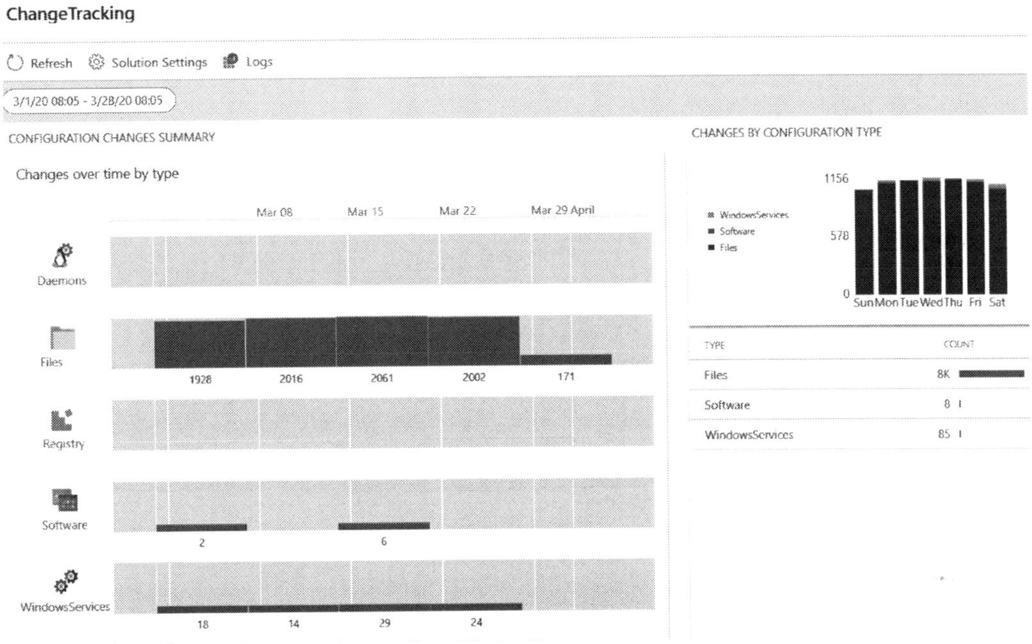

Figure 11.19 – The ChangeTracking solution in Log Analytics

> **Tip**
> To automatically onboard all available and future machines to **ChangeTracking**, choose **Enable on all available and future machines** under the **Manage Machines** option of **ChangeTracking** from your Automation account.

More information about the **ChangeTracking** solution can be found at https://docs.microsoft.com/en-us/azure/automation/change-tracking.

Next, let's look at using **ServiceMap** to enable a visualized map to look at processes in real time.

Using ServiceMap

The **ServiceMap** solution helps you visually conceptualize your systems as a network of connected services, processes, and connections. It can be useful to identify application and system dependencies across all your systems through a holistic view of your systems' interconnectivity. This has great value as a troubleshooting tool in diagnosing problems that historically required deploying many types of monitoring systems in order to gain these insights. In the following screenshot, you can see all the connections that have been established by the source system:

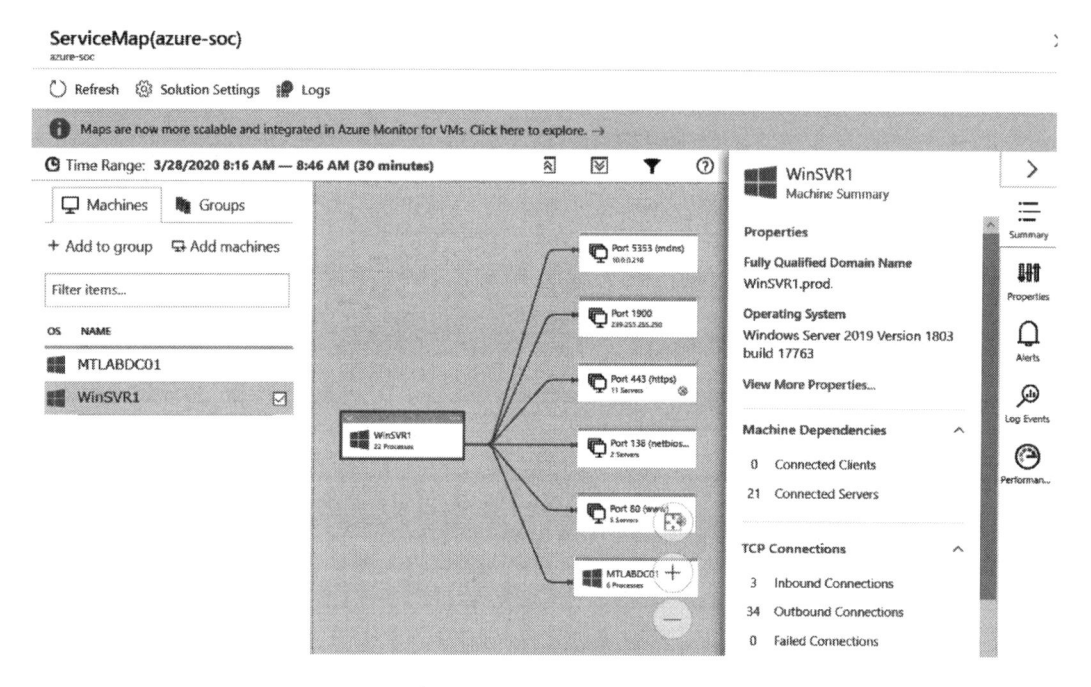

Figure 11.20 – The ServiceMap solution in Log Analytics

The **ServiceMap** solution requires Windows **Dependency agent** to be installed on the system in order to collect the required data.

More information about the **ServiceMap** solution can be found at the documentation page at https://docs.microsoft.com/en-us/azure/azure-monitor/insights/service-map.

Next, let's look at a network traffic analysis solution called Wire Data 2.0.

Using Wire Data 2.0

The **Wire Data 2.0** solution is used to analyze network traffic without the need to configure additional captures on your physical or virtual network devices. The types of information that **Wire Data** analyzes include the following:

- Inbound and outbound connections
- Total data flows over your subnets
- Application-level protocol transmissions

This solution includes out-of-the-box queries to be used with Log Analytics. The following screenshot shows a KQL query in Log Analytics used to pull up all the application-level protocol information. The results can be turned into a visual pie chart and pinned to a dashboard for real-time monitoring. The chart shows the percentage of all the application protocol traffic over the last 24 hours from the combined source systems:

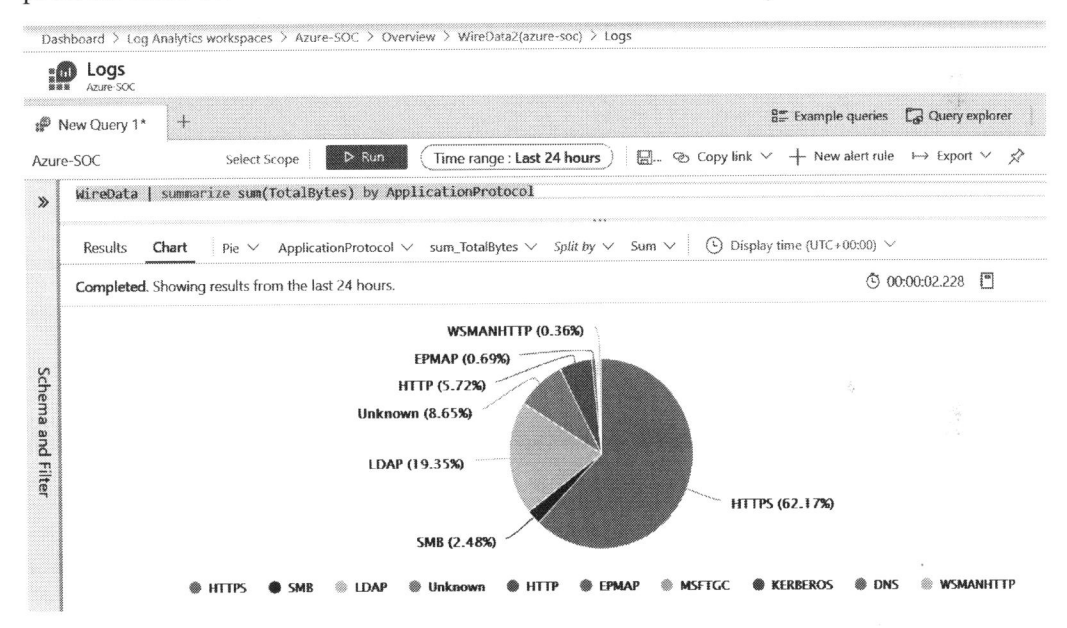

Figure 11.21 – A KQL query in Log Analytics

The **Wire Data 2.0** solution also requires Windows **Dependency agent to be** installed on your servers.

> **Tip**
> Windows **Dependency agent** can be installed systemically using Configuration Manager or through a virtual machine extension. It can also be configured with ARM templates during resource deployments.

Next, let's look at using Azure Monitor to analyze the telemetry data stored in Log Analytics.

Monitoring with Azure Monitor and activity logs

Azure Monitor provides a single place in Azure that can be used to monitor most Azure resources and services. Using telemetry collected from a variety of sources, it provides insights into applications, virtual machines, storage accounts, containers, networks, and more. Virtual machines can be onboarded individually or at scale using Azure Policy. Azure Monitor can provide near-real-time monitoring, which is invaluable for setting up critical alerts and notifications. Through action groups, you can create custom actions that are triggered based on alerts. These actions include email, SMS, push, or voice notifications, custom webhooks, and triggering an Azure Automation runbook for advanced remediation. There are also solutions in Azure Monitor that are prepackaged with the necessary logic to query data and provide rich visualizations and custom dashboards. Dashboards with metrics can be created and shared out to the appropriate teams responsible for operational monitoring. The following screenshot shows the processor performance metrics for virtual machines in a resource group. Using the pin icon, this chart can be pinned to a dashboard for quick access:

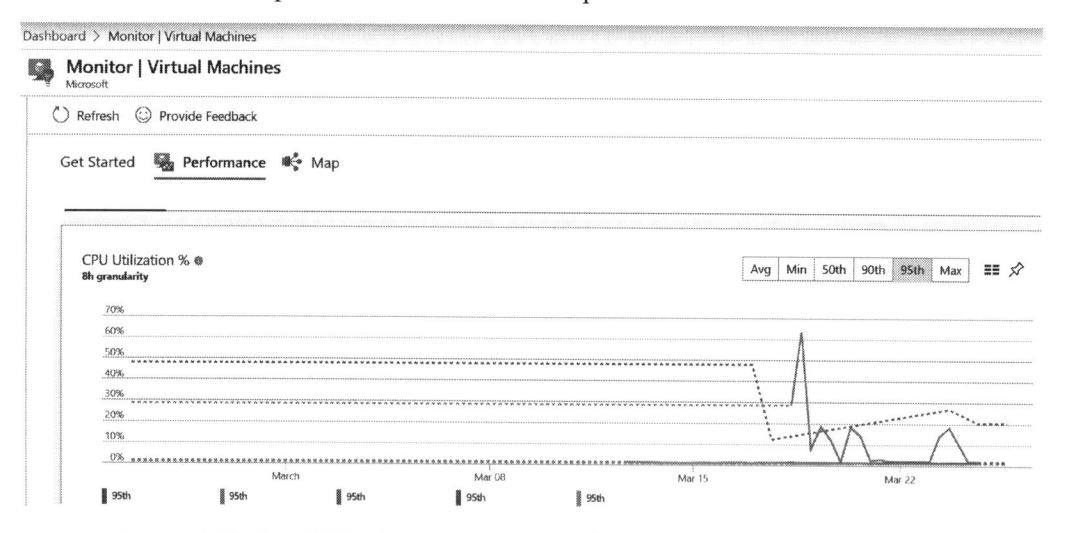

Figure 11.22 – The CPU utilization percentage of virtual machines in Azure Monitor

Using the power of the cloud, organizations can scale up resources during periods of high demand and scale them back during low activity to reduce costs. By leveraging Azure Monitor, resources can be added, removed, or scaled out based on a set of conditions that are triggered by the data analyzed with Azure Monitor.

These monitoring capabilities can be extended to on-premises servers by deploying the MMA. When deploying the MMA, the following data sources can be configured:

- Custom logs
- **Internet Information Services (IIS)** logs
- Performance counters
- Windows event logs

More information about the data sources that can be collected with MMA can be found at `https://docs.microsoft.com/en-us/azure/azure-monitor/platform/agent-data-sources`.

Secure access to Azure Monitor

In some instances, it's important to restrict the data in Azure Monitor to only the appropriate teams. Like most other Azure resources, Azure Monitor can leverage **Role-Based Access Control (RBAC)** for resource-level access. There are two built-in roles created for Azure Monitor:

- **Monitoring Reader**: Can read all monitoring data
- **Monitoring Contributor**: Can read, create, or modify the monitoring settings

Additional information about built-in Azure roles can be found at `https://docs.microsoft.com/en-us/azure/role-based-access-control/built-in-roles`.

Access to metrics logs can further be restricted at a storage account level or directly on the Log Analytics workspace scope.

Monitoring Azure activity logs

In addition to monitoring Azure resources and services directly for performance and changes, it's also important to monitor the activity as it relates to the operations carried out on these resources. For this, the Azure activity log is the place to go. These activity logs include information about the who, what, and when of an operation that occurred and also keeps a history of changes in JSON format if further research needs to occur as a result of an operation that may have caused issues.

Azure activity logs are kept for 90 days within your account and can be queried at any date within this period. Activity log insights can be pinned to a custom-built dashboard and scoped to a specific resource if you need to keep an eye on any operations performed against them. There is also a PowerBI content pack available to build shareable reports and dashboards.

To view the Azure activity logs, follow these steps:

1. Log in to the Azure portal at `https://portal.azure.com`.
2. Search for **Activity Log** and select it.

You can also open Azure activity logs from Azure Monitor, just under the **Overview** blade. The following screenshot shows the Azure activity log with information about events and operations that occurred against certain resources. You can see the actor who initiated the event and correlate them with the time that the event happened:

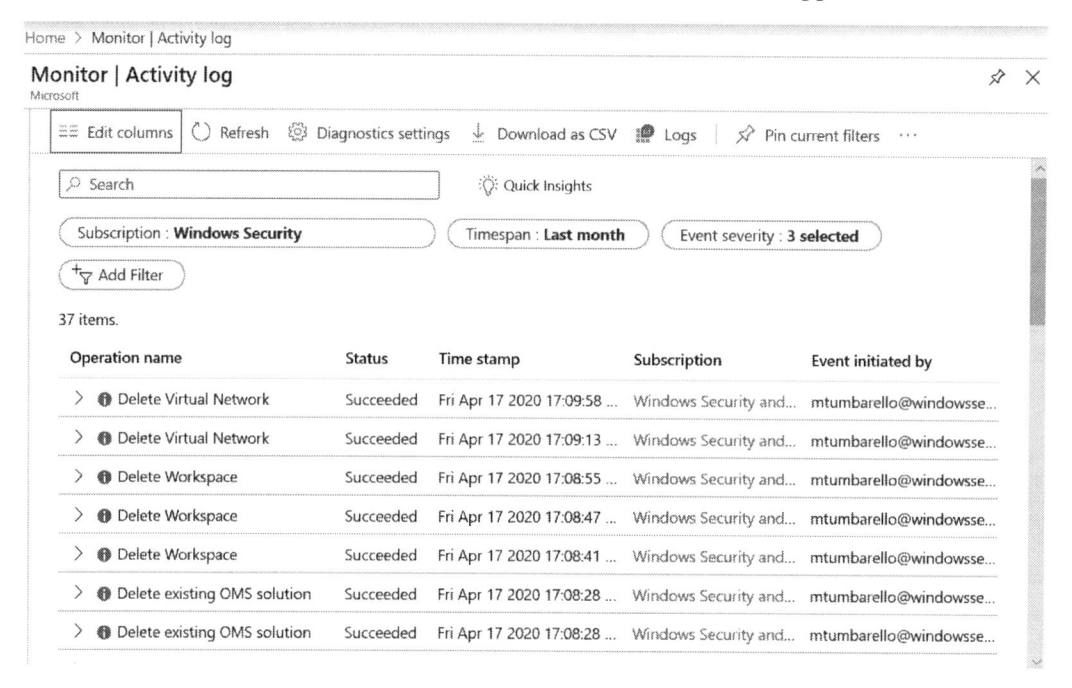

Figure 11.23 – An Azure activity log

Now that we have discussed using Azure Monitor, including reviewing Azure activity logs, let's look at how to configure ASC. To configure ASC, use a pre-configured Log Analytics workspace to analyze existing security log data, or create a new one during setup.

Configuring ASC

ASC is a next-generation security-management service provided by Azure that offers ATP to your environment for both cloud and on-premises resources. ASC leverages Microsoft's cloud ecosystem to process trillions of signals using machine learning to help detect and protect against many different threats.

Both the Windows and Linux operating systems are supported by ASC. In addition, integration with MDATP is available with Windows Server 2008 R2, 2012 R2, and 2016. For information about the most current supported platforms, visit https://docs.microsoft.com/en-us/azure/security-center/security-center-os-coverage.

> **Tip**
> To view the list of features for virtual machines and servers, visit https://docs.microsoft.com/en-us/azure/security-center/security-center-services?tabs=features-windows. To view the list of Azure PaaS services, visit https://docs.microsoft.com/en-us/azure/security-center/features-paas.

To access ASC and view the console, follow these steps:

1. Log in to https://portal.azure.com.
2. Search for **Security Center** and open it:

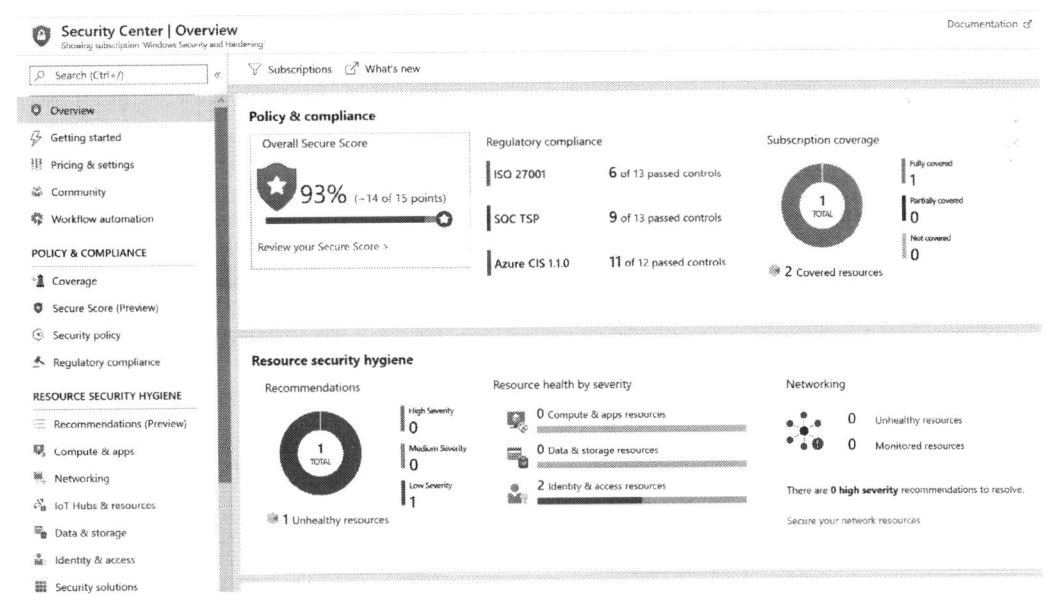

Figure 11.24 – The ASC console

One of the significant benefits of ASC is its ease of use. By default, ASC is enabled with your subscription and you will receive the benefits of the Free tier for your Azure resources. The Standard tier option provides many more features, including extending the capabilities to an on-premises environment and other clouds. To enable the Standard tier option within your subscription and to view the different features available with each tier, follow these steps:

1. Log in to `https://portal.azure.com`.
2. Search for **Security Center** and open it.
3. Click on **Pricing & Settings**.
4. Click on your subscription (you will need to enable **Standard** for each subscription).
5. Within **Pricing tier**, you will see the available features for each option. Simply click on the **Standard** option, and then click **Save** to enable it:

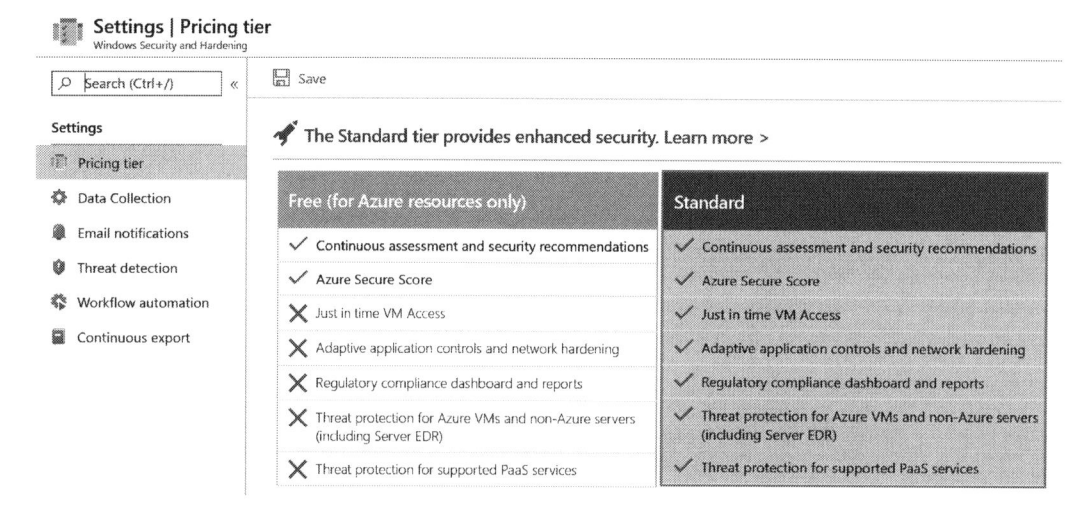

Figure 11.25 – The ASC tiers with their features listed

6. To view the current supported resources that are covered with the **Standard** tier, scroll down on the same page. Here, you can disable or enable the desired resources to be monitored. New resources are added as the service evolves:

Resource Type	Resource Quantity	Pricing	Plan
Virtual machines	0 VMs and VMSS instances	$15/Server/Month	Enabled Disabled
App Service	0 instances	$15/Instance/M...	Enabled Disabled
PaaS SQL servers	0 resources	$15/Server/Month	Enabled Disabled
SQL servers on VMs (Preview)	0 SQL servers on VMs	FREE during prev...	Enabled Disabled
Storage accounts	0 Storage acounts	$0.02/10K Transactions	Enabled Disabled
Kubernetes Services	0 Kubernetes services' cores	$2/VM core/Mo...	Enabled Disabled
Container Registries	0 Container registries	$0.29/Image	Enabled Disabled
Key Vaults (Preview)	1 Key vaults	$0.02/10K Transactions	Enabled Disabled

Figure 11.26 – The ASC resources that can be monitored

7. The pricing shown in the preceding screenshot may change, and you can find the most current by visiting https://azure.microsoft.com/en-us/pricing/details/security-center/.

Within **Settings**, under the **Pricing tier** option (see *Figure 11.25*), there are several other configurations available:

- **Data Collection** is where you can enable auto-provisioning for your virtual machines. Here, you can configure the Log Analytics workspace to collect your data configuration if you would like to collect Windows Security events.

- **Email notifications** is where you can configure who should receive email notifications and you can configure the notifications settings.

- **Threat detection** allows you to configure integrations with other Microsoft security services, such as **Microsoft Cloud App Security** (**MCAS**) and MDATP.

- **Workflow automation** is where you can set up automation based on events that occur; for example, customizing notifications to specific users and applying remediation steps.

- **Continuous export** is where you can configure the export of data into Event Hub or Log Analytics and configure integration with a third-party **Security information and event management solution** (**SIEM**).

To onboard non-Azure Windows or Linux servers, you will need to install the MMA manually and configure it to the Log Analytics workspace managed by ASC. We covered onboarding a non-Azure Windows server in the *The Update Management solution* section of *Chapter 10, Keeping Your Windows Server Secure*.

Once ASC Standard is enabled on your subscription and the resources reporting in, you can browse the menu on the left on the ASC console to view the recommendations for your resources:

1. Log in to `https://portal.azure.com`.
2. Search for **Security Center** and open it.
3. Within **Resource Security Hygiene**, select the area that you would like to view more details for. As an example, click on **Compute & Apps**.
4. Here, you will see an overview of the resources, along with each of the resource types:

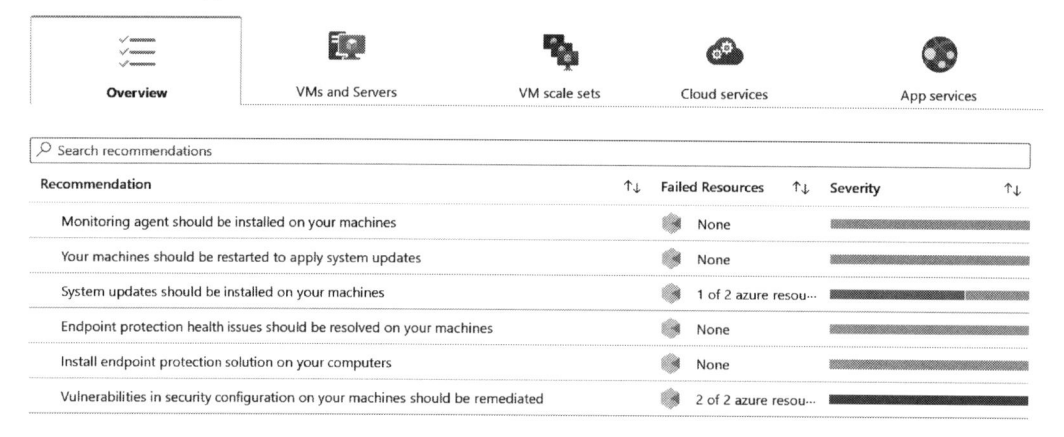

Recommendation	Failed Resources	Severity
Monitoring agent should be installed on your machines	None	
Your machines should be restarted to apply system updates	None	
System updates should be installed on your machines	1 of 2 azure resou…	
Endpoint protection health issues should be resolved on your machines	None	
Install endpoint protection solution on your computers	None	
Vulnerabilities in security configuration on your machines should be remediated	2 of 2 azure resou…	

Figure 11.27 – Computer and apps recommendations

> **Important note**
> The following link provides information about all the alerts you may see within ASC:
> `https://docs.microsoft.com/en-us/azure/security-center/alerts-reference`

Throughout this book, we have discussed building security baselines. Another type of baseline to consider is performance baselines. The tools we just covered, such as Azure Monitor and Log Analytics, are also helpful in this area. Next, let's review why you should also implement these types of baselines.

Creating performance baselines

Apart from the normal operational monitoring of your servers, it's important to build and document performance baselines of your server workloads. A performance baseline can be as simple as a set of metrics for the processor percentage, overall processor usage, memory, disk space, and network throughput observed and documented over a time period during peak and off peak business hours. Performance baselines should be captured on a recurring schedule and the frequency dictated by the business criticality and/or workload type. Once established, you can compare real-time performance metrics against the captured baseline for comparison. Not only is this useful for diagnosing issues and for cost tracking and optimization, but the ability to observe any odd performance metrics also helps with identifying potential security attacks. The benefits of performance baselining include the following:

- Risk mitigation
- Capacity planning
- Improvement opportunities
- Cost management
- Identifying bottlenecks
- Security risk mitigation

Windows has a built-in tool called **Performance Monitor** that is useful for capturing metrics over a period of time using custom or predefined data collector sets. **Performance Monitor** can be a useful tool for building performance baselines and can also be used to browse the network for domain or remote computers to track performance counters across multiple systems:

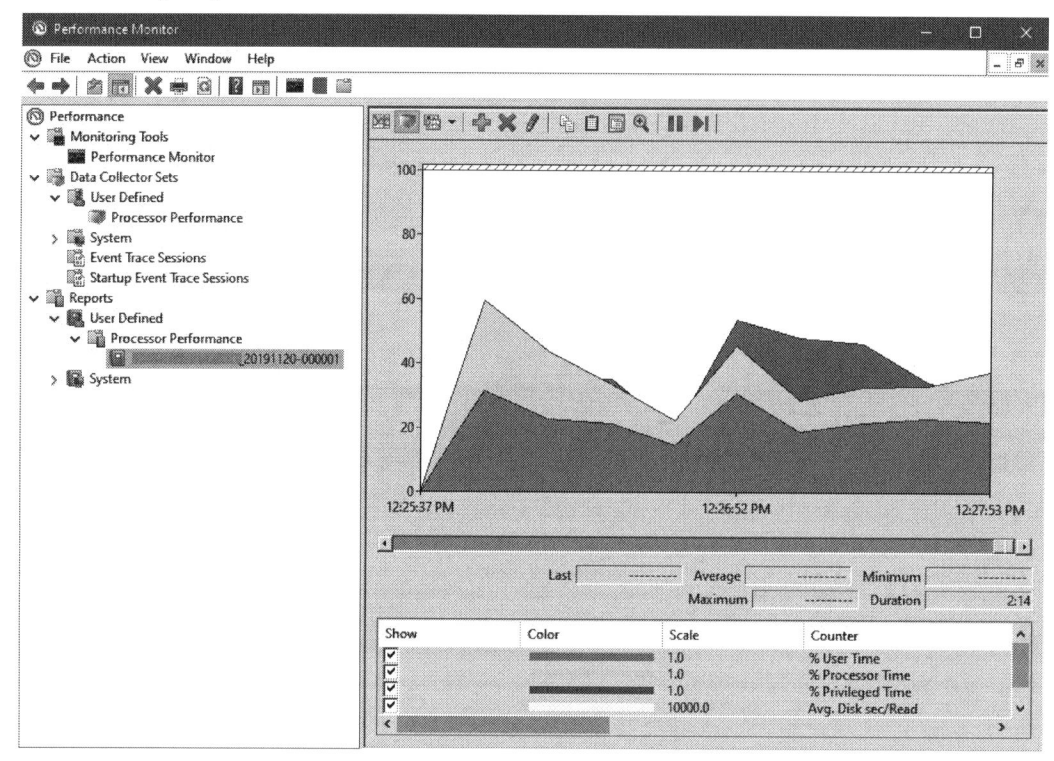

Figure 11.28 – Performance Monitor in Windows

By using Log Analytics workspaces, you can also view historical performance data for servers that have been onboarded with the MMA. The following screenshot shows the maximum CPU consumption and average memory consumption by process name for a group of servers:

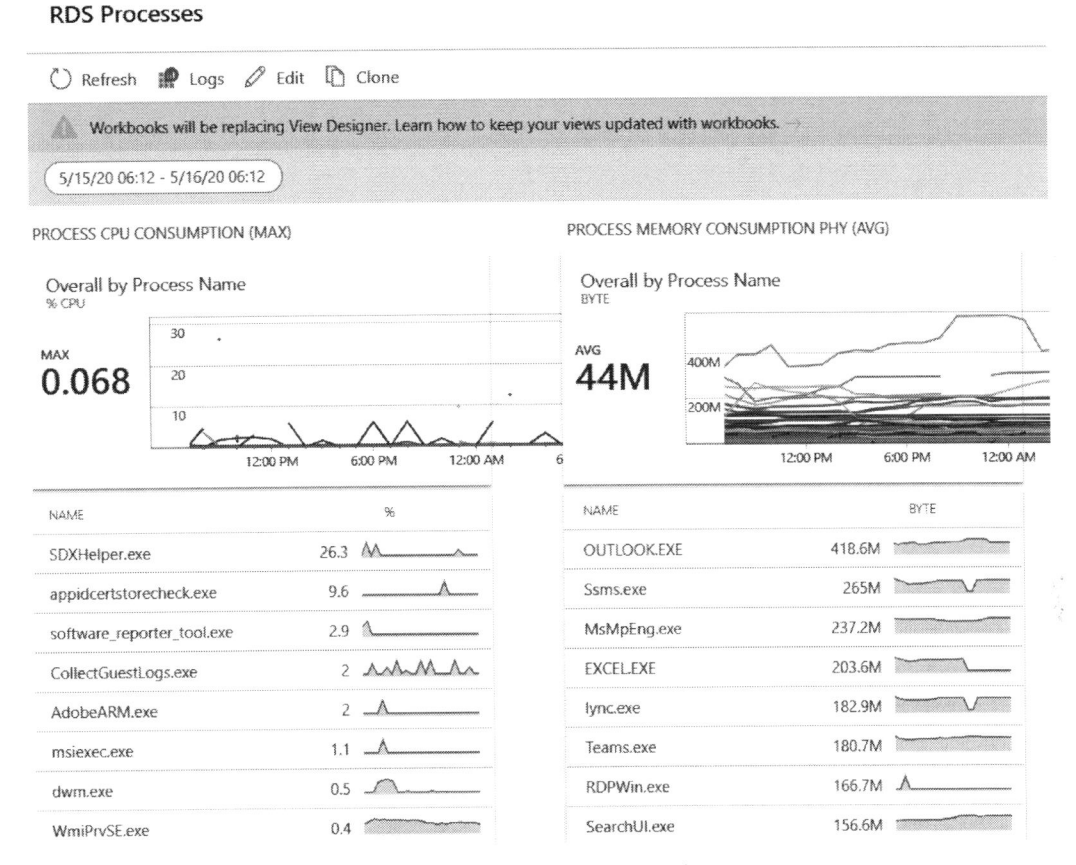

Figure 11.29 – A Log Analytics solution workspace summary

Using the tools described in this chapter can help you succeed in building performance baselines. In addition, Windows also has several built-in tools, such as **Performance Monitor**, that can be helpful when building a performance baseline for an individual server.

Summary

In this chapter, we covered monitoring with MDATP. We learned how to investigate an alert and reviewed the threat analytics, **Threat & Vulnerability Management**, and machine health and compliance dashboards. We covered how to onboard Windows 10 endpoints and create a machine risk compliance policy in Intune from the MDATP Intune connector. Next, we learned how to use Azure Log Analytics. We covered installing gallery solutions, such as **ServiceMap** and **Wire Data 2.0**, which help to quantify the data being captured with charts and visuals. We also provided an overview of Azure Monitor, including using Azure activity logs to audit operations taken on your resources.

In the next section, we discussed ASC and provided the steps to enable advanced features and to onboard machines. Finally, we discussed the importance of capturing performance baselines in addition to building security baselines. Now that we have learned how to configure telemetry to capture performance and security data, let's look at how this data can be used in the SOC.

In *Chapter 12*, *Security Operations*, we will provide an overview of the SOC and its place within an organization. We will review the Microsoft 365 security portal and the various Microsoft tools used to detect, protect, classify, and send alerts based on your data. We will also discuss using Secure Score to create a security posture and act on improvement recommendations.

12
Security Operations

In this chapter, we will cover security operations and exactly what it entails. Like a technical operations team, it is just as important to have a security operations team or **Security Operations Center** (**SOC**) and program in place. This team's day-to-day responsibilities include 24/7 monitoring and responding to any security-related incidents within your environment or with your users. This is a critical component and a necessity of the overall security program today.

In this chapter, we will focus on the Microsoft technologies available that can support your SOC and provide the insights needed to ensure your servers, end user devices, and users are safe. We will first cover an introduction to a SOC and provide an overview of what is needed to make this a successful operation. We will then review the **Microsoft 365** (**M365**) security center, which provides a centralized place for monitoring Microsoft security solutions. Next, we will cover **Microsoft Cloud App Security** (**MCAS**) and how to configure and use Azure **Advanced Threat Protection** (**ATP**).

In the following section, we will review Azure Security Center alerts and incidents, before providing an overview of Azure Sentinel, Microsoft's cloud **Security Information and Event Management** (**SIEM**) tool. We will then review Windows Defender ATP alerts and incidents, and review automated investigations before finishing off with a brief overview of **Business Continuity Planning** (**BCP**) and **Disaster Recovery** (**DR**) and its place within the security program. To recap, this chapter will cover the following topics:

- Introducing the SOC
- Using the M365 security portal

- Using MCAS
- Configuring Azure ATP
- Investigating threats with Azure Security Center
- Introducing Azure Sentinel
- Microsoft Defender Security Center
- Planning for business continuity and DR

Technical requirements

In order to follow along with the overviews in this chapter and complete the how-to instructions, the following requirements are recommended:

- An Azure subscription with contributor rights: https://azure.microsoft.com/en-us/free/
- MCAS (trial/MCAS + EMS E3 or E5): https://query.prod.cms.rt.microsoft.com/cms/api/am/binary/RE2NXYO
- Azure ATP: https://docs.microsoft.com/en-us/azure-advanced-threat-protection/atp-prerequisites
- Azure Security Center (free/standard): https://docs.microsoft.com/en-us/azure/security-center/security-center-pricing
- Azure Sentinel (per-capacity or pay-as-you-go): https://azure.microsoft.com/en-us/pricing/details/azure-sentinel/
- Microsoft Defender ATP (Windows 10 E5/M365 E5): https://docs.microsoft.com/en-us/windows/security/threat-protection/microsoft-defender-atp/minimum-requirements

In addition to these products, we will also discuss an overview of Microsoft's data loss prevention technology using **Azure Information Protection** (**AIP**). AIP requires at least Azure AD Premium P1 to configure. Many of the services mentioned in the preceding bullet points also allow you to set up a trial or include free versions to help you get started. We recommend working with a sales representative at Microsoft to understand the best options regarding licensing these products for your organization.

Introducing the SOC

Operations within the technical world have become a very standard and mature process. This function is core to the ongoing success of ensuring your users, systems, and applications are always available and running efficiently for your business. If there is an outage or an issue, operations teams typically follow very strict **Service Level Agreements** (**SLAs**) to return the service back to normal. This same concept is applicable to the security world. The concept of a SOC has grown exponentially over recent years, to the point where it is a necessity for maintaining normal business operations.

In short, a SOC manages and overlooks the day-to-day functions of your security operations for your organization. They typically operate 24/7 to monitor and detect potential security risks and alerts within your organization. If any alerts are detected, it is the SOC's responsibility to investigate and remediate them. A major part of this process also includes identifying the impact and potential damage your organization may face as a result of a security incident.

When looking at the security incident response life cycle, there are a few different variations, but they mostly overlap and follow a similar process. When referencing the *NIST Special Publication 800-61, Revision 2, Computer Security Incident Handling* guide, a four-step process is used for the incident response life cycle:

1. Preparation
2. Detection and analysis
3. Containment, eradication, and recovery
4. Post-incident activity

To learn more about the NIST incident response life cycle, visit the NIST *Computer Security and Incident Handling* guide at `https://nvlpubs.nist.gov/nistpubs/SpecialPublications/NIST.SP.800-61r2.pdf`.

One important document that needs to be clearly stated after any incident is the **Root Cause Analysis** (**RCA**) document. Ensuring a root cause is found is critical to not only ensure that the threat has been contained but also that the vulnerability that caused the incident has been remediated. In addition, and sometimes dictated by the severity of the incident, the RCA may need to be provided to the leadership team for review. For this reason, the RCA must clearly define why there was an incident, what the impact or damage was, how the incident was remediated, and a long-term resolution to ensure it doesn't happen again and that the risk is mitigated.

There are different variations of SOC models that can be adopted within your organization. Different factors will come into play as you decide on which model makes sense. These factors may include the size of your organization, the type of industry of the business, regulatory reasons, and budget considerations, to name a few. In general, an internal SOC can be created that is managed and operated by internal staff in the organization. This is most likely the case for large enterprises with bigger budgets who can afford to recruit top talent. Commonly, organizations opt for a fully outsourced model where you contract your SOC services to an external vendor who specializes in security services. This is referred to as a **Managed Security Service Provider** (**MSSP**). The MSSP model is an attractive service for medium to smaller sized businesses who may not have the budget to implement a fully functioning in-house SOC. Hybrid models also exist that maintain some functions of the SOC internally and outsource a subset of specialty services to the MSSP.

An additional service that needs to be accounted for when implementing a SOC program is a **Digital Forensic Incident Response** (**DFIR**) service. This is a very specialized service that requires detailed analysis for an investigation into breaches. Because this is a very specialized service and skillset, internal resources on staff or the MSSP may not provide this as part of their standard service offering. With the increasing amounts of active breaches that organizations face today, having a DFIR service available to engage quickly is beneficial to providing detailed forensic analysis of what has been (if anything) impacted. If your business has purchased a cyber insurance policy, the cyber insurance company should have an approved list of vendors who they will allow you to engage with for any DFIR services.

A SOC's ability to be efficient will depend on the tools it has at its disposal to allow the best visibility into your environment and the activities taking place. Throughout this chapter, we will be reviewing many of the Microsoft tools that make up a well-rounded and extremely robust security operations program to best protect your users, Windows devices, and Windows servers. We will first look at the M365 security portal as part of your security operations.

Using the M365 security portal

With all of the security tools that are deployed these days and all the different data points, it becomes challenging to keep up with different management consoles and ongoing feature enhancements. With Microsoft, there is a whole suite of security features and functionality that can be enabled for your organization. To help centralize and manage your security with Microsoft, they have provided the **M365 security center**, which is a place to view, manage, access, and monitor all the M365 security features. This is a very powerful tool for your security operations team and one that will be constantly accessed by that team. To access the M365 security center, browse to `https://security.microsoft.com` and log in to the management console:

Figure 12.1 – The M365 security center

> **Tip**
> To access the M365 security center, you will need to be either a global administrator, security administrator, security operator, or security reader within **Azure Active Directory** (**AD**).

Within the M365 security center, you can manage the following from the menu:

- **Home** provides an overview of the security center and a dashboard that can be customized with different dashboards.
- **Incidents** will have a consolidated list of all your incidents, which can be sorted based on status, severity, service source, and so on.
- **Alerts** from all your active Microsoft security tools will be consolidated here for viewing. Some examples include Office 365 ATP and Windows Defender ATP.
- **Action Center** shows any current or historical investigations within your environment. Some remediation actions may require manual approval or rejection and others may be automatic.

- **Reports** is a consolidated place to view and access all activity reports for all active security features.
- **Secure score** provides insight into all your Secure Score metrics across the environment.
- **Hunting** is where you can perform deep analysis and search for threats within your environment.
- **Classification** is where you will find **Data Loss Protection** (**DLP**) features, which include **Sensitivity labels, Retention labels, Sensitive info types,** and **Label analytics**.
- **Policies** provides links to all the security policies that can be managed within your environment.
- **Permissions** is where admins can manage roles and access to the M365 security center.
- **Settings** will show any configurable M365 settings.
- **More resources** provides links to all other Microsoft security consoles within your environment.
- **Customize navigation** is where you can customize what you would like to view within the navigation pane.

Expanding the **More resources** section will show you all the different management consoles that make up most of the security and compliance portfolio for Microsoft and include quick links. For more information about the Microsoft security portals and admin centers, visit `https://docs.microsoft.com/en-us/microsoft-365/security/mtp/portals?view=o365-worldwide`.

Next, we will provide more detail about Microsoft Secure Score and the benefits it provides to help with your overall security posture.

Understanding Microsoft Secure Score

One important area that will help with providing a more secure environment is Microsoft Secure Score. Microsoft Secure Score provides a numeric score of your environment based on an analysis of the current settings and configurations. It will provide recommendations based on your current state to help improve your overall security posture. Each recommendation has a different impact on your secure score and the higher the score, the more secure your environment is considered.

The current data sources used to build Secure Score reports include Office 365 (Exchange Online, OneDrive for Business, SharePoint Online, and Microsoft Information Protection), Azure AD, Microsoft Defender ATP, and Cloud App Security. Microsoft continues to add more data sources as the product evolves. Secure Score is currently broken down into five different categories: **Identity**, **Data**, **Device**, **Apps**, and **Infrastructure**. To access Microsoft Secure Store, follow these steps:

1. Browse to `https://security.microsoft.com` and log in.
2. Click on **Secure Score** in the left menu.
3. You will be presented with the Secure Score dashboard with an overview of the different device category scores:

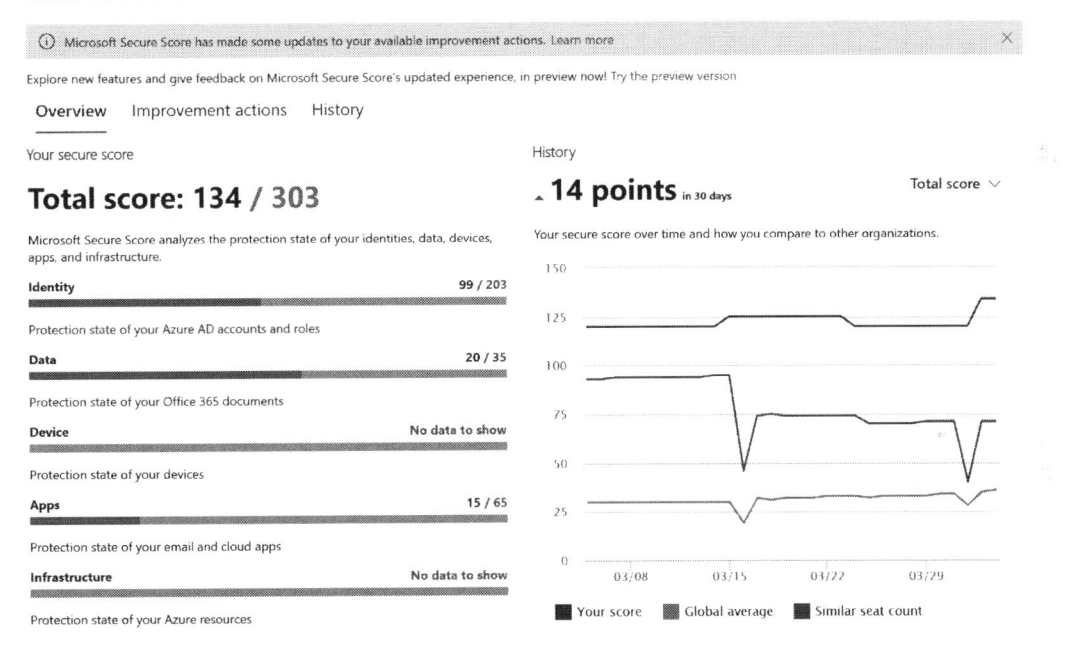

Figure 12.2 – The Secure Score dashboard

To improve your score, click on the **Improvement actions** option at the top of the page to view a list of all the recommendations from Microsoft. From here, you can click on a recommendation to view more details on why Microsoft is providing the recommendation, along with how this recommendation will better protect you with the next steps to take. Once the action has been taken, your Secure Score dashboard will reflect the changes and add the points to your score for that specific category group, as well as the overall score. If you are using a third-party tool to manage any of the recommendations, you can click on **Resolved through third-party** to also receive the points.

In the following example, Microsoft recommends **Turn on user risk policy**, which will help detect against potentially compromised accounts, allowing actions to be taken:

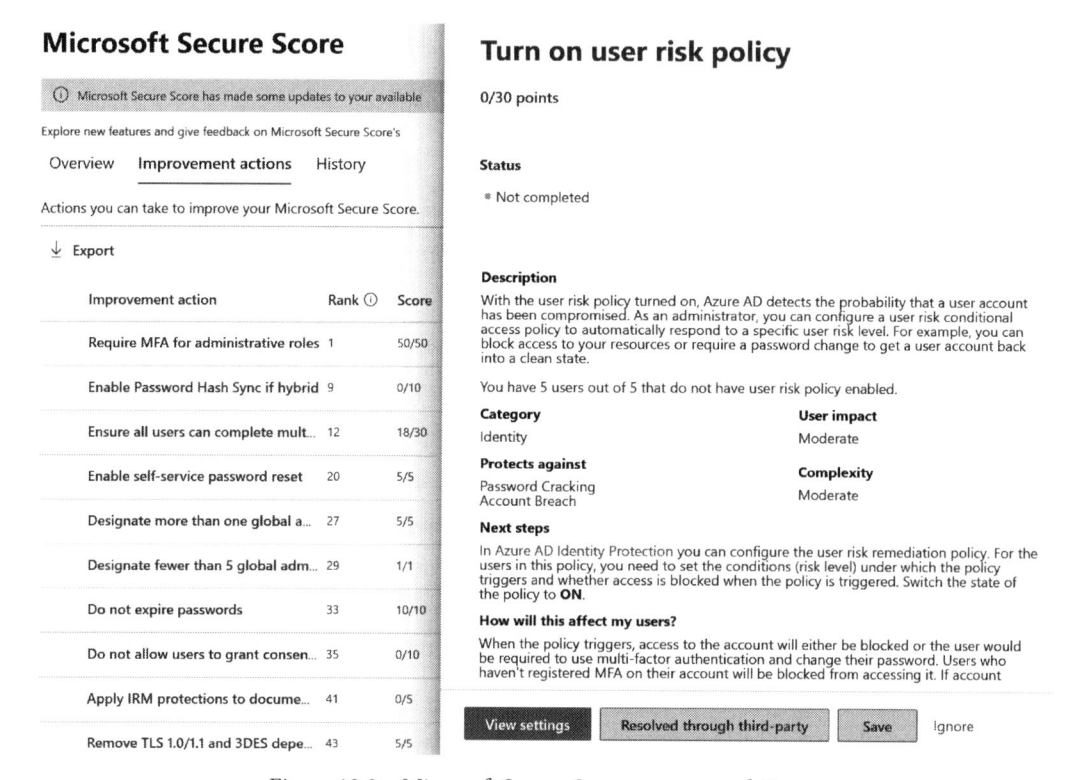

Figure 12.3 – Microsoft Secure Score recommendations

> **Tip**
> Recommendations for Azure ATP and Microsoft Defender ATP will be available soon within Microsoft Secure Score.

Next, we will take a high-level look at some DLP tools and the importance of data protection for your users and organization.

Classifying your data

Expand the **Classification** menu item or open **Office 365 Security & Compliance Center** (`https://protection.office.com/`) within the **More resources** menu item. These are the data protection tools for your organization. Although they are not directly related to hardening your Windows 10 device or Windows servers, it is critical that you are aware of the tools that will help protect the data your users are accessing from their Windows 10 devices and any data stored on Windows servers. There are three primary technologies to be familiar with to better protect your company data:

- **DLP**
- **AIP**
- **Windows Information Protection (WIP)**

These technologies can be used as separate products from Microsoft and may appear to provide some overlap, but they all have their unique usages as well as complementing each other to provide additional protection for your company's data. Let's look at each of these technologies.

DLP

DLP tools have been around for a while and provide great benefits to help protect against data exfiltration in your environment. With Microsoft DLP, you can protect sensitive information within Office 365 environments (Exchange Online, SharePoint Online, OneDrive for Business, and Microsoft Teams) from leaking out of your environment. Within the DLP engine, you can create policies that allow you to select which type of data you would like to protect. With the data type, you can select from many pre-defined templates that scan for **Personal Identifiable Information** (**PII**), finance, health, and GDPR types of information. You can then define the technology that you would like to search within, along with the rules and conditions, and actions on how to handle sensitive data if detected.

To access Microsoft's DLP, log in to the Office 365 Security & Compliance console at `https://protection.office.com/homepage`, and select **Data Loss Prevention**. Click on **Policy** to set up and review your policies.

> **Tip**
> The licensing requirements constantly change with Microsoft, so it's always good to confirm what the current licensing is. You can view the latest Security & Compliance licensing at `https://docs.microsoft.com/en-us/office365/servicedescriptions/office-365-platform-service-description/office-365-securitycompliance-center`.

Next, we will look at the **AIP** technology.

AIP

AIP, in short, is a technology that provides the ability to classify data by applying both sensitivity and retention labels. You can then enforce protection mechanisms such as encryption against the data based on the label type and sensitivity of that data. Data can be classified manually by users or automated depending on your license type. In addition, you can expand the labeling on to your on-premise files using the AIP scanner. You can view the different functionalities based on license type at `https://azure.microsoft.com/en-au/pricing/details/information-protection/`.

To access Microsoft's AIP, access the Office 365 Security & Compliance console by logging in to `https://protection.office.com/homepage`, then select **Classification**. Here, you can manage **Sensitivity labels**, **Retention labels**, and **Sensitive info types**.

WIP

The final technology we will review is WIP. WIP is the technology available to help prevent the accidental leakage or loss of data from your enterprise documents in Windows 10 version 1607 and later. With WIP, you can create policies that prevent data from being moved out of your environment, such as preventing data from being copied to USB drives. WIP also helps bridge the gap between users bringing their own devices and isolating corporate and personal data without impacting the user experience. In addition to running Windows 10 version 1607 or later, you will also need to be licensed for Intune or to run Microsoft Endpoint Configuration Manager. Third-party solutions can also apply WIP policies through the `EnterpriseDataProtection` **Configuration Service Provider** (**CSP**). Information about the CSP can be found at `https://docs.microsoft.com/en-us/windows/client-management/mdm/enterprisedataprotection-csp?redirectedfrom=MSDN`.

To access Microsoft's WIP, log in to the Microsoft Endpoint Manager admin center at `https://devicemanagement.microsoft.com` and click on **Apps**. Then, click on **App Protection Policies** under the **Policy** menu. Here, you can create and manage your WIP policies, including MAM policies for iOS and Android. For more information about creating a WIP policy using MDM, visit `https://docs.microsoft.com/en-us/windows/security/information-protection/windows-information-protection/create-wip-policy-using-intune-azure`.

We have just reviewed the M365 security center and highlighted an overview of important areas. This management resource provides a centralized view of Microsoft's security, including links to many additional security resources. The M365 365 security center is an essential resource for your security operations team. Next, we will review MCAS and the benefits it provides to protect your environment.

Using MCAS

MCAS is a **Cloud Access Security Broker (CASB)**. In short, a CASB is a service and/or tool that can extend your security footprint from on-premises into the cloud and provide better visibility and control over your data across a multitude of services. Additionally, it helps to add visibility through the discovery of shadow IT processes, which is traditionally a challenge for many organizations. One of the major benefits of MCAS is its native and simple integration with Microsoft security technologies. In addition, MCAS also integrates with other cloud providers for visibility into all your combined cloud environments in a single console.

As with any security tool, it will take time to fully configure all the MCAS features, implement your monitoring and policies correctly, and ensure that ongoing maintenance and operations are running efficiently. At a high level, you can set up MCAS relatively quickly to start gaining visibility with your environment. To access MCAS, follow these steps:

1. Browse to `http://portal.cloudappsecurity.com/`. You can also access it through the M365 security portal. Then, log in.

   You will be presented with the general dashboard. Here, you will be provided with an overview of all the environments that are being monitored. From the dashboard, you will be able to link to other app or risk-type dashboards, alerts, activity or content matches, and any of your investigative activities:

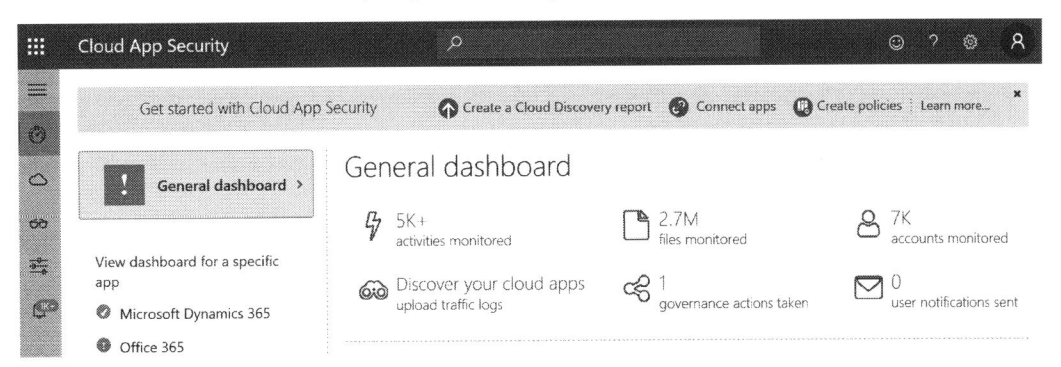

Figure 12.4 – The MCAS console's General dashboard

> **Tip:**
> MCAS requires the correct per-user licensing assignments depending on the features you wish to enable. Visit the following link to view more information about license requirements:
>
> https://query.prod.cms.rt.microsoft.com/cms/api/am/binary/RE2NXYO

2. The first thing to do is to connect your apps by clicking on the **Connect apps** option at the top of the dashboard. Once you are on the **Connected apps** page, click on the + sign to connect to an app, then follow the instructions to add the app:

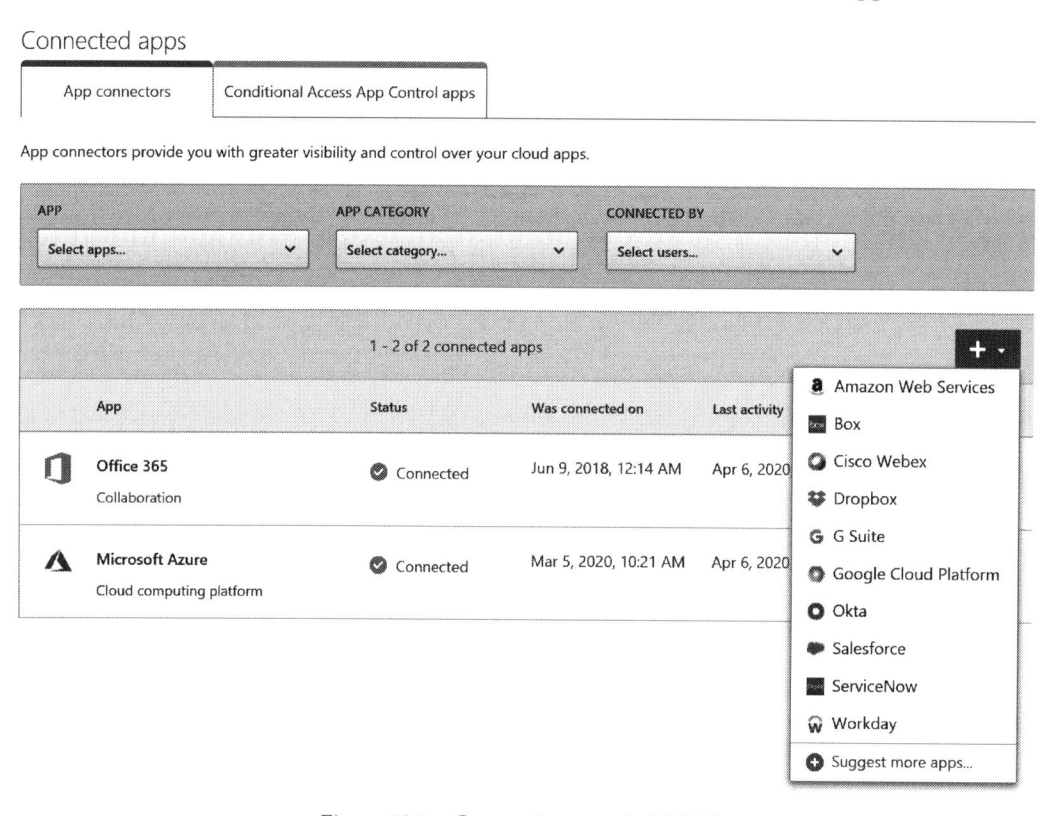

Figure 12.5 – Connecting apps in MCAS

3. The next step is to set up policies based on the provided templates. To access polices and templates, click on the **Control** menu item in the left-side navigation pane. Depending on the apps you have connected, there may already be predefined policies with the **Policy severity** and **Category** options configured. To set up alerts on any policy, go to the **Policies** page and click on the **Edit policy** cog, then configure your notifications within the **Alerts** section.

> Tip:
> The following article provides instructions to integrate Microsoft Defender ATP with MCAS for device alerts:
> `https://docs.microsoft.com/en-us/cloud-app-security/wdatp-integration`

There is a lot more involved in the setup of MCAS. To access the documentation library available from Microsoft, which contains more details on MCAS, visit `https://docs.microsoft.com/en-us/cloud-app-security/`.

Next, let's go into further detail about MCAS by reviewing the activity log.

Reviewing the activity log

The activity log in MCAS shows all the activities that have been performed by your users. The SOC can use these logs during an investigation to identify sign-ins and anomalous behavior and to review activity throughout Azure, Office, and all your connected apps to help identify risky behavior. Activity logs can be filtered to help narrow down the scope of an action if you are trying to identify a specific activity. Some examples of filterable queries include the following:

- **Admin activities**
- **Failed log in**
- **Impersonation activities**
- **Security risks**
- **Password changes and reset requests**

The following screenshot is filtered to **Failed log in**. One way in which the SOC team can use this query is to see which user accounts may be a target for brute-force login attempts. The results return a list of the activity performed, the user account, the application with which the activity originated, the IP address, the location, the device type, and the date:

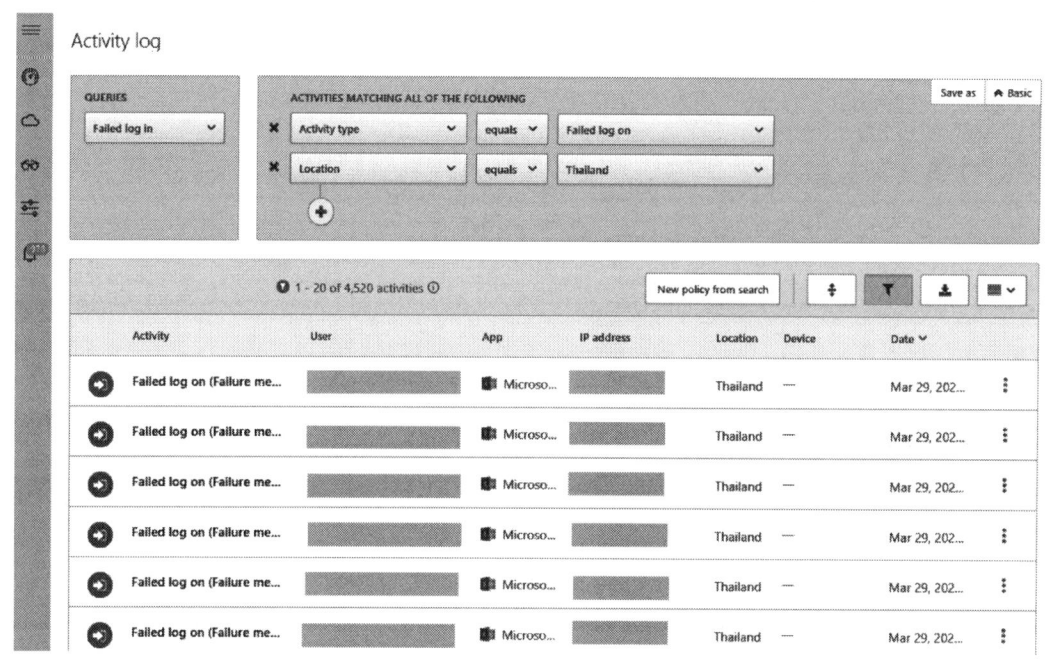

Figure 12.6 – Activity logs in MCAS

When investigating the query results, we find that the SOC team identified a failed login attempt to Microsoft Exchange Online originating from Thailand. The users are blanked out for privacy reasons, but the SOC team is aware that their users have never visited Thailand, so the failed log on activity from that location seems suspicious. Using the filtering options, the SOC adds an additional condition to scope the location to Thailand and try to understand more about the source of these login attempts. After the filter is added, multiple failed login attempts to Microsoft Exchange Online are presented, all originating from Thailand with activities being logged every few minutes.

Clicking on a specific activity will open the activity drawer, which provides additional details about the alert, as well as insights about the user and IP in question. The SOC analyst clicks to open the activity drawer and then selects the **User** tab to return more details, such as the ones in the following screenshot. Here, they can see a map view of the user's frequent locations, which only includes the United States. This further confirms the activity from Thailand as suspicious:

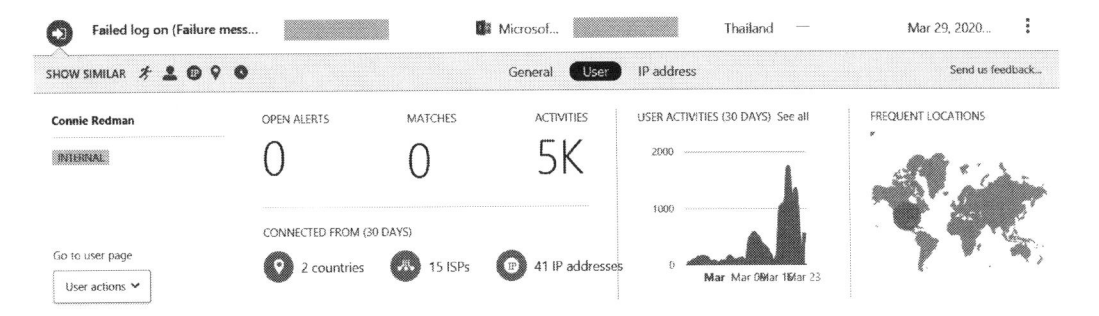

Figure 12.7 – The activity drawer in the activity log in MCAS

The activity log is a great way to look at all the activities from your connected apps to identify potential security risks and suspicious activity. More information about the MCAS activity logs, including the activity drawer, can be found at `https://docs.microsoft.com/en-us/cloud-app-security/activity-filters`.

Next, let's look at investigating user accounts to get more comprehensive details about a user's activity.

Looking at a user's activity

The **Users and accounts** page in MCAS lets you view activity relating to a user whose information is gathered from your connected apps. This is helpful for SOC teams as it allows a unified view of the identity across all the applications without needing to look at various monitoring systems. The landing page of **Users and accounts** returns all the users by the most recent and includes the username, investigation priority, type of account, email address, apps, groups, and the last seen information.

474   Security Operations

Users and accounts is filterable by username, affiliation, or account type, or you can select a specific connected app or user group. Affiliation filters include internal accounts as well as external accounts, such as **Business-to-Business (B2B)**-invited guests, and are denoted by green and yellow icons. Any user who has admin privileges in your environment also has a red tie on their icon, as seen in the User name column in the following screenshot:

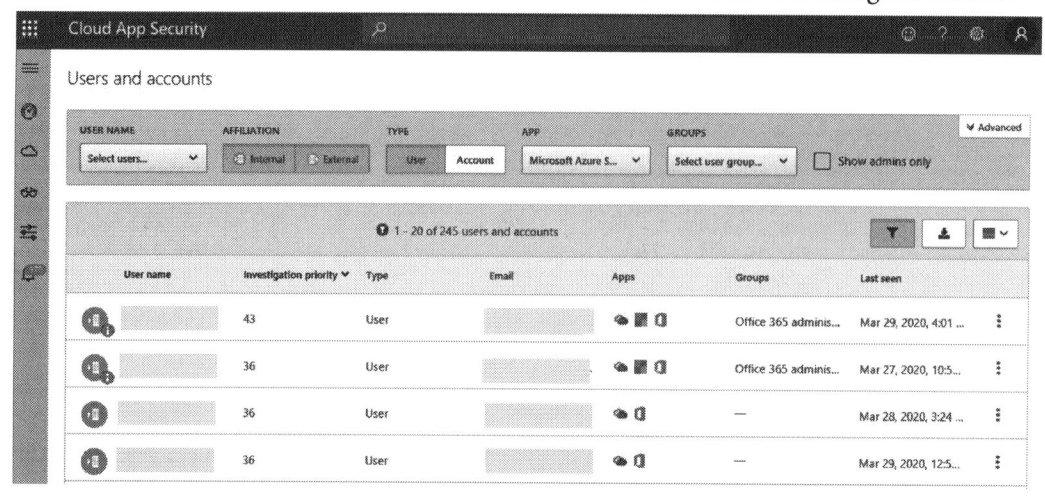

Figure 12.8 – Users and accounts in MCAS

By selecting the **Investigation priority** column to filter from highest to lowest, you can sort the users by their **Investigation priority** score. This score is a point-value system that is comprised of alerts and risky activities based on what MCAS sees as anomalous behavior for the user over a period of the past 7 days. A higher number indicates that the account should have investigation priority and could indicate a compromise or even an internal employee behaving maliciously.

Clicking on the username will bring up a summary of the connected apps where the identity exists. Click on **View User** to see more detailed information about the user. The following screenshot contains the user summary from MCAS. You can see a timeline of the user score over the past 2 weeks, which days accrued points that led to the increased score, and a timeline view with the summary of actions deemed anomalous:

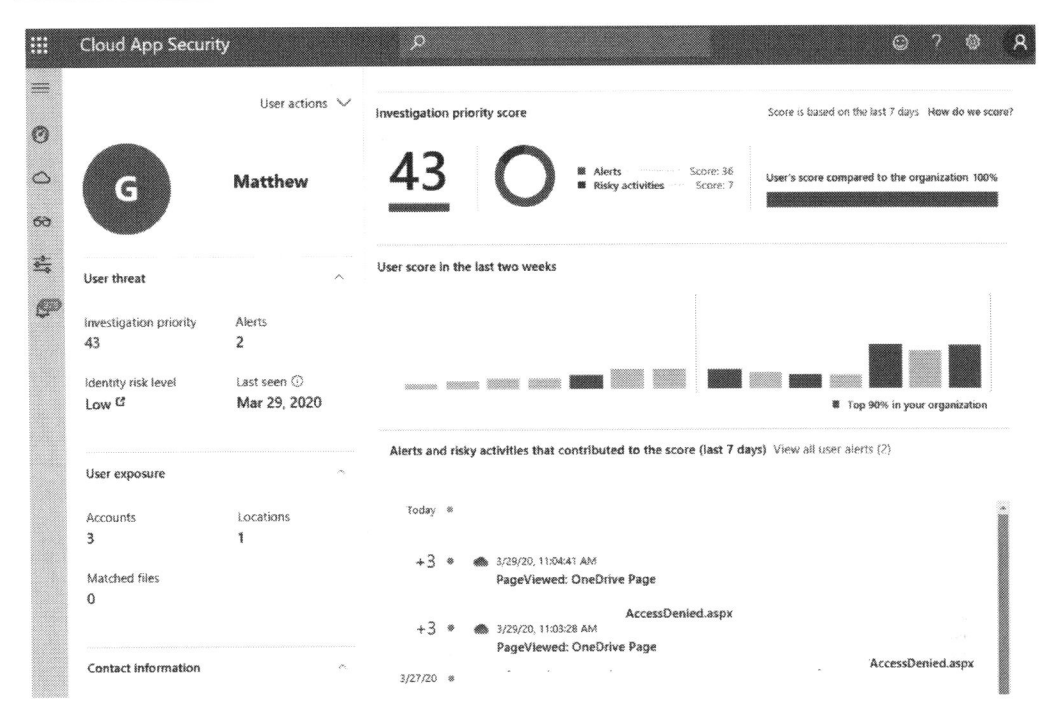

Figure 12.9 – User summary in MCAS

After the SOC analyst performs their analysis and considers that the account may have been compromised, there are remediation actions under the **User actions** dropdown that can be taken for immediate remediation. These include the **Sign in again**, **Suspend user**, or **Confirm user compromised** requirements for the user. Selecting **Confirm user compromised** will raise their user risk level to high and any Azure AD directory policy set for high-risk users will apply.

Clicking on **View all user alerts** from the user summary will bring up all the alerts associated with the user, which can be reviewed and either dismissed or resolved:

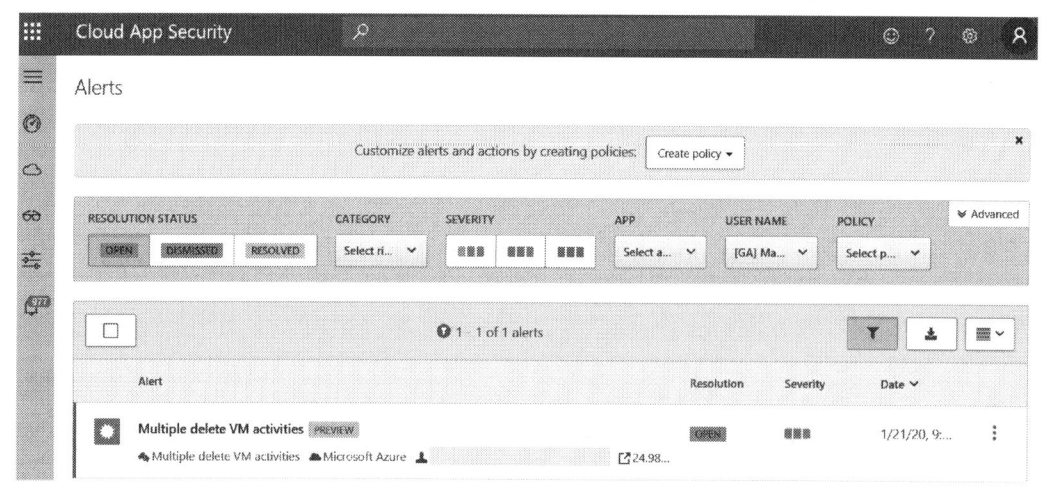

Fig 12.10 – Investigating alerts associated with the user

For more information about investigating risky users using MCAS, visit https://docs.microsoft.com/en-us/cloud-app-security/tutorial-ueba.

Next, we will review how to configure Azure ATP to monitor domain network traffic in your AD environment.

Configuring Azure ATP

Azure ATP is a cloud security service from Microsoft that's used to analyze domain network traffic. This solution is helpful for the SOC to identify attacks and malicious movements in your AD environment. Telemetry data is collected by installing the ATP sensor on a domain controller, which forwards that information to the Azure ATP cloud service for investigation using the ATP portal. The ATP portal is a unique instance to your tenant and has a similar style and feel to the other cloud-based security portals that Microsoft offers. The SOC team can use the portal to investigate alerts in a timeline view to correlate activity throughout different phases of the attack kill chain. The ATP sensor will capture the following information and forward it to the ATP service:

- Domain controller network traffic
- Windows events

- **Remote Authenticaion Dial-In User Service (RADIUS)** account information for a VPN
- User and computer data from AD

> **Tip:**
> In order to use the ATP service, the **Forest Functional Level** (FFL) of your AD domain must be Windows 2003 or higher.

For more detailed information about the Azure ATP architecture, visit `https://docs.microsoft.com/en-us/azure-advanced-threat-protection/atp-architecture`.

Planning for Azure ATP

There are a few pre-requisites required before using Azure ATP, which include the following:

- An Azure tenant with global or security administrator privileges to configure the ATP instance
- Enterprise Mobility + Security 5 (EMS E5) or a standalone Azure ATP license: `https://www.microsoft.com/cloud-platform/enterprise-mobility-security-pricing`
- Rights to install the ATP sensor on a domain controller with internet connectivity to the Azure ATP cloud service

For more detailed information about the technical prerequisites, including network configuration, proxy setup, and portal requirements, visit `https://docs.microsoft.com/en-us/azure-advanced-threat-protection/atp-prerequisites`.

Microsoft also has a capacity planning guide and tool that can help you determine the number of sensors recommended for a rollout. To download the ATP sensor tool and for more information about the CPU and memory requirements, visit `https://docs.microsoft.com/en-us/azure-advanced-threat-protection/atp-capacity-planning`.

Activating your instance

The activation of the Azure ATP portal instance is straightforward. Once you have verified the prerequisites and understand the capacity planning, installation can be achieved by following these high-level steps:

1. Using an Azure global administrator or security administrator account, activate your instance of the Azure ATP portal by logging into `https://portal.atp.azure.com`. Follow the onscreen instructions to confirm the activation.
2. From your AD, configure a read-only (domain user) account and password.
3. In the ATP portal, click on the **Directory Services** section of the Azure ATP portal. Enter the username and password of the account created previously. Enter the **FQDN** of your domain.
4. Click on the **Sensors** tab under **System**. Download and install the sensor on a domain controller using the access key provided in the portal.
5. Once the sensor is installed, it will show up in the **Sensors** section after you next refresh the page.

For more information about installing the Azure ATP sensor, visit the following link. There are also instructions for a silent installation if you need to deploy the sensor to more than one system using a tool such as Configuration Manager:

`https://docs.microsoft.com/en-us/azure-advanced-threat-protection/install-atp-step4`

Next, let's look at how Azure ATP recognizes sequences of events to identify the attack kill chain.

Understanding the kill chain

Once the sensor is installed, the information that is monitored is relayed back to the cloud service for analysis. Azure ATP is designed to detect common attack methodologies within the cyber kill chain. The kill chain is defined as a sequence of events typically followed by a malicious actor to gain knowledge of your environment to ultimately gain domain dominance. Azure ATP recognizes these in the following sequences:

- Reconnaissance
- Compromised credentials
- Lateral movements

- Domain dominance
- Exfiltration

Having a solution to correlate events and identify these stages in the attack kill chain will help the SOC increase their chances of stopping an attack. This is the real value of adding Azure ATP as a security enhancement to your AD environment. The following table lists the types of alerts that Azure ATP will report on during each stage of the kill chain:

Attack Phase	Alert
Reconnaissance	Account enumeration reconnaissance.
	Network mapping reconnaissance (DNS).
	Security principal reconnaissance (LDAP).
	User and IP address reconnaissance (SMB).
	User and group membership reconnaissance (SAMR).
Compromised Credential	Honeytoken activity.
	Suspected brute-force attack (Kerberos, NTLM, LDAP, and SMB).
	Suspected WannaCry ransomware attack.
	Suspected use of Metasploit hacking framework.
	Suspicious VPN connection.
Lateral Movements	Remote code execution over DNS.
	Suspected identity theft (pass-the-hash or pass-the-ticket).
	Suspected NTLM authentication tampering.
	Suspected NTLM relay attack.
	Suspected overpass-the-hash attack (encryption downgrade and Kerberos).
	Suspected SMB packet manipulation (CVSE-2020-0796 exploit).
Domain Dominance	Malicious request of the data protection API master key.
	Remote code execution attempt
	Suspected DCShadow attack (domain controller promotion and replication requests).
	Suspected DCSync attack (replication of directory services).
	Suspected Golden Ticket usage (encryption downgrade, forged authorization, nonexistent account, ticket anomaly, and time anomaly).
	Suspected Skeleton Key attack (encryption downgrade).
	Suspicious additions to sensitive groups.
	Suspicious service creation.
Exfiltration	Suspicious communication of DNS.
	Data exfiltration over SMB.

Figure 12.11 – Alerts issued by ATP during the kill chain

Azure ATP can be integrated with additional security solutions, such as Microsoft Defender ATP, and can forward alerts to MCAS. Combining these solutions creates a robust suite of security tools. Microsoft Defender ATP handles endpoint protection and antivirus with the real-time detection of files and processes, while Azure ATP analyzes the traffic and activity through your domain. These solutions can all be monitored through the MCAS portal, creating a unified view for the SOC. As covered earlier in this chapter, adding MCAS allows organizations to analyze signals from many sources, including Microsoft Online Services apps, such as SharePoint, Exchange, and OneDrive, Microsoft Azure, Defender ATP, Azure ATP, and other third-party app providers, such as Box, Amazon Web Services, Salesforce, and Google Cloud, to name a few. For more information about enabling Azure ATP integration with Microsoft Defender ATP, visit https://docs.microsoft.com/en-us/azure-advanced-threat-protection/integrate-wd-atp.

For more information about using Azure ATP with MCAS, visit https://docs.microsoft.com/en-us/azure-advanced-threat-protection/atp-mcas-integration.

Next, let's look at using the security alert timeline of the Azure ATP portal to investigate alerts.

Looking at alerts

After logging in to the ATP portal, you are taken to the timeline view, where alerts are listed in chronological order with the latest opened alert first. The filter options allow you to view the alert status by **Open**, **Closed**, and **Suppressed**, as well as by **High**, **Medium**, and **Low** severity. Clicking on the three dots, you can choose to close, suppress, or download the alert details. Clicking on the alert heading will open the alert details page. In the following screenshot, the ATP security timeline shows two open alerts that were flagged with medium severity. The first is for the use of a Honeytoken account and the other is for a user and IP address reconnaissance activity:

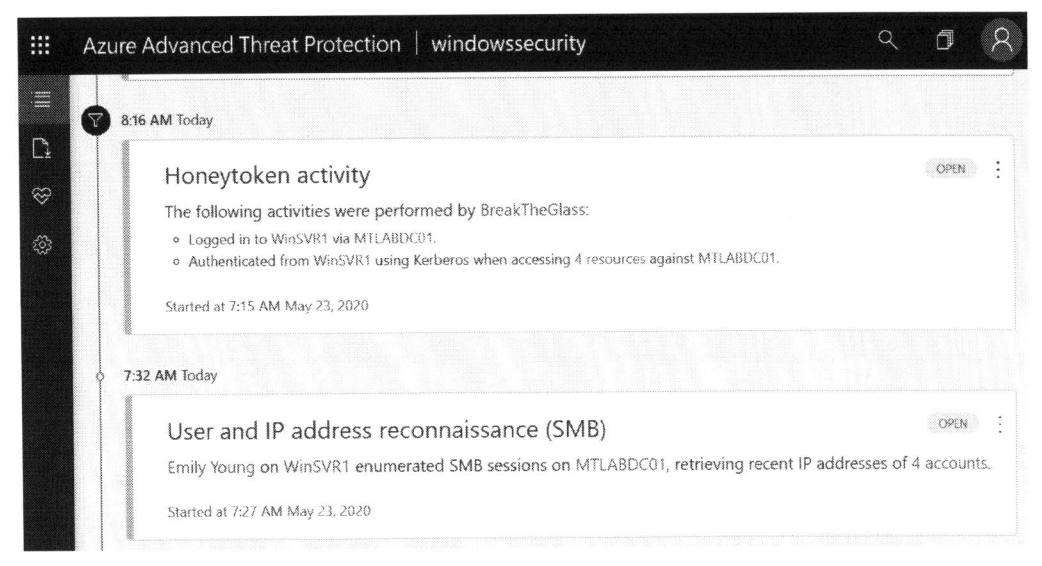

Figure 12.12 – A security timeline in the Azure ATP portal

Let's look at the Honeytoken activity first. Honeytoken accounts are useful detection mechanisms to lure attackers. They can help identify whether there is potentially active reconnaissance going on inside the domain that may have malicious intent. In the Azure ATP portal, a Honeytoken account can be configured from the **Configuration** menu in the **Entity tags** settings, under **Detection**:

Figure 12.13 – Configuring entity tags in the ATP portal

In the preceding screenshot, a Honeytoken account named **BreakTheGlass** could be used to entice an attacker as it may have high privileges.

In the **Sensitive** section of **Entity tags**, you can add additional accounts, groups, or servers that are considered sensitive and easily identifiable and are tagged in the Azure ATP portal. By default, sensitive entities already include domain admins, administrators, domain controllers, enterprise admins, and other privileged objects. The following screenshot shows the **Domain Admins** security group labeled as **sensitive**. Any sensitive entity that shows up in an alert will have an **S** icon beside it:

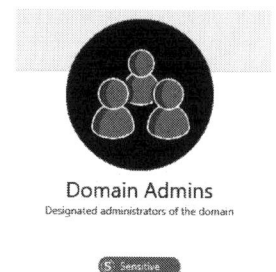

Figure 12.14 – The Domain Admins security group depicted as Sensitive

Heading back to the security alert timeline, let's look at the second alert for **User and IP address reconnaissance (SMB)**. Clicking on the heading will bring up more information about the activity. In the following screenshot, you can see that **Emily Young** enumerated SMB session details on the `MTLABDC01` domain controller from the `WinSVR1` source system. This activity could potentially indicate malicious intent and that the account has been compromised. Using this reconnaissance technique, the actor successfully enumerated the SMB session details, as shown at the bottom of the alert and now has access to a list of network locations and accounts to be targeted:

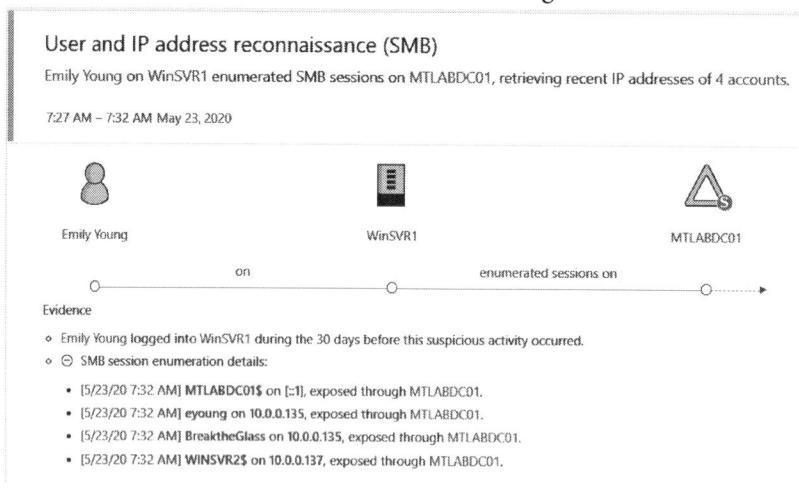

Figure 12.15 – Investigating the alert in the ATP portal

Now that the user accounts and locations have been discovered, further reconnaissance can be carried out. The `BreakTheGlass` account looks enticing, and more information can be found by running a `net user "BreakTheGlass" /domain` command. If the user is a member of a highly privileged group, such as **Domain Admins** or **Enterprise Admins**, they now have a viable target that is worth going after. Let's look into this a little further by clicking on the user in the alert to pull up the user-specific activity log. As seen in the following screenshot of the user activities list, there are multiple entries that show successful **Security Account Manager Remote Procedure Call (SAMR)** queries for all domain groups and the **Domain Admins** security group:

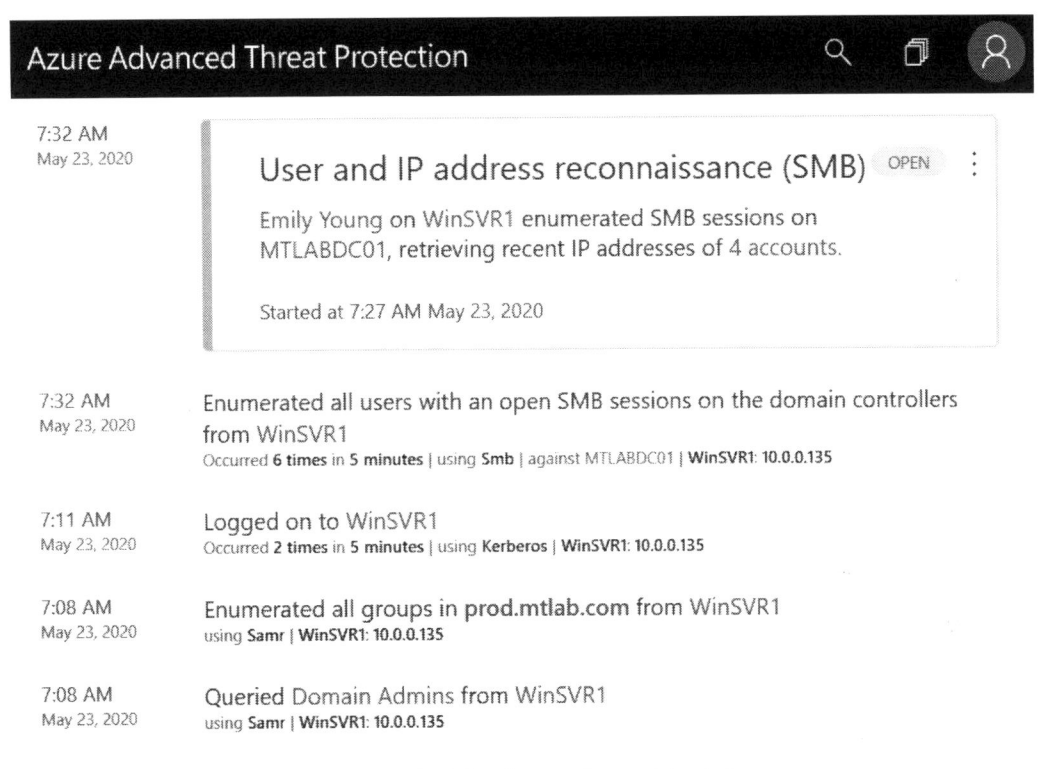

Figure 12.16 – Activity alert on the machine info page

Based on the preceding example, it's highly probable that the account in question has been compromised and is currently in the reconnaissance phase of the kill chain. The SOC team should reach out to the user and attempt to stop the attack by changing the user's password or blocking sign-ins all together. If they are using MCAS or if integration with Microsoft Defender ATP has been configured, they can check for additional alerts triggered from the user's PC and perform advanced hunting to try and identify the source of the compromise.

It's important to understand that once a user's account is compromised, the attacker may have the ability and skills to move laterally throughout systems. Using publicly available tools, such as `mimikatz`, attackers can attempt to dump credentials stored in memory on the compromised system. If the NTLM hashes are successfully captured, the attacker can use the **overpass-the-hash** technique to acquire a **Ticket-Granting Ticket (TGT)** of another user who may have logged into the system and gain further access by acting on their behalf. As shown in the following screenshot, the attacker was able to dump the `BreakTheGlass` account's NTML hash and acquire a TGT. Luckily, Azure ATP has flagged it as a suspected overpass-the-hash attack:

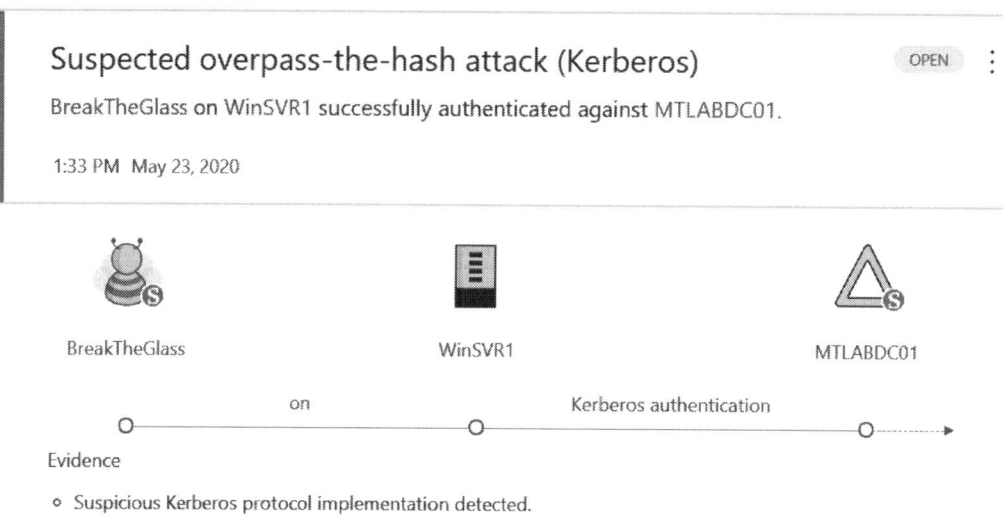

Suspected overpass-the-hash attack (Kerberos)   OPEN

BreakTheGlass on WinSVR1 successfully authenticated against MTLABDC01.

1:33 PM May 23, 2020

BreakTheGlass —on→ WinSVR1 —Kerberos authentication→ MTLABDC01

Evidence

- Suspicious Kerberos protocol implementation detected.
- BreakTheGlass logged into WinSVR1 during the 30 days before this suspicious activity occurred.

Figure 12.17 – An Azure ATP alert for a suspected overpass-the-hash attack

Assuming `BreakTheGlass` has elevated permissions on many systems, the attacker can move laterally by executing code remotely with tools such as `PSExec` and `mimikatz` to dump credentials from remote systems. If successful, this will allow them to gain more knowledge of the environment. Azure ATP will also flag attempts to execute services remotely by creating a **Remote code execution attempt** alert, as in the following screenshot:

2:30 PM Today

Remote code execution attempt   OPEN

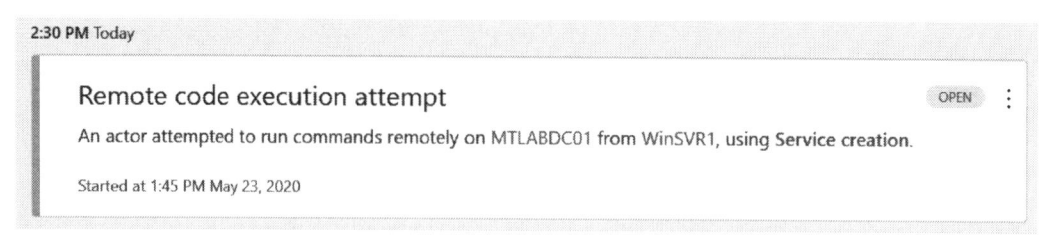

An actor attempted to run commands remotely on MTLABDC01 from WinSVR1, using **Service creation**.

Started at 1:45 PM May 23, 2020

Figure 12.18 – A Remote code execution attempt alert

Now that the attacker has successfully been able to dump credentials from a remote system and use similar reconnaissance techniques, they have acquired a new user account, who is a member of **Domain Admins**. In the next phase, the attacker will use the **Domain Admins** privileges to dump all credentials from AD using the `Mimikatz DCSync` command or a similar sdomain-replication technique. The following screenshot is of an Azure ATP alert for a suspected DCSync replication:

2:26 PM Yesterday

Suspected DCSync attack (replication of directory services) OPEN

Matt Tumbarello on WinSVR1 sent 1 replication request to MTLABDC01.

Figure 12.19 – Suspected domain replication alert

If the replication is successful, the **Kerberos Ticket-Granting Ticket Account (KRBTGT)** password hash could become compromised and be used in a **golden ticket** attack. The KRBTGT account is the master service account used in Kerberos distributions. Once collected, it can be used to forge TGTs for any accounts. The attacker now has everything they need to gain domain dominance and exfiltrate data quite easily. As the following screenshot shows, an Azure ATP alert was generated for a suspected golden ticket attack:

Suspected Golden Ticket usage (time anomaly) OPEN

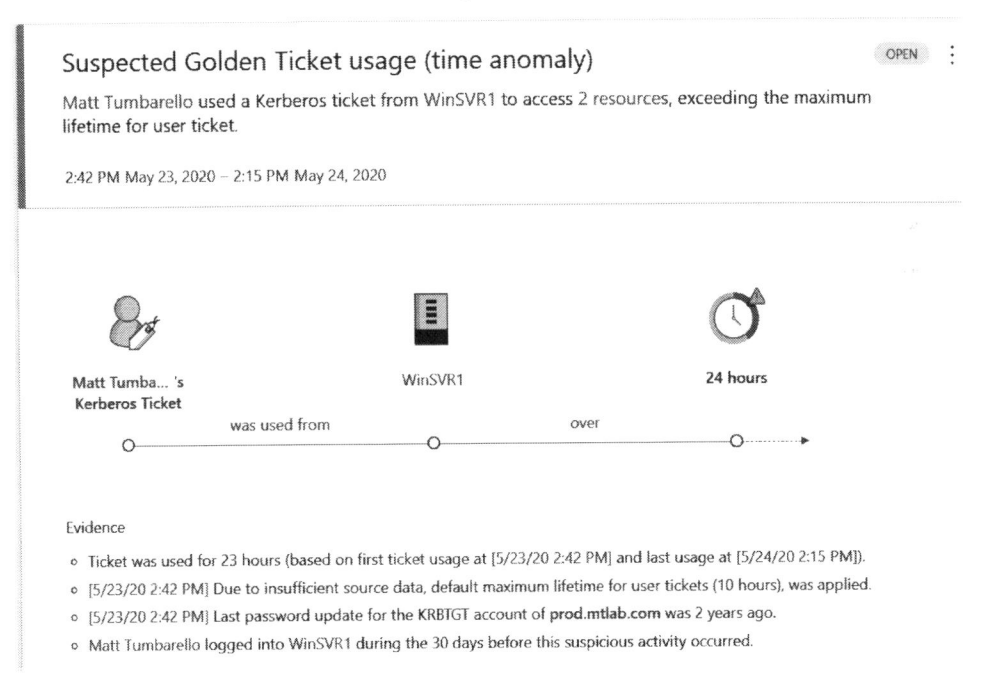

Matt Tumbarello used a Kerberos ticket from WinSVR1 to access 2 resources, exceeding the maximum lifetime for user ticket.

2:42 PM May 23, 2020 – 2:15 PM May 24, 2020

Matt Tumba... 's Kerberos Ticket — was used from — WinSVR1 — over — 24 hours

Evidence

- Ticket was used for 23 hours (based on first ticket usage at [5/23/20 2:42 PM] and last usage at [5/24/20 2:15 PM]).
- [5/23/20 2:42 PM] Due to insufficient source data, default maximum lifetime for user tickets (10 hours), was applied.
- [5/23/20 2:42 PM] Last password update for the KRBTGT account of **prod.mtlab.com** was 2 years ago.
- Matt Tumbarello logged into WinSVR1 during the 30 days before this suspicious activity occurred.

Figure 12.20 – Alert for a suspected golden ticket attack

Once this level of access has been obtained, the attacker has control over resources that rely on Kerberos tickets for authentication. Even if a compromised user's password has changed, the attacker can still impersonate the account by using the KRBTGT account. The best protection against these types of attacks is to adopt the recommendations given in these chapters to prevent them from occurring and have monitoring in place to detect and alert you on these intrusions. Ensure that privileged accounts are limited and that appropriate access management solutions are in place. Enforcing security baselines and enabling endpoint protection will allow you to lock down the use of PowerShell scripts and hacking tools commonly loaded into malicious payloads. If the KRBTGT account has become compromised, it is recommended to reset it twice to remove any passwords stored in the password history. Resetting the KRBTGT password will be disruptive and invalidate tickets that have been issued to systems. They will likely need to be rebooted, allowing a new ticket to be issued. Users that have active sessions to resources may be required to re-authenticate to services. For more information on resetting the KRBTGT account password, visit `https://docs.microsoft.com/en-us/windows-server/identity/ad-ds/manage/ad-forest-recovery-resetting-the-krbtgt-password`.

This was just one example of a potential kill chain within an attack of an AD environment. Hopefully, it shows the value of implementing security solutions such as Azure ATP. It gives the security team valuable insights to hopefully help stop these attacks before domain dominance is obtained. For more information about the security alerts in the Azure ATP portal, visit `https://docs.microsoft.com/en-us/azure-advanced-threat-protection/understanding-security-alerts`.

Next, we will review how to view and investigate any threats with Azure Security Center.

Investigating threats with Azure Security Center

In *Chapter 11*, *Security Monitoring and Reporting*, we enabled and configured the standard version of Azure Security Center to gain the benefits of all the available premium features. ATP is part of the standard feature for your Azure environment, including your Windows machines. To view and investigate any threats that have been triggered by Azure Security Center, do the following:

1. Log in to `https://portal.azure.com`.
2. Search for **Security Center** and open it.
3. Click on **Security Alerts** within the **Threat Protection** section.
4. Here, you will see all the generated alerts from your environment:

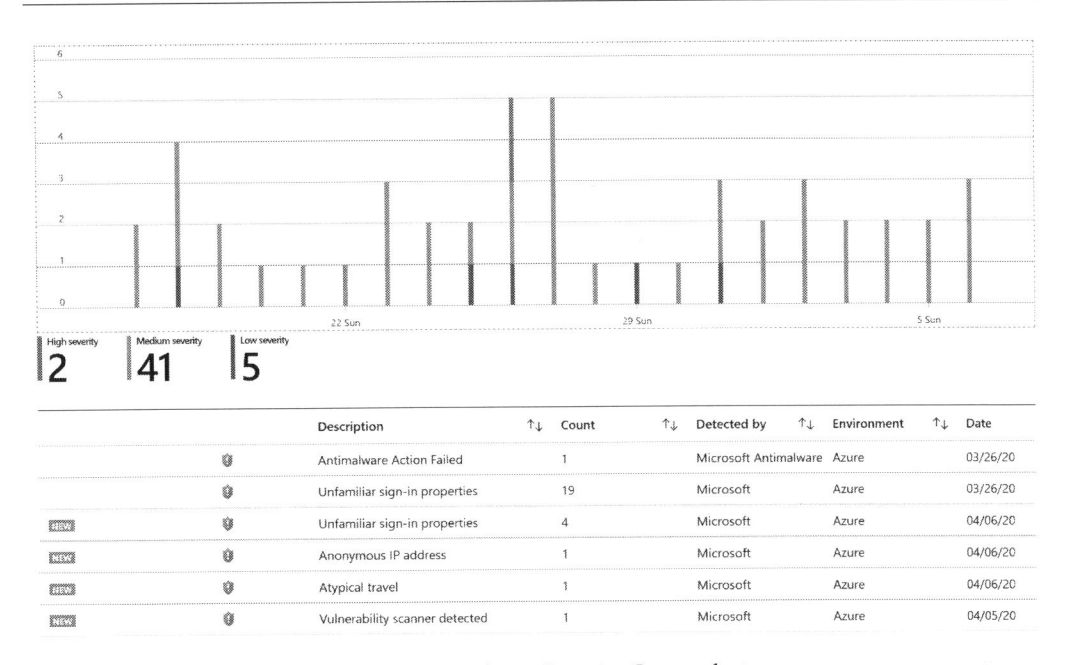

		Description	↑↓	Count	↑↓	Detected by	↑↓	Environment	↑↓	Date
		Antimalware Action Failed		1		Microsoft Antimalware		Azure		03/26/20
		Unfamiliar sign-in properties		19		Microsoft		Azure		03/26/20
NEW		Unfamiliar sign-in properties		4		Microsoft		Azure		04/06/20
NEW		Anonymous IP address		1		Microsoft		Azure		04/06/20
NEW		Atypical travel		1		Microsoft		Azure		04/06/20
NEW		Vulnerability scanner detected		1		Microsoft		Azure		04/05/20

Figure 12.21 – Azure Security Center alerts

To further investigate an alert, simply click on the alert and you are provided with additional details. In addition, you will be provided with any available remediation steps by scrolling further down the details page. The following is an example of the details page of an **Antimalware Action Failed** alert:

Antimalware Action Failed

General information

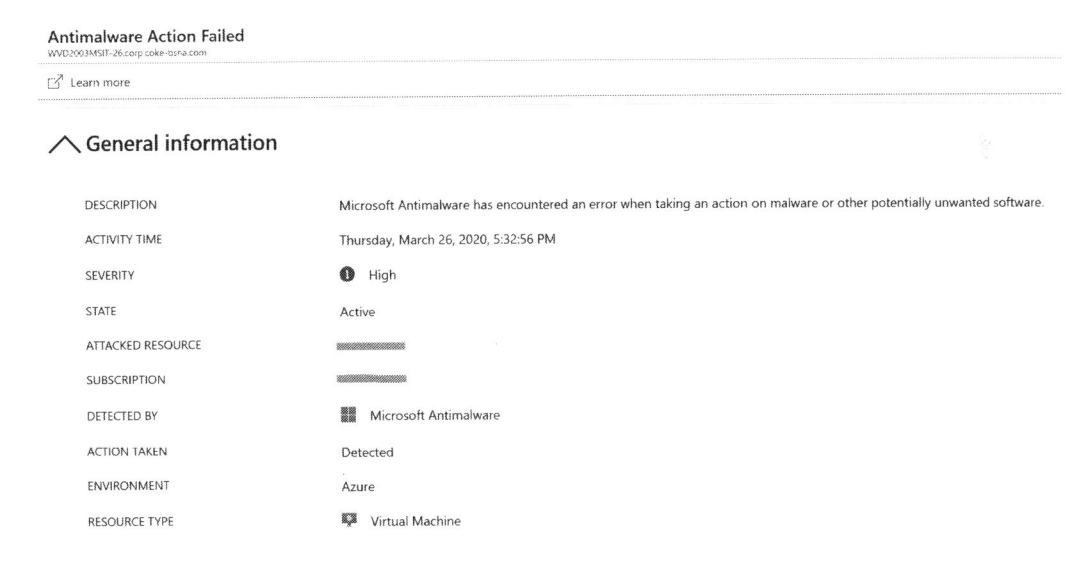

DESCRIPTION	Microsoft Antimalware has encountered an error when taking an action on malware or other potentially unwanted software.
ACTIVITY TIME	Thursday, March 26, 2020, 5:32:56 PM
SEVERITY	High
STATE	Active
ATTACKED RESOURCE	
SUBSCRIPTION	
DETECTED BY	Microsoft Antimalware
ACTION TAKEN	Detected
ENVIRONMENT	Azure
RESOURCE TYPE	Virtual Machine

Figure 12.22 – Azure Security Center alert details

To ensure you receive alerts to your SOC, within the Azure Security Center management console, click on **Pricing & Settings** in the left-side navigation panel, click on your subscription name, then click on **Email notifications** to configure an email notification for high-severity alerts. You can also use the **Workflow automation** section to provide additional dynamics for your alerts, in addition to using the **Continuous export** section to export alerts to a SIEM.

A nice benefit to provide additional insight into your alerts is the security alert map, which provides a visual of where your alerts are being generated from. To access the map, browse to **Security alerts map** within the **Threat Protection** section and click on it. Within the map, you can click on the circles to view details on the alert:

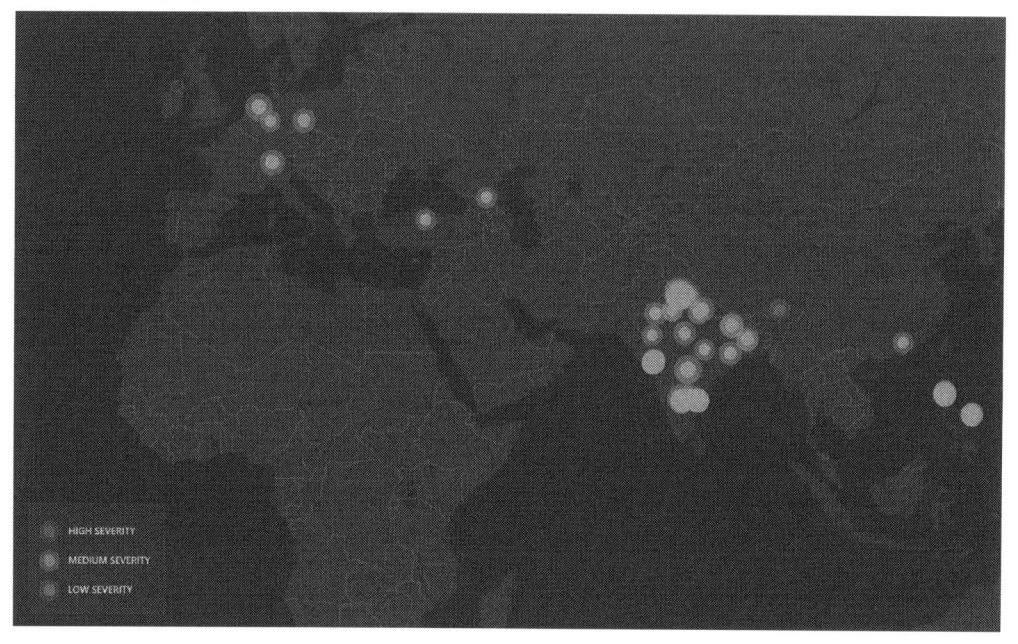

Figure 12.23 – The Azure Security Center security alert map

In the next section, we will provide an overview of Microsoft's cloud-built SIEM service.

Introducing Azure Sentinel

Azure Sentinel is a modernized **SIEM** and **Security Orchestration Automated Response** (**SOAR**) that is built on Microsoft cloud technology. Azure Sentinel is a centralized SIEM solution that provides an intelligent robust life cycle to allow the collection of data, the detection of threats, the investigation of threats, and responses to incidents. Because Azure Sentinel is a cloud-built solution, the ease of setup and integration makes this service an extremely attractive and powerful service for your security needs, especially compared to a traditional SIEM, which typically requires massive amounts of infrastructure and storage to efficiently support the ongoing log collection and compute power to analyze data.

Creating the connection

To set up Azure Sentinel within Azure, follow these steps:

1. Log in to `https://portal.azure.com`.
2. Search for **Azure Sentinel** and open it.
3. Click on **Add** or **Connect Workspace**.
4. Select a workspace to connect to, then click on **Add Azure Sentinel** or click on **Create a new workspace** to build a new Log Analytics workspace to add to Azure Sentinel.
5. It will take a few minutes to create, then you will be redirected to the Azure Sentinel console:

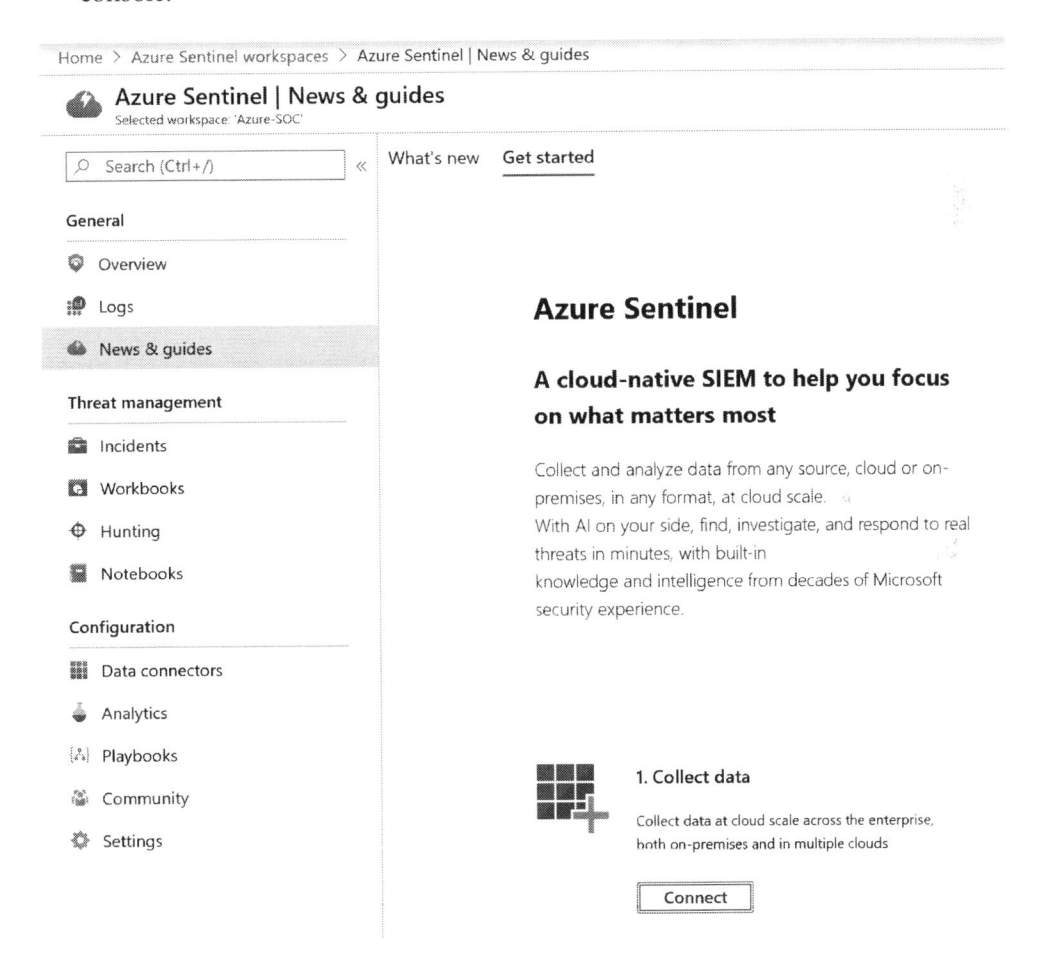

Figure 12.24 – The Azure Sentinel console

As you will have just experienced, your cloud SIEM was deployed within minutes. This goes to show the power of cloud technology and, even more, the benefits for security. Now that Azure Sentinel is set up and ready to use, first, you will need to set up your data sources to begin collecting your data. To do this, follow these steps:

1. Ensure **Azure Sentinel** is open.
2. Click on **Data Connectors** within **Configuration**.
3. Within **Connector name**, select the connector you would like to connect, then click on **Open connector page**. As an example, search for **Azure Security Center** and select the connector, then click on **Open connector page**.
4. Follow the instructions to set up the connector. For Security Center, click on **Select All** or select the individual subscriptions to connect to by clicking on **Connect**. You can also allow the automatic creation of incidents by clicking on **Enable** under **Create incidents**.
5. Click on **Next steps** to review any recommended workbooks, query samples, or relevant analytic templates.
6. Once configured, you have just successfully set up a connector to collect logs within Azure Sentinel:

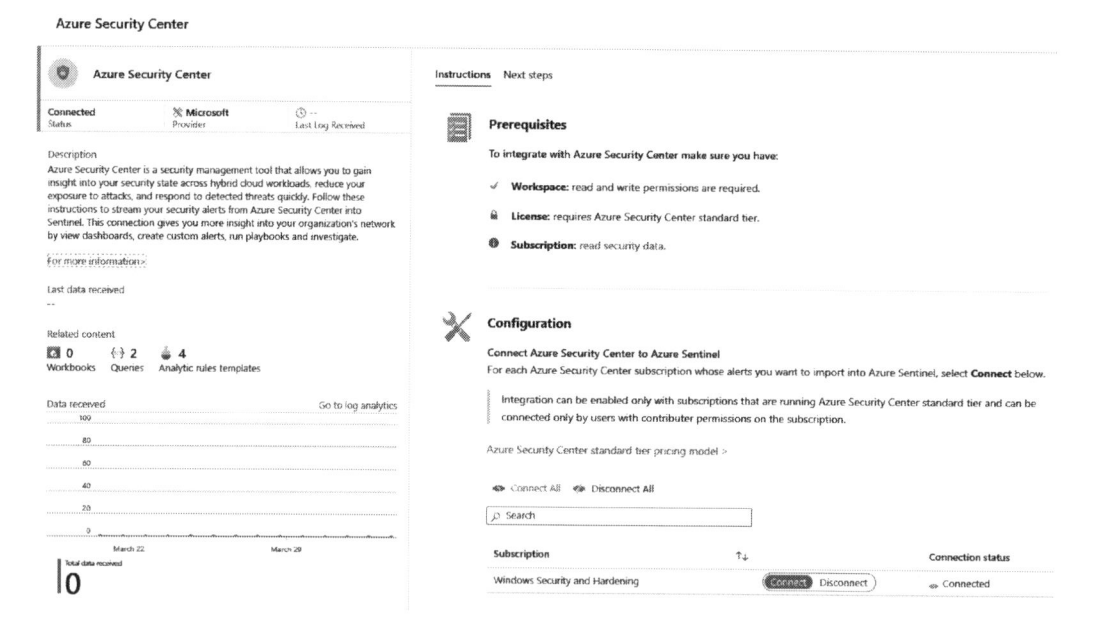

Figure 12.25 – The Azure Security Center connector setup within Azure Sentinel

You can go back to set up any other relevant connectors for your environment. Some more important connectors to provide insight to your users and servers include security events, Azure AD, and Office 365, to name a few.

> **Tip:**
> You can view the latest pricing for Azure Sentinel at `https://azure.microsoft.com/en-us/pricing/details/azure-sentinel/`.

Now that you have your data sources connected, you can get a high-level overview of your environment by accessing the **Overview** menu item within the left-side navigation pane:

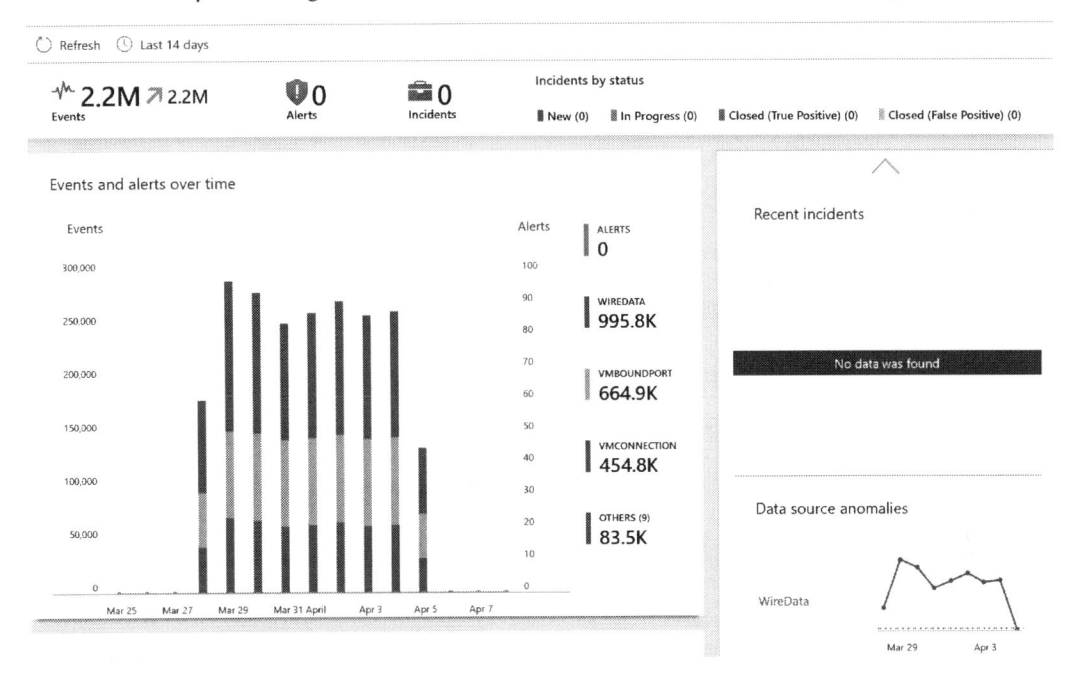

Figure 12.26 – The Azure Sentinel Overview view

Next, you will want to set up **Workbooks** to allow enhanced visibility into your environment and data, along with configuring detections to investigate threats. Both of these can be accessed and configured from the navigation pane on the left within the **Workbooks** and **Analytics** menu items. There is a lot more to learn with Azure Sentinel than what we have covered here, so visit the Azure Sentinel documentation library to learn more:

`https://docs.microsoft.com/en-us/azure/sentinel/`

In the next section, we will review Microsoft Defender Security Center and how it can best help with operational activities.

Microsoft Defender Security Center

The Microsoft Defender Security Center portal is used to investigate and monitor threats directly impacting your Windows devices. To log in to Defender Security Center, visit `https://securitycenter.windows.com`.

Security Center is useful for SOC teams to monitor, track, and respond to security threats using multiple analysis dashboards, automated investigations, real-time remediation actions, and threat-tracking with an incident management system. The landing page after logging in to Security Center takes you to the **Security Operations** dashboard. This dashboard provides a high-level overview for the SOC analyst to quickly explore active alerts, investigations, workstations, and users at risk over the last 30 days. The left column in the portal includes the navigation links to all the features of the ATP service. For more information about the Security Center portal, visit the official Microsoft Docs page at `https://docs.microsoft.com/en-us/windows/security/threat-protection/microsoft-defender-atp/portal-overview`.

Assigning permissions and machine groups

By design, access to view the Security Center portal is locked due to the sensitivity of information available through it. Access to the portal can be managed by using **Role-Based Access Control** (**RBAC**) or by using basic permissions and assigning Azure AD roles. For basic permissions, the following Azure AD roles can be assigned directly to users:

- **Security Administrator** allows full access to the portal, including all system information, alerts, and administrative functions.
- **Security Reader** allows read-only access to log in and view all alerts and other information. You will not be able to perform administrative functions.

For more granular control and to separate permissions based on the SOC job role, use RBAC or roles from the Security Center portal. For example, your organization's SOC may need to read all the data and act on the remediation actions, but they don't need administrative access to change the security settings of your tenant or to enable any features.

> **Tip:**
> If you are using roles for RBAC, any user assigned the **Security Reader** role will be denied access to the portal until they are assigned to a role.

To create a role, go to the settings icon in the navigation pane and select **Roles** under the **Permissions** menu. Click on **+ Add Role** to create a new role. The following screenshot provides an example of a role that a level 3 SOC analyst could be assigned. It would enable permissions to perform almost all actions inside the Security Center portal, except managing the security settings:

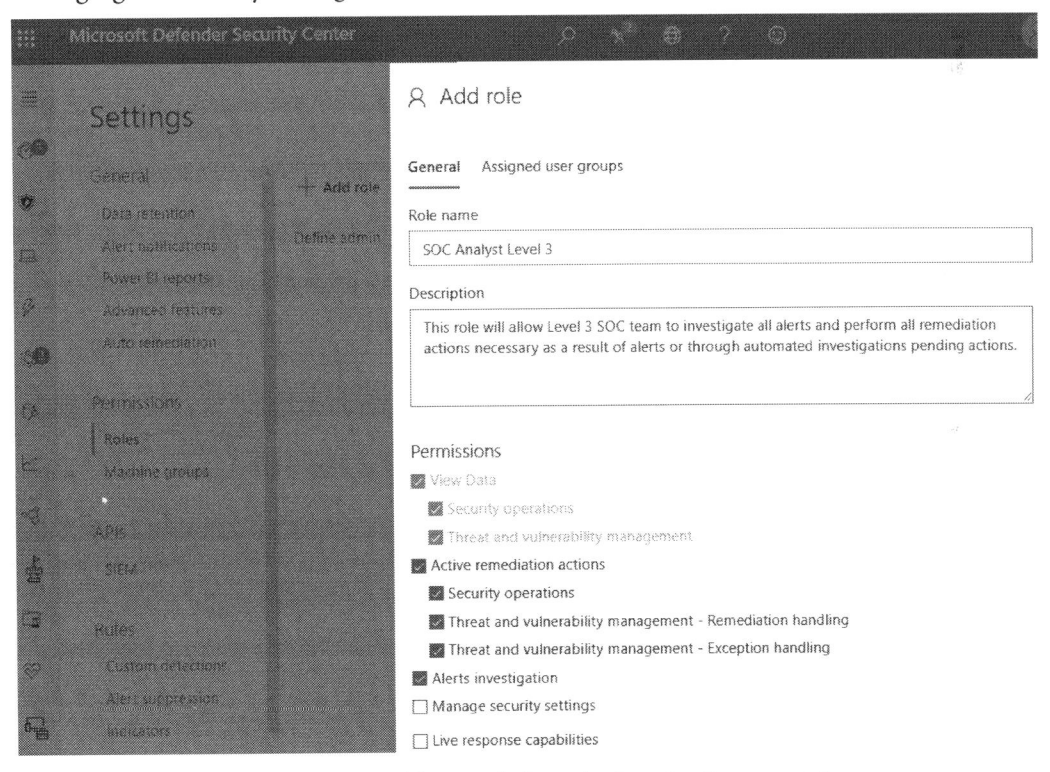

Figure 12.27 – Adding a role from the Security Center portal

Hovering your mouse over each of the **Permissions** settings will provide additional details about what each setting is scoped to include within the portal. More information about managing portal access using RBAC can be found at `https://docs.microsoft.com/en-us/windows/security/threat-protection/microsoft-defender-atp/rbac`.

In addition to creating Microsoft Defender ATP roles for RBAC to the portal, creating machine groups allows you to organize your workstations and devices into groups and assign users access to manage them. Machine groups also allow setting the automation level for remediation actions from the action center and automated investigations, which we will discuss next.

A use case for creating machine groups is if workstations are in different regions or if there is a need to separate servers from Windows 10 workstations. Different teams may be responsible for security remediation on servers compared to workstations or PCs in another region. To grant permissions to manage a machine group, an Azure AD security group must be assigned a role in Microsoft Defender ATP. To create a machine group in the Security Center portal, go to **Settings** and choose **Machine groups** under **Permissions**. Currently, the criteria for members include the following conditions:

- Name
- Domain
- Tag
- OS

Click on the **User access** tag to select an ATP role group that would be responsible for managing this machine group. In the following screenshot, you can see the conditions, as well as the different automation levels that can be set for investigations for the group:

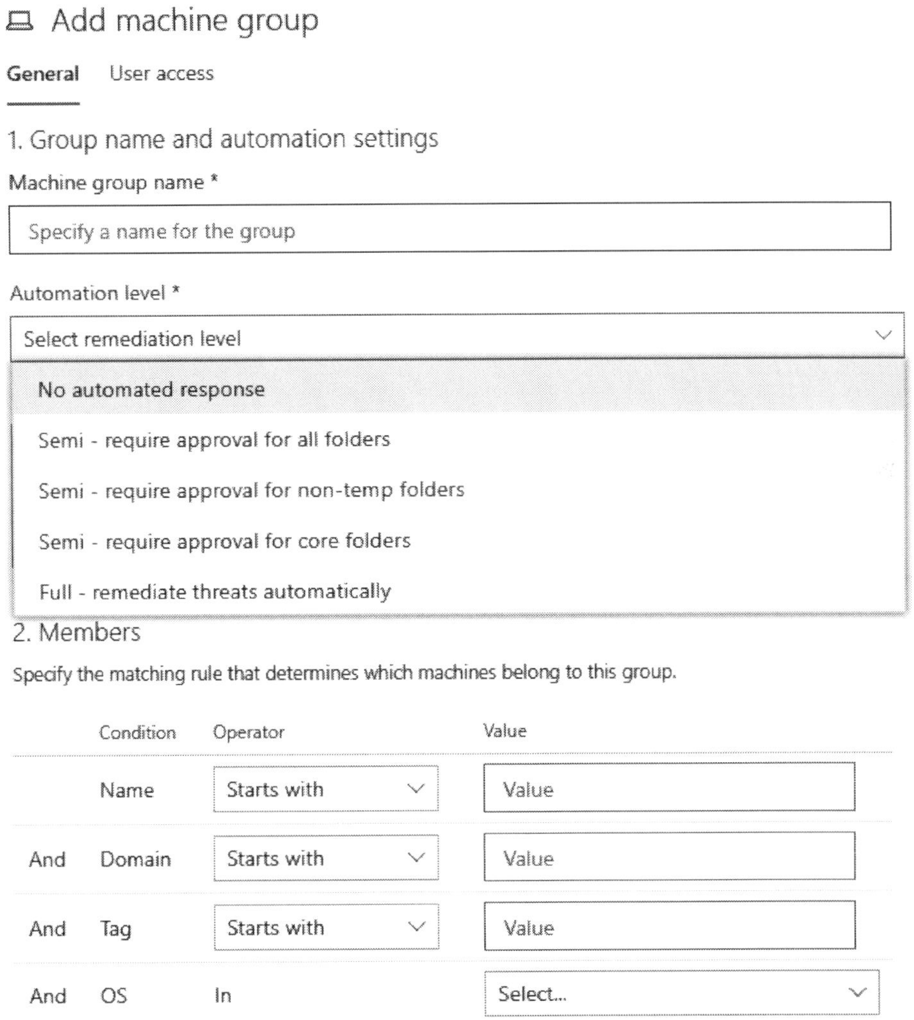

Figure 12.28 – Creating a machine group in Security Center

After specifying the member criteria, there is a preview button to show up to 10 machines that match the conditions specified before saving. In order to better organize your workstations based on the conditions when creating a machine group, it is recommended to leverage tags. Tags are a useful way to create logical groups and provide additional identification that may be limited by the member criteria. Tags can be set manually through the Security Center portal or the `HKEY_LOCAL_MACHINE\SOFTWARE\Policies\Microsoft\Windows Advanced Threat Protection\DeviceTagging` registry key:

- Registry key value (`REG_SZ`): `Group`
- Registry data: `Name of tag`

The registry keys can be deployed through Group Policy or with a Configuration Manager baseline applied to specific collections of devices. Then, use the **Tag** condition when creating a machine group to create the logical grouping in Security Center. More information on managing machine groups and tags can be read at `https://docs.microsoft.com/en-us/windows/security/threat-protection/microsoft-defender-atp/machine-tags`.

Next, let's look at reviewing the alerts queue from the portal.

Reviewing the alerts queue

The alerts queue lists the most recent events that were detected by Microsoft Defender ATP signals over the last 30 days. It's a good place for the SOC team to get a holistic view of all the alerts that were triggered by Defender. The ability to filter the alerts by severity helps to understand any current high-priority risks that devices may pose to the organization. The alerts queue also contains a category column, which Microsoft uses to label the alert type by analyzing the signals against the Enterprise Tactics definitions by MITRE. More information about the Enterprise Tactics categories can be found at `https://attack.mitre.org/tactics/enterprise/`.

The following screenshot is of the Microsoft Defender ATP alerts queue filtered by severity over the last 30 days:

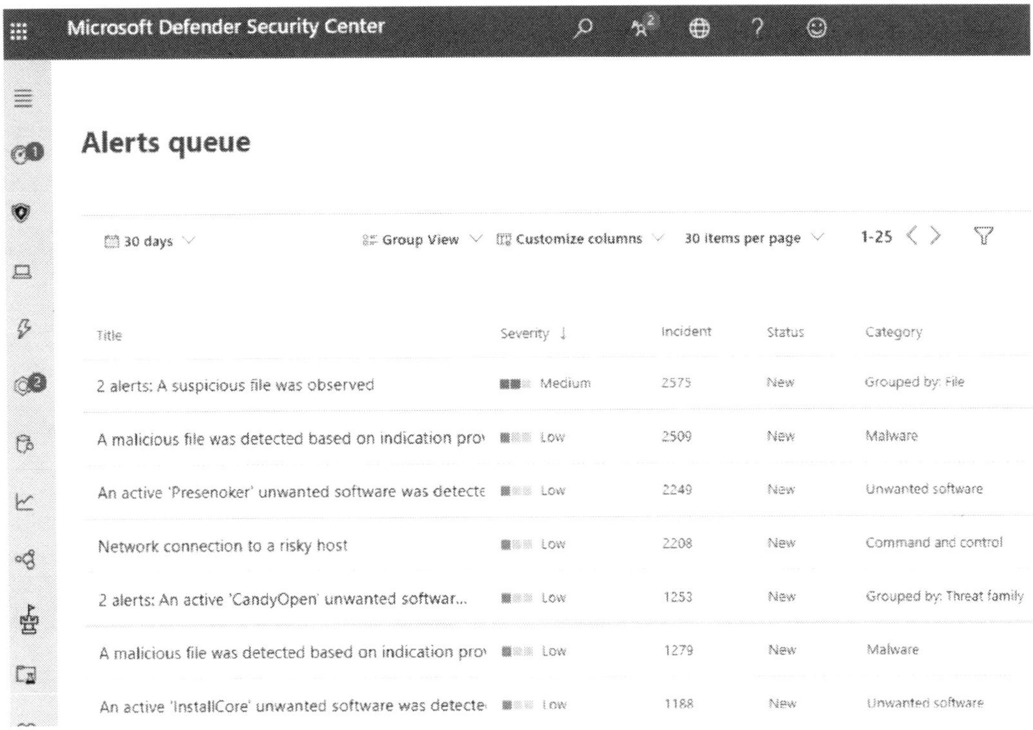

Figure 12.29 – The Microsoft Defender ATP alerts queue

Clicking on each alert will bring up the alert investigation page with additional details and real-time remediation actions. Depending on the number of devices in your organization, the alerts queue can be noisy and can make it difficult for the SOC team to investigate. To help with this, Microsoft Defender ATP includes a feature known as **Automated Investigations**.

Automated Investigations

Automated investigation and remediation in Defender ATP is a feature that can help keep the noise down on alerts and reduce the volume so that the SOC team can focus more on higher-priority incidents that require immediate action. An automated investigation is initially triggered by an alert analyzed by a series of algorithms known as security playbooks. Once the investigation begins, it is automatically placed in the investigations queue for categorization. Here, the analyst can see additional information, such as the alert that triggered the investigation, the assigned investigation ID, the detection source, and entities such as the workstation's PC name. In the following screenshot, you can see an investigation that has a **Pending approval** status and needs to take action from the action center:

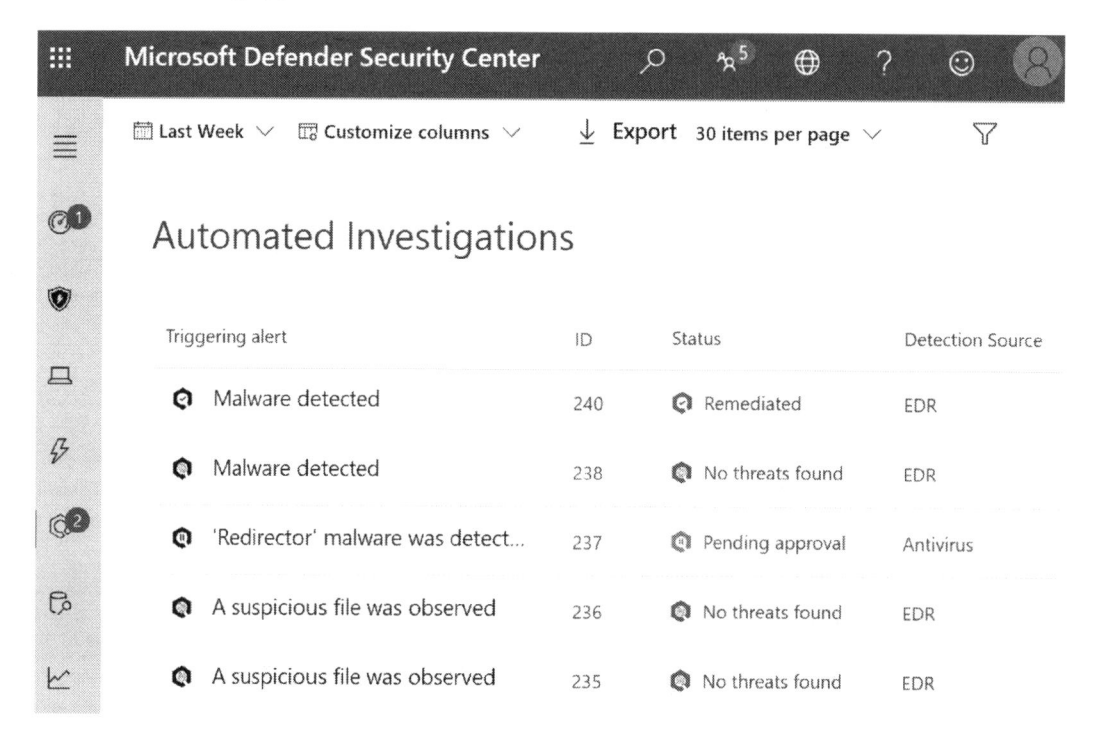

Figure 12.30 – Automated Investigations in the MDATP portal

During an open investigation, any additional alerts generated from the compromised device or similar alerts detected on other workstations will automatically be grouped under the initial investigation.

From the customized column's dropdown, select the **Remediation Actions** option. That will show the number of actions required to perform the recommended remediation, which is determined by the automation level configured for the machine groups. To view the pending actions, open the action center from the **Automated Investigations** menu in the left-side navigation pane. Here, you can view all the pending remediation actions and the remediation history of past actions. In the following screenshot, the investigation ID correlates with the ID from the **Automated Investigations** dashboard:

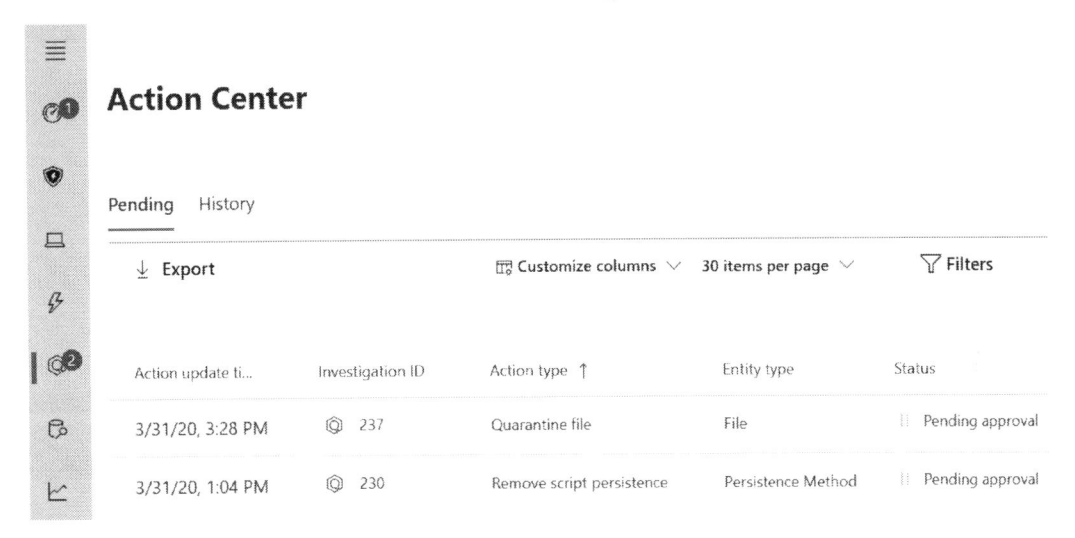

Figure 12.31 – Action Center in the MDATP portal

The action center contains the actions that require user approval before a remediation action can occur. By default, all onboarded machines are placed into an ungrouped machines group, which has the automation level set to require approval. As a result, any investigation that requires action will be placed under a **Pending approval** status and into the action center for review. By setting the automation level to **Full – remediate threats automatically**, all remediation actions will be performed automatically and no approval is needed from the SOC team. To view more information about how threats are remediated with **Automated Investigations**, visit `https://docs.microsoft.com/en-us/windows/security/threat-protection/microsoft-defender-atp/automated-investigations`.

Reviewing the incidents queue

The incidents queue is another place where the SOC analyst can go and review all the incidents that were created in the Security Center portal. Using the incidents system allows an additional view to sort the incidents by severity, the number of active alerts included in the incident, the detection source, and how many machines are affected. The queue also contains the categories based on the MITRE enterprise tactics for each incident. The following screenshot shows the incidents queue in the Security Center portal. By default, only 30 days worth of incidents are shown:

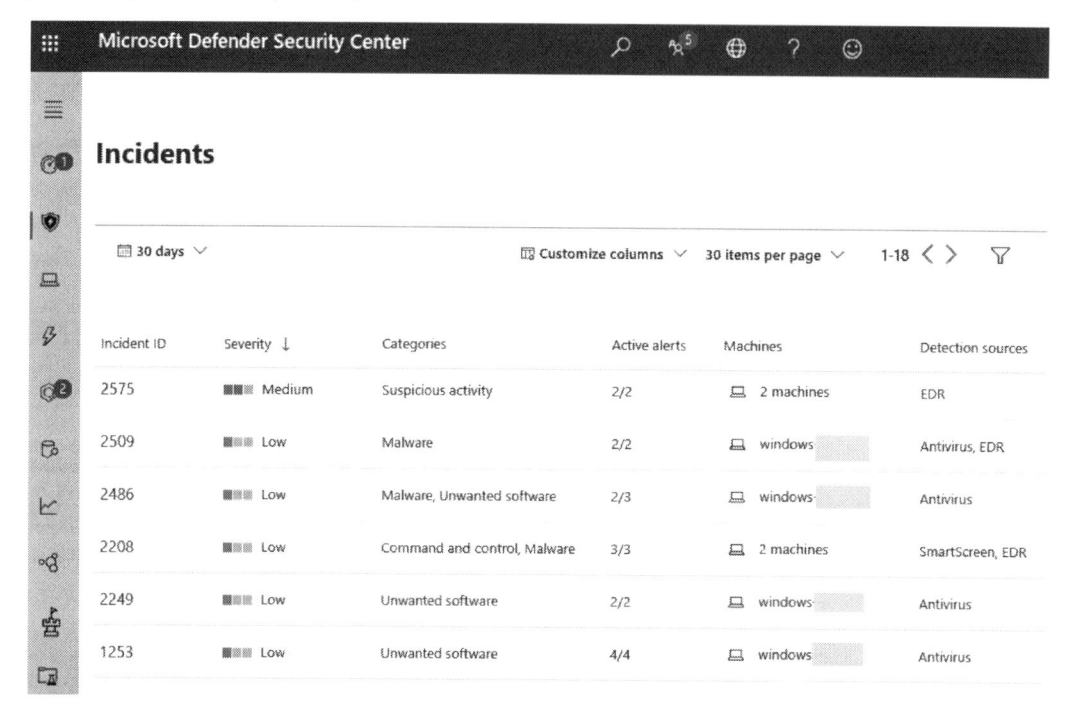

Incident ID	Severity ↓	Categories	Active alerts	Machines	Detection sources
2575	Medium	Suspicious activity	2/2	2 machines	EDR
2509	Low	Malware	2/2	windows-	Antivirus, EDR
2486	Low	Malware, Unwanted software	2/3	windows-	Antivirus
2208	Low	Command and control, Malware	3/3	2 machines	SmartScreen, EDR
2249	Low	Unwanted software	2/2	windows-	Antivirus
1253	Low	Unwanted software	4/4	windows-	Antivirus

Figure 12.32 – The incidents queue in Microsoft Defender ATP

Additional value that the incidents queue provides comes from a service management perspective. Each incident can be assigned an owner for a follow-up and additional investigation. Here, the SOC analyst can set the incident status to an active or resolved state and determine whether the alert is real by setting the classification label as **true** or **false**. Setting the alert classification label helps Microsoft Security Center learn from the alerts and improve the efficiencies of the alert-identifying algorithms and security playbooks.

Selecting an incident will open the quick summary incident management pane in the web browser. This quick view lets you perform actions such as viewing all the alerts tied to the incident, assigning an owner, or quickly setting a classification:

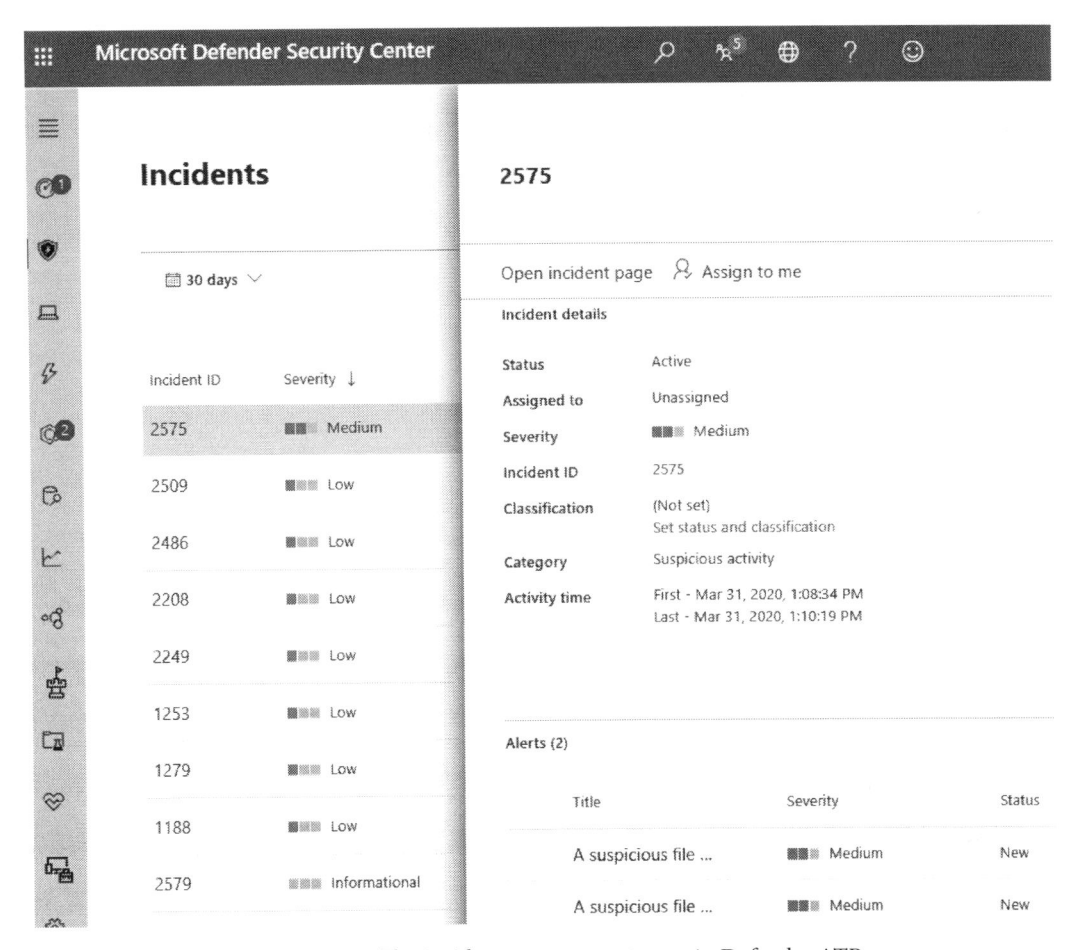

Figure 12.33 – The incident management pane in Defender ATP

Click on **Open incident page** to view the full incident details. The incident page view further breaks down what comprises each incident by sorting alerts, machines, the number of investigations, the evidence that triggered the alerts, and a visual graph to help understand the attack from a graphical perspective. The following screenshot shows the evidence summary that lists all files, processes, and persistence methods that correlated to trigger an alert in Microsoft Defender ATP:

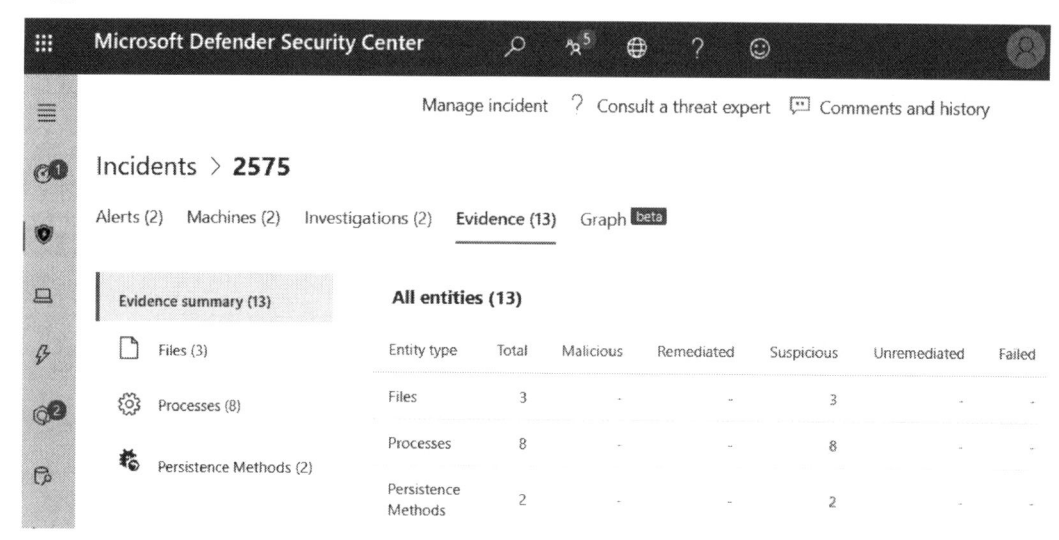

Figure 12.34 – The evidence summary of an incident

Select the **Graph** option to visually show how the attack played out. Clicking on each circle will pull up additional information about the machine, file, or process identified in the graphical view:

Figure 12.35 – A graphical view of an incident

> **Important note**
> The **Graph** option is currently in beta release at the time of writing.

Additional information about investigating and managing incidents in the Security Center incidents queue can be found at https://docs.microsoft.com/en-us/windows/security/threat-protection/microsoft-defender-atp/view-incidents-queue.

We have just covered an overview of how the SOC can leverage Microsoft Defender Security Center for daily operational security tasks. Next, let's look at how organizations can approach BCP and DR.

Planning for business continuity and DR

To finish this chapter, we are going to cover BCP and DR and the importance they play as they relate to security. When we look at BCP and DR, it is important to understand that these are separate functions that serve different purposes. BCP is a business-specific function that focuses on the business as a whole to ensure the continued operation of the business. The DR function is technical in nature and focuses on the recovery of IT infrastructure and systems. The DR plan falls within the larger BCP plan for the entire organization.

BCP is not a simple plan to build and put in place as it requires a lot of time and resources to build the plan. In addition to building a well-documented plan, it is just as important to ensure that everyone is familiar with the plan and that it has been coordinated and tested in some way. When it comes to executing the BCP plan in a real-world scenario, you don't want to be doing so for the first time without at least being familiar with the process and steps involved. An example of a situation that could require the execution of BCP includes a natural disaster, such as hurricanes, earthquakes, and floods. Depending on the severity, fires or power outages are also examples of incidents that could cause a BCP plan to execute, as well as the more common threats that we see today, such as cyberattacks, which can easily bring a business to a halt based on their dependency on technology.

At the time of writing, we are currently undergoing one of the biggest BCP exercises of our lifetime—the COVID-19 pandemic. This situation has forced most of the world to shift to a fully remote workplace almost overnight, a situation that most companies were certainly not prepared for. Fortunately, technology has enabled many businesses to continue their operations, but the situation has revealed a major gap for many—that of security. There will be a lot of lessons learned from this situation, and it is one that I'm sure will have many companies re-visiting their BCP strategy and looking at security very closely. This situation alone will bring more visibility to the importance of BCP and this will be an area of focus for many companies for years to come.

As we look at today's threats in the security space, there has been an increase in advanced cyberattacks, and we are seeing more sophisticated attacks around ransomware, which is preventing businesses from operating efficiently, or even at all in some instances. Many businesses aren't prepared for these levels of attacks and it could take them days, weeks, or even months to get back to normal operation. There's a chance that if a business isn't prepared for these types of attacks, they could even lose business-critical data and in some instances, go out of business, depending on the damage. Therefore, it is critical that your organization fully understands the possible threats to your organization and how you should best deal with them with a well-defined BCP plan that allows ongoing operations in the event of a cyberattack. One important part of this process as it relates to security is to ensure your leadership team has gone through some form of cyber-incident tabletop or simulation exercise. These types of exercises will show the importance of having a good BCP plan and will provide insight into some of the difficult decisions that may need to be made as part of an actual event.

When we look at DR, it's just as important to have a well-defined and documented plan specifically for DR based on its specialty. This plan will fall within the overall BCP program, but the execution of a DR plan will be unique and based on the situation, it may not impact the entire business. As stated, DR is focused on the technical aspects and ensuring that the technology, systems, and applications that support the business continue to operate in an outage. As mentioned earlier, events that impact BCP will most likely have some form of impact on your systems and may require the execution of DR. Some examples include a natural disaster, such as a hurricane or a fire taking out a data center, as well as a cyber incident that could take down all your systems.

Your DR plan may not need to be fully executed depending on the situation. If a business-critical application becomes corrupted, you may only need to execute DR for that specific application to ensure restoration. There are many different instances that could cause DR to be required, so it's critical to account for each of these scenarios and make sure you are able to accommodate recovery for individual systems or entire data centers. An important part of your DR plan is understanding the impact of a service or function and the **Maximum Tolerable Downtime** (**MTD**) a service or function can withstand before your business is negatively impacted. Two other important factors that also come into play are the **Recovery Time Objective** (**RTO**) and **Recovery Point Objective** (**RPO**). The RTO is the maximum amount of time a system can be unavailable for before negatively impacting a service or function within the business and preventing it from being able to operate normally again. The RPO is the point in time in which the service or function can afford to lose data without being negatively impacted.

As you build out your recovery plan and understand the expected restoration of each system based on the RTO and RPO, you are going to need to ensure that you have the technology and proper planning in place to meet those requirements. A few examples of considerations include the following:

- Having **High-Availability (HA)** configurations for systems may help restoration from any local issues within a data center but will come at a cost.
- Understanding your backup strategy as it relates to full backups, incremental backups, and differential backups, as well as considering how often each backup needs to be taken and retained.
- Considering what type of failover is needed for a complete restoration of a data center should you have a cold, warm, or hot site available.

All of these considerations will depend on the business requirements and needs, along with the cost. Having a hot site on standby will come at a much greater cost than that of a warm or cold site. More importantly, as you implement your DR plan and backup strategies, the role security plays in each should be understood. Ensuring that your data is backed up securely, that any off-site storage of data is secure, and that your standby data centers maintain the same level of security as your primary data centers should all be taken into consideration. Referring back to the ransomware cyberattack creates new challenges for DR, also. These types of attacks can make your entire network and systems inoperable and unrecoverable, so having an offline back-up system that is isolated from your production system will be critical. If you rely on highly available technologies only and have back-up systems connected to your network without the correct measures in place, a well-executed ransomware attack could also impact your back-up or failover systems. For many, a full, clean restoration may be the only option in some cyberattack situations.

Thorough BCP and DR planning requires a lot of thought and collaboration between both the IT architecture and the operations and security teams, as well as the business stakeholders. We want to ensure that the importance of these activities is called out and accounted for as they influence the structure of your overall security program. One of the biggest advantages of having an effective BCP and DR plan today is the use of the cloud. The cloud allows the enablement of services at a pace not seen before. The ability to span your data center, services, and applications regionally or even geographically all over the globe allows the true redundancy of services, including isolated backups of your data.

There are many frameworks available to assist with your BCP/DR programs. Since we've referenced NIST throughout this book, we will also reference the *SP 800-34 Rev. 1, Contingency Planning Guide for Federal Information Systems* NIST framework publication as a great resource for your BCP/DR planning:

```
https://csrc.nist.gov/publications/detail/sp/800-34/rev-1/final
```

Summary

In this chapter, we covered security operations and reviewed the tools and technologies available from Microsoft that offer enterprise-class protection. We began the chapter with an introduction to the SOC and the importance of its place in an enterprise. We then introduced the M365 security portal and provided an overview of the feature. Next, we reviewed Microsoft's version of a CASB, known as MCAS. Then, we learned how to activate an instance of Azure ATP and review alerts throughout the cyber kill chain.

Other tools and features reviewed in this chapter included Azure Security Center to review and investigate alerts, Microsoft's SIEM, known as Azure Sentinel, and Microsoft Defender Security Center for alert and incident management. We finished off the chapter with an overview of BCP and DR.

In the next chapter, *Chapter 13*, *Testing and Auditing*, we will review validating controls to ensure the security measures that have been agreed on are actually in place. We will then review vulnerability scanning and testing to ensure your controls are working correctly, before finishing off with an overview of penetration testing and remediation.

13
Testing and Auditing

In this chapter, we will provide the details around testing and auditing your environment that will help validate and ensure that due diligence has been executed within your security program. The challenge we face when deploying recommendations, hardening, and baselines is proving that they are in place and doing what they are designed to do. The IT department as a program may have obligations to leadership, board stakeholders, shareholders, and regulators to prove that you have implemented the recommended controls depending on your business or industry. Helping with providing evidence is where testing and auditing comes into play. To prove that controls are in place is why we audit, and it is even better to have a third-party company execute the audit. We test to ensure that our controls are doing what they are designed to do. Without testing, we fail to validate whether the controls work.

The first section we will cover in this chapter is validating that the controls that you have implemented are in place. We will review audits and assessments and what they are, along with reviewing the different types of audits. We will also discuss vendor management and the importance of ensuring vendors are following the agreed-upon controls. This process will also require due diligence around collecting and reviewing audits and questionnaires for validation.

In the following section, we will review vulnerability scanning and testing to help ensure your implemented controls and configurations are working correctly. We will look at the different scanning types, including scanning options, within Azure. Next, we will provide an overview of penetration testing and cover the different methods and steps taken as part of a test. Finally, we will review security awareness and training and the importance of this program within your environment.

In this chapter, we will cover the following topics:

- Validating controls
- Vulnerability scanning
- Planning for penetration testing
- Security awareness and training

Technical requirements

In order to follow along with the overviews in this chapter and complete the how-to instructions, the following requirements are recommended:

- A Microsoft cloud services account to access the Service Trust portal: `https://servicetrust.microsoft.com/`
- An Azure subscription with contributor rights: `https://azure.microsoft.com/en-us/free/`
- Azure Security Center (free/standard): `https://docs.microsoft.com/en-us/azure/security-center/security-center-pricing`
- Microsoft Defender **Advanced Threat Protection** (**ATP**) (Windows 10 E5/M365 E5): `https://docs.microsoft.com/en-us/windows/security/threat-protection/microsoft-defender-atp/minimum-requirements`
- An Office 365 ATP Plan 2 license: `https://docs.microsoft.com/en-us/office365/servicedescriptions/office-365-advanced-threat-protection-service-description`

Let's start by looking at validating your environment controls.

Validating controls

Validating the controls put in place is a very important task and one that must not be overlooked. Enforcing some form of validation program to ensure the controls you documented as part of your policies and baselines are enforced will help provide additional certainty and peace of mind. Having a second set of eyes to review anything you implement in the IT and security fields is always a good idea. This doesn't necessarily mean an incident will never happen, but it does show that you are executing due diligence and doing what is right.

In addition, it's important to validate that the vendors you partner with also maintain the same level of detail in protecting their environment as you do. The more we move data to vendor-managed cloud and SaaS services, the more due diligence is needed regarding making sure auditing access and validating controls are also in place in the vendor's environment. This is changing the dynamic of how we work in IT and security compared to the traditional world of on-premises. Having a detailed onboarding process for vendors with collaboration from other teams, such as legal and procurement, is critical to ensure that nothing is missed.

> **Important note**
> Validating controls—both internal and external—requires time and, in many cases, collaboration with different teams.

First, let's look at auditing and what it entails. An audit is a process that checks the intended controls are in place. At a high level, you will typically see two types of audits:

- An **internal audit** is typically completed by an internal team employed by the organization to conduct audits within the business.

- An **external audit** is completed by a third-party company. The idea behind an external audit is to avoid any conflict of interest within the organization and to have an independent party with no ties to the organization complete the audit. Depending on your organization and the industry it operates in, this could be a requirement.

Typically, in an internal audit scenario, the auditing team will report directly to the CEO or the board of directors and not internally to the IT department or security. Having an audit team report to the same executive as the team that implements the controls is not a good idea. This helps ensure accountability, checks, and balances and avoids conflict of interest.

When looking at audits, one of the more common practices and well-known reporting offerings is that of **System and Organization Controls** (**SOC**)—not to be confused with the security operating center. The SOC services are part of the **American Institute of Certified Public Accountants** (**AICPA**). It's a good idea to become more accustomed with SOC and other auditing standards within the industry, especially as you look to adopt more cloud services. As you meet with vendors and subscribe to services, you are going
to want to ensure that these types of reports have been completed and are in place for your vendors.

There are three different SOC reports to be familiar with:

- **SOC 1** reports focus on the financial aspect of an organization, ensuring the correct financial controls and reporting are in place. This report comes with two types of reports:

    --**Type 1** reports are based on the feedback and description of controls provided by management, completed at a specific point

    --**Type 2** reports are more involved and look to test the effectiveness of the controls in place over a period of time

- **SOC 2** reports are focused more on the technology and security aspects of an organization to better protect users' data and reduce risk. The specific controls measured include security, availability, processing integrity, confidentiality, and privacy. Like SOC 1, there is a type 1 and type 2 report that follows the same format. SOC 2 reports are intended for internal use only and vendors will require a **Non-Disclosure Agreement** (**NDA**) to be signed in order to view them.

- **SOC 3** reports take the output of SOC 2 reports and write them in a more readable format that is less technical. This allows them to be made available for anyone to access and view.

You can view more information about the AICPA SOC services at `https://www.aicpa.org/soc`.

> **Important note**
>
> ISO 27000 is another common certification family to validate that controls from the ISO framework have been implemented. The ISO certification is used more widely (internationally) than SOC. You can view more information about the ISO standards at `https://www.iso.org/isoiec-27001-information-security.html`.

Even if your business is not required to complete an audit, it may be a good idea to go through the process of an SOC engagement to ensure that you are maintaining the highest level of standards for the organization.

The job of managing vendors is becoming a lot more challenging than it was in the past. Onboarding vendors has always been a thorough and lengthy process, involving teams such as legal and procurement to ensure contracts are written and executed correctly to reduce any liability. As more services are shifting to the cloud and we are moving our users and customer data onto third-party systems and environments, the onboarding process has become significantly more rigorous with additional requirements needed. This is only becoming more challenging as you need to deal with current and new privacy requirements that must be followed. As part of this onboarding process, it is crucial that you include the right personnel from both the technical and security teams for review. Nowadays, there are probably very few contracts that don't include some use of technology and I'd imagine that at some point, all contracts with vendors will involve some form of technology that needs to be reviewed by the technical and security teams.

From a technical and security standpoint, one recommendation is to implement a security questionnaire or risk assessment that will help assess and better understand the vendor being onboarded. A couple of third-party questionnaires that are commonly used include the following:

- The **Consensus Assessment Initiative Questionnaire (CAIQ)**, which is made available by the **Cloud Security Alliance (CSA)**: `https://cloudsecurityalliance.org/artifacts/consensus-assessments-initiative-questionnaire-v3-1/`
- The **Standardized Information Gathering (SIG)** questionnaire, provided by SFG Shared Assessments: `https://sharedassessments.org/sig/`

In addition to collecting a questionnaire, you will need to request additional documents to ensure that a thorough review and assessment has been completed. Additional items to request include the following:

- Third-party audit reports—for example, an SOC 2 report or ISO 27001 certification
- Any penetration testing results or those that have been flagged as critical/high-risk findings
- If available, an information security management program policy or overview
- A business continuity plan and disaster recovery plan
- Any other supporting audit/risk/security documentation for review

> **Important note**
> It's important to remember that this process is not just a one-time exercise but one that needs a life cycle attached to it. At a minimum, annual reviews of your vendors should be occurring as audits and certifications expire.

As a Microsoft customer, the same due diligence is required as with any other vendor. To help with this, Microsoft has a public portal dedicated to providing audit and compliance reports for all of its cloud services, known as the Service Trust portal. To visit the Service Trust portal, go to https://servicetrust.microsoft.com/:

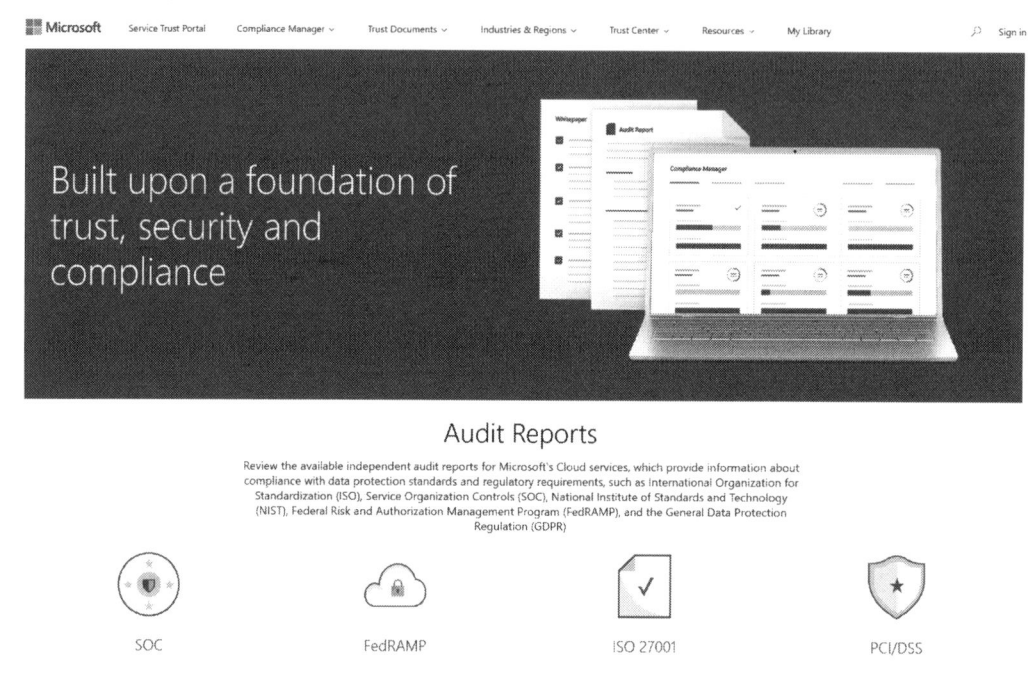

Figure 13.1 – The Microsoft Service Trust portal

If you browse through the menu at the top of the web page, you will see several sub-menu options that provide access to different resources. To access the audit-specific documents, take the following steps:

1. Ensure you are on the Service Trust portal home page, found at https://servicetrust.microsoft.com/.
2. Click on **Trust Documents**.

3. Click on **Audit Reports**.
4. Scroll down and you will see the different reports and certificates available.
5. Click on **SOC Reports** to view the SOC-specific reports from Microsoft.
6. Select the report you would like to view, and then sign in with your Microsoft account to access it:

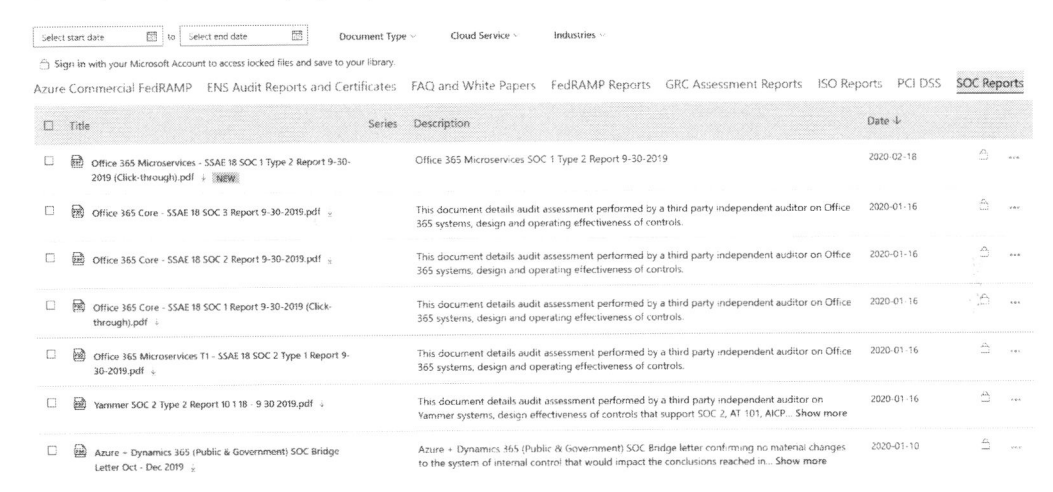

Figure 13.2 – SOC reports for Microsoft

In addition to viewing the reports provided by Microsoft, you can also assess your own cloud environment from within Azure. As part of the Security Center service within Azure, there is a **Regulatory compliance** section that will check your environment against the compliances available. Not all the controls will be automated, but the feature continues to be enhanced and it is a great tool to help ensure you strive for a compliant cloud environment. There are many regulatory compliances available for reference. To access the **Regulatory compliance** section, take the following steps:

1. Log in to `https://portal.azure.com`.
2. Search for **Security Center** and open it.

3. Click on **Regulatory compliance** in the left-side menu within the **POLICY & COMPLIANCE** section:

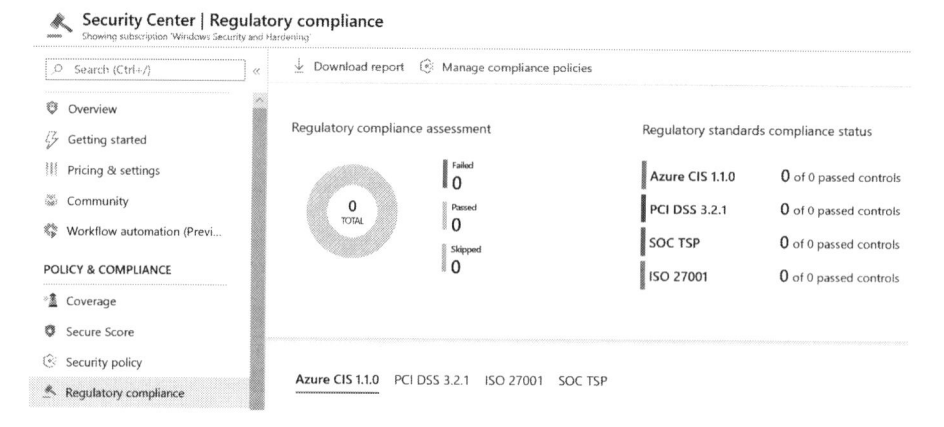

Figure 13.3 – The Azure Regulatory compliance console

> **Important note**
>
> In order to use the **Regulatory compliance** feature, you will need to upgrade your Security Center plan from Free to Standard, which will add an additional cost to your subscription. The current costs can be found at `https://azure.microsoft.com/en-us/pricing/details/security-center/`.

The following screenshot shows the ISO 27001 compliance outline and some controls that are specific to your Windows virtual machines to ensure they are best protected:

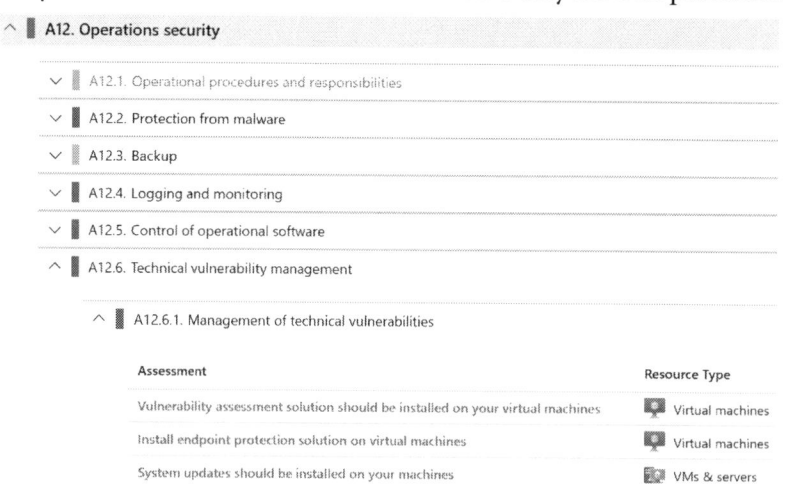

Figure 13.4 – Example of the ISO 27001 compliance outline within Azure

In this section, we reviewed what is needed to validate controls, primarily focusing on auditing, and then we looked at what resources Microsoft provides for review. In the next section, we will look at vulnerability scanning and testing tools to ensure the hardening of your Windows devices.

Vulnerability scanning

In addition to auditing, which only validates controls, you need to ensure you have an on-going vulnerability scanning program. This will provide a lot of insight into your environment and will help to surface any vulnerabilities or weaknesses that exist. Let's take a look at what a vulnerability scan involves.

Preparing for a vulnerability scan

These scans or assessments look for, and identify, known vulnerabilities within your environment or systems. For example, a vulnerability scan may detect that a version and/or file that has been identified has a known vulnerability. Once a scan is complete, a report is generated that highlights any identified vulnerabilities and improvement actions. They are typically scheduled to run automatically. The following is a list of common types of vulnerability assessments that are used:

- Network/wireless assessments
- Web application assessments
- Application assessments
- Database assessments
- Host-based assessments

There are many vulnerability assessment tools available at your disposal. Some of the more common tools that you may be familiar with include the following:

- Qualys: `https://www.qualys.com/`
- Nessus: `https://www.tenable.com/products/nessus`
- OpenVAS: `https://www.openvas.org/`
- Nikto: `https://cirt.net/nikto2`

Included with Azure Security Center, which was covered in detail in *Chapter 11*, *Security Monitoring and Reporting*, and *Chapter 12*, *Security Operations*, is the ability to enable a built-in vulnerability assessment for your Azure virtual machines, including on Windows and multiple Linux versions. This assessment is part of the Standard offering and is powered by Qualys. If you can't take advantage of the Security Center scanner because you are not a Microsoft Azure customer, you will need to review other third-party tools, signposted in the preceding list, to execute an assessment on your Windows servers and other resources.

The following article provides additional information about the vulnerability scanner, including the supported operating systems:

https://docs.microsoft.com/en-us/azure/security-center/built-in-vulnerability-assessment

To enable the assessment for your virtual machines, follow these steps:

1. Log in to https://portal.azure.com.
2. Search for **Security Center** and open it.
3. Click on **Compute & apps** in the left-side menu under the **Resource Security Hygiene** section.
4. Search for **Enable the built-in vulnerability assessment solution on virtual machines (powered by Qualys)** and click to open it.
5. Select the virtual machines you would like to deploy to, and then click on **Remediate**:

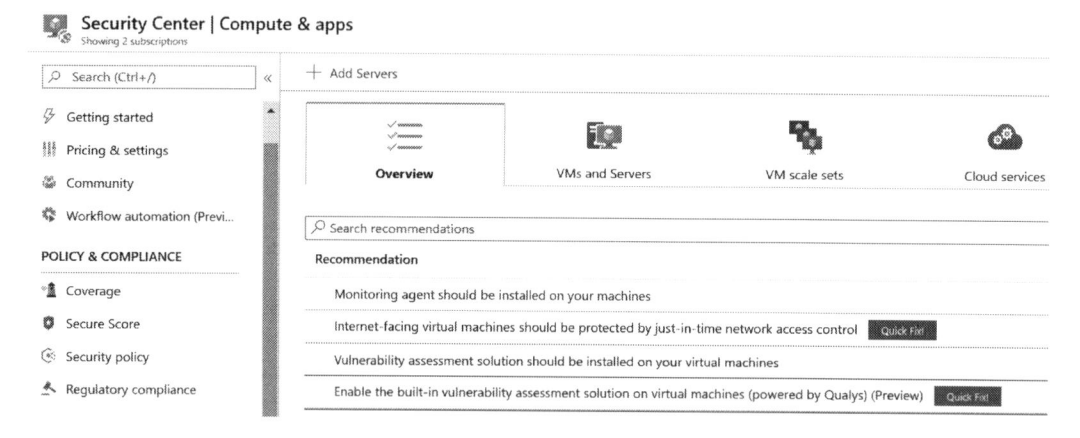

Figure 13.5 – Enabling a vulnerability assessment on your virtual machines

Once the virtual machines have been remediated to receive the vulnerability assessment, you will be able to view any discovered vulnerabilities by following these steps:

1. From the Azure portal, browse to Security Center.
2. Click on **Recommendations** from the left-side menu.
3. Within the main screen, look for **Remediate vulnerabilities** and expand the section.
4. Click on **Remediate vulnerabilities found on your virtual machines (powered by Qualys)** to view all the findings, as in the following screenshot:

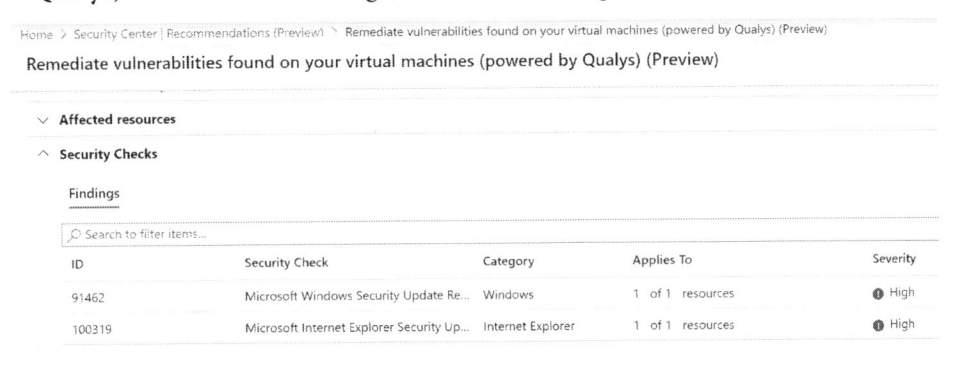

Figure 13.6 – Viewing vulnerabilities found on your virtual machines

The following article provides additional information on the vulnerability assessment, along with options to deploy it as part of the Free tier:

```
https://docs.microsoft.com/en-us/azure/security-center/
security-center-vulnerability-assessment-recommendations
```

> **Tip**
>
> The following reference guide provides a list of the recommendations that you may see within the **Compute and app recommendations** section from the scans within Azure Security Center:
>
> ```
> https://docs.microsoft.com/en-us/azure/security-
> center/recommendations-reference
> ```

For your Windows clients, you can access the **Threat & Vulnerability Management** feature included with Microsoft Defender ATP to view any vulnerabilities on your devices. To access this feature, take the following steps:

1. Log in to the Microsoft Defender ATP portal by going to `https://securitycenter.windows.com`.
2. Click on the menu at the top left, and then expand **Threat & Vulnerability Management**.
3. Click on the **Weakness** option to view all the identified vulnerabilities:

Weaknesses

131 Vulnerabilities

Name	Severity	CVSS	Related Software	Age	Published on	Updated on	Threats	Expose
CVE-2020-0772	High	7.8	Windows Server 2008 (+13 more)	a day	3/10/20	3/10/20		N/A
CVE-2020-0834	High	7.8	Windows Server 1909 (+9 more)	a day	3/10/20	3/10/20		N/A
CVE-2020-0822	High	7.8	Windows Server 2008 (+13 more)	a day	3/10/20	3/10/20		N/A
CVE-2020-0800	High	7.8	Windows Rt 8.1 (+9 more)	a day	3/10/20	3/10/20		N/A
CVE-2020-0791	High	7.8	Windows Server 2008 (+13 more)	a day	3/10/20	3/10/20		N/A
CVE-2020-0866	High	7.8	Windows Rt 8.1 (+9 more)	a day	3/10/20	3/10/20		N/A
CVE-2020-0684	High	8.8	Windows Server 2008 (+13 more)	a day	3/10/20	3/10/20		N/A
CVE-2020-0779	High	7.0	Windows Server 2008 (+13 more)	a day	3/10/20	3/10/20		N/A

Figure 13.7 – The Microsoft Defender ATP threat and vulnerability console

Next, we will look at the different methods used for tests within your environment.

Planning for penetration testing

Penetration testing is an extremely important function of your security program that shouldn't be overlooked these days. In general, penetration testing validates whether a risk exists by performing a specific task within your environment against systems, applications, devices, users, and so on to exploit the identified vulnerability and prove success. It is typically executed by a security professional who is skilled in hacking techniques and is commonly referred to as ethical hacking. The ethical hacker's role is to try and replicate what a malicious hacker would try to accomplish.

Penetration tests can be executed externally, to simulate an outside threat trying to break in, or internally, to simulate an insider threat and replicate a breach of your environment. There are many different types of penetration tests and they will typically cover the following areas:

- Systems and servers
- Web applications
- Databases
- Networks (internal/external/DMZ), including wireless
- Social engineering, such as phishing simulations
- Physical security tests against facility access and data center controls

> **Tip**
> A separate type of testing that is also very critical as part of your security program is software testing. This type of testing is most likely executed in conjunction with your developers and programmers. The types include static and dynamic testing, misuse case testing, fuzz testing or fuzzing, interface testing against APIs and user interfaces, and more. One excellent resource used in this type of testing is OWASP (https://www.owasp.org/index.php/Main_Page), which was reviewed in *Chapter 1, Fundamentals of Windows Security*.

There are a few different testing types that can be used as part of penetration testing, known as **black box**, **gray box**, and **white box**.

- **Black box** testing is also referred to as no- or zero-knowledge testing, where the ethical hacker is provided with no information about your environment upfront. This best represents an actual hacker.
- **Gray box** testing is also referred to as some- or partial-knowledge testing, where the ethical hacker is provided with limited information on the environment.
- **White box** testing is also referred to as complete- or full-knowledge testing. The ethical hacker is provided with complete knowledge of the environment.

Depending on the size of your organization and the maturity of your overall security program, it may make more sense to outsource your penetration service to a third-party company. These services are more widely adopted these days as organizations continuously work toward building a secure environment. There are many third-party companies available to execute a penetration test; a few examples include the following:

- Secureworks: https://www.secureworks.com/services/adversarial-security-testing/penetration-testing
- FireEye: https://www.fireeye.com/services/penetration-testing.html
- Rapid7: https://www.rapid7.com/services/security-consulting/penetration-testing-services/

If your organization is well-staffed and has the expertise available to execute its own internal penetration test through a red team (offensive), you should also adopt a blue team (defensive), which would most likely be your SOC. These teams work together to address the risks in an organization and are often complemented with purple team (red and blue) exercises. For example, the red team will execute an attack on the organization and the blue team will attempt to validate whether they were able to detect the attack and respond to it. If the attack was detected, the blue team was successful with their role. If they didn't identify the attack, they then work out how can this be addressed.

There are many tools available to conduct your own tests within your environment. A few of the more common tools you may be familiar with include the following:

- Metaspoilt: https://www.metasploit.com/
- Wireshark: https://www.wireshark.org/
- NMAP: https://nmap.org/

Building an internal program is not easy and successfully deploying an internal penetration testing program will require great effort, experience, and skilled experts to execute efficiently. We have barely touched on what is included in a penetration testing program, but we wanted to ensure you are aware of its importance in today's landscape. Next, we will briefly cover the steps included in executing a penetration test.

Executing a penetration test

Whether you conduct a penetration test internally or outsource it to a third-party company, you will need to ensure you follow a rigid process as part of its execution. Simply deploying some tools and trying to uncover vulnerabilities without a plan and proper approval can be extremely risky and potentially disruptive. The penetration test needs to be carefully planned out with the correct approval in place before executing it. There may be slight variations or some different approaches, but the following process for executing a penetration test can be considered standard:

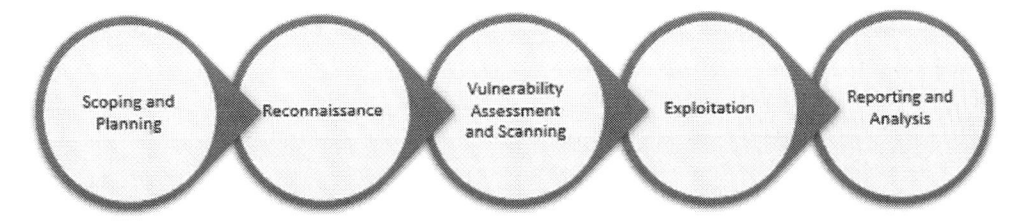

Figure 13.8 – The penetration testing process

The following provides a brief description of each phase:

- The **Scoping and Planning** phase is where you will plan and define the scope for the penetration test. This is where contracts will be signed and the rules of engagement document is agreed on.
- **Reconnaissance** is the phase where information about the company or environment being targeted is gathered.
- In the **Vulnerability Assessment and Scanning** phase, you will scan the environment and search for any weaknesses and vulnerabilities.
- **Exploitation** is where you will attempt to exploit the environment with any of the identified vulnerabilities.
- **Reporting and Analysis** is the final stage, where you will receive a report with an overview and detailed analysis of the test.

> **Tip**
> One particular phase of importance is to ensure that a **rules of engagement** document has been created with clear language, and that signoff has been provided by leadership before any work is started.

When you conduct a penetration test, you also need to be aware of any rules of engagement with other environments you operate your services in. For example, Microsoft has a rules of engagement document that you will need to review when you are ready to test your environment with Azure, if applicable. You can find the Microsoft rules of engagement at `https://www.microsoft.com/en-us/msrc/pentest-rules-of-engagement`. The following screenshot shows the Microsoft rules of engagement introduction and scope:

Figure 13.9 – The Microsoft rules of engagement

Make sure you scroll down to the section with the activities prohibited by Microsoft; the list is quite lengthy.

> **Tip**
> You should plan to execute a penetration test annually, at a minimum, within your environment.

Next, let's look at what the penetration test report findings may look like.

Reviewing the findings

The penetration test report will typically provide any identified vulnerabilities or concerns within four different categories: **Low**, **Medium**, **High**, and **Critical**. You may also see an information category that provides details on an item, but that may not be of concern to you. Once you have the report, your work doesn't stop there. It is just as important that you take the report and build a plan around the remediation of those items. Once you build a plan, it is critical that you work to remediate the identified items and set deadlines to ensure their completion. If critical or high-risk items are identified, you will need to action them straightaway. Once remediation has occurred, you will need to ensure you carry out retesting to validate that the controls put in place work as designed. In some instances, you may accept a risk if the cost to remediate outweighs the value of the data or the type of information at risk. In any case, building a remediation report that can be shared with leadership to show resolution and closure to any identified vulnerabilities from a penetration test is highly recommended. The following screenshot is an example of what could be used to document a vulnerability with a resolution:

Title of Vulnerability Identified

Findings	Resolution	Status: Risk Accepted or Remediated
Severity: Low or Medium or High or Critical		
Description: Description of vulnerability uncovered.	Here you will detail the steps taken to remediate the identified vulnerability or provide justification as to why the risk has been accepted.	
Systems/Applications Effected: List any systems or applications that were affected from this finding.		
Recommendation: Provide recommendation to remediate vulnerability.		

Figure 13.10 – Example of vulnerability remediation report

In addition to tracking the risks as part of the penetration test, you will most likely have a risk register for your organization that will track all known risks. If you don't have a risk register, it is highly recommended that you build one for visibility at the leadership level. Having a risk register is a great way for organizations to view all the known risks within their environment, as well as document the risk owners and those who accept risk. Something as simple as an Excel spreadsheet could meet your needs, to begin with.

To recap, we just provided details on penetration testing and remediation and the importance of this activity within your environment. Ensure you understand these technologies and concepts and apply them efficiently within your environment.

Next, we will review security awareness and training and the importance of this within your overall security program.

Security awareness and training

One specific area of importance in the process is to ensure that you don't forget to test your users and provide them with training and an awareness of vulnerabilities. The human factor is one of the weakest links when it comes to security, and providing awareness is critical and something that is quite often overlooked.

There are three important components to consider for a robust employee security program. The first is **testing**, most commonly completed through phishing campaigns or an attack simulator. Secondly, we need to ensure that we provide a robust **training** program and keep a record of employees who have taken and passed the training. This shouldn't be a one-time event, but rather an ongoing event. Lastly, you need to provide **awareness** to your users as needed. Sending a weekly security communication with tips, tricks, and recommendations, or providing somewhere for users to learn more, such as on an internal portal, will help strengthen your users' mindsets.

> **Tip**
> As already mentioned, security awareness and training is a critical component of your overall security program and should not be overlooked. There is a chance that you will be required to show evidence of this program in the event of a breach or as part of an audit.

Like all technologies, there are many vendors who can provide you with security and awareness services and tools. A couple of the more familiar vendors include the following:

- **Proofpoint**: `https://www.proofpoint.com/us/wombat-security-is-proofpoint`
- **KnowBe4**: `https://www.knowbe4.com/`

Microsoft also has a tool that you can use to test your users, named **Attack Simulator**. There is no accompanying training or awareness provided with **Attack Simulator** at the time of writing, but it does provide a great offering to test your users, especially if you have it as part of your licensing. To use **Attack Simulator**, you will need to be a global administrator or security administrator and have an Office 365 ATP Plan 2 license. To access **Attack Simulator**, take the following steps:

1. Log in to `https://protection.office.com/`.
2. From the left-side menu, click on **Threat Management**.
3. Select **Attack Simulator** to access the simulation options:

    --**Spear Phishing (Credentials Harvest)**: This email attack is designed to target a specific individual or organization by tricking the user into clicking on a URL to submit information, such as their username and password.

    --**Spear Phishing (Attachment)**: This email attack is designed to target a specific individual or organization by tricking the user into opening an attachment that contains malware.

    --**Brute Force Password (Dictionary Attack)**: This attack references a file containing passwords and uses the passwords to attempt to log in to a user's account. This helps identify commonly used passwords by a user.

    --**Password Spray Attack**: This attack will allow you to specify one password and attempt to log in to many user accounts. Using only one attempt will not likely trigger the lock-out policy, allowing the attacker to possibly find one account using that password. This helps identify commonly used passwords by users.

> **Tip**
> It is highly recommended that you run these tests often against all active user accounts within your environment, not just for your full-time employees but also for any contractors, temporary workers, interns, and so on.

4. Click **Launch Attack** on the desired simulation to set up your campaign:

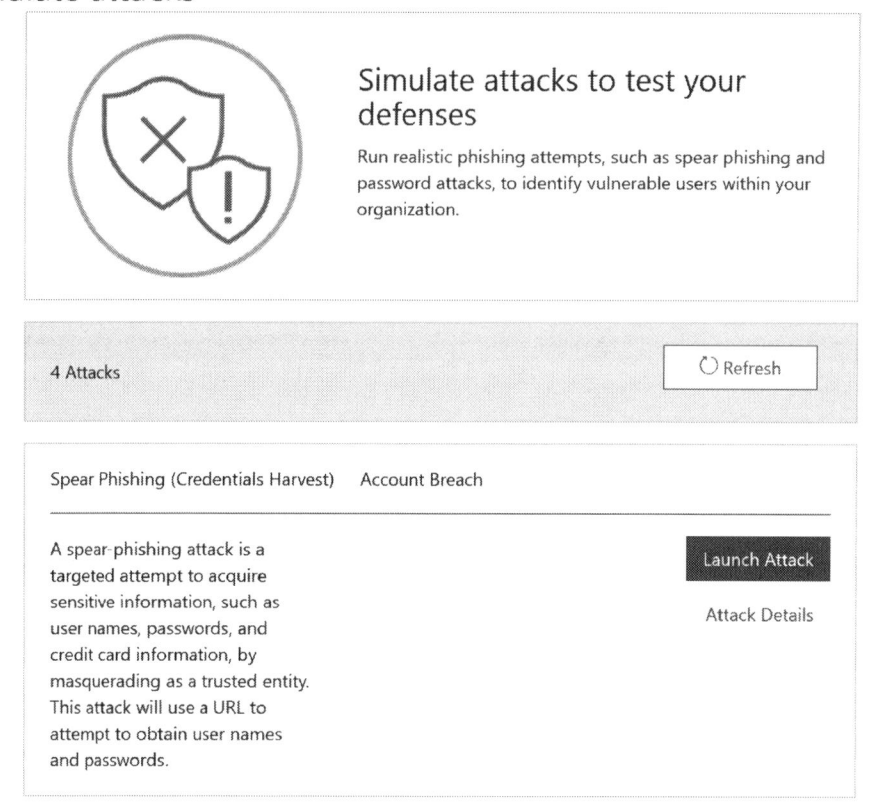

Figure 13.11 – Office 365 Attack Simulator

You can learn more about **Attack Simulator** by visiting `https://docs.microsoft.com/en-gb/microsoft-365/security/office-365-security/attack-simulator?view=o365-worldwide`.

> **Important note**
> NIST has a very detailed document on security testing and assessment. You can view the *SP 800-115, Technical Guide to Information Security Testing and Assessment* publication at `https://csrc.nist.gov/publications/detail/sp/800-115/final`.

Summary

In this chapter, we have covered validating controls within your environment. This includes looking at both internal auditing as well as external auditing. We then reviewed what SOC is and the different types, before reviewing the importance of vendor assessments as part of your vendor onboarding process. Next, we reviewed the Microsoft Service Trust portal, which is a place to view all of Microsoft's audits and assessments. We then finished the section with an overview of the regulatory compliance center within Azure Security Center.

In the next section, we covered vulnerability scanning, which included a detailed review of what scanning and assessments are and how Security Center can help with running assessments. We then reviewed penetration testing and remediation, which involved reviewing the different types of penetration tests, the process to execute, the importance of remediation, and an overview of the rules of engagement that Microsoft has published. In the final section, we covered security awareness and training and reviewed the phishing simulation options within Microsoft.

Moving on to *Chapter 14*, *Top 10 Recommendations and the Future*, we will finish off the book by covering the 10 most important takeaways and to-dos after reading through this book. We will then look at the future of device security and management, before looking at an overview of security and what the future holds.

14
Top 10 Recommendations and the Future

You made it to the final chapter! We hope that, up to this point, you have been able to gain a much better understanding of not just the tools needed to protect your Windows operating systems, but of everything involved in an overall security program to ensure your users and devices are secure. The primary focus of this book has been on the cloud technology that is at your disposal today. We often hear of the challenges of keeping up to date with today's fast-growing technology and cloud environments. Hopefully, we have been able to provide you with the necessary knowledge to better understand the fundamentals of shifting to a cloud-managed environment and, more importantly, the security tools to support and maintain that transition.

In this chapter, we will provide an overview of what we believe to be the 10 most important topics that were covered in this book. We hope these top 10 recommendations will provide you with an actionable list and that you will ensure these specific recommendations are in place. If they aren't, this book contains the knowledge that you require to plan and implement the appropriate protection for your organization and its users. Following our 10 recommendations, we will also provide a few additional recommendations that we feel are of importance and should be considered to strengthen your security program even further.

At the end of this chapter, we will provide an overview of our thoughts as they relate to the future of security and device management, and how the shift toward an anywhere-at-any-time access model is forcing enterprises to modernize their access strategies with cloud technologies. We will then finish the chapter with our thoughts on security in the future in an increasingly connected world. We will discuss how everyday interactions need well-defined security models, and a more autonomous world will require the right governance and security put in place.

In this chapter, we will cover the following topics:

- The 10 most important to-dos
- The future of device security and management
- Security and the future

The 10 most important to-dos

To finish the book, we wanted to highlight what we believe to be 10 of the most important areas covered within this book. These items are not listed in any priority order, but we feel they should be the focus of attention for your security program.

Implementing identity protection and privileged access

In a world that has shifted to the internet for an anywhere-at-any-time access model, identities have become the target of attention and are fundamental for gaining access to your environment. Because of this, it is critical that your identity protection program has multiple layers of protection and preventative measures in place.

Proper identity protection will require implementing account and access management tools and enforcing the principle of least privilege. A user must only be provided access to the specific data, applications, and systems that are necessary for their job role. Use **role-based access control** (**RBAC**) to streamline access and enforce strong passwords. Require **multi-factor authentication** (**MFA**) for all users, and implement conditional access controls that allow MFA to be bypassed if on a compliant company device for a better user experience. Enable biometric authentication when available, and consider an end goal of working toward a passwordless-authentication world.

> **Tip**
> Of all the recommendations, if you don't have MFA for your users enabled, ensure this is your highest priority. According to Microsoft, enabling MFA can prevent over 99.9% of account compromise attacks: `https://www.microsoft.com/security/blog/2019/08/20/one-simple-action-you-can-take-to-prevent-99-9-percent-of-account-attacks/`.

To access more information, we covered identity protection in detail in *Chapter 7, Identity and Access Management*.

Additionally, we covered privileged access models in both *Chapter 3, Server Infrastructure Management*, and *Chapter 7, Identity and Access Management*. The important areas to focus on include adopting a tiered model for privileged access in your Active Directory environment. Additionally, implement a Bastion or enhanced security administrative environment to administer your production workloads if applicable. Always enforce the principle of least privileged when assigning permissions to users. This includes Active Directory's built-in roles as well as Azure Active Directory roles. To manage access to resources in Azure, use Azure RBAC. Furthermore, enhance access security for your privileged users by deploying the following solutions:

- **Privileged Access Management (PAM)**
- **Just-in-Time Access (JIT)**
- **Privileged Identity Management (PIM)**

These solutions will provide a well-rounded privileged access administration program for both your traditional on-premises environment and cloud environment. If you don't have any privileged management tools available, create a secondary account for these purposes and ensure you educate your users not to use the same passwords between accounts.

Enact a Zero Trust access model

Ensure you adopt a Zero Trust access architecture for your systems, identities, applications, and infrastructure where applicable. In *Chapter 1*, *Fundamentals of Windows Security*, we touched on Zero Trust access and its value in securing your environment. This is a model where we trust no one until we can validate who they are, where they are coming from, and whether they have authorization. This approach will require an access model that consists of multiple layers and can evaluate several facets in the authentication and authorization chain from the network and firewall to the physical devices, down to the user's identity. Implementing cloud-based security technologies will significantly help if you are looking to adopt a Zero Trust access model. You can read more about the Zero Trust access model at Microsoft here:

`https://www.microsoft.com/en-us/itshowcase/implementing-a-zero-trust-security-model-at-microsoft`

Define a security framework

In *Chapter 2*, *Building a Baseline*, we covered the adoption of a security framework to serve as the foundation of your organization's security program. It should consist of recommendations from widely adopted frameworks such as the following:

- **Control Objectives for Information and Related Technology (COBIT)**: `http://www.isaca.org/cobit/pages/default.aspx`
- **ISO (International Standards Organization)** 27000 standards: `https://www.iso.org/isoiec-27001-information-security.html`
- **NIST (National Institute of Standards and Technology) Framework for Improving Critical Infrastructure Cybersecurity**: `https://www.nist.gov/cyberframework`

We also covered the importance of including well-documented policies, standards, procedures, and guidelines as part of your security program. The framework should also consist of one or more security baselines that outline a minimum set of configurations for your devices. The security program should be sponsored by leadership and promoted throughout the organization to help educate users about the importance of security and the part they play.

Get current and stay current

Get current and stay current with the latest feature builds and security updates for your Windows 10 and Server operating systems. In *Chapter 3, Server Infrastructure Management*, and *Chapter 4, End User Device Management*, we cover infrastructure and end user device management tools that assist with keeping your devices up to date. In *Chapter 8, Administration and Remote Management*, we review how to administer your devices to ensure they remain current and compliant. For example, enforcing a compliance evaluation to ensure your devices meet a minimum operating system build version is helpful for flagging non-updated devices that might be at risk. You can even enforce additional security controls such as the requirement of MFA based on this compliance evaluation using a conditional access policy. Configure **Windows Update for Business** (**WufB**) on Windows 10 devices and **Windows Server Update Services** (**WSUS**) or Azure Update Management for Windows servers to keep your devices patched. This will help ensure that your devices are as secure as possible against ongoing threats. In addition to updating the Windows operating system, other business applications such as Google Chrome, Microsoft Office, and Adobe products need to be kept up to date as well. Incorporate third-party applications into your update strategy.

Make use of modern management tools

Use modern management tools to enforce security configurations and for the overall administration of devices. Enterprise-grade solutions such as Microsoft Endpoint Configuration Manager and Intune can enforce security baselines, perform compliance evaluations, deploy applications, apply device configurations, and manage software updates. Use tools such as the **Microsoft Deployment Toolkit (MDT)** and Configuration Manager to build hardened images and deploy task sequences for in-place upgrades or migrations. Reduce the number of tools, if applicable, to avoid complexities in your environment. Simplicity with a reduced footprint will also helps to reduce the number of vulnerabilities. We primarily covered the management of your server infrastructure and end user devices in *Chapter 3, Server Infrastructure Management*, and *Chapter 4, End User Device Management*.

Certify your physical hardware devices

For end user physical devices and any physical servers within your environment, ensure the hardware specifications pass a hardware certification program and can support virtualization-based security features. In addition to this, ensure a process to securely update hardware and device firmware is built into your documented baseline procedures. In *Chapter 5, Hardware and Virtualization*, we covered hardware certification in more detail. As a reminder, make sure you review the **Windows Server Catalog** and **Windows Hardware Compatibility List** before procuring any hardware for your Windows operating systems from the following links:

- `https://www.windowsservercatalog.com/`
- `https://partner.microsoft.com/en-us/dashboard/hardware/search/cpl`

Administer network security

In *Chapter 6, Network Fundamentals for Hardening Windows*, we covered network security for your Windows environment. Although there has been a shift in the focus of security towards the user device and identity, network security still plays a pivotal role. The function of network security is not just for your network devices, offices, and data centers. Ensure network-specific security configurations are included in the security baselines for end user devices and servers. Communications to devices can be locked down by configuring Windows Defender Firewall with Group Policy, Intune, or Configuration Manager. For additional protection against connections to risky hosts, deploy a proxy server or service or use Windows Defender Exploit Guard network protection. For servers running in Azure, apply a network security group to the subnet or network interface resource, and only allow the necessary communications to pass through. As your users become more decentralized, ensure you implement a reliable and secure VPN service, such as Microsoft's Always On VPN, which we covered in *Chapter 6, Network Fundamentals for Hardening Windows*.

Always encrypt your devices

The use of encryption should always be enabled for end user workstations and servers. In the past, encryption was a challenge to deploy and manage. Fortunately, the process has become much easier with Microsoft's encryption technology, BitLocker. Enforce BitLocker encryption on workstations and servers using Group Policy or Intune and leverage Azure Active Directory or Configuration Manager to store and manage encryption keys. For virtual machines in Azure, leverage Azure Disk Encryption and Key Vault for key storage. Additionally, ensure that you configure backups when necessary. We covered encryption in detail for both end user devices and servers in *Chapter 9, Keeping Your Windows Client Secure*, and *Chapter 10, Keeping Your Windows Server Secure*.

Enable endpoint protection

Endpoint protection has typically been a standard over the years. Deploying solutions such as Microsoft Defender enhanced with the **Advanced Threat Protection (ATP)** service extends the antivirus to the cloud and provides next-generation endpoint protection with behavioral detection, native cloud-based analytics, and threat intelligence. Ensure you onboard workstations and servers to Microsoft Defender ATP for real-time protection and monitoring. In *Chapter 9, Keeping Your Windows Client Secure*, and *Chapter 10, Keeping Your Windows Server Secure*, we covered the onboarding process. In *Chapter 11, Security Monitoring and Reporting*, and *Chapter 12, Security Operations*, we discussed, in more detail, the monitoring and security operations aspects of Microsoft Defender ATP and how to review and investigate alerts and incidents.

Deploy security monitoring solutions

Having the right security tools in place is a critical part of your security program. But if you don't have a well-implemented operations and monitoring security program, the value of your security tools diminishes. Being a Microsoft customer means taking advantage of the security operations and monitoring products to allow instant reaction and remediation on any detected incidents within your environment. Ensure you deploy enterprise-class security monitoring and reporting solutions that include Log Analytics, Microsoft Defender ATP, Microsoft Cloud App Security, Azure Security Center, and Azure Sentinel. Many of these solutions allow integration with a third-party SIEM solution if you are outsourcing your security operations center. In *Chapter 11, Security Monitoring and Reporting*, and *Chapter 12, Security Operations*, we covered security operations and security monitoring and reporting in detail.

Other important items

Although we have compiled a top 10 list to consider when building a plan for hardening Windows devices, we want to highlight a few additional and important items of the overall security program.

Stay educated

Stay current on the ever-evolving threat landscape of today's world. It is important as a security professional that you are aware of and understand the current threats to ensure you are applying any remediations that will help to reduce the risk of a compromise. The following is a list of the resources referenced in *Chapter 1, Fundamentals of Windows Security*, and are great places to visit for up-to-date cybersecurity trends and new and emerging threats:

1. *DarkReading*: https://www.darkreading.com/
2. *Microsoft Patch Tuesday Dashboard*: https://patchtuesdaydashboard.com/
3. *Common Vulnerabilities and Exposures (CVE) List*: https://cve.mitre.org/cgi-bin/cvekey.cgi?keyword=Windows

Validate controls

In *Chapter 13, Testing and Auditing*, we covered, in detail, the testing and auditing of your environment. It is critical to validate that your controls are in place by regularly scheduling audits. Additionally, schedule yearly vulnerability assessments and penetration tests to help find and mitigate any new risks discovered in your environment. Don't exclude validating controls from your security program, as it could be a fatal mistake.

Application controls

Ensure you are only allowing access to applications you trust within your environment. Plan for and deploy **Windows Defender Application Control** (**WDAC**) policies for full fine-grained control over what applications can run on your systems for your users. We covered WDAC in more detail in *Chapter 9, Keeping Your Windows Client Secure*.

Security baselines and hardening

Ensure you harden your end user devices and servers by configuring Microsoft's recommended security baselines or by referencing the CIS Benchmarks. You don't need to build your own baselines from the ground up. The hard work has already been done by Microsoft and a community of others, providing the recommended controls that you should be deploying within your environment. Security baselines can be enforced using Group Policy, Intune, and/or Configuration Manager. Leverage reporting and auditing features with device compliance policies and configuration profiles in Intune or by deploying configuration baselines in Configuration Manager. Don't forget to include security baseline policies for other enterprise-based apps such as Microsoft Office, Google Chrome, Edge, and other web browsers. We covered the fundamentals of security baselines and hardening in *Chapter 2, Building a Baseline*. In *Chapter 9, Keeping Your Windows Client Secure*, and *Chapter 10, Keeping Your Windows Server Secure*, we reviewed how to implement these baselines and hardening controls into your workstations and servers.

Business continuity and disaster recovery

Having a well-defined business continuity plan and disaster recovery plan for your organization is critical. This is not only from a business operations perspective but also because of the ongoing and evolving security threats that can have catastrophic ramifications. Threats such as ransomware can prevent organizations from being able to operate normally and have the potential for large amounts of data loss. We briefly covered business continuity and disaster recovery in *Chapter 12, Security Operations*.

We have provided an overview summarizing the important takeaways from this book. Hopefully, this guide will help to provide you with insights into the critical components that you should focus on to best protect your Windows workstations and servers. Next, we will provide some personal insight into the future of security and device management.

The future of device security and management

As the technology we consume continues to evolve, and the access model continues to become more internet-centric, the better our security posture and defense must be. Not only does our security need to be better, but a complete shift needs to occur in the way security has been implemented in the past. Protecting our users within a traditional network is no longer the norm, as our users are far more dynamic today than they were in the past. With accessibility to the internet available from almost anywhere, we are being forced to change our security strategies from within the four walls of the office towards an anywhere at anytime access model. Not only are we challenged with users accessing data from corporate devices, but also from personally owned mobile devices in addition to a **bring-your-own** (**BYO**) laptop/tablet model. Ensuring that your corporate data is protected and is not exfiltrating from your environment requires many security tools and a well-defined security program. At the same time, it's important to ensure we don't inhibit end user productivity; otherwise, they will look to circumvent the controls put in place and create a more vulnerable environment.

In order to be more successful with your overall security strategy, you need to start by simplifying where you can. Traditionally, it takes numerous tools to secure your environment. This is to a point where maintaining and keeping all of these tools and services becomes unsustainable and, in certain instances, can open you up to more vulnerabilities because of their complexity. Because of this, you need to review what you have in place and understand where you can reduce products and services to consolidate your security footprint. Simplicity is key to a successful program, and Microsoft has done a great job in this regard, having evolved its security presence over the years.

Another direction you should be striving for is that of next-generation security tools. Traditional security tools will no longer suffice in today's modernized world. Next-generation security tools are those that can drive the security portfolio around that of the cloud data centers with unlimited scale, limited or zero infrastructure required, and always up-to-date apps, services, and platforms. You need to ensure that the tools and services you are deploying support a level of automation, can leverage artificial intelligence, analyze big data, and incorporate behavioral analytics. Without these features of next-generation protection, organizations will miss out on valuable security insights that can help to mitigate risk as opposed to reacting to a breach.

As we have mentioned throughout this book, your protection strategy needs to continue to shift toward identity- and device-based protection. As ATP tools continue to improve, it is critical that you continue to assess and enable these tools. They will be able to provide intelligent security insights such as cloud telemetry to analyze your users and devices based on their location along with any atypical travel, and identify anomalies based on user activity. Layering automation to automatically remediate incidents based on these anomalies is also a huge step in the right direction for security operations and to better secure your organization. In addition, devices are becoming biometric-enabled and can leverage finger scans and face recognition. These technologies are pivotal in creating a path to a passwordless world for your users and devices. If you haven't already heard of FIDO2, you should quickly become familiar with it, as this specification is currently driving the passwordless initiative.

> **Tip**
> Windows Hello also promotes the use of PINs for Windows 10 devices. Read more about why a PIN is better than a password here: `https://docs.microsoft.com/en-us/windows/security/identity-protection/hello-for-business/hello-why-pin-is-better-than-password`.

In addition to the focus on identity- and device-based protection is the protection of your data. To protect data in an available-anywhere-from-any-device strategy, additional protection needs to be considered to prevent leakages. To do this, continue to evolve your **Data Loss Prevention** (**DLP**) strategy into cloud-based technologies and enhance your protection with information rights management and data classification tools such as Azure Information Protection and Windows Information Protection. Your organization's data should be automatically labeled and classified based on industry-standard privacy regulations along with custom rules used to identify sensitive data. Depending on the classification applied, there should be auto-protection features that include the ability to enforce encryption, require authentication, restrict the data from leaving your devices, and block copy and paste to non-protected apps.

Moving beyond the classic Windows and server operating system is the **Internet of Things (IoT)**. IoT has grown exponentially over recent years and continues to grow as devices are now being built for anything imaginable. Microsoft also has a presence in this space with its Windows for IoT platform, which includes multiple versions for building out your IoT infrastructure:

- Windows 10 IoT Core
- Windows 10 IoT Enterprise
- Windows Server IoT 2019
- SQL Server IoT 2019

> **Tip**
> You can learn more about Windows IoT here: `https://www.microsoft.com/en-us/windowsforbusiness/windows-iot`.

As IoT continues to grow, the conversation of both standard device management and security continues to surface as a serious concern as we depend more and more on IoT devices. As we look ahead to develop and deploy more IoT within the enterprise, we need a unified standard to govern, manage, and secure these devices. In an ideal world, we would want to be able to unify the management of all our devices to allow for unified governance and a standard security approach. Currently, we are not aware of a true unified model. However, hopefully, this is something we can see become available as the adoption of IoT continues to grow. The following is a diagram of the ideal future unified management model:

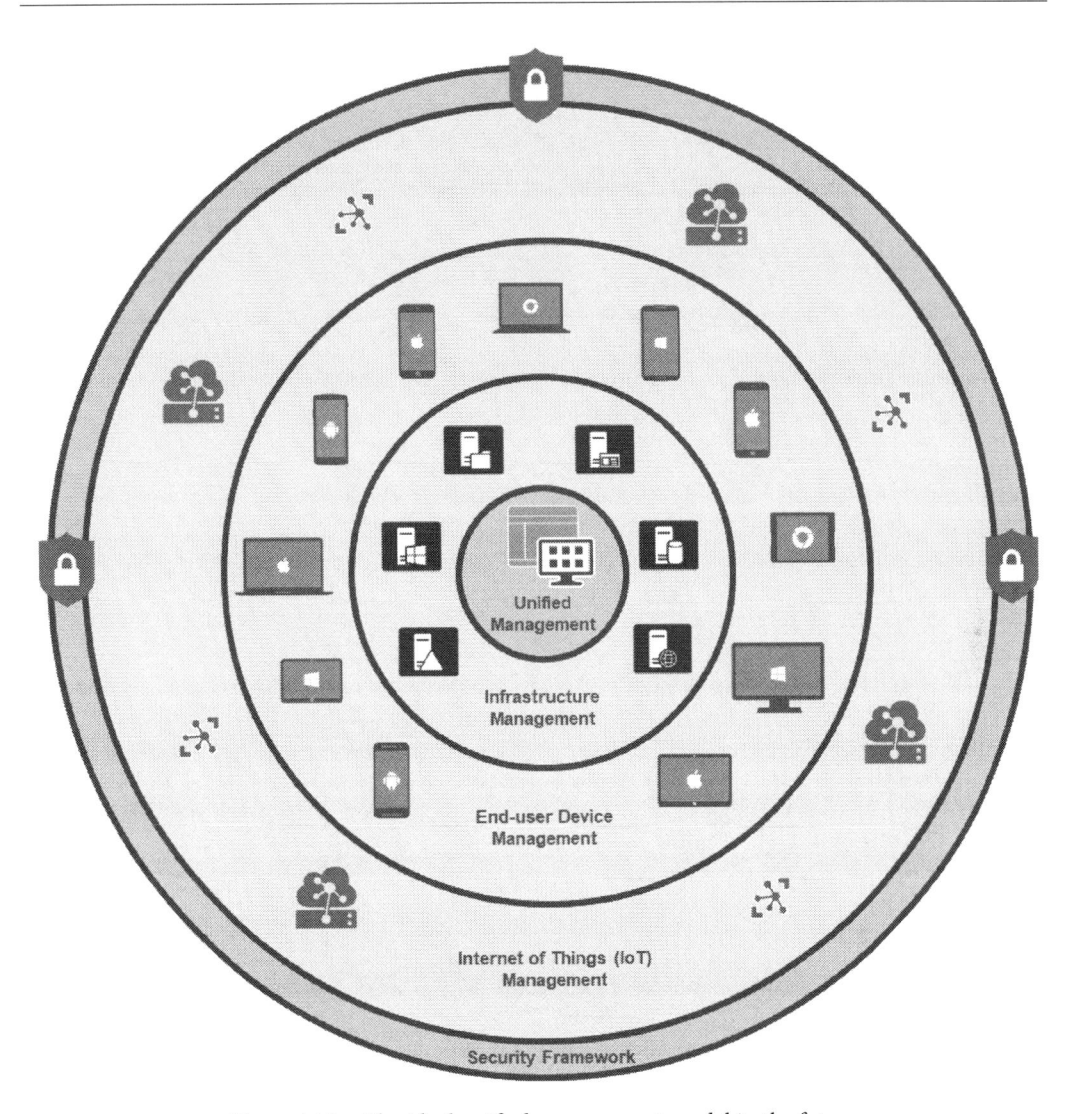

Figure 14.1 – The ideal unified management model in the future

So, we have provided some insights regarding the direction of device security and management along with the ideal future of better-unified management to simplify security for all devices within your organization. Next, we will discuss security and the future.

Security and the future

In this section, we will provide some thoughts on the growth and future of security and the role it will play in a world that becomes more connected every day. Technology continues to evolve at a significant pace and, as this technology grows, we need to get ahead of security, not only within the enterprise but also within the consumer space. Devices, gadgets, household items, entertainment, automobiles, accessories, and drones are all examples of the types of internet-connected "things" we are able to consume today. Unfortunately, security has been an afterthought for a lot of these items as usability becomes the focus and exposes a significant gap. Hopefully, as we continue to evolve in this space, we will see the creation of a more universal standardization that can be followed with some form of certification showing whether a device meets the minimum-security specifications for both enterprise and consumer usage. A few standardized examples include that of a PIN number for debit cards, fingerprint/face ID to unlock your phone, and the adoption of MFA across many services.

As highlighted several times throughout this book, your security strategy needs to shift toward leveraging cloud technologies in order to be more efficient in the future. By adopting next-generation cloud-based security technologies, you will be gaining the benefit of an environment that has little-to-zero self-managed infrastructure, is scalable, allows for automation, leverages the power of big data, makes use of artificial intelligence, and incorporates behavioral analytics. This model aligns better to companies going through a digital transformation to cloud-based infrastructure and offers greater support for a decentralized user base that requires work access from both corporate and personally owned devices.

As we move into the future, no matter the size of your organization or business, it is strongly recommended that you incorporate some form of a security presence. For a smaller business, security in the form of an outsourced model that leverages a **Managed Security Service Provider** (**MSSP**) may make more sense over hiring in house. Having an MSSP available will give you the necessary resources to provide the expertise needed to handle security-related incidents. Larger organizations may opt for an in-house security team, but many MSSPs can cater to larger organizations as well. There will be an increase in demand for security and services such as MSSPs as we continue to be challenged by more threats.

As we mentioned in the previous section, almost every powered device around us is becoming internet-connected. If we look in our homes alone, everything including alarm systems, video cameras, home entertainment systems, thermostats, light bulbs/switches, phones, smart TVs, doorbells, power outlets, appliances, and much more are becoming internet-enabled. The same also applies to the business world. As this trend continues to grow, we need to ensure our security standards are solidified and that a mature foundation is being provided in order to protect these items.

Critical infrastructure is one area that should be at the forefront of adopting and spearheading the development of security-based technologies. Examples include the energy sector, emergency services, chemical and nuclear factories, the transportation sector, and the government sector. These are essential services that support our daily lives and even a minor disruption in these services can be catastrophic. We need to ensure a secure future around these critical components of everyday life.

Cars, planes, trains, drones, autonomous vehicles, and even space travel all involve technology and have some form of external connectivity. These services are used by millions of people daily, and a compromise that can diminish the safe operation of these vehicles can result in severe damage or loss of life. We have already heard of cars being breached over the years as they continue to become more dependent on technology; one example is that of the Jeep hack incident: `https://www.wired.com/2015/07/hackers-remotely-kill-jeep-highway/`. We are also seeing a massive increase in drone usage by consumers and its adoption for military purposes. We cannot afford security to be an afterthought in these technologies.

Although discussed several times, the personal "digital" identity continues to evolve and be enhanced. As FIDO2 usage continues to grow and we continue into a passwordless world, where do we go beyond this? Do we get to a place where an item we carry represents our entire identity without the need to carry car keys, a wallet, a license, or even a passport? Although considered a controversial topic, where will the future go with microchip implants? Will this ever become a reality or requirement for humans? Perhaps we will live in a world where a microchip can be considered mandatory, such as requiring an inoculation to enroll kids into certain schools or to board an airplane. As with all conversations around identity, we are faced with the ongoing concern with privacy and how it is handled and protected. Maintaining this balance with future technological opportunities will be interesting as this exciting space continues to evolve.

The final topic of discussion is that of robots and autonomy, what the future holds, and where do we draw the line in terms of how far and intelligent robots can become? We have all most likely watched some kind of futuristic movie that entails robots becoming smarter than humans, with the strength to overpower humanity. Could this ever become a reality? And could robots become programmed to do more harm than good? These are conversations that will continue and it's critical that we build a solid, core security model that includes protection against these threats as robotic technology continues to evolve. There should be no failure of security in this space.

From our discussion, the importance of security from a holistic approach should be clear; that is, one that does not overlook any area of the infrastructure, the physical device, or the underlying software down to the user identity. Security should be at the forefront when designing any solution and should be natively embedded into the product from the beginning. Nothing should be built without security, and failure to do this can result in a negative outcome.

Summary

In this chapter, we provided an overview of the 10 most important to-do's and takeaways from this book. In addition to the 10 most important to-do's, we covered some additional items to remind you of as you continue to harden and secure your Windows workstations and servers. Each of these items includes a reference back to the original chapter where you can review the material to gain more understanding.

We then provided an overview, using our personal insights, of the future of device security and management. Here, we covered a few essential areas that relate to device security along with a brief overview of IoT and the importance of security management as this space evolves. We finished the chapter with more personal insights on security and the future, especially as they relate to the ever-evolving innovation of new and futuristic technologies.

This chapter concludes the content of this book and Windows security and hardening. We hope you enjoyed the content provided and that you were able to take away the necessary knowledge to help secure and strengthen your environment.

Other Books You May Enjoy

If you enjoyed this book, you may be interested in these other books by Packt:

Learn Computer Forensics

William Oettinger

ISBN: 978-1-83864-817-6

- Understand investigative processes, the rules of evidence, and ethical guidelines
- Recognize and document different types of computer hardware
- Understand the boot process covering BIOS, UEFI, and the boot sequence
- Validate forensic hardware and software
- Discover the locations of common Windows artifacts
- Document your findings using technically correct terminology

Metasploit 5.0 for Beginners - Second Edition

Sagar Rahalkar

ISBN: 978-1-83898-266-9

- Set up the environment for Metasploit
- Understand how to gather sensitive information and exploit vulnerabilities
- Get up to speed with client-side attacks and web application scanning using Metasploit
- Leverage the latest features of Metasploit 5.0 to evade anti-virus
- Delve into cyber attack management using Armitage
- Understand exploit development and explore real-world case studies

Leave a review - let other readers know what you think

Please share your thoughts on this book with others by leaving a review on the site that you bought it from. If you purchased the book from Amazon, please leave us an honest review on this book's Amazon page. This is vital so that other potential readers can see and use your unbiased opinion to make purchasing decisions, we can understand what our customers think about our products, and our authors can see your feedback on the title that they have worked with Packt to create. It will only take a few minutes of your time, but is valuable to other potential customers, our authors, and Packt. Thank you!

Index

A

access management
  best practices 75
  implementing, in Windows servers 68
account and access management
  implementing 225
Active Directory (AD) 199, 436
Active Directory Domain (AD) 273
Active Directory Federation
    Services (AD FS) 228
Administrative Templates
  using 291, 292
Advanced Threat Protection
    (ATP) 27, 45, 285, 537
advanced Windows hardening
    configurations 327
AICPA SOC services
  URL 512
Alert process tree
  used, for viewing alert 428
Always on VPN 197
Always on VPN configuration,
    for Windows 10 clients
  reference link 197
American Institute of Certified Public
    Accountants (AICPA) 512

ApplicationControl CSP
  reference link 174
application security group (ASGs) 213
AppLocker
  considerations 366
Artificial Intelligence (AI) 26
attack surface reduction events
  reference link 208
audit
  about 511
  external audit 511
  internal audit 511
Authentication, Authorization, and
    Accountability (AAA) 221
Azure
  network security groups (NSG),
    creating 214-217
Azure Active Directory (AAD) 108, 273
Azure activity logs
  monitoring 449, 450
Azure AD B2B
  reference link 233
Azure AD joined devices
  versus domain joined devices 273
  versus hybrid joined devices 273

240   Index

Azure AD pass-through
    authentication 255
Azure AD password hash
    synchronization 255
Azure AD PIM
  admins, enabling 242-244
Azure AD Seamless SSO
  using 254-256
Azure ATP
  alerts, viewing 480-486
  architecture, reference link 477
  configuring 476, 477
  instance, activating 478
  kill chain 478, 480
  planning 477
  reference link 478
  technical prerequisites,
    reference link 477
Azure ATP sensor
  installation link 478
Azure Backup
  about 91
  Application-Consistent Backup 92
  Crash-Consistent Backup 92
  reference link 91
  requisites 92
  securing 93
Azure Backup RBAC
  reference link 93
Azure Backup, RBAC roles
  Backup Contributor 93
  Backup Operator 93
  Backup Reader 93
Azure Bastion
  about 311
  connecting with 311-313
Azure cloud administrative roles 236

Azure Desired State Configuration
    (DSC) 402
Azure Disk Encryption
  enabling, on virtual machine 412-415
  reference link 414
  using 409
Azure external user access (B2B)
  managing 233-236
Azure Information Protection (AIP)
  about 468
  pricing, reference link 468
Azure Key Vault
  creating 410, 411
Azure Marketplace
  URL 87
  using 87
Azure Monitor
  access, securing 449
  built-in roles 449
  monitoring with 448, 449
Azure network security 211
Azure PIM service
  reference link 242
Azure portal
  about 86
  URL 86
  virtual servers, accessing 86
Azure RBAC
  using 245
Azure Resource Manager (ARM) 91, 440
Azure Resource Manager templates
  reference link 91
Azure resources
  reference link 98
Azure Security Center
  used, for investigating threats 486-488

Azure Security Center (ASC)
  about 307, 393
  configuring 451-455
Azure Security Center JIT access
  reference link 308
  using 307-311
Azure Sentinel
  about 488
  setting up, within Azure 489-492
Azure services
  used, for managing Windows servers 85
Azure Site Recovery (ASR)
  leveraging 97
  reference link 97
Azure Site Recovery (ASR), components
  Backup Services 97
  Site Recovery Services 97
Azure SSO
  configuring 257, 258
Azure Update Management
  about 94-96
  deploying 387-392
  deployment requisites 94
  reference link 96
Azure virtual machines 149, 150

B

baseline
  implementing 54
baseline controls
  building 52
baselining 42, 43
Basic Input/Output System (BIOS)
  about 158
  NIST security guidelines,
    reference link 159
  protecting, guidelines 158

Best Practices Analyzer (BPA)
  using 78
BitLocker CSP
  reference link 131
BitLocker Device Encryption, Windows 10
  reference link 331
BitLocker encryption
  managing 331-333
BitLocker Encryption Key (BEK) 410, 414
black box testing 521
Bluebugging 196
Bluejacking 196
Bluesnarfing 196
Bluetooth 196
book kit 158
breaches
  recognizing 34-36
bring your own device (BYOD)
  scenario 104
Business Continuity Planning
  (BCP) 504, 505
Business-to-Business
  (B2B)-invited guests 474

C

California Consumer Privacy
  Act (CCPA) 42
Center for Internet Security
  (CIS) 361, 400
Center for Internet Security (CIS®)
  about 52
  reference link 53
Central Administration Site (CAS) 119
Central Store for Group Policy
    Administrative Templates,
    in Windows
  reference link 208

change management 48
ChangeTracking solution
    deploying 445
    reference link 445
Chief Executive Officer (CEO) 22
Chief Information Security
        Officer (CISO) 22
CIS benchmarks
    downloading 54-56
CIS cybersecurity best practices
    reference link 53
CIS hardened images
    reference link 56
CIS home page
    reference link 52
Classless Inter-Domain
        Routing (CIDR) 312
client deployments best practices,
        Configuration Manager
    reference link 120
client management operations
    reference link 126
cloud
    hardware and virtualization 154
    overview 62, 63
Cloud Access Security Broker (CASB) 469
Cloud Management Gateway
    reference link 122
cloud model
    about 64
    example 65
Cloud Security Alliance (CSA) 513
cloud solutions, primary services
    Platform as a Service (PaaS) 65
    Software as a Service (SaaS) 66
collections, Configuration Manager
    reference link 124

Command-Line Interface (CLI) 86
Common Platform Enumeration
        (CPE) 32
Common Vulnerabilities and
        Exposures (CVE)
    about 32
    reference link 32
Common Vulnerability Scoring
        System (CVSS) 32
Common Weakness Enumeration
        (CWE) 32
compliance policies
    creating, with Intune 286, 287
compliance settings
    creating, with Configuration
        Manager 275, 276
Component Object Model (COM) 364
Conditional Access
    about 264
    reference link 264
Conditional Access policy
    setting up 265, 266
Configurable Code Integrity
        (CCI) policy 415
Configuration Baseline
    building 280-283
    creating, from GPO 301-305
    reporting 283, 284
Configuration Item
    about 276, 278
    creating 279, 280
    setting types 276
Configuration Manager
    used, for creating compliance
        settings 275
    used, for onboarding Windows
        Server 2019 397-399

Configuration Manager
    workloads, to Intune
  reference link 291
Configuration Service Provider (CSP)
  about 444
  reference link 468
configuration service providers
  reference link 131
Consensus Assessment Initiative
    Questionnaire (CAIQ)
  reference link 513
Control Objectives for Information and
    Related Technology (COBIT)
  reference link 49
controls
  validating 511-517
Credential Guard
  about 166, 167
  enabling 167
  enabling, with Group Policy 169-171
  enabling, with MDM (Intune) 168, 169
  reference link 167
Cybersecurity and Infrastructure
    Security Agency (CISA) 32
Cyber Supply Chain Risk Management
  project and risks, reference link 152
cyber threats 28
cyber threat sources
  reference link 28

D

data center
  cloud model 64
  hybrid model 67
  on-premise 64
  overview 62, 63
Data Loss Prevention (DLP) 190, 467, 541

Data Loss Protection (DLP) 464
Defender ATP
  reference link 480
demilitarized zone (DMZ) 153, 199
denial of service (DoS) attack 407
deployment rings, Windows 10
  reference link 323
device administration 273
device compliance policy
  configuring 288
device configuration profile
  configuring 289, 290
Device Firmware Configuration
    Interface (DFCI) 289
Device Guard
  about 171, 415
  enabling, with Group Policy 172-174
device imaging 104, 105
device management
  evolution 103, 104
devices
  encrypting 536
device security and management
  future 540-543
Digital Forensic Incident
    Response (DFIR) 462
digital transformation 26
digital world 24-27
Direct Memory Access (DMA) 169
directory services
  integrating 227-230
Disaster Recovery (DR)
  planning 505, 506
Domain Controller (DC) 58, 378
domain joined devices
  versus Azure AD joined devices 273
  versus hybrid joined devices 273

Domain Services 199
Dynamic Root of Trust
    measurement (DRTM) 181

E

Endpoint Detection and
    Response (EDR) 426
Endpoint Protection
  assigning 285, 286
  enabling 537
enhanced security administrative
    environment (ESAE) 74
Enterprise State Roaming 108
Ethernet 199
Event Viewer
  using 79-81
exchange key (KEK) 160
extensions
  whitelisting 362, 363
external audit 511

F

Fast ID Online (FIDO) v2.0 262
Fast ID Online v2 (FIDO) 328
Federal Information Security
    Management Act (FISMA) 42
fine-grained password policies 407
Forefront Identity Manager (FIM) 227
Forest Functional Level (FFL) 477
Full-Time Employee (FTE) 225
Fully Qualified Domain Name
    (FQDN) 301

G

General Data Protection
    Regulation (GDPR) 42
geo-redundant (GRS) 91
globally unique identifiers (GUID) 296
golden ticket attack 485
Google Chrome
  hardening 360-362
Google Chrome Enterprise bundle
  download link 360
Google Chrome mDNS
  disabling 346-351
Graphical User Interface (GUI) 377
gray box testing 521
Group Policy
  reference link 173
  used, for onboarding Windows
    Server 2019 393-396
Group Policy Management
    Console (GPMC) 169
Group Policy Objects (GPOs) 42, 273
  guidelines 46, 47
GUID Partition Table (GPT) 159

H

hardware certification 154-157
hardware security
  concerns, addressing 151, 152
  recommendations and best
    practices 182
Hardware Security Modules (HSMs) 411
Health Information Trust
    Alliance Common Security
    Framework (HITRUST)
  reference link 50

Health Insurance Portability and
    Accountability Act (HIPAA) 42
high availability (HA) 143
Homeland Security
    reference link 195
HR, and identity management 226
hybrid joined devices
    versus Azure AD joined devices 273
    versus domain joined devices 273
hybrid model 67
Hyper-V
    about 145-148, 201, 202
    additional methods, reference link 148
    installing, through Windows UI 147
    on Windows 10, requisites 147
    on Windows Server, requisites 146
    operating systems, reference link 146
    platform, requisites 145
    reference link 145
    tools, requisites 145
Hypervisor-Protected Code
        Integrity (HVCI)
    about 177, 178
    enabling 179, 180
    reference link 178
Hyper-V networking, in Windows Server
    reference link 201
Hyper-V security, for Windows Server
    reference link 201

I

Identification, Authentication,
        Authorization, and
        Accountability (IAAA) 221
identity and access management
    accountability 223, 224
    authentication 222

authorization 223
identity 221
overview 221
Identity Protection
    about 267
    accessing 267
    implementing 532, 533
Information Technology
        Infrastructure Library (ITIL)
    reference link 48
Infrastructure as a Service (IaaS)
    about 65, 149
    reference link 65
internal audit 511
International Standards Organization
        (ISO) 27000 Family
    reference link 49
Internet Assigned Numbers
        Authority (IANA) 189
Internet Information Services
        (IIS) 377, 449
Internet of Things (IoT) 542
Intrusion Detection Systems (IDS) 190
Intrusion Prevention Systems (IPS) 190
Intune
    used, for creating compliance
        policies 286, 287
    Windows updates, configuring 323-325
Intune Mobile Device Management
        (MDM) 129
Intune roles
    using 238
Intune security baselines
    enforcing 293, 294
ISO standards
    reference link 512

J

JSON
  reference link 90
Just-In-Time (JIT) access 69, 241

K

Kerberos Ticket Granting Ticket
    Account (KRBTGT) 485
key encryption key (KEK) 410
  creating 411, 412
Kusto Query Language
    (KQL) 207, 365, 427

L

least-privilege 221, 223
Light Touch Installation (LTI)
    deployments 113
Link-Local Multicast Name Resolution
    Poisoning (LLMNRP) 232
Link-Local Multicast Resolution
    (LLMNR)
  about 338
  disabling, with Group Policy 339
  disabling, with registry keys 339
local administrative accounts
  using 231, 232
Local Admin Password Solution
    (LAPS) 73, 232
Local Area Network (LAN) 194, 199
Local Group Policy Object (LGPO) 295
locally redundant (LRS) 91
Local Security Authority
    Subsystem (LSASS) 166

Log Analytics
  deploying 439-441
  gallery solutions, installing 441
  reference link 441
Log Analytics, gallery solutions
  ChangeTracking solution, deploying 445
  ServiceMap solution, using 446
  Update Compliance solution,
    for Windows 10 441-443
  Windows workstations,
    onboarding 443, 444
  Wire Data 2.0 solution, using 447
Long-Term Servicing Channel
    (LTSC) 377

M

M365 security center
  reference link 462
  using 462
M365 security portal
  data, classifying 467
  data, classifying with AIP 468
  data, classifying with DLP 467, 468
  data, classifying with WIP 468, 469
  Microsoft Secure Score 464-466
  reference link 464
  using 462-464
Machine health and compliance
    report, MDATP
  reference link 432
machine risk compliance policy
  creating 436-438
main distribution frame (MDF) 191
malware 29
Managed Security Service Provider
    (MSSP) 462, 544

Index   247

Man-in-the-Middle (MITM) attacks 327
Maximum Tolerable Downtime
    (MTD) 505
MDATP service
  workstations, onboarding to 433-435
MFA
  configuring 258-261
Microsoft BitLocker Administration and
    Monitoring (MBAM) 331, 409
Microsoft Cloud App Security (MCAS)
  about 453
  activity log, reference link 473
  activity log, reviewing 471-473
  Microsoft Defender ATP integration,
    reference link 471
  reference link 470, 471
  user's activity, viewing 473-476
  using 469
Microsoft Defender Advanced
    Threat Protection (MDATP)
  advanced features, enabling 439
  alert, investigating 427-430
  capabilities 427
  Machine health and
    compliance report 432
  machine risk compliance policy,
    creating 436-438
  Microsoft Intune connection,
    enabling 435, 436
  monitoring with 426
  software inventory report 432
  Threat analytics dashboard 430
  Threat & Vulnerability Management
    dashboard 431
Microsoft Defender ATP
  connecting to 392, 393

Microsoft Defender ATP, features
  reference link 393
Microsoft Defender Security Center
  about 492
  alerts queue, reviewing 496, 497
  Automated Investigations 498, 499
  incidents management and
    investigation, reference link 503
  incidents queue, reviewing 500-503
  permissions and machine groups,
    assigning 492-496
  reference link 492
Microsoft Defender Security
    Center, machine status
  reference link 397
Microsoft Defender SmartScreen
  enabling 336, 337
Microsoft Deployment Toolkit (MDT)
  about 110, 113
  reference link 113, 115
  security features 113
  task sequence 114
Microsoft Deployment Toolkit
    (MDT) 535
Microsoft Desktop Optimization
    Pack (MDOP) 331
Microsoft Edge
  privacy settings 372, 373
Microsoft Edge for business
  download link 373
Microsoft Endpoint Configuration
    Manager (MECM) 103, 105
Microsoft Endpoint Configuration
    Manager (SCCM)
  about 113, 119
  client collections 123, 124

client communication 127, 128
clients, deploying for 120-123
client settings 125, 126
Microsoft Endpoint Manager 134-137
Microsoft Endpoint Manager Admin
    Center (EMAC) 134, 433
Microsoft Endpoint Manager
    admin center login page
  reference link 134
Microsoft Intune connection
  enabling, on MDATP 435, 436
Microsoft Message Analyzer (MMA) 202
Microsoft Monitoring Agent (MMA) 440
Microsoft SCT
  about 57, 58
  reference link 59
Microsoft Secure Score
  about 464
  accessing 465, 466
Microsoft Security Compliance Toolkit
  GPO, creating from baseline
      recommendation 298-300
  policies, comparing with Policy
      Analyzer tool 296, 297
  using 295, 296
Microsoft Security Response
    Center (MSRC)
  reference link 30
MIM
  reference link 227
Mobile Application Management
    (MAM) 129
Mobile Device Management (MDM) 42
  about 129
  Configuration Service Provider
      (CSP) 129-131
  versus Mobile Application
      Management 132

modern device management
    (MDM), policies
  enforcing 275
modern management tools 535
Multi-Factor Authentication
    (MFA) 44, 129, 532
Multi-Factor Authorization (MFA) 436

N

name resolution poisoning
  preventing 338
Nano Server 2019
  installing 379, 380
National Institute of Standards
    and Technology (NIST)
  reference link 30, 49, 195
National Vulnerability
    Database (NVD) 32
NetBIOS Name Service (NBT-
    NS) 340-345
NetMarketShare
  URL 25
Network Access Control (NAC) 190
networking 201, 202
network security
  administering 536
network security fundamentals 187-191
Network Security Group (NSG)
  about 211, 307
  creating, in Azure 214-217
  service tag 213
network troubleshooting 202
network virtual appliances (NVA) 211
Nintex Promapp
  URL 46

NIST cybersecurity framework
    core functions
        reference link 51
NIST Cyber Supply Chain best practices
    reference link 152
NIST framework
    Protect function 51
NIST SP 800-53
    reference link 50
NIST SP 800-171
    reference link 50
NIST Special Publication
        800-121 Revision 2
    reference link 196
Non-Disclosure Agreement (NDA) 512
non-virtual secure mode 165

O

Office 365 admin roles 237
Office 365 ProPlus ADMX files
    download link 356
Office 365 Security and
        Compliance activity list
    for file deletions, from OneDrive 106
Office security baselines
    configuring 354, 355
OneDrive Group Policy
    reference link 107
OneDrive safeguards
    reference link 106
on-premise data center 64
Open Systems Interconnection (OSI) 187
Open Web Application Security
        Project (OWASP)
    about 33
    reference link 33

Organizational Units (OUs) 228
Out-of-Box Experience (OOBE) 118
overpass-the-hash technique 484
OWASP Top 10 34
OWASP Top 10 2017
    reference link 34

P

PAM
    using 240, 241
PAM security tools
    implementing 240
Pass-the-Hash (PtH) 167
Pass-the-Ticket (PtT) 167
passwordless
    about 262
    configuration screen 263
    enabling 263
password policy
    implementing, fine-grained
        password policy used 248, 249
    implementing, Group Policy used 248
passwords
    securing 247-250
Password Settings Object (PSOs) 407
PatchManagement.org
    reference link 31
Patch Tuesday Dashboard
    reference link 31
Payment Card Industry Data Security
        Standard (PCI DSS) 42
penetration testing
    black box testing 521
    executing 523, 524
    findings, reviewing 525, 526
    gray box testing 521
    planning for 520, 522

types 521
white box testing 521
penetration testing, tools
   reference links 522
performance baselines
   creating 455-457
Personal Identifiable
      Information (PII) 227
physical hardware devices
   certifying 536
physical security 68
physical servers 143, 144
PKI certificate
   reference link 127
Platform as a Service (PaaS)
   about 65, 119
   reference link 65
platform key (PK) 160
policies
   defining 44, 45
   enforcing, with modern device
      management (MDM) 275
PowerShell constrained language mode
   using 315
PowerShell Desired State
      Configuration (DSC) 440
PowerShell, language modes
   reference link 315
PowerShell logging
   configuring 314, 315
PowerShell scripts
   deploying 291
PowerShell scripts, in Intune
   reference link 291
PowerShell security
   about 313
   script execution, enabling 316, 317

Preboot Execution Environment
      (PXE) 110, 115
privileged access
   implementing 532, 533
Privileged Access Management
      (PAM) 69, 231
privileged access, securing
   reference link 76
Privileged Access Workstation
      (PAW) 43, 72
Privileged Identity Management (PIM) 69
procedures
   creating 46
   example 46
process hollowing 428
Provisioning packages (PPKG) 111
public cloud, versus private cloud
   reference link 64
Public Key Infrastructure (PKI) 190, 416

Q

queries, Configuration Manager
   reference link 123

R

RBAC, for Azure resources
   reference link 245
Recovery Point Objective (RPO) 97, 505
Recovery Time Objective (RTO) 97, 505
registry
   user access, preventing to 363, 364
Regulatory compliance section 515
Remote Authentication Dial-In User
      Service (RADIUS) 477
Remote Desktop Connect (MSTSC) 311
Remote Desktop Protocol (RDP) 306

remote interactive 404
remotely servers
  secure connection 306
remote management 306
remote procedure calls (RPC) 166
Remote Server Administration
    Tools (RSAT)
  about 76, 379
  reference link 306
request for proposal (RFP) 155
Reset password link, for Windows clients
  reference link 253
resource policy providers
  reference link 307
resource provider operations
  reference link 90
Responder
  reference link 338
Resultant Set of Policies (RSOP) 299
revoked signature (DBX) 160
Role-Based Access Control (RBAC)
  about 69, 85, 223, 307, 449, 532
  implementing 87-90
role-based administration,
    Configuration Manager
  reference link 124
role definition structure
  reference link 88
Root of Trust for Update (RTU) 158
Root of Trust Management (RTM) 180
runtime (RT) processes 159

S

Second Level Address
    Translation (SLA) 165
security
  challenges 36-39

  future 544, 545
security alerts, Azure ATP portal
  reference link 486
security and compliance admin roles 239
Security Assertion Markup
    Language (SAML) 257
security awareness and training 526-528
security baselines
  about 293
  building 295
Security & Compliance Center
  reference link 467
Security Compliance Manager (SCM) 401
security framework
  defining 534
  implementing 49-51
Security Information and
    Event Management
    (SIEM) 82, 190, 315, 454, 488
security monitoring solutions
  deploying 537
Security Operations Center
    (SOC) 82, 426, 461, 462
Security Orchestration Automated
    Response (SOAR) 488
Security Phase (SEC) 159
security transformation 22-24
Self-Service Password Reset (SSPR)
  configuring 250, 251
  implementing, for Windows
    10 login 252
Semi-Annual Channel (SAC) 377
Server Manager
  about 76, 78
  remote servers, adding 77
  tasks 76

ServiceMap solution
  reference link 446
  using 446
service tag 212, 213
Service Trust portal
  URL 514
Shielded Virtual Machines (VMs)
  about 378
  features required 146
  reference link 147
small office home networks (SOHOs) 203
SMTP Server 200
SOC 1 reports 512
SOC 2 reports 512
SOC 3 reports 512
Software as a Service (SaaS)
  about 66
  reference link 66
Software-Defined Networking (SDN) 378
software development kit (SDK) 91
software inventory report, MDATP
  reference link 432
software update point
  reference link 121
Standardized Information Gathering (SIG)
  URL 513
standards
  setting 45
Static RTM (SRTM) 181
Storage Service Encryption (SSE) 93
Sysprep 113
sysprepping 113
System and Organization
    Controls (SOC) 512
System Center Configuration
    Manager (SCCM) 103

T

TCP/IP 187
Telerik Fiddler
  URL 202
The (ISC)² Cybersecurity Workforce Study
  reference link 23
The Sarbanes-Oxley Act 42
The U.S. Department of Homeland
    Security (DHS) 32
Threat analytics dashboard
  reference link 431
threats
  about 29
  investigating, with Azure
      Security Center 486-488
Threat & Vulnerability
    Management dashboard
  reference link 431
Ticket-Granting Ticket (TGT) 484
tiered model, for privileged access
  considerations 72, 73
  tier 0 70
  tier 1 71
  tier 2 71, 72
  using 70
trusted boot process 159
Trusted Computing Base (TCB) 181
Trusted Computing Group (TCG) 181
Trusted Platform Module (TPM) 287, 328
Trusted Platform Module (TPM 2.0)
  about 162-164
  reference link 163

Index

U

UEFI Secure Boot
  about 160
  configuring 161, 162
Unified Extensible Firmware
    Interface (UEFI)
  about 159, 160
  security features 159
update deployments
  managing 325
  monitoring 326
upgrade paths, Windows 10
  reference link 105
user access
  preventing, to registry 363, 364
user access security 68
user-based office policies
  deploying 355-359
user-defined routing (UDR) 211
User Mode Code Integrity (UMCI) 315
User State Migration Tool (USMT)
  reference link 106

V

Virtual Desktop Environment (VDI) 440
virtualization
  about 143
  security concerns, addressing 153
Virtualization-Based Security (VBS) 364
  Credential Guard 166, 167
  Device Guard 171
  hardware requirements,
      reference link 165
  Hypervisor-Protected Code
      Integrity (HVCI) 177
  used, for system protection 164-166
  Windows Defender Application
      Guard 175
  Windows Defender System Guard 180
virtualization technologies, Microsoft
  about 144
  Azure virtual machines 149, 150
  Hyper-V 145-148
  Windows Virtual Desktop 151
virtual machine
  Azure Disk Encryption,
      enabling 412-415
virtual network service tags
  reference link 212
Virtual Private Network (VPN) 190, 197
virtual secure mode 165
VPN connection, from
    Windows 10 device
  reference link 197
vulnerabilities
  identifying 30-34
vulnerability assessment
  reference link 519
vulnerability scan
  about 517
  preparing for 517-519

W

WDAC policy rules options
  reference link 417
Web Proxy Autodiscovery
    Protocol (WPAD)
  disabling 352, 353
Web Server (IIS) 200
white box testing 521
white glove OOBE 118
whitelist (DB) 160
Wi-Fi 194

Windows 10
　Network & Internet management
　　console, reviewing 193, 194
　Update Compliance solution
　　for 441-443
Windows 10 login
　SSPR, implementing for 252
Windows 10 login page
　Password Reset link, enabling 253
Windows 10, network connections
　Bluetooth 196
　Virtual Private Network (VPN) 197
　Wireless Local Area Network
　　(WLAN)/Wi-Fi 194, 195
Windows 10 privacy
　about 366
　privacy settings 368-370
　privacy settings, controlling
　　for app 367, 368
Windows Admin Center
　about 84
　Azure services 84
Windows as a Service
　reference link 321
Windows as a Service (WaaS) 321
Windows Assessment and Deployment
　　Kit (Windows ADK)
　about 110
　functionalities 110
Windows Autopilot
　about 105, 117
　deployment scenarios 118
　reference link 117
　steps 117
　using 117
Windows clients
　securing 320

Windows Configuration Designer (WCD)
　about 111
　features 112
　reference link 112
　settings 111
Windows Defender Antivirus 83
Windows Defender Application Control
　about 364
　considerations 366
Windows Defender Application
　　Control (WDAC)
　about 171, 315, 415
　deploying 415-422
　enabling, with Group Policy 172-174
Windows Defender Application Guard
　about 175-177
　used, for protecting from attacks 175
Windows Defender AV
　configuring 334, 335
Windows Defender AV, scanning options
　reference link 334
Windows Defender Exploit Guard
　　Network Protection
　about 207, 208
　configuring, with Group Policy 209, 210
Windows Defender Firewall
　about 202-204
　firewall rule, configuring with
　　Group Policy 204-206
　with Advanced Security 202-204
Windows Defender Firewall,
　　network profile types
　domain profile 203
　private profile 203
　public profile 203
Windows Defender System
　　Guard 180-182

Index   255

Windows Deployment Services (WDS)
　about 115
　images, securing 115
Windows Domain Controller
　　(DC) server 43
Windows enrollment methods
　about 133
　administrator enrollment scenarios 133
　reference link 133
　user self-enrollment scenarios 133
Windows Hardware Compatibility List
　reference link 536
Windows Hardware
　　Compatibility Program
　reference link 156
Windows Hello 262
Windows Hello biometrics
　reference link 328
Windows Hello for Business
　enabling 328, 329
Windows Information
　　Protection (WIP) 468
Windows IoT
　reference link 542
Windows Management Framework
　　(WMF) 5.1 84
Windows Management
　　Instrumentation (WMI) 313
Windows Network Security
　about 191
　Hyper-V 201, 202
　network baselining 192
　networking 201, 202
　network troubleshooting 202
Windows Operating System (OS) 24
Windows PowerShell Desired State
　　Configuration (DSC) 401

Windows Preinstallation
　　Environment (WinPE) 110
Windows security baselines
　about 53
　reference link 54
Windows Server
　about 198, 199
　Azure Disk Encryption, using 409
　Azure Key Vault, creating 411
　hardening 400
　key encryption key (KEK), creating 412
　Local Area Network (LAN)/
　　ethernet 199
　roles and features 199-201
　supported hardware, reference link 156
Windows Server 2019
　onboarding, with Configuration
　　Manager 397-399
　onboarding, with Group Policy 393-396
　roles 378
　security options 378
Windows Server 2019, features
　reference link 378
Windows Server 2019, installation options
　Desktop Experience 377
Windows Server 2019, roles and features
　installing 378
　reference link 379
Windows Server Catalog
　reference link 536
Windows Server Core, roles and features
　reference link 379
Windows Server footprint
　reducing 379
Windows Server Internet Information
　　Services (IIS) 43

Windows Server management tools 76
Windows servers
  access management, implementing 68
  managing, with Azure services 85
Windows Server, security baseline
    implementation
  about 400-402
  account policies, configuring 406, 407
  Accounts settings, configuring 404
  fine-grained password policies,
    implementing 408
  Interactive Logon, configuring 404, 405
  logon process, securing 409
  Remote Desktop Protocol session
    time limits, setting 405
  User Rights Assignment,
    controlling 402, 403
Windows Server Update Services (WSUS)
  about 45, 320, 321, 381
  implementing 383-387
  installing, on Windows Server
    2019 Core edition 380
  using 82, 83
Windows Server versions 377
Windows Server versions, life cycle
  reference link 377
Windows Update for Business (WUfB)
  about 321, 441
  Driver Updates 322
  Feature Updates 321
  Microsoft Product Updates 322
  Quality Updates 321
Windows updates
  configuring 381
  configuring, in Intune 323-325

Windows Virtual Desktop
  about 151
  reference link 151
Wire Data 2.0 solution
  using 447
Wired Equivalent Privacy (WEP) 194
Wireless Local Area Network
    (WLAN) 194
Wireshark
  URL 202
WPA2-Enterprise, with EAP-TLS
  reference link 194
wpad.dat file 352

Z

Zero touch Installation (ZTI) 113
Zero Trust access model
  about 534
  reference link 534
Zero Trust approach
  implementing 39
Zero Trust Microsoft model
  reference link 39

Printed in Poland
by Amazon Fulfillment
Poland Sp. z o.o., Wrocław